ANCIENT GREECE

WILLIAM E. DUNSTAN
NORTH CAROLINA STATE UNIVERSITY

HARCOURT COLLEGE PUBLISHERS

FORT WORTH   PHILADELPHIA   SAN DIEGO   NEW YORK   ORLANDO   AUSTIN   SAN ANTONIO

TORONTO   MONTREAL   LONDON   SYDNEY   TOKYO

Publisher	Earl McPeek
Acquisitions Editor	David Tatom
Market Strategist	Steve Drummond
Developmental Editor	Christine Abshire
Project Editor	G. Parrish Glover
Art Director	Vicki Whistler
Production Manager	Diane Gray

Cover photo: *Marathon Boy, c.* 340 BCE. Praxitelean-style bronze. National Museum, Athens/ Art Resource.

ISBN: 0-15-507383-4
Library of Congress Catalog Card Number: 99-069432

Address for Domestic Orders
Harcourt College Publishers, 6277 Sea Harbor Drive, Orlando, FL 32887-6777
800-782-4479

Address for International Orders
International Customer Service
Harcourt, Inc., 6277 Sea Harbor Drive, Orlando, FL 32887-6777
407-345-3800
(fax) 407-345-4060
(e-mail) hbintl@harcourtbrace.com

Address for Editorial Correspondence
Harcourt College Publishers, 301 Commerce Street, Suite 3700, Fort Worth, TX 76102

Web Site Address
http://www.harcourtcollege.com

Printed in the United States of America

9 0 1 2 3 4 5 6 7 8 016 9 8 7 6 5 4 3 2 1

Harcourt College Publishers

To my brother and sisters, David Fuller Dunstan, Virginia Herrington Dunstan Tyndall, Susan Mangun Dunstan Ward

CONTENTS

PREFACE

We remain under the spell of the ancient Greeks, whose stunning civilization has inspired and shaped so much of western science, art, architecture, literature, and philosophy. They inhabited a deceptively beautiful world broken by mountains into narrow plains, making the sea of primary importance for communications. The sea presses deeply into the long coastline of the Greek peninsula and encircles innumerable islands that beckon traders and sea travelers. This sparse environment divided the Hellenic world into countless independent states and helped spawn jealous competitiveness and debilitating wars of Greeks against Greeks. Other striking Greek blemishes included slavery, the subordination of women, and harsh imperialism. Yet the Greeks were united by common customs and religion. They gave birth to philosophy, theatrical tragedy and comedy, narrative history, biological study, and political theory. They inaugurated and argued about democracy. They introduced the alphabet—borrowed from the Phoenicians—to Europe. In sculpture, they excelled in portraying the human body. Their splendid architectural styles remain commonplace in the western world, which has also inherited their enthusiasm for athletic competition and physical fitness. In geometry, their terminology and theorems endure to the present day. Guardians of dazzling myths and great libraries, the Greeks also probed fundamental questions in works of literature that have survived through the ages.

This study serves as the middle volume of the Harcourt College Publishers series on ancient civilizations, taking its place, chronologically, between *The Ancient Near East* and *Ancient Rome*. Designed for students and general readers, *Ancient Greece* brings together the findings of archaeologists, historians, and other specialists. Its chapters explore the notable history of ancient Greece, beginning with the Bronze Age and ending with the Hellenistic period. The Bronze Age witnessed the flowering of two distinctive palace civilizations in turn, that of the non-Greek-speaking Minoans on the island of Crete and the Greek-speaking Mycenaeans on the mainland. The brilliant Minoan culture, inspired partly from contact with the east, heavily influenced Mycenaean Greece. The prosperous monarchies of these civilizations collapsed before a mysterious series of destructions, ushering in a measure of depopulation and a poorly understood period generally termed the Dark Age (c. 1150–750 BCE), when the Greeks produced no written records to help illuminate the nature of their world. Yet archaeological discoveries and other evidence suggest the Dark Age gave rise to important cultural developments shaping the Archaic period (c. 750–480 BCE). Of special note, the late Dark Age and the Archaic period saw the independent polis, or city-state, settling into its classic form as a vital political, social, and religious institution. Although influenced by many cultures, the Greeks created their own distinctive civilization. The fifth and fourth centuries BCE produced Classical Greece, famous for its subtle minds, sophisticated art, and military struggles. This period also witnessed the remarkable transformation of the northern kingdom of Macedonia into a great power, with King Philip II (reigned 359–336 BCE) creating a powerful army and imposing his will on most Greek cities. His daring son Alexander the Great (reigned 336–323 BCE) conquered the entire Persian Empire with astonishing speed, ruling a vast domain stretching from the Adriatic Sea to ancient India. The Hellenistic period after Alexander's premature death saw his generals carving up his empire for themselves. Their descendants were autocratic monarchs who exploited native populations in huge states and dominated the history of the Greek world. The Greco-Macedonian ruling class spread Greek culture widely in the east, borrowing only modestly from long-established indigenous traditions. Remarkable Hellenistic cultural activity centered on great royal cities like Alexandria and Pergamum. Meanwhile the Hellenistic monarchs held sway in the eastern Mediterranean until their kingdoms fell before the victorious march of Rome. Yet Hellenistic culture ultimately triumphed over its conqueror, for the Romans were quick to appreciate and absorb the cultural tradition of the Greeks. Ruling the Mediterranean world and much of continental Europe for centuries, Rome firmly implanted the core of Greek civilization in the western world.

Focusing on social and cultural themes while broadly outlining political and military developments, *Ancient Greece* is intended to be thought-provoking and does not shy away from controversial issues and topics. The aim throughout is to kindle the reader's interest in examining more specialized works, a number of which are listed in the bibliography. Regarding the spelling of ancient Greek names, the more familiar system follows Latin rather than Greek practice (for example, Aeschylus rather than Aiskhylos, Apollo rather than Apollon). On behalf of clarity, this book retains firmly rooted latinized forms of personal names and geographical places, with Greek transliterations adopted for most of the rest.

ACKNOWLEDGMENTS

Many colleagues, friends, and students deserve my warmest appreciation for their enthusiasm and valuable suggestions, especially Professors S. Thomas Parker and John M. Riddle of North Carolina State University. The reviewers of the manuscript merit particular recognition for their vigilance and reliable guidance: Jack Balcer, Ohio State University; David Cherry, Montana State University; John W. Dahmus, Stephen F. Austin State University; Eleanor G. Huzar, Professor Emeritus, Michigan State University; Frederick M. Lauritsen, Eastern Washington University; Anthony J. Papalas, East Carolina University; Thomas Turley, Santa Clara University; Allen M. Ward, Professor Emeritus, University of Connecticut; Richard D. Weigel, Western Kentucky University. Their advice contributed immensely to the quality of the book, though any faults or omissions are my own. Access to the superb holdings of the Widener Library at Harvard University and the Walter Royal Davis Library at the University of North Carolina at Chapel Hill greatly aided in preparing the text. Finally, I must express grateful thanks to the dedicated team at Harcourt: David C. Tatom, Christine Abshire, Steve Stembridge, Fritz Schanz, Steve Drummond, Parrish Glover, Vicki Whistler, and Diane Gray.

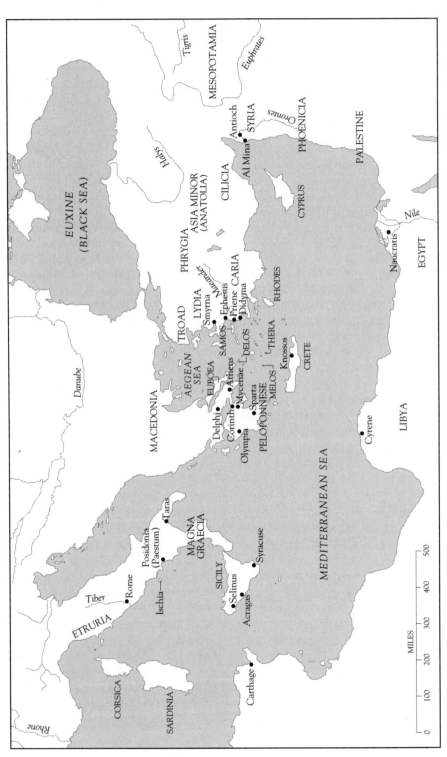

The eastern Mediterranean.

CHAPTER I

THE AEGEAN CIVILIZATION OF MINOAN CRETE

We are heirs of many ancient civilizations but owe a particular debt to the Greeks and Romans. The Greeks warrant being studied in their own right. Although they borrowed heavily from the cultural traditions of the Near East and elsewhere, they fashioned these elements into an extraordinary culture, the keystone of western civilization. The ancient Greeks gave birth to philosophy and scientific thought and also created noble poetry and brilliant art. Yet they were a quarrelsome, competitive lot, prone to both destructive and constructive behavior. Their story begins with the first major European civilizations, that of the Minoans on the island of Crete and that of the Mycenaeans on the Greek mainland.

THE GEOGRAPHY OF THE AEGEAN WORLD

Greece is famous for the remarkable visual effects created by its intense sunlight, with surfaces often taking on an apparent golden glow. This sea-dominated realm has cast its spell and influence upon people through the ages. Mainland Greece is washed on the east by the Aegean Sea, an arm of the Mediterranean. Studded with islands, the Aegean extends from mainland Greece to Asia Minor, or Anatolia, thus embracing seacoasts in both Europe and Asia. The shores and islands of the Aegean were the first parts of Greece to become civilized, for this world lay open to influence from the advanced cultures of the Near East.

The ancient Greeks referred to their home as Hellas. The term did not signify a unified country with distinct boundaries but referred collectively to the places they had settled, including the mainland of Greece, the islands of the Aegean, and the western coast of Asia Minor. The geographic center of this extensive realm was not located on a body of land but in the Aegean Sea. Hellas enjoyed a total land area of about 50,000 square miles, approximately the size of England, most of which was on the Greek mainland.

THE GREEK MAINLAND

The mainland, or Greek peninsula, is famous for its beauty, complexity, and variety. This landscape is ribbed by mountains—more than forty per cent of the surface rises above 1,650 feet—and is indented by long gulfs and innumerable bays. Such

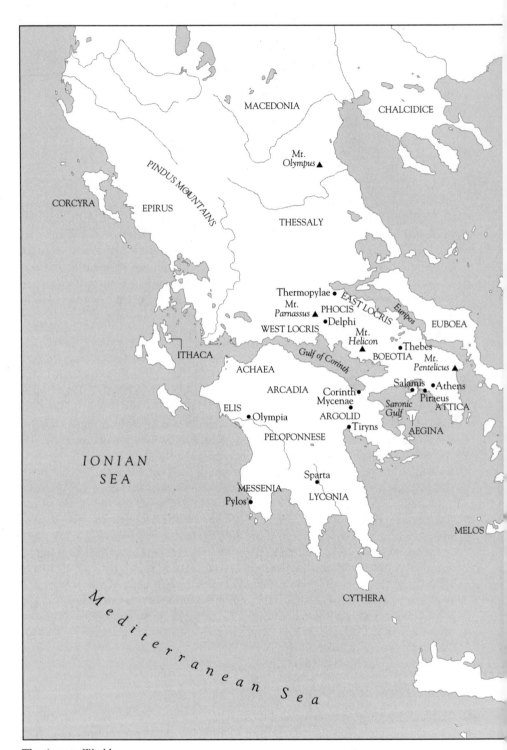

The Aegean World.

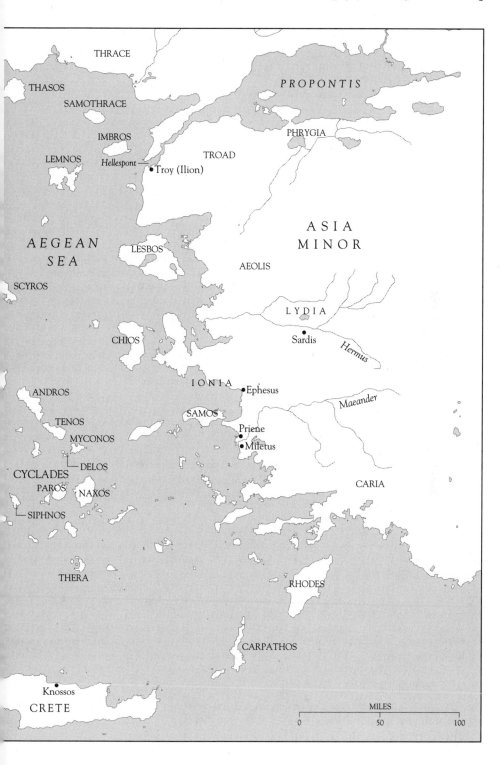

THRACE

THASOS

SAMOTHRACE

PROPONTIS

IMBROS

PHRYGIA

LEMNOS *Hellespont*

TROAD

•Troy (Ilion)

AEGEAN
SEA

LESBOS

ASIA
MINOR

AEOLIS

SCYROS

LYDIA

CHIOS

•Sardis *Hermus*

ANDROS

IONIA •Ephesus

Maeander

SAMOS

TENOS

Priene
•
•Miletus

MYCONOS

DELOS

CYCLADES

CARIA

PAROS NAXOS

SIPHNOS

THERA

RHODES

CARPATHOS

•Knossos

CRETE

MILES

0   50   100

natural barriers cut the mainland into countless small segments, thereby impeding communications and keeping settlements politically and culturally isolated. Except under extreme political pressure, ancient Greece remained fragmented into hundreds of small states.

Northern Greece.   The mainland falls into three natural divisions of unequal importance, namely, northern, central, and southern Greece, the last usually called the Peloponnese. In antiquity northern Greece embraced the region called Thessaly and, loosely, the regions of Epirus, Macedonia, and Thrace. Bordering the Aegean, Thessaly enjoyed the most extensive and fertile plains of ancient Greece but contributed little to Greek intellectual life. Thessaly is bounded on the west by the formidable Pindus Mountains. This range separates Thessaly from its rugged, inaccessible western neighbor called Epirus, a sparsely populated region making slight impact upon classical Greece. The region of Thrace is located far to the northeast of Thessaly. Forming the extreme northeastern limb of modern Greece, Thrace was a popular site for ancient Greek colonization. Immediately north of Thessaly lies the relatively remote region of Macedonia, which became an aggressive kingdom during the classical period. Western Macedonia is fractured by mountains, while its eastern expanse enjoys fertile plains facing the Aegean. The border separating Macedonia and Thessaly is marked by a vast range of rugged mountains, including Mount Olympus—the highest peak in Greece—identified by ancients as the seat of the gods.

Central Greece.   Central Greece embraces the territory between the northern division and the Gulf of Corinth. Although quite mountainous in the west, central Greece enjoys many small plains in the east. These stretches offered ancient travelers easy access to its various regions or even to the Peloponnese in the south. A number of the great landmarks and centers of ancient Greece stood in the central division on a conspicuous spur pointing southeast to the Aegean Sea. Listed from the northwest, these include the famed pass at Thermopylae leading from Thessaly into the region of Eastern Locris, the holy site of Delphi on Mount Parnassus in the region of Phocis, the beautiful mountain called Helicon—sacred to the Muses—in the region of Boeotia, and the important Boeotian city of Thebes, made famous by Greek saga. The southeastern extremity of the spur supported marble-rich Mount Pentelicus and the celebrated city of Athens, both embraced by the important region of Attica. The indented southern coast of Attica faces the great Saronic Gulf, which offers a safe inlet in Piraeus, the harbor of Athens, while the noteworthy island of Salamis stands only a mile offshore. North of Attica lies the large, generally mountainous island of Euboea.

The Peloponnese.   Mainland Greece is nearly divided into two parts by the Saronic Gulf and the Corinthian Gulf. Below these bodies of water is the large expanse of southern Greece—the Peloponnese—linked to the rest of the mainland only by the slender Isthmus of Corinth. Today the isthmus is cut by a small canal, but in ancient times ships were dragged across on a stone causeway. The most important region of the Peloponnese is the Argolid in the northeast. This was the heart of the first high civilization on the mainland, now called Mycenaean from its famous

Bronze Age center of Mycenae. The triangular Argolid is bounded on the west by the hills of land-locked Arcadia. Immediately west of Arcadia lies Elis, the region that produced the settlement of Olympia and the famed Olympic Games. The southeastern expanse of the Peloponnese is known as Laconia, the region of the ancient militaristic city of Sparta. After gaining domination over Laconia, Sparta subjected the most southwesterly region, Messenia, which was celebrated in antiquity for its large tracts of fertile soil.

SEA AND ISLANDS

Pressing deep into the mainland, the wine-dark sea is always close, never over thirty-three miles away in the Peloponnese, thirty-eight in central Greece. The majority of the ancient Greeks lived within sight of the sea, and most others could catch a glimpse of its shimmer from a nearby hill. Travel was often easier by sea than by land. Although only a small proportion of the ancient Greeks earned their living by fishing, they soon became the best sailors in the Mediterranean. The cities they built facing the sea—exemplified by Athens—usually gained considerable importance and played a major role in Greek destinies.

Two seas embrace the Greek mainland. As noted, its heavily indented eastern and southern shores face the Aegean. The relatively smooth western coast is bounded by the Ionian Sea—another arm of the Mediterranean—which supports a number of fairly important islands, including Ithaca, the legendary home of Homer's hero Odysseus. In terms of the economic, political, and cultural life of Greece, however, the Aegean Sea has always exercised far greater influence than the Ionian. The Aegean is liberally dotted with islands forming distinct geographical clusters. One small group lies off Thessaly. Another cluster, Euboea and the Cyclades, are actually partially submerged extensions of the mountain chains on the mainland. The large island of Euboea hugs the mainland regions of Attica and Boeotia, while the Cyclades lie southeast of Attica and Euboea. An archipelago of twenty-four islands, the Cyclades (meaning *circular*) were so named because they were thought to revolve around the sacred island of Delos, the mythical birthplace of Apollo and the site of one of his great shrines. Lying across the southern extremity of the Aegean is the long island of Crete, the largest of all the Greek islands and the home of the great Minoan civilization. Finally, several fairly large islands are located along the Asian coast, including, from north to south, Lesbos, Chios, Samos, and Rhodes, the last becoming a prosperous trading port.

ASIA MINOR

Hellas also included the western shore of Asia Minor, now belonging to Turkey, physically similar to the Greek seaboard on the opposite side of the Aegean but enjoying a somewhat more moderate climate, especially in the south-central section known as Ionia. The extensive coastal plains of Asia Minor, well watered by rivers such as the Hermus and the Maeander, formed a hospitable world attracting Greek settlement.

Natural Resources and Climate

As noted, arable land was scarce except on the coastal plains, whose soil was adequate for the cultivation of grapes and olives, eventually leading to the export of considerable wine and oil, but less suited to the growing of vital grain. Greece would grow increasingly dependent on imports of grain to feed its expanding population. Ships to transport the grain depended upon the accessibility of timber. The once plentiful forests growing on the mountain slopes of the mainland had been overcut by the classical period, though good quantities of timber were still available in northwestern Greece and Macedonia. Meanwhile silver was mined in Attica and iron in Laconia, part of the explanation for the eventual rise to power of Athens and Sparta. Other sources of silver included Macedonia and Thrace. Some gold was available on the island of Thasos, and both silver and gold were extracted from the island of Siphnos. The glass-like black lava called obsidian was quarried from very early times on the Aegean island of Melos. The ancient Greeks were famous for their magnificent marble, obtaining yellow-white Pentelic in Attica, white on the Aegean islands of Paros and Naxos, red in the southern Peloponnese, and green in Thessaly. An abundance of potter's clay permitted the manufacture of vases for many purposes and eventually led to the creation of exquisite pottery expressing Greek artistic genius.

The Aegean world as a whole has a Mediterranean climate of mild wet winters and hot dry summers, with regional variations caused by the great physical diversity. Inhabitants experience extremes of heat and cold, rain and drought. The short, tortuous rivers of mainland Greece virtually dry up in the summer. In July and August a strong Mediterranean gale—known to the ancients as the Etesian winds—blows steadily from the northeast, tempering the dry summer heat of the islands and the eastern coast of mainland Greece but hindering the growth of trees. Winter produces violent, changeable winds. Both the winter and Etesian winds posed extreme danger for the small seagoing vessels of the ancient Greeks and thus rendered Aegean navigation seasonal.

The sea helped to moderate the climate of the southern coasts and islands—though not the interior regions or mountainous terrain—by cooling summer air and warming that of winter. These sea-girt areas enjoyed a subtropical climate. Here people could live simply and required only modest clothing and shelter for survival. Thus many of the ancient Greeks were not obsessed with the struggle for existence. A number of the men were able to spend many of their waking hours together in the open air, enjoying all sorts of activities, including asking questions and clarifying ideas.

DISCOVERY OF THE AEGEAN BRONZE AGE

Before 1870 historians generally made a marked distinction between legendary and historical Greece. Most identified the year 776 BCE, the traditional date for the first Olympic Games, as the symbolic beginning of a period of transition from myth and legend to actual history. They realized the Aegean world was inhabited before that

Heinrich Schliemann (1822–1890) reaped a fortune in trade and turned to archaeology, realizing his childhood dream of finding the Homeric world of Troy and Mycenae.

date but considered earlier events lost beyond recovery. Yet some perceptive investigators thought that the heroic tales enshrined in Greek legends, particularly the famous epics preserved under the name of Homer, the *Iliad* and *Odyssey*, were distorted images of a real past rather than mere fiction. The German Heinrich Schliemann was one of these.

Schliemann will always be remembered for his pioneering archaeological work at Bronze Age sites in the Aegean region. His excavations from 1870 to 1890 at Troy on the northwest coast of Asia Minor, where limited explorations had already been undertaken by earlier investigators, and at Mycenae and other sites on the Greek mainland demonstrated the existence of powerful states in the Aegean world centuries before 776 BCE. His finds at Mycenae were extraordinary, and archaeologists were soon referring to the culminating period of the mainland-based culture as Mycenaean. Following Schliemann's stunning discoveries, the English archaeologist Sir Arthur Evans excavated at the Bronze Age site of Knossos in northern Crete and brought to light the first major civilization of the Aegean world, which he named Minoan, after its legendary king Minos.

HEINRICH SCHLIEMANN

As noted, Heinrich Schliemann (1822–1890) was highly influenced by the Homeric epics. Most contemporary scholars suggest the *Iliad* and *Odyssey* were shaped over many centuries and transmitted orally by nonliterate poets chanting to the accompaniment of music and sometimes adding their own lines of verse. Written down in the eighth century BCE, the epics were attributed to Homer, whose identity remains elusive. These literary masterpieces, describing an era when weapons were usually of bronze, seem to preserve some memory of the distant Greek Bronze Age, though they contain many details reflecting society of later times, particularly the period in which they were written.

As a young boy in Germany, Schliemann was captivated by stories in the *Iliad* about the victory of mainland Greeks (Homer called them Achaeans), led by a king named Agamemnon, against the city of Troy in northwest Asia Minor and in the *Odyssey* about the fantastic adventures of another Greek hero, Odysseus, on his wandering return from the Trojan War to rejoin his faithful wife, Penelope, on their island home of Ithaca. Young Heinrich became convinced that the epics, especially the *Iliad*, were based on actual events. Unable to complete his classical studies because of poverty, the indomitable Schliemann set out to accumulate a fortune that would enable him to discover the Troy of Homer. He was a brilliant linguist and built a commercial empire stretching from Russia to California. Retiring from business to devote the rest of his life to prehistoric archaeology, he settled in Athens in 1868. The following year Schliemann, approaching fifty, married a seventeen-year-old Athenian school girl named Sophia Engastromenos, who shared her husband's enthusiasm for Homer and took an active part in his archaeological explorations.

Troy.   In 1870 Schliemann began preliminary excavations at the mound of Hissarlik in northwest Asia Minor, a site he correctly identified as ancient Troy (also called Ilion by Homer). Yet Schliemann discovered that the mound contained the remains of several different ancient cities, each built upon the ruins of its predecessor. Nine main layers with subdivisions were eventually revealed. Schliemann's concern was the Troy of the Trojan War, traditionally dated in the thirteenth century BCE, which he erroneously identified as the second layer from the bottom. Later archaeologists established that the layer Schliemann had unearthed (Troy II)

Nineteenth-century engraving of Schliemann's effort to uncover Troy, beginning in October 1871.

represented the period around 2300 BCE, a thousand years older than the likely date of Homeric Troy, and that he had hastily dug through and seriously damaged the actual city of his quest (now generally regarded as Troy VI).

Schliemann discovered a dazzling collection of gold, silver, and bronze objects at Hissarlik in 1873. He named the horde the Treasure of Priam, mistakenly associating the artifacts with Priam, identified in the *Iliad* as the king of Troy during the Trojan War. The rich array, later shown to predate Homeric Troy by a millennium, was placed on exhibition in Berlin but disappeared at the end of World War II, confiscated by Russian soldiers and sent to the Pushkin Museum in Moscow, where the treasure was kept hidden until its seizure was officially acknowledged in 1993.

Wilhelm Dörpfeld at Troy. Schliemann continued his operations at Troy at intervals for twenty years. Beginning in 1882, a brilliant young German archaeologist named Wilhelm Dörpfeld served as Schliemann's colleague at the site and brought more precision to the identification of the stratified settlements.

Mycenae and Tiryns. Schliemann's investigation of Bronze Age settlements was not limited to Troy. He turned his attention to the Greek mainland and began excavating at Mycenae in 1874 and at Tiryns in 1884. Mycenae was described in the *Iliad* as a city "rich in gold" as well as the home of the legendary king Agamemnon. Schliemann opened the now famous Shaft Graves at Mycenae and found an immense treasure of gold, silver, bronze, and ivory objects but impulsively identified a

Sophia Schliemann shared her husband's enthusiasm for archaeology and frequently played an active role in the epoch-making excavations. She is shown here wearing an assortment of jewelry from the so-called Treasure of Priam, Heinrich Schliemann's most celebrated find at Troy.

gold funerary mask as that of King Agamemnon. He immediately telegraphed the king of Greece: "I have gazed upon the face of Agamemnon!" Later archaeologists determined that the burials in the royal graves of Mycenae predated Homeric Troy by some four hundred years. Excavating at Tiryns, Schliemann mistakenly assumed the ruins of the great palace there were from the period of the expedition against Troy, for his overriding concern was to verify his beloved Homer.

Crete.   Schliemann also sought archaeological evidence for the ancient tradition that a king named Minos once ruled a mighty maritime empire from the city of Knossos on the island of Crete. Although Schliemann conducted some preliminary work at the site, his quest was blocked because the Turks, who then governed Crete, would not permit the excavations. Schliemann soon turned to carrying out additional explorations at Troy but died suddenly in 1890. Much of the academic establishment of the day had scorned him as a self-taught archaeologist or even labeled him a fraud.

Scholars still regard him in a variety of lights. Although he was blundering and irascible, prone to exaggeration, and not fully aware of the scope of his discoveries, we should not lose sight of his trailblazing accomplishments. Schliemann was the founder of prehistoric Greek archaeology. He demonstrated that two powerful states, Troy and Mycenae, had flourished in the Aegean long before the accepted beginnings of Greek history, and he pointed to a third on the island of Crete.

CRETE IN MYTH AND LEGEND

In a famous passage in the nineteenth book of the *Odyssey*, Homer sings, "There is a land called Crete in the midst of the wine-dark sea, a fair land and a rich, begirt with water. . . ." Continuing, Homer relates that the island supports innumerable people and ninety cities, among which is mighty Knossos, where Minos ruled and conversed with great Zeus, the king of the gods. Any quest for the real Cretan Bronze Age will inevitably be shaped to some extent by such legendary and mythic images. One famous myth tells that Zeus was captivated by the beauty of a mortal named Europa, a princess from Phoenicia who gave her name to a continent. Disguised as a beautiful white bull, Zeus came from the waves into the presence of Europa as she played by the seashore, enticing her by his gentleness to climb upon his back as he knelt before her. Without warning, he leapt into the sea and swam with Europa on his back to his cave on Crete. Here the bull-god made love to Europa, and she bore him several famous sons, including Minos, who is said to have ruled a powerful kingdom from his palace at Knossos. The Greeks told haunting legends about Minos. They said he was inspired by Zeus to give the first laws to humanity. The notable Greek historians Herodotus and Thucydides, writing in the fifth century BCE, relate that he swept the sea of pirates with his powerful fleet and imposed his rule upon the peoples living along the coasts of the Aegean.

We read in one incredible legend that the wife of Minos, Pasiphae, mated with a beautiful bull sent by Poseidon, god of the sea, and gave birth to a monstrous creature called the Minotaur, having the head of a bull and the body of a man. Minos imprisoned the Minotaur beneath his palace at Knossos in a great maze called the Labyrinth. Built by the mythical artisan and architect Daedalus, the Labyrinth was so diabolically intricate with its tangle of dark passages that no one who entered could hope to escape alive from the monster.

When a son of Minos was murdered in Athens on the Greek mainland, so the story goes, the king sought revenge. He defeated the Athenians in a punitive campaign and compelled them to send an annual tribute of seven boys and seven girls to be fed to the Minotaur in the Labyrinth. Finally, the sixteen-year-old Athenian prince Theseus volunteered to go to Crete as one of the fourteen victims. Theseus assured his father, the legendary Athenian king Aegeus, that he would change the sails on his ship from black to white for the homeward journey if he succeeded in slaying the bull-monster.

After Theseus landed on Crete, one of Minos' daughters, Ariadne, was enraptured by his courage and beauty and vowed to save him from the Minotaur. She secretly gave the boy-hero a ball of thread he could unwind through the twisting passages and then use to find his way out after slaying the monster. After killing the Minotaur with a magic sword Ariadne had presented him, Theseus made his escape by following the trail of string. The two young lovers fled from Knossos by sea, but one version of the legend relates that Theseus abandoned Ariadne on an Aegean island. In some versions she is rescued by the god Dionysus and becomes his consort, while in others she commits suicide. Meanwhile Theseus, forgetting the agreement with his father, failed to change the sails from black to white. When Aegeus saw the ship approaching with black sails, he supposed his son had perished. The grief-stricken king threw himself from a cliff into the sea, thereby giving his name to the Aegean.

Sir Arthur Evans

After Heinrich Schliemann demonstrated that the ancient legends had some factual basis, other investigators rushed to the Aegean. The most important of these was the remarkable English archaeologist Sir Arthur Evans (1851–1941). An eccentric but highly respected scholar of great wealth, Evans was attracted by the persistent tradition of antiquity that a king named Minos once ruled the Aegean world from Knossos on the island of Crete. His interest in Knossos was also stimulated by the presence of beautifully carved sealstones, which left an image behind when pressed into clay, and by evidence of a primitive form of writing. In 1898 Crete became free of its two-century Turkish yoke, and the following year Evans purchased land at Knossos. He spent a fortune and half his lifetime re-creating—some would say virtually inventing—the rich civilization of Bronze Age Crete, considerably older than that of the Greek mainland. He conducted his principal work here over six seasons from 1900 to 1905 but continued exploring at intervals until 1932. Ruling like a prince from his Villa Ariadne, Evans excavated and, in part, reconstituted the massive palace complex of Knossos, which he termed the Palace of Minos. He spent many years writing his account and interpretation of his discoveries, published in four volumes between 1921 and 1935 as *The Palace of Minos*.

Writing in the Aegean Bronze Age

Knossos yielded thousands of clay tablets and other remains revealing several systems of writing. The earliest, dated from roughly 1850 BCE, is a kind of pictographic writing employing signs to represent animals or things in the manner of Egyptian hieroglyphics. On the analogy of the oldest Egyptian script, Evans termed this still undeciphered Cretan writing system Hieroglyphic. The second script Evans distinguished, Linear A, probably developed from Hieroglyphic. Characterized by its simple linear signs, Linear A was regularly used in Crete between the eighteenth and sixteenth centuries BCE. Archaeologists have discovered examples of Linear A throughout Crete and beyond, though the paucity of these documents has prevented much progress toward decipherment. Many of the signs of Linear A were employed to develop a new script that Evans termed Linear B, used from the sixteenth century BCE at Knossos (fragments have also been found in western Crete) and later at the major sites on the mainland. Linear B defied decipherment for half a century.

Michael Ventris and the Decipherment of Linear B.   In 1936 the eighty-four-year-old Evans delivered a lecture in London, telling of wrestling for over three decades with the strange Bronze Age scripts he had named but not deciphered. In the audience was a spellbound fourteen-year-old English schoolboy, Michael Ventris, who vowed to accept Sir Arthur's challenge of decipherment. Becoming a London architect and an amateur cryptographer, the young man used his spare time to make a serious study of the problem. In 1952 the Linear B tablets finally yielded to his genius. Ventris demonstrated that the script expressed an archaic form of Greek— usually termed Mycenaean Greek—predating Homer by hundreds of years. Ventris's brilliant work was cut short when he was tragically killed in an automobile accident in 1957 at the age of thirty-four.

Apparently most of the signs of Linear A represent the syllables of the Minoan language, still unidentified but clearly not Greek. Most of the signs of Linear B also represent syllables, though these were used to write words in Mycenaean Greek. Why had Linear A, expressing the Minoan language, undergone a modification into Linear B, expressing an archaic form of Greek? The favored theory suggests that Greek-speaking mainlanders, or Mycenaeans, established themselves on Crete during the second millennium BCE, whereupon Minoan scribes altered Linear A into Linear B to write the intruding language. Later, according to this view, Linear B was carried to the mainland.

The parallels between Linear A and Linear B show that the tablets in both scripts are chiefly annual inventories of people, animals, and produce. Apparently the ability to write Mycenaean Greek was the exclusive possession of a small number of scribes keeping administrative records. Writing seems to have been far more widespread in Crete than on the mainland, however, and some Minoan sacred objects bear inscriptions showing Linear A had religious purposes in addition to its administrative uses. Moreover, the archaeological record offers tantalizing hints that certain Minoan texts may have been written with ink on perishable materials such as parchment or papyrus. Possibly myths, hymns, prayers, and other important texts were so inscribed, while the sun-dried clay tablets, which could be softened in water and used over and over again, were reserved for inventories. The only surviving clay documents are those that were baked by chance in fires that destroyed various archives.

MINOAN CRETE

About 160 miles long and six to thirty-five miles wide, Crete flanks the southern limits of the Aegean and served in ancient times as an important anchorage for voyagers from the coasts of Asia, Africa, and Europe. The island was receptive to external influences but sufficiently isolated to form a distinctive way of life. Roughly two-thirds of Crete is covered by conspicuously rugged mountains, with the highest

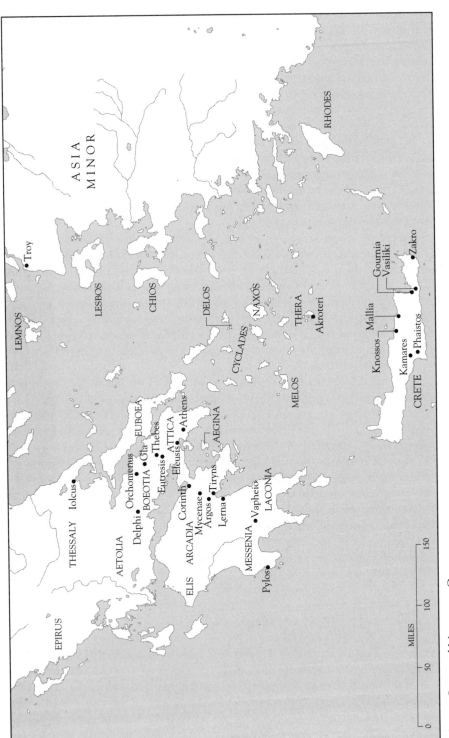

Minoan Crete and Mycenaean Greece.

peak—centrally located Mount Ida (modern Mount Psiloriti)—rising more than 8,000 feet. Yet the central and eastern regions of ancient Crete enjoyed lowlands blessed not only with arable portions suitable for the cultivation of crops such as olives and vines but also with fair meadows and pastoral highlands. A series of sheltered harbors on the northern and eastern coasts offered protection for a large number of seagoing vessels.

Neolithic Farming Settlements (c. 7000–3500 bce)

Space permits only a brief summary of the earlier cultural phases in the Aegean world, encompassing Crete, the Greek mainland, and the Cyclades. The predecessor to the Minoan civilization in Crete was the Neolithic (or New Stone) Age, the period of Cretan prehistory beginning with the first establishment of settled farming communities. After having evolved in the ancient Near East, farming slowly spread across Europe, from southeast to northwest, during a three-thousand-year period beginning around the opening of the seventh millennium bce. The initial farming communities in the Aegean region were established in Crete after seaborne settlers, probably from the coast of Asia Minor, arrived about 7000 bce to colonize a landscape that was probably largely empty of people. Cretan farmers and herders produced their own varieties of decorated pottery as well as naked female figurines of the type known as mother-goddesses, apparently conceived as magical purveyors of fertility. The Cretans dwelt in caves and in small communities of rough houses. Their oldest known settlement was at Knossos in north-central Crete.

Bronze Age Crete before the Palaces (c. 3500–2000 bce)

The transition from the Neolithic to the Early Bronze Age in the Aegean world is now estimated to have occurred about the middle of the fourth millennium bce. Perhaps new settlers had arrived from civilized regions in the east such as Asia Minor or Syria, bringing the use of metal, first copper and later bronze. Molten bronze flowed easily into molds for the casting of intricate objects. An extraordinary improvement over copper, bronze yielded harder and more durable tools, weapons, and ornaments. The flourishing Bronze Age cultures on Crete and elsewhere in the Aegean permitted local rulers to accumulate remarkable treasures of gold and silver. In Crete, the desire to exploit fully both metallurgy and a growing farming economy must have been an impetus for the gradual development of large towns, the first on European soil. Four settlements in the central and eastern portion of the island—Knossos, Phaistos, Mallia, and Zakro—quickly forged ahead of others both in size and in population. Apparently the ruling authorities in each town managed to establish control over adjacent territory, dominating its agricultural production and religious practices. Cretan farming—devoted largely to the famous Mediterranean triad of olive, grape, and grain—produced an agricultural surplus supporting a complex, probably socially ranked population. This stable and prosperous development of Early Bronze Age society in Crete led to the emergence of the first high civilization on European soil.

Period of the Old Palaces (c. 2000–1800 bce)

The Palaces.   Sir Arthur Evans divided the Cretan Bronze Age into three periods—Early, Middle, and Late Minoan—each of which was subdivided three times and then further subdivided. Many later scholars found this system, based chiefly on changes in pottery styles, entirely too artificial and inflexible. Most archaeologists now combine Evans's chronological scheme with a system revolving around the building and rebuilding on Crete of imposing architectural complexes, conveniently termed palaces. The palaces were constructed around 2000 bce, the beginning of the Old Palace period, but required extensive renovations after a series of destructions—perhaps resulting from earthquakes—around 1800 bce, the beginning of the New Palace period.

Although by the end of the third millennium bce the Minoans had produced the most advanced culture of the Aegean, with eastern and central Crete blossoming into an elusive but polished urban civilization, nothing in the archaeological record of the island prepares us for the astonishing palaces of the Old Palace period. The most important of the great complexes were constructed within a comparatively short time at the leading centers of Knossos, Phaistos, and Mallia. The ruins we see today are chiefly from the New Palace period because of the serious damage to the original buildings around 1800 bce.

The palaces are subject to varying interpretations, for a lack of textual evidence seriously limits our understanding of the roles they played in society. Like the temples of the Near East, the palaces were designed to serve a variety of purposes. The Minoan complexes contained dozens or even hundreds of rooms and must have been conceived not only as residences for rulers and their retinues but also as administrative centers of regional importance, storehouses for food and goods, manufacturing centers, and great sacred buildings. Clearly, every palace controlled a distinct geographical region and exploited its agriculture. Pack animals and wagons regularly brought produce from the hinterland to the palace. An exceptionally large area of the complex was devoted to the storage of food, required for feeding the ruling family and staff and perhaps made available to the population during periods of lean crop yields. The palace also used the stored food as an important medium in foreign trade. Every complex included shrines. Numerous workshops accommodated a large body of artisans such as sculptors, potters, gem cutters, smiths, painters, and weavers. Thus the palaces were clearly at the heart of a system of economic, political, religious, and cultural centralization.

All the palaces were constructed on a similar plan. Each contained a monumental central courtyard—an appropriate setting for pageants, ceremonies, and games—around which was built a complex of rooms at least two stories high. The palace at Knossos was located in rolling country in central Crete near the north coast. The complex is thought to have received fresh water from an outlying area via a great aqueduct. An elaborate drainage system running throughout the interior of the Knossos palace was built with fired clay pipes, each being tapered at one end to fit into the next. This palace served as the focal point of a substantial town having a network of streets and probably provided with fortifications.

Popular shapes for the highly original Kamares ware included the one-handled cup, the spouted jar, and the beak-spouted pitcher. The intricate decoration ranged from sweeping spirals to abstract natural forms, with white paint and vibrant shades of yellow, red, and orange applied to a dark surface. This beak-spouted pitcher from Phaistos, dated about 1800 BCE, carries an energetic, curvilinear design featuring a play of spirals. Archaeological Museum, Heraklion, Crete.

Pottery.   Much of our knowledge of the life of the Minoans comes from pottery. Although vases are easily broken, pottery fragments—potsherds—are virtually indestructible. When thrown away, potsherds often become embedded in stratified layers and help to establish a chronological framework. Among the remarkable technical advances of the Old Palace period was the use of the fast potter's wheel, probably an import from Asia Minor, which was introduced about the same time on the Cyclades, the mainland, and Crete. The fast wheel, spindle-mounted and freely rotating, enabled the Minoans to produce great quantities of thin-walled pottery. Artists customarily applied red, orange, and white paint to a lustrous black background, thereby creating a striking polychrome effect. This style of pottery is known as Kamares ware, named after its first discovery in the Kamares Cave on the south slope of Mount Ida. Made in various shapes, particularly beak-spouted jugs, spouted jars, and one-handled cups, Kamares ware remains the most famous genre of the smaller arts during the period. The pieces of the highest quality and refinement were fashioned with almost eggshell thinness in imitation of metalware.

Sealstones.   The Minoans also produced a great quantity of sealstones. Another sign of eastern influence, sealstones had begun to appear throughout the Aegean around the middle of the third millennium BCE. Seal cutters in the Old Palace period fashioned semiprecious stones such as amethyst and agate into disks, lenses, cylinders, prisms, cones, or other shapes, engraving patterns on one or more faces. Designs of the period include simple geometrical patterns, depictions of mythical beasts, and naturalistic scenes featuring animals, birds, or insects. Seals offered a means of identifying and preventing access to property long before the invention of locks. If stamped by the owner's personal seal, a lump of clay over the lid of a vessel or over the loop of cord securing a wooden chest or a door could not be removed and replaced without detection.

Maritime Trade and Writing.   The classical Greeks told colorful stories of Cretan seafaring exploits in a distant past. The Minoans of the Old Palace period inherited a long Cretan tradition of maritime trade. They heavily influenced—perhaps even colonized—a number of islands of the southern Aegean, notably Cythera, Ceos, Melos, Thera, and Rhodes. The need to better organize trade and production led to the inauguration of writing. By this period the Minoans had learned to use a system of pictographic writing—the so-called Hieroglyphic—from which developed a script known as Linear A, regularly used in the New Palace period. All efforts to decipher the pictographic writing and Linear A have been unsatisfactory.

In addition to their trade with the Aegean islands, the Minoans exported their goods to the Greek mainland, the Levant (countries bordering the Eastern Mediterranean), and Egypt. This exchange increased under the impetus of the flourishing palace economies. In return for copper, gold, ivory, and semiprecious stones for seals, the palace workshops traded superb stone vases, Kamares ware, and probably metalwork such as silver and bronze cups. An important spur to long-distance trade was the need for tin, for tin-bronze had come into general use, replacing the earlier method of making bronze by alloying copper with arsenic. Approximately one part of tin was required for every nine of copper to produce optimum bronze. Tin was difficult to obtain and may have been imported from western Asia Minor.

PERIOD OF THE NEW PALACES (c. 1800–1550 BCE)

The destructions around 1800 BCE prompted the authorities to undertake large-scale renovations, the beginning of the so-called New Palace period. The palaces at Knossos, Phaistos, and Mallia were repaired or rebuilt on a truly splendid scale, while the important palace at Zakro was either rebuilt or first constructed. The Minoan civilization reached the height of its power and influence during this period. Beyond the palaces were large towns with cobbled streets, traversed by horses and oxen slowly pulling carts and by horses clipping along drawing chariots. The light, two-wheeled chariot with spoked wheels, originating in the Near East, had been adopted by Minoan aristocrats as a symbol of power and prestige.

The Palace at Knossos.   The relatively well preserved New Palaces not only reflect the talents of the creating architects and artisans but also provide clues to the complexity of Minoan society during the period. All known Cretan palaces share a

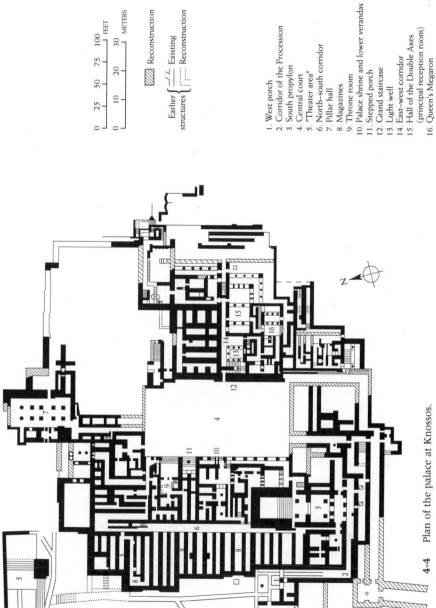

FEET

METERS

Reconstruction

Existing
Reconstruction

Earlier
structures

100

75

50

25

0

30

20

10

0

1. West porch
2. Corridor of the Procession
3. South propylon
4. Central court
5. "Theater area"
6. North–south corridor
7. Pillar hall
8. Magazines
9. Throne room
10. Palace shrine and lower verandas
11. Stepped porch
12. Grand staircase
13. Light well
14. East–west corridor
15. Hall of the Double Axes
    (principal reception room)
16. Queen's Megaron

4-4   Plan of the palace at Knossos.

Plan of the palace at Knossos.

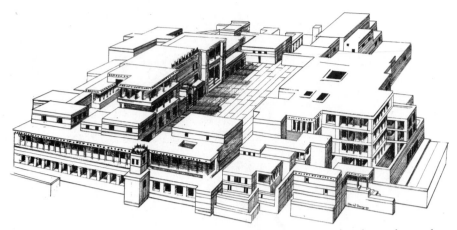

Reconstruction of the sprawling palace at Knossos, an intricate complex clustered around a huge central courtyard and containing residential quarters, shrines, storerooms, and workshops. The palace, the seat of Minoan rulers, served as the political, economic, and administrative center of the region and as the focal point for its religious and state ceremonies.

number of common features. The largest, the immense Knossos palace, is a complicated structure that does not seem to have been planned as a whole but simply continued to expand over time. The entire fabric covers some six acres and represents a marvel of engineering and artistic skill. Perhaps the winding passages of the palace survived in folk memory beyond the Bronze Age and lay behind the myth of the Labyrinth. The word labyrinth itself may be of Bronze Age date and apparently means the House of the Double Axe. The double axe was a potent sacred emblem in the Minoan religion and was frequently emblazoned on the walls and columns of the Knossos palace.

Evans partly reconstructed the palace to an extent now considered excessive and made a number of unfortunate mistakes along the way, but his effort helps one visualize the scale and grandeur of the original. Set on a low hill, the colonnaded palace at Knossos was built around a huge central courtyard, as in the Old Palace period. Wide flights of stairs led from the courtyard to upper stories. The interior staircases of the palace were arranged around light wells, or shafts extending vertically through the building. These and other light wells provided reflected sunlight and ventilation for the interior chambers grouped around them. The use of light wells meant the Minoans could make extensions to the palace without sacrificing illumination or fresh air.

The walls of the palace were constructed of stone and were framed with large horizontal and vertical wooden beams, possibly to provide resilience against the shock of earthquake. Most of the walls were plastered, but the more important ones were often veneered with large sheets of gypsum. Interior floors were fashioned with slabs of gypsum. Because gypsum is soluble in water, exposed pavements were of limestone.

Stairwell in the residential
quarters of the palace at
Knossos.

The floors and flat roofs of the Knossos palace were supported by downward-tapering
wooden columns resting upon gypsum bases. Evans restored the columns in stone,
perhaps with overly bulky proportions, and gave each a cushion-shaped capital, or
crowning part, on the basis of wall paintings. The columns supported hefty beams,
which carried ceilings of stone slabs.

As noted, the important components of each palace looked inward to the rectangular central courtyard. This huge uncovered space at Knossos measured about
two hundred feet long by one hundred feet wide. The western side of the Knossos
courtyard faced the west wing, which encompassed three floor levels, all joined by a
monumental staircase. Except for a few fragments suggesting their original magnificence, the rooms of the upper stories of the west wing have vanished. The ground
floor of this wing contained a set of long and narrow rooms used for storing the
wealth of the palace. Enormous clay jars—now called pithoi—held olive oil, wine,
grain, and other produce collected by the authorities as taxes. Some of the pithoi
were deposited in stone-lined pits that kept the contents cool. Lead-lined chests
were set into the floors, probably for securing treasures.

The ground floor of the west wing also encompassed a complex of rooms that
were probably designed for the practice of religion. Evans termed one of these the

Reconstruction of part of the west wing of the palace at Knossos, as seen from the central courtyard. On the extreme right was the entrance to the antechamber of the Throne Room. To the left of the staircase stood small shrines, one with a cult pillar. This reconstruction reflects the ideas of Sir Arthur Evans, the original excavator. Although most of the details are conjectural, they are soundly based on archaeological evidence.

Throne Room. This is a modest chamber, dark and mysterious, containing a high-backed carved chair of gypsum. Evans sometimes speculated that perhaps the stone chair served as a throne in an audience chamber, though this is unlikely. Two griffins—creatures combining the features of birds and mammals—were painted on the wall to guard the occupant of the chair, perhaps a priestess. Evans interpreted the nearby sunken area as a lustral basin, or place for ritual purification.

The east wing was served by a grand staircase, which connected no less than five stories, two above the level of the court, two below. A large part of the east wing consisted of magnificent suites of rooms that Evans called the Domestic Quarter, which he regarded as apartments reserved for the ruling family. At the lowest level are two well-known chambers. Evans named the larger the Hall of the Double Axes, after the design inscribed on the walls of its light well. This room contained multiple doorways and opened onto a porch that may have faced a garden. He thought the smaller room, celebrated for its splendid wall painting of dolphins, must have been the queen's apartment. Next to the Hall of the Double Axes were several workshops, while the northern part of the east wing housed additional storerooms. Evans decided that a chamber adjacent to what he identified as the queen's apartment was a bathroom and placed a clay bathtub here that he had uncovered nearby. The elaborate sanitation system at Knossos incorporated the equivalent of flush toilets, connected to an efficient drainage system beneath the palace. Running water from hillside springs entered the palace through skillfully joined clay pipes.

Frescoes.   The walls of the more important rooms at Knossos were vividly decorated with wall paintings that are usually termed frescoes. True fresco is created by applying pigments directly to wet plaster, which absorbs the colors and dries, resulting in a very durable painting. Studies indicate that many Minoan and other Aegean murals were painted on a final thin coat of wet plaster, similar to the true fresco technique, and in this respect they were distinct from the wall paintings of Egypt or anywhere else in the Near East. We should keep in mind that only fragments of Minoan wall paintings survived by the time Evans began his excavations at Knossos. Undeterred, he commissioned artists to reconstruct several of them, though these attempts are now considered somewhat imaginative and inaccurate.

The Minoans borrowed certain painting techniques from Egypt, but they developed a distinctive style, fresh, vibrant, and intensely naturalistic. Whereas Egyptian creations usually exhibit an aura of stability and permanence, Minoan art shows an enchantment with undulating motion and rhythm. Although a number of the Minoan wall paintings were merely decorative, exemplified by long friezes with spiral or other designs, many others portray sophisticated and elegant compositions of human, animal, and plant life. Scenes from nature often depict frolicking dolphins and other sprightly creatures of the sea. We also see brightly painted birds, powerful bulls, mythological beasts, monkeys imported from Egypt, and native wild goats, all in the midst of luxuriant and sometimes imaginary vegetation. Paintings of palace life abound, offering tantalizing hints of the social and religious life of Minoan Crete at its height. The norm is Minoan youthful beauty. Death and the disabilities of aging are never shown, and many of the frescoes seem devoid of much serious purpose or concern for the frailties of life. Instead we find vigorous, seemingly carefree young men and women engaged in festivals, sacred dances, religious ceremonies, and athletic events.

Young men appear unbelievably wasp-waisted in the frescoes and wear the customary Minoan male costume, namely, high-laced boots, a dagger at the waist, an abbreviated loincloth cut to expose the thighs and often turned up at the back like an animal's tail, a prominent and exposed codpiece resembling a narrow, stiff jockstrap, and sometimes for more formal occasions an intricately patterned short skirt that left the codpiece uncovered. The formfitting codpiece, a genital guard, was frequently worn without a loincloth. Occasionally young men went about naked. Bare-chested and slender, youthful males wore their hair in flowing dark locks falling over their shoulders and were usually beardless.

Both men and women dressed to reveal rather than to conceal their bodies. Women, who always appear in the frescoes with prominent, completely exposed breasts, wore long flounced skirts, apron-girdles, high open bodices, and sometimes highly elaborate coiffures. They also used pigments for facial cosmetics. Men and women wore jewelry such as necklaces, earrings, armlets, bracelets, and anklets. Clothes were usually made of wool, but wealthier Minoans may have worn linen garments imported from Egypt. As in Egyptian art, males are shown in frescoes with red-brown skin, females with much lighter skin.

Dated about 1550 BCE, this considerably restored fresco from the palace at Knossos shows a young male walking in a flower garden. Evans identified the figure as the Minoan "Priest-King," though without convincing evidence that the figure was a priest or king. Archaeological Museum, Heraklion, Crete.

Drawing of the celebrated Minoan female figure known as *La Parisienne*, the best-preserved portion of a fresco depicting a ceremonial scene of uncertain significance discovered at the Knossos palace. The young woman wears a kind of sacred knot at the back of her neck, perhaps signifying that she is a priestess or even a goddess. The original, dated about 1550 BCE, is one of the treasures of the Archaeological Museum at Heraklion, Crete.

Despite the exuberant revelry and pageantry of the frescoes, some of them suggest a darker side in Minoan life. The famous *Bull-Leaping Fresco*, found at Knossos, depicts the acrobatic spectacle now termed bull-leaping, in which supple young men and women seem to have taken turns—probably in the central courtyards of palaces—facing the flaring nostrils and unbridled power of a massive bull. In this fresco we encounter a youth, painted red-brown, and two maidens, dressed as males and painted white, all of whom appear to be barely past puberty. This and other surviving images of the acrobatic feat, perhaps exaggerated, suggest that the leaper grasped the lowered horns of a fully charging bull and, as the mighty head came up, somersaulted—or was vigorously thrown—over the horns, landing on the animal's back either hands or feet first before somersaulting into the arms of a companion. The *Bull-Leaping Fresco* shows an airborne male in the process of making a tremendous vaulting leap over an enormous bull, while a female at the rear of the animal holds her arms out to assist him and another female grasps the bull's horns in the breathtaking instant before being thrown over the animal's back herself.

Minoan Religion.   In the absence of detailed textual evidence, the wealth of relevant artifacts and cult places discovered in Crete are subject to different interpretations, though they clearly indicate Minoan life was steeped in religion. Representations on sealstones and other objects suggest that Cretan worship was dominated by female divinity, closely connected with natural forces and fertility. Evans argued that female divinity was expressed by a single great goddess taking various manifestations, but many scholars now think the evidence hints at distinct goddesses reflecting a developed

The Minoans were by no means entirely pacific and enjoyed dangerous athletic contests in palace courtyards, reflected in this famous *Bull-Leaping Fresco, c.* 1550 BCE, from the palace at Knossos. Both males and females participated in the perilous acrobatic feat. Archaeological Museum, Heraklion, Crete.

polytheistic religion. Apparently Minoan religion was closely associated with the concept of a great mother-goddess, a figure worshipped throughout the Near East from earliest times as a promoter of crop, animal, and human fertility. Probably arriving on the island with the first farmers, the Minoan mother-goddess seems to have been connected with the moon and other heavenly bodies and to have lived on the high places, where she tamed animals. She had much in common with the later Greek goddess of the wild called Artemis, another deity associated with the moon. Homer describes Artemis as Mistress of the Animals because of her role in protecting game. The Cretan mother-goddess, whom the Minoans probably addressed as Artemis, also played the role of a Mistress of Animals and is often depicted on sealstones in the presence of wild animals. Apparently her authority extended over the palace and the home, the mountain and the field, the sky and the sea, and even life and death. Perhaps as an expression of her cult, the Minoans produced large numbers of objects used as offerings. The surviving examples were generally made of clay and include male and female figurines, parts of the body, animals, and small vessels. Many of these were burned in sacred bonfires on mountain peaks. The later Greek worship of Artemis also involved similar bonfires on high places. At least a substratum of the complex Cretan belief system probably survived in Greek religion.

Images on sealstones suggest the Minoan mother-goddess, or possibly a separate deity, was a dominant figure in association with a young male deity—her son or consort—known to archaeologists as the Cretan Zeus. The later Greeks believed Crete was the place of Zeus' birth and boyhood. Yet the Cretan Zeus—possibly a descendant of the thunder-god worshipped in early Asia Minor—differs in many respects from the mature Zeus of the traditional Greek pantheon. Unlike immortal

Drawing of the upper part of a Minoan figurine representing a goddess, or perhaps one of her human attendants, who holds writhing snakes in her hands and supports a spotted feline on her head. The figure wears the Minoan court costume depicted in the frescoes, with wide flounce skirt (not shown) and open bodice. Discovered at the Knossos palace and dated about 1600 BCE, the original figurine was made of a type of glazed earthenware known as faïence and is now displayed in the Archaeological Museum at Heraklion, Crete.

Zeus, the divine youth dies and is resurrected each year in the spring to ensure the renewal of the vegetation cycle. Perhaps in Crete, like the Near East, the fertility of humans and crops was thought to depend upon the sexual union of the mother-goddess and the young male. In certain respects the Cretan Zeus seems to resemble the later Greek fertility god Dionysus, also a dying god.

    Sometimes the mother-goddess, or perhaps a separate deity, appears with doves, proverbially the most sexually active of birds. She may have been either identified with or distinct from a goddess shown with snakes writhing in her uplifted hands or draped about her body. Later Greek women often carried snakes coiled around their hands and arms as a practice of the ecstatic cult of Dionysus, who could appear in the form of a snake. Shedding its old skin and promptly developing a new one, the snake in ancient times was considered a manifestation of resurrection and thus of immortality and fertility. These characteristics, combined with its phallic nature, rendered the snake a potent religio-sexual symbol. Other sacred Minoan symbols include the single pillar—perhaps regarded as an emblem of procreation based on the phallic associations of the post—and the bucranium, a bull's head with horns.

The two symbols most closely associated with Minoan religion are the double axe and horns, both perhaps imports from Asia Minor. The walls and columns of the Knossos palace were adorned with images of the double axe, probably an ornamental form of the implement used for animal sacrifice. The double axe never appears in the hands of a male figure in Minoan art and seems to have been reserved as a symbol of the great power of female divinity. The Minoans also placed monumental stylized bull horns of stone—Evans called them horns of consecration—around their shrines and palaces as religious symbols. Some investigators regard them as the horns of a sacred bull, while others interpret them as the raised hands of the mother-goddess or compare them to the horns associated with the Egyptian goddesses Isis and Hathor. Thus both the double axe and the horns of consecration may have symbolized female divinity.

The Minoans worshiped at various places. Images on sealstones and rings suggest they considered all elements of nature holy and especially venerated trees, pillars, and boulders. Certain of their cult practices were conducted at small sanctuaries on mountain peaks. We saw that devotees employed great bonfires at these sites to burn clay figurines of animals and humans. They also offered agricultural produce and made animal sacrifices at the peak sanctuaries, apparently to propitiate and honor the mother-goddess. The Minoans treated many caves as sacred places, and they built small temples in the towns and the countryside. They also set aside special rooms of palaces and larger houses as shrines. Among these chambers were those now called pillar crypts, for each was designed with a central rectangular pillar. The ashes of animal sacrifices were deposited under the floors of the pillar crypts in the west wing of the Knossos palace, while the prominent pillars bore engraved double axes.

Apparently much of Cretan worship centered on the palaces. Clearly, the west wing of each was reserved for religious rites, suggesting to some investigators that the Minoans had a theocratic administration. The willingness of the people to participate in the stupendous outlay of effort required to build a palace may have stemmed from the belief that they were building a great divine home for the mother-goddess, a complex where the ruler would reside as her representative.

The meaning and scope of Minoan religious rites are poorly understood. A priestly class provided intermediaries between the community and the divine powers. A fresco at Knossos shows priestesses, in addition to priests in feminine costume, carrying a chalice to figures probably signifying deities. This ceremony may represent a sacred communion. As noted, some scholars suggest the Minoans accorded divine status to the bull, a powerful symbol of fertility in an agricultural community. The significance of bull-leaping in Minoan society is not comprehended but may have been part of a central religious ritual witnessed by the public from the courtyard of the palace. The unarmed acrobats must have been gored to death at times, and a number of investigators argue that the game was a form of human sacrifice, possibly to a bull-god. Perhaps the story of the terrible sacrifice of the Athenian youths and maidens to the bull-monster in the Theseus myth was based upon knowledge of the fearsome activity of bull-leaping. Although Evans portrayed the Minoans as a pacific and life-loving people, archaeologists exploring a temple south of Knossos found the remains of a youth offered as a human sacrifice. We are uncertain whether such rites were frequent or were reserved for times of extraordinary crisis. Excavators at the Minoan town of Knossos discovered a mass of children's bones bearing many knife marks, possible evidence of an interment ritual, or of sacrifice and cannibalism.

Diet.   As noted, the Minoan economy depended primarily upon the cultivation of the famous Mediterranean triad of grain, grape, and olive. The last named served the multiple purposes of cooking, cleaning the body, and lighting. The staple Cretan grains were wheat and barley. Popular fruits besides grapes included figs, apples, pears, and pomegranates. Wine was produced from the fermented juice of grapes, and honey served as a sweetener. Fish and meat supplemented the diet. Various animals were hunted for food, hides, and furs. Domestic animals were bred for wool, milk, meat, and other products, as well as for sacrifices and pulling loads.

Prominence of Women.   The supreme position of female divinity suggests the importance of women in Minoan society. Women of elite status received many honors in their own right. Wall paintings portray them serving as priestesses. As such, they must have exercised considerable influence in courtly circles. Evans discovered a number of miniature frescoes at Knossos depicting women on a larger scale and in more elaborate detail than men. Overall, Minoan art indicates women played a prominent role in Crete.

Minoan Rulers.   Later Greek tradition tells of a powerful Cretan kingship, but Minoan artistic representations seem to portray an elite class made up of both men and women. While some historians speculate that the Minoans were ruled by queens or queen–high priestesses, others argue for kings, the latter hypothesis based partly on Minoan paintings depicting a male wearing what appears to be kingly costume. Yet Minoan art never shows a kingly figure presiding over ceremonial scenes. Although clear evidence is lacking, some scholars propose that perhaps a shadowy king served merely as the queen's consort, or that perhaps he was dominated by other officials and functioned as a ceremonial figure without real monarchical power. Each of the great administrative centers in Crete—Knossos, Phaistos, Mallia, and Zakro—probably had its own ruler, whether a man or a woman, who apparently exercised considerable political and spiritual authority over the surrounding area and conducted sacred ceremonies in the palace. As noted, Cretan palaces seem to have served not only as dwellings for rulers and their retinues but also as administrative centers of

Drawing of a Minoan marine-style octopus jar, from Gournia, with the vivid tentacles of the sea creature embracing the curving surface of the vessel, providing a sense of continuous movement and suggesting a relationship between the decoration and the shape of a vase. Dated about 1550 BCE, the original is now in the Archaeological Museum at Heraklion, Crete.

regional importance, manufacturing concerns, storehouses for food and goods, and religious complexes. The palace at Knossos was by far the largest during this period. Its ruler must have played an important role throughout Crete and perhaps even dominated the entire island.

Social Organization.   One might make the reasonable inference from palace architecture and art that Minoan society was highly stratified. Ranking below the ruler must have been a vast array of local leaders and nobles, scribes and bureaucrats, and religious functionaries. Artisans of all kinds formed another group, with traders and merchants providing them with imported raw materials. A large class of agricultural workers supplied the palaces with produce. Apparently slaves were bought and sold to serve in various capacities such as agricultural workers, domestics, and rowers on ships. The palace officials—perhaps drawn from the members of the ruling family and the nobility—must have directed the duties not only of the agricultural workers but also of other groups, exemplified by the scribes and traders and the artisans producing luxury items.

Pottery.   Baked clay vessels were used for many purposes, from the preparation and storage of food and drink to the practice of religion. By the New Palace period potters were painting dark forms on a light background in a manner reflecting Minoan fascination with the dynamics of nature. Besides producing vases of a lively plant style exhibiting floral motifs, Minoan potters made others decorated in a sprightly marine style incorporating a great variety of sea creatures such as dolphins or octopuses, the latter seemingly spreading their dark tentacles over the curving surfaces of a vessel and thereby serving to emphasize its elastic volume.

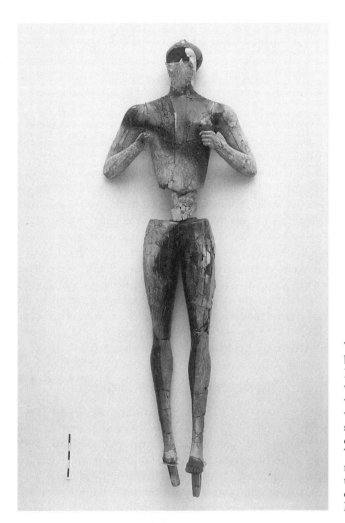

This ivory statuette of a boy in motion, found at Palaikastro, originally wore garments of gold, while the head and eyes were crafted of gray serpentine and rock crystal, *c.* 1550 BCE. The rich array of materials suggests that the figure served as a cult image. Sitía Museum, Crete.

Jewelry. Talented Minoan jewelers, patronized by persons of high status, produced gold diadems, beads, hair ornaments, pendants, bracelets, and other pieces. The jewelers were masters of the art of hard soldering, a technique used to ornament a surface with either patterns of fine wire (filigree) or minute globules of gold (granulation). They also excelled in the inlaying of decorative materials in metal cells (cloisonné) and in the embossing of sheet gold with designs and figures by means of punches or with molds or stamps (repoussé).

Sculpture. Minoan sculptors produced brightly colored clay figurines of humans and animals, most apparently used in the service of religion. These pieces tend to be stiff but reasonably lifelike. The artisans creating the figurines echoed an artistic convention of ancient Egypt by depicting males with a red-brown complexion and females with a much lighter one. Archaeologists have found other varieties of sculpture such as fragments of large clay statues at the sites of certain peak sanctuaries. Minoan sculptors sometimes crafted statuettes of ivory and gold, exemplified by a boy in motion, possibly the Cretan Zeus, found at Palaikastro. The naturalistic treatment and anatomical accuracy of the young male—reflected in the lifelike carving of tendons, veins, and even fingernails—prefigures the realistic art of the Greeks by a thousand years.

Shipbuilding and Trade.   Apparently the palace bureaucracy oversaw the building of seagoing ships for long Aegean trading voyages. A Minoan sailing vessel—often attended by friendly, frolicking dolphins—was a masterpiece of nautical design with its rounded hull, lofty mast, and unornamented prow and stern. Slender and sleek, each was propelled by oars and a square sail, and the larger merchant ships were decked. The Minoans were so artistically and technically skilled that their products were in demand beyond the Aegean. Goods for the overseas trade—wine, olive oil, metalware, and pottery—were shipped from palace storehouses. We know that Crete continued to enjoy a flourishing trade with Egypt, for long-haired Minoans appear on the murals of a number of fifteenth-century BCE Egyptian tombs, and several Egyptian inscriptions of the period refer to trading relations with "the land of Keftiu [usually identified as Crete] and the isles, which are in the midst of the sea." Minoan artistic influence was widespread in the Aegean world. Excavation near the modern village of Akrotiri on the Cycladic island of ancient Thera (now called Santorini) has revealed a thriving ancient town, with buildings three stories high and frescoed walls decorated in Minoan style.

DECLINE OF THE MINOAN CIVILIZATION (c. 1630–1150 BCE)

Major Eruption on Thera (c. 1630 BCE).   The volcano on the island of Thera— roughly seventy miles north of Crete—erupted about 1630 BCE, burying the settlements of that small island under many feet of fine ash, then pumice. This date is based on the scientific techniques of radiocarbon dating (calculating the time elapsing since the death of organic matter by measuring its remaining radioactive carbon) and dendrochronology (determining the age of timber remains by studying the sequences and differences of its growth rings). The evidence suggests that the conventional date for the Thera eruption, about 1500 BCE, and the entire framework of traditional Aegean chronology is roughly a century too late and requires adjustment, a tentative scheme followed here.

The cataclysmic seventeenth-century BCE eruption on ancient Thera was one of the largest in recorded history and may have caused heavy destruction and loss of life on Crete, possibly by triggering earthquakes. Perhaps many Minoan ships at sea or in exposed harbors on the north coast of Crete suffered damage or capsized. Some scholars speculate that the wind-borne ash falling on Crete impoverished agricultural production for a number of years until washed and blown away by rain and wind. Although terrifying, the eruption of Thera was followed by a period of extensive rebuilding in Crete.

Increasing Influence in Crete of Mycenaean Greeks (c. 1550–1500 BCE).   In the sixteenth century BCE the Minoans began to lose their ascendancy in Aegean and eastern

Mediterranean trade to the Mycenaean Greeks, now taking to the sea and spreading their products from Egypt to the Levant. After fifteen centuries of spectacular evolution, the Minoan civilization entered a period of declining prosperity and splendor. About 1550 BCE disaster struck the Minoan palaces, towns, and country houses, though Knossos escaped extensive damage. Most sites were destroyed by intense fire and abandoned for many years. The cause of the devastation remains uncertain and controversial. A group of Mycenaean Greeks may have conquered Crete, or perhaps they took control following calamitous earthquake activity or some other catastrophe. Mainland influence in Crete during this period is clear. The Mycenaean Greek language made inroads and eventually tended to prevail. Tablets in the Linear B script soon replaced those of Linear A, providing the clearest indication of Mycenaean presence and suggesting that the mainlanders, centered at Knossos, now managed the production and distribution of goods. The later Greek traditions about King Minos may refer to a ruler or a dynasty of rulers imposed by the Mycenaeans on the Minoans. The probable Mycenaean rulers were preoccupied with war and built up stores of military equipment. We also find changes in pottery as well as the introduction of mainland-style chamber tombs and the burial customs associated with them. During this period prosperity and settled conditions were gradually restored on the island. Meanwhile Cretan skills, harnessed to Mycenaean needs, made major contributions to the cultural life of the mainland.

Fall of Mycenaean Knossos (c. 1500 BCE).   About 1500 BCE the palace at Knossos was mysteriously destroyed by fire and never rebuilt, possibly by rebellious Cretans or by rival Mycenaeans from the mainland. Mycenaean influence after the fall of Knossos seems to have been slight. Apparently the various geographical regions of Crete were left to function under local rulers, and for many years the island exercised only marginal technical and artistic influence in the Aegean. By the thirteenth century BCE, however, Crete seems to have reclaimed a degree of its old external cultural activity, indicated by pottery exports, and was enjoying a relatively prosperous and peaceful existence.

The Destruction of Cretan Settlements and the Arrival of Another Wave of Mycenaeans (c. 1200–1150 BCE).   This tranquil scene was disturbed about 1200 BCE, when many Cretan settlements were again destroyed and abandoned. New Mycenaean influences suddenly appear in pottery, apparently the result of refugees escaping from serious but poorly understood disruptions on the Greek mainland. Wealthy Mycenaean citadels were burned, possibly by rival mainlanders, and trade was disrupted. The troubles on the Greek mainland did not represent an isolated phenomenon. Contemporary cultures in the eastern Mediterranean were also experiencing widespread destruction at the time, apparently victims of a dramatic movement of ruthless maritime raiders. The archaeological record suggests that these invaders—the Egyptians termed them the Sea Peoples—were a mixed population and possibly included Mycenaean Greeks in flight from collapsing mainland kingdoms. The tumultuous Sea Peoples overran the states bordering the eastern shores of the Mediterranean, inflicting death blows on the great empire of the Hittites of Asia Minor and severely battering ancient Egypt.

The Dark Age in Crete (c. 1150–750 bce)

The collapse of the old Bronze Age civilizations of the eastern Mediterranean resulted in severe depopulation and decline. The Greek world experienced the so-called Dark Age between roughly 1150 and 750 bce, with a lowering of material culture, but also with a modest degree of cultural continuity linking the Bronze Age to both the Iron Age and the historic period. Although elusive newcomers in Crete may have disrupted the social structure and caused various other disorders sometime during this period, the island passed through the Dark Age in a more prosperous condition than the other Aegean regions and also preserved a greater degree of its Bronze Age traditions, notably its mythological and religious fabric. Such surviving elements, rooted in the splendid Cretan civilization that first flowered about 3500 bce, enriched the cultural life of historic Greece.

CHAPTER II

MYCENAEAN GREECE

The Bronze Age civilization of the Greek mainland is now called Mycenaean, from its famous center of Mycenae in the Argolid, the ancient triangular region in the northeastern Peloponnese. Other notable centers included Tiryns and Pylos in the Peloponnese and Thebes and Athens in central Greece. The rulers at these powerful centers lived in imposing palace-fortresses, from which they controlled the surrounding territory and dominated the Mycenaean warrior civilization both politically and economically. Ruling families enjoyed immense wealth, reflected in the dazzling array of gold and other precious objects uncovered in their tombs and in the records of their many possessions, inscribed in the syllabic script called Linear B. The Mycenaeans were not only redoubtable warriors but also bold seafarers whose markets and outposts dotted the eastern Mediterranean and reached westward as far as southern Italy, Sicily, and Sardinia. The amazing exploits of these Achaeans, as Homer called them, left a lasting imprint on the Greek consciousness.

ORIGINS AND HISTORY OF MYCENAEAN GREECE

NEOLITHIC FARMING SETTLEMENTS (c. 7000–3500 BCE)

Bands of hunter-gatherers roamed the Greek mainland following their sources of food during the many millennia of the Paleolithic (Old Stone) Age. With the establishment of Neolithic societies about 7000 BCE, the mainland supported a mosaic of farming villages enjoying agricultural staples from outside Europe, including wheats and barleys, sheep and goats. This transition to farming may have been the result of groups entering Greece from Asia Minor or, less likely, of native societies adopting staples and skills from contact with peoples to the east. The farmers produced simple pottery without the wheel, initially plain in style but later decorated with a variety of geometric designs. They surrounded several of their settlements in Thessaly with defensive walls or ditches, but the typical agricultural village lacked fortifications. Apparently the Neolithic farmers believed the power to give or withhold fertility lay in a force having a woman's form, for they made numerous figurines of the type known as mother-goddesses, usually interpreted as cult objects. During this period mainland farmers established numerous agricultural communities on the fertile plains of Thessaly, central Greece, and the northeastern Peloponnese.

THE EARLY BRONZE AGE (c. 3500–2100 BCE)

The Bronze Age culture of mainland Greece is distinguished from the Minoan of Crete by the term *Helladic*, a word manufactured from *Hellas*, the ancient name of Greece. The chronology is divided into Early, Middle, and Late Helladic, of which the last is generally labeled Mycenaean, after the important site of Mycenae. Similarly, the Bronze Age culture of the central islands of the Aegean is conventionally termed Cycladic.

A number of settlements of the Early Bronze Age (Early Helladic) were surrounded by massive walls with projecting towers, notably the seacoast village of Lerna in the northeastern Peloponnese. Several houses of substantial size were erected at Lerna, each having a series of large rooms laid out in a basically rectangular plan. The so-called House of the Tiles, one of the largest examples, was provided with many rooms and corridors, staircases to an upper floor, a pitched roof with stone and fired clay tiles, a stone foundation, and walls of sun-dried brick covered with yellow stucco. An abundance of imported items discovered here indicates mainland trade with the Cyclades and with Crete. Lerna was destroyed by fire at the end of the Early Bronze Age.

THE MIDDLE BRONZE AGE: EVIDENCE OF NEWCOMERS (c. 2100–1700 BCE)

The three Aegean Early Bronze Age cultures developed along similar lines, though there is no evidence the populations spoke a common language. We find clear signs of immigrants, probably a mixed stock largely from Asia Minor, pushing into mainland Greece sometime during the period extending from roughly 2100 to 1700 BCE. The newcomers are thought to have spoken an Indo-European language that developed into the Greek language (first attested in the syllabic script known as Linear B dating from about the sixteenth century BCE at Knossos). They may have been responsible for plundering and burning Lerna and other mainland centers at the end of the Early Bronze Age, or perhaps they arrived in the wake of the ruinous damage. Apparently the intruders superimposed themselves on the earlier Bronze Age population through superior military techniques. By the Late Bronze Age southern and central Greece had produced a distinctive culture, now called Mycenaean, which incorporated features from the heritage of the newcomers, the Helladic culture of the mainland, and the Minoan civilization of Crete. We should keep in mind, however, that ancient writers did not use the designation *Mycenaean* or *Mycenaeans*. The Greeks referred to their early mainland ancestors by several names. As noted, Homer usually spoke of them as the Achaeans. To the classical Greeks, the early history of their homeland was veiled in mystery, and somewhat contradictory accounts about the past came down to them in the form of epics and legends. One of the main centers about which such legends were told was Mycenae, the strongest settlement of the early Greek speakers. Strategically located, Mycenae overlooked a rich agricultural plain to the south and controlled passage from the narrow Isthmus of Corinth to the north, the only land route to the southern half of Greece.

Reconstruction of Grave Circle A, Mycenae, famous for its rich shaft grave containing multiple burials, presumably all belonging to a single royal family. The massive fortification walls of the citadel were extended around 1300 BCE to enclose the site, though the grave circle and burials are a few hundred years older.

The Early Mycenaean Period: The Age of the Shaft Graves at Mycenae (c. 1700–1600 BCE)

We find a notable increase in wealth and prosperity on the mainland by the opening of the Late Bronze Age (Late Helladic, synonymous with Mycenaean). Many scholars suggest this flowering was tied to the infusion of energetic Greek-speaking rulers who managed to reap rewards through trade or warfare. The dramatic change in culture is clearly reflected in the elaboration of funerary architecture, which signifies the emergence of an elite class. The greatest achievements took place at Mycenae. The scholarly world was astonished when Heinrich Schliemann, excavating in 1876, discovered an imposing cemetery of the Middle and Late Bronze Ages at the site. Here he uncovered a double ring of upright limestone slabs—known today as Grave Circle A—encompassing six deep burial shafts, now called shaft graves. His excavations revealed an opulent array of grave goods, including solemn masks of beaten gold placed over the faces of the men. As noted, Schliemann assigned these treasures to the period of the Trojan War, traditionally set in the thirteenth century BCE, though later archaeologists determined that the shaft graves were centuries older than the reputed date of the expedition to Troy.

The original appearance of Grave Circle A is unknown because important changes took place a few hundred years after the last burial, such as extending the fortification wall of Mycenae to enclose the grave circle and erecting the present splendid ring of limestone slabs to mark the circle. These alterations indicate that Grave Circle A was regarded with particular veneration by the later Mycenaeans. In 1951, excavators at Mycenae discovered an older grave circle—Grave Circle B—whose double ring of upright stones encompasses twenty-four graves, of which fourteen are shaft graves. Set over special graves in both circles were massive rectangular limestone grave markers, some bearing carved scenes of warfare, hunting, and fierce animals.

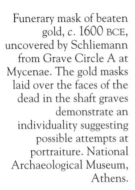

Funerary mask of beaten gold, *c.* 1600 BCE, uncovered by Schliemann from Grave Circle A at Mycenae. The gold masks laid over the faces of the dead in the shaft graves demonstrate an individuality suggesting possible attempts at portraiture. National Archaeological Museum, Athens.

The wealthy and powerful families buried in the shaft graves of both circles are generally identified as early Greek speakers, that is, Mycenaeans. The lower sides of the deep rectangular shafts were lined with stone walls, the floors were spread with a layer of pebbles, and each tomb was closed by a roof. A deceased man was placed on the pebble-lined floor fully clothed, his face covered with a gold death mask, his clothing and body adorned with fine gold ornaments and jewelry. Such shaft graves also contained swords and other weapons of the warrior as well as many gold vessels. The women were buried with bejeweled clothing and grave goods of equal opulence. Many exquisite ornaments in the shaft graves were created or inspired by Minoan artisans, while inlaid daggers and other pieces indicate Mycenaean manufacture. The individuals buried at Mycenae stood at the top of a highly stratified social structure unlike any known on the mainland at an earlier time. The men were nearly six feet tall—giants for their day—and were probably the warrior rulers of Mycenae at the beginning of the Late Bronze Age.

The Period of Mycenaean Expansion: The Age of the Early Tholos Tombs (*c.* 1600–1500 BCE)

Early Mycenaean settlements were widespread in southern, central, and northeastern Greece. These communities were usually located around defensible hilltops or promontories and depended on nearby tracts of agricultural land. Architectural traces suggest the rulers lived in palaces and controlled artisans as well as warriors. Their tombs reflected their wealth and power. The members of a ruling family were no longer buried in a shaft grave but in the much larger beehive tomb, or tholos, from the ancient Greek word for a round building. Although tholoi had first appeared about 1700 BCE in the region of Messenia—possibly inspired by a long tradition of circular communal tombs on the island of Crete—they did not appear at Mycenae until the sixteenth century BCE, when an initial group of nine were constructed.

Most of the tholos tombs in Greece were built into hills. A spacious and deep vertical shaft was dug from the top of the hill to provide room for the actual tomb, a soaring chamber constructed of great blocks of cut stone and shaped like a pointed dome. This domed vault was created by corbeling, that is, by overlapping the courses of stone, so that the diameter of the circle gradually decreased, the final opening at the apex of the tholos being closed with a capstone. When the top of the tomb was then covered with earth, the result was an imposing mound. The covering mound provided sufficient pressure to counteract the structure's outward thrust, thereby preventing its collapse. The tholos was approached by a long passageway known as a dromos, dug horizontally into the side of the hill and generally faced with massive stone walls. The dromos led to a tall doorway topped with a horizontal beam, or lintel. Usually a triangular opening, or relieving triangle, was placed above the doorway to relieve the lintel of weight. Inside the tholos, bodies could be deposited either on the floor or perhaps in shallow interior pits. The majority of these family tombs were used for several generations.

Mycenaean Domination of Minoan Crete and the Aegean.   The few unplundered tholos tombs demonstrate that local rulers were buried with a rich array of grave goods such as Minoan and Mycenaean sealstones, pottery, bronze and stone vessels, exquisite gold jewelry, swords and daggers, ivory boxes, and necklaces of amber beads. Designs during the first half of the sixteenth century BCE indicate that many of the objects were imported from Crete, but a fusion of Minoan and Mycenaean styles becomes apparent during the latter half of the century, reflecting the Mycenaean expansion then taking place. The century witnessed the Mycenaean Greeks successfully challenging Minoan ascendancy in Aegean and eastern Mediterranean trade. As noted in chapter 1, about 1550 BCE most of the sites in Minoan Crete were burned, yet Knossos escaped extensive damage. Although the underlying cause of the destruction is not certain, a group of Mycenaeans occupied the island at the time or soon thereafter. Archaeological evidence suggests the Mycenaeans took up residence at Knossos, organized Crete under their own control, and persuaded or coerced scribes at Knossos to keep records (some still survive as Linear B tablets) in Mycenaean Greek. During their domination of Crete the Mycenaeans learned from the Minoans how to organize and manage a great palace civilization based on written records. The Mycenaeans also took advantage of Minoan technical achievement and artistic skills to intensify the development of their own mainland-based culture. Clearly, Minoan Crete exerted the greatest cultural influence on Bronze Age Greece, though the Mycenaeans also borrowed from the cultures of Egypt, the Levant, and Europe.

The Age of the Great Palace-Fortresses (c. 1500–1200 BCE)

After the shift of power from the Minoans to the Mycenaeans, the latter were the most powerful force in the Aegean, the rulers of an aggressive warrior civilization characterized by massive fortifications and innumerable weapons. Mycenaean exploits left an indelible imprint on the Greek consciousness, and Homer gave their culture the famous epithet "rich in gold." The emphasis in Mycenaean architecture now shifts dramatically from monumental burial chambers to palace-fortresses crowning hills. This network of palaces must have served not only as royal residences but also as administrative, military, and ceremonial centers. Each contained rooms for manufacturing and for the storage of agricultural products and goods. In short, the palaces seem to have duplicated on a smaller scale certain functions of Minoan palaces. Major mainland palace and town sites included Mycenae and Tiryns in the northeast Peloponnese, Pylos in the southwest Peloponnese, Athens in Attica, Thebes and Gla in Boeotia, and Iolcus on the coast of Thessaly. Yet other important settlements, exemplified by Argos located near both Tiryns and Mycenae, were without fortifications or palaces.

Government and Society.   As noted, mainland Greece was divided by geography into distinct compartments. Thus the rugged landscape made political unification unfeasible during the Mycenaean period, but early rulers established monarchies within the various geographical divisions. Their kingdoms took the form of city-states, each consisting of a chief settlement and its surrounding territory. The kings of major centers such as Mycenae and Pylos probably exercised considerable control over lesser rulers. The elusive and scanty documentary evidence concerning the mainland kingdoms comes mainly from tablets discovered at Pylos. The Pylian state, roughly the southwestern quarter of the Peloponnese, seems to have enjoyed a stable society, with an established hierarchy headed by a king, or *wanax*. Apparently each of the Mycenaean kings was known as a *wanax*. The kings of some states—notably Mycenae and Pylos—controlled rather powerful fleets, an important asset considering the difficulty of land travel in much of mountainous Greece. Judging from excavated finds, the mainland kings enjoyed immense wealth. Their treasures probably came from local manufacture and long-distance trade and perhaps also from raiding and piracy.

The *wanax* oversaw a hierarchy of state officials, from great royal lieutenants to lesser officeholders exercising authority in a single town or village. At least some of these officials must have been drawn from a relatively small class of major landholders, or nobles, who may have been obligated to provide agricultural products for the king and to serve him in war. The nobles' rank in society was reflected by their use of chariots. The Mycenaean rulers also called upon the specialized skills of a handful of palace scribes. Writing, inscribed in the Linear B script, is thought to have been far from widespread during the Mycenaean period and used entirely for administrative purposes. The Linear B tablets and material remains suggest that the palaces exercised direct authority over trade and manufacturing by supervising the merchant class and the artisans creating luxury items. Apparently the largest por-

The monumental outer walls of the heavily fortified citadel at Tiryns were hollow in places to accommodate imposing galleries, or passageways, *c.* 1350 BCE. As illustrated here, the roof of each gallery was not constructed as a true arch but was corbeled, with enormous irregular Cyclopean blocks piled in horizontal courses and then overlapped inward until the two walls met at the top.

tion of the population consisted of agricultural workers living in small villages and producing staples such as wheat, barley, olive oil, flax, and wool. The Pylian tablets also indicate the existence of an important class of priests and priestesses serving the various deities. The bottom end of the social scale was occupied by slaves, most of whom seem to have been women. Slaves were numerous and performed various assigned tasks. Some were domestic workers, while others served as artisans. Apparently most were engaged in textile production, chiefly spinning and weaving.

Cyclopean Walls and Other Fortifications at Mycenae.   Apparently the kingdom ruled from Mycenae became increasingly powerful and began to dominate the Argolid, the ancient region in the northeast Peloponnese. This development meant that the smaller citadels and towns in the Argolid—notably Argos, Tiryns, and Corinth—became subordinate to the kings at Mycenae. Who would dare question the authority of a ruler from such a great palace-fortress? Its walls were built of such enormous

The monumental Lion Gate at Mycenae, built *c.* 1250 BCE, supports a carved limestone slab of religious and heraldic significance, with two animals resembling lions (now missing their heads) flanking a pillar.

limestone blocks that the classical Greeks believed them to have been supernaturally created by the Cyclopes, a mythical family of one-eyed giants. Thus the massive stone walls at Mycenae and other Mycenaean sites are termed Cyclopean.

The Lion Gate.   The famous Lion Gate served as the main entrance through the fortification walls at Mycenae. Erected about 1250 BCE, the Lion Gate was fashioned from two huge monoliths topped with a massive lintel, above which the courses of stone form a corbeled arch, leaving a triangular opening serving to lighten the load carried by the lintel. This relieving triangle holds one of the few pieces of monumental sculpture surviving from the Aegean Bronze Age and one of the oldest from mainland Greece. Carved from a single block of gray limestone, this remarkable work takes the form of high relief, that is, sculpture strongly projecting from a flat background. The triangular relief depicts two animals resembling lions on opposite sides of a typical Minoan-style tapering pillar. The heads of the beasts are now missing, for originally they were made separately and attached to the bodies with wooden pegs. Accordingly, scholars are uncertain whether the animals were actually intended to be lions, and their exact form is the focus of endless debate. The pillar and the forepaws of the animals rest upon two altars placed side by side. The subject and the arrangement were frequently used on Minoan sealstones and carved ivories, but here a miniature theme has been translated into a monumental sculptural ensemble expressing the Mycenaean culture. The heraldic beasts, who probably symbolize the ruler of Mycenae, are shown guarding the pillar, possibly an emblem of deity. Clearly of religious and heraldic significance, the sculpture invokes divine power to protect Mycenae and reflects the close association of its kingship with supernatural authority.

The Palaces.   Although the Mycenaean culture differed in many respects from the Minoan civilization, we noted that Mycenaean palaces served as administrative centers on the Cretan model. Visitors to Mycenaean palace-fortresses must have been impressed by the stupendous walls and monumental gates. The palaces themselves were considerably smaller than the courtyard-centered Cretan examples, but each is thought to have contained storerooms, workshops, and living quarters for the ruling family and officials. The often precipitous character of the landscape meant that the buildings were usually erected on artificial terraces, with communication between the different levels afforded by stepped streets or ramps.

All the Mycenaean palaces were based on a relatively rigid plan differing from the more flexible and expansive designs of the Minoan palaces. The focal point of each was the megaron, typically consisting of a columned entrance porch, vestibule, and great central hall. Clearly, the hall served as a throne room and contained a wooden throne, a central circular hearth, and usually four columns supporting the roof. The vestibule joining the porch and the hall bustled with activity during the day because people could gain access to the rest of the palace through its side doors. The few windows on the first floor of the Mycenaean palace meant that much of the building was only dimly illuminated, though additional light was provided by hearths and stone lamps. The typical palace was decorated with wall paintings executed by Minoan artists or in the Minoan style. Some of these resemble the earlier Cretan frescoes, though many depict non-Minoan subjects such as hunting and battle.

Pylos is the best preserved of the major palaces. Uncovered by the American archaeologist Carl Blegen in 1939, Pylos is the traditional home of King Nestor, wise old hero of Homer's *Iliad*. A small entrance courtyard at Pylos led to the megaron, of typical design with its porch, vestibule, and central hall. Apparently the wooden columns in the center of the hall supported a balcony over the hearth, presumably permitting people in upstairs apartments to view activities below and admitting light from a lantern, or windowed structure crowning a roof. The central hall of the megaron provided an appropriate setting for the king to entertain exalted guests and dignitaries. Smoke from the hearth escaped through a chimney

A reconstruction of the highly decorated central hall of the megaron of the palace at Pylos, showing columns, hearth, and throne, c. 1400 BCE.

above the balcony. The floor, hearth, beams, and ceiling were brightly painted with designs such as flames and spirals. The stuccoed surfaces of the walls at Pylos were enlivened with colorful scenes of hunting and battle, perhaps reflecting legendary tales sung by a court bard, and the throne was flanked by painted griffins.

The Mycenaeans demonstrated remarkable ingenuity in obtaining water. They tunneled through rock to reach water sources at Mycenae, Tiryns, and Athens. At Pylos water was brought from a spring by a wooden aqueduct. Archaeologists found a clay bathtub at the same site, recalling Homer's memorable description of fair Polycaste bathing Telemachus in King Nestor's palace. Evidence of an effective drainage system was discovered at Pylos, Mycenae, and Tiryns.

The general population of Mycenaean Greece lived in hillside villages and looked to the palace-fortress as a place of refuge in time of attack. As noted, the citadel was the indispensable focal point of each Mycenaean kingdom, providing for its administration, prosperity, and defense. The descriptions of sumptuous palace-fortresses in Homer seem to be based upon distant memories of Mycenae and the other great citadels of mainland Greece.

The Treasury of Atreus.   The spectacular tholos tombs at Mycenae range in date from roughly 1600 to 1225 BCE. The tholoi became increasingly large and elabo-

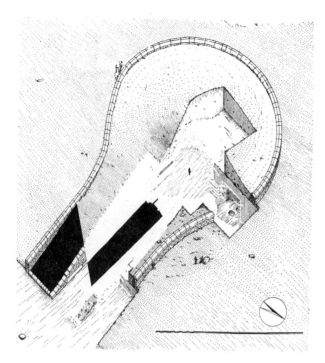

Architecturally, the Treasury of Atreus, dated about 1300 BCE, is the finest of the spectacular tholos tombs at Mycenae. This cutaway view demonstrates how such tombs were constructed. A wide vertical shaft was dug from the top of a hill to accommodate the actual tomb, a soaring corbeled vault, which was covered with earth to form an imposing mound. The tomb was approached by a great passageway driven into the hillside.

rate, culminating in the magnificent thirteenth-century BCE monument known by local villagers as the Tomb of Agamemnon and to scholars as the Treasury of Atreus. Both designations seem to lack historical foundation. Heinrich Schliemann popularized the latter name, though his misunderstanding was based upon an account of Pausanias, a Greek traveler and writer of the second century CE who visited Mycenae and was told that the tholoi were strongholds where Atreus and his sons safeguarded their treasures, not the final resting places of powerful kings and their families.

The so-called Treasury of Atreus at Mycenae, the best preserved and most famous of the tholoi, demonstrates the skill that Mycenaean architects and engineers had attained by this period and proclaims the importance of some powerful king. The approach by its dromos of huge dressed stone blocks is almost 120 feet long and ends at a monumental doorway over seventeen feet high. Apparently the doors of the tomb were made of bronze-clad wood. The massive stone lintel over the doorway was made in two sections, of which the inner has been calculated to weigh over one hundred tons. The splendid façade is some thirty-four feet high and was faced originally with colored, elaborately carved marble, pieces of which survive in the British Museum. The huge relieving triangle above the doorway was once masked by a decorative slab of red marble carved with spirals, and the doorway was flanked by half-columns of green marble carved with crisp zigzag patterns. The capitals on these columns appear to be directly ancestral to the Doric capital of the later Greeks.

The long approach passageway of the Treasury of Atreus at Mycenae ends at a monumental doorway. Today the façade looks bare, stripped of its marble facing, half-columns, great doors, and decorative slab masking the overhead relieving triangle.

The huge vault of the tomb is overwhelming in its grandeur and precision. Approximately forty-eight feet in diameter and forty-three in height, this vault is the largest unsupported, covered space constructed anywhere until the Pantheon was erected in Rome roughly 1,400 years later. The now austere surface of the vault was originally decorated with bronze rosettes, some of which remained in place as late as the early nineteenth century. A unique feature of the Treasury of Atreus is its rectangular side chamber cut into the hillside, perhaps to house previous burials.

Other Mycenaeans were buried in smaller tombs cut into sloping hillsides and entered down a dromos. These chambers were used over and over again, the older skeletons simply being pushed aside. Objects thought to be needed in the afterlife—exemplified by figurines, jewelry, weapons, and pottery—were placed in the burial chamber, and aromatic substances were heated to fumigate the tomb at the time of a new burial. Apart from the tholoi and chamber tombs, we also find some mainland burials in rectangular graves cut in the earth and lined with stone slabs.

Religion.   Apparently the Mycenaeans adopted certain elements of Minoan religion, especially symbols. Minoan and Mycenaean religious scenes engraved on sealstones and gold rings are almost identical and include goddesses and attendants, flowers and animals, and sacred trees. Yet Mycenaean Greece, unlike Minoan Crete, has few identifiable cult sites. An important discovery was made at Mycenae, where an entire cult center of buildings stood in a cramped space within the massive forti-

Nineteenth-century depiction of the interior of the Treasury of Atreus at Mycenae, its great dome created by corbeling, or overlapping courses of stone.

fication walls. The complex includes what appears to be a shrine or temple, with a central offering table as well as platforms of varying heights along the walls to support statues. Excavators found a crudely modeled female clay figure here. Other rooms contained a single female statue portrayed with elegantly painted jewelry and robe, many coiled clay snakes, the remains of a cult fresco featuring female figures, and large numbers of tall male and female clay statues having grotesque heads and outstretched arms. The last named are now generally interpreted as representations of worshipers rather than deities. Perhaps at least some cult statues were made of wood and thus have disintegrated. Thousands of much smaller clay figures— mainly of standing women—have been found throughout Greece. Although such figurines probably had a religious function, scholars disagree about their significance. The popularity of female figurines may reflect belief in a great goddess or perhaps several goddesses.

The Pylos tablets indicate that Mycenaean Greece was characterized by a fully developed polytheism. A number of divine names are known from the tablets, including Zeus, Hera, Poseidon, Athena, Artemis, and Hermes, possibly among the greater deities of the Mycenaean world. These names were borne by several notable divinities honored by the later Greeks, though we should not assume the Mycenaean gods and goddesses approached the forms of the like-named classical deities. The Pylos tablets also include the names or titles of a number of elusive divine figures. Male deities are prominent in the Mycenaean texts, though rarely represented in art.

The Pylos tablets refer to a class of priests and priestesses, with males and females presumably serving deities of their respective genders. One aspect of worship involved making offerings of various kinds. Animal sacrifice was an important feature of the Mycenaean religion, and the blood of a victim was apparently collected for libations, that is, pouring liquid offerings during sacred ceremonies. Other offerings seem to have included agricultural products such as honey, olive oil, fruit, grain, and wool. Human sacrifice—a familiar element in the Homeric epics—may have been practiced as an extraordinary measure in times of extreme crisis, for the Pylos tablets mention an offering of thirteen gold vessels and eight human beings to a series of deities. Plausibly, many scholars suggest the great circular hearth of the palace megaron had a sacred function. The classical Greeks revered the hearth as an offering place for libations and small gifts of food.

Dress.   Mycenaean frescoes indicate that aristocratic women generally dressed in Minoan style, with bare breasts, embroidered tight bodice, and multicolored flounced skirt. Cooler weather witnessed high-ranking women covering their shoulders with fine shawls bordered with a fringe of tassels. They adorned both their bodies and clothing with gold ornaments and other jewelry, while decking their hair with ribbons and huge embossed diadems of gold. Aristocratic men wore comparatively little jewelry, though they were buried with gold armlets and pectorals. They usually kept their hair shoulder length and often grew beards, customarily shaving the upper lip. In warm weather men donned only a loin cloth or a short kilt, but for formal dress they clothed themselves in a short tunic—woolen in the winter and linen in the summer—and often wore leggings as well.

The Exploitation of Animals and the Diet.   Animals were employed for food and many other purposes. Domestic animals included oxen for plowing, sheep for wool, pigs for sacrifice, goats for hair and horns, and small horses for pulling light chariots. Apparently ordinary Mycenaeans ate little meat, chiefly after special occasions such as a sacrifice. Yet vivid scenes on frescoes and inlaid daggers depict aristocratic Mycenaeans, accompanied by their hounds, hunting game such as wild boar, red deer, lions, geese, and ducks. Wild animals were killed to protect livestock from attack and to obtain hides, tusks, furs, and meat. Apparently fish supplemented the diet. The Mycenaeans ate some cheese, presumably made from the milk of goats and sheep. Cultivated crops served as the mainstay of the diet. The Mycenaeans enjoyed peas, beans, and lentils, but their chief crops were wheat, barley, figs, olives, and grapes. Food was enhanced by spices such as cumin and coriander, and honey served as a sweetener. The tablets indicate that women ground wheat or barley into flour and that men baked it into bread. Wine was made from grapes, and the red poppy was a source of the narcotic opium.

Weapons and Warfare.   In classical times the Mycenaeans were remembered as warriors who had attacked Troy. Frescoes and other remains strongly suggest they were quite militaristic. Aristocratic Mycenaean warriors wore basically conical helmets, each covered with small plates of boar's tusk or faced with bronze and having bronze cheek pieces. A warrior protected his shins with a pair of greaves, his upper body with a figure-eight shield made of hide stretched over a wooden frame. Archaeologists excavating at Dendra near Mycenae opened a chamber tomb, datable to about 1400 BCE, which contained the astonishing remains of a warrior wearing not only a complete suit of bronze armor but also a helmet plated with boar's tusk and having bronze cheek pieces. This panoply reminds us of Homer's description of "bronze-clad Achaeans." The Dendra armor—though of ungainly appearance and requiring heavy internal padding—shielded the body from head to thighs with its fitted cuirass (breastplate and backplate), separate high collar, hinged shoulder guards, and encircling bands of flexible bronze to protect the abdomen and groin. This unique find notwithstanding, bronze armor does not seem to have been widely used. Most Mycenaean warriors probably wore leather tunics, sometimes reinforced with bronze strips or plates.

The principal offensive weapons of this warrior civilization were bows, heavy thrusting spears, short two-edged swords, and decorated daggers of all descriptions. The military equipment of Mycenaean kings included fleets of costly war chariots. Although the axled, two-wheeled Mycenaean chariot was of high prestige value and played an important role in ceremonial settings, its practical military value must have been quite limited. Pulled by two horses, the chariot was unsuitable for massed formation on the broken terrain of the mainland but perhaps was used—as in the *Iliad*—for conveying heavily armed elite warriors to and from battlefields, while the large mass of regular soldiers presumably moved on foot. All fighting was not on land, for some Mycenaean kings could mount great seaborne expeditions with their powerful fleets of warships, each vessel of which carried a crew of rowers.

Frescoes.   Turning to art, the walls, floors, and ceilings of Mycenaean palaces were heavily decorated. Palaces and some houses were provided with frescoes in Minoan style and technique, though these paintings often lack a spontaneous and fluid quality. Popular themes from the Cretan pictorial repertoire include religious processions of richly dressed women, but we also find scenes alien to the Minoans, notably of battle and hunting. Following a convention originating in Egypt but derived from Crete, Mycenaean frescoes usually depict males with a red-brown complexion and females with a much lighter one. The most brilliant Mycenaean fresco finds come from Mycenae. A private house within its fortification walls yielded a well-known fresco fragment showing the expressionless face of an elegant woman—perhaps a goddess—whose exquisitely rendered hand seems poised to touch her necklace.

Pottery.   Much of our knowledge of the Mycenaeans comes from their pottery. Pottery workshops hummed with activity at all the chief Mycenaean centers, producing ware in quantity not only for home use but also for export. Mycenaean pottery has been found all over the eastern half of the Mediterranean and westward at least to southern Italy. The decoration of early Mycenaean pottery shows great Cretan influence, but the spirited marine and plant motifs favored by the Minoans gradually became simplified beyond recognition. The Mycenaeans also developed a crude pictorial style that gives the impression of reproducing on pottery various subjects from wall painting. Belonging to this style were specially decorated vessels—many for export to Cyprus and the Near East—featuring animals, humans, or riders in chariots. Scenes of bulls were especially popular, and painters occasionally show a bird vigorously picking parasites from the back of a bull.

The basic shapes of Mycenaean pottery generally represent developments of earlier forms. For storing liquids, the Mycenaeans favored the stirrup jar, a closed vase with a cylindrical spout on the shoulder. For drinking, they preferred the kylix, an elegant cup in the shape of a shallow bowl, which was also the most common form of drinking vessel in the later Greek world. They produced a large mixing bowl known as the krater, a shape common to Crete as well. The classical Greeks used kraters for mixing wine and water, their usual beverage. In addition to basic shapes, the Mycenaean potters made specialized pieces such as the rhyton, a ritual vessel with a normal mouth or opening, in addition to a small hole for pouring liquid offerings. Adopted from the Minoans and usually made of clay or fine stone, rhytons were often conical in shape or took the form of the head of an animal.

Figurines and Sculpture in Relief.   As noted, the potters created tall clay statues for the Mycenaean religion. They also made clay figurines of animals and humans, including great numbers of abstract standing females painted with vivid red patterns. Such works, many of which were deposited in tombs, represent the most common types of Mycenaean freestanding sculpture. As for relief sculpture, we saw that the most famous example is provided by the two lions in the relieving triangle of Mycenae's Lion Gate.

Stonework, Jewelry, and Metalwork.   Artisans on the Greek mainland carved graceful vases from amethyst, agate, alabaster, and other fine stones. Engraved sealstones and gold rings were also in demand. Although Mycenaean jewelers frequently made beads of glass or brightly colored stones, the typical necklace was fashioned of gold, with decorative patterns imposed on the linked gold beads by means of repoussé, granulation, and enameling. Meanwhile metalworkers created exceptionally fine pieces. As noted, Schliemann's excavation of the shaft graves at Mycenae yielded a dazzling array of objects in gold and other metals, notably the famous funerary masks. The Mycenaean metal industry—many of its techniques acquired from the Minoans—produced not only tools, weapons, and body armor but also handsome vessels of bronze, silver, and gold.

The Mycenaean warrior kings highly valued their swords and daggers. Archaeologists have uncovered superb examples, especially daggers, brilliantly decorated with precious metals and rare stones. Cutouts of figures in silver or gold were hammered into the prepared surface of the blade and engraved with details. The incisions of the engravings were then filled with a black decorative compound, which was burned in with heat. Such techniques were developed during the shaft grave period, probably by skilled metalworkers from elsewhere, perhaps as far away as

This splendid bronze inlaid dagger blade, c. 1600 BCE, comes from Grave Circle A at Mycenae. The scene depicts a spirited battle of men against lions, with four hunters lunging toward a lion that has struck down a fifth hunter, while two other lions turn tail and flee. After the figures used for the inlay were prepared in gold and silver, engraved details were filled with niello (a black enamel-like compound of copper, lead, sulphur, and borax), a technique borrowed from the Near East. National Archaeological Museum, Athens.

Syria. One famous example is a bronze dagger blade discovered at Mycenae. Lavishly inlaid with cutouts of figures and landscape elements in gold and silver, the blade depicts lunging hunters carrying huge shields and battling lions, a scene of unprecedented spirited movement.

The Vapheio Cups. Even more beautiful than the dagger blade are two gold cups, the so-called Vapheio Cups, dating to about 1500 BCE and found in an unplundered tholos tomb at Vapheio in the Peloponnese. Each has a plain lining but a magnificently embossed outer case and a handle attached with rivets. Ranked among the masterpieces of ancient art, the Vapheio Cups may have come from a Minoan workshop. Both the subject—the capture of wild bulls—and the style are unmistakably Minoan. The rendering is relatively peaceful on one cup, which portrays three different episodes in the capture of a wild bull by means of a decoy cow. In the third scene, one of his legs has been tied by a youth dressed in the typical Minoan manner. The capture is more violent on the other cup, which shows a bull brought to the ground in a net, his body distorted in agony, while on either side a bull flees in fright. One of the hunted animals impales a youth and tramples another. Both cups splendidly convey the excitement of the moment, and the modeling of the figures is firm. Moreover, the two highly naturalistic reliefs create a richly textured play of light and shade.

Ivories. Mycenaean artisans employed imported elephant tusks to produce many exquisite carved ivories, including boxes and handles as well as relief plaques used to ornament furniture and various objects of wood. They also created small ivory figures in the round, exemplified by the famous carving from Mycenae of two women with a small boy across their knees, perhaps representing a divine group. The two women, their breasts exposed in the Minoan fashion, and the boy are affectionately grouped together with arms over shoulders in a fluid, almost playful pose.

Commercial Expansion. A balance of power prevailed between the Hittites of Asia Minor and the Egyptians during the age of the great Mycenaean palaces, permitting the eastern Mediterranean to enjoy relative peace. After the Mycenaeans occupied

Detail of one of the two magnificent cups found at Vapheio in southern Greece, with a highly naturalistic scene portraying a youth tying the hind leg of a wild bull he has lured with a decoy cow on the right, c. 1500 BCE. Gold with repoussé decoration. National Archaeological Museum, Athens.

Knossos around 1550 BCE, they expanded their trading ventures and either established settlements or left merchants behind at sites in the eastern and central Mediterranean. Trade was important to their palace economies as a means of obtaining both raw materials and luxury goods and seems to have reached a high point in the fourteenth and thirteenth centuries BCE. Mycenaean pottery went to the Aegean islands, Cyprus, Asia Minor, Syria-Palestine, Egypt, and the central Mediterranean, including Albania, Italy and Sicily, and Sardinia. Some bronze knives and swords were exported to Albania. The Mycenaeans sought metal above all else, especially copper and tin, in exchange for their goods. Much of the copper probably came from Cyprus or Asia Minor in the form of oxhide–shaped ingots. The Mycenaeans also traded with their neighbors for luxury items such as gold, ivory, amber, and gemstones.

The Trojan War and Its Aftermath in Later Greek Literature.   Few literary works have won greater admiration than the *Iliad* and *Odyssey*, which were shaped over many centuries and handed down in song by nonliterate poets until committed to writing in the eighth century BCE. Clearly, the origin of these epics lies in an age when poetry was oral, not written. Oral poetry is characterized by recurring verbal formulas, making the work easier to memorize and refreshing the memories of listeners. Thus we find frequent repetition of epithets, similes, speeches, and episodes in the genre. For an audience, much of the enjoyment came from hearing a bard repeatedly sing such formulaic elements, binding the work together.

As noted, the classical Greeks attributed the *Iliad* and *Odyssey* to a poet named Homer, whose identity remains elusive. Scholars generally approach Homer with

An exquisite ivory triad from Mycenae, generally interpreted as two goddesses with a young god, *c.* 1400–1300 BCE. National Archaeological Museum, Athens.

extreme caution in terms of the history of Bronze Age Greece. Although the *Iliad* and *Odyssey* seem to preserve distorted images of the distant Mycenaean past, the epics are pervaded with powerful gods interfering in human life and contain numerous details portraying society from later centuries.

Greek tradition and the *Iliad* report that the Mycenaeans became involved in a lengthy military engagement against the ancient walled city of Troy in northwestern Asia Minor. The later Greeks considered the Trojan War an actual event in the history of their ancestors. With mounting archaeological evidence of Mycenaean presence in Asia Minor, the possibility of a Trojan War—traditionally dated in the thirteenth century BCE—has become increasingly acceptable to scholars. At this time Troy was a prosperous city overlooking a fertile plain in the strategic northwest corner of Asia Minor. Its rulers must have exercised some control over the

Hellespont (ancient name of the Dardanelles), the vital narrow strait providing convenient passage between Europe and Asia and serving as the water route between the Aegean and the Black Sea. Some scholars suggest the Trojan War tradition stemmed from Mycenaean military activity designed to seize Trojan wealth or from conflicts between the Mycenaeans and the Trojans over access to the Hellespont or fishing rights, but such proposals have been met with healthy skepticism. We have no way of knowing if a kernel of truth lies behind the Homeric and the classical Greek view that war erupted over a mysterious Mycenaean queen.

Although the Greek legend of the Trojan War interweaves divine and human elements, the tale makes sense on a purely human level. We are told that Mycenaeans from all over Greece—Homer usually calls them the Achaeans—are roused to avenge an injury to Menelaus, legendary king of Sparta. His wife, Helen, said to be the most beautiful woman in the world, has been seduced and abducted by Paris, prince of Troy. The Achaean leaders embark for Troy to recover Helen, "the face that launched a thousand ships." When the Trojans refuse to surrender her, the invaders respond by besieging Troy for ten years.

The *Iliad* covers only a few eventful weeks in the tenth year of the conflict. The Achaean Greeks are under the general command of Agamemnon, brother of Menelaus. They enjoy a remarkable asset in the most formidable of all Greek warriors, Achilles, whose mother, the sea deity Thetis, had dipped him in the River Styx at birth, rendering every part of his body invulnerable, except the part of the heel she held. Much of the action of the epic hinges on a disastrous quarrel Achilles has with Agamemnon for taking from him a concubine, part of his legitimate spoils of war. His honor wounded, headstrong Achilles withdraws his men from battle and remains in his tent. This pride and wrath will bring disaster to many of his confederates.

Achilles implores his divine mother to petition Zeus to aid the Trojans, so the Achaeans will realize how much they need him. Except when distracted, Zeus helps the Trojans gain advantage on the battlefield. The Trojan hero Hector soon kills Achilles' beloved friend Patroclus. Grief-stricken Achilles, his own actions responsible for the death of his companion, returns to battle and slays Hector in frenzied fury, dragging the corpse behind his chariot to the Achaean camp. Late at night, the aged ruler of Troy, Priam, comes to Achilles to beg for the return of his dead son. Achilles takes pity on the old king and gives him the body. With the funeral rites of noble Hector—not the fall of Troy—the Homeric epic closes.

Although the *Iliad* ends at this point, the Greek legend continues. Paris soon strikes Achilles' vulnerable heel with an arrow. With the loss of their greatest warrior, the Achaeans attempt to bring about the downfall of Troy by artifice. They sail off to hide behind a nearby island, leaving behind a huge wooden horse, its hollow belly filled with warriors. The Trojans—tricked into believing the mysterious horse is an offering to Athena—pull the gigantic figure inside their walls. That night the Achaean warriors emerge from the fabricated horse to kill the sentries and open the gates. The Achaean army then destroys the city, massacring its men and carrying off its women into slavery.

The second Homeric epic, the *Odyssey*, describes the long-delayed return of valiant Odysseus, legendary king of Ithaca, to his native land. After fighting for ten years at Troy, the Achaean hero is compelled to wander for a decade, undergoing a series of fantastic adventures. Meanwhile his kingdom is being devoured by the many suitors seeking the hand of his faithful wife, Penelope, and plotting the death of his young son, Telemachus. Aided by the goddess Athena, Odysseus finally returns to Ithaca, slays the suitors, and reestablishes himself as king.

The *Odyssey* tells us that many of the other Achaean heroes, having offended the gods, find their return from Troy beset by difficulties. Menelaus, for example, experiences a series of misadventures on his travels back to Sparta. Although Agamemnon reaches Mycenae easily, he is treacherously murdered by his wife, Clytemnestra, and her lover, Aegisthus. Thus Homer pictures the period after the Trojan War as a confused time on the Greek mainland.

The Collapse of the Mycenaean Civilization at the End of the Bronze Age (c. 1250–1150 bce)

The period from about 1250 to 1150 BCE was one of general cataclysm in the eastern Mediterranean. We know that the elusive Sea Peoples—as the Egyptians termed this mixed population—made a series of violent surges through the region at the end of the thirteenth and the beginning of the twelfth centuries BCE. By the time these raiders were finally repulsed from the borders of a battered Egypt in the early years of the twelfth century, they had mortally wounded the great Hittite Empire in Asia Minor, devastated Syria and Palestine, and severely undermined trade in the region. The throng may have included groups of Mycenaeans in flight from collapsing mainland kingdoms.

The Greek mainland shows signs of confusion and disturbances during this period. Pointing to anxiety concerning the threat of attack, the rulers of some centers had embarked on a program of enlarging and extending palace fortification walls by the mid-thirteenth century BCE. Moreover, the authorities at Mycenae threw up a defensive wall across the Isthmus of Corinth, suggesting preparations to protect the Peloponnese against agents of destruction from the north. Some mainland centers were burned in the second half of the thirteenth century, though a much greater wave of destruction took place around 1200 BCE. The destroyed palaces were never rebuilt. The military and political organization of the palace economy disappeared, along with attendant arts such as writing and fresco painting. Meanwhile the remains of palaces lay roofless and disintegrating under the devastating forces of sun and rain.

The cause or causes of the Mycenaean downward spiral remain much disputed, and suggested explanations are always subject to revision in the light of additional evidence or new proposals. Perhaps the collapse was precipitated by developments that were both external and internal, human and natural. Although no archaeological trace indicates incursion by the ferocious Sea Peoples or other outside raiders, we may reasonably suppose that the ruinous damage the Sea Peoples effected in the Near East severely disrupted Mycenaean foreign trade. Some scholars speculate that the disintegration in Greece was tied to deadly epidemics, climatic changes impeding agricultural productivity, or earthquakes and other natural disasters. Others theorize that the various kingdoms were beset by internal social antagonisms or intense stress on their centralized administrative systems. Ancient authorities and a number of modern scholars argue that the major cause was rivalry among the Mycenaean powers, an explanation that cannot be ruled out.

Many settlements and areas were abandoned or severely depopulated in the wake of the destructions of about 1200 BCE, particularly in the southern Peloponnese. Yet Mycenaean civilization survived for nearly a century. Sites such as Mycenae, Tiryns, and Athens continued to be occupied, though in much reduced circumstances. Greek tradition affirms that Athens became a haven for refugees during this period of difficulties at the end of the Bronze Age. Archaeology indicates that many Mycenaeans migrated to or took refuge in remote and hilly mainland regions. Countless others sailed to Crete, the Aegean islands, the west coast of Asia Minor, and Cyprus.

THE DARK AGE (c. 1150–750 BCE)

These widespread migrations mark the early Iron Age, traditionally called the Dark Age, an obscure period of material poverty extending from about 1150 to 750 BCE. Conditions had worsened on the mainland by the late twelfth century BCE, with many of the remaining centers being abandoned, though Athens shows signs of unbroken habitation from the Bronze Age to the classical period. The archaeological picture of this disturbed period remains quite incomplete, leading to clashing scholarly opinions. We know that the political vacuum left by the obliteration of the Mycenaean kingdoms was eventually filled by the Dorians, speakers of a distinctive Greek dialect called Doric. Greek tradition held that they were expelled from the Peloponnese and went north, later returning as invaders of southern Greece, thus far unproven archaeologically. If the Dorians were newcomers, or newly returned, perhaps they filtered in over a long period, or perhaps they were there all along as members of the lower class, seizing opportunities in the wake of the precipitous decline of the Mycenaean world. All we can say with certainty is that by the end of the Dark Age a Doric-speaking population occupied the old Mycenaean heartland of southern Greece, from where they had spread to Crete and other southern islands as well as the southwest corner of Asia Minor.

Although the Dark Age witnessed the eradication of writing and many artistic skills, certain important elements of the Mycenaean culture survived in the classical Greek civilization. The first of these was the basic structure of the Greek language, an unrivaled instrument for the vigorous and precise exchange of ideas. Second, many aspects of classical religion clearly stem from the Bronze Age, including the names of about half of the Mycenaean deities. Finally, myths and legends were passed down in oral poetry to inspire sublime Greek literature and art, for Dark Age bards sang of a former illustrious age characterized by vast fleets, fortified palaces, and mighty monarchs, a time when deities walked with heroes upon the face of the earth. We can hardly doubt that the famous epics preserved for us under the name of Homer reflect, in part, a substratum from the days of Mycenaean warrior princes.

CHAPTER III

THE DARK AGE

We saw in chapter 2 that unknown agents of destruction engulfed the Mycenaean civilization in the late thirteenth and early twelfth centuries BCE. The great palaces were destroyed or deserted, and with them went the ruling classes as well as the scribes and artisans. The scattering of palace bureaucracies meant the loss of writing. Several centuries elapsed between the last Linear B texts, functioning solely as Mycenaean royal records, and the first inscriptions in the alphabetic scripts of the later Greeks. After the collapse of the Mycenaean kingdoms, Greece experienced drastic depopulation, mass migrations to the Aegean islands and coastal Asia Minor, and declining foreign contacts, though certain important elements of the Mycenaean culture were preserved at a reduced level. This period from roughly 1150 to 750 BCE is aptly termed the Dark Age, its swift cultural decline revealed by archaeological exploration. Our knowledge of Greece remains extremely murky until the crystallization of the Greek polis, or city-state, in the eighth century BCE. Yet the Greece known to history was gradually emerging during the long centuries of the Dark Age, culminating at its close with the momentous Archaic period, which witnessed the reintroduction of writing, a vast colonizing movement, and the acceleration of political, artistic, and intellectual developments.

HOMER AND OTHER SOURCES

One major source for the Greek Dark Age is archaeology, which is fraught with problems and provides relatively meager evidence for the period. Another is the monumental epics preserved under the name of Homer, the *Iliad* and *Odyssey*. After the use of writing disappeared on the mainland in the decades following 1200 BCE, transmission of information about the past depended on human memory. Oral poets, using formulaic expressions and other devices to facilitate memory, composed and recited from a stock of legendary material about the exploits of heroes at the close of the Mycenaean period. The Homeric epics are part of this oral tradition. Although rooted in some dim memory of the distant Mycenaean civilization, the *Iliad* and *Odyssey* were shaped over many centuries and contain substantial detail reflecting society in later times, principally the end of the Dark Age. With the development of the Greek alphabet in the eighth century BCE, the Homeric epics were written down, providing us with an amalgamated portrayal drawn from widely separated periods and describing society from an aristocratic point of view.

The Greeks of the fifth century BCE regarded Homer as a blind poet from Ionia, though differing about when he lived and details of his life. Scholars today offer several theories concerning Homer. Some suggest an oral poet dictating verse to a scribe, while others propose an oral poet who had learned to write. Most consider Homer simply a proper name for an oral tradition embracing many poets singing from memory the first great epics of Western literature. Linguistic evidence suggests the Homeric epics were captured in writing at the close of the Dark Age by Ionian Greeks on the Aegean coast of Asia Minor. Whatever the truth may be about Homer, the *Iliad* and *Odyssey* form the bedrock of Western literature, their poetic power lying in the directness of the narrative, the nobility of the characters, and the vividness of the action. Except for the works of the poet Hesiod, active around 700 BCE and concerned with routine farming life, we have no other detailed written documentation of the Greeks until about 650 BCE.

THE DORIAN TRADITION AND THE MIGRATIONS

As noted in chapter 2, colorful Greek legends held that Greek speakers known as Dorians invaded southern Greece from the north at the close of the Bronze Age, destroying the great Mycenaean centers and seizing territories for themselves. Many scholars deny the reality of a Dorian invasion from the north because archaeological evidence is lacking. Historians acknowledge that the Dorians existed, however, and have brough forth various theories to explain their prescence. Some suggest that the Dorians filtered in over a long period or arrived much later. Others think that the Dorians were already in Greece as members of the lower class, perhaps employing force to subjugate the remnants of the upper-class Mycenaean population. Whatever the cause or causes, most of the old Mycenaean centers were destroyed or abandoned, and the few that survived, notably Athens, clearly experienced a pronounced reduction in the scale of life. Apparently Athens and the surrounding triangular peninsula, the region known as Attica, afforded refuge for people escaping collapsing Mycenaean kingdoms. In the meantime the Dorians became dominant in the southern and eastern Peloponnese.

Greek tradition also tells of great numbers of mainlanders fleeing the collapse of Mycenaean civilization by crossing the Aegean to settle on islands and the west coast of Asia Minor. Archaeology indicates that a series of eastward migrations actually took place, beginning around 1100 BCE. Greeks from Thessaly and Boeotia in northern and central Greece, described as Aeolians, sought places of refuge by migrating directly across the Aegean to the island of Lesbos and then to the northwest coast of Asia Minor. Their new territory, including Lesbos, became known as Aeolis. According to tradition, refugees from the Peloponnese were joined by many Athenians in settling on the Cyclades and then on the central west coast of Asia Minor. These Greeks are described as Ionians, and their region in Asia Minor became known as Ionia, later the home of a brilliant Greek culture. The Ionians played such a major part in Greek history that the entire west coast of Asia Minor is frequently called Ionia. Apparently, the intellectual preeminence of both Ionia and Athens in historical times was connected to the migration of many Mycenaeans to these areas during the era of upheavals. The Dorians migrated also during the Dark Age, spreading eastward from the Peloponnese to Crete and other southern islands as well as to southwest Asia Minor and its offshore islands.

THE GREEK DIALECTS

The distribution of Greek dialects in the Classical period is consistent with the tradition of the migrations. Although the dialects differed in peculiarities of pronunciation, grammar, and vocabulary, they were mutually intelligible. The ancient Greeks classified them as Aeolic (the speech of the Aeolians), Ionic (the speech of the Ionians), and Doric (the speech of the Dorians), amended by modern linguists to include Arcado-Cypriot. The last named was an archaic form of Greek surviving in two remote enclaves, Arcadia in the central Peloponnese and the distant island of Cyprus. The Aeolic dialect was spoken in Thessaly and Boeotia, with varying elements of other dialects, and in Aeolis, including Lesbos. The Ionic dialect was spoken, with local variations, in Attica, the long island of Euboea, the Cyclades, and Ionia. The Doric dialect was spoken in the southern and eastern Peloponnese, Crete, and other southern islands as well as the southwest corner of Asia Minor and adjacent islands such as Rhodes.

ECONOMIC, POLITICAL, SOCIAL, AND CULTURAL DEVELOPMENTS

The Economy

Agriculture was the basis of the Greek economy in the Dark Age and subsequent periods of antiquity. After the Mycenaean kingdoms collapsed, Greece was dotted with simple agricultural villages reflecting the reduced circumstances of life. Farmers depended upon small fertile plains and mountain valleys for growing their crops, principally the famous Mediterranean triad of olive, grape, and grain. The typical settlement was located near a high, easily defended hill, providing a place of refuge in times of enemy attack and serving also as a site for shrines of deities and homes of political leaders. Along with writing, monumental stone architecture had vanished, replaced by huts and modest structures made of sun-dried bricks, timber, and thatch. Yet we also find the first signs of a reawakening. The technology of iron smelting was introduced around 1050 BCE. The difficulty of obtaining tin for alloying with copper to produce bronze led the Greeks to turn to iron—which was fairly plentiful in Greece—for making many objects. The complex process of smelting and working iron had been developed earlier in the east and was probably conveyed to Greece from Cyprus and Asia Minor. Iron implements, though not as beautiful as those of bronze, were harder and thus kept their sharp edges longer. Iron became the principal metal for making tools and weapons,

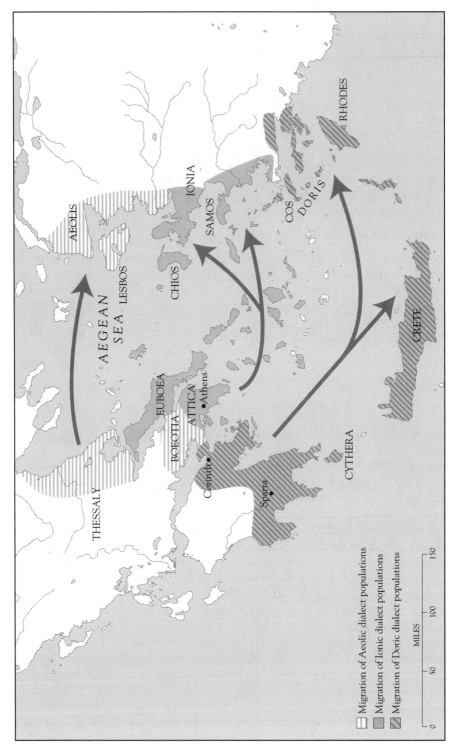

Greek dialects and the pattern of post-Mycenaean settlement.

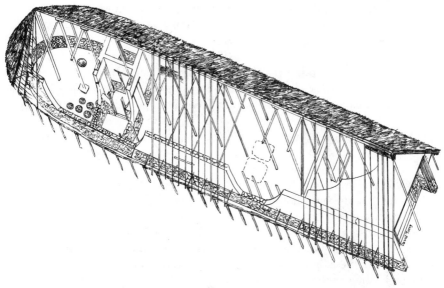

Reconstruction of a cult building at Lefkandi, modern village and archaeological site on the island of Euboea off the east coast of Greece. Buried within this large structure, the center of a cemetery, were a warrior (cremated), a woman, and a number of horses. The size of this tenth-century-BCE building, almost fifty-five yards long and eleven yards wide, suggests a place of heroic worship.

though bronze was still widely used for all sorts of decorative objects. Meanwhile communities of the Greek world formed loose associations to ensure survival, encourage worship, and promote prosperity. The communities of central Greece, which shared a common culture, collaborated to some degree during this period. Scholarly interest in central Greece has been heightened by archaeological exploration on the island of Euboea at the site of Lefkandi, a settlement that enjoyed contact with faraway Cyprus and the Levant and a remarkable level of prosperity in the depth of the Dark Age. Indications of social hierarchy are unmistakable in the sumptuous graves of a man and woman buried about the middle of the tenth century BCE under a large colonnaded building that prefigures later Greek temple design.

The Political and Social Structure

The Basileus.   Political power shifted in the Dark Age from strong centralized monarchies to a nobility composed of a small group of influential families. Although certain local leaders bore the ill-defined title *basileus*, normally meaning king in later Greek, they lacked the sweeping prerogatives usually associated with monarchy and were much closer in function to high nobles. The *basileus* held an uneasy position of supremacy within a small political unit consisting mainly of villages clustered around his house, built more often than not upon a defensive outcrop.

His primary responsibility was providing military protection when danger threatened. He also functioned as a priest, offering sacrifices on behalf of the community to calm the anger of the gods.

The *basileus* knew how to plow his own fields and perform many other tasks, thereby getting his hands dirty like an ordinary farmer. The kings described in Homer are thought to be closer portrayals of the limited rulers of the late Dark Age than the exalted monarchs of the distant Mycenaean period. The king's effective power in the Dark Age must have depended largely on the forcefulness of his personality, his persuasive ability, and his skill in protecting the population during warfare.

The Nobles and the Implied Kinship Groups.   The Dark Age kings faced increasing rivalry from their noble followers. The nobility wielded political power through an intricate pattern of poorly understood social associations based mainly on supposed blood relationship. The Greeks at the beginning of the historical period inherited a number of these implied kinship groups, which were incorporated in their city-states. Clearly, these divisions developed at different times, but apparently all had been established by the Archaic period. Listed from largest to smallest, these included the tribe (*phyle*), brotherhood (*phratria*), clan (*genos*), and household (*oikos*). Other social units were common, such as aristocratic associations of male companions (*hetaireiai*).

The term tribe, or *phyle,* denoted not only a number of large, shadowy groups based on supposed ties of kinship—subdivisions principally of the Dorians and Ionians—but also a later grouping of the citizens of a state into administrative units, about which more will be said in connection with political developments in Athens (see chapter 5). The tribes were often subdivided into the widespread kinship associations known as brotherhoods. The brotherhood, or phratry (*phratria*), probably originated as a military band drawn from allied noble families, its members theoretically kinsmen and worshiping protective deities. By the beginning of historical times the phratry, though dominated by nobles, embraced a much larger segment of society and played a political, religious, and social role in civilian life. The clan, or *genos*, was a subdivision of a phratry and consisted of a group of families claiming descent from a common hero or god. Apparently such unions were formed in the Dark Age by wealthy landowning families to increase their social, economic, and political strength. We know that the clans in early historical Athens were dominated by the aristocracy.

The basic social and economic unit of the farming villages of the Dark Age was the single household, or *oikos*, consisting of husband and wife with their children, dependent relatives, livestock, and lands and buildings. The overriding concern of each household was to maintain self-sufficiency by producing enough food and textiles to feed and clothe its members. If adequately wealthy, the *oikos* was supplemented by tenant farmers, hired laborers, and slaves.

The patriarch, or male head of the household, enjoyed great authority over its members. He represented the household both to the other households of the community and to the gods. Only a male could carry out the religious ceremonies signifying the unity of the family. For this and other reasons, the Greeks considered the birth and survival of a son of supreme importance.

Aristocratic men gained status if successful in attracting male companions, or *hetaireiai*, from their class to join them in typical activities such as warfare, raiding, and piracy. A noble drew these followers through his personal reputation and by offering them lavish entertainments and feasts in his house. Likewise, the power of the nobility was bolstered by the institution of guest-friendship and its prized gift. Traveling aristocratic strangers were cordially welcomed by men of their own class with board and lodging and were presented upon departure with valuable gifts, particularly of metalwork, from the household treasures. The gift-giver expected the guest to bestow similar hospitality upon him or his sons at some future time. The network of relationships formed in such a manner became hereditary, with guest-friendship ties serving almost as rudimentary political alliances among great families.

The Lower Classes.   Besides the small group of aristocratic families, the society of Dark Age Greece was made up of the masses of ordinary people. Most free men were occupied with agriculture and herding, though a few specialists functioned as seers, bards, and healers. Artisans were important but not plentiful, their number restricted by the goal of each household to be as self-sufficient as possible. Barter was the only method of exchange, and a merchant class would not emerge until later.

The *oikos* of the noble surpassed that of the smaller farmer by both the size of its land and the number of its retainers. The noble's house was surrounded by the smaller dwellings of his tenant farmers, who were permitted to keep a portion of their produce but turned the bulk over to their lord. The Greek noble ran his estate with the help of slaves and hired laborers, employing the latter principally during busy agricultural seasons. The hired laborers, lacking land or profession, were the most despised and downtrodden social group of the period. By contrast, slaves occupied a valued place in society, though their lot varied from place to place. Women were relatively common as household slaves, for the traditional practice in Greek raiding and warfare was to kill the males and enslave the women and children. Female slaves served as concubines, weavers, and domestics. The tasks of adult male slaves often involved heavy labor such as agricultural work. A few highly regarded male slaves ran farms and were permitted to have their own wives and children.

Free Women.   Homer suggests there was a time when women from noble families enjoyed a relatively high social status. Sometimes outspoken, they freely participated in festive and religious events. Yet the free woman in the late Dark Age— even those representing the aristocracy—were of low social standing and legally under the care of a male. Besides their other duties, women were responsible for grinding grain and preparing food, producing textiles and clothing, and supervising the children and female slaves. Respectable women in later Greek society were generally confined to their own quarters and excluded from male social activities.

Political Organization.   The *basileus* could not hope to maintain his authority without the support of his nobles. Presumably he summoned a council of nobles to meet with him in an advisory capacity. Judging from Homer, individual members of the council often rebuked the king or disobeyed his commands. Under weaker kings, the council might gain greater authority or even the right to compel obedience to its will. Apparently major decisions of the king and council were announced to an assembly of the fighting men, a body seemingly having no formal power but existing to test the support of the people, for the political system recognized the importance of public opinion.

The Legal System: Regulation of Disputes.   Neither the king nor the council enacted or enforced law. Conduct was supposed to be guided by custom and religious conceptions. Dark Age Greeks would have been mystified by the modern understanding of crime as a violation of a body of law, nor did they have any machinery of justice for inflicting punishments on behalf of the community. The administration of justice was the responsibility of families. Even homicide was a private affair, the murderer forced either to go into exile or to face the vengeance of the victim's family. Choosing the latter course often led to a disastrous cycle of killings and reprisals threatening the entire community. For that reason kings or nobles might be called upon to mediate in disputes between individuals, their principal task to determine the compensation due for injuries. The murderer was exiled if unable to pay the price. The decisions of the mediators gradually produced an oral body of precedent providing the basis for the later development of Greek law.

RELIGION

Mythology.   Through the ages people have created traditional stories called myths about gods and heroes and the creation of the world. The ancient Greeks produced a mythology making a priceless contribution to western civilization. Its rich imagery and esthetic quality has inspired a host of ancient and modern artists, philosophers, poets, and dramatists. Greek mythology is set in an earlier day, when the gods were playing a more aggressive role in human affairs. The myths tell of deities who were fully anthropomorphic with clearly defined personalities and human form. All of the great deities—with the exception of the lame metalworker Hephaestus—were models of beauty. The gods and goddesses appeared in the guise of immortal human beings, though their stature, physical perfection, and power were incomparably greater than that of ordinary men and women. Yet like mortals, the deities were susceptible to the foibles of ungovernable appetites and tender emotions. They needed sleep, suffered pain, and often fell prey to seduction or flattery.

A nineteenth-century engraving of Mount Olympus, celestial home of Zeus and most of the other major gods.

The abode of the great divinities was the summit of Mount Olympus, where they feasted on ambrosia and nectar under the watchful eye of Zeus but were subject to constant quarrels among themselves. Limited by ethical shortcomings similar to those plaguing mortals, the gods could be capricious in their relationships with humans, aiding those they loved and distressing others. Yet divine society sanctioned prominent aristocratic ideals such as justice and honor. The deities occasionally protected the righteous or avenged evil, as when Zeus sent rainstorms upon the unjust during the harvest season. Moreover, the gods could be influenced by humans through sacrifices and oaths.

The Afterlife.   Many elements of Dark Age religion were inherited from Minoan-Mycenaean practice and belief. Apparently the notion of Elysium, also known as the Elysian Fields, was passed down from the Minoans. Homer describes Elysium as a beautiful place without pain or suffering located at the ends of the earth. The gods sent favored heroes here after death and made them immortal. Later epic poets were more generous and opened Elysium also to the virtuous.

A completely different Greek conception of the afterlife was that of a murky underworld, known in later mythology as the realm of Hades. Shades, or ghosts, were thought to survive temporarily in this subterranean land of the dead. Following the death and cremation of their bodies, shades were carried by the aged ferryman

Charon over the rivers of the lower world. They experienced a bodiless and joyless existence in gravelike Hades. Thus in Book XI of the *Odyssey* the shade of Achilles cries out, "Better be a hired man on a poor farm on earth than king over all the strengthless dead." Convinced that life on earth was worth living for its own sake, the early Greeks regarded death as a terrible boundary for most mortals, not a paradisiacal release from life.

Homer.   Although every Greek activity was linked to the cult of some deity, the Greeks had no settled body of doctrine concerning faith or ethics. Yet they could turn to the epics of Homer for guidance in conduct and for information about the world of the gods. Not unjustly, the epics have been called the bible of the ancient Greeks. In fifth-century BCE Athens, as reported in the conversations of Socrates by Plato, ethical questions were settled with quotations from Homer, and for centuries the epics provided moral instruction for the young.

VILLAGE EXPANSION IN THE LATE DARK AGE

In contrast to the wealthy Mycenaean centers of an earlier day, the Greek villages in the late Dark Age were small and scattered. The king in Homeric society served as the leader of a small political unit, enjoying far less exalted status than the rulers of major Mycenaean centers. Homer describes kings digging their own gardens and aristocratic women washing their own laundry. Yet at least some villages were beginning to expand, a development exemplified by Old Smyrna (modern Izmir) on the west coast of Asia Minor. Here archaeologists discovered a small oval house consisting of one room. Built around the end of the tenth century BCE, this dwelling was provided with walls of sun-dried bricks and a roof of thatch, typifying the simple architecture of the period. The ninth century BCE witnessed Old Smyrna coming under the control of the Ionian Greeks, who fortified the settlement with a surrounding wall of sun-dried bricks that boasted an outer facing of large stones. The densely populated town was dotted with rectangular stone houses of several rooms. The brilliant culture of later Ionia would emerge from such beginnings.

CULTURAL PHASES

The Protogeometric Style (c. 1050–900 BCE).   As noted, archaeology indicates that the Dark Age witnessed a general pattern of deterioration followed by gradual recovery of material culture. Most evidence of artistic change in the period comes from pottery. The earlier part of the Dark Age, ending around the middle of the eleventh century BCE, was marked by a declining Mycenaean style known as Sub-Mycenaean. While skills for working in gold, frescoes, ivories, and monumental architecture were lost for centuries, pottery was necessary for survival and continued to be produced after the collapse of the Mycenaean civilization, though Sub-Mycenaean ware was awkwardly shaped and decorated.

Archaeologists commonly divide the remainder of the Dark Age into two main cultural phases, the Protogeometric and the Geometric, both named after pottery styles.

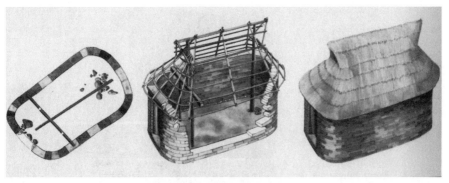

Plan and reconstruction of a small late-tenth-century BCE house at Smyrna, near modern Izmir on the west coast of Turkey. This oval structure of sun-dried brick contained one room and probably supported a thatched roof.

The pottery now called Protogeometric grew out of the Sub-Mycenaean style around 1050 BCE, the beginning of a long span of creativity leading to the astonishing cultural developments of Archaic and Classical Greece. Protogeometric vases seem to have originated in Attica. Such Attic ware demonstrates a noteworthy advance in proportional harmony. Attic and other Protogeometric vases are also characterized by the simplicity and rhythm of their decoration. Artists beautifully adorned the pottery with repeated geometric patterns, notably wavy lines, thin horizontal lines, crosshatching, lozenges, and compass-drawn concentric circles and semicircles. They created the geometric decoration by applying bold and dark glossy patterns over a lighter clay body, a technique handed down from Mycenaean times. They added to the dynamic quality by leaving much of the surface blank or by providing broad bands of dark and light.

Most of the discovered pieces of the Protogeometric style come from the Ceramicus cemetery, the main burial ground in ancient Athens. Here the dead were cremated and then buried singly in stone-lined pit graves—archaeologists call them cists—replacing the communal family tombs so common in the Mycenaean world. Cremation was, for adults, almost universal in the cemetery from the early Protogeometric phase until about 800 BCE, when inhumation came into fashion once more. Protogeometric pottery was interred in graves to hold the human ashes. The graves in the Ceramicus cemetery were graced also with several varieties of bronze ornamental pins, or fibulae, used to fasten garments, and they contained iron swords and daggers, for ironworking had been introduced in Athens during the eleventh century BCE, about the same time that cremation became the general burial custom in the city. Although bronze was still the principal metal for many objects, Greece was slowly passing into the Iron Age. Perhaps indicating a return to the sea by some Greeks, archaeologists have discovered Attic Protogeometric vases over much of the eastern Mediterranean. Thus the Aegean world—despite its poverty—was again becoming economically interlinked.

The Geometric Style (c. 900–750 BCE).   Geometric art, which developed out of the Protogeometric style, belongs to the ninth and eighth centuries BCE. The term

Around the middle of the eleventh century BCE a new style of pottery, now called Protogeometric, was developed in Athens and spread swiftly through Greece. The ware was beautifully ornamented with simple linear decoration. Various types of Protogeometric amphoras, or two-handled vases, were employed in graves to hold the ashes of the deceased. The early tenth-century-BCE amphora shown here was discovered in the main Athenian cemetery of the period. Kerameikos Museum, Athens.

Geometric refers to the tendency of the painter to shift from circular to angular and rectilinear ornamentation. Unlike Protogeometric artists, Geometric painters left no blank spaces and employed zigzags and interlaced patterns called fretwork to cover the entire vessel. Other prominent geometric motifs included diamonds, dots, lozenges, and slender black lines. By the early eight century BCE Geometric painters were regularly inserting files of abstract animals and birds around the vase, though retaining the field of tight geometric patterns. Severely stylized silhouettes of human figures also show up as decorative themes, usually within the conspicuous central bands ringing the vase. Thus painters were already incorporating what became the focus of later Greek art: representations of humans, deities, and animals. Although Geometric pottery was produced throughout the Greek world, Attica was the most prolific manufacturer.

The Dipylon Master.   After inhumation replaced cremation as the prevailing funerary custom in Athens about 800 BCE, mourners regularly placed two-handled storage vessels—amphoras—over graves. These huge vases had perforated bottoms, permitting rainwater to drain off and offerings of oil or wine to seep down to the remains of the deceased. Of great elegance, a typical Geometric grave amphora was full-bodied and often supported a lofty neck and slightly flaring lip. Many of these

The predominant style of pottery produced in the ninth and eighth centuries BCE, now termed Geometric, was covered with abundant ornamentation. After inhumation replaced cremation as the main funerary custom of Athens around 800 BCE, monumental amphoras served as grave markers. This superb Geometric amphora by the so-called Dipylon Master was placed over an Athenian burial of about 750 BCE. The artist conveys the complicated scene of a grand funeral with the simplest design, introducing human figures constructed of triangular torsos with attached heads and limbs. A small panel at the handle level shows the deceased (whose gender is uncertain) on a bier, which rests on a cart for transportation to the grave, while the mourners show their grief by ritually tearing their hair. Roughly five feet tall, the vase reflects not only the skill of the potter but also the prosperity of the bereft family. National Archaeological Museum, Athens.

pieces were found outside Athens in a small eighth-century burial ground called the Dipylon Cemetery, from its location beyond the later Dipylon Gate. A talented artist conventionally known as the Dipylon Master and perhaps a small group of artists working in the same style produced many monumental vases to adorn the graves. The Dipylon Master depicted battle scenes on land and sea, survivors mourning corpses on biers, and funeral processions with chariots and marching warriors. Standing five to six feet high, the vases attributed to the Dipylon Master excel both technically and artistically.

CHAPTER IV

THE FERMENT OF ARCHAIC GREECE

The Dark Age ended with an accelerated artistic, political, and intellectual flowering associated with the period known as Archaic, lasting from about 750 to 480 BCE. Despite the static connotation of the designation *Archaic,* this was a revolutionary age of cultural ferment and experiment. The Archaic period, while leaving both triumphs and failures in its wake, was marked by the emergence of many of the institutions that would shape Greece. One of the first signs of the closing of the Dark Age was a renewal of trade between the Greek mainland and the Near East in the ninth century BCE. Another was the return of writing to Greece, the earliest recovered example coming from a pottery inscription of around 750 BCE. A momentous achievement, the reintroduction of writing was based on the use of an alphabet borrowed with modifications from the Phoenicians, great seafarers inhabiting a narrow coastal plain along the eastern Mediterranean in what is now Syria and Lebanon. The new alphabet permitted the individual representation of all the main speech sounds—vowels and consonants—of the Greek language. A third indication of the dissipation of the Dark Age was the famous colonization movement, beginning in the eighth century BCE.

THE EXPANSION OF THE GREEK WORLD

SOCIOECONOMIC CONDITIONS PROMPTING THE COLONIZATION MOVEMENT

Hesiod Details the Impoverishment of Farmers. The colonizing movement was related to the plight of Greek farmers. The first farmer known by name in European history, Hesiod, is also one of the earliest known Greek poets. Probably active around 700 BCE, Hesiod tells us in his verse that his father had settled in the village of Ascra in Boeotia. Hesiod spoke for the ordinary person, though the nobility still dominated Greek society. Unlike Homer, concerned with the immortal deeds of mythical heroes in a departed glorious age, Hesiod presents an account of routine farming life in his lengthy poem called *Works and Days.* The title comes from the two main sections of the poem, in which Hesiod describes the yearly *works* of the farmer and lists lucky and unlucky *days* for various activities during the lunar month. Partly written as a warning to nobles that their activities are undermining society, *Works and Days* is addressed to Hesiod's unethical brother, Perses. Hesiod

PHOENICIAN *Letter-Name*		GREEK *Letter-Name*		ROMAN
ALEPH	𐤀	ALPHA	A	A
BETH	𝟅	BETA	B	B
GIMEL	𐤂	GAMMA	Γ	C
DALETH	𐤃	DELTA	Δ	D
HE	𐤄	EPSILON	E	E
VAV	𐤅			F
				G
HETH	𐤇	ETA	H	H
TETH	⊕	THETA	Θ	
YOD	𐤉	IOTA	I	I
KAPH	𐤊	KAPPA	K	K
LAMED	𐤋	LAMBDA	Λ	L
MEM	𐤌	MU	M	M
NUN	𐤍	NU	N	N
SAMEK	𐤎	XI	Ξ	
AYIN	O	OMICRON	O	O
PE	𐤐	PI	Π	P
SADE	𐤑			
KOPH	𐤒			Q
RESH	𐤓	RHO	P	R
SHIN	W	SIGMA	Σ	S
TAW	Τ	TAU	T	T
		UPSILON	V	V
		PHI	Φ	
		CHI	X	X
		PSI	Ψ	
				Y
ZAYIN	I	ZETA	Z	Z
		OMEGA	Ω	

About 775 BCE the Greeks adapted their versatile alphabet from the Phoenician alphabet, a northern Semitic script. They employed letters from the Phoenician alphabet to represent the consonant sounds of Greek and used other Phoenician letters for the vowel sounds, which the Phoenician alphabet lacked, thereby creating the earliest truly phonetic alphabet. Later, the Romans and other Italian peoples adapted Greek signs for their own alphabets. The Phoenicians employed twenty-two letters, the Greeks twenty-four, and the Romans twenty-three. During the medieval and modern periods the letters J, U, and W came to be clearly distinguished from other signs, thereby completing the twenty-six letter alphabet used in this book.

tells us that Perses had bribed the nobles to gain more than his rightful share of the farm left to them by their father. Hesiod rails against the nobles for ignoring justice and settling disputes to the advantage of their own class. The poet insists that Zeus is an ethical god concerned with justice, an idea influencing the later development of Greek religious thought.

After Hesiod denounces the judges and invokes the eternal justice of Zeus to punish wrongdoers, he devotes most of the rest of the poem to ordinary farming, advising Perses—who by this time has squandered much of his ill-gotten gains—how to survive by honest agricultural labor. Thus the poem develops into an account of how farmwork should be tackled throughout the year. Hesiod presents a rather grim view of agricultural life. Although Hesiod's own farm supported an ox and a few slaves, the poet insists that farmers cannot reap even a bare living without exercising tight-fisted thrift and performing constant physical labor. He advises farmers to limit themselves to one son, for few in the agricultural calling can accumulate sufficient wealth to support two male offspring.

Seeking a general explanation for the harshness of life and the tribulations befalling men, Hesiod presents a famous misogynist myth in *Works and Days*. He tells us that Zeus had first brought evil into the world by creating woman. The first woman, Pandora, was molded from "water and clay" to become the mother of the disastrous order of women. Her mind was infected with "a dog's shamelessness and the deceit of a thief." She was created as "an object of painful love and exhausting desire" to punish men—present and future—for transgressing Zeus' laws. Pandora crushed the former state of earthly bliss by releasing the evils and diseases of the world from a great jar, often incorrectly identified as a box. The misogyny voiced in Hesiod was a common attitude in the Archaic period and remained so throughout Greek antiquity.

Hesiod relates that humanity has passed through five distinct ages—Gold, Silver, Bronze, Heroic, and Iron—each representing a progressive decline over its predecessor. In the faraway Golden Age humans had lived almost like gods without care or trouble, but in Hesiod's day they struggled to survive in a harsh era of anxiety and pain, the age of "the black metal iron. . . ."

Displacement of Farmers.   Hesiod lived at a time when the patriarchal head of each Greek farming household oversaw the duties of all its members. After the patriarch died, his land was divided equally among his sons. The successive divisions of land brought numerous problems—especially for larger families—because the inheritances of land became increasingly smaller. In a few generations many farmers were reduced to a mere subsistence level or, even worse, driven from their farms altogether. A large number of impoverished former farmers resorted to piracy or were incapacitated by burdensome debt. The nobles, on the other hand, entered into profitable marriages, seized the best land for themselves, and made considerable gains from their mediation of disputes. They took bribes and administered the customary law to their own advantage. They increased their wealth by lending their surplus food at high rates of interest to their less advantaged neighbors. When debtors were unable to pay, the nobles annexed their lands or sold the unfortunates into slavery. Many displaced farmers wandered about as beggars, hired laborers, or mercenary soldiers.

Growth of Manufacturing and Trade.   The nobles' acquisition of wealth permitted them to obtain better manufactured goods. To help meet this demand, some of the urban poor began manufacturing articles on a small scale, competing with the domestic economy based on the family. Eventually the more successful artisans were able to take on assistants and set up workshops. Other individuals became full-time traders or merchants, some ultimately rivaling the nobles for wealth and political power.

The principal impetus for industrial growth came from Ionia on the west coast of Asia Minor. The Ionians, who employed the inland Anatolian Plateau for the herding of sheep, rapidly developed an important textile industry in their coastal cities. The textile producers in city of Miletus, for example, were praised for weaving fine woolens beautifully dyed in hues of scarlet, violet, purple, and saffron. The Milesians were also celebrated for their elaborate embroideries used in decorating hats and robes. Milesian furniture, notably beds, represented another highly valued export.

Later, but across the Aegean, we find additional developments in manufacturing and trade. The island of Aegina off the southeast Greek coast and the settlement of Chalcis on the island of Euboea earned distinguished reputations for their excellent bronze work. In the meantime Attica, though still overwhelmingly agricultural, exported oil, wine, and fine pottery. Geography helped make the city of Corinth in the northeast Peloponnese a major trading center. Located on the narrow isthmus connecting southern and central Greece, Corinth dominated the trade route over this land bridge. Moreover, the city took advantage of its two harbors—one on the Saronic Gulf and the other on the Corinthian Gulf—to control communications between the eastern and western seas. Above the Isthmus of Corinth stood the city of Megara, whose rocky soil spurred the impoverished inhabitants to turn to the manufacture of coarse woolens and heavy vases.

By the mid-eighth century BCE the Greek world embraced a contrasting and complex society of wealth and poverty, nobles and slaves, farmers and beggars, plus a new merchant and trading class. Travelers visiting any city found a seething mass of human misery, a condition ultimately producing the class hatred characteristic of subsequent Greek history. The nobles heightened the tension by denying political rights to the lower classes. Yet Greek seafarers were becoming increasingly skilled, and their ventures opened the way for large numbers of Greeks to overcome the misfortunes at home by migrating to new lands.

COLONIZATION (c. 750–550 BCE)

The eighth century BCE seems to have been a period of dramatic population increase, one notable result being insufficient land to support all the Greeks. While much of the soil was barren or stone-infested, the richer land was either unbearably crowded or in the hands of aristocratic landlords. By 750 BCE many inhabitants of the settlements on the mainland's east coast faced virtual starvation. The vexing problem of overpopulation was relieved by the colonization of lands outside Greece. At this time the Mediterranean and Black seas sustained a number of thinly populated islands and coastal regions not altogether different geographically and climatically from Greece. With the mists of the Aegean beckoning, some of the more

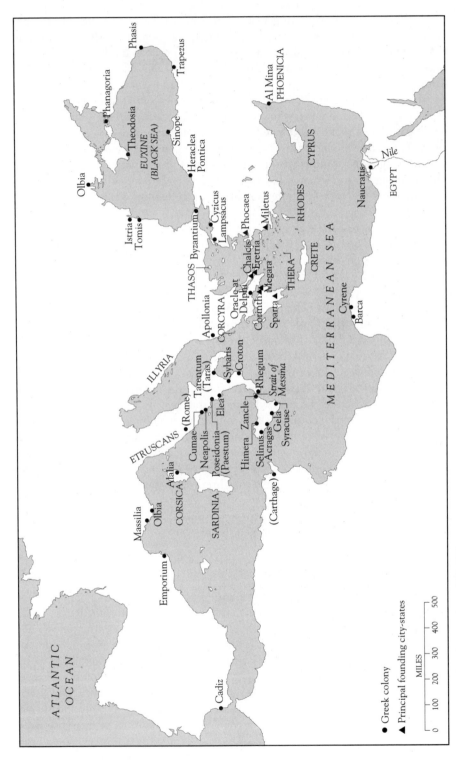

Principal Greek colonies, about 750–550 BCE.

daring sailed abroad to found colonies extending from the straits of Gibraltar to the shores of the Black Sea.

Exploration and Trade.   A host of Greek seafaring adventurers had already explored this long stretch, beginning in the ninth century BCE. When such mariners ex-plored distant waters, no doubt they carried Greek wine, olive oil, textiles, metal-work, woodwork, and pottery—exports enabling them to return home with the luxury goods and metal demanded by the nobility. The use of manufactured goods for payments in trading ventures encouraged the further development of Greek in-dustry. Meanwhile Greek traders were discouraged from sailing along the Mediter-ranean coast of Africa, the route to the great Phoenician colony of Carthage. Phoenician power generally restricted them to the northern Aegean, the Black Sea, southern Italy, and eastern Sicily.

Al Mina.   One notable exception was the famous international trading post at the site of Al Mina—its ancient name is unknown—near the mouth of the Orontes River in northern Syria (now part of Turkey). The Greeks established a presence at Al Mina by the early eighth century BCE, living and trading alongside Cypriots, Phoenicians, and others from the eastern Mediterranean. The Greeks carried home many examples of eastern metalwork and other wares decorated with motifs utterly unlike the then prevalent Geometric style. Soon eastern influence caused a virtual revolution in Greek art (commonly called the Orientalizing style), especially on decorated pottery. Meanwhile the Greeks at Al Mina and similar sites in the region became acquainted with the Phoenician writing system. We saw that by the eighth century BCE the Greeks had learned to express their ideas in an alphabet based on that of the Phoenicians. This period of relative tranquility along the north Syrian coast ended when the reinvigorated Assyrian Empire raided to the west and con-quered the region in the second half of the eighth century BCE, though the Greek merchants were allowed to remain at Al Mina. Apparently the Phoenicians, ha-rassed at home by the Assyrians, turned to concentrate on trade with the more peaceful markets in the western Mediterranean.

Procedure for Establishing a Colony.   Between about 750 and 550 BCE thousands of Greeks migrated to establish scores of colonies in places where no power was suffi-ciently entrenched to stop them, namely the coasts of the northern Aegean, the Black Sea, eastern Sicily and southern Italy, southern France, northeastern Spain, and Libya. The first settlements were designed principally to further trade, but Greece soon began planting colonies to obtain much needed agricultural land to feed its growing popula-tion. Every Greek colony was sponsored by a mother city. Eventually the procedure for organizing a colonizing venture became traditional. The mother city first sought di-vine sanction for the project from the god Apollo through his oracle at Delphi. An or-acle was a deity's utterance issued through a human intermediary in response to an inquiry. Whenever an inquirer at Delphi—the most sacred oracular shrine in Greece—asked a question, Apollo spoke through the frenzied reply of his priestess. Apollo's per-mission having been gained, a leader called the *oikistes* (founder), usually an ambitious noble, led the expedition and selected the site. The powerful *oikistes* brought fire from the altars of the home state and some of its soil to the new settlement. He assigned land to the colonists, established the laws and religious cults of the mother city, and set the political machinery in motion. Although the colonies were usually politically independent, they remained closely linked by commercial and cultural ties to their mother cities. Meanwhile the new settlers helped spread Greek speech, customs, and wares over a large part of the Mediterranean world.

The Aegean Colonies.   The nearest potential area of Greek settlement was the north Aegean. The earliest colonies here were founded in the eighth century BCE on a distinctive three-fingered peninsula pointing downward. Because most of the settlers were natives of Chalcis on the island of Euboea, the triple peninsula became known as Chalcidice. The colonists prospered in this land of many harbors and fertile plains. The seventh century BCE witnessed migrating islanders from Paros in the Cyclades planting a colony on the island of Thasos, northeast of Chalcidice, a rich prize blessed with important gold and silver mines. Meanwhile various mother cities established colonies along the coast of Thrace.

Colonies on the Black Sea and Its Entrance.   The Greeks began securing the approach to the Black Sea in the early seventh century BCE by planting settlements, particularly from Megara. This colonizing effort took place along the three connecting bodies of water separating the Aegean from the Black Sea and Europe from Asia: the Hellespont (a narrow strait now called the Dardanelles), the Propontis (an intermediate sea now called the Sea of Marmara), and the Bosporus (a second narrow strait). The Megarians, perhaps assisted by other Greeks, soon founded the important colony of Byzantium (renamed Constantinople by the Romans, Istanbul by the Turks) on the European side of the Bosporus. Eventually rising to great importance as a trading port, Byzantium became wealthy from its plentiful supply of migrating tuna, used both for domestic consumption and for export. Additionally, the city commanded the entrance to the Bosporus and, consequently, to the Black Sea because powerful currents forced ancient vessels toward its excellent harbor, enabling the inhabitants to levy tolls. A thousand years after its founding, Byzantium—under the celebrated name Constantinople—became the capital of the Roman Empire.

The Greeks called the Black Sea the Euxine (Friendly to Strangers) in a vain attempt to placate the evil spirit of its stormy and unpredictable waters. Seafarers from Miletus brought tuna home from the Black Sea and soon created a trading empire in this foggy region. Their principal settlement on the warm southern shore was Sinope, which eventually became strong enough to send out its own colonists. A number of other Milesian foundations flourished on this coast, each serving as the terminus of a trade route from the interior. The northern shore of the Black Sea, though harsh and cold, offered a rich black soil capable of producing abundant harvests of grain. The first settlement on this coast was the Milesian foundation of Olbia, enjoying river access to the hinterland. The Milesians consolidated their holdings around the northern reach of the sea by founding cities in the Crimean area of southern Russia toward the end of the seventh century BCE. The Scythians, who occupied fertile plains in southern Russia and Ukraine, transported grain and raw materials hundreds of miles from the interior on great rivers emptying on the northern shore, trading for Ionian exports such as metalware and textiles. Eventually most of the desirable coastal lands of the sea were dotted with colonies. In return for wine, olive oil, and manufactured products, the colonies shipped huge amounts of wheat and barley to Greek cities. This bountiful food supply from the Black Sea made possible the scintillating cultural expansion of sixth-century BCE Ionia and fifth-century BCE Athens.

The Colony at Cyrene in Libya and the Trading Port at Naucratis in Egypt.   At the time the Black Sea trade was developing, the Greeks made important contacts with Libya and Egypt. The first Greek settlement in North Africa was at the site of Cyrene in Libya, founded by colonists from the drought-stricken island of Thera about 630 BCE. Although Cyrene grew slowly at first, successive waves of settlers from the mainland and the Aegean eventually occupied the city or the adjoining coastal region, a massive rounded promontory. Fertile Cyrene grew prosperous by exporting grain, fruit, sheep, and horses. A unique, wealth-producing export was silphium, a now-extinct plant apparently used not only as a medicine but also as a contraceptive and an abortifacient.

Kings of Egypt often campaigned with large numbers of Greek mercenaries. In the seventh century BCE the Egyptian monarchy permitted a contingent of Greeks, principally from Ionia, to establish a trading post at Naucratis on a branch of the Nile in the Delta. The Greek residents were free to observe their own customs and to build temples to their gods. Although most of the inhabitants were Ionians, various Greek naval powers maintained quarters here, notably Miletus, Samos, Aegina, Corinth, Athens, and Rhodes. This commercial settlement, not a colony, served principally as a port of exchange, with Egyptian products traded for Greek goods. From Naucratis, Greece received great quantities of grain and specialized articles such as linen, papyrus, and jewelry. Greek artisans at Naucratis gained valuable manufacturing and artistic skills through association with the Egyptians. Greek sculptors, for example, were soon imitating Egyptian models by producing life-size statues. Meanwhile the importation of papyrus (the "paper" of antiquity) into Greece made writing material more plentiful and less expensive. Greek travelers in the Nile Valley—exemplified by Solon in the sixth century BCE and Herodotus in the next—brought back knowledge of Egyptian medicine, mathematics, and astronomy, a stimulus for the birth of Greek philosophy and science among the Ionians and later the Athenians. Without doubt the astounding cultural awakening of Archaic Greece was partly related to the opening of Egypt, though contacts with the Levant and Asia Minor were just as important. We noted, for example, that the Greeks adapted the Phoenician alphabet to express their language.

Colonies in Italy and Sicily.   As in the east, colonists in the west were pulled by trade routes. Here the most important areas of Greek settlement were the coastal plains and hill valleys of southern Italy and eastern Sicily. By 750 BCE Greeks from the two major cities of Euboea—Chalcis and Eretria—had jointly established a trading post on the island of Ischia in the Bay of Naples, where arguably they traded textiles and wine for Italian iron and copper. About twenty years later Greeks planted a colony on the mainland at Cyme—usually known by its Latin name Cumae—just north of the Bay of Naples. This joint venture of settlers from various Ionian centers also included a Boeotian group known as the *Graioi*. Apparently this Graian element in the population was the basis for the name the later Romans used for the Hellenic people, *Graii* or *Graeci*, still preserved in the anglicized word *Greeks*. Greek colonies became so thick in southern Italy that the Romans eventually termed this aggregate Magna Graecia, or Great Greece.

Cumae was the northernmost Greek colony on the Italian west coast. Many scholars suggest the Romans became acquainted with the Greek alphabet and many Greek deities through contact with Cumae. The settlement functioned as the main trading center with both the native Italian populations and the elusive Etruscans of western central Italy. The Etruscans, speakers of a puzzling non-Indo-European language, developed a remarkable civilization in their metal-rich home in western central Italy between around 800 and 300 BCE. They had become a major producer of copper, tin, and iron by the period of Greek colonization. One reason for Greek settlement in the area must have been to trade for the valuable metals. Greek merchants shipped wares not only from Greece but also from Syria and Phoenicia to the wealthy Etruscan settlements. The Etruscans adapted artistic techniques and other elements of Greek culture, an early stage in the Hellenization of Italy.

Cumae soon sent out colonists of its own to plant the nearby settlement of Neapolis, or New Town, now called Naples. Before long Cumae and its mother city of Chalcis seized important sites on the Strait of Messina between Sicily and Italy, founding Rhegium on the Italian shore and Zancle—later renamed Messana (modern Messina)—on the Sicilian side. The two newly colonized cities controlled the traffic through the strait, adding to the prosperity of both Cumae and Chalcis.

Sparta's sole colony was Tarentum (Greek Taras, modern Taranto), planted in the corner of the heel of the bootlike Italian peninsula. A persistent tradition claims the city was founded in 706 BCE by disowned and exiled illegitimate sons born to Spartan women while their husbands were away at war, one version asserting the offspring were fathered by males too young to serve with the army. Tarentum stood on a promising site commanding an excellent enclosed harbor. An exporter of fine metalware, woolens, and pottery, Tarentum became known for its wealth and commercial importance.

In the meantime Greeks from Achaea in the northern Peloponnese founded Sybaris on the instep of the boot about 720 BCE. Around twenty years later settlers from Sybaris colonized Poseidonia, better known by its Latin name Paestum, on the coast of southwestern Italy. The prosperity of this Sybarite establishment is attested today by the ruins of two great Archaic temples. Sybaris itself was blessed with agricultural fertility. Trade was another source of the growing prosperity of the city, which commanded the land route across the toe of Italy. The unpredictable hazards of the Strait of Messina prompted merchants to unload their wares at Sybaris, carrying them overland to the Tyrrhenian Sea on the opposite coast. The name Sybaris still remains a synonym for untold luxury and wealth.

One of the greatest colonizing cities was Corinth, enjoying an easy route through the Gulf of Corinth to the Ionian Sea and then up the coast of western

Greece to the island of Corcyra (modern Corfu), which served as a stepping stone between mainland Greece and the riches of Italy. The Corinthians expelled a group of Eretrians and established a settlement on the island about 735 BCE. Other Corinthians proceeded to eastern Sicily and founded Syracuse on the little island of Ortygia in 734 or 733 BCE. Soon the city outgrew its island and expanded to the nearby mainland, where the Greeks began dominating the native Sicels living in the area. Syracuse eventually became the richest Greek colony in the western Mediterranean. Meanwhile other flourishing settlements were planted in Sicily by Corinth, Chalcis, and Megara. Such Greek foundations gradually expanded along the shore of the island, bringing them into conflict with the Carthaginian settlements in the west.

The Carthaginians resented the loss of fertile fields and good markets in Sicily. They became a constant source of trouble for the Greeks, plagued also by the hostility of the substantial native population living beyond the coastal hills. Moreover, the Greeks in Sicily, as elsewhere in Greek colonized lands, were often embroiled in bitter rivalries among themselves, with class fighting class, city attacking city. Their many troubles notwithstanding, the Greeks prospered in Sicily. They continued the process of colonization until the eastern half of the island was dotted with their settlements. Colonization was especially beneficial for Corinth, now exporting its fine vases and other wares to Italy and Sicily, while importing countless shiploads of Sicilian grain.

Trading Ports in France and Spain.   The powerful Phoenician trading network stretched from the Levant across the southern Mediterranean to the northwestern corner of Sicily and to the opposite promontory of Africa—Carthage—and then on to Sardinia, the Balearic Islands, and the coasts of Spain. The Phoenician quest in Spain was for tin and copper, metals much in demand for the production of bronze.

Some of the Ionians began to risk Phoenician displeasure by planting outposts on the coasts of southern France and northeastern Spain to compete for the Spanish metal trade. The small Ionian settlement of Phocaea on the west coast of Asia Minor pioneered in this perilous and distant colonizing venture. About 600 BCE the daring Phocaeans planted a trading outpost at Massilia (Greek Massalia, modern Marseilles) in southern France near the mouth of the river Rhone, not easily navigable. The Phocaean colonists at Massilia—soon the chief center of Greek culture west of Magna Graecia—introduced the grape and olive to southern France. Massilia founded its own settlements as far away as the Spanish coast, exemplified by magnificently sited Emporium (modern Ampurias), whose ancient name signified a trading port and market. Moreover, the energetic Phocaeans sailed beyond the straits of Gibraltar to the region of Tartessus on the Atlantic coast of Spain, where they traded for rare metals such as tin and silver. At Massilia they loaded their ships with amber, furs, slaves, and other northern products brought overland, and they picked up Italian iron at Etruria in central Italy. The Phocaean traders of Ionia were active until the middle of the sixth century BCE, when their city was besieged and taken during the Persian conquest of Ionia. To avoid Persian rule, most of the Phocaeans fled, finally finding refuge in Italy below Neapolis. Although the entrenched Carthaginians were able to bar the Greeks from Tartessus by the opening of the fifth century BCE, Massilia continued to trade with and influence the inhabitants of the upper Rhone valley.

The Effects of Colonization.   Many of the colonies—especially those of Magna Graecia—became wealthier than their mother cities. Free to adjust to new circumstances, the foundations experimented with novel political institutions, extended the frontiers of knowledge, and patronized artists and philosophers, thus contributing to the cultural enrichment of the Greek world. The far-flung Greek trading empire also prompted the development of improved sailing craft. By the sixth century BCE naval architects were fashioning long, slender warships. The standard warship of the Archaic period was the penteconter, so named because the craft carried fifty rowers, twenty-five per side. The vessel was armed with a deadly beak, sheathed in bronze, for ramming opponents. Having a relatively flat bottom and propelled not only by the fifty oarsmen but also by sail, the penteconter was a fast-moving, menacing instrument of war, but the design was too long and slender for good maneuverability. Shipbuilders also produced remarkable cargo vessels that frequently carried over a hundred tons, making possible a significant increase in bulk trade.

The extensive network of colonies greatly benefited the mother cities. The pressing problem of Greek overpopulation was temporarily solved by colonization and the importation of grain from abroad. Moreover, the foundations provided the mother cities with outlets for manufactured goods. The colonies received pottery from Corinth, textiles from Samos and Miletus, metalware from Chalcis and Samos, and wine and olive oil from mainland Greece. In turn, the mother cities imported vital grain from Sicily, Egypt, and the Black Sea region. They also procured important metals from overseas, notably iron from Italy, tin from Spain and possibly even Britain, and copper from Cyprus and Spain. Among the many additional prized imports were timber, tar, gold, and silver from Macedonia and Thrace, salted fish and slaves from the Black Sea region, hides from Magna Graecia, amber from the Baltic (carried overland to the Black Sea ports), ivory and papyrus from Egypt, glass and linen from Egypt and Phoenicia, and horses and drugs from Cyrene. Although ancient Greek industry would remain economically and socially subordinate to agriculture, successful traders and artisans were gaining wealth. An important new medium of exchange—coined money—became closely connected with their international commercial ambitions.

EARLY GREEK COINAGE

The use of precious metals as a medium of exchange was common in the Near East by the third millennium BCE, and the system made inroads on the barter economy of Dark Age Greece. The most common forms were metal lumps, gold and silver ingots, gold dust, and iron spits. The metal required testing and weighing for each transaction to determine purity and weight, an inconvenience eliminated with the invention of true coinage about 625 BCE. At this time Ionia was economically linked with its eastern neighbor Lydia. Apparently the kings of Lydia conceived the

Overseas trade was of great economic importance for the Greek cities. This sixth-century BCE Attic black-figure vase shows a dramatic scene on the high seas: a warship, slimmed-down and equipped with two levels of oars, attacking a merchant vessel, round-bellied and essentially driven by sail. Perhaps the ramming vessel is a pirate ship. British Museum, London.

revolutionary idea of minting coins to facilitate trade between the Ionians and the Lydians. Accordingly, lumps of electrum (a natural alloy of gold and silver mined in Lydia) were cast in uniform size and then stamped with a royal seal as an official guarantee of their value and weight. Made easily negotiable by the official guarantee, coins were also quickly counted and easily transported.

The Ionians soon began minting both electrum and gold coins. The invention quickly spread across the Aegean, yet gold was scarce on both the Greek mainland and the islands. Early coins on the mainland were limited to silver—mined in Attica and on the islands of Thasos and Siphnos—with Aegina minting the earliest examples about 540 BCE, followed by Corinth, Athens, and other states. Greece remained on a silver standard throughout most of its history. Each government stamped its coins with a distinctive design. While the Lydian coins were stamped with the royal insignia of the kingdom—a lion's head—the Ionians and other Greeks generally employed symbols relating to the legends and religious cults of their cities. At first Greek coinage carried only an obverse design, often a representation of the patron god of the city and part or all of the city's name.

The invention of coinage facilitated international trade and major governmental purposes such as payments on public works. Local commerce, fines, and certain other transactions still relied on barter because early coins were minted in large denominations, making them virtually useless as everyday currencies. Until the inauguration of token coinage in base metal in the late fifth century BCE, local transactions were confined to barter. Early Greek silver coins were minted in denominations of two, four, or

These Archaic Greek silver coins, from the period 520–480 BCE, suggest the wide range of design. At Athens (A), the celebrated "owl" coinage appeared around 520–510 BCE, with the helmeted head of the patron goddess stamped on the obverse and the owl, olive branch, and first three letters of the city's name on the reverse. At Corinth (B), the head of Athena the Bridler accompanies the flying horse Pegasus, captured by the mythical Corinthian hero Bellerophon with the goddess's aid. At Delphi (C), a ceiling of decorative sunken panels (coffers), perhaps representing that of the rebuilt temple of Apollo, accompanies two drinking horns in the shape of rams' heads. The fourth coin (D), from Caulonia, an Achaean colony on the toe of Italy, is wafer-thin and shows on each side the god Apollo carrying a branch and a small running figure, with a stag before him, images undoubtedly associated with the mythology of the city. Ashmolean Museum, Oxford.

more drachmas. We saw that the iron spit had been a common medium of exchange in an earlier day, with six iron spits constituting a measure of value called a drachma, literally "a handful." When the Greeks adopted a system of coinage, the drachma remained a standard value. In the last decades of fifth-century Athens a drachma was the customary daily wage for a laborer, a convenient standard against which we can measure prices at the time.

While the Italian and Sicilian Greeks began at an early date to strike neatly executed coins, the Athenian coins never attained a comparable excellence of design. Yet the Athenian four-drachma piece, introduced in the late sixth century BCE and stamped on the obverse with a rather crude head of Athena and on the reverse with an equally ungainly but appealing owl, acquired a reputation for purity and honest weight, becoming the standard coin throughout the Greek world. The owl was an emblem of Athena as well as a symbol of Athens, whose famous silver coins bearing its image became known as owls. Because other cities were seldom quite so honest as Athens in guaranteeing purity and weight, their coins frequently found acceptance only within their own territories.

RISE OF THE POLIS (c. 750–500 BCE)

The institution most closely connected with Greek history is the polis, or city-state, which gradually crystallized in the centuries after 1000 BCE. Thus the early steps in the formation of the polis (the plural is poleis) seem to have preceded the beginning of the colonization movement. Although developing in widely different ways, the polis generally originated with the unification of the old farming villages. Each consisted of a small autonomous state dominated by a single city, which was walled and strategically located and surrounded by farmland.

Eventually Greece was divided into a host of these tiny, mutually suspicious, sovereign political units. Although the city-states shared a common culture and sometimes cooperated against an outside invader, they were characterized by constant rivalry and frequent hostility. Generally speaking, the free adult males, who were the only full citizens, made and carried out political decisions. Citizens of other states were admitted to a polis only as inferiors with drastically curtailed privileges. While women enjoyed an important role in religious life, they were completely barred from participation in the political process and usually led extremely restricted lives. Moreover, we saw that ancient Greece was divided by geography into numerous natural compartments, discouraging political unification. Thus the Greeks became accustomed to functioning both politically and religiously in small units.

AMPHICTYONIES AND LEAGUES

Despite their usual jealousies, neighboring city-states sometimes combined to form a league, the members meeting to worship at the temple of a deity common to the represented communities. Leagues concerned ostensibly with the administration of shrines were known as amphictyonies. One of the most important was a twelve-state amphictyony located in central Greece, originally organized around the temple of the agricultural goddess Demeter near Thermopylae, later the temple of Apollo at Delphi. The twelve states of this association—the Delphic Amphictyony—pledged to administer and protect the shrine and its celebrated oracle. Such religious combinations could become political, especially when the membership included an aggressive superior power. The Boeotian Amphictyony, for example, whose deities were Poseidon and Athena, was eventually converted into a political league by the city of Thebes, the principal city of Boeotia. Unlike a polis, a political league did not provide a common citizenship throughout a designated area and thus represented a less effective way of achieving unity.

KINGSHIP REDUCED IN FUNCTION

As noted, the society depicted in the Homeric epics was headed by kings. The king of old sought advice from a deliberative council, composed of the heads of the most powerful noble families. Apparently major decisions of the king and council were announced to an assembly of the fighting men, a body lacking formal power and existing primarily to test the support of the people. The king could not hope to maintain his authority without the backing of the council. When the king was weak or unpopular, the council frequently acted to end the royal system of government, sometimes violently.

By the eighth century BCE the nobles had superseded the kings everywhere—except at Sparta, Argos, and a few other places—either by outright usurpation or by reducing the old patriarchal monarchy to an elective office with only priestly or judicial functions. Yet the royal office was seldom abolished outright, for the typical Greek city-state retained a subordinate king until relatively late in its history. The chief reason for keeping the monarchical title involved religion. The deities expected a king to offer the sacrifices and prayers made on behalf of the state; otherwise such acts might lack effectiveness. Thus at Athens a lesser official known as the king (*basileus*) was elected annually to conduct sacrifices and preside over religious services.

ARISTOCRATIC RULE

The nobles gaining control of the developing city-states in the eighth century BCE ruled for several generations in some places, for centuries in others. They controlled the old royal advisory body—the council—and gave it additional prerogatives. They confined membership in the high offices of state, or magistracies, to their own landowning class. Clearly, participation in the government of the early polis was restricted to the aristocratic families, all of whom justified their status by emphasizing their high birth and illustrious ancestry. They claimed descent from gods and heroes, proudly proclaiming they could trace their genealogies for fifteen or twenty generations. They believed they were the best—the *aristoi*—and thus the government they headed in each city is known as an aristocracy, the rule of the best.

The council, customarily small, remained the most important governing authority. The body appointed a number of magistrates, who took over most functions of the old king in many states. Included among the magistrates were the civil head of state and the army commander—the former usually called the archon and the latter the polemarch—as well as judicial and religious officers. The magistrates became members of the council after their term of office, commonly a year. Apparently councilors held office for life.

MILITARY REORGANIZATION

The nature of warfare also changed with the development of the polis. All the Homeric heroes are depicted as aristocratic champions challenging one another to individual combat. Comparatively small in number, such warriors entered battle armed with shield, breastplate, greaves (shin guards), and helmet. Their chief offensive weapons were swords and spears, the latter used for throwing or thrusting. Because only the aristocrats could afford the elaborate and expensive military equipment, other members of the army were armed with little more than their daggers and the stones they found on the field of battle. Homer portrays them hovering on the sidelines and playing the minor role of slinging stones and shouting encouragement to the dueling champions. We are uncertain to what extent the poems depict real warfare. Although Homer, perhaps for dramatic effect, stresses encounters between individual warrior-heroes, some passages seem to imply occasional massed charges.

Many historians suggest that some sort of mass formation was employed in Greece from an early date. We know that heavily equipped foot soldiers called hop-

The Archaic period witnessed major changes in military equipment and tactics. By the mid-seventh century BCE, Greek land battles depended on heavily armored foot soldiers called hoplites, arranged in a tightly packed formation known as the phalanx. This scene shows a hoplite engagement, with the piper on the left playing to help the soldiers keep in step. Detail from the Protocorinthian Chigi Vase, c. 640 BCE. Villa Giulia, Rome.

lites, who were organized in a rectangular formation called a phalanx, had evolved by the middle of the seventh century BCE. The phalanx was arranged in a long battle line, usually eight ranks deep. As hoplites moving at double time neared the enemy in open formation, ranks closed, with the men lining up almost shoulder to shoulder. The two opposing phalanxes, bristling with spears, charged one another and collided. The hoplites jabbed at vulnerable spots with their long heavy spears until there was no room for such thrusting and then turned to fight with their short slashing swords. Besides their weapons, warriors required excellent defensive armor: closed helmet, breastplate, greaves, and a large round shield (*hoplon*), the most distinctive piece of equipment and probably the source of the name hoplite. Each hoplite carried his shield by slipping his left forearm under a central metal armband and then grasping a handle on the inner rim. His left side was protected by his own shield, his right by the shield of the hoplite to his immediate right. Thus the advancing phalanx presented a formidable wall of overlapping shields.

The ranks behind pushed with great force against those in front, employing their tremendous combined weight to break the enemy's ranks. Anyone fleeing battle was held in contempt. As a rule, men summoned the extraordinary courage and resolve to hold their ground, "biting their lip with their teeth," in the words of the mid-seventh-century BCE Spartan poet Tyrtaeus. Blood spattered warriors, bearing equipment weighing up to seventy-five pounds, were often dismally hot inside their heavy armor. Ears rang with the clash of metal and the ghastly sounds of death, including the trampling of warriors underfoot.

Yet battles seldom lasted more than an hour. Apparently a winning side could expect to lose around five percent of its men, the defeated side at least double or triple that. If the hoplites of one side took fright and fled, the victors generally refrained from pursuing and massacring them. In the meantime the aristocratic cavalry typically played a subordinate role, their chief mission being to guard the vulnerable wings of the army.

Once the superiority of a hoplite army had been established, the more powerful states adopted the new system. The phalanx required large numbers of infantrymen, usually equipped at their own expense. The commercial revolution of the eighth and seventh centuries BCE had produced a new prosperous class of merchants, traders, and farmers enjoying the means to equip themselves for proper infantry engagements. These men were called upon to field the hoplite armies. They served the city-states, not the landed aristocracy, now rapidly ebbing in power. Although political and social status remained tied to landholding, the hoplite defenders of the state were on their way to achieving political recognition, for trade and manufacturing increasingly undermined the aristocratic monopolization of power.

GRADUAL CHANGE FROM ARISTOCRACIES TO TIMOCRACIES

As the economic revolution of colonization, commerce, mining, and manufacturing progressed and provided new sources of wealth, non-aristocrats gradually rose in political status. Birth-based aristocratic regimes survived only in remote rural areas and in certain special cases. Although the nobles continued to influence the city-states, the old aristocracy was gradually transformed into timocracy, a mild form of oligarchic government, whose qualification for political office was no longer birth but a degree of wealth. In the typical timocracy the most affluent citizens, who made up the cavalry, could hold any office of state or membership on the council. Those of moderate wealth, the men with the means to equip themselves as hoplites, could hold minor posts and meet in assembly. Thus in a Greek timocracy political rights were granted in proportion to wealth—whether landed or movable—regardless of ancestry.

The development of the Greek timocracies was related to the colonization movement. We saw that because ancient Greece lacked natural resources, the importation of raw materials and foodstuffs was essential to support its growing population. Enterprising Greeks developed products for export to pay for the numerous imports. The great expansion of trade provided Greek manufacturers with growing markets and led to a rapid development of industry. The new traders and merchants often enjoyed a more prosperous way of life than the old agrarian nobles.

The evolution of timocracy was also related to the nobles' unpopularity for constantly promoting the interests of their own class. The land not under their control was owned and worked by a large group of modest to poor farmers. Small-scale farmers often fared badly, for many could not compete with the large estates of their aristocratic neighbors. Although poorer farmers might mortgage their small plots, they were frequently unable to liquidate their debts and thus were enslaved. In the meantime wealthy landowners reduced other poor farmers to a serflike existence.

WRITTEN LAW

An important step in undermining the privileged position of the nobles came with a movement to reduce the customary law to writing. Because the laws were unwritten and unavailable for perusal by ordinary citizens, they were enforced to the advantage of the aristocrats. Yet the new wealthy traders and merchants allied themselves with the small-scale farmers against the landed nobility in demanding the establishment of written law. In the seventh century BCE many of the Greek cities authorized special legislators known as lawgivers (*nomothetai*) to publish the customary laws of the community. The lawgivers carried out their task by making public proclamations or introducing a series of laws in the new alphabetic writing. The written law could be inscribed on tablets of wood, bronze, or stone, or entered on the walls of temples or public buildings.

The colonial world produced the first lawgiver, Zaleucus, who compiled laws for the Greek city of Locri in southern Italy around 675 BCE. Written enactments were particularly needed in the new cities in the west to avoid a clash of customs among heterogeneous citizens coming from a variety of places. We hear that Zaleucus' legislation was notoriously severe, though virtually no undisputed information survives about his effort. Apparently the earliest lawgivers—themselves aristocrats—simply published the customary laws to restrict license and to safeguard their own interests. Thus early legislation not only prevented the alienation of family land by sale or bequest but also required an heiress to marry her nearest male relative, both provisions designed to prevent property from passing from the control of the family. Regulations concerning the treatment of slaves probably signify that slavery was increasing in importance during the seventh and sixth centuries BCE. Although the early written laws reflected aristocratic interests, they provided ordinary citizens with an idea of their rights, and the magistrates could not easily distort the written laws to promote class interests. With their loss of exclusive knowledge of the laws, the aristocrats experienced a severe blow to their old monopoly of political power.

REVOLUTIONS AND THE ESTABLISHMENT OF TYRANNIES

The written laws seldom quieted the misery of the masses or the ambitions of the new socioeconomic class rising with the growth of trade and industry. Repeated disagreements occurred between the two timocratic factions—the aristocrats and the merchants and traders—with the bitterness often sparking revolutions. From the middle of the seventh century BCE a series of forceful leaders seized many of the mercantile cities from aristocratic governments. These men were occasionally commoners but more frequently dissidents of noble birth who joined the discontented to gain power. The Greeks used a word of eastern origin, *tyrannos* (from which the modern term *tyrant* derives), as an informal title meaning lord or leader, to denote such an autocratic ruler who gained control of a city without any hereditary or official right. Because the early tyrants seized power through popular support, the designation *tyrannos* was benign at first but acquired a sinister connotation by the time the Greek philosophers Plato and Aristotle were writing in the fourth century BCE. The two portray a tyrant as a man grasping power by force and governing despotically.

Although tyrannies existed in later periods of Greek history, they are especially prevalent from about 650 to 500 BCE. Once in control the early tyrants curtailed the social and economic prerogatives of their aristocratic peers in numerous ways. For example, they sometimes exiled the great landowners, dividing up their large estates to gain the support of the small-scale farmers. They unfailingly advanced the interests of the new mercantile class. Several of the early tyrants were associated with the hoplites, whose emergence helped to undercut aristocratic domination. Many of the tyrants weakened aristocratic influence by promoting written codes. They additionally aided the rising mercantile class by fostering trade and manufacturing.

Most of the tyrants prudently drew attention away from their own power by sponsoring popular festivals, patronizing poets and artists, and beautifying their cities with great building projects. The typical tyrant held no political office but worked behind the scenes to place his candidates in the magistracies and the council. Despite their initial popularity, the tyrants were never really secure, partly because the office stood outside the Greek constitutional tradition of council and assembly, partly because the tyrants maintained supreme power with an armed bodyguard. They usually tried to make their rule hereditary, yet their overindulged successors of the second and third generations became increasingly arbitrary and were also despised for their corruption, excessive wealth, and frequent failure to address grievances. These sons and grandsons of the early tyrants had not won popularity through a successful rebellion, and many of them resorted to brutality to maintain power.

Pheidon of Argos.   The earliest tyrant on record is the shadowy Pheidon of Argos. Aristotle describes Pheidon—whose dates are disputed—as a hereditary king who made himself a tyrant. He is said to have imposed autocratic control over the city of Argos in the northeast Peloponnese, perhaps about 675 BCE, because the monarchical office had lost influence under the inroads of the aristocracy. Argos became a powerful state in the second quarter of the seventh century, probably under the leadership of Pheidon. Credited with early employment of hoplite warfare, the king-tyrant seems to have extended his sovereignty over several neighboring states of the northern Peloponnese. The Argives, plausibly led by Pheidon, marched south in 669 BCE, defeating the Spartans at the battle of Hysiae and thereby gaining control over the plains between Argos and Sparta for more than a century. Apparently Pheidon also extended his influence over his northern neighbors, Corinth and Sicyon, and as far west as the Olympic sanctuary of Zeus within the territory of Elis, but the Eleans soon defeated the Argives with the aid of Sparta. Tradition associates Pheidon with establishing standard weights and measures, which became prevalent in many Peloponnesian states and ultimately throughout Greece.

The Cypselids of Corinth.   Not long after the rise of Argos, the Dorian city of Corinth came under a dynasty of tyrants. The founder of the house, Cypselus, seized power about 657 BCE by overthrowing the exclusive aristocracy of the Bacchiads, slaying or expelling members of the clan, and distributing their lands among his supporters. Legend credits the rise of Cypselus to divine intervention, probably indicative that he was a popular leader. Famous stories of this type, thought to be derived from Mesopotamian mythology, were common in the Near East and Europe, with notable versions surrounding the birth and upbringing of Cyrus the Great, Moses, Jesus, and others. Under Cypselus, who allied himself with the new mercantile class, Corinth became the greatest sea power of Greece. The important colony on Corcyra had wrested its independence from Corinth, but Cypselus furthered Corinthian expansion by establishing new ports of call on the west coast of Greece.

Cypselus died about 627 BCE and was succeeded by his son Periander. Legend makes Periander bloodthirsty, but he was clearly an able ruler, counted in antiquity among the Seven Sages, a varying list of notables from the late seventh and early sixth centuries known for their wisdom. He enlarged the Corinthian colonial empire by founding Potidaea in Chalcidice and regaining control of Corcyra. Besides conquering the island of Aegina and the Pelopp city of Epidaurus, Periander established many colonies in the region of Epirus in northwest Greece. To afford passage for his strong navy between the Saronic Gulf and the Gulf of Corinth, he constructed the *diolkos,* a system of rails over which ships were pulled across the Isthmus. Periander established trading relations with Egypt by bringing Corinth into the new center at Naucratis. Corinthian exports were prized also by the Lydian king Alyattes and the tyrant Thrasybulus of Miletus. Periander extolled the primacy of Corinth by making sumptuous gifts to Delphi and by developing a sanctuary to Poseidon, lord of the sea, on the Isthmus of Corinth, where the popular Isthmian Games were held in the god's honor to attract visitors from other states. Maintaining the poet Arion at his court, Periander was also a patron of arts and letters. Industry flourished, and splendid Corinthian pottery served as a leading export.

Periander died after a long reign and was succeeded by his nephew Psammetichus, who was soon murdered. Wealthy merchant families then established an oligarchic government based on property qualifications, a form surviving almost two centuries, but this administration was unable to maintain the primacy Corinth had enjoyed under the Cypselids. Corinthian pottery was yielding to Attic competition in both quantity and quality by the early sixth century BCE. The latter part of the century witnessed Corinth joining the famous league of Peloponnesian states dominated by Dorian Sparta.

The Orthagorids of Sicyon.   The previously obscure city of Sicyon, about eleven miles northwest of Corinth on the Corinthian Gulf, emerged from political dependence on Dorian Argos under a tyranny founded by Orthagoras about 655 BCE. Surviving a full century, longer than any other tyranny in Greece, the house of Orthagoras seems to have owed its success to the support of the non-Dorian residents.

Sicyon attained its greatest power under Orthagoras' descendant Cleisthenes (c. 600–570 BCE), who was popular with the non-Dorian element. According to a doubtful story told by Herodotus, Cleisthenes invented offensive new names for the traditional Dorian tribes. Three tribes were found in many states occupied by Dorian speakers (*Hylleis*, *Pamphyloi*, and *Dymanes*), along with one or more tribes of the non-Dorian population. Cleisthenes is said to have renamed his non-Dorian tribe the Rulers (*Archelaoi*), while giving the three traditional Dorian tribes the offensive new names Pigites (*Hyatae*), Assites (*Oneatae*), and Swinites (*Choereatae*).

According to an amusing story in Herodotus, when Cleisthenes sought a bridegroom for his daughter Agariste, young nobles came as prospective suitors from far and wide to be entertained in munificence at Sicyon. Cleisthenes kept them at court for a year to inspect their athletic prowess and social skills. At a magnificent banquet held for the announcement of Cleisthenes' choice, the favored suitor drank too much wine and stood on his head, giving a riotous dance with his legs in the air. The irritated Cleisthenes cried out, "You have danced away your marriage," and presented his daughter to Megacles, scion of the illustrious Alcmaeonid clan of Athens. Descendants of that union included three of the most famous Athenian notables: Cleisthenes, Pericles, and Alcibiades.

Cleisthenes of Sicyon is remembered also for taking a leading part in the First Sacred War, a successful crusade to prevent the town of Cirrha from levying tolls on pilgrims making their way to the shrine at nearby Delphi. Soon after the death of the flamboyant Cleisthenes, Sparta terminated the tyranny of the Orthagorids— now replaced by a moderate oligarchy—and brought Sicyon into its Peloponnesian League.

Tyrannies of Ionia.   Usurpers seized power in Ionia during the seventh and sixth centuries BCE, with tyrannies arising at Miletus, Ephesus, and Samos. Among the most famous Ionian tyrants was Polycrates, who overthrew an aristocratic regime about 535 BCE on the island of Samos, the center of an important but small maritime empire. The reign of the exceptionally powerful Polycrates is associated with the patronage of poets and magnificent building projects. Yet his success brought him to the attention of the Persians, who arranged his murder in 527 BCE and brought Samos under their control.

The Role of the Tyrants.   The tyrants represent a unique tradition in Greek political development. After overthrowing the old political monopolies, they provided a measure of political stability during a transitional period. Generally, their power was based on the support of the mercantile and lower classes against the monopoly of the old birth-based landed aristocracies. We saw that most tyrants diverted attention from their exercise of unconstitutional power by sponsoring popular festivals, patronizing poets and artists, and beautifying their cities with great building projects. The last offered employment for the population, whose approval the tyrants needed to maintain their power.

One major defect of tyranny was not providing an outlet for political rivalry, with the exception of conspiracy and assassination. Their early popularity notwithstanding, the tyrants eventually began losing support, partly because their office was unconstitutional, partly because their power was backed by an armed bodyguard. As their overindulged successors of the second and third generations became increasingly ruthless and corrupt, many of the tyrannies were overthrown by various means, often with assistance from Sparta. Sometimes exiled aristocrats deposed the tyrants, but on other occasions they simply lost the backing of their traditional supporters. Yet any Greek state might revert to a tyranny in a time of stress, as many did during the fifth and fourth centuries, especially in western Greece.

The tyrants' achievement of bending the nobles to their will paved the way for the development of various forms of constitutional government. Although the tyrants ruled outside the customary law and the conventions of political life, they helped to raise the political consciousness of the *demos*, the people as a whole. After the *demos* gained confidence, some states entrusted rule to them, the basis of the political system known as democracy.

THE POLIS IN THE ARCHAIC PERIOD

We saw that the polis, or city-state, the characteristic form of Greek political organization, existed in all essential aspects by the beginning of the Archaic period. Each polis was a tiny autonomous state dominated by a single city. The small size of the polis resulted from the division of the Greek landscape into countless geographical units, the division of the Greek people into numerous tribes, and the division of the Greek religion into many local cults. The dependent territory surrounding the city served mainly as farmland. Citizens might live in the country or walk to fields and pastures from their homes in the urban center. Except in the smallest city-states, the surrounding territory also supported villages subordinate to the governing city.

The word *polis* originally denoted a citadel, reflecting the early Greeks' practice of choosing a defensible rocky hill as a place of refuge when they settled an area. Later, the Greeks usually referred to a citadel as an acropolis, or high town. They strengthened an acropolis with stone walls, if necessary, and constructed temples on its crest for the housing of gods. Prominent among these was the temple sacred to the patron deity of the city-state. Thus the acropolis served as the religious center of the polis.

A residential and commercial city arose at the foot of the acropolis. The sixth century BCE frequently witnessed the extension of the fortification walls of the acropolis to encompass the homes of the city, a practice encouraging the construction of monumental architecture as well. The political and commercial life of the urban center and the polis as a whole revolved around the city's agora, an open square employed not only as a meeting place for the citizens but also as a market. The agora was bordered by a number of civic buildings and stoas, the latter serving as the center of economic life in the city. Generally, an ancient Greek stoa consisted of a back wall from which a roof sloped to a long colonnade, or line of columns, at the front. The stoa offered a sheltered, shaded promenade and a welcome place for merchants and peddlers to display their goods. The general-purpose building of the Greeks, the stoa was used not only as a strolling area and marketplace but also as a court house, council chamber, classroom, and pleasant setting for informal conversations. The Greeks adapted the principle of the stoa to create handsome enclosed courts—colonnaded on all sides—in shrines, gymnasiums, and other structures.

The Greek world embraced several hundred city-states, of which many were colonies founded by mother cities. Important examples include Athens and Thebes in central Greece, Sparta and Corinth in the Peloponnese, and Miletus on the shore of Ionia. The development of the poleis was always in flux, and no two were identical. Moreover, the Greek city-states varied considerably in both area and population. The two largest were Sparta, more than 3,000 square miles, and Athens, about 1,060, the others averaging less than 100. Even Athens, whose territory included both Attica and the island of Salamis, was barely larger than the Grand Duchy of Luxembourg and was smaller than the state of Rhode Island.

CHAPTER V

Sparta and Athens

Words cannot convey the Greeks' attitude of transcendent patriotism and reverence for their cities scattered around the shores of the Mediterranean. They conceived the polis as a sacred site providing shrines for their patron gods. Each citizen viewed his fellow citizens as kinsmen but sometimes regarded citizens from other cities as descendants of hated hereditary enemies his ancestors had bloodied on the battlefield. By the close of the sixth century BCE several states on the eastern Greek mainland—Athens, Sparta, Corinth, Thebes, and Argos—enjoyed great political, military, and economic strength. Of these, Athens and Sparta played preeminent roles during the two-hundred-year period extending from around 550 to 350 BCE. Representing two extremes, Athens and Sparta produced especially interesting histories. While Athens enacted reforms leading to the development of democracy for its citizens, Sparta strongly resisted change and kept power in the hands of its ruling class.

SPARTA

Early Sparta

Pleasantly nestled beside the banks of the slowly winding Eurotas River, Sparta became the principal city of fertile Laconia, comprising the southeast region of the Peloponnese. Formed by the long river valley of the Eurotas, Laconia is bordered by the sea in the south, the Argolid in the north, Arcadia in the northwest, and Messenia in the west. The majestic Taygetus range flanks the western edge of the rich valley, while the Parnon range lies on the eastern side. Laconia had been important in Mycenaean times, the home of the legendary royal couple Menelaus and Helen of Troy. Sometime in the tenth century BCE the territory came under the domination of a particularly aggressive group of Dorians, who established a number of settlements. Three miles above the ancient citadel of Amyclae they founded a group of villages coming to be known collectively as Sparta. Soon Sparta began to grab the territories of neighboring towns and villages. Amyclae temporarily barred the Spartans from southward expansion, but by the eighth century BCE they had absorbed the town.

The Dual Kingship. Perhaps this union of communities (or an even earlier unification) explains why the Spartans always retained two kings, for the dual hereditary

The Peloponnese.

monarchy may have been the result of some ancient compromise. Each of the two royal families—the Agiads and the Eurypontids—furnished one king, with both monarchs claiming descent from Heracles, the most popular of all mythical heroes. During the Archaic period the dual kings enjoyed command of warfare and considerable power over foreign policy, though sometimes demonstrating extreme difficulty reaching joint decisions. Besides the two kings, the early government of Sparta probably included a council of aristocrats and an assembly of weapon-bearing citizens.

Perioikoi and Helots.   The Spartans' policy of expansion in Laconia during the ninth and eighth centuries BCE led to a larger than usual Greek state, with their neighbors reduced to dependent status. Sparta granted a measure of independence over domestic affairs to perhaps thirty favored Dorian communities in the subjected area but retained control over foreign relations. The free men in such communities were required to pay taxes to Sparta and were liable to military service. They were known as the *perioikoi* (dwellers around), the neighbors of Sparta. Although people in various Greek territories bore the designation *perioikoi,* those in Laconia are best known. A second group of inferiors, the helots, existed as a servile class in Laconia and certain other Greek lands. While the helots of Laconia, the best attested, were not slaves who could be bought and sold, they were permanently attached to the soil and worked the farms of their Spartan overlords as virtual serfs of the state.

First Messenian War (c. 735–715 BCE).   During the eighth century BCE, when the city-states of Greece were solving their overpopulation problem by founding colonies, the Spartans embarked upon a different course, securing additional territory without the necessity of settling overseas. They established but one colony— Tarentum in southern Italy—and satisfied their land hunger by turning to conquest. About 735 BCE they poured westward across the Taygetus range and struggled bitterly for twenty years to conquer Messenia, making helots of its people. The socioeconomic basis of classical Sparta stemmed from this expansion into the neighboring region.

Literary and Artistic Awakening.   Almost overnight Sparta had gained the wealth that other cities acquired only gradually through years of trade and colonization. Although militaristic from the beginning, Sparta developed its austere and dictatorial character later, and an early cultural blossoming took place in the seventh century BCE. The Spartans themselves produced few poets, yet they encouraged the efforts of foreign ones, many of whom competed at the great festival of the Carnea held at Sparta early in the fall in honor of Apollo. Later tradition reports the Spartans played a leading role in the development of Greek music. Their lyric poet Alcman—said by some sources to have been a Lydian taken as a slave from Sardis to Sparta—arranged choral dances and composed music and lyrics for religious festivals. The Laconian poet Tyrtaeus, who served as a military commander, seems to have come from the Spartan nobility. Tyrtaeus' martial verse is remembered for exhorting the Spartans against the Messenians.

Archaeologists excavating at the temple of Artemis Orthia in Sparta uncovered fine bronze work as well as a distinctive style of Spartan vase painting, with figured drawing largely confined to dance and horse scenes. Having gained considerable wealth with the conquest of Messenia, Spartan aristocrats imported quantities of luxuries such as eastern ivory, northern amber, and Egyptian scarabs. Yet by 600 BCE these importations had nearly ceased, and the state was becoming culturally stagnant. One reason for the change was a growing Spartan rigidity and militarism sparked by a revolt in Messenia.

Second Messenian War (c. 650–620 BCE).   About 650 BCE the Messenians enlisted the aid of Argos and launched a revolt against Sparta—commonly called the Second Messenian War—and persevered for perhaps three decades. Fighting desperately to regain their freedom, the Messenians invaded Laconia itself. The Spartans were saved by the untimely death of the Argive commander and by the rousing pleas of the firebrand poet Tyrtaeus, who proclaimed the Messenians should serve

their Spartan masters "like asses under great burden. . . ." Eventually the highly disciplined and tactically superior Spartan hoplites crushed the Messenians, forcing
them back into helotry, but the latter never forgot their brief period of freedom.

THE SPARTAN CONSTITUTION

Lycurgus.   The Spartans initiated a number of drastic political changes to prevent
any future helot uprising, unwittingly enslaving themselves with a constitution
that virtually blocked peaceful change. The later Spartans claimed their political
and social institutions stemmed from the legislation of a shadowy lawgiver named
Lycurgus. In his *Life of Lycurgus*, the Greek philosopher and biographer Plutarch,
writing in the early second century CE, admits at the outset that no one knew for
certain who the lawgiver was or when he lived. Most historians suggest the complicated Spartan constitution was not the work of a single lawgiver but evolved in
stages over many generations.

Government of Two Kings, Council, Assembly, and Ephors.   Later Greek thinkers regarded the Spartan constitution as superior to the others of Greece because the system combined monarchical, aristocratic, and democratic elements. Sparta preserved
its hereditary kingship after the Messenian revolt, though with somewhat diminished influence. The reigning dual kings retained religious duties, numerous prerogatives and honors, and authority over some judicial functions. Their principal
power was command of the army, with one king dispatched for each campaign. The
existence of two kings meant that each one could prevent the other from becoming
too powerful. A second organ of government was the council of elders, the Gerousia, consisting of the two kings and twenty-eight men aged sixty and above, elected
for life by the assembly of citizens from a restricted circle of noble families. The
councilors advised the kings, served as a court in capital cases, and probably prepared measures to be presented to the assembly. The third organ of government was
the assembly, or *ekklesia*, composed of all adult male citizens of at least thirty years
of age. In theory, the assembly was the supreme decision-making body for matters
of policy, but the body lacked the right to discuss proposed motions and was em-
powered only to confirm or deny them. Moreover, no measure could be brought before the *ekklesia* until fully deliberated by the members of the aristocratic Gerousia.
Although a powerful Spartan nobility continued to function above the ordinary
citizens, the *ekklesia* represented a groping toward democracy, at least for the adult
Spartan males, who described themselves as the *homoioi* (equals or similar ones) because in theory all were equal in military and governmental affairs. Numbering up
to nine thousand men, the citizen body of equals was divided into administrative
units based upon residential areas.

Kingship, council, and assembly were traditional in early Greek city-states, but
the Spartans added a fourth organ of government known as the ephorate, a powerful board of five magistrates set up beside the monarchy and exercising the chief administrative authority in the state. The ephors, or overseers, were chosen annually

in the assembly to represent the five villages of Sparta. Drawn from the equals, the ephors exploited the rivalry between the two kings to strengthen their own position. The ephors exchanged monthly oaths with the kings, the latter pledging to uphold the established laws, the former promising to preserve the privileges of the kings as long as they honored their oaths. Two ephors accompanied kings into battle. Every ninth year they selected a clear and moonless night to observe the heavens for signs of displeasure with the kings. If they saw a meteor, the ephors had the right to suspend the kings from office. They enjoyed extensive police powers, used in part to hold down the helots. They transacted much of the daily business of government and supervised the social system. Moreover, the ephors presided at meetings of the assembly and probably also at the council. They conducted prosecutions before the council, controlled the distribution of property, exercised a veto over all legislation, and received foreign envoys.

THE RIGID SOCIAL HIERARCHY

Spartans.   The population of the Spartan state continued to be divided into three main social classes under the kings: Spartans, *perioikoi,* and helots. With the exception of helots, the inhabitants of the state were called Lacedaemonians. Male Spartans—the equals—functioned as the ruling class and numbered perhaps one in every fifteen or twenty of the total population. Each possessed a plot of state land (*kleros*) in Laconia or Messenia that was cultivated by helots, thereby freeing the full Spartan citizen for military training and warfare. All Spartan males became warriors and were indoctrinated to serve the state without question. Thus they functioned as a perpetual army and spent most of their lives in military training. The Lycurgan constitution strictly prohibited them from engaging in industry or trade.

Perioikoi.   Next in rank were the *perioikoi,* who enjoyed local autonomy in Laconia but not full citizenship. The *perioikoi* were liable to service in the Spartan army and subject to Spartan supervision but otherwise lived as ordinary Greeks. Some members of the class monopolized industry and trade. These *perioikoi* produced armor, tools, pottery, woolen cloth, furniture, and other goods. They employed money in the form of unwieldy iron bars—prohibited for use by full Spartan citizens—when trading with outsiders. Consequently, foreigners' access to the Spartan economy was only through the *perioikoi* or state officials. Apparently the *perioikoi* were content with their lot, for they held a privileged position monopolizing important economic activities that were essential to the state yet prohibited to the Spartans.

Helots.   The helots at the bottom of the social scale were bound to the land and performed all agricultural labor for the Spartans. They were also required to accompany their masters on campaigns as personal attendants. Harshly treated to compel obedience, they were whipped annually and forced to wear distinctive garments. The relatively small population of full Spartan citizens could never escape the haunting fear of helot revolt.

Education and Training in the Service of the State

Exposure (Abandonment) of Unhealthy Infants.   The strident Spartan system of training was a reaction to this fear. Every Spartan was brought up to become a hardened, rigid warrior who demonstrated unquestioning loyalty to the state. The process started at birth. Elsewhere in Greece each father decided on grounds of health whether a newborn should be reared or put to death, but in Sparta a board of state officials inspected infants to determine which were physically fit to survive, the unhealthy or puny being thrown into a deserted mountain ravine.

Harsh Early Training.   Education and training were rigidly controlled to foster devotion to the state, with Spartans developing an attitude of obedience at an early age. A Spartan boy was taken from his mother in his seventh year and assigned to a barracks, organized in "packs," where he progressed through a series of age grades bearing archaic-sounding names. Under the zealous command of teenage leaders, who were supervised by a camp commandant, the boys were introduced to the harshness of Spartan life. They went barefoot and wore but one thin tunic in summer and winter, slept upon bedding of reeds without covers, learned traditional war songs and dances inculcating patriotism, and recited verse enjoining absolute obedience and bravery. Encouraged to supplement their meager diet by stealing from farms, they were severely beaten if caught to improve their skill at living off the countryside. Although boys were taught the rudiments of reading and writing, the Spartan system emphasized physical prowess rather than intellectual development. Most training was designed to make the boys accept commands without hesitation. They were flogged without mercy to harden them for war and compelled to participate in brutal fights.

Scourging at the Altar of Artemis Orthia.   Upon reaching puberty, the Spartan male underwent various tests and initiations into military manhood. The boys participated in a famous public religious ceremony at the temple dedicated to the goddess Artemis Orthia, a cult closely associated with the state training of young males. Each boy ran naked to the altar of the goddess and was whipped severely, his body bloodied. Those enduring the longest gained the greatest respect. Having been indoctrinated to endure the flogging with pride, many boys died under the lash rather than utter the slightest whimper. The survivors experienced other Spartan initiations, probably including anal intercourse from the older youths, who then selected their favorite boys from the initiates to become their lovers. Such relationships were explicitly recognized and formed powerful bonds of mutual support, with each older youth held accountable for the performance and behavior of his beloved.

The Messes.   The training of older youths was increasingly directed toward military service. At the age of twenty the male became an active warrior in the army and sought election to one of the famous Spartan messes serving as military clubs. Belonging to a mess, each with about fifteen members, was requisite for full Spartan citizenship. The entire social and military organization of the state was closely tied

Flogging at the altar of Artemis Orthia, where the initiates into Spartan military manhood risked death.

to the messes, though a single adverse vote vetoed or postponed election. To be denied admission in a military mess, a rare occurrence, meant social and political death. The members of a mess ate together, shared the same sleeping quarters, and fought side by side in battle. The Spartan warriors in the messes were the only Greeks who consistently ate meat. From his land allotment cultivated by helots, every member contributed his share of the simple diet of barley bread, cheese, figs, grapes, olives, and wine, plus the famous Spartan black broth, a strong concoction of blood, vinegar, salt, and pork.

Spartan Homosexual Ethos and Marriage Customs.   The Spartan army depended on the comradeship of messmates, who lived and fought together. The soldiers were commonly allied by affection based on homosexual ties, stronger than those to wives and children. Although a young warrior was encouraged to marry about the age of twenty for the sake of procreation—unmarried males suffered legal disabilities—family life was kept to a minimum. Women were generally left to themselves and typically married when about eighteen to twenty years old, later than in most Greek states. The chief wedding rite was a ritual seizure, with the groom symbolically capturing and carrying off the bride, a survival of the primitive custom of marriage by actual capture. Perhaps reflecting the prevailing homosexual way of life in Sparta, the bride was then dressed for her wedding in male clothing, her head shaved (a similar custom prevailed at Argos, where the bride wore a beard on her wedding night). She was left alone in a darkened room on a hard bed, whereupon the bridegroom entered and briefly engaged in sexual intercourse with her before hastily retreating to his customary male companionship. Until the age of thirty the married male was severely restricted in performing the role of a husband, not residing with his wife and seeing her only on rare and secret visits. Plutarch reports in his *Life of Lycurgus*, written long after the demise of classical Sparta, that men sometimes "had children before they ever saw their wives' faces in daylight." Upon reaching the age of thirty the Spartans were finally considered mature men. Even after their thirtieth year, however, warriors still ate in their messes and spent much time in military exercises, not retiring from armed service until they were sixty.

Secret Police.   One of the most sinister aspects of the Spartan method of training warriors was the *krypteia* (secret police). Originating perhaps in a primitive rite of passage in which young men demonstrated feats of courage or shed human blood before initiation into manhood, the notorious secret police terrorized the helots as a means of discouraging revolts. The ephors declared war on the helots every year at the beginning of their term of office, thereby legalizing murder of members of the serflike class. A picked body of young Spartans then went out to live secretly in the countryside with no more than a few morsels of food and a dagger, enjoined to remain hidden by day but to come out at night and kill any helots they could find.

Women.   A society centering on male relationships had implications for the position of women. A board of state officials examined female infants at birth, permitting the survival of those deemed physically fit to become mothers of vigorous and courageous children. The upbringing of females—they were educated at state expense—was designed to ensure the success of their all-important reproductive function. Although free from military service, girls underwent vigorous athletic training, including running and wrestling, possibly in the nude, to produce the well-developed bodies believed to yield strong offspring. They mixed freely with the boys, sharing their athletic activities. Such a practice was unthinkable in Athens, where females were secluded in houses. Some sources indicate that homoeroticism was part of female upbringing. Plutach reports in his *Life of Lycurgus* that "respectable women would in fact have love affairs with unmarried girls," and we find explicitly erotic language in the songs of female choruses. The other Greeks were shocked by the appearance of women in Sparta, for they were forbidden to adorn themselves with jewelry or cosmetics and wore a slit dress baring their thighs, the Dorian peplos, unlike the voluminous female garments elsewhere. Even more scandalous was the unique Spartan practice of wifeborrowing, which made one woman's fertility available to more than one man (including younger men when her husband was old). Plutarch mentions in his *Life of Lycurgus* that it was "honorable for men to give the use of their wives to those whom they should think fit, so that they might have children by them. . . ."

Women were outspokenly loyal to Sparta, as reflected in the proverbial story of the mother who bade her son to return from battle either with or upon his shield. They enjoyed far more freedom than elsewhere in Greece. Although adult females were excluded from most official institutions of the polis—except processions and festivals—they managed their absent husbands' affairs. Moreover, women were free to abstain from the domestic chores of spinning and weaving, thereby gaining more time for physical exercise in the service of the state. Apparently they enjoyed the right of owning and disposing of property in their own right. Many of them seem to have accumulated considerable wealth through inheritances and dowries.

Clearly, the entirety of the Spartan program was designed to transfer to the polis the primary loyalty and devotion usually accorded the family, for the principal goal was creating stalwart soldiers. The training produced tough, unyielding fighting men, the most effective warriors of Greece, with nothing permitted that might compete with the obligation of defending Sparta.

THE PELOPONNESIAN LEAGUE

With Messenia firmly in their grasp, Spartan kings employed superior military might in the sixth century BCE to extend Spartan influence over most of the remainder of the Peloponnese. First they attacked the Arcadian city of Tegea near their northern border, fighting a long war designed to reduce its inhabitants to helotry. Yet the brave Tegeans defeated the Spartans, probably early in the century. Later, on advice from an oracle at Delphi, the Spartans removed by stealth from Tegea the reputed bones of the old Mycenaean hero Orestes, son of Agamemnon, and gave them burial in Sparta with proper honors. This served not only as an expression of respect for the ancient traditions revered by the non-Dorian population in the Peloponnese but also as an assertion that Sparta was the successor of the Achaeans in providing leadership for the entire region. Accordingly, Sparta shifted from a policy of conquest and subjection to alliance. Tegea came to terms and accepted a defensive alliance about 550 BCE, with the obligation of furnishing military aid when required. Shortly thereafter Sparta began negotiating alliances with other neighboring city-states, suppressing wherever possible the autocratic rulers known as tyrants in favor of a network of friendly aristocratic and oligarchic governments.

From the forged alliances, Sparta gradually constructed an organization now called the Peloponnesian League, though the ancient name was "the Lacedaemonians [Spartans] and their allies." The Peloponnesian League, which could field fifty thousand men, was a defensive and offensive alliance bringing all the states of the Peloponnese, except hostile Argos and the cities of Achaea, under Spartan leadership. Sparta now stood at the head of the most powerful land force in Greece.

No common agreement existed among the members, for individual treaties with Sparta provided the principal link among them. Each state pledged to furnish military aid when the league waged war, and Spartan kings held the command of the combined allied forces. Members of the league were bound by a majority vote in an assembly meeting at Sparta or at Corinth, with each state having one vote. By now the strongest state in Greece, Sparta alone had the authority to call meetings of the all-important assembly.

Cleomenes I Pushes Spartan Influence beyond the Peloponnese.   Spartan foreign policy was forcefully pursued by King Cleomenes I (*c.* 519–490 BCE) of the Agiad line, a talented but perhaps mentally unstable ruler. Seeking to extend Spartan control beyond the Peloponnese, Cleomenes expelled the tyrant Hippias from Athens but failed to coerce the state to join the Peloponnesian League, owing to the opposition of Corinth and his coruler Demaratus. Cleomenes then savagely crushed Sparta's traditional enemy Argos about 494 BCE, thereby eliminating its role as a major power in the Peloponnese. Various internal disputes eventually led to his disgrace and exile. The king was recalled to Sparta but, according to Herodotus, soon went mad and stabbed himself to death, possibly a disguised assassination.

Cleomenes had pursued a policy of blocking the expansion of the Persian Empire, now threatening the old powers of the Mediterranean. When the Persians launched great onslaughts against Greece shortly after 500 BCE, the population looked to Sparta for military leadership on land, while calling on Athens to resist the enemy by sea.

ATHENS

Athens was the great rival of Sparta. Whereas Sparta developed into a conservative land power, the Athenian city-state was destined to become a great sea power, remembered for experimenting with democratic institutions and launching a militant imperialism. Athens lies near the sea in the southwest part of Attica, a triangular peninsula constituting the easternmost region of central Greece, bordering Boeotia in the north, Megara in the west, the Saronic Gulf in the south, and the Aegean in the east. Smaller and less fertile than Laconia, Attica forms a natural geographic unit of hills and plains separated from Boeotia by Mounts Parnes and Cithaeron and from Megara by Mount Cerata. Although plagued by relatively meager rainfall and many tracts of barely arable soil, Attica was suited to the cultivation of olives, grapes, and figs. The potential for commercial and industrial ventures was far more promising, however, for fine marble and clay were available northeast and east of Athens in Mounts Pentelicus and Hymettus, and after 500 BCE rich silver deposits were mined throughout the hilly district in the southeast known as Laurium. Among the chief natural assets of Attica were harbors at Marathon and at Phaleron, the latter a relatively ill-protected open beach near Athens. Yet Phaleron was replaced in the early fifth century BCE by an excellent harbor called Piraeus, four miles southwest of Athens.

EARLY ATHENS

The Athenians never tired of boasting they were autochthonous, or native, to Attica rather than late arrivers. Archaeology confirms that view, at least to the extent that Athens shows uninterrupted settlement from the Neolithic period. Athens may have exercised some control over the various communities of Attica during the Mycenaean epoch. Tradition credits the mythical hero-king Theseus, kinsman and rival of Heracles, with unifying Attica into a single state in the distant past. As noted, Athens was one of the rare Mycenaean settlements escaping destruction during the upheavals of the Late Bronze Age. Apparently Ionian Attica became a haven for refugees escaping collapsing Mycenaean kingdoms in the late thirteenth and twelfth centuries BCE. Tradition declares they were fleeing from onslaughts of Dorians.

Unification of Attica.   Eighth-century BCE Athens began unifying Attica by bringing the small outlying kingdoms under its control, completing the process around

Attica.

675 BCE with the addition of the important sanctuary town of Eleusis and its rich Thriasian plain. Eleusis was famous for its Eleusinian Mysteries, celebrated in honor of the agricultural-goddess Demeter and her daughter Persephone, attracting visitors from the entire Greek world. After this unification into one state—or synoecism, to use the Greek term for grouping communities into a single unit—the inhabitants of Attica called themselves Athenians, not Atticans. Of great significance, every freeborn native male of Attica, whether from Athens or an outlying territory, was henceforth a full Athenian citizen.

From Monarchy to Aristocratic Rule.   Like Greek states elsewhere, Dark Age Athens was governed by a hereditary king, or *basileus*. Apparently the rise of a nobility, based upon ownership of inalienable tracts of land and descent from presumed divine ancestors, led to the piecemeal curtailment of royal authority, though the transition from monarchy to aristocratic rule is poorly understood. By the latter half of the eighth century BCE the Athenian nobles, who were called the Eupatrids (men of good birth), had set up two magistrates from their ranks to share monarchical power, namely, the polemarch (leader in war) and the archon (ruler), both subsequently appointed annually. The polemarch originally served as the commander of the army, formerly a prerogative of the king. The most important of the two new magistrates was the archon, later called the first archon, the holder of principal power.

The title *archon* was employed at Athens and elsewhere in central Greece to designate the chief state officials. Initially, Athens had three archons: the (first) archon, the polemarch, and the king. Subsequently, the kingship was reduced from a hereditary lifelong office to an elected magistracy with a one-year term, though the designated official retained the title king, *basileus,* and the significant right of supervising state religious practices. Meanwhile the first archon served as the chief executive of the state for civil affairs and enjoyed great administrative and judicial powers. The first archon was also known as the archon eponymous because the calendar year was named after him (the *eponymoi* were gods or people who gave their name to something).

By the late seventh century BCE the three archons had been supplemented by six others, the *thesmothetai* (lawmakers), who recorded legal decisions and served as judges, thereby relieving the great burdens on the first archon. The six *thesmothetai,* the polemarch, the first archon, and the *basileus* formed an executive board of annually elected members.

The nine archons were advised by a council of nobles, the Areopagus, a name derived from its usual meeting place on the Hill of Ares just northwest of the Acropolis. Originally possessing vast powers in the aristocratic state, the Areopagus probably scrutinized magistrates and exerted at least indirect control over their elections. The councilors enjoyed great prestige and held office for life. By the early sixth century BCE, perhaps earlier, the Areopagus included the former archons in its membership. Another organ of government was the assembly, or *ekklesia,* composed of all citizens, though its influence and role in early Athens remains shadowy.

Kinship Associations.   The population was still grouped in a hierarchical series of ancient kinship groups based on supposed blood relationship. Accordingly, the Athenians were organized in four so-called tribes, or *phylai,* large associations probably having some political and military functions. The tribes were subdivided into smaller kinship associations known as brotherhoods, or phratries, originally probably aristocratic military bands, now open to ordinary citizens. The phratry dominated citizens' social and religious life. Phratries of Athens and other Ionian states characteristically celebrated a three-day festival every autumn, the Apaturia, with carefully conducted rites of passage and sacrifices that reinforced the bonds of the group. The Apaturia is known chiefly from Athens, where every Athenian citizen was duly presented to his phratry, first in early infancy and again as a young adult (this time with his hair shorn for Zeus Phratrios), and where each new husband presented an offering on behalf of his bride.

Phratries were subdivided into clans, or *gene,* dominated by nobles. The nobility exercised great power over the state through the clans during the period of aristocratic rule. Thus the clans were a constant irritant to ordinary Athenians—hired laborers (*thetes*), petty farmers, and artisans—numbering at least three-quarters of the population.

THE SOCIAL CRISIS

Impoverishment of Small-Scale Farmers.   Landownership was concentrated in the hands of the nobles, now growing mainly olives and vines, which provided olive oil and wine, easily traded for grain and even luxury items. Both grapevines and olive trees require patience and years of cultivation before reaching full maturity, a considerable long-term investment that was beyond the reach of small farmers. With the wealthy minority not only holding most of the fertile land but also continuing to expand their estates, agricultural distress became increasingly common for ordinary farmers, who struggled to survive on generally unproductive, marginal land. Reduced to borrowing grain from the nobles, the poorer farmers pledged as security their labor, their land, their families, and themselves. By the late seventh century BCE many were unable to pay their debts, obliging them under Athenian law to hand over one-sixth of their scarce produce to aristocratic creditors. Meanwhile the humble class of hired laborers, the *thetes*, lacked land to mortgage and were sold into slavery abroad.

The social crisis was also linked to the plight of Athenian potters in the late eighth and most of the seventh centuries BCE, now losing their earlier favored position to Corinthian competition. This was the great age of Greek colonization, with Corinth playing a leading role, though Athens was not yet participating. Presumably, the population was growing in Attica, like the rest of Greece, and the failure to found colonies may indicate political ineptitude and weakness.

Military Reorganization.   About this time the Dorian phalanx was introduced in the Athenian army, the heavily armed hoplites now becoming the mainstay of warfare. The insufficiency of Eupatrids to fill the hoplite units resulted in the recruitment of common landowners having the means to equip themselves with arms. To determine which men were obligated to serve in the military and what duties they would perform, the entire population was divided by a census into three classes based on property. The aristocratic horsemen (*hippeis*) were the wealthy landowners constituting the cavalry. The hoplites (*zeugitai*) were the ordinary farmers making up the phalanx. The landless poor of laborers and petty artisans (*thetes*) were either exempt from service or served as poorly armed militia. This reorganization of the military, based on wealth rather than birth, offered a clear challenge to aristocratic power.

Cylon.   The social and political tensions made Athens fertile soil for turmoil. A prominent young nobleman named Cylon, a former Olympic victor and son-in-law of Theagenes, the powerful tyrant of Megara, attempted to establish a tyranny about 632 BCE. Supported by a pronouncement from the Delphic oracle and backed by a military force from his father-in-law, Cylon seized the Acropolis with the help of a small band of friends from his clan and proclaimed himself tyrant. The Athenian masses, probably incensed at the presence of Megarian soldiers, then poured in from the countryside to besiege the rebels and support the established authorities. Cylon himself escaped. We hear that his followers took sanctuary at the altar of Athena on the Acropolis but were butchered on the spot by that year's first archon, Megacles, the head of the powerful Alcmaeonid clan. Delphi, having backed Cylon, now placed Megacles and the aristocratic Alcmaeonids under a famous curse for this act of impiety. The Alcmaeonids were banished but soon returned. The scandal of the bloodguilt would be revived more than once against their descendants. Meanwhile Athens had been profoundly weakened. Alienated Megara began raiding Athenian territory, and an orgy of blood feuding broke out among the clans.

Draco.   Athens was plagued not only by the deadly feuds among the noble families but also by a struggle between the nobles and the ordinary Athenians, of whom the men in arms posed a serious threat to aristocratic rule. Perhaps as a response of the ruling class to popular demands for protection against the arbitrary decisions of aristocratic judges, Draco was appointed to prepare the first written Athenian laws. Published around 621 BCE, these enactments struck a blow at aristocratic privilege by depriving judges of their right to declare what the law was. Tradition labels Draco's laws notoriously harsh—thus the English adjective draconian—and in later times the Athenian orator Demades remarked that they were written in blood instead of ink. The only surviving part of Draco's work involves homicide, and these provisions marked a great advance in criminal law. We saw that Athens was cursed at the time by the blood feud—sometimes lasting for generations—with the kindred of the victim avenging their injuries upon the perpetrator or the relatives of the perpetrator. Customary law made no distinction between premeditated murder and involuntary homicide, but Draco introduced the concept of intention. Thus his laws provided a different procedure for each kind of homicide. An individual falsely accused of killing another, for example, could flee to a sanctuary and swear innocence before the relatives of the slain. Unless supernatural evidence pointed to the falsity of the oath, the accused was immune from further prosecution. On the other hand, an individual who killed another unintentionally was judged by a court, provided the accused had managed to flee to a sanctuary. In the event the court accepted the plea, the relatives of the victim could then grant pardon by unanimous vote, but if they declined to do so, the state provided the accused with a safe-conduct to the border. These provisions represented a significant step toward eliminating the ruinous blood feuds among the various clans. The code of Solon about a generation later left Draco's laws on homicide essentially intact.

THE REFORMS OF SOLON

Draco's laws did not address economic problems. Agricultural distress and other calamities mounted in the early sixth century BCE, bringing Attica to the brink of revolution. The ruling Eupatrids sought a solution by fighting a fitful war with Megara for possession of the neighboring island of Salamis. Meanwhile problems concerning debt intensified, and many Athenians clamored for reform. In 594 BCE a statesman of noble descent but moderate wealth named Solon was elected first archon and granted extraordinary powers to resolve the dangerous conflicts between social classes by inaugurating reform legislation. Solon is the earliest Greek political leader whose own words are known to us, surviving in the fragments of his forceful poems that paint a picture of harsh antagonisms between rich and poor. Solon was well known as a military leader, for he had commanded the expedition conquering the island of Salamis. Despite his noble birth, Solon is said to have been an experienced merchant with a judicious temperament—an avoider of extremes—and later admirers identified his favorite motto as "Nothing in excess."

Social and Economic Measures.   Athenian tradition remembered Solon as one of the Seven Sages and credited him with embarking on a program of social justice. A man of unimpeachable honesty, he was trusted by both the Eupatrids and the commoners. Solon employed his great power to hold the state together while mediating between rich and poor. His series of compromises set the Athenian state on a course followed for the next two centuries. Solon began by striking at the problem of ruinous debt, enacting bold emergency legislation known as the *seisachtheia*, or "shaking off of burdens," which cancelled all debts contracted on the security of land or liberty. These measures released poor farmers from their serflike existence, restored their farms, secured the emancipation of many citizens who had been sold into slavery abroad (scholars are uncertain how he raised sufficient funds to compensate their owners), and forbade once and for all the enslavement of any Athenian for debt. Thus Solon gave the poor a new start, though refusing to redistribute the land as proposed by more radical reformers.

In Solon's day Athens suffered from a shortage of grain and a surplus of olive oil. He prohibited the export of all agricultural products from Attica except its prized olive oil, shipped in painted vases to foreign markets in exchange for grain and raw materials. This measure, besides preventing grain from going abroad, encouraged not only the development of trade and industry but also a diversification of the economy. Yet as the production of olive oil became increasingly profitable, additional land was withdrawn from producing precious grain, resulting in greater Athenian dependence on grain imports. Moreover, we saw that poorer farmers could not afford the required long-term investment in olive trees, which require fifteen or twenty years to bear fully.

Solon further lessened economic burdens, while also encouraging industry, by offering Athenian citizenship to foreign artisans willing to settle in Attica to produce wares both for local consumption and export. Apparently a number of Corinthian potters responded to his invitation and contributed to a swift improvement in Attic pottery. By 550 BCE Athens had overtaken formerly dominant Corinth in the Mediterranean pottery trade.

The Constitution and the Law.   Solon reformed the constitution by shifting political privilege from birth to wealth, a process already in progress. He regrouped the citizenry into four income classes on the basis of wealth, calculated according to the annual production of units of grain, oil, and wine. Citizens of each income class were assigned proportionate political rights. The wealthiest farmers were known as the *pentakosiomedimnoi* (five-hundred measure men), for their land produced at least five hundred agricultural units. Members of the second class were known as the *hippeis* (mounted warriors)—the term formerly designating the uppermost rank—and consisted of men whose land produced at least three hundred units. Members of the third class were known as the *zeugitai* (men of the yoke,)—probably because they could afford to own a team of oxen—and consisted of men whose land produced at least two hundred units. The *zeugitai* constituted the majority of the farmers and artisans of Athens. While the citizens of the first two classes could afford to serve in the cavalry, the *zeugitai* provided the bulk of the hoplites. Members of the fourth class were known as the *thetes* (hired laborers), and consisted of citizens who did not own land producing as much as two hundred units. Only men in the first two income classes could hold major state offices, though individuals in the upper three could fill minor posts. The *thetes*, too poor to provide their own arms and armor, were barred from all offices of state but were at least theoretically entitled to a voice in the assembly. By admitting men to government posts on the basis of wealth rather than birth, Solon created a timocracy and breached the Eupatrid monopoly of power.

Both Aristotle and Plutarch report that Solon set up a Council of Four Hundred, drawing a hundred members from each tribe, though we are uncertain how this people's council functioned. Meanwhile the assembly, or *ekklesia*, seems to have flourished under Solon's pragmatic leadership. Although not permitted to initiate legislation, the assembly elected all magistrates. Closely linked with the body was a popular court of appeal, the *heliaea*, which heard appeals by citizens from the decisions of state officials. Thus the *heliaea* provided an effective check on the power of the magistrates and elevated the citizens themselves as a court of appeal. The decisions of the Council of the Areopagus could not be appealed to the *heliaea*. The Areopagus, whose membership now included wealthy non-Eupatrids, continued to enjoy wide powers, functioning as the guardian of the constitution and retaining extensive judicial powers.

Athenians of later generations honored the memory of Solon as the great lawgiver. His laws, inscribed on stelae and rotating pieces of wood, supplanted many of the legal measures of Draco. Although Athenian tradition often credits Solon with laws that were enacted in later times, analysis of the scattered remaining evidence provides a fairly reliable picture of the essentially Solonian measures. His laws encompassed a wide range of human activity and cannot be reviewed in any depth here. Many of his enactments concerned family and inheritance, including adoption. To prevent a family from dying out, Solon permitted a man without legitimate sons to adopt a male as his heir. We saw that Solon left the homicide laws of Draco substantially intact, with continuing traces of the right to conduct a blood feud. Of particular interest, Solon enacted legislation permitting any citizen to institute legal proceedings to satisfy wrongs inflicted on himself or others. Granting citizens the right to seek justice on behalf of those wronged—formerly restricted to victims and their families—reflects an important contribution to the Athenian justice system. Although Solon's laws carefully guarded family and property rights, many of their provisions had far-reaching consequences for the evolution of Athenian society.

Solon had freed the poor farmers of Attica from a serflike existence, attacked agricultural distress, provided constitutional compromise substituting wealth for birth as the qualification for office, and bound the community to modified laws. After completing his momentous year in office, according to tradition, Solon went abroad for ten years. Yet soon after he left Athens new political struggles erupted, for the poor reached for additional privileges, while the Eupatrids agonized over the cancellation of debts and loss of their absolute ruling monopoly.

PISISTRATUS AND HIS SONS

Political Factions.   Strife finally broke out again in Athens, not between economic classes but between noble factions supported by strong client interests. Aristotle says the discontent led to such bitter feuds that no archon could be chosen in 590 and 586 BCE. The archon of 582 refused to relinquish his post for more than two years, until expelled by force. Classical writers mention three main factions, all led by aristocrats, arising in the assembly. The three groups, each loosely connected with a region, later became known as the Plain, the Coast, and the Hill. The Plain, which was dominated by many of the old noble families, challenged the Solonian reforms and opposed the Coast, made up of moderates supporting those reforms. The Coast seems to have included the bulk of the artisans and merchants and was led by Megacles of the Alcmaeonid clan, the successful suitor for the hand of Agariste of Sicyon and descendant of the archon of the same name who had butchered Cylon's associates. Apparently the Hill included certain discontented elements, perhaps the landless agricultural workers employed on large estates, and was led by Pisistratus. A noble distantly related to Solon, Pisistratus had won popularity by his command of a successful campaign against Megara.

The Tyranny of Pisistratus.   Colorful ancient sources report that Pisistratus deliberately inflicted wounds on himself and his mules, blaming the injuries on his political foes. The deceived assembly granted him a bodyguard of fifty club bearers, with whose help he seized the Acropolis and made himself tyrant in 561 BCE. Although the Plain and the Coast soon united to eject him from Athens, Pisistratus subsequently profited from renewed squabbles between the two factions to reach an accord with Megacles, leader of the Alcmaeonids, who offered to restore him to power if he would marry his daughter. Herodotus tells a picturesque story, perhaps true, that the two new allies devised an ingenious scheme about 558 BCE for smoothing Pisistratus' return. They disguised a tall, striking woman as the goddess Athena, placing her on a chariot in full armor, and she rode with Pisistratus to the Acropolis, where the enthusiastic people rejoiced and welcomed the deity-sponsored leader. Yet Herodotus reports that Pisistratus and Megacles soon fell out because the restored tyrant refused to consummate the marriage with his new wife, for he did not want to complicate the rights of his existing sons with additional offspring.

The enraged Megacles succeeded in driving Pisistratus from Athens again. The exiled tyrant lived abroad for about a decade, settling first in Macedonia and then in southwest Thrace, where he gained sufficient wealth from silver and gold mines to put together a large force of mercenaries for the purpose of seizing power in Athens. In 546 BCE, with important assistance from various states, Pisistratus defeated his foes in battle and restored his tyranny. He maintained his power through the ample use of mercenary soldiers and ruled Athens until his death in 527 BCE, with his sons succeeding him until 510 BCE.

Despite all his fulminations against tyrants, Aristotle emphasizes in his *Constitution of the Athenians* that the rule of Pisistratus was characterized by mildness and popularity. Pisistratus continued the Solonian policy of curtailing Eupatrid power. He banished his leading noble opponents but eased strained relations with other aristocratic families. He pleased the poor by establishing a modest tax on agricultural produce employing part of the revenue for granting loans to small-scale farmers, presumably on easy terms, so they could purchase adequate seed, draft animals, and plows. He undertook building projects in Athens to provide work for the unemployed and to beautify the city, creating a new agora, an aqueduct, and several additional temples.

Famed as a patron of culture, Pisistratus attracted artisans, poets, and philosophers to Athens. He courted additional popularity by supporting public festivals, including the City Dionysia held in the spring in honor of Dionysus, god of fertility, wine, and drama. The theatrical contests performed at the City Dionysia evolved into tragedy, the literary and theatrical glory of Athens in the next century. Likewise, Pisistratus expanded the magnificence of the great Panathenaic festival honoring Athena, the main event of which was the long sacrificial procession to the Acropolis, culminating with the presentation to the goddess of a new robe embroidered for her by young Athenian women. Thus he enhanced one of the major religious festivals of Greece.

Pisistratus is credited also with instituting traveling judges to settle minor lawsuits throughout Attica, another step in breaking the power of rural nobles and enforcing the jurisdiction of the state in distant territories. Much of Pisistratus' achievement stemmed from his willingness to spend from his considerable personal fortune, which came from his holdings in the mining area of Thrace, on the public interest. His policies improved the lot of the ordinary Athenian while vastly increasing the importance of Athens among the Greek states.

Lastly, Pisistratus' foreign policy fired Athens to increase its alliances in the Aegean world. The tyrant cultivated friendly relations with his neighbors—including Thessaly, Argos, and the cities of Boeotia—and with other states likely to increase Athenian commerce. The city of Thebes in Boeotia, for example, became an ally and helped to protect the northern frontier of Attica. The Athenians wrestled the adjacent island of Salamis from Megara while forging closer links with other Aegean islands. Pisistratus' policies anticipated the future claim of Athens to be the mother and leader of all Ionian Greeks. He enjoyed good relations with the marble-rich Cycladic island of Naxos, whose artists were prominent in the development of early monumental sculpture and architecture. Moreover, Pisistratus actively promoted colonial expansion. He secured partial control over the Hellespont by capturing Sigeum in the Troad (the northwest corner of Asia Minor), thereby protecting the vital grain route from the Black Sea. Another colony protecting Athenian trading interests in the northern Aegean and Black Sea regions was Thracian Chersonesus, the slender wheat-growing peninsula projecting southwest from Thrace and strategically positioned between Europe and Asia. Thus under Pisistratus' leadership Athens acquired not only important colonies but also vital markets for its pottery and other products.

Hippias and Hipparchus.   Pisistratus died peacefully in 527 BCE. The tyranny then passed to his eldest son, Hippias, while one of the younger sons, Hipparchus, shared in the rule by managing public works and the arts. Apparently the sons governed along the mild lines established by their father, but the Athenians were becoming restless under the rule of tyrants. The nobles resented the loss of their former privileges, while the lower classes grumbled over their exclusion from the magistracies.

Meanwhile, according to Thucydides, a handsome youth named Harmodius rejected the romantic advances of Hipparchus, who retaliated by arranging a public insult to the boy's sister. Harmodius and his lover—an older adolescent male named Aristogiton—were outraged by the insult and assassinated Hipparchus in 514 BCE. The sources suggest the assassins also hoped to rouse the citizens in rebellion against the tyranny. Although Harmodius and Aristogiton paid for the deed with their lives, the two young tyrant-slayers were celebrated by the nobles as heroic martyrs in a struggle to destroy Pisistratid rule. Later Athenians toasted the pair of lovers in drinking songs and honored them with statues and cult.

The immediate effect of the assassination was to thoroughly frighten the surviving brother, Hippias, now convinced that dangerous discontent was widespread. He abandoned enlightened rule in favor of harsh despotism. About 513 BCE, not long after the assassination, his regime was beset with a staggering economic recession, for westward-encroaching Persia captured Thrace, including the gold and silver mines that had enriched the Pisistratids. In the meantime the Alcmaeonids, again in exile, attempted to invade Attica but were repulsed by Hippias' forces. Turning to diplomacy to accomplish their schemes, the Alcmaeonids succeeded in persuading Delphi to urge the Spartans to overthrow Hippias.

The command of Apollo reinforced the old Spartan policy of supporting conservative governments and thus opposing tyrannies. The aggressive new Spartan king Cleomenes I and his hoplites invaded Attica in 510 BCE and besieged Hippias on the Acropolis. When the children of the Pisistratid family were captured as they were being smuggled from Athens, Hippias surrendered to recover them, on condition of retiring from the country. The tyranny of the Pisistratids was finished. After first withdrawing to Sigeum in the Troad, Hippias sought refuge at the court of King Darius I of Persia. There he looked to the extension of Persian power to restore his position in Athens, and twenty years later the aged Hippias accompanied the Persians on their invasion of his native land.

The Reforms of Cleisthenes

With the downfall of Hippias, the long-suppressed nobles regained political control in Athens, though their struggle for power resulted in furious party strife. Isagoras, leader of a conservative noble faction, was elected first archon in 508 BCE, against the wishes of Cleisthenes, the head of the Alcmaeonid family. The grandson of the great tyrant of Sicyon bearing the same name, Cleisthenes had fled with the Alcmaeonids into exile during Hippias' reign, eventually settling at Delphi, where he rebuilt the recently burned temple of Apollo. We hear that he persuaded Delphi, in return for generously exceeding the terms of the building contract, to urge the Spartans to overthrow Hippias.

Cleisthenes turned the tables on his rival Isagoras when he forged an alliance with the masses—the *demos*—by proposing major reforms. The frightened Isagoras then appealed to Sparta for military intervention, a step with clear risks of reducing Athens to a dependency of the powerful southern state. Spartan king Cleomenes, who had fallen out with Cleisthenes, soon arrived in Athens with a small force. Invoking the old hereditary curse tainting the Alcmaeonids at the time of the Cylonian massacre, Cleomenes banished Cleisthenes and his followers. The Spartan ruler announced that the government of Athens would be entrusted to a council of three hundred Athenian aristocrats headed by Isagoras. The indignant Athenians rose up and besieged Cleomenes and Isagoras on the Acropolis, forcing them to surrender and leave the country, whereupon Cleisthenes and his Alcmaeonid followers returned in triumph.

The Ten New Tribes.   Cleisthenes then seized the opportunity to institute far-reaching reforms, thereby establishing the essential framework for the later Athenian democracy. The basis of his reorganization was a complicated and variously interpreted new tribal system. Much of the dissention in Attica stemmed from the old tribal organization, with loyalty to tribe taking priority over duty to state. Cleisthenes drastically curtailed the noble-dominated, four hereditary Ionian tribes—they were retained only for religious purposes—and divided the citizens into ten new tribes, named for legendary Athenian heroes selected by the Delphic oracle.

The Demes and the Trittyes.   The ten new tribes served as the basic administrative and military units of the state. The old tribes were closely linked to birth, the new to geography. Now tribal membership was based on residence in the demes—corresponding to existing villages or other small districts—of which there were more than one hundred in Attica at the time. A new tribe was constructed of three groups of demes, one group from each of the three new regions: the city (Athens and its immediate vicinity), the coast, and the inland. This principle of the thirds, or *trittyes*, meant that each tribe included residents from each region and thus represented a cross-section of interests and a mixture of citizens, a principle breaking up the old privileged position of the aristocrats. Because each tribe contained three *trittyes*, thirty *trittyes* were required to make up the ten new tribes. The number of demes was increased as Athens grew, but the number of *trittyes* and tribes remained constant.

The people of the demes worshiped their own local patron gods and enjoyed a measure of local self-government. Each deme annually elected its own mayor (or *demarchos*), maintained its own assembly, and kept an official membership list, admitting new males at the age of eighteen. Inclusion on the deme rolls guaranteed citizenship, formerly based upon membership in a clan or a phratry. Membership in the deme eventually became hereditary, and a male retained his original registration even if moving to another. He automatically belonged to the tribe of his deme and participated in the government as a member of one of the ten new tribes. By introducing the new tribal system, Cleisthenes encouraged the Athenians to shift their basic allegiance from the clans or the traditional tribes to the polis. Moreover, he increased the participation of ordinary Athenians in the government by making residence rather than birth the qualification for citizenship.

The Council of Five Hundred.   Cleisthenes reconstituted the Solonian Council of Four Hundred as the Council of Five Hundred, or *boule*, the common name for the main council in Greek states. The Cleisthenic *boule* represents a keystone in the development of the Athenian democracy, which reached full fruition in the fifth century BCE. The new council was made up of five hundred members—fifty from each of the ten tribes—with all citizens over thirty eligible for membership, though the poor could not afford to serve until pay was introduced in the fifth century BCE. The fifty members from each tribe were chosen annually by lot from among candidates elected as proposed councilors by the demes. An early example of proportional legislation, the fifty positions for the council were distributed among the demes in accordance with the population of each. No citizen could serve as a member of the *boule* more than twice in his lifetime, ensuring that thousands of Athenians gained some experience in the administration of the state. The Council of Five Hundred met in the council house, or Bouleuterion, in the agora, with responsibilities for managing financial and foreign affairs and for preparing business destined to come before the assembly.

The Prytanies.   A body of five hundred men was far too large for overseeing daily affairs. Thus fifty councilors from each tribe took turns serving as an executive committee of the *boule*. Known as the prytanies (Greek *prytaneis*), the executive committees were responsible for managing the council's day-to-day business. Each prytany served for one-tenth of the year. This period was called a prytany, and came to be used as a measure of time. The official Athenian year was divided into ten prytanies (the prytany calendar). A different councilor was chosen daily by lot to act as president of a prytany, another application of the rotation principle. In the fifth century BCE an office building called the Tholos, from its circular shape, was built for the prytanies next to the Bouleuterion. A third of the prytany always remained in the Tholos, on call day or night.

The Archons and the Areopagus.   The archons—still key magistrates—continued to be elected from the upper class and to pass after their year of office into the conservative Areopagus, which retained considerable, though ill-defined, powers and duties. Although its responsibilities were reduced by the creation of Cleisthenes' new

Council of Five Hundred, the Areopagus certainly exercised numerous judicial functions, prosecuting those magistrates and others who violated the laws.

The Assembly.   We saw that the Council of Five Hundred prepared business for the assembly, though any citizen was entitled to speak in the *ekklesia* and to make or amend a proposal. The assembly, which met regularly on a hill in Athens called the Pnyx, retained the rights and prerogatives granted by Solon of passing decrees or laws, electing magistrates, and imposing judicial penalties through the *heliaea*. The final legislative authority in the state, the assembly consisted of all male citizens over eighteen. Its meetings were potentially very large, though actual attendance tended to be restricted to urban males, and the leisured aristocratic class probably dominated proceedings. A noteworthy feature was a rule prohibiting men from addressing the body if they were in debt to the state or had thrown away their shields during battle.

Ostracism.   Aristotle, probably correctly, attributes to Cleisthenes the extraordinary institution of ostracism, apparently intended to prevent the recurrence of dangerous factional warfare but evolving into a device for banishing unpopular citizens and destroying political careers. Every year the members of the assembly voted whether they wanted to proceed with an ostracism. An affirmative vote gave them the right to inscribe on a piece of broken pottery—an *ostrakon*—the name of a man they viewed as a threat to the security of the community. If the responses exceeded six thousand, the man with the greatest number of votes was exiled for ten years without loss of citizenship or property. (An alternate but less likely idea suggests an ostracism went into effect only when a man received at least six thousand votes.) Surprisingly, the mechanism was not put into effect until 487 BCE—two decades after the reforms of Cleisthenes—possibly because a quorum of six thousand votes was not obtained until that date.

Military Reorganization and the Strategoi.   The new tribes of Cleisthenes resulted in an important change in the military organization. Each of the ten tribes was required to provide a regiment of hoplites. Henceforth the ten tribal regiments of hoplites formed the primary Athenian land force. Meanwhile Cleisthenes or an immediate successor set up a new board of ten generals, or *strategoi*, normally one from each tribe, who became more important than the archons. At an uncertain date, perhaps 487 BCE, the decision was made to appoint the archons—including the polemarch—by lot from a select list, thereby seriously eroding their political significance. The polemarch ceased commanding forces on the field of battle after Marathon in 490 BCE, his duties becoming largely ceremonial.

The vital and specialized duties of the *strategoi* precluded choosing them by lot. They were elected annually in the assembly and could be reelected repeatedly in recognition of the ongoing need for their military expertise. Accordingly, ambitious Athenian politicians desired this prize as an avenue of continuing authority. The *strategoi* served as the highest military offices in the state, commanding both the army and navy. As the fifth century BCE progressed, Athens embarked on an imperialistic policy that resulted in numerous crises and wars, and the generalship—usually the preserve of aristocratic families—became increasingly powerful. Thus the *strategoi* tempered the democratic thrust of the Cleisthenic reforms. They strongly influenced the Council of Five Hundred and probably gained the right to send supplemental proposals to the assembly. The most able among them clearly dominated both domestic and foreign affairs.

Notwithstanding the emergence of the powerful *strategoi*, Cleisthenes' reforms had carried Athens one step closer to the democracy of the fifth century BCE. His new ten-tribe system introduced residence in the deme, not birth, as the sole test of citizenship. Although all the traditional organizations remained intact—including the four tribes, the many clans, the ancient phratries, and the customary priesthoods—they were reduced to social and religious functions. Yet conservative checks remained in place, exemplified by the absence of pay for public service, which kept the poorest citizens from continuous participation in either the assembly or the courts, and aristocrats usually continued to occupy the great offices of state.

Thus Cleisthenes inaugurated a political system combining conservative and liberal principles, a trend that would continue throughout Athenian history. His genius was to pair aristocratic and popular participation in the government, giving ordinary citizens experience in the political process for the first time in history, and his progressive framework endured for centuries. After creating his new social order, Cleisthenes passed from the scene in silence, whether from death or loss of approval remains unknown.

The Return of Cleomenes

In 506 BCE Spartan ruler Cleomenes attempted to avenge his recent humiliation at the hands of the Athenians by restoring Isagoras. The Spartans and their allies marched into Attica from the south, while the Thebans and their Boeotian allies and the Chalcidians threatened from the north. Although the reason for Chalcis' presence remains unknown, the city of Thebes in Boeotia had become hostile to Athens several years earlier when the small state of Plataea—a Boeotian town near the frontier of Attica—had refused to join the Theban-dominated Boeotian League, instead seeking and receiving Athenian protection. Cleomenes' attempted coercion was thwarted at the last minute, for he was abandoned by his fellow king Demaratus and obstructed by his Corinthian ally. When Cleomenes and the Peloponnesian forces withdrew, the Athenians turned and won a complete victory over the Boeotian army. Then on the same day, according to Herodotus, they followed and defeated the retreating Chalcidians in Euboea. These impressive dual victories are said to have given the Athenians great confidence in their new form of government. We hear that about two years later Cleomenes proposed the restoration of the exiled tyrant Hippias but failed because once again the Corinthians opposed intervention in Athens.

Overtures to Persia.   King Cleomenes' invasion in 506 BCE prompted Athens to make overtures to Persia for protection. The extremely steep terms demanded surrender of all Athenian territory to Persian overlordship. Although the desperate

Athenian ambassadors acquiesced, the crisis had passed by the time they returned home, and the terms were repudiated. Yet threats were now coming from Thebes, Sparta, and elsewhere. The Athenians again sued for a Persian alliance, breaking off negotiations when the eastern giant made the restoration of Hippias a condition. The Athenians wanted to forget the entire episode, but unfolding events, covered in chapter 8, show the Persians had a long memory indeed. Meanwhile Athens, though less powerful than Sparta, was enjoying considerable commercial success, and Cleisthenes' remarkably reorganized state had demonstrated its effectiveness in times of war as well as peace.

CHAPTER VI

RELIGION IN ARCHAIC GREECE

The Archaic period, from about 750 to 480 BCE, witnessed not only revolutionary change in Greek social and political life but also accelerated artistic and intellectual development, attested by a wealth of material evidence and literary remains. Religion pervades many of the greatest works of Archaic art and literature, for honoring the gods and goddesses was an essential element of Greek existence. By the middle of the eighth century BCE Greek civilization had already revealed the potential of its grandeur through the passion and stately verse of the *Iliad* and *Odyssey*. During the following centuries the ancient Greeks remained under the spell of Homer, who saw the world through the eyes of the nobility, endowing his heroes with aristocratically applauded virtues such as courage and honor. We saw that the poet Hesiod, who flourished around 700 BCE, extolled contrasting ideals, exemplified by the practical farming values of thrift and hard work. Meanwhile the new social classes arising in the seventh and sixth centuries BCE stressed yet another cardinal virtue—moderation—as indicated by Solon's reported favorite motto, "Nothing in excess," later inscribed on the wall of the temple of Apollo at Delphi. Notwithstanding the hallowedness of this principle, the Greeks would always find the ideal of moderation extraordinarily difficult to attain.

THE INFLUENCE OF HOMER AND HESIOD

Sacred practices and beliefs were fundamental to the culture of the ancient Greeks. Their religious institutions were of diverse origins. We saw that the Greeks were an Indo-European-speaking people who had settled in the Aegean world, inheriting composite sacred traditions from their predecessors and from the remarkable civilizations of the ancient Near East. Only one of their gods, Zeus, king of the gods and lord of the sky, possessed a name proving certain descent from an Indo-European deity. As noted in chapter 2, a number of divine names mentioned in Mycenaean texts were borne by great gods and goddesses of the later Greeks. Zeus, Hera, Poseidon, Athena, Artemis, Hermes, and Ares are clearly attested. Allusion to Dionysus is probable, to Demeter possible. Moreover, many functions of Archaic Greek deities were inherited from Minoan-Mycenaean and other pantheons.

Homer and Hesiod are credited with the considerable achievement of standardizing the gods for the Greeks. Although rooted in memory of the distant Mycenaean civilization, the Homeric epics generally reflect religious beliefs of the eighth century BCE. The *Iliad* and *Odyssey* were widely venerated among Archaic Greeks, partly because of their epic grandeur, but were not regarded as revelations of unchangeable divine truth. Homer presents the gods as anthropomorphic beings with fully defined personalities. While clearly subject to humanlike passions and failings, the Homeric deities are distinct from humankind in their immortality and superhuman power. Immortality certainly set them aside from the old gods of vegetation who lived in the dark earth, who grew old and died. The Greeks believed a divinity subject to death and rebirth every year was less than immortal and refused to include such beings among their greatest gods.

In Homer the major deities lead an existence paralleling in many ways that of the earthly nobility. Although the warrior-nobles are supported or opposed at every turn by heaven, they regard their relations with the gods as those between a lesser and a greater order of beings. Homer sings of humans attempting to propitiate the gods through prayers, sacrifices, and oaths, for each deity controlled a particular province of human activity and could quickly bestow either favor or harm. He tells scandalous tales of divine quarrels and treachery and points out that the gods, though majestic, could be raucous, deceitful, and petty. Yet both Zeus and Apollo frequently demonstrate certain exalted qualities separating them from the others.

Homer describes an age when the gods still walked upon the face of the earth, but what of a previous state of affairs? The poet Hesiod composed his epic known as the *Theogony* to account for the origin of the universe and the descent of the gods. Hesiod, who says his father moved to Boeotia from Asia Minor, borrows heavily from the myths of western Asia and Mesopotamia.

MYTHS OF CREATION

Chaos Produces Gaea and Other Beings.   Hesiod declares that in the beginning the empty void of Chaos was the first power to arise. Out of Chaos came both Erebus, the darkness of the netherworld, and Night, the darkness over the earth. Then Erebus slept with Night, and the latter gave birth to Ether, the heavenly light, and to Day, the earthly light. Thus light was created before the sun, as in the biblical book of Genesis. Chaos also bore Earth, or Gaea, who conceived alone to bring forth Heaven, or Uranus. Gaea represents the creation of the female principle, Uranus the male principle.

Cronus Castrates Uranus.   Gaea became the consort of her son, Uranus, the first ruling deity, and the divine pair produced many beings, including the Hecatonchires (three monsters each having fifty heads and one hundred powerful arms) and the older generation of gods—the Titans—of whom twelve are named. Uranus hated and feared the Titans and kept them (as well as the Hecatonshires) captive within the womb of Gaea, who could not give birth and writhed in agony. She persuaded Cronus, the youngest of the Titans, to castrate Uranus with a jagged metal sickle. Cronus carried out the deed while Uranus was sexually united with Gaea. This is Hesiod's device for explaining the primeval separation of Heaven (Uranus) and Earth (Gaea). Cronus then threw the severed genitals behind him with great force. Blood from them fell upon Gaea, from which she produced several groups of

Zeus attacks a Titan or a Giant, pedimental figures from the Temple of Artemis on Corcyra (modern Corfu), early sixth century BCE. Violent scenes of Olympian power were popular for decorating early Greek temples. Corfu Museum.

offspring, including the Erinyes (the Roman Furies), spirits of vengeance upholding the rights of parents against their children, and the Giants, described by Homer as monstrous savages but by Hesiod as huge valiant warriors. The Giants emerged from Gaea, Hesiod says, "dressed in resplendent armor and holding long spears in their hands. . . ." In the meantime Uranus' castrated genitals fell into the sea. From the foam gathering round them rose a beautiful deity called Aphrodite, the goddess of erotic love, whose name derives from the Greek word for foam (*aphros*).

Zeus Dethrones Cronus.   Hesiod declares that the Titans, ruled by Cronus, held sway for a while. Cronus and his sister-consort Rhea produced six of the majestic deities known as the Olympians: Hestia, Demeter, Hera, Hades, Poseidon, and Zeus. Like Uranus before him, Cronus feared a usurper. He attempted to prevent his children from seizing the throne by swallowing them, but Rhea saved Zeus—the youngest son—by substituting for him a stone dressed in infant's clothing. After growing to manhood on the island of Crete, the disguised Zeus gave an emetic potion to Cronus, who vomited up the swallowed children fully grown. Zeus and his disgorged siblings then defeated Cronus and relegated him to the earthly paradise of the Isles of the Blest, where the vanquished god reigned over some favored heroes. A new threat arose when the Titans rebelled against the powerful upstart gods, but Zeus and the other Olympians eventually triumphed after a cosmos-shaking battle of ten years (the Titanomachy). Later, the Giants fought the Olympians in a famous war (the Gigantomachy), piling mountain upon mountain to dislodge the gods from the summit of Mount Olympus. Aided by the mortal Heracles, the gods eventually triumphed, and the Giants were buried under mountains and volcanos in various parts of Greece and Italy. Now Zeus and the other Olympians wielded undisputed authority.

THE GREEK PANTHEON

The Twelve Olympian Gods

Although Homer and Hesiod describe deities who simply taper off in importance from almighty Zeus to the quite minor spirits of field and stream, the later Greeks conventionally distinguished Twelve Gods above all others: Zeus, Hera, Poseidon, Hephaestus, Ares, Apollo, Artemis, Demeter, Aphrodite, Athena, Hermes, and Dionysus. These were the Olympians, the most exalted gods and goddesses of Greek religion. Most of the Olympians were thought to dwell on the highest peak of the heavenly mountain Olympus in Thessaly, where they passed their days in the radiance of eternal youth. Homer depicts them as world rulers living together in Zeus' sprawling palace.

Zeus.   First among the Olympians stood Zeus, god of sky and weather, hurler of the thunderbolts by which he destroyed foes and made all the world tremble. An old Indo-European sky god worshiped under cognate names in India, Iran, and elsewhere, Zeus entered the Aegean world with early Greek-speaking settlers. Here he tended to merge with other deities, ultimately taking their cults, their myths, and their powers. Zeus served as the supreme god of all the Greeks, his numerous titles indicating his dominion over the entire range of human life and conduct.

A Homeric phrase acknowledges Zeus as "Father of gods and men." His epithet *Father* should not be understood to mean special creator of deities or humans but protector and ruler of heaven and earth. Although Zeus furiously struck down enemies with his thunderbolt, he was also a god of healing and protector of the weak. Moreover, he was the wrathful god of justice and virtue who had established the moral order of the universe and continued to uphold what was holy and sacred. Eventually the Greek philosophers elevated him from his old position of fatherly concern to the austere dignity of an impersonal cosmic force. Zeus appears in art as a kingly, bearded figure, majestically robed in the Archaic period, later sometimes shown in heroic nudity. He may be accompanied by his attributes of crown, throne, scepter, thunderbolt, and eagle. The Romans identified Zeus with the Italian sky-god Jupiter.

Hera.   Zeus' consort was Hera, queen of the gods, worshiped in pre-Hellenic times at Argos and elsewhere as a powerful fertility goddess. The early Greeks yielded to the popularity of her cult and adopted the goddess as the sister-wife of their chief god. Mythologically, Hera was the daughter of Cronus and Rhea. As goddess of marriage, she exhibited particular concern for protecting wives and mothers. Hera was famous for her jealousy, aroused by Zeus' inexhaustible promiscuity. She mercilessly persecuted many of his mistresses and lovers, even seeking vengeance upon their descendants. In art she is often depicted as a stately woman, sometimes wearing an elaborate crown and holding a scepter surmounted by a cuckoo, the emblem of the deceived spouse. Her costume may include the magic girdle of Aphrodite, known for making its wearer irresistibly desirable. At times she appears in her chariot drawn by a pair of peacocks. The Romans identified Hera with the Italian goddess Juno.

Poseidon.   Zeus' brother Poseidon, another of the Twelve, is an ancient and important god whose name appears in Mycenaean tablets. As god of water, he fertilized the earth and became the ruler of waves. His connection with the sea gave him a natural popularity among the Greeks. Poseidon was famous for siring the horse, one version of the myth declaring that he spilled his semen on a rock from which the first horse sprang forth. Poseidon embodied elemental forces. Accordingly, he was responsible for earthquakes, on occasion violently shaking the lands and seas under the dome of heaven. He was a wrathful, moody figure who carried a trident, or three-pronged spear, and traveled in the company of sea nymphs and monsters of the deep. His seductions, like those of Zeus, included mortals of both sexes. An important Archaic stone temple of Poseidon—later replaced by a new sanctuary after a fire—stood on the Isthmus of Corinth. Poseidon appears in art as an older but majestic god, usually easily recognized by his trident. He may be depicted astride a dolphin, sacred to him in antiquity, or riding his chariot pulled by sea creatures. The Romans identified Poseidon with the Italian water-god Neptune.

Hephaestus.   Another of the Twelve, Hephaestus, god of fire, apparently originated as a non-Greek deity of volcanic fire. His cult seems to have spread from the volcanic region of Asia Minor to Greece via the island of Lemnos, the center of his cult. In mythology, Hephaestus was a son of Zeus and Hera or, according to another version, of Hera alone. Because he was misshapen and lame, his mother hurled him from heaven at birth, but he became a talented metalsmith and was later brought back to Olympus, where he created splendid works for the gods. As god of fire in its creative aspect, Hephaestus produced many magic devices. He took revenge on his mother by ensnaring her in an artfully constructed golden throne that gripped her with invisible bands. Despite his ugliness, Hephaestus became the husband of the erotic Aphrodite, who was unfaithful to him, especially with the virile war-god

Ares. After the outraged Hephaestus set up a net and caught the two making love, he called the other deities to come and have a hearty laugh at the naked pair. Hephaestus is a favorite subject in art, often showing up in scenes with Aphrodite or other deities. He is frequently depicted as a robust smith at his anvil, sometimes standing awkwardly because of his twisted feet. He may be accompanied by his assistants, the one-eyed giants known as the Cyclopes, though they usually appear as brawny men with normal eyes. The Romans identified Hephaestus with the Italian fire-god Volcanus (Vulcan).

Ares.   The name of another Olympian, Ares, god of war, is attested in Linear B tablets. An offspring of Zeus and Hera, Ares exhibited an insatiable appetite for bloodshed, producing untold carnage on the battlefield. His brutal nature made him unpopular with the other Olympians, except for his lover Aphrodite. In the *Iliad* his bombastic, murderous nature is frequently contrasted with the wisdom of his female counterpart, the warrior goddess Athena. Ares appears in art as an ordinary Greek warrior, with helmet, shield, sword, and spear. He is far less significant than his Roman equivalent Mars.

Apollo.   One of the supremely important Olympians was the young god Apollo, possibly non-Greek in both name and origin. Perhaps he was a recent arrival. There is no clear evidence for Apollo in Mycenaean tablets, though he was not necessarily unknown. His cult was widespread in Greece by the time the Homeric epics were committed to writing. His two great centers of worship were his Cycladic island birthplace of Delos and his famous oracular shrine of Delphi, which ancient pilgrims must have approached with reverence and exaltation. God of light, prophecy, healing, archery, music, and youthful male beauty, Apollo—like Zeus and others—became a composite deity in Greece with multiple functions and a complex character. As a solar deity, he was god of light, the ripener of the fruits of the earth, and his radiant beauty gave him the epithet Phoebus, or shining. He enjoyed jurisdiction over the rites of purification by which the Greeks sought to maintain peace with the gods. Apollo was known also for his dual nature, at once beneficent and terrible. He healed illness yet sent raging plagues. He inculcated high moral principles yet killed without mercy by shooting his terrible arrows.

Apollo pursued numerous romantic adventures, though most proved tragic or unsuccessful. When the Trojan princess Cassandra rejected his advances after he had given her the power of prophecy, he doomed her to foretell in vain, for no one would believe her utterances. The nymph Daphne was changed by Gaea into a laurel tree before Apollo could ravish her. Apollo consoled himself by placing a wreath fashioned from the tree in his hair, the mythological explanation of why laurel was sacred to him. Apollo also sought romantic relationships with boys, exemplified by his devotion to the Spartan Hyacinthus. A famous version of the story tells us that Apollo aroused the jealousy of Zephyrus, the West Wind, who had fallen in love with the boy himself. One day when Apollo was instructing his beloved in discus throwing, Zephyrus diverted the missile to strike Hyacinthus on the head with a killing blow. From his blood on the ground sprang the hyacinth, a brilliant lily-shaped purple flower. Apollo is a very popular figure in art, appearing as an idealized youth of rare beauty—usually nude—and often holding a bow or a lyre and wearing a crown of laurel leaves. Roman Apollo is identical with his Greek counterpart.

Artemis.   Long worshiped in Greece, Artemis, goddess of hunting, was another pre-Hellenic deity, one with Near Eastern and Minoan connections. Her name is attested on Linear B tablets. Mythologically, Artemis was the daughter of Zeus and the goddess Leto, and she was born on the island of Delos with her twin brother Apollo. Artemis remained an unapproachable virgin, an inviolable goddess with the dual function of taking and giving life. She served both as a huntress and a guardian of animals. Homer describes her as the Mistress of the Animals, an eastern motif, from her responsibility to protect game. Artemis also guarded forests and hills. She was strongly linked with the moon, perhaps an association with the monthly cycle and the menstruation period. Because her mother, Leto, had delivered her without pain, Artemis was called upon to aid women in childbirth. Yet she often used her arrows to strike down young girls with sudden death, as Apollo did to young boys. In contrast to the lustful pleasures of Aphrodite, Artemis insisted upon absolute purity and chastity, utterly rejecting sensual love. She was accompanied by a devoted troop of virgin woodland nymphs. When one of them, Callisto, was hunting, Zeus suddenly appeared in the guise of Artemis herself and made love to her. In one version of the story Artemis discovers the unfortunate nymph is pregnant and prepares to kill her, whereupon Zeus transforms Callisto into the constellation of the Great Bear (Ursa Major). In art Artemis usually appears as a huntress armed with her bow and quiver. Occasionally winged, she is commonly depicted with crescent moonlike horns. The Romans identified Artemis with the Italian goddess Diana.

Demeter.   Zeus' sister Demeter, goddess of grain and the fruits of the earth, was honored throughout Greece as one of the Twelve. There are possible references to her in the Linear B tablets. The mythology of Demeter revolves around a group of chthonian deities, those of the earth and the underworld, as opposed to the celestial Olympians. The chthonian gods exhibited a double concern with the dead and the fertility of the earth. In myth, Demeter adored her daughter, Persephone, often called simply Kore, or the Maiden. Because of the very close association of mother and daughter, they are frequently described as the Two Goddesses. Their story reflects the recurring theme in antiquity of the death and rebirth of vegetation. Fathered by Zeus and strikingly beautiful, Persephone went out one day to gather flowers from a secluded meadow. As she bent down to pick a flower, the earth opened up at her feet and Hades—god of the underworld—charged out to snatch her away and make her the queen of the dead. Hearing Persephone cry out as she was being abducted, grief-stricken Demeter abandoned Olympus and came to live on the earth disguised as an old woman, eventually arriving in Eleusis, where she later established her Eleusinian Mysteries. In her anguish over the loss of Persephone, Demeter withheld the fruits of the earth and made every plant wither. Thus Zeus was forced to send for Persephone, and thereafter Hades released the goddess from the underworld each spring for two-thirds of the year, prompting Demeter to

Demeter and Persephone with Triptolemus, detail of a marble relief from
Eleusis, c. 440 BCE. Originally this superb representation was colored and
included ears of wheat and a crown, both fashioned of metal, probably gold.
Demeter, goddess of grain and the fruits of the earth, offers the ears of wheat
to the naked youth Triptolemus, while her daughter Persephone places the
crown on his head. In myth, Demeter sent Triptolemus to spread the arts of
agriculture throughout the world. National Museum, Athens.

send forth fresh crops. In art the mother and daughter often appear together, sometimes wearing crowns and carrying torches or sheaves of grain. The Romans identified Demeter with the Italian grain-goddess Ceres.

Aphrodite.   The erotic Aphrodite acquired important traits from ancient Near Eastern love goddesses such as the Phoenician Astarte and may have been an eastern import from the post-Mycenaean period. Primarily a goddess of fertility and beguilement, Aphrodite presided over beauty and the act of love. She is familiar in epic poetry for her many sexual unions. In myth, Aphrodite won the golden apple in the beauty contest with Hera and Athena by promising the Trojan prince Paris fair Helen. Paris carried Helen off from Sparta during her husband's absence, leading to the outbreak of the Trojan War, during which Aphrodite sided with the Trojans. Aphrodite often appears in art rising from the sea, frequently accompanied by her attributes, including paired doves or swans (either may draw her chariot), scallop shells or dolphins (each signifies her birth from the sea), and her magic girdle or a flaming torch (both kindle love). She may show up standing by the side of her son, Eros, who presides over sexual desire. While her earlier images are normally majestic, her fourth-century BCE representations are usually characterized by sensuality, as exemplified by Praxiteles' renowned nude statue *Aphrodite of Cnidus*, surviving only in inferior Roman copies. The Romans identified Aphrodite with the Italian goddess Venus.

Athena.   Probably pre-Hellenic in origin, Athena or a precursor is mentioned in a Linear B tablet at Knossos as a "Lady of Athena." The later Greeks worshiped her not only as goddess of war but also as the personification of wisdom, the patron of crafts, especially the work of women in spinning and weaving, and the guardian of Athens and other cities. She shows up in Homer as an armored female warrior befriending the Greeks against the Trojans. Hesiod, in telling the story of her birth, says the first wife of Zeus, the goddess Metis, became pregnant with Athena, whereupon the almighty Olympian swallowed his consort, for fear she carried a son who would overthrow him. Later, bright-eyed Athena sprang from Zeus' head fully armed with his aegis, a shield with miraculous protective powers. The story of her birth symbolizes the unique bond between the divine father and his favorite daughter, famous for her prowess, wisdom, and masculinity. The nature of this fierce warrior maiden relates to her birth from a father rather than a mother. One of her many titles is Pallas, possibly meaning *maiden* and signifying the goddess' chastity. She was honored foremost by the Greeks as Athena Polias, protector of cities.

Athena is closely linked by name and sphere of influence with Athens. Around the late sixth century BCE the Athenians inaugurated their famous silver coinage bearing the head of Athena and an image of her owl. The sixth-century tyrant Pisistratus exalted Athena. He initiated an ambitious project of crowning the steep hill of the Acropolis with gleaming monuments. About this time the Athenians built on the Acropolis a large temple called the Parthenon, a name betraying its dedication to Athena Parthenos (the Virgin Athena). A century later this temple was replaced by an even more magnificent Parthenon, whose imposing ruins have come to symbolize Greek art and Athenian splendor. Pisistratus also enhanced the great annual festival in Athens known as the Panathenaea, celebrated with particular magnificence every fourth year—the Greater Panathenaea—when contestants were invited from every part of Greece to compete in music, poetry, and athletics. Prisoners were

This marble relief from Athens, *c.* 470 BCE, shows the goddess Athena mourning as she leans on a spear and gazes at what was probably a list of Athenians killed in battle. Acropolis Museum, Athens.

set free, slaves were permitted to feast with their masters, and the Homeric epics were recited. One of the principal features every fourth year was the Panathenaic procession of the free population, the participants making their way from the streets of Athens to the Acropolis to present the goddess with a new embroidered robe (*peplos*) for her statue. The splendid spectacle of the Panathenaic procession is depicted on the famous Elgin Marbles, once gracing the frieze of the Parthenon and now displayed in the British Museum. Clearly, Athens and Athena were wedded in

Marble herm from Siphnos, late sixth century BCE. Herms were pillars topped with the head of the god Hermes and usually adorned with an erect phallus on the front. The pillars were set up at crossroads, sanctuaries, gates of private houses, and other prominent places. As representations of Hermes, they were thought to offer protection. Other deities were occasionally represented in herm form, and the Romans employed the same kind of mount to display portrait busts. National Archaeological Museum, Athens.

a holy and inseparable bond. The goddess often shows up in art bearing her military array of helmet, spear, and aegis (on which the head of the Gorgon Medusa may appear). The Romans identified Athena with the Italian goddess Minerva.

Hermes. Another of the Twelve, Hermes, the messenger of the gods, seems to be one of the oldest. An almost certain reference to him occurs in a Linear B tablet from Pylos. At first Hermes was simply a phallic deity dwelling in heaps of stones and pillars erected along roadsides to mark boundaries, but he was transformed over time into an Olympian. In myth Hermes was the son of Zeus and the nymph Maia, the pair having united while Hera slept. On the first day of his life Hermes left his cradle and sang to the accompaniment of his newly invented lyre, fashioned from a tortoise shell, thereby lulling his mother to sleep. A cunning and playful thief, the infant promptly went out and stole the cattle of his elder brother, Apollo, but the two became fast friends after Hermes gave his lyre to the irate god as a peace offering. The mischief-maker quickly found favor with Zeus, who made Hermes his herald. Thereafter Hermes was employed by the greater gods, especially Zeus, as their swift messenger. Hermes also escorted the bloodless dead to the underworld.

Personally masculine, Hermes united with the voluptuous Aphrodite to produce the androgynous god Hermaphroditus, who had the physical characteristics of both sexes. A god of great sexual power, Hermes multiplied herds of sheep and goats. Moreover, he served as the god of athletic youths exercising in the homoerotic environment of the Greek gymnasium. Hermes was famous as a god of phallic display. Before houses and at crossroads and marketplaces stood a representation of Hermes known as a herm, a pillar surmounted by the bearded head of Hermes and adorned, halfway down, with male genitals, the penis fully erect. Herms were sacred and thought to provide protection and good fortune. They were often set up along roads to invoke Hermes' protection for travelers. Accordingly, he was the god not only of travelers and merchants but also of the thieves preying on them. Besides his characteristic emblem of the herm, Hermes often appears in art as a herald, wearing a broad-rimmed traveler's hat and winged sandals and bearing his magical snake-entwined staff (the caduceus), which caused people to sleep or wake as he willed. The Romans identified Hermes with Mercury, the god of traders.

Dionysus.   Myth and literature treat Dionysus as a newcomer from Lydia, a prosperous kingdom in Asia Minor during the seventh and sixth centuries BCE, but there are probable references to him in Linear B tablets from Pylos. Mythologically, Dionysus was the son of Zeus and the mortal Semele. While Semele was carrying Dionysus in her womb, the jealous Hera came disguised and enticed the woman to petition Zeus to appear in his full majesty. Semele instantly burst into flame when her Olympian lover revealed his splendor through a flash of lightning. Yet Zeus sewed his unborn son up inside his own thigh, a part of the body having erotic associations, until the proper time for the birth. Hera's wrath continued, however, and Dionysus grew to manhood in some distant place, where he learned to change the juice of the grape into the exhilarating beverage of wine.

God of ecstasy and wine, Dionysus delighted mortals with the fermented juice of the grape. After spreading the mysteries and rites of vine cultivation far and wide, the god brought prosperity and rapturous release to his worshipers but madness and death to his opponents. In myth, Dionysus was accompanied by a retinue of Satyrs and most emphatically Maenads (the Romans called them Bacchae), frenzied female devotees carrying wands tipped with pine cones. The lecherous Satyrs—each was part man and part animal—remained in a perpetual state of sexual excitement and often chased the Maenads through the woods. The Maenads wandered and danced in the mountains, where they tore apart live boys and animals and ate them raw, for Dionysus himself was present in the bleeding flesh. The Maenads possessed their god by consuming him, a sort of ritual communion having parallels in many other religions. Mentioned below, actual Greek women known as Maenads enjoyed ecstatic revels in honor of Dionysus.

Maenads dancing for Dionysus, scene on an Attic red-figure cup by the painter Macron, *c.* 490 BCE. The maenads have been seized with Dionysiac frenzy while worshiping their god, portrayed as a human-headed pillar attired in a fine garment and sprouting vines with globes attached. Staatliche Museum, Berlin.

Thus through intoxication and orgy, Dionysus provided release and ecstasy. In contrast to the reason of Apollo, Dionysus appealed to the sensual side of human nature. In mythology he could take various forms such as a bull, lion, ram, goat, or serpent. When, in one famous story, Dionysus was captured by pirates, he caused wine to flow through their ship and a grape-laden vine to entangle the mast and sail. Dionysus himself assumed the form of a fearful lion, and he turned the terrified pirates into dolphins as they leapt into the sea. Dionysus and his followers were popular subjects for artists. He shows up in the seventh and sixth centuries BCE as an elderly bearded man dressed in a long robe, later as a beautiful naked youth. The god frequently holds a sacred wand bound with ivy and topped with a pine cone, wears an ivy wreath, and carries an upturned wine cup. The Maenads, who also are depicted carrying the wands, wear the skins of animals they have killed during the rites. Their headbands are of ivy or even snakes. The Satyrs show up as men with horse tails, pointed ears, and erect penises, symbolizing the freed impulses offered by Dionysus. The cult spread to Italy under Dionysus' other name, Bacchus.

ADDITIONAL MAJOR DEITIES

Hades.   The twelve Olympians and two others, Hades and Hestia, are generally recognized as the major deities of Classical Greece. The subterranean ruler Hades, brother to Zeus, is usually excluded from lists of the Olympians, for he belongs to the class of chthonian gods. The name Hades (the unseen one) reflects the myth that the god wore a helmet making him invisible. The Greeks dreaded pronouncing his name and usually called him by various euphemistic titles, the best known being

Pluto (the wealthy one). Essentially a god of terror and dark mystery, Hades was seldom venerated under his own name, but he received more homage as Pluto, guardian of the riches of the lower earth and provider of agricultural abundance on its surface.

In myth, Hades and his wife, Persephone, were enthroned in a great palace in the underworld. The idea that the dead dwell together in this terrifying realm found its classic expression in the Homeric epics. In Homer the shade, or ghostly image, of the mortal departs the body at the moment of death and begins its journey to the underworld. Hermes, the messenger of the gods, was said to escort shades from the upper world to the subterranean River Styx. Following the introduction of coinage, a small coin was placed under the tongue of every corpse to pay the mythological figure Charon to ferry the deceased across the Styx to the entrance of the underworld, guarded by the monstrous watchdog Cerberus, who permitted all to pass, none to return. The Greeks believed the living need not fear the dead, mere phantoms lacking vital force and confined to the gravelike kingdom of Hades. In art Hades may be depicted as a helmeted old man with white hair or as a younger man with dark hair. He never appears as an evil being (Greek religion had no Satan-like figure). Hades is often represented seated on his throne or wearing a crown or riding in his chariot. The emblem of his power was the staff he used to drive the shades into the lower world. In a period of strong Greek influence, the Romans adopted Pluto (also called Dis Pater) as the wealthy ruler of the dead.

Hestia.   Zeus' sister Hestia, the virgin goddess of the hearth, was the last of the six children of Cronus and Rhea. The name Hestia (hearth) evokes an image of the focal point of house and family. Hestia guarded the hearth and its vital fire as well as the house, family, and community. Equating her fire with life, the Greeks ritually received a newborn infant into the family at the hearth. The ceremony included a purification rite, with a member of the family carrying the baby while running naked around the hearth and Hestia's holy fire. Although a place in the Greek religion was assured for Hestia because of the need to maintain the hearth fire for survival, she was the least personalized of the major deities and enjoyed almost no mythology. A goddess with few shrines, Hestia rarely appears in art. The Roman hearth-goddess Vesta is her etymological equivalent.

Moira

Zeus is sometimes said to be the father of the Fates, or the Moirai, three female divinities responsible for the destiny of every newborn infant. Yet Fate is frequently conceived in the singular, Moira, an inescapable destiny to which mortals and the gods themselves are subject. Some ancient sources insist that even powerful Zeus must yield to Fate's irrevocable decrees. The strong interrelation of Fate, gods, and mortals is fundamental to the Greek religion.

Lesser Gods and Heroes

Epithets.   The Greeks honored countless lesser gods and beings who enjoyed cults and were worshiped in small shrines. In time many of them became identified with the great deities. The name of the lesser figure often survived as an attachment to the greater name. An example of such a survival is related to Hyacinthus, honored by a shrine at Amyclae near Sparta, where Apollo absorbed his beloved's attributes and was called Apollo Hyacinthus. Frequently the Greeks attached an adjective to the name of a deity, indicating an appeal for aid of some sort, thereby creating a special function or domain of the god. Athena, for example, was worshiped in Athens under several epithets expressing hope for her divine intervention, including Athena Polias, guardian of the city, and Athena Hygeia, giver of health. The practice of assigning each god a host of epithets led to a considerable overlapping of divine functions from one location to another.

Eros and Pan.   One of the lesser gods, Eros, god of sexual passion, was a customary companion of Aphrodite and a favorite subject of Greek poets and artists. Eros enjoyed a wide variety of genealogies in early Greek mythology but was most widely described as the son of Aphrodite. Poets sang of the pranks he played on humans and deities alike. Eros was thought to produce unmanageable sexual desire in his victims, causing them to lose control not only of their bodies but also their minds. In art he appears in his familiar guise as a winged boy. From the fifth century BCE onward, his weapon for striking his victims with tormenting passion was the bow and arrow. The Roman equivalent of Eros was Cupid.

Another popular lesser god, Pan, protector of shepherds, was regarded as indispensable for fertilizing flocks. The center of his cult was mountainous Arcadia. Although partly human in shape, Pan had the legs, ears, and horns of a goat, and he was often portrayed with an erect penis. Pan embodied strong sexual powers and made love to both youths and maidens. Noted for his love of music, the god invented the high-pitched panpipe, consisting of a series of pipes bound side by side, the tones being produced by blowing across the upper ends. The Romans identified Pan with Faunus, the Italian god of shepherds.

Helios, Selene, and Eos.   The lesser gods Helios, Selene, and Eos were children of the Titan Hyperion. Helios, called Sol by the Romans, was the personification of the sun itself. Mythologically, the sun-god was said to drive westward across the sky each day in his four-horse chariot and then to float back in a great vessel over the ocean to his palace in the east. Helios enjoyed an important cult on the island of Rhodes, where the Greeks later represented him with their largest statue in bronze—the Colossus of Rhodes—its tremendous height permitting ships to pass between the legs. In antiquity the spectacular Colossus was regarded as one of the Seven Wonders of the World. Helios' sister Selene, identified as Luna by the Romans, was goddess of the moon. Dressing herself in brilliant shining robes, beautiful Selene of the broad wings began her nocturnal journey across the sky on a great chariot when her brother completed his drive. Selene's sister Eos, rosy-fingered dawn, brought mortals their first glimmer of daylight every morning by rising into the sky. The Romans identified Eos with Aurora.

Asclepius.   Apollo's son Asclepius, god of healing, was greatly venerated in the Greek world by the fifth century BCE. His most important center was at Epidaurus, though others were founded at Athens, Pergamum, and elsewhere. The usual method of treatment was by incubation, that is, the patient slept in the temple complex, and the god appeared in a dream to perform a miraculous cure or to prescribe methods of treatment such as exercising, bathing, and changes in diet. As an offspring of the god of light, Asclepius also restored to the sick the precious warmth lost through illness. The latinized form of his name is Aesculapius.

Heracles.   Greek mythology includes a class of semidivine mortals called heroes. The Homeric epics refer to any noble performing distinguished feats as a hero, but in later usage the word signifies a deceased man possessing the capacity either to help or hurt the living from his grave. Heroes enjoyed their own legends and cults. The cult of a hero tended to be local, centered on his grave, and was performed with libations and sacrifices. The Greek devotion to the hero was somewhat analogous to the early Christian veneration of saints. Yet the Greek hero was not famous for extraordinary virtue or absolute obedience to heaven, for normally his outstanding qualities were superhuman strength and exceptional personal powers.

The most popular and widely worshiped of all mythical heroes, Heracles, personified strength and courage by performing feats requiring stupendous power. The son of Zeus and the virtuous mortal woman Alcmene, whom the almighty Olympian had visited in the form of her absent husband, Heracles was constantly plagued by the malice of Hera. After Heracles brutally killed his wife and children under a spell of madness induced by Hera, he was sent by the Delphic oracle to serve King Eurystheus of Tiryns in penance. The ruler commanded him to perform a series of virtually impossible tasks—the famous Twelve Labors—most of which involved vanquishing various monsters. Heracles completed the Labors successfully and performed many other glorious deeds, protecting humans and serving the gods. When Heracles died, Zeus rewarded his great exploits by raising him to Mount Olympus as a god and giving him the task of guarding the Olympian gates. He was worshiped at Rome as Hercules.

GROUP DIVINITIES

Muses, Charites, Erinyes, and Nymphs.   The Greeks recognized a class of divine collective beings. Among the group divinities—most are female—some are little more than abstract concepts, exemplified by the Charites, the Erinyes, and the Muses, the last being nine deities presiding over literature and the arts. The Muses collectively inspired poets, musicians, and writers, but in Roman times each was thought to enjoy special dominion over a distinct art or science. The Charites— the Romans called them the Gratiae (Graces)—were normally regarded as three divinities fathered by Zeus. Personifying grace and beauty, they danced and sang on special occasions. From the end of the fourth century BCE they were represented as three nude young women holding each other by the shoulder. Hesiod tells us the Erinyes—the Romans knew them as the Furiae (Furies)—were daughters of Gaea and the spilled blood of the castrated Uranus. Fearsome goddesses of vengeance who barked like dogs, they relentlessly punished crimes, especially when someone killed a parent or close relative. Usually the Erinyes drove their victims mad.

Other group divinities, such as the nymphs, are more concrete. Minor nature deities, the nymphs were beautiful young maidens enjoying some superhuman powers but not necessarily immortality. Hunting, dancing, and playing, they inhabited waters, meadows, glens, forests, trees, mountains, large rocks, and many other places. They were usually hospitable to strangers, though many were lascivious and known to abduct handsome youths. The nymphs, in turn, were frequently pursued by the Satyrs and courted by men and gods alike. In legend they become the brides of innumerable gods and heroes.

Gorgons.   Among the most famous of the group divinities were the winged Gorgons, three sister monsters (Stheno, Euryale, and Medusa), with writhing snakes instead of hair and tusklike fangs in place of teeth. Their frightful appearance and terrifying eyes transformed anyone glancing at them into stone. Medusa, the only mortal of the three, was the most important Gorgon. When the hero Perseus beheaded Medusa, whom Poseidon had impregnated, a winged horse, Pegasus, and an armed warrior, Chrysaor, leapt from her corpse. The Gorgons were a favorite theme of Greek art, especially in the early period, when their hideous masklike faces exhibit menacing smirks, though they were humanized somewhat by Classical artists.

The Greek religion penetrated every aspect of life and permeated all the world with spiritual power. The entirety of nature was divine, for spirits inhabited all parts of the earth. Divinity also revealed itself in the sun, moon, stars, and sky, in the breezes of morning and evening, in the winds and thunderstorms. Likewise, all daily activities from work to gymnastics were of religious significance. Greek religion offered security in a threatening world, and the population gave thanks to their deities in times of joy and turned to them for comfort in times of sorrow.

PUBLIC RELIGION

FESTIVALS

Apart from the mystery cults, Greek religion did not develop a body of doctrine or impose an orthodoxy. Worshiping the gods was chiefly a matter of correctly observing sacred rituals. Public festivals assumed both a religious and a political character, for all citizens were expected to participate as a sign of loyalty to the polis. Thus every Greek was integrated into the community through public religion. Regular religious festivals were fixed according to a state calendar. The total number was quite high. At least a third of the days of the year at Athens were devoted to their observance. Celebrated to win the favor of the gods, the civic festivals might include sacrifices, athletic contests, processions, choruses, hymns, prayers, and dramatic performances. Frequently the most honored poets and musicians of the day composed the hymns and prayers for the occasion.

This scene of sacrifice to Apollo shows a statue of the god holding a bow and laurel branch while watching the sacred procedure from his slender pillar behind the bloodstained altar. The priest before the altar offers bones and some inedible portions of the animal, due to the gods. The edible meat from the sacrifice, carried on spits by the naked boy behind the priest, will be cooked for human consumption. Note the man putting his hand on the shoulder of the boy, probably a sexual approach. Detail from an Attic red-figure krater (wide-necked bowl for mixing wine and water), *c.* 440 BCE. Museum für Vorund Frühgeschichte, Frankfurt.

ANIMAL SACRIFICE

The most essential element of Greek religion was sacrifice at an altar. All sacred shrines included an altar in the open air, where both public and private religious celebrations took place. Hymns and prayers were offered just prior to the sacrifice, regarded as a gift for a deity. Meanwhile an animal—less commonly vegetable matter—was prepared in an elaborate ritual prescribed by ancestral tradition. In one form of animal sacrifice the victim was butchered, its thighbones wrapped in fat and burned on the altar, and its edible meat cooked and eaten by the worshipers. Thus the deity permitted worshipers to join the sacred feast, which functioned as a shared communion joining humans with the divine. The communion-meal included the sacrificial meat, sacred cakes, and wine—poured out as libations—and was certainly a memorable occasion because the Greeks seldom ate meat. In contrast, sacrifices to chthonian deities involved burning the entire animal as an act of propitiation.

Priests

Reflecting the close link between the religious and the secular life of the community, the vast majority of Greek priests were simply public officials whose duties included religious activity. A magistrate of high standing usually assumed the chief role during public worship and offered official sacrifices on behalf of the people, but any father with the means could act as a priest on behalf of the household by making private sacrifices on an altar in the courtyard of his house. Most priesthoods lasted for one year or another predetermined period. Some exceptional priesthoods were hereditary, as those administering the sanctuary at Eleusis. A number of priests and priestesses were attached to particular cults or temples, with the males commonly officiating for gods and the females for goddesses, though priestesses were relegated to a subordinate role in the male-dominated Greek religion.

Greek Temples

Sacrifices for civic festivals usually took place at altars before temples. Participants faced the east, with the temple behind them. The temple, opening to the east, served as the house of the deity and was built on holy ground where a divine manifestation was thought to have occurred. The early temples were small modest structures with wooden or sun-dried brick walls, thatched roofs, and a simple porch. Around 700 BCE the Greeks began building stone temples, which eventually evolved into mammoth edifices. A central hall, the naos (or cella), housed the anthropomorphic cult statue. Some of these holy images were said to move their eyes or to become covered with perspiration, important signs of miraculous power. A vase containing holy water—purified by the addition of a little salt—was kept near the door of the naos. The temple also housed relics of heroes, which might cure certain illnesses or offer protection to worshipers. Admission to the interior of temples were forbidden to all except priests, priestesses, and attendants because these holy dwellings were not to be violated by ordinary human presence.

Divination

The Greeks employed various means to communicate with their deities. From eastern cultures they adopted the practice of divination, or the interpretation of divinely given signs expressing the will of the gods or even foretelling future events. One method of divination involved examining the entrails (particularly the liver) of a newly sacrificed animal. In another form, augury, observers interpreted the flights and acts of birds, regarded as the messengers of almighty Zeus. The Greeks also believed that all sorts of omens could portend future events. Certain specialists interpreted dreams, while others explained meteorological phenomena such as storms and meteorites. We saw that the Greeks sought advice from the resident deity of an oracular shrine, a practice with west Asian and Egyptian precedents.

Primarily, an oracle is a response of a god to a question, though the term may also signify the mode or medium of such a response or the oracular shrine itself. There were many places in Greece where gods were consulted and gave responses to questions of a private and public nature. The most notable oracular shrines were at Delphi in Phocis and Dodona in Epirus. Apollo made his will known at Delphi through the utterances of a priestess, while Zeus spoke at Dodona through the rustling of oak leaves.

The Great Centers of Worship

Certain shrines of the preeminent deities became centers of worship for the entire Greek world and are therefore referred to as Panhellenic. Among the most important Panhellenic centers were Olympia in Elis, sacred to Zeus, and Delphi in Phocis, chief shrine of Apollo. Each became the place of important international religious festivals, featuring the Olympic Games of Zeus at Olympia and the Pythian Games of Apollo at Delphi.

Zeus and the Olympic Festival.   One of the driving forces in Greek religion was the concept of competition for divine favor. The Greeks turned a large number of skills and personal assets into contests, including poetry, song and dance, drama, art, disputation, male beauty, and athletics. The most famous of these were athletic contests, perhaps originating with Late Bronze Age games associated with funerary rites. While every state sponsored local games, the Olympic Games represented the pinnacle of Panhellenic sporting contests. Olympia in the rugged region of Elis in the western Peloponnese was not a polis but a sacred place administered by local officials. A great temple to Zeus stood here, a reminder that the athletic contests at Olympia were only part of a great religious festival honoring the god and that the contestants were seeking his glory.

Every four years heralds traveled throughout the ancient Greek world proclaiming a sacred truce, guaranteeing safe passage to contestants and spectators on their way to the Olympic Games. The period of four years from one festival to another became known as an Olympiad, and Greek historians dated events by Olympiads and intermediate years. According to Greek tradition the first festival occurred at Olympia in 776 BCE. Initially, the festival was humble, drawing contestants and spectators only from Elis, but by the beginning of the fifth century BCE visitors were coming from all over the Greek world, though women were barred from attending on pain of death (the priestesses of Demeter excepted). The Olympic Games continued as a religious festival in honor of Zeus until the very end, and for that reason were abolished by the Christian emperor Theodosius I in 393 CE, well over a millennium after their traditional inauguration.

All freeborn Greek males of unsullied character were eligible to compete in the Olympic Games, though success depended on having ample leisure and finances for training and travel. The contestants trained rigorously for ten months and then spent a final month of preparation at Elis. Held in late summer and evolving into a five-day event, the festival at Olympia opened with the contestants standing with

The fiercely competitive nature of the young Greek aristocrat is reflected in this representation of a footrace, painted by an artist excelling in positioning figures and showing their long strides and swinging arms. Detail from a black-figure Panathenaic prize amphora, c. 530 BCE. Metropolitan Museum of Art, New York.

their fathers and trainers before the altar of Zeus and swearing to compete fairly. This first day was one of elaborate rites and sacrifices to honor Zeus. The competition actually started on the second day with horse and chariot races. Only the very rich could enter these equestrian events, and the owners—not the drivers—were declared the victors. The games included various footraces, with swift runners competing barefoot and entirely naked (only chariot drivers were clothed). Powerful athletes participated in boxing and wrestling contests or matched their strength in the brutal pankration, a combination of the two. Participants in the pankration were free to punch, kick, choke, break fingers, and strike the genitals but forbidden to bite or gouge eyes. The popular pentathlon featured competitions in five events: footrace, long jump, discus throw, javelin throw, and wrestling. The winners of the various contests were crowned with a wreath of olive leaves cut from Zeus' sacred grove. Feasted and feted by kinsmen and countrymen at Olympia, the victorious athletes returned to triumphal receptions in their home cities, where they were greeted with banquets and orations and regaled with poems composed in their honor. At Athens they were even rewarded with a purse of gold or silver and meals at public expense. Statues were sometimes set up in their honor, and over time local veneration for a native victor could reach the level of a hero cult. Clearly, the Greeks looked with awe upon a victorious athlete, one blessed by heaven.

Apollo and the Delphic Oracle.   In mythology, Apollo descended from Mount Olympus to establish his oracle at Delphi, a magnificent site on the slopes of Mount Parnassus above the Gulf of Corinth. He destroyed a great dragon guarding the place, the Python, thereby earning the title Pythian Apollo. From the sixth to the third centuries BCE, Delphi was the greatest of the Panhellenic religious centers. The

This scene of inspired utterance shows Themis, a mythical forerunner of the Pythia, seated on a tripod and holding a spray of the laurel of Delphi. She responds to a question asked of Apollo by Aegeus, mythical king of Athens, who is inquiring about his lack of children. Aegeus later fathered the Athenian hero Theseus. Drawing of an Attic red-figure vase, *c.* 440 BCE. The original graces the collection of the Staatliche Museum, Berlin.

Pythian Games were celebrated at Delphi every fourth year in honor of Apollo and were almost as popular as those at Olympia. We saw that Delphi owed its original fame to the oracular shrine of Apollo. The prestige of the Delphic oracle extended to the most remote corners of the Greek world and even beyond, for individuals came from faraway places in search of Apollo's counsel before embarking on major undertakings. A suppliant approached the oracle as a private person or as a representative of a community, with questions covering a wide range of personal, religious, or political concerns. Apollo settled disputes involving territory, assisted states in the writing of their laws, sanctioned the founding of colonies, and established rites of purification to salve troubled consciences. The god gave his responses through the mouth of a priestess known as the Pythia—an office held by a succession of local women—who sat upon a tripod in the temple of Apollo. Details about the procedure the Pythia followed in answering questions remain poorly understood. Although excavation has rendered improbable the story that her tripod was suspended over a fissure issuing intoxicating volcanic fumes, apparently the Pythia fell into a trance and uttered inarticulate sounds, interpreted by the priests of Delphi and given to the inquirer in verse. The priests were closely identified with two pronouncements of Apollo engraved over the doors of his temple, "Know Thyself" and "Nothing in Excess."

The answers to questions were often so ambiguous that subsequent events could not impugn their validity. Herodotus says King Croesus of Lydia misinterpreted the reply that "if he made war on the Persians he would destroy a mighty empire," discovering all too late the empire was his own. Clearly, the stakes were high in seeking divine sanction for human projects. Apollo's domain over political questions

The temple of Apollo at Delphi, completed about 330 BCE. These ruins represent the third temple built to Apollo at the site in historical times, the first being destroyed by fire in 548 BCE and the second by earthquake in 373 BCE. The temple enjoyed great length to make room for the innermost sanctuary, where the oracular consultation took place.

gave the establishment at Delphi enormous sway over the affairs of the various Greek states. Yet some replies proved altogether untrue and eventually damaged Delphi's political power, though not its religious influence.

The Apollo temple at Delphi was destroyed by fire in the sixth century BCE and rebuilt on a larger scale. Although this new structure was toppled by an earthquake in 373 BCE, its replacement survived until Roman times. The grave of Dionysus was said to be inside the great temple of Apollo. Also inside was a sacred stone of navel shape, the *omphalos,* thought to mark the center of the earth. A stadium and theater stood nearby. Along the serpentine Sacred Way leading to the temple from the holy spring, whose water purified worshipers, the Greek states constructed some twenty treasuries, small but magnificent templelike structures housing gifts to Apollo.

By 600 BCE the shrine had come under the protection of a religious league of twelve states known as the Delphic Amphictyony. Member states pledged to protect the sanctuary from attack and sent delegates to a meeting of their council twice each year. Although principally concerned with the upkeep of the temple and cult of Apollo, the members of the amphictyony often adopted a plan of unified action in political and diplomatic matters. A notable example of their concerted action was the Sacred War, a successful venture fought by the Delphic Amphictyony in association with Cleisthenes of Sicyon to protect the oracle from the economic encroachment of the nearby town of Cirrha, then levying tolls on pilgrims journeying to Delphi.

The Nemean and Isthmian Games and Other Festivals. The early sixth century BCE witnessed the development of two additional Panhellenic festivals, the Nemean and Isthmian games, modeled on the Olympic and Pythian games. The Nemean Games took place every second year in Nemea, a valley in the northern Peloponnese, and were centered on the worship of Zeus. The Isthmian Games were held every two years at the Isthmus of Corinth in honor of Poseidon. Thus by the sixth century BCE the Greek world celebrated four great Panhellenic festivals: the Olympic, Pythian, Nemean, and Isthmian games. Important local festivals included the sacred rites that the Ionians held annually in honor of Apollo at Delos—the traditional birthplace of the god and his twin sister, Artemis—with music, dances, and games. The Apollo temple on Delos featured a colossal gilded statue of the god. We saw that the Panathenaic festival in Athens honored the goddess Athena. The other Greek states, fearing the power of Athens, blocked Athenian attempts to elevate the Panathenaea to a Panhellenic festival.

THE GREEK MYSTERIES

Although fulfilling both religious and patriotic obligations, the Panhellenic and local festivals did not entirely satisfy the spiritual longings of all Greeks. Many sought outlets for their religious devotion beyond the traditional festivals and sacrificial rites. While never rejecting the public worship of the Olympians, a large number of ordinary Greeks participated in certain mysteries, which were supplemental cults focusing on secret rites and requiring formal initiation for admission. Besides stressing secrecy, the mysteries promised a better lot in the afterlife. In this context they taught the doctrine of immortality, for the most part ignored by traditional Greek cults, and provided sacrament-like ceremonies ensuring worshipers a safe passage to the next world. Our knowledge of the observances, conducted in private and shrouded in mystery, remains sketchy.

THE ELEUSINIAN MYSTERIES

The most important mysteries honored the grain goddess Demeter and her daughter, Persephone, at Eleusis near Athens. We noted the famous myth portraying Persephone's abduction by Hades and the arrival of her mother, wildly grieving, at Eleusis in search of her. When Demeter withheld the fruits of the earth, Persephone was permitted to return to the upper world for part of the year. Thereupon, Demeter restored earthly fertility. The story reflects the Greek belief that seed must die in the earth to be reborn as grain and that sperm must die in the womb to be reborn in animal or human form. This concept makes death the center of life and thus regards existence as constant renewal. Persephone, whose return to the earth suggests resurrection, released those honoring her to a blissful eternal life.

The Eleusinian cult was of great antiquity, probably enjoying Mycenaean antecedents. Initiation was open to all Greek-speaking men, women, children, and slaves, provided they were untainted by homicide. The mysteries began with the initiates—the *mystai*—making an exhausting pilgrimage for fifteen miles along the Sacred Way from Athens to Demeter's magnificent temple at Eleusis. They crowded into the darkened Telesterion, or the Hall of Initiation, where the hereditary priests revealed the secrets of the cult. Our fragmentary evidence suggests the initiates underwent a solemn purification, participated in special sacrament-like ceremonies, touched and fit together objects in the shape of sexual organs, and watched sacred dramas acting out the rape of Persephone and the arrival of her mother at Eleusis. Apparently the rites closed with the brandishing of torches, revealing statues of the Two Goddesses and a priest holding a cut ear of grain, which signified the cycle of life through death. The joyous initiates thus came to understand a pattern of death and rebirth applying to their own salvation.

THE DIONYSIAC MYSTERIES

In contrast to the Eleusinian rites, the mysteries of Dionysus, giver of wine, provided ecstasy through intoxication and eroticism. Dionysus was associated with fertility, and huge erect phalluses were carried in his processions. In myth, the god was accompanied by a retinue of frenzied male and female figures. His rites quickly won a large number of actual followers, particularly women, providing them with temporary escape from domestic confinement and male domination. Yet the celebrations confirmed the male view of women as irrational, erratic beings requiring strict supervision. The women devotees—the Maenads—came at night from the towns and cities scantily dressed in fawn skins and followed their intoxicating god to the mountains. Yelling and brandishing torches, they danced and surrendered to him in a state of frenzy. At the height of their abandon, the Maenads are said to have seized wild animals, torn them to pieces, and devoured the flesh raw. The Dionysiac rites were tinged with eroticism, and some celebrations may have included wine-induced orgies. Even in Greek states not practicing unrestrained mountain flights, Dionysiac festivals included various forms of intoxicated license, allowing followers to enjoy a sacred union with their god in ecstasy. If they could be unified with him, could they not rise from the dead as he had done and enjoy a blessed eternal life?

The Dionysia.   Dionysus was honored throughout Greece in various festivals, most notably the splendid Dionysia, celebrations featuring dramatic performances. Dionysia were instituted virtually everywhere, though the best known were staged in Athens: the City and the Rural Dionysia. Pisistratus introduced or reorganized the City Dionysia in the sixth century BCE, when a small temple of Dionysus was constructed on the southern slope of the Acropolis. The lavish City Dionysia were conducted with great pomp in the spring and included a procession of Dionysiac fertility symbols—huge erect phalluses—and an ancient statue of the god, to the accompaniment of sacrifices. Various entertainments were offered from the Dionysiac orchestra (space allotted to choruses), where individuals or choruses appeared as Satyrs or in other guises. In this context masked choirs performed a song and dance to Dionysus called a dithyramb. Tragic drama was gradually grafted on the cult of Dionysus through changes in the dithyramb, beginning about 534 BCE, when a speaker came forward at intervals during the performance to address and answer the chorus or its leader in verse, thus adding a prologue and a dialogue. The members of the chorus appeared as characters portraying the scenes described in their songs, while the speaker assumed the part of Dionysus or some other figure in the story. Thus he clarified the narrative by conducting a dialogue with the chorus. The speaker might be thought of as an actor performing the first play.

According to tradition, a composer of odes named Thespis was responsible for combining the chorus with a speaking actor and creating what has been called the first dramatic tragedy. The words of the actor were probably spoken, not sung, though accompanied by a musical instrument, and he could play several roles by changing masks. This was the nucleus around which later tragedy developed. Thereafter Athenian tragedies were enacted at the Dionysia, but later poets added stories besides those involving Dionysus. By the early fifth century BCE the plays had assumed their familiar form, with three actors and a chorus. Thus the elaborate choral performance of the festival had evolved into drama, of which Dionysus served as the patron god.

Orphism

In the sixth century BCE one phase of Dionysiac worship crystallized into the remarkable other-worldly Orphic cult. Orphism took its name from a legendary Thracian singer-poet named Orpheus, famed for enchanting even animals and trees with his lyrics. In one myth he was torn to pieces by the Maenads, yet his head was saved and continued to speak. Poems attributed to him and his head were actually the work of many poets living over several centuries. These poetic compositions—which take the form of hymns, prayers, and myths—constitute an Orphic sacred literature explaining the origin of the world and the ethical obligations of humanity. The Orphics drew from the Dionysus story a key to the mystery of the universe and the destiny of humankind. There were many Greek myths telling of the god's birth. A famous Orphic version has newborn Dionysus slaughtered and eaten by the wicked Titans, though later he would rise again. After Zeus destroyed the Titans with a thunderbolt, their ashes gave birth to humans, who inherited an evil element—a sort of original sin—from the monstrous beings but also a divine element from the Titan-devoured flesh of Dionysus. The chief obligation of humans is to dispel the evil element and preserve the divine by following Orphic principles.

The Orphics regarded the soul as immortal but imprisoned within the body, able to escape temporarily in dreams and permanently at death. They advocated the practice of moral purity to preserve the soul from defilement by the contaminated body. The Orphics prohibited the shedding of blood and the eating of meat, for they believed in the sanctity of life and the transmigration of souls, or the passing of a soul at death to an animal appropriate to an individual's character. Accordingly, the Orphics regarded the eating of meat as a form of cannibalism. Purged of guilt by practicing Orphic rites and righteousness, the soul will eventually escape the cycle of rebirths and find rest in heaven. Meanwhile the wicked will suffer punishments in the netherworld. Thus the Orphics expanded upon the teachings of the other mysteries regarding a future life, dividing the next world into a heaven and hell, and they insisted upon justice and personal holiness. Although some of the Orphics were charlatans preying on the gullible, most seem to have been sincerely devout. Plato denounced the former, yet he took many of his fundamental ideas from the Orphic movement. Centuries later when Christianity had almost demolished the older religions of antiquity, Platonic philosophers bravely continued to support Orphism as a noble and divine teaching.

CHAPTER VII

LITERATURE, PHILOSOPHY, AND
ART IN ARCHAIC GREECE:
A CULTURAL RENAISSANCE

The turbulent Archaic period witnessed an artistic and intellectual acceleration producing a highly sophisticated and refined culture that was much influenced by contact with the ancient Near East. The Greek world during this time was greatly transformed by developments not only in architecture, sculpture, and painting but also in literature and philosophy. In this context the Archaic period—often called the Greek Renaissance—eventually ushered in the flowering of Classical Greece.

LITERATURE

GREEK ALPHABETIC WRITING

All modern western alphabets are Greek derived. In the eighth century BCE, judging from the earliest preserved inscriptions, the Greeks began to write their language in a new alphabetic script, having adapted the Phoenician alphabet (aleph, beth, gimel, etc.) to form their own (alpha, beta, gamma, etc.). The Phoenician signs were virtually all consonants, leaving the reader to fill in the vowels mentally. The Greeks took the final great step in the development of alphabetic writing by employing specific symbols for vowels. Their alphabet, first presumably used for commercial purposes, was eventually applied to the writing of verse. Although initially there was much experimentation and considerable local variation, the basic elements were the same, and eventually an alphabet of twenty-four characters became standard. Early inscriptions, exemplified by laws and treaties, were displayed on wooden or stone tablets in the various city-states and later were cast in bronze. Other writing materials included parchment and papyrus (the latter coming into use after a flourishing trade was cemented with Egypt), making possible the circulation of long literary texts. By the Classical and Hellenistic periods literacy had become widespread among the male population, and many women could read as well.

EPIC POETRY

The Iliad *and* Odyssey.   Poetry was the normal medium for literary expression. For centuries before the development of the Greek alphabet, bards drew from a storehouse of metrical formulas they memorized, combining and extending these elements at will to produce freshly improvised accounts of the exploits and values of legendary warriors. We saw that the *Iliad* and *Odyssey*, representing the culmination of this oral tradition, were handed down under the name of Homer. Shaped over a long period, the Homeric epics reflect the aristocratic behavioral code fostered in the Dark Age. The extraordinary power of Homer was captured in writing in the eighth century BCE, forming the bedrock of western literature. The *Iliad* and *Odyssey* were composed in the stately meter of epic poetry, the dactylic hexameter, which like all Greek meters was essentially quantitative, or based on repeated patterns of long and short syllables, in contrast to our own traditional meters based on stressed and unstressed syllables.

The Homeric Hymns.   The epic style is represented also by a collection called the *Homeric Hymns,* poems addressed to various deities of the Olympian pantheon. This verse, often ascribed to Homer in antiquity, was composed over a broad period of time by poets whose names are lost. Probably serving as preludes to longer epic recitations at public festivals, the *Homeric Hymns* feature myths praising divine deeds and attributes. The four major surviving pieces are dedicated to Aphrodite, Apollo, Demeter, and Hermes.

Hesiod.   We saw that Hesiod, a Boeotian poet active around 700 BCE, wrote two major poems in epic meter: the *Theogony* and the *Works and Days.* The former describes the genealogy of the gods and the formation of the world, while the latter condemns the same aristocratic class lauded by Homer and speaks out passionately for justice on behalf of the oppressed.

IAMBIC POETRY

Epic poetry steadily lost ground to a variety of novel meters in the seventh and sixth centuries BCE. This was a time of intellectual ferment in the wealthy cities of Ionia on the central west coast of Asia Minor, where political and economic forces were modifying traditions, while contact with brilliant eastern cultures was fostering new ideas. The Ionians took the lead in developing literature in the seventh century and philosophy in the sixth. One of the new written poetic forms appearing in the seventh century BCE was iambic, whose sharp rhythms sounded to the Greeks much like ordinary speech. This verse, which seems to have been recited rather than sung, was composed on the basis of metrical units known as iambs. In Greek verse an iamb is a metrical foot consisting of two syllables, the first short and the second long, a pattern well adaptable to satire and to strong utterances of human passion ranging from extreme eroticism to stinging images of hate.

Archilochus.   Probably living around the middle of the seventh century BCE, Archilochus of Paros elevated iambic poetry to literary respectability, though he was also a genius at producing an astounding variety of other metrical forms. Growing up as the illegitimate son of a noble and a slave on the Cycladic island of Paros, he lacked a recognized place in society and grew to detest the aristocracy. Yet the impoverished young man longed to marry the daughter of a local aristocrat. When her father forbade the match, Archilochus sought revenge by attacking him in a series of hideously scathing poems. The verse also explicitly detailed the sexual experiences Archilochus and others had enjoyed with the daughter. The resulting shame, according to tradition, drove both father and daughter to suicide. Apparently the reckless Archilochus was then forced to leave Paros. Like many disgruntled men before him, he adopted the life of a mercenary and became involved in numerous escapades such as the Parian attempt to colonize the island of Thasos about 670 BCE.

Archilochus' strong individualism is indicated by his practice of scoffing at the conventions of aristocratic society. In contrast to the Homeric heroes, he threw away his shield and ran for his life during a battle on Thrace between the Parian colonists and Thracian natives. To abandon the field of battle was the height of dishonor in the aristocratic code, yet Archilochus boasted of the deed poetically: "I saved my skin, so good riddance to the shield! I'll soon have a better one." He wandered far and wide as a mercenary until meeting his death in battle. Although he produced a prolific body of verse with countless themes—religion, seduction, satire, wine, and shipwreck—only fragments of his poems survive. He was the first Greek writer composing almost entirely from what he claims are personal experiences and emotions rather than from traditional material. Thus he set a precedent for personal expression in poetry. The Greeks regarded Archilochus as one of their greatest poets.

ELEGIAC POETRY

Another popular new form was the elegy, composed in couplets, in which the meter of epic is modified by shortening every second line. Elegiac poetry is often described as a line of epic hexameter of six metrical feet alternating with a pentameter of five metrical feet, thereby creating an agreeable rhythm. Elegy was customarily accompanied by a reed pipe known as the aulos (often mistakenly identified as a flute), which resembled a double oboe and made a mournful sound. The verse served as a vehicle for expressing political and social concerns, erotic themes, religious devotion, lamentation, and war songs. An important function of elegy was to inspire troops entering battle, the singers recounting the glorious deeds of fabled heroes. The form seems to have evolved among the Ionians sometime before the beginning of the seventh century BCE and was soon established on both sides of the Aegean.

Callinus, Archilochus, Tyrtaeus, and Mimnermus.   The first known elegiac specialist was Callinus of Ephesus, a shadowy figure whose career seems to have fallen within the seventh century BCE. Archilochus of Paros, discussed above, was one of the first great composers of elegy. His elegiac verse is remarkable for its strong personal note. The earliest elegiac poet on the mainland of Greece was Tyrtaeus of Sparta, the general who roused the Spartans to stand and fight during their desperate struggle with the Messenian rebels in the years after 650 BCE. In contrast to the martial fire of Tyrtaeus, the Ionian poet Mimnermus of Colophon sang of eroticism, love, and the fleeting quality of youth. His melancholy music and spirit influenced the Hellenistic writers who revived the elegy in the third and second centuries BCE.

Solon and Theognis.   The Athenian statesman Solon, discussed in chapter 5, used elegy and other poetic forms to defend his political beliefs and actions to the Athenians. The surviving fragments of his verse provide a glimpse of Solon's earnest devotion to the affairs of state and his strong belief that the gods will preserve his city. Another composer of elegy was Theognis of Megara, an aristocratic poet active in the second part of the sixth century BCE. He had no illusions about the decline of his class but insisted on maintaining aristocratic standards. Some of his poems reflect his open contempt for lower-class rulers. Others are love poems to the boy Cyrnus. Theognis wrote about his passionate devotion and longing for Cyrnus in much of his verse and counseled the boy with the moral admonitions he had learned from the old aristocratic code of his forebears.

Lyric Poetry

In the later Hellenistic period the Greek scholars of Alexandria—the great city founded on the Nile Delta by Alexander the Great in the fourth century BCE—distinguished several classifications of poetry: epic (narrative and didactic), iambic (abusive or satirical lampoons), elegiac (associated with lamentation, war songs, and personal verse), dramatic (dialogue presenting a story intended to be acted out in a theater), and melic (sung with musical accompaniment). These designations were not new. Melic poetry, for example, was traditional, and writers before the Hellenistic period referred to a poem meant to be sung with musical accompaniment as a *melos*, or song. Because the harplike instrument known as the lyre was most commonly used, the Alexandrian scholars also termed melic poetry *lyric*.

Monodic Lyric: Sappho and Alcaeus.   To avoid the current imprecision surrounding the terms *lyric* and *lyrical* when used in reference to either modern or ancient poetry, we divide ancient Greek lyric into monodic lyric and choral lyric, each broadly corresponding to forms appearing in Homer. In monody the words of a poet were sung solo and accompanied by a lyre, while in choral lyric the poetry was sung by a trained choir. Monodic lyric, usually performed on private occasions, celebrated the personal feelings of the composer through a wide range of poems, including drinking songs, appeals to the gods, and addresses to friends. About the beginning of the sixth century BCE monodic lyric reached a new height of distinction in the Aeolic areas of Asia Minor, particularly the island of Lesbos, with members of the turbulent aristocracy composing in their native Aeolic dialect. The earliest and greatest representatives of the genre—Sappho and Alcaeus—were born on Lesbos. The more famous of the two, Sappho, the daughter of a prominent family on the island, is the only known woman poet from the Archaic period. One of the greatest lyric poets of all time, she seems to have enjoyed a personal freedom experienced by few women of mainland Greece. On the Lesbos of her day aristocratic women often came together in informal societies for the practice of graceful endeavors, including the composition and singing of poetry. Sappho gathered about her such a circle of young women and girls, perhaps in the form of a religious association dedicated to the worship of Aphrodite, a goddess frequently addressed in her verse. Love was Sappho's paramount theme. Apparently she found the chief inspiration for her poetry in the members of her group, who formed her audience, for she sings to them with burning descriptions of passionate desire. Sappho even experienced psychological effects because of her personal longings for her companions. Provoked by the sight of a girl speaking with a man, not only did her ears buzz, she became speechless and pale. The aristocratic code of Archaic Greece sanctioned homosexual love among males. Perhaps a similar attitude prevailed toward aristocratic females on Lesbos. Although Sappho's exact relationship with the girls and women in her group remains uncertain, she was superbly gifted at expressing homoerotic yearnings, and the English word *lesbian* is derived from the name of her island.

Sappho imbued much of her verse with the intertwined ecstasy and agony often springing from the fierce attraction of one human being to another. We can only lament that Christians destroyed most of her works in the eleventh century CE, though a few remnants survive: a number of quotations by later writers and some fragments of verse found on papyri lining Egyptian coffins. The papyri, dating from the early centuries of the Christian era, indicate how widely she was read and admired throughout antiquity. We hear that Plato himself, inspired by Sappho's vivid imagination and melodic cadences, referred to her as "the tenth Muse."

Her slightly younger contemporary Alcaeus, son of aristocratic parents, became actively engaged in a political struggle against the tyrants in his native city on Lesbos and endured several periods of exile. A noble, a warrior, and a traveler, he lived on the island during a period of intense political strife. His poems describe his fierce hatred for political opponents, the joys of sensual gratification, and the pleasures of wine. As a member of the nobility, Alcaeus passionately believed the welfare of his native city was tied to the success of his own class.

Choral Lyric: Alcman and Pindar.   Choral lyric was presented at public festivals and private ceremonies to honor the gods or to celebrate marriages, funerals, athletic victories, and other important events. Performed by a chorus of costumed men, boys, or girls singing and dancing to instrumental accompaniment, choral lyric affirmed the sentiments of the Greek polis and its traditions rather than the personal feelings of the poet. Accordingly, the genre was more formal and stately than monody. Choral lyric was composed in stanzas, and its meter varied with almost every composition. The verse retained its standard form for centuries, with the choir telling a story about gods or heroes, enjoining moral maxims, and introducing personal remarks about the participants in the festival. Popular forms of choral lyric included the dirge (lament for the dead), the dithyramb (song in honor of Dionysus), the paean (hymn to Apollo), and the *epinikion* (song honoring a victor in the games).

Alcman distinguished himself as a choral poet in Sparta before 600 BCE, composing for the dances and songs of girls at religious festivals. The most extraordinary figure in choral lyric—perhaps the greatest lyric poet of antiquity—was a creative genius named Pindar (518–438 BCE), who is discussed here even though he belongs to the Classical period. Born to a noble family living near Thebes in Boeotia, Pindar was the only non-Athenian among the great literary figures of Classical Greece. His verse celebrates the grandeur of an already waning aristocratic tradition. Yet Pindar's contemporaries, recognizing his brilliance, regarded him as a special favorite of Apollo, god of song, and a special seat was reserved for him at Delphi. He composed long victory odes (*epinikia*)—a category of choral lyric mentioned above—in honor of the triumphant athletes of the four great Panhellenic games (Olympic, Pythian, Nemean, and Isthmian). His dazzling images in the victory odes express his view that the victors represented the flower of aristocratic manhood. In this corpus he also sings the praises of the gods—Pindar believed he wrote under divine inspiration—while telling of the lineage of his heroes and recounting the glorious deeds of their forebears. Moreover, the poet composed other poetic forms—all sparkling with brilliant phrases—including elegies to kings and tyrants. His fame and prestige continued to increase after his lifetime. Over a century after Pindar's death, his house was the only one spared by Alexander the Great when he destroyed Thebes.

PRE-SOCRATIC PHILOSOPHY

THE MILESIAN TRADITION

The Greek philosophers before the great Socrates of the Classical period are customarily called the pre-Socratics. The earliest pre-Socratics were active in the sixth century BCE in two widely separated parts of the Greek world: Ionia to the east and southern Italy and Sicily to the west. The initial group of pre-Socratics came from the prosperous Ionian seaport of Miletus and are thus termed the Milesians. Thinkers in Miletus began to speculate about the nature of the world, the problem of human existence, and the composition of matter, thereby embarking on a search that is basic to both science and philosophy. Although the Milesians did not call themselves scientists or philosophers—neither word had been coined—apparently they were the first to view the universe an orderly system governed by laws capable of discovery by reason and observation. They borrowed heavily from the accumulated knowledge of Babylonian and Egyptian mathematicians and astronomers, but they were not dominated by a priestly monopoly, as in the ancient Near East. The Milesians charted a new course by seeking natural causes to explain the phenomena around them, thus breaking with inherited assumptions and introducing the Greeks to reasoned theories. After a century or so the word *philosophia* (love of wisdom) came into general use to describe the reduction of available information about the world to a logical system, a concept embracing the disciplines now called philosophy and science.

Thales.   European science and philosophy began with Thales of Miletus, an intellectual forebear of Socrates, Plato, and Aristotle. Thales, whose activity embraced the first half of the sixth century BCE, was listed among the venerated Seven Sages. Because he left no writings to posterity, we are uncertain of the factual basis for the extraordinary achievements credited to him in antiquity, including the prediction of the solar eclipse of 585 BCE. Regarded by Aristotle as the first real philosopher, Thales is also said to have been the founder of Greek geometry and astronomy. Thales and the other Milesian philosophers believed all material things could be reduced to some primary substance, from which all matter had developed. Thales identified water as the underlying constituent of the universe. Perhaps his notion was inspired by an ancient Near Eastern myth common to the Hebrews, Babylonians, and Egyptians. This famous story tells of a creator fashioning the earth and all life from primeval waters. Yet Thales expressed his concept as a statement of fact, not mythology. He conceived of the earth as a disk floating on the surface of the primordial waters, and he imagined that eventually all substances would return to their original watery form. By providing a natural explanation for the origin of the world, Thales took an essential step in advancing science and philosophy and dislodging the exalted status of theology and mythology.

Anaximander.   Said to be Thales' younger associate or pupil, Anaximander of Miletus was active about the middle of the sixth century BCE. He is credited with setting up the first sundial in Ionia and making the initial Greek attempt to map the world, supplying details from information gathered by dauntless Ionian mariners. Anaximander wrote the earliest known prose book, *On the Nature of Things*, a philosophical treatise surviving only in a few words and part of a sentence. His explanation of world origins was far more complex than Thales' theory of different forms of matter springing from a single underlying constituent. Anaximander identified the source of all things as the *Apeiron*—the Infinite or Boundless—which he regarded as divine, eternal, and timeless. Anaximander envisioned this ungenerated principle with unlimited capacity for assuming different forms. He held that a number of pairs of familiar opposite qualities separated from the *Apeiron* (for example, wet and dry, hot and cold, liquid and solid, light and dark, male and female) and then struggled with one another to produce the ordered world. Accordingly, the heavens and earth took shape through the motion of the pairs of contrasting opposites.

Anaximander visualized the earth as a drumlike body—with people living on its flat top—floating in the center of the universe. What we see as heavenly bodies are actually great rings of fire encircling the earth, but they are enveloped by mist, except for holes permitting the fire to shine through as the sun, moon, and stars. Earthly life, which is closely bound up with moisture, originated in the sea. Perhaps Anaximander had examined fossil remains, for he even advanced a rudimentary theory of evolution, arguing that prehistoric humans had descended from fishlike creatures. He held that by the end of time moisture will have been gradually evaporated, resulting in all things returning to the *Apeiron*.

Anaximenes.   Said to have flourished around 546 BCE, Anaximenes of Miletus followed the same intellectual tradition by theorizing about an underlying principle from which all things originate. He selected *aer*, usually translated *air* but actually meaning *mist* or *breath* (the Greeks had not yet developed the concept of air as a gaseous atmosphere). Anaximenes gives *aer* the all-encompassing and divine qualities of the *Apeiron*. He credits *aer* with producing all visible matter through a process of condensation and rarefaction, or thickening and thinning. Accordingly, *aer* changes by condensation into wind, cloud, water, earth, and rock, and by rarefaction into fire. The flat earth is supported by *aer*. Mists rising from the earth become rarified and form fiery discs—the heavenly bodies—which revolve around but not under the earth. *Aer*, the source of all life and movement, circulates and serves as a soul for the cosmos. The ancient world regarded the soul, which was associated with breath, as the animating force of the human body, and Anaximenes draws a parallel between the life of the universe and that of the human animated by the breath of life.

THE DIVERGENCE OF LATER IONIAN THOUGHT

Pythagoras and the Pythagoreans.   Persian pressure on Ionia from 546 BCE onward prompted many Ionians to sail west. Some migrated to Greek colonies in southern Italy and Sicily, where a different orientation in philosophy developed during the late sixth century BCE. The most important pre-Socratic philosophers in the region, Pythagoras and Xenophanes, were both natives of Ionia. Pythagoras, born about 580 BCE on the island of Samos, was one of the most important, albeit elusive, thinkers of the ancient world. At the age of fifty he left Samos and settled at the seaport of Croton in southern Italy. Acquiring a reputation as a mystic and prophet, Pythagoras persuaded many Greeks in southern Italy—women included—to join him in a religious community devoted to his teachings. His disciples, who were known as the Pythagoreans, were essentially ascetics living by strict rules governing every aspect of life.

Unfortunately Pythagoras never committed his philosophy to writing, thus inviting later misunderstandings of his actual teachings. Clearly, he affirmed the kinship of all life and advocated vegetarianism. Like the Orphics (discussed in chapter 6), he regarded the soul as divine and immortal, imprisoned within the body, and doomed to a cycle of transmigration. Accordingly, the soul survives at death to enter another human, an animal, or even a plant. The soul's impurities can be cleansed away and final release attained by the observance of ritual purity, as taught by Pythagoras, who claimed to possess astounding psychic powers and to remember vividly his own former incarnations. Each of his followers wore white robes and practiced meditation, modesty, sexual abstinence, silence, and purification rites. Pythagoras also issued a series of dogmatic prohibitions smacking of old religious taboos, including injunctions against eating flesh or beans, practicing animal sacrifice, stirring a fire with iron, and wearing rings. The rule against eating beans probably arose from the belief that beans contain little souls, whose attempts to escape cause the eater's flatulence. Adopting Anaximander's doctrine of opposites, Pythagoras taught—Aristotle reports—that the universe is organized according to contrasting pairs such as form and order, odd and even, male and female, rest and motion, light and darkness, and good and evil. Yet he gave the doctrine of opposites a new twist, for the male principle (form) is good and the opposite female principle (matter) is evil. This doctrine corresponds with the notion that the divine soul is imprisoned within and polluted by the mate-rial body. Such ideas substantially influenced many later thinkers and played an important role in the development of Greek dualism.

Pythagoras is famous also for his speculations about numbers. He is often credited with discovering the geometric theorem still bearing his name—namely, the square of the length of the hypotenuse of a right triangle equals the sum of the squares of the lengths of the other two sides—though the Egyptians and Babylonians had demonstrated the proposition more than a millennium earlier. Pythagoras theorized that "all things are numbers," meaning the entirety of the world is explicable through numbers. Number represents the divine essence of the universe for him, occupying the place of water, the *Apeiron,* or *aer* for the Milesians. He assigned mystic properties to numbers and geometric figures. Pythagoras identified the number 10 as sacred and a key to knowledge, chiefly because 10 is the sum of the first four integers: $1+2+3+4$. The Pythagoreans employed a mystic symbol of 10 dots arranged to form an equilateral triangle, by which they swore oaths. Pythagoras held that the harmonious interrelation of numbers regulates the cosmos, and he saw in numbers the primary cause of all things, whether the nature of the gods, abstract ideas, or musical harmonies.

His concept concerning numbers was inspired, in part, by the realization that music rests upon a mathematical basis, for Pythagoras experimented with the lyre and discovered that the pitch of the instrument varies inversely with the length of strings. He found that a string exactly half as long as another produces the same note as the first string but an octave higher. Thus simple numerical proportions exist between intervals of the musical scale (the octave, the fifth, and the fourth). Additionally, Pythagoras speculated that each of the celestial bodies produces a distinct tone—inaudible to the human ear—corresponding to the notes on a musical scale. Drawn from various traditions, Pythogoreanism substantially influenced the development of philosophy and the sciences. Its suggestion that the earth is a revolving sphere, for example, influenced Copernicus in the sixteenth century of our era.

Pythagoras' movement was politically active and dominated a number of the city-states of southern Italy for several generations, until a catastrophic revolt broke out about 450 BCE. A number of its adherents emigrated to nearby Tarentum, where they made an impact on Plato when he visited the city. Plato was deeply influenced by the Pythagoreans' principle of Justice, which they regarded as the basis of all virtue, and he borrowed from their mathematical conception of nature and other doctrines.

Xenophanes.   One thinker seeking a new religious direction was the poet-philosopher Xenophanes of Colophon, born about 570 BCE. He left Ionia after the Persians moved to capture Colophon in 545 BCE and spent the rest of his life in exile, mostly in the Greek colonies of Sicily. Xenophanes, who lived well into his nineties, traveled about reciting his poems, but his independent spirit did not always win him friends. Like the other pre-Socratics, he speculated about the nature of the universe. After observing marine fossils in rocks high above the water, he concluded that the land periodically rises from and sinks into the sea, subjecting humankind to successive rebirths and destructions. Additionally, Xenophanes held that matter is indestructible and that the universe has always existed. He advanced the novel theory that a different sun rises every morning and moves in a straight line beyond the earth until disappearing from sight, the setting of the sun on the western horizon being merely an optical illusion.

The philosopher remorselessly criticized the Greek religion for its anthropomorphic conception of deity, particularly as expressed by Homer and Hesiod, remarking that the two poets had "attributed to the gods all things that are shameful and a reproach among mankind: theft, adultery, and mutual deception." Xenophanes imagined one supreme and eternal god ruling the universe by reason, arguing that "without toil" the sole deity "moves everything by the thought of his mind." Thus he regarded the divine power as an eternal consciousness exercising its will without motion (anticipating the Unmoved Mover of Aristotle). He blamed the desire of humans to represent divinity in their own image for the traditional misrepresentation of the one god. Noting that the gods of Ethiopia were depicted with black skin and the deities of Thrace with red hair, Xenophanes argued that if oxen, horses, and lions had hands, they would create divine images in their own forms.

Heraclitus.   The last of the great philosophers actually living in Ionia was Heraclitus of Ephesus, active at the end of the sixth century BCE. Lonely and aloof by nature and unhappy with the decline of his aristocratic class, Heraclitus tended to be strident and bitter. He imagined the primary form of matter to be "ever-living fire," not to be confused with the visible fire we know. Because the eternal fire changes one element into another, everything in the universe is in a perpetual state of flux. Accordingly, Heraclitus saw the cosmos as a raging torrent of change and held that we cannot step in the same river twice, for different waters are flowing by us the second time. Following Anaximander, he viewed the world as a perpetual battleground between opposites. Yet each pair of apparently contradictory opposite qualities is essentially unified and can change into the other, as hot into cold, sleep into waking, good into evil, life into death, or youth into age.

Heraclitus scorned the theories of other philosophers, including Xenophanes, though the two thinkers shared certain concepts, most notably the idea of a governing divine intelligence. Heraclitus imagined a universe ruled by divine reason—Logos—the one stable element in existence. Somehow connected with the creative fire, the Logos is the divine rational principle bringing harmonious order to the universe. Yet this regulating principle, which unifies all opposites, can be understood only by a few wise men, while the masses are doomed to perpetual ignorance and folly. Although philosophers and Christian theologians have given the word Logos a wide variety of meanings, Heraclitus spoke of the concept as the rational principle behind the cosmos. Thus in his view the world was not governed by arbitrary gods but by divine reason.

The thought of the pre-Socratics after the Milesians betrays a strong religious undercurrent. Their mystical ideas were diffused from Ionia to mainland Greece and the western colonies, forming a significant element in the emerging common Greek civilization. Yet philosophical thought, the province of a relatively few educated Greeks, did not undermine the religious outlook of ordinary Greeks for generations. Most Greeks must have remained committed to the great Olympian gods, the guardian deities of the city-states, and the sacred practices handed down by their ancestors.

HISTORY AND GEOGRAPHY

HECATAEUS

Greek historical writing was derived, in part, from the desire of leading families to prove divine or heroic ancestry. Accordingly, the first works in the field began with genealogists who expressed themselves in prose and called upon both myth and tradition in constructing lines of descent for their patrons. These pioneers in Greek historical writing are commonly called logographers. Most did not hesitate to fabricate names and incidents, but Hecataeus of Miletus, who flourished around 500 BCE, applied critical principles to the tracing of genealogies. Although Hecataeus included mythical epochs to explain the family origins of his patrons, he attempted to weave these stories into a chronological system based on a rational conception of history. In the opening to his work telling the legends of families claiming a divine origin—the *Genealogies*—Hecataeus expresses a growing awareness of the distinction between myth and fact: "I write here what I think is true, for many stories of the Greeks are, in my opinion, ridiculous." Herodotus, who was active in the next generation, built upon this groundbreaking step toward a critical approach to historical evidence.

Greek historical writing also found expression in mariners' handbooks, or texts listing the ports and peoples of the Mediterranean and providing details about local history and customs. Hecataeus wrote the *Description of the Earth,* based on his own and others' travels, to record information about the far-flung lands with which the Greeks had established trading links. The work was divided into two books, one for Europe and one for Asia (which included Africa). Thus Hecataeus was a pioneering prose writer in both history and geography, though his works survive only in a few fragments.

ART

Archaic artists refined their techniques and forms, many of which were inherited from the Dark Age or earlier. As noted, Greek culture of the period was permeated with religious concerns, and artistic production was generally related to religion, except for functional objects made for public or household use. Contrary to popular opinion, Greek artists were not blessed with miraculous creative gifts. They struggled diligently through trial and error to produce their first great successes, which appeared under aristocratic patronage in the seventh century BCE. Thus their stunning achievements resulted partly from experimenting with techniques. Moreover, the artists—like the philosophers—were motivated by the desire to express eternal truths. Many of their works demonstrate both artistic and intellectual brilliance.

Painting

From literary sources we know that Archaic Greek painters created murals on large surfaces such as public porticoes. Yet no painting has survived from the period, except for examples on vases of fired clay. Greek pottery is a primary source of evidence for artistic development from the Dark Age to the end of the Archaic period. After a lingering end to an earlier pottery tradition about the middle of the eleventh century BCE, the remainder of the Dark Age witnessed the production of fired clay vessels showing two successive styles of painted decoration, now called Protogeometric and Geometric, discussed in chapter 3. Protogeometric pottery with its geometric patterns and large blank spaces emerged about 1050 BCE and was superseded around 900 BCE by the Geometric style, characterized by geometric patterns deployed in bands around the vase, disdain for empty space, and rigidly stylized figures of humans and animals composed of triangles, squares, circles, and other patterns.

The Orientalizing Style.   The resurgence in seagoing trade around the middle of the eighth century BCE resulted in a dramatic increase of imports from the cultured cities of the Near East (especially Syria). We find evidence of tapestries, carved ivories, jewelry, and bowls made of gold, silver, and bronze. The severe linear patterns of the Geometric style began to yield to a strong eastern, or oriental, influence. This new style—now called Orientalizing—was established by the beginning of the Archaic period, about 750 BCE, with Near Eastern motifs on imported metalwork and textiles blossoming into a painting tradition. Eastern animal designs abound on Orientalizing pottery. The lion was a favorite subject, and the Greeks also prized hybrid monsters such as sphinxes and griffins. A whole range of curvilinear eastern patterns—most inspired by vegetation—also show up, notably alternating lotus flowers and buds, palmettes, and rosettes. The new Orientalizing motifs first appear on pottery made from the pale, yellowish clay of Corinth, the leading commercial center of Greece from around 750 to 575 BCE. The appealing Corinthian vases were prized throughout the Mediterranean world.

The Black-Figure Technique.   The Corinthian potter-painters took an important step in the development of figure drawing. Geometric painters had created figures in full silhouette, eventually learning to show minor details by leaving reserved (that is, unpainted) areas. The Orientalizing Corinthian artists, finding silhouetted figure painting inadequate for depicting details such as eyes or muscles or the vigorous movement of overlapping figures, invented a new technique around 720 BCE. While continuing to paint silhouetted figures against the light background of the natural clay, they incised inner details with a fine point, thereby producing thin clear lines revealing the underlying pale clay, a technique now called black-figure. They enlivened figures with touches of white and red paint, the former gradually becoming customary for

Corinthian black-figure jug with animal friezes, c. 625–600 BCE. Corinthian vases of the period, decorated with Orientalizing animals and motifs, enjoyed widespread circulation in the Mediterranean area. This example was found on the island of Rhodes, lying on the opposite side of the Aegean from mainland Corinth. British Museum, London.

portraying female flesh, the latter for male hair and beards. The result lacked the refinement of shading, yet figures were drawn with a remarkable level of naturalism.

Although the most popular Greek pottery in the export trade during the seventh century BCE was Corinthian, the orange-red vases of Athens became increasingly prized after about 600 BCE, by which time Athenian painters had fully adopted the black-figure technique. The Athenian artists established a dignified narrative style moving away from eastern motifs and concentrating instead on the human figure. They turned their growing technical skill to representations from Greek myth and heroic legends. In the meantime Corinthian pottery degenerated into an inferior product of mass production, and the Attic (that is, Athenian) ware was regularly transported far from its point of manufacture. The Attic silhouettes were increasingly refined, and this pottery attained a preeminence in the pottery trade soon after 550 BCE.

The brilliant Athenian potter-painter Exekias demonstrated subtlety and skill in his *Dionysus in a Warship*, a scene on the interior of an Attic black-figure kylix (wine cup), *c.* 550–525 BCE, illustrating the myth that the god of wine was captured by Etruscan pirates. Staatliche Antikensammlungen und Glyptothek, Munich.

The potter began the process of creating a black-figure vase by shaping clay on the wheel. After the piece had been dried and its surface polished, the figures were drawn in outline and filled in with paint to produce the black silhouette against the clay background. The paint consisted of a solution of finely sifted clay that became deprived of oxygen and permanently black during the complicated three-stage firing process.

The Attic black-figure vase is notable for its lively and fluid human representations. We find black or red silhouettes for males and white flesh for females, with additional touches of purple paint added for garments and accessories. Sometimes the figures tell a story—often drawn from heroic legends—or they may portray scenes of human activity ranging from the great religious festivals to everyday life. Inscriptions painted on the vase identify the gods and heroes by name. Meanwhile, beginning with the Corinthians, many potters signed their works, and thus the names of some of the greatest are still known.

The height of the black-figure technique was achieved about 540 BCE by the potter-painter Exekias of Athens, who produced richly incised vases portraying human figures with a restrained and almost Classical presence. In his striking scene showing *Dionysus in a Warship*, which was painted on the interior of a kylix, or wine cup, Exekias leaves an expanse of natural clay beneath the glossy silhouetted figures, who thus seem to exist in a timeless realm, an appropriate setting for the depiction of divine events. Now in Munich, the kylix portrays the wine-god Dionysus reclining on a handsome warship, around whose mast he has miraculously entwined a grape-laden vine, thereby terrifying pirates who had captured him for ransom. They have leaped overboard and been transformed into dolphins. Dionysus then sails over the sea carrying his gift of wine to humanity. Exekias demonstrates a new

An unequaled Athenian genius of the black-figure technique, Exekias decorated a vase with this elegant yet forceful scene of Ajax and Achilles playing a board game. In the legend of the Trojan War, Achilles is the greatest of the Greek warriors, Ajax the second. No doubt the scene is set during a lull in the fighting at Troy, but a helmeted Achilles on one side and Ajax on the other—each holding spears—are ready to spring into action at a moment's notice. Seemingly calm, the scene is pervaded by foreboding of the dire events to follow for the two. After Achilles' death, his armor was awarded to Odysseus rather than Ajax. Maddened with shame, Ajax committed suicide by throwing himself on a sword. From a black-figure amphora, *c.* 540–530 BCE, decorated in Athens and exported to the Etruscan city of Vulci. Vatican Museums, Rome.

awareness of the physical presence of nature in this masterpiece through such details as the beautiful billowing of the sail.

The Red-Figure Technique.   The black-figure technique was limited, in part, because the stiff line made by the engraving tool was adequate for producing ornament but not for suggesting movement or emotion. Exekias' successors sought a clearer representation of anatomy. The solution came about 530 BCE in Athens with the inauguration of a new painting method reversing black-figure by making the background a lustrous black and leaving the figures reserved in the clay's natural color (often reddish). This technique, called red-figure, produced luminous figures. Details were supplied with fine black lines, and the paint could be diluted to a golden brown for occasional shading or minor lines. Only the lightest touches of red and white appear, for painters now distinguish men and women by features of dress and anatomy rather than by complexion. Moreover, they have replaced the incising point with the supple brush. A talented painter could create beautifully

One of the more daring exponents of the new red-figure technique was the Athenian painter Euphronius. A panel on one of his mixing bowls shows Heracles struggling with Antaeus. In myth, the famous Greek hero Heracles journeyed across northern Africa and encountered the dangerous giant Antaeus, son of Poseiden and Earth, who ruled over Libya and killed all comers by wrestling. Antaeus derived his seeming invincibility from contact with his mother, but Heracles destroyed the giant by holding him aloft and crushing him while no part of his body touched Earth. Euphronius depicts an apparently serene Heracles struggling with the giant, now facing death, in a complicated pose reflecting the painter's fame for stressing anatomical detail. Antaeus' face is a mask of pain and his arm hangs limp, while his unkempt hair and beard contrast with the groomed curls of his opponent. From an Attic red-figure krater, c. 510 BCE. Louvre, Paris.

flowing lines with the fine, single-hair brush that was employed for outlining both figures and ornament. Drawing skills improved greatly with time, leading to an increasing variety of scenes reflecting the expanding richness of Greek life.

Although the old black-figure technique lingered for another two generations, the vigorous red-figure technique soon dominated the field. Leading red-figure artists included Euphronius and Euthymides—both active in the late sixth century BCE—and the anonymous Berlin Painter (named for the present location of one of his most notable pieces), who flourished early in the next century. Demonstrating a fuller understanding of the subtleties of anatomy, the three artists broke with the old frontal-profile conventions and opened the way to the full naturalism of the Classical period. Painters had learned before the middle of the fifth century BCE to employ bold foreshortening (the reduction or distortion of a represented object to produce the illusion of three dimensions), making possible, for example, the depiction of a foot seen from in front rather than in profile. Moreover, they were using pose and gesture to convey the impression of convincing movement and emotion, and they were moving toward a naturalistic use of color and shading. Such advances meant the red-figure style had reached a plateau. Thus the most talented artists soon turned from the decoration of pottery to the production of monumental paintings.

ARCHITECTURE

The Temple.   Although the Archaic city was not yet a metropolis adorned with a vast array of gleaming limestone or marble structures, much energy was expended on the construction of public buildings, especially temples, the earliest Greek monumental architecture. Some temples were constructed in lowland sites, while others were set upon commanding heights such as the Acropolis in Athens. The revival of monumental architecture was linked to the expansion of the polis, whose chief symbol of unity was the worship of a common anthropomorphic deity requiring a temple as a dwelling. Initially of modest dimensions, the Greek temple never approached the mammoth size of an Egyptian temple and was truly impressive only on its exterior. Yet the Greeks created increasingly harmonious and beautiful temples by refining the balance and proportion of the architectural elements. The usual plan for the Greek temple was the Mycenaean central hall, or megaron. Thus the heart of the temple was a large rectangular hall called the naos (or cella in Latin) housing the image of the deity and entered through a porch, or portico, known as the pronaos, which was supported by two columns. Serving as the façade, or front, of the temple, the porch was created by extending the sidewalls of the naos beyond its portal, or doorway. A number of Archaic temples also included a rear porch (*opisthodomos*), usually without a doorway into the naos.

The first provable Greek temples are from the eighth century, though not much survives before the sixth century BCE. Long, low, and narrow, the early temples were brightly painted structures with sun-dried brick walls and wooden columns and beams, stone being reserved for the foundations. The temple also included a pitched gable roof built upon wooden beams. Fired clay roof tiles remained standard throughout the Archaic period. Between the eighth and sixth centuries BCE Greek architects steadily widened the temple, replaced its wood with stone, and extended its roof to create a deeper porch. They finally gained the ability to surround the larger and more prestigious temples with a great colonnade known as a peristyle (*peristylon*), the roof resting upon the colonnade rather than the walls. Such an edifice, described as a peripteral temple, reminds us of the preeminence of the column in Greek monumental architecture. The peristyle created a covered walk around the temple between the columns and the naos, thereby attracting Greeks for strolling, escaping from sun and rain, and discussing philosophy, business, or politics.

Stone for the Archaic temple was carefully cut and polished into sharp-edged blocks, which were held together only with dowels of wood or bronze. The practical Greeks translating the old wooden construction into stone—a feat accomplished by the Egyptians in the distant past—constructed the roof of wood rather than stone to ease the spanning of a wide naos. The architects used limestone for building the temple in the sixth century BCE, turning in the next century to marble, if readily available, for the entire building, including the ceiling and tiles. The customary orientation of the edifice was east to west, and the cult statue was placed at the westward end of the naos. The image of the god was thought to look eastward through the open door at the offering of sacrifices on the altar outside the temple. Both the temple and altar stood on demarcated sacred land (*temenos*). Clearly, the Greeks put forth extraordinary effort in creating a temple. Perhaps believing the qualities of the deity were embodied in the very building itself, the architects regarded a temple almost as sculpture and thus lavished far more attention on the exterior than on the dimly lit naos.

The Legacy of Greek Temple Architecture.   Certain characteristic features of early Greek temples persisted long after antiquity. Architects provided the temple with a platform of three steps, of which the topmost (stylobate) supported the columns. They crowned the shaft of each column with a capital, a transition member carrying the weight of the entablature (the part of the building above the columns). The instability of sun-dried brick construction prompted builders of early Greek temples to top the naos wall with a broad wooden beam, the architrave, supporting the upper entablature. The architrave spread the weight of the superstructure evenly and prevented the rafters from damaging the wall. The architrave persisted in stone temples as a distinct stone beam resting on the naos wall or, in the case of a peripteral temple, on the colonnade.

The architrave supported the upper parts of the entablature: the frieze, cornices, and pediments. The frieze—a horizontal course above the architrave—originated with the wooden cross beams resting upon the architrave in early temples to prevent the roof from spreading and collapsing. The ends of the wooden cross beams were visible from the outside. Between the beam ends were openings, each of which was probably filled with a block of painted wood. Eventually both the beam ends and the wooden slabs between them were translated into stone to form the frieze, itself protected by an overhanging cornice. The triangular space enclosed by the cornice and the slopes of the roof formed the pediment, which was set back to create a shelf, regularly used to hold freestanding sculpture that heightened the sculpturesque effect of the exterior.

In time the ancient Greeks developed a number of representative plans for their temples. The simplest form consisted of a naos and a porch of two columns, the latter created by extending the side walls of the naos and setting two columns between their ends (*antae* in Latin). Such a temple is said, in Latin, to be *in antis*. An alternate architectural plan was the *prostyle* temple, with the antae shortened to make room for a row of four columns across the front. A later development was the *amphiprostyle* temple, with porches at both ends. Next architects designed the *peripteral* temple, with a single colonnade running around the entire naos, and eventually they created the *dipteral* temple, with a double colonnade surrounding the naos.

Although the Greeks always retained the traditional post and lintel construction, they developed three orders, or styles of buildings: Doric, Ionic, and Corinthian. Doric and Ionic emerged earlier, while Corinthian—actually a form of Ionic—remained exceptional until the Roman period. The relatively severe Doric order prevailed in mainland Greece and the western colonies in Sicily and southern Italy. The Ionic order, more ornamental and variable, originated in Ionia in

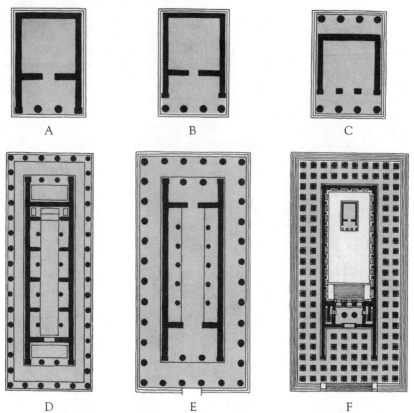

Six representative plans of the Greek temple: (A) treasury of the Athenians at Delphi, a temple *in antis*, its porch formed by the projecting side walls with two columns set between their ends (*antae* in Latin); (B) temple B at Selinus, Sicily, a *prostyle* temple, with the *antae* shortened to provide space for a row of four columns across the front; (C) temple of Athena Nike on the Athenian Acropolis, an *amphiprostyle* temple, in which the *prostyle* plan has a porch added at the rear; (D) temple of Hera at Olympia and (E) temple of Aphaea on the island of Aegina, both *peripteral* temples, with a single colonnade surrounding the naos; and (F) temple of Apollo at Didyma, a *dipteral* temple, with a double colonnade surrounding the naos. Drawings are not to scale.

Asia Minor, where the tendency to borrow forms from the Near East was naturally stronger. The Doric order took definite form by the end of the sixth century BCE, but the Ionic was not well established until the Athenian Acropolis was rebuilt in the late fifth century BCE. The orders differ not only in the shape of their capitals, the most easily recognizable feature, but also in the proportion and design of other elements. Yet the orders have many common features. In each, for example, the shaft of the column gently tapers upward and swells slightly in the middle, thereby providing the profile with a subtle curve (entasis). Moreover, the shafts were made of cylindrical blocks called drums, which were turned on a lathe and held together by metal dowels.

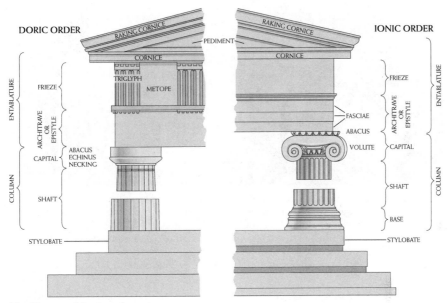

The Doric and Ionic orders.

The Doric Order.   Ancient writers contrasted the Doric and Ionic orders as masculine and feminine. The Doric order is characterized by its massiveness, its severely plain columns, and its unique frieze. The sturdy Doric column, being without a base, rests on the top step (stylobate) or floor of the temple. Its shaft is fluted, resulting in shallow vertical channels that were divided by a knife-sharp edge. The Doric capital consists of a cushion-shaped block (the echinus) surmounted by a square block (the abacus). The columns of early Doric temples appear squat and bulky, but Greek architects learned to create increasingly taller and less massive columns as the Archaic period passed into the Classical.

The frieze of the Doric order is formed by a horizontal course of alternating triglyphs and metopes. The triglyph (from a Greek word meaning three grooves) is a block with three narrow vertical bands separated by grooves. Triglyphs were derived from the beam ends of wooden buildings, with the beam ends represented by grooved blocks of stone. The metopes are blank panels representing the old wooden slabs between the beams, though in the more elaborate temples they were adorned with paintings or sculpture in relief. The scenes usually depict a series of episodes in a connected story such as the battle of the gods and Giants.

The Ionic and Corinthian Orders.   The shaft of the Ionic column, unlike the Doric, rests upon a base. Moreover, its flutes are more numerous and deeper than those on a Doric shaft, and each is separated by a flat band of stone. The elaborate Ionic capital consists of a richly ornamented echinus separated from a delicate abacus by a volute, a graceful ornament resembling a double-rolled scroll. Occasionally architects employed luxuriously carved female figures—caryatids—in place of columns

Our prime example of early Greek Doric design is the temple of Hera I (eighteenth-century investigators erroneously termed the structure the Basilica after the Roman building type), erected at the colony of Poseidonia/Paestum in southern Italy, *c*. 550 BCE. The great peripteral colonnade of this huge (80 by 170 feet) temple remains standing, showing the pronounced bulge and taper of Archaic Doric columns. Inscriptions and other evidence identify the principal diety as Hera, though her consort Zeus also may have been the object of a cult here.

on an Ionic temple. The Ionic frieze, instead of alternating triglyphs and metopes in Doric fashion, consists of a continuous band running around the temple. The Ionic frieze is usually decorated with relief. The Corinthian order, a form of Ionic, developed in the fifth century BCE but was not popular until Hellenistic times. The Corinthian order is characterized by its bell-shaped capital decorated with acanthus leaves gracefully reaching up from the base.

Artisans painted parts of the stone temples to highlight architectural de-tails, a practice echoing the decoration of the old wooden temples. They em-ployed red and blue on the triglyphs and many of the moldings while usually spreading solid coats of red or blue on the backgrounds of metopes, friezes, and pediments. They accentuated the sculpture with touches of various other colors, though they left the shafts of the columns and the walls of the naos in the nat-ural color of the stone. The contrast between the luminous white of the building and its vividly painted surfaces must have been dramatic in the intense Mediter-ranean sunlight.

Notable Archaic Temples.   The Greeks erected several exceptionally large temples in the Archaic period, including a Doric example completed around the middle of the sixth century BCE in the colony of Poseidonia (later called Paestum) in south-ern Italy. Misnamed the Basilica by eighteenth-century investigators, the temple was probably dedicated to Hera, wife of Zeus and queen of the gods. Its great peri-style still stands. The oldest Doric temple on the Greek mainland with some stand-ing columns is the temple of Apollo at Corinth, also erected in the mid-sixth century BCE. An early example of Ionic architecture on the mainland is provided by the treasury of the Siphnians at Delphi, a refined small building constructed about 530 BCE. In place of columns the architects incorporated two graceful cary-atids, harmonious female figures seeming to carry the weight of the entablature ef-

A conjectural view through the pronaos, or front porch, of the Archaic temple of
Artemis at Ephesus, erected over a long period from the mid-sixth century BCE.
This gigantic Ionic temple, measuring 181 by 378 feet, enjoyed a triple row of
columns on the façade. After burning down in the fourth century BCE, the
temple was rebuilt on the same plan and was designated in the Hellenistic
period as one of the Seven Wonders of the World.

fortlessly. The immense yet magnificent Ionic temple of Artemis at Ephesus was designed in the 540s BCE and completed about a century later. Destroyed by fire in
the fourth century BCE, the temple was replaced by a still larger version that was
reckoned among the Seven Wonders of the World.

Reconstruction of the Treasury of the Siphnians at Delphi, built about 530 BCE, of which little remains standing. This small Ionic marble masterpiece was erected at Delphi by the island-state of Siphnos to store its gifts to Apollo, an exuberant architectural expression of civic pride. The structure is celebrated for its symmetrically posed caryatids (female figures functioning as columns), sculpted frieze, and ornate moldings.

Other Architecture.   Although temples were the most important buildings in ancient Greece, various other specialized structures dotted the landscape. To store their gifts to a particular deity at the great sanctuaries such as Delphi and Olympia, city-states erected treasuries, which took the form of miniature temples *in antis*. All sorts of buildings were needed in the rapidly developing city-states of the Greek world. In chapter 4 we encountered the stoa, essentially a long covered colonnade, with many possible elaborations. The most characteristic form contained a back wall from which a roof sloped to a row of columns on the front. Eventually architects designed stoas with back rooms and second stories. Affording cover at sanctuaries and marketplaces, stoas were popular for such uses as shops, courts of law, and council chambers. They also served as convenient gathering places for business or personal discussions. As a rule the Greek marketplace—the agora—took the form of a large open space surrounded by stoas. A central institution in all Greek cities was the gymnasium, which originated as an athletic field and developed into a school for boys and a club for men. Associated with the gymnasium was a place for exercise called the palaestra, eventually taking the form of a courtyard surrounded by a colonnade and rooms for bathing, changing, and athletics. Youths trained at the palaestra in wrestling, jumping, boxing, and ball games.

While lavishing attention on public buildings, the Greeks regarded their houses as relatively unimportant. Our evidence for the Archaic period remains scanty, though archaeology suggests the Greeks built simple freestanding houses of one or two rooms, some with porches. Apparently none had refinements such as decorated walls or floors. The floor consisted of beaten mud or pebbles, and the walls were constructed of sun-dried bricks on a stone foundation. The extensive use of perishable materials for dwellings has left little trace of their former existence.

Sculpture

Greece is blessed by an abundant supply of stone, much of which is suitable for both architecture and sculpture. From Mounts Hymettus and Pentelicus near Athens and from the Greek islands, notably Paros, came marble of dazzling luminosity. Greek marble, famous for its clarity, was far more suitable for convincing representations of human flesh than the dark diorite or speckled granite used in Egypt. The production of monumental sculpture in the great centers of civilization in the ancient Near East was controlled by a priestly autocracy and thus restricted to conventional boundaries. Most major works of Greek sculpture were produced also to express eternal religious truths, with notable examples including statues in the temples depicting gods and goddesses and statues in the temple precincts serving as thank offerings for success in athletics, war, or commerce. Yet the Greek religion was not strictly controlled by powerful priesthoods, and Greek sculptors were free to experiment. They seem to have experienced a growing awareness that art is valuable for its own sake, not simply for its religious expression. This aesthetic approach led to important innovations in both technique and style

Examples of Greek sculpture date from the beginning of the ninth century BCE and consist of tiny representations of animals and humans fashioned from materials such as terra cotta, copper, bronze, lead, and ivory, all showing the clear simplification of the Geometric period. When trading and colonizing ventures in the eighth century BCE brought eastern influences, Greek sculptors imposed Near Eastern monsters and other motifs on seals and small figures in the round. Not much is known about larger works produced in this period, though literary sources mention sizable wooden cult statues (the so-called *xoana*).

The Daedalic Style.   One technique introduced from the east was the use of the mold for producing clay plaques and statuettes. This promoted standardized proportions for figures and led to a style now called Daedalic, after a legendary Cretan artist. In the Daedalic style, clearly a descendant of eastern prototypes, figures were rendered in a flat, planklike fashion with schematized musculature. The style was enlisted to create, besides molded clay figures, small works in ivory or metal and occasionally large stone statuettes, which were usually less than life-size. Almost all the Daedalic figures in stone depict naked youths or draped women, both having long triangular faces and commonly wearing broad belts.

As noted in chapter 4, a number of Greek traders settled at the town of Naucratis in the western Delta during the second half of the seventh century BCE. Thus

Greek travelers and traders encountered the age-old massive stone statuary of Egypt. Greek sculptors were inspired to produce their own monumental pieces—initially in the Daedalic style—and white marble was the preferred medium. They easily worked the stone with iron tools such as chisels, gouges, and drills. Sculpture was smoothed with soft stones and emery, though the practice of polishing surfaces did not develop until after the Archaic period.

Kouroi and Korai.   A new series of large-scale standing statues became popular in the late seventh century BCE, and an exceptionally large number survive from the following century. There were two types—the nude standing youth and the draped standing maiden—whose exact functions and significance remain unclear. Scholars use Greek words to describe them: *kouros* (youth) for the naked young male figure and *kore* (maiden) for the draped young female figure. The kouroi and the korai reflect a continuation of aristocratic wealth and prestige in Greece, for they represent the sons and daughters of noble families.

Art historians generally consider the naked young male figure more significant than the draped female figure for understanding the development of Greek art. The kouros was adapted from the walking Egyptian male statue and reflects its strong frontal emphasis. The early kouros is stiffly upright and is easily recognized by its advanced left leg, rigid arms at the sides, and clenched fists by the thighs. The somewhat abstract body lacks convincing musculature, especially in the first examples, and its hair is stylized and wiglike. While the gaze of the statue is frontal and fixed, its lips are customarily turned upward in a conventional shallow smile, the so-called Archaic smile, which was probably intended to animate the face rather than indicate any particular state of mind.

Clear similarities exist between a celebrated early Greek kouros, dated about 600 BCE, in the Metropolitan Museum of Art at New York, and an Egyptian free-standing statue of Vizier Bakenrenef, dated about 625 BCE, in the Museum of Fine Arts at Boston. Of these, the New York kouros appears less realistic with its patterned geometrical surface, intense stiffness, cubical head, and large flat eyes. Yet its face seems alert, and the entire body suggests tension and pent-up energy. The Egyptian figure, with its mood of passive stillness, recalls works of the Old Kingdom (c. 2647–2124 BCE) and retains stylistically fixed forms of art preserved along the Nile for millennia. Moreover, the Egyptians almost invariably clothed their statues, whereas the Greeks preferred theirs nude. The Greeks were preoccupied with youthful male beauty and took male nudity—an important mark of Greek aristocracy—for granted. In Greece men and boys spent much of their time exercising naked at the gymnasium, warriors trained for battle without clothing, and youths appeared naked in religious rituals and initiations (see chapter 10 for a fuller discussion of public male nudity).

Like the pre-Socratic philosophers who observed the world to speculate on the nature of reality, Greek sculptors examined the body to render increasingly convincing human representations. Throughout the sixth century BCE they retained the basic form of the kouros but advanced greatly in their ability to render the body in a naturalistic manner. They were on the verge of an artistic break-

The ancient Egyptians preserved stylistic conventions governing figurative portrayal for thousands of years. On the left, the green schist standing statue of Vizier Bakenrenef, *c.* 625 BCE, now in the Museum of Fine Arts at Boson, recalls works of the Old Kingdom (*c.* 2647–2124 BCE), with its rigid stance, arms pressed against the sides, left leg advanced, kiltlike costume, and mood of passive stillness. The Greeks adapted their *kouros* (youth) type from such Egyptian male figures. On the right, the marble kouros from Attica, *c.* 600 BCE, now in the Metropolitan Museum of Art at New York, shows many similarities with the timeless Egyptian works, but contrasts notably in its nudity and suggestion of pent-up energy. Such Greek statues replaced the huge amphoras and kraters used earlier as grave markers or served as gifts to the gods.

through, and in the next century Greek sculptors pushed the kouros beyond naturalism to produce a male image reflecting the essence of divinity, thus blurring the distinction between mortal hero and immortal god. Although, as mentioned, the precise significance of the kouroi remains elusive, they stood as representatives of youthful male beauty on graves or served as gifts to the gods at sanctuaries.

Sculptors made the kouros figures more lifelike by devoting attention to the natural depiction of human anatomy, and they enlivened the kore figures also by giving them pretty faces and beautifully carved drapery. For men, nudity was divine and beautiful, a source of strength, but taboo for women. Respectable women always appeared completely clothed in ancient Greece, and thus the korai are shown fully draped. Like the kouroi, the korai served as gifts to the gods or as grave markers. Apparently most were created to attend deities as votive figures in permanent poses of

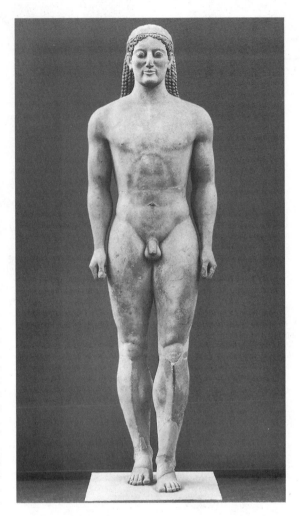

The Greeks kept the basic form of the kouros throughout the sixth century BCE but portrayed the body in an increasingly naturalistic manner. This kouros, c. 530 BCE, was found near the village of Anavysos, not far from Athens. Set up as a grave marker for a young man, an inscription on the base invites the passerby (cemeteries frequently lined roadsides) to pause and grieve for a certain Kroisos, who had died in the front line of battle. The work retains the blissful Archaic smile and the old frontal stance, but the modeling demonstrates an increasing ability to render anatomical details realistically. Traces of the original paint add to the naturalism. National Archaeological Museum, Athens.

worship. A host of these maidens stood on the Acropolis at Athens—archaeologists found them among the broken statues buried after the Persian sack of the city in 480 BCE—often executed with patterns of decorative folds fanning out across their bodies. Archaic sculptors generally ignored the study of female anatomy, and there is little hint of the shape of the body under the clothing. Yet artists took increasing delight in the ornamental treatment of the drapery, which they enhanced through incision and color. Gradual changes in Archaic fashion are reflected in the costume of the korai from one century to another. The well-known *Peplos Kore*, as she is affectionately known, dating about 580 BCE, was discovered on the Athenian Acropolis and is now exhibited in the Acropolis Museum. She wears simple dress. Standing rather stiffly, the kore is one of the last known to be shown wearing an outer garment known as a peplos, a heavy woolen garment—often richly embroidered—that was thrown over the body and pinned at the shoulders. Her left hand originally ex-

A parallel development was taking place in Archaic statues of young female figures, termed *kore* (maiden), which were always clothed. Typically, a kore was commissioned by a wealthy family to serve as a grave marker or a dedicatory offering in a temple. Some may represent goddesses. Early examples demonstrate considerable variety in the treatment of detail, especially the dress. This well-known piece, dubbed the *Peplos Kore, c.* 530 BCE, is one of the last shown wearing the heavy woolen peplos as her main garment. Originally brightly painted, she stood on the Athenian Acropolis, probably an offering to a deity. Acropolis Museum, Athens.

tended forward, perhaps offering a votive gift such as a libation of wine. The *Peplos Kore* and some others still bear traces of color, for the Greeks painted their sculptures in order to enhance drapery patterns and to accentuate hair, lips, eyes, and other parts of the body.

Local schools of sculpture flourished in the early Archaic period. Peloponnesian sculpture was characterized by its massiveness, while that of Ionia was more graceful and ornate, as reflected in the elaborate eastern costumes of its korai. Archaic sculptors gradually spread their techniques and styles by accepting commissions beyond their native city-states. The elaborate decorative quality and ornamental drapery of a number of the late-sixth-century BCE korai on the Athenian Acropolis exemplify the Ionian school, the sculptors probably having come to Athens after the Persians occupied their homeland in Asia Minor in 540 BCE. Athenian sculptors greatly benefited from the influx of Ionian artists, which led to a blending of the Peloponnesian

Another kore from the Athenian Acropolis, usually dated about 510 BCE, was carved by an artist excelling in producing cascading folds of drapery and elaborately styled hair. This celebrated figure, her face softly modeled, wears the light linen chiton of Ionia with a short himation on top, both once richly painted. The sculptor, probably an Ionian, expresses a certain sensitivity to the contours of the body below. Acropolis Museum, Athens.

and Ionian styles by the end of the Archaic period. By that time Athenian sculpture excelled in modeling and line, enabling them to permeate their works with a spirit of power, grace, and beauty.

Temple Sculpture.   When the Greeks began erecting stone temples, they adopted the age-old tradition of architectural sculpture. For many centuries the Egyptians had covered their walls and columns with shallow reliefs, but the Greeks used sculpture only in the empty spaces of their temples. Thus they filled the metopes of the Doric temple and the frieze of the Ionic temple with relief. Moreover, they regularly placed ornaments—acroteria—on the corners and crowns of pediments, thereby silhouetting sculpture against the sky. Acroteria were used on both Doric

Reconstruction of the west end of the great Doric temple of Artemis on Corcyra (modern Corfu), a prosperous island off the western coast of Greece and a major stop on the vital trade route between the mainland and the Greek settlements in Italy. This poorly preserved temple, built around 580 BCE, is famous for its ambitious architecture and lavish sculptural decoration. The east pediment is fragmentary. Most of the center of the better preserved west pediment is taken up by a huge limestone figure of snake-haired Medusa—hideous female monster upon whom none looked without turning to stone—now displayed at the Corfu Museum.

and Ionic buildings and took the form of abstract ornaments, human figures, or hybrid monsters such as sphinxes, griffins, or Gorgons. Winged creatures were very popular in this lofty position.

Perhaps the most important avenue for temple sculpture was the pediments, which could be filled with figures carved in much greater depth than those on the metopes or friezes. Sometimes the figures were entirely in the round and set on the pedimental floor. An early pedimental composition was created at the sixth-century BCE temple of Artemis at Corcyra (modern Corfu) off the Greek west coast. The central space was dominated by a huge limestone Medusa with a frightful grin, bared teeth, protruding tongue, and snakes for hair. Flanked not only by her offspring Pegasus and Chrysaor—both of whom sprang from Medusa's blood when Perseus cut off her head—but also by fierce lion-panthers, the fearsome Gorgon was probably intended to scare away evil influences.

Archaic pedimental architecture reached its culmination with the Doric temple honoring the local goddess Aphaea, a pre-Greek deity with similarities to Artemis, on the island of Aegina in the Gulf of Athens. Built about 510 BCE, the temple of Aphaea is well preserved and beautifully situated on a hilltop. Art historians are baffled that two sets of pedimental sculpture were carved for its east end, the earlier of which was soon replaced. The surviving sets—now mostly in the

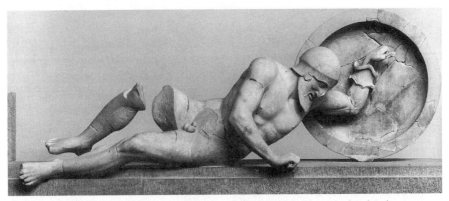

This marble figure of a fallen warrior from the east pediment of the temple of Aphaea at Aegina, 490–480 BCE, reflects a radical change in outlook and expression. The Archaic smile has vanished, replaced by the earliest known Greek attempt to suggest the pain and despair of death. Staatliche Antikensammlungen und Glyptothek, Munich.

Glyptothek in Munich—show two styles: the solidity preferred by Peloponnesian sculptors on the west pediment and the grace of the Attic-Ionic sculptors on the later east pediment. The fragments of the sculptural ensembles from both pediments show a central Athena presiding over a battle scene. The height of the figures varies with the sloping and decreasing triangular space. In the extraordinary east pediment, Greek sculptors finally achieve a unity of composition, scale, and subject matter, exemplified by the figure of a fallen warrior, whose superb rounded forms demonstrate an increasing reach for naturalism. He seems to accept what fate has decreed with tremendous dignity and resolve. Magnificently calm and showing only a hint of pain at the moment of violent death, the fallen warrior embodies the heroic grandeur of the Homeric epics and prefigures the astounding harmony typifying Early Classical art. Thus the Greek sculptors active at the close of the Archaic period were on the threshold of achieving the illusion of inner movement and life through the medium of inert stone.

GREEK UNITY AND SEPARATISM

Although the city-states jealously guarded their sovereignty in an attitude of defiant separatism, by the eve of the Persian Wars the Greeks acknowledged a vague uniform culture characterized by its common language, religion, and traditions. The popular Olympic Games and the venerable Delphic oracle, for example, served as loose bonds despite the political fragmentation of the Greek world. With the growing awareness of their cultural identity, the Greeks began to refer to those sharing their civilization as Hellenes and to all others as barbarians. We do not find the word barbarian (barbaros) in the Homeric epics, except in the form of a compound adjective. Homer refers to the Carians in southwestern Asia Minor as "strange-speaking [barbaro-phonoi] Carians," but at that time and long afterward the designation *barbarian* did not imply cultural or social crudity. The term simply meant a speaker of an incomprehensible language. To Homer, Carian speech sounded like "bar-bar-bar," meaningless sounds similar to the bleating of sheep; thus the origin of the word *barbaros*. Although the Greeks came to regard people who expressed themselves by making such sounds as uneducated, in the seventh and sixth centuries BCE hostility among the Greeks themselves figured far more prominently than antagonism toward foreigners. After the Persian Wars, however, and especially by the fourth century BCE, the Greeks consistently viewed the so-called barbarians with hatred and contempt. Foreigners were regarded not only as non-Greeks but also as inferior and uncivilized. The attitude of ethnic superiority helped to mold cohesiveness and national patriotism, though Greek loyalty to the autonomous city-states was fiercely guarded and paramount except in times of severe crisis. Such a crisis came during the well-known period of robust Persian aggression, which prompted the Greeks to form a war coalition and to expand their culture through remarkable new achievements. We turn in the next chapter to the powerful Persian assault against Ionia and the Greek mainland. The ultimate Greek response testifies to the vigor and vitality of the civilization lying behind factional Hellenism during the closing years of the Archaic period.

CHAPTER VIII

THE PERSIAN WARS

Although the Greeks had developed a relatively uniform culture by the end of the Archaic period, their world remained a constellation of small powers whose citizens supported their own individual states at the expense of Panhellenic unity. Yet the opening years of the fifth century BCE witnessed many of the Greek city-states temporarily suspending their rivalries and joining together for defense against attacks from Persia. The Persian Wars not only frustrated the attempts of the greatest imperial power the world had ever known to expand into Greece but also liberated the Greek cities in Asia Minor from Persian control. The conflict with the Persians represented a monumental, though temporary, triumph of Greek civilization.

The age of the Persian Wars lasted from 499 to 479 BCE. Our main source for the period is Herodotus (c. 484–420 BCE), born in Halicarnassus on the Carian coast of Asia Minor just as the conflict was ending. Years later in Athens he wrote a history of the conflict between Greece and Persia, producing a narrative of epic dimensions recounting the stirring events of his youth. Herodotus had traveled far and wide, partly on business, to gather information for his work. He shows remarkable objectivity toward the Persians while finding much to criticize about the Greeks. His material generally seems reliable, though he often came to erroneous conclusions when depending on the accounts of others, and he includes many dubious but colorful tales. His strengths and weaknesses as a historian are more fully discussed in chapter 13 against the background of fifth-century BCE Greek civilization.

PERSIA AND IONIA

While the Greeks were caught up in the ferment of the Archaic period, the great Persian Empire was developing in the east. The Persians erected their empire on the foundations laid by the closely related Medes, once their overlords. The core of the kingdom of Media lay in what is now the northwestern part of modern Iran. The Medes had helped bring about the downfall of dreaded Assyria in 621 BCE and then carved out a vast realm reaching from Iran to central Asia Minor. Their holdings included the heartland of Persia in what is now southwestern Iran. The Persian Empire took shape when Cyrus of Persia organized the Persians in a successful rebellion against Media and welded the Medes and Persians into a single state. The Greeks regarded Medes and Persians as the same and described any act favoring the Persians as *medizing*. Cyrus, justifiably called the Great, ruled from 599 to 530 BCE. The empire he forged steadily expanded in the sixth century and the beginning of

This limestone relief from Persepolis, *c.* 490 BCE, shows the enthroned Darius I and his heir apparent Xerxes receiving in audience a high court official, who touches his hand to lips in a gesture of respect and stands behind a pair of incense burners. Both king and prince wear crowns as well as the long, square-tipped beards signifying royalty. Because Persian society viewed the king as a descendent of the gods, he was surrounded by an elaborate court ceremonial. Archaeological Museum, Tehran.

the fifth, becoming the most powerful state in the ancient world and dominating the Near East from Mesopotamia to the Black Sea. Persian rulers, who were members of the famous Achaemenid dynasty, were surrounded by elaborate ceremony and protocol and bore the imposing title King of Kings. They drew on the achievements of subject people to foster a rich cultural tradition.

King Cyrus defeated Croesus and conquered his kingdom of Lydia in western Asia Minor just after the mid-sixth century BCE. The Lydians had gained control of the Greek cities in Asia Minor, and one of Cyrus' most trusted generals, Harpagus, pushed to the Aegean coast and annexed the Greek cities and adjoining islands to the Persian Empire. In the meantime the states on the Greek mainland showed little concern for the Asian Greeks, though Sparta is said to have sent a protest to Cyrus, who mockingly asked, "Who are the Spartans?" Sparta did not follow up its protest with effective action, and the other mainland Greeks also failed to provide military aid.

Cyrus and his successors required moderate tribute and warriors from all their subjects, including the Greeks of Asia Minor, but did not impose cultural uniformity on them. The Persians exerted loose control by organizing western Asia Minor, like the rest of the empire, into satrapies (provinces) and appointing leading local men as satraps (governors). The Greeks experienced considerable freedom under Persian rule and offered scant opposition. Ionian traders profited from the overlordship, in part because the unification of western Asia made overland trade and travel far easier. They enjoyed access to the Anatolian plateau on the great Royal Road, the first long highway in the world, which ran from the Persian winter capital of Susa to Sardis in Lydia and was later extended to Ephesus on the Aegean coast, a total length of about seventeen hundred miles. The prosperity of the Asian Greeks increased under Darius I (ruled 522–486 BCE), who inaugurated the famous Persian daric—a handsome gold coin minted with Lydian gold—which served as the basis of his currency. The government guaranteed the worth of the daric, and the coin helped to unify the entire commercial world of the day.

Yet not all the Greeks in Asia Minor were content with Persian rule. The Ionian cities had been experimenting with more democratic forms of government before annexation to the Persian Empire, and a number of poets, philosophers, and artists had sought refuge from Persian rule by sailing to mainland Greece or southern Italy. Moreover, many of the Phocaeans, as noted in chapter 4, had abandoned their homes in northern Ionia and settled in the western Mediterranean rather than submit to the Persians, while some of the inhabitants of the Ionian city of Teos had sought a haven on the north Aegean coast. In the meantime King Darius adopted a policy of expanding to the western shore of the Aegean.

THE CONFLICT

THE OUTBREAK OF HOSTILITIES

Darius' Scythian Expedition (c. 513–512 BCE). Besides his quest for additional land, Darius seems to have been motivated by a long-range economic policy of undermining mainland Greece as a trading rival in the Mediterranean. He turned north to subdue the Scythian nomads inhabiting an extensive area above the Black Sea. Apparently Darius thought that a successful engagement would cut off supplies of grain and shipbuilding timber coming out of the Balkan hinterland, imports of which were essential to the prosperity of mainland Greece. After his engineers constructed a remarkable floating bridge over the Bosporus about 513 BCE, the first organized military invasion of Europe by Asians commenced. Darius had assembled a huge army, though few modern historians believe the Persian forces equaled Herodotus' figure of seven hundred thousand infantry and cavalry. Darius' effort to conquer the Scythians collapsed on the vast plains of southern Russia and Ukraine, where the nomads were able to avoid an open battle and to draw the Persians deeper and deeper into the interior. The Persian army lost heavily and barely managed to make its way back to another floating bridge—this one on the lower Danube (the Greeks called the river the Ister)—thus avoiding the vengeance of the pursuing Scythians. Although Darius returned to Asia Minor, he ordered his army to subject southern Thrace, and the troops marched westward and successfully extended Persian rule along the northern shore of the Aegean to Macedonia. Now a power in Europe, the Persian Empire had reached its greatest extent. In the meantime Thrace was organized as a satrapy, leading to considerable disquiet among the European Greeks, who interpreted the Persian presence in Thrace as a prelude to an invasion of the entire Greek peninsula.

The Ionian Revolt (499–493 BCE).   Shortly after the Scythian campaign, Darius began to doubt the loyalty of Histiaeus, Persian-sponsored tyrant of Miletus, and summoned him to reside at Susa. Histiaeus left behind as ruler his ambitious relative Aristagoras. The new tyrant persuaded the Persians to undertake a military expedition against the island of Naxos, then engulfed in civil strife, as a means of extending Persian domination over the Aegean. When the assault failed—in part because the warring Naxian factions united in resistance—Aristagoras faced political disgrace,

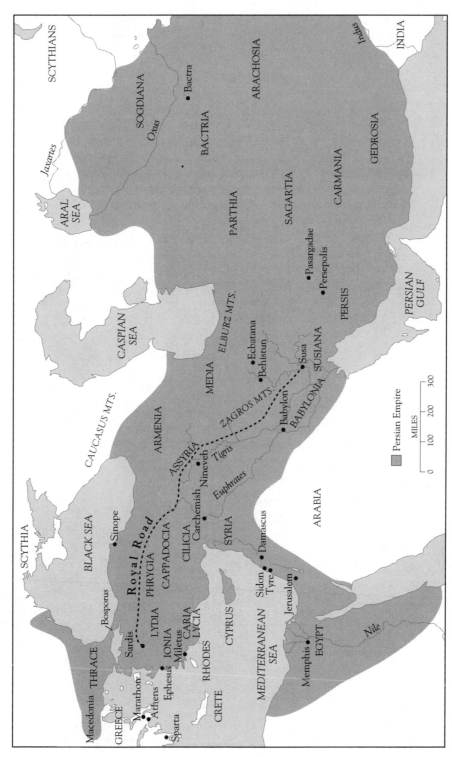

The Persian Empire under Darius I, about 490 BCE.

but he attempted to save himself upon returning to Miletus in 499 BCE by raising the standard of rebellion against Persia. The rebels proclaimed their support of democracy to secure wider Ionian backing. Accordingly, Aristagoras and other Ionian tyrants abdicated their tyrannical offices. The rebel leader then hastened to mainland Greece in search of military assistance. Aristagoras sailed first to Sparta, the strongest of the Greek states, where King Cleomenes ignored his pleas because of the danger of opposing Persia, but Athens furnished twenty ships, while the Euboean city of Eretria provided five. Perhaps Athenian help was spurred less by a sense of kinship with the Ionian Greeks than by the fact that the former tyrant of Athens, Hippias, was intriguing from his refuge in Asia Minor for Persian aid.

The military action commenced in 498 BCE with an initial victory by the Ionian, Athenian, and Eretrian forces at Sardis. The rebels burned part of the city, but its satrap, Artaphernes, succeeded in holding the citadel. Later, his forces defeated the Ionians near Ephesus. Although the Athenians and Eretrians then withdrew their contingents, leaving the Ionians to face the Persians alone, the rebels continued to fight vigorously. When Thrace, Caria, and the states of the Propontis joined the uprising, Darius understood the gravity of the rebellion and began to act decisively. By 495 BCE Persia had mobilized an overwhelming army, which eventually laid siege to Miletus. Meanwhile the Ionian Greeks, who had marshaled a fleet of some 350 warships, encountered the Persian naval force near the little island of Lade, off Miletus, and made a last stand. As the Persian flotilla approached, however, the ships of Samos and Lesbos deserted the Ionian line, leaving the remaining rebel vessels to be scattered or destroyed. Miletus was sacked and burned to discourage additional resistance and its population deported to Persia.

Darius was too shrewd, notwithstanding his severity toward Miletus, to attempt to restore the unpopular tyrants. Instead, he reconciled the Ionian Greeks to Persian rule by permitting them to enjoy democratic governments in their various cities. Meanwhile he dispatched his son-in-law Mardonius with a large fleet intended to consolidate Persian rule along the northern coast of the Aegean. Then, if possible, Mardonius was to push southward to punish two cities that had insulted the king's authority, namely Athens and Eretria. Although Mardonius accomplished the first part of his mission of returning the coastal cities of Thrace to the Persian fold, he lost the fleet in a storm while rounding Mount Athos and was forced to return home.

A little earlier—while the Persians were reestablishing their rule over the northern Aegean—the tyrant of Thracian Chersonesus, Miltiades, fled to his native Athens. Formerly a vassal of Darius, Miltiades had become an enemy of the Persian king by siding with the Greeks in the Ionian Revolt. Instead of finding the safety that he had expected in Athens, however, Miltiades was brought to trial on the charge of having ruled as a tyrant in the Chersonesus. Acquitted, Miltiades remained bitterly anti-Persian and would play a major role in the coming hostilities between Athens and the Persian Empire.

Darius' Forces Attack Attica: The Battle of Marathon (490 BCE).   Darius was convinced that Persia could not expect peace in Ionia as long as mainland Greece encouraged revolutionary movements. He set out to subject the European Greeks

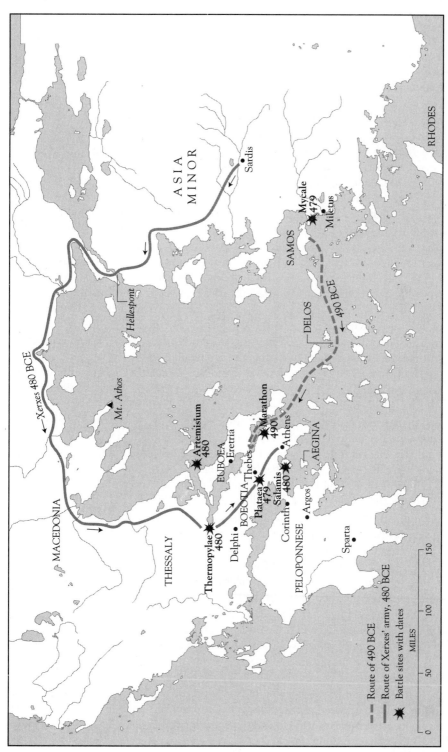

The Persian Wars, 490–479 BCE.

and thus preclude their interference in the eastern Aegean. The mainland Greeks realized the Persian king wanted to settle a score with Athens and Eretria but were uncertain what action he might take. Meanwhile in Athens foreign policy reflected internal discord, with political leaders vacillating and exchanging mutual recriminations over the involvement of Athens in the Ionian Revolt. The city had prospered under the Pisistratids, and a strong peace party favored the restoration of the old exiled tyrant Hippias as a means of coming to terms with Persia. The opposing war party was led by Themistocles, a radical democrat, who advocated a policy of building up Athenian naval power to resist any Persian attack. Probably inspired by Themistocles, the early dramatic poet Phrynichus wrote *The Capture of Miletus*, a sensational play produced, perhaps, in the spring of 493 BCE to lament the recent Persian ravaging of the city. Herodotus reports the performance aroused such sorrow and shame among the Athenian audience that Phrynichus was heavily fined. Yet the fear and hatred of Persia was increasing, and Themistocles was elected chief archon for 493–492 BCE. He used his year in office to strengthen Athens by fortifying the harbor of Piraeus and initiating the development of a powerful Athenian navy. The resistance to Persia continued to gain momentum, and the citizens swept the brilliant tactician Miltiades into office as a general (*strategos*). Miltiades' familiarity with the Persian methods of fighting—he had accompanied Darius on the Scythian expedition—made him invaluable to the war party. Themistocles found the conservative and aristocratic Miltiades a useful, though not altogether congenial, ally.

In 491 BCE Darius tested the resolve of the Greeks by sending envoys to the main islands and the cities of Greece to demand earth and water as tokens of submission. Most states complied—or *medized*, as the Greeks put it—but not Athens and Sparta. According to fanciful stories told later by Herodotus, the Athenians threw the Persian envoys into a pit and commanded them to dig their own earth, while the Spartans pushed them into a well and instructed them to collect their own water. Rejecting the exaggerated account of Herodotus, we may assume that the heralds were roughly handled both in Athens and in Sparta. Yet the island of Aegina, a maritime power chronically feuding with Athens, gave the tokens of submission, an indication that naval resistance to the coming attack would depend chiefly on Athens. Meanwhile although Athens, Sparta, and Eretria were united in their determination to resist, the three cities failed to work out plans for joint action. Darius became convinced the Greeks were too divided to offer a strong defense, and Hippias, the former tyrant, held out the prospect of a betrayal by his supporters in Athens on behalf of the Persian king.

Darius, deciding to send his ships directly against Athens and Eretria, placed his relatively small Persian force under the command of two generals—Datis and Artaphernes—and the aged Hippias accompanied the expedition, for Persian success would mean his restoration in Athens. The fleet and fighting men—the latter numbering perhaps twenty thousand—crossed the Aegean without mishap in 490 BCE, ravaging the resisting island of Naxos on the way but honoring the island of Delos because Apollo had often shown favor to the Persians. Upon reaching Eretria in Euboea, the Persians were forced to begin siege operations. The Eretrians fought alone, no help having come from Athens. The city fell after a few days and was reduced to a heap of smoldering ruins in revenge for the destruction at Sardis, while its inhabitants were taken away as slaves, an example to Athens of the dreadful price of resistance.

Several days later Datis and Artaphernes anchored their fleet in the bay of Marathon off the northeastern coast of Attica. They safely disembarked on the plain of Marathon, intending eventually to march overland to Athens. The Athenians, who had awakened to the impending danger, appealed to Sparta and to the small city of Plataea for assistance. The Athenians had come to the aid of Plataea against Thebes in the last quarter of the sixth century BCE, and the Plataeans soon dispatched all their troops, a loyalty never forgotten.

Sparta had been deeply divided politically for several years prior to the Persian invasion, in part because Cleomenes and his fellow king, Demaratus, were at odds on almost every issue. Cleomenes opposed Persian interference in Greece, for example, but Demaratus advocated accepting Persian suzerainty to avoid possible catastrophe. Soon Cleomenes started spreading rumors that his fellow king was illegitimate, and in 491 BCE Demaratus fled to Persia. By the time of the Persian invasion, the Spartans were fairly unified in their opposition to medizing. When the runner from Athens arrived in Sparta seeking immediate help, however, they were in the midst of a religious festival and thus forbidden by sacred mandate from marching until the day after the full moon, or the gods would be grievously offended and probably vengeful as well.

Fortune favored the Athenians by providing them with the superb strategist Miltiades, who seized the initiative by marching twenty-six miles eastward to the plain of Marathon rather than risking a battle at Athens. After crossing the spurs of Mount Pentelicus, ten thousand Greek hoplites positioned themselves in the hills overlooking the Persian camp on the semicircular plain of Marathon, which was hemmed in by both mountains and sea. For some days the Greek and Persian armies faced one another as the Athenians waited for the arrival of the Spartans. When the small Plataean force arrived, Miltiades convinced his fellow commanders to attack without the Spartans.

The battle of Marathon is one of the earliest in recorded history that was won by tactical skill against superior numbers. Because the Persian army was considerably larger than the combined forces of the Athenians and the Plataeans, the Greeks ran the risk of being outflanked on both wings by the longer line of the Persians. To prevent this, Miltiades thinned and thus lengthened his center rank and reinforced the wings, a masterstroke of strategy. When the Greek hoplites came within range of enemy arrows, they charged on the run. The lightly armed Persians fought valiantly and broke through the center of the Greek line but were then encircled between the powerful wings of their heavily armed opponents. Soon they were in full retreat. Herodotus reports that the Greeks "followed the Persians in their flight, cutting them to pieces," and upon reaching the shore even splashed into the water after them to grab the anchor cables and the ornaments of their ships, thereby capturing seven of the vessels. The Persians, he says, lost 6,400 men in the battle of Marathon but the Athenians only 192. Nothing is known about the casualties among the Plataeans and the slaves.

Miltiades immediately dispatched a runner to Athens with news of the victory. He then marched the exhausted Athenians back to Athens on the double during the night to intercept any Persian move on the city. When the Persian fleet sailed up to the beach at Phaleron to anchor the next morning, they saw that the Athenian army was waiting. Not willing to risk another engagement, the Persians turned their ships around and sailed back across the Aegean. The Athenians were jubilant, for their small city-state had almost single-handedly won a battle against the great Persian Empire. Meanwhile the Spartan advance guard arrived and, upon hearing of the Athenian victory, continued their march to Marathon to study both the carnage on the field and the Persian weapons. They saw that the Persians had worn padded clothing, carried wicker shields, and were armed with short spears, giving the Greeks a great advantage with their longer spears and bronze-clad armor. The Spartans returned to congratulate the Athenians and then marched another 140 miles home. Yet only the most sanguine Greeks, of whom there were many, believed that the Persian threat had ended. In the meantime wiser heads realized the victory had bought time to prepare for another Persian thrust.

The Aftermath of Victory in Athens (490–481 BCE)

Factionalism.   Athens, enjoying a new confidence after the celebrated victory against the Persians, struck at Aegina, Paros, and other islands that had medized. Miltiades realized they could serve as enemy military bases in a renewed attack against the Greek mainland and decided to compel the islands to renounce their allegiance to the Persian king. The action against Aegina was abortive. Cleomenes of Sparta—who cooperated with Athens in the failed expedition—met a violent end about 489 BCE. According to Herodotus, the king killed himself in a fit of insanity. Athens and Aegina began an ineffective war of mutual raiding parties and noisy diplomatic disputes. Meanwhile Miltiades persuaded the assembly to put him in command of a fleet on a secret mission, promising to lead his fellow countrymen to a place where they could enrich themselves and win huge rewards for the state. He sailed to the island of Paros to punish and fine its inhabitants for medizing, though the undertaking failed miserably. Miltiades was wounded during the siege of Paros and abandoned the venture—some suspected he had been bribed by the Parians—and when he returned to Athens his many enemies seized upon his temporary unpopularity to indict him for "deceiving the people." Now gravely ill, Miltiades was brought to trial on a stretcher, unable to speak, and the death sentence was proposed, but the court rejected that punishment in favor of a heavy fine in recognition of his former services to the state. Thus the great tactician at Marathon had become one of the victims of his own campaign against medizers. His fame tarnished, he died soon thereafter of gangrene, and his young son Cimon was left to pay the financially crippling fine. The prosecutor of the trial was Xanthippus, the father of Pericles, which explains the origin of the famous feud between Cimon and Pericles dominating Athenian politics around the mid-fifth century BCE.

New Naval Policy and Constitutional Changes.   In the meantime the Persian question polarized Athenian politics, though cutting across factional lines. Apparently

In a practice known as ostracism unique to fifth-century BCE Athenian democracy, the citizens could vote to banish any citizen for ten years by writing his name on a fragment of pottery (*ostrakon*), the ancient equivalent of scrap paper. If a quorum of six thousand votes was reached, the man receiving the most votes was compelled to leave Athens. A large number of *ostraka* have been discovered in the Athenian Agora. The *ostraka* illustrated here bear the names of Aristides, son of Lysimachus, and Themistocles, son of Neocles. The years after the Battle of Marathon (490 BCE) saw political turmoil and a rash of ostracisms in Athens. During this period the citizens voted to banish Aristides, though the vote to banish Themistocles failed.

many Athenians thought the Persian danger had ended, yet Themistocles knew better. He wanted to create a powerful naval force, believing that nothing short of a strong fleet could effectively stop the Persian war machine, but his plan was opposed by the bulk of the conservative family of the Alcmaeonids, for they advocated a strong land defense. Most of the Alcmaeonids wanted to get rid of Themistocles—who was not of full noble birth—but he engaged in tough political fighting to weaken his opposition. He may have been behind the prosecution of the great Marathon victor Miltiades. About this time Themistocles is said to have dusted off a statute attributed to Cleisthenes that authorized a hitherto unused device known as ostracism, a method by which the citizen body could send anyone into political exile for ten years without loss of citizenship or property. Apparently an ostracism could take place only if the citizens cast a total of at least six thousand votes, each participant writing on a potsherd (*ostrakon*) the name of his candidate for expulsion. The individual receiving the greatest number of votes was required to leave Athens within ten days. Themistocles and his supporters skillfully manipulated public opinion to force several leading conservatives—men who were potential collaborators with Persia—into exile through the device. Megacles, the Alcmaeonid nephew of Cleisthenes and brother-in-law of Xanthippus, was banished, and soon Xanthippus himself—an Alcmaeonid by marriage—was expelled. Yet more than a third of the *ostraka* that have been found carry the name of Themistocles, indicating that he too was at risk every year. Year after year, however, Themistocles unsuccessfully maneuvered to escape the ostracism, but not his enemies.

New democratic constitutional reforms were enacted in Athens, though suggestions that Themistocles was behind them have no foundation in the surviving documents. In 487 BCE the lot was inaugurated as the method of choosing archons, whose political importance thus ended. Moreover, the polemarch—one of the nine archons—was now divested of his military duties and relegated to judiciary functions in civil cases. Naturally these constitutional changes had an impact on the Council of the Areopagus. Recruited exclusively from former archons, the council eventually lost much of its influence. Meanwhile the leadership of the state passed into the hands of the board of generals (*strategoi*), one of whom might be given

Greek naval warfare was greatly altered by the invention of the superior warship known as the trireme, built to ram enemy vessels. Under the leadership of Themistocles, Athens amassed two hundred swift triremes and was acknowledged as the dominant Greek naval power. Athenian triremes, after inflicting repeated rammings, defeated the navy of Xerxes at the battle of Salamis in 480 BCE. This detail of a relief from the Erechtheum, Athens, c. 400 BCE, shows the forward hull section of the starboard side of a trireme. Acropolis Museum, Athens.

supreme command. When Themistocles was chosen as *strategos* in 483 BCE, his victory over the conservative opposition was almost complete.

In the meantime a fortunate discovery was made in 483 BCE, a rich vein of silver at the state mines in the Laurium region of southeastern Attica. The conservative leader Aristides, who had served as a general at Marathon and had been elected chief archon in 489 BCE, argued that the resulting profits should be distributed among the citizens of Athens. Themistocles, however, persuaded the Athenians that the windfall should be used to build a modern fleet of two hundred triremes, ostensibly for the war being waged with Aegina, but his true purpose was to create a powerful navy for the impending conflict with Persia. The trireme was the standard warship of the time, a narrow vessel built for speed and propelled in battle by rowers. The origins of the trireme remain uncertain, though modern authorities usually credit its development to either the Phoenicians or the Egyptians and date its invention to the second half of the sixth century BCE. The trireme provided close quarters for its crew of one hundred and seventy oarsmen and also typically carried ten hoplite warriors and four archers to engage enemy crews in hand to hand combat when warships became entangled. Officers and other crew, including the helmsman, brought the total on board to two hundred. Although the arrangement of the oarsmen has been much debated, for the ancient evidence is obscure, modern scholarship suggests the one hundred and seventy oarsmen sat on three levels (sixty-two oarsmen on the top level, fifty-four on the middle, and fifty-four on the lowest). The positioning of the rowers on more than one level is confirmed by Aristophanes, who spoke in his comedy the *Frogs* of one oarsman in a trireme making wind and worse in the face of another. The quarters were extremely cramped, and the customary practice was to go ashore for meals and sleeping. In naval battles the trireme fought by battering enemy ships with a bronze-clad ram attached to the bow at the waterline, the rectangular main sail being unfurled and usually left ashore when engagement was imminent. Trials of a modern reconstruction of an Athenian trireme demonstrated speeds in excess of nine knots. The Athenians required thirty-four thousand oarsmen and a highly trained crew to operate two hundred triremes, a costly venture backed by the new source of mining wealth. Rowing being an arduous occupation not appealing to the upper classes, oarsmen were drawn from the poorer population. The importance of the navy made the rowers essential and thus gave them influence and helped to bring about further democratic developments. Indeed, the navy came to be associated with democracy. After Themistocles' crash program of shipbuilding, Athens ranked as the dominant Greek naval power and enjoyed sufficient power to fight the Persians at sea.

Full-Scale Persian Invasion

Xerxes Prepares to Invade Greece (481 BCE).   Before completing preparations for a new invasion of Greece, Darius died in 486 BCE. His favorite son and successor Xerxes (486–465 BCE) inherited a revolt in Egypt but quickly quelled the uprising along the Nile and turned his attention to Greece. By 481 BCE Xerxes was at Sardis preparing to launch his vast forces against the Greek mainland. Soon Persian heralds came to all the Greek states except Athens and Sparta to demand submission. About a third of the states complied, especially the islanders and the inhabitants of northern and central Greece, who feared that the Athenians and the Spartans were too far away to offer them much protection. Even the Delphic oracle counseled against resisting Persian might.

Formation of the Hellenic League (481 BCE).   Meanwhile a congress of deputies from the small number of poleis that were determined to resist—a total of thirty-one—met in the fall of 481 BCE, probably at Sparta. In attendance were not only Athens and Sparta but also the Spartan allies such as Aegina and Corinth as well as a number of smaller states. The assembled deputies formed a new league, which modern historians usually call the Hellenic League, and selected Sparta—the foremost military power in Greece—as its leader. Sparta enjoyed the right of furnishing both the generals and the admirals for the army and navy of the league. King Leonidas of Sparta, the young successor of Cleomenes, took charge of the land forces and a Spartan nobleman named Eurybiades was given command of the Greek fleet, but Themistocles seems to have been granted an influential role in planning strategy. The members of the league quickly pledged to end their destructive quarrels—most notably that between Athens and Aegina—for the duration of the Persian threat. Yet the members of the league were disheartened that other states refused to join the alliance. The Sicilian Greeks, for example, would not send aid because they feared retaliation from Persia's Carthaginian allies, while Argos refused to join because of its hatred for Sparta.

The Spartan plan was to hold fast at the Isthmus of Corinth—their overriding concern was to protect the Peloponnese—but Themistocles realized this would result in ceding all of northern and central Greece to Persia, and he pressed for a defense at the northern mountain passes. The members of the Hellenic League were finally swayed by Themistocles' arguments, for the Athenian fleet was vital to the Greek cause, and they decided to take a stand at the narrow pass of Tempe in northeastern Thessaly, which formed the easiest route between Macedonia and Thessaly.

Xerxes' Invasion of Greece (480 BCE).   Meanwhile the Persian route of invasion was being prepared. Xerxes bridged the Hellespont—the ancient name of the strait now called the Dardanelles—with a vast number of boats lashed together, and he ordered the establishment of supply depots along the projected line of march at convenient intervals. He had already provided for the cutting of a canal through the peninsula of Mount Athos, for he was aware of the disastrous storm damage to Mardonius' fleet off the rocky coast in 492 BCE. Such preparations were part of Xerxes' grand scheme of subjugating the entire Greek peninsula by striking from the satrapy of Thrace in the north. He planned for his great army and navy to advance in close proximity because the former was too large to live off the land and had to be supported and supplied by the fleet. Thus the fleet was expected to serve for supply and communications, not to engage in naval warfare. Yet Themistocles had seized upon the weakness of Xerxes' plan, realizing that if the Greek navy could somehow inflict a decisive defeat on the great Persian fleet—perhaps by luring its ships into treacherous narrow waters—the Persian army would be forced to retire.

Meanwhile Xerxes moved down the coast. His naval forces had been levied from the Phoenicians, Egyptians, and Ionian Greeks, while his army of archers and cavalry had been drawn from the various peoples of the Persian Empire. The mainland Greeks were terrified by the size of the enemy expedition. They heard dreadful tales of thirsty troops and horses drinking dry entire lakes and streams. Xerxes commanded an enormous force of perhaps two hundred thousand fighting men and six to seven hundred warships, outnumbering the allied Greeks on both land and sea.

The Greeks Attempt to Halt the Persian Advance: Thermopylae and Artemisium (480 BCE).
The Persians entered Macedonia in July 480 BCE. As the great army moved relentlessly onward, the Hellenic League attempted to stop the advance at the pass of Tempe, which could not be defended without full Thessalian loyalty. When the Thessalians showed signs of joining the enemy, the Greek allies decided to abandon Tempe and instead take a stand on Thessaly's southern frontier at the pass of Thermopylae. In the meantime the states of Thessaly went over to Xerxes' side without offering resistance.

The narrow coastal pass at Thermopylae—hemmed in between mountains and sea—was about seventy-five miles northwest of Athens on an extension of the northern Euboean strait and carried the main land route from northern to central Greece. This was a natural defensive position against armies invading central Greece from the north. The plan of the Greek allies was for a small land force of six or seven thousand hoplites under King Leonidas to hold the pass while the Greek fleet of three hundred ships (with its nucleus of new Athenian triremes) stationed itself off Cape Artemisium at the northern tip of the island of Euboea, a naval position chosen to separate the enemy's fleet and army. The Greek army, the allies hoped, could hold the Persians in check until the sea battle had been fought in the narrow waters off Artemisium.

Leonidas knew the situation was desperate—he refused to take any men without sons to succeed them—but he held his position for three days. Eventually Leonidas and his forces were betrayed by an act of treachery, for a Greek from southern Thessaly agreed to lead a detachment of Persians up a mountain path to a point behind them. When scouts informed Leonidas of the enemy movement, he sent many of his troops south. True to the Spartan ideal of defending a post until death, however, he and a small band of three hundred followers remained behind and were sacrificed to the last man. The fame of Leonidas' heroic stand overwhelmed the Greeks. Copied by Herodotus, the simple epitaph raised over the tomb of Leonidas and his men at Thermopylae characterizes Spartan resolve and bravery: "Go tell the Spartans, O passerby, that here we lie, complying with their orders."

The Battle of Salamis (480 BCE).   The defeat at Thermopylae left the Boeotian plain open to the onslaught of the Persians, and the Thebans welcomed Xerxes. Central Greece had been lost. Only a timely violent storm had saved Delphi from destruction. Earlier, the Delphic oracle had advised the Athenians that safety lay in trusting "a wooden wall" of their city. Themistocles had persuaded the Athenians that the divine message meant their fleet. After the fall of Thermopylae and the death of Leonidas, the Greek fleet immediately sailed down the length of Euboea and took station near Piraeus in the narrow strait of Salamis in the Saronic Gulf. The odds at sea had been narrowed because raging storms had dashed a large number of Persian ships against reefs. In the meantime most of the noncombatant Athenian population had been evacuated to the Peloponnese or to the island of Salamis just offshore from Athens. The Persians easily occupied Athens and burned the Acropolis, defended by a few stalwarts, while the horrified refugees on Salamis watched the smoke rising from their beloved monuments. Although the Greek fleet had taken up a position in the strait of Salamis, the Spartans were urging all their allies to sail to the Isthmus of Corinth and take refuge behind a wall being built as a bulwark against the Persians, but no barrier could stop the invaders if the Greeks lost control of the sea.

Desperate to force an immediate battle because so many Greeks were clamoring to retreat, the cunning Themistocles sent a secret message to Xerxes, purporting to be on the king's side and urging him to attack in the strait before the Greeks could escape. Xerxes fell for the ruse and ordered a naval battle. As he sat on a throne on Mount Aegaleos to gain a panoramic view of the engagement below, the Greek triremes quickly demonstrated their superior maneuverability. The crowded Persian ships were helpless before repeated Greek rammings. Thus the Greeks won a dramatic reversal at Salamis, and the battle—the turning point of the war—was one of the most famous naval victories of all times. The stunning triumph was a vindication of the naval policy Themistocles had advocated for years. His old rivals Aristides and Xanthippus, both of whom had been recalled from exile just before the invasion, had participated in the battle.

Xerxes foolishly beheaded the Phoenician sea captains, and the furious Phoenician and Egyptian crews sailed home, leaving the King of Kings with the unreliable

In the years around 480 BCE, Athenian painters decorated numerous vases with the popular representation of a Greek hoplite triumphing over a Persian adversary. The scene illustrated here is from a red-figure Attic amphora, c. 480–470 BCE. Metropolitan Museum of Art, New York.

Ionians. Although much of his fleet and all of his land forces remained intact, Xerxes was fearful for his own safety. Moreover, the naval engagement had been fought in September, too late in the year to try again. The allies now gained control of the sea, for the Persian fleet retired to the Hellespont to protect the crossing point from Europe into Asia. With a large portion of his army, Xerxes marched to the Hellespont and then on to Sardis, leaving Mardonius in Thessaly with the remainder of the Persian forces to renew the war the following spring.

Lacking a fleet, Mardonius was powerless to advance and could only hope to retain control of central Greece. Yet he devised a plan to detach Athens from the Hellenic League. He proposed to make peace with Athens and then, with the assistance of the Athenian fleet, to crush Sparta. Alexander, the vassal king of Macedonia, was sent to Athens to promise Athenian independence and Persian aid in rebuilding the city in return for help against the Peloponnesians. These were tempting terms, but the Athenians refused to desert the allied cause. When Alexander reported to Mardonius that the Athenians would not medize, the Persians soon marched southward from Thessaly toward Athens.

Victories at Plataea and Mycale (479 BCE). The issue was finally decided in 479 BCE. When Mardonius invaded Athens a second time—probably in June—the Athenians abandoned their city for the island of Salamis and sent envoys to Sparta demanding that Spartan troops be dispatched immediately for Attica, or the Athenians might come to terms with the Persians. The Spartans finally put aside their insistence that the stand should be made against the Persians at the Isthmus of Corinth and marched northward. Meanwhile Mardonius had destroyed whatever was left of Athens and withdrawn to southern Boeotia.

The Persians were joined in Boeotia by troops from their allies of Thebes, Thessaly, and Macedonia. The Greek opposition force, spearheaded by the Spartans, gathered on the northern foothills of Mount Cithaeron near Plataea in southern Boeotia. Supported by both the Athenians and the Megarians and under the command of Pausanias—acting as regent for the young son of Leonidas—the Spartans endured three weeks of cavalry assaults from the Persians near Plataea. When the Persian cavalry blocked their water supply, however, the Greeks decided to withdraw to higher ground during the night. This perilous maneuver caused some disarray, and at the first light of day the Greek army was still widely spread out. Mardonius, now overconfident, committed his lightly clad Persians against the well armored hoplites. Then the Greeks charged downhill on the double and dashed through the Persian line, which was defended by a mere fence of wicker shields, maiming and killing both the Persians and their Greek allies. Mardonius was among the victims in the battle of Plataea—the greatest land engagement the Greeks had ever fought—and the surviving Persians reeled in retreat and panic. The remnant of the once great Persian army faced disease and starvation while retreating through northern Greece to Asia, with only a few troops actually making their way back to Persia. Meanwhile the Greek allies successfully besieged Thebes, executing the leaders of the city who had collaborated with Persia and disbanding the Boeotian League. Greece had been saved, for the Persians were never to return. While the Athenians had been primarily responsible for preserving Greek security at Salamis, the Spartans and other Peloponnesians played the same role at Plataea.

In the meantime the allied naval force had taken the offensive. Envoys came from Samos to Delos, where the Greek fleet under the command of Spartan King Leotychides (the successor of the exiled Demaratus) was keeping an eye out for the Persian fleet. After the envoys persuaded the king to sail to Asia to liberate Persian-dominated Ionia by assuring him of help from both Samos and Chios, Leotychides led the allied fleet across the Aegean. Meanwhile, not trusting their Asian Greek crews, the Persian admirals landed on the rocky coast at Mycale—the promontory on the mainland opposite Samos—where they beached their ships and built a barricade around the vessels. Supported by a Persian army, they awaited the Greek attack, but their fate was sealed when many Ionians and Aeolians turned against them. The battle of Mycale was fought, according to tradition, on the same late August day as that of Plataea and was an overwhelming Greek victory. The victory at Mycale wiped out the last remnant of Persian naval strength in the Aegean, along with a substantial ground force, and led to the revolt of most of the Greek cities on the coast of Asia Minor. The Spartans proposed that the allies should protect the Asian Greeks from Persian vengeance by settling them in mainland Greece on the lands of the medizing Greeks, who themselves should be expelled, but the plan was opposed by the Ionians and the Athenians. The Spartans did not wish to pursue the war in the Aegean—summer was ending—and they and the other Peloponnesians returned home. The Athenians, on the other hand, were anxious to liberate the Greek cities of Asia Minor and regain access to the Black Sea. Thus the Athenians and the islanders sailed northward to besiege Sestos, the main Persian base on the Hellespont and the most important crossing point from Europe. By the end of winter Sestos had been starved into submission. The opposing goals of Athens and Sparta in Asia Minor, however, reveal a fundamental difference in viewpoint that would lead ultimately to rivalry and bitter conflict between the two states.

War in the West (480–474 BCE).   While the Greeks in the Aegean were busy defeating Xerxes, their kindred in Sicily were engaged in an equally fierce struggle against Carthage. The Carthaginians were Phoenicians who had occupied Carthage in the ninth century BCE, thus gaining the best harbor on the coast of North Africa. The Phoenicians had also colonized western Sicily, while the Greeks had occupied the eastern part of the island. Eventually Carthage became a great mercantile power and gained leadership of the Phoenician settlements planted in western Sicily. Over a period of several centuries the Carthaginians competed in Sicily with the Greeks, and now they sought to control the eastern, Greek-dominated part of the island. Although no known evidence links the Carthaginian campaign in Sicily with the Persian invasion of Greece, perhaps some arrangement had been made for concerted action. After all, the Persian fleet consisted largely of Phoenician ships and men.

A succession of dictator-generals had dominated the Greek colonies in Sicily, the most powerful being Gelon, who made his capital at Syracuse in 486 BCE and gained control of most of Greek Sicily. One of the small towns that Gelon had gobbled up, Himera, appealed to the Carthaginians to free the eastern part of the island from domination by Syracuse, and Carthage—perhaps encouraged by Xerxes—sent a large fleet of warships to Sicily. Gelon met and defeated the Carthaginians in 480 BCE at Himera, however, and eastern Sicily remained free from another Carthaginian invasion for more than seven decades. After the battle of Himera, Gelon became the most powerful man in the Greek world, but he died two years after his great victory. He was succeeded by his brother Hieron I, who welcomed to his brilliant court the notable poets Pindar, Simonides, Bacchylides, and Aeschylus, and the famous philosopher Xenophanes.

CHAPTER IX

THE ATHENIAN EMPIRE

The struggle against Persian invasion had produced a rare period of Greek cooperation. With the ending of hostilities, the Greek states turned to pursue their own
particular interests. Athens was remarkable for its restless artistic and intellectual
brilliance and its celebrated democratic movement, highlights of an era now called
the Age of Pericles after the leading Athenian statesman of the day. The stunning
civilization of fifth-century BCE Athens was in many ways the envy of the Greek
world, but Athenian creativity was paralleled by its greedy imperialism. The same
Athenian navy that helped to stem the tide of Persian aggression became a ruthless
tool for forging what today we call the Athenian Empire. The Greeks had failed to
learn from the Persian Wars to curb their rivalries, and near the end of the century
Athens and Sparta embarked on a devastating struggle against one another that ultimately led to the ruin of Athens and cast long shadows across all of Greece.
Clearly, the fifth century BCE is of great importance in the story of ancient Greece
and is divided chronologically into three nearly equal parts: the first belonging to
the Persian Wars, the second to the Age of Pericles, and the third to the Peloponnesian War between Athens and Sparta. This chapter and the next trace the explo-
sive misunderstandings leading to the Peloponnesian War, while chapters 11–13
examine Athenian civilization during the Periclean epoch.

SPARTA FALTERS AS LEADER OF THE HELLENIC
LEAGUE (479–470 BCE)

The Persian invasion had been repulsed by the cooperative efforts of the two most
powerful city-states, Athens and Sparta, assisted by several of the others. Athens
justly claimed credit for the victories of Marathon and Salamis, while Sparta glo-
ried in the decisive triumph at Plataea. The events of the Persian Wars had brought
to the fore the hope for a possible unification of the Hellenic world in a federation.
Although the policies of Sparta during the wars had often been provincial, the battle of Plataea vindicated confidence in Spartan leadership of the Hellenic League.
Yet the wisdom of Themistocles' strategy and the naval victories at Salamis and
Mycale had brought acclaim to Athens and recognition of the importance of warfare on the sea.

Friction and jealousies quickly arose between Sparta and Athens after the battle of Plataea. For one thing, the Spartans had asked the Athenians to refrain from
rebuilding their city walls to prevent the Persians—if they returned—from using

Athens as a fortified base against the Greek allies. This rather transparent scheme would have put the Athenians at the mercy of the Spartan army, but Themistocles managed to mislead the Lacedaemonians. Going to Sparta as an envoy, he relied on deliberate falsehoods to conceal the truth from the Spartans that all able-bodied Athenian citizens were hurriedly rebuilding the walls. When the Spartans learned the construction was nearly complete, they reluctantly gave way.

Sparta made other attempts to extend its power on the mainland. In 478 BCE the Spartans sent an army under King Leotychides to Thessaly, but the Thessalian states saved their independence by bribing him. Upon returning to Sparta rich with his ill-gotten gold and silver, the king was driven into exile for life. Another misfortune of Sparta involved a decision of the members of the Hellenic League to clear the Persians from the eastern Aegean. All too quickly the Spartan leaders in this venture proved susceptible to corruption and arrogance. Pausanias was sent in 478 BCE to take charge of the campaign in Asia Minor as commander in chief of an allied fleet supplied by the members of the Hellenic League. Pausanias had succumbed to vanity after his feats at Plataea and then demonstrated his arrogance by commissioning an inscription for the base of the thank-offering at Delphi—a tripod of gold mounted on a bronze pillar—in which he named only himself as destroyer of the enemy, but the Spartan government had ordered the offending words erased, substituting the names of the thirty-one allied cities opposing the Persians.

Leading a force to Cyprus, Pausanias and his troops drove the Persians off the island. From Cyprus the fleet sailed up to Byzantium (modern Istanbul), which commanded the entry to the Euxine (the Greek name for the Black Sea). Byzantium was captured and the grain route to the Black Sea opened, but Pausanias' dictatorial arrogance and his adoption of Persian dress made him increasingly unpopular with the allies. Suspected of plotting with the Persian commanders in northern Asia Minor and accused of negotiating with Xerxes for the hand of one of his daughters, the general was recalled to Sparta and tried for misconduct. Acquitted, he left Sparta and set up a tyranny in Byzantium, from which he was expelled by the Athenians and settled in the Troad. Here rumors circulated that he was involved in treasonable negotiations with the Persians. Upon being recalled to Sparta again—this time about 470 BCE—he was tried and acquitted once more, but then Pausanias is said to have become involved in a plot to incite a revolt among the helots. Although the ephors hesitated for a while to lay hands upon the hero of Plataea, they finally decided to arrest him. Pausanias faced almost certain condemnation. To escape arrest he fled into the shrine of Athena for sanctuary. The ephors then had the temple walled up and left Pausanias to suffer starvation, dragging him out only when he was at the point of death so he would die on unconsecrated ground, lest he defile the shrine by expiring under its roof. We are unable to determine whether the charges of treason against Pausanias were justified or merely a pretext by his enemies to destroy him.

Meanwhile the Ionians—who had found Pausanias so disagreeable—decided they wanted no more Spartan commanders and invited the head of the Athenian contingent, Aristides, to take over leadership of the fleet of the Hellenic League. Thus command in the Hellespont fell to Athens. The Spartans then returned home and abandoned all additional participation in the struggle against Persia, a move marking their temporary eclipse. Through Aristides' initiative, the Athenians and their allies began to establish an organization that modern scholars call the Delian League, thereby further straining the Hellenic League and creating additional mistrust between Athens and Sparta.

FROM DELIAN LEAGUE TO ATHENIAN EMPIRE (478–431 BCE)

THE DELIAN LEAGUE AND THE RISE OF ATHENS

Many Athenians thought their strategy and fleet had delivered the Hellenic world. Now they reasoned that their kindred the Ionians should be freed by Athenian initiatives. Themistocles, whose policies had made Athens the foremost sea power in the Aegean, had long urged the formation of a Greek confederacy based on naval might, but it was Aristides who forged the Delian League. As for Themistocles, he had become involved in party struggles between the growing commercial forces in the city—whose champion he was—and the more conservative wing of politics led by Aristides and Cimon. Over the years Themistocles had offended many Athenians through his pride and austerity. Persistent rumors that he had received and given bribes also helped to undermine his popularity. Finally he was ostracized and went into exile at Argos about 472 BCE. Later, he was implicated in the plot of Pausanias, but upon being recalled to Athens for trial, he fled to Persian-controlled Asia Minor for refuge and was rewarded with the governorship of Magnesia and several other towns. Rejected by his fellow Athenians, he defiantly spent his final years in the service of his old enemy. The tradition he committed suicide is dubious. After his death, at least some Greeks remembered that his foresight and strategy had saved Hellas in its great moment of peril.

During the winter of 478–477 BCE the Athenians began to plan the formation of the new Delian League, conceived at first as the military arm of the larger Hellenic League. They chose the island of Delos, sacred to all Ionians, and its temple of Apollo as the meeting place and treasury of the new confederation. In the summer of 477 BCE the chief organizer, Aristides, persuaded representatives from the islands and the coast of Asia Minor to join with the Athenians at Delos to form the league as an offensive and defensive confederation against Persia. The fleet of the confederation was expected to protect the Aegean from the Persians and to conduct annual attacks on Persia until all Greek cities were free. To symbolize the permanence of the league, representatives dropped iron weights into the sea and exchanged binding oaths in the name of Athena to remain faithful to the association until the metal should rise and float on the surface.

From the outset, the leadership of Athens was paramount. Although an assembly of representatives met annually on Delos—where each member-state enjoyed the right of casting one vote—the determination of policy depended on the agreement of Athens. Moreover, apparently an Athenian always served as the chairman of the league meetings. The fleet was composed of Athenian vessels and additional ships provided by other member states under a quota system. Yet those members preferring not to construct ships could take the easier option of paying a contribution to the common treasury, and by midcentury the only ship contributors were the large islands of Lesbos, Chios, and Samos, three states with a naval tradition. Although the money was deposited in the shrine of Apollo on the island, the treasurers of the league were Athenian officials, and the purse was spent at the sole discretion of Athens. Yet apparently the allies welcomed these arrangements, for they feared that without Athenian support and leadership they would fall again under Persian domination.

Cimon.   The commander of the fleet was to be an Athenian. Cimon was the first to gain this important office. The son of a Thracian princess and the Miltiades—the famous victor at Marathon—Cimon had been forced to pay the heavy fine imposed on his father after the disgrace at Paros. Cimon, who had served with distinction at Salamis, was known in Athens for his upright political conduct. He acquired great wealth from the dowry of his Alcmaeonid bride, and his sister was married to Callias, the wealthiest man in Athens. Allied with many of the Alcmaeonids, Cimon became the leader in Athens of the conservatives opposing Themistocles and later Pericles and other democrats. His simple policy of stable conservatism, sincere friendship with Sparta, open hostility toward Persia, and ambitious imperialism appealed to the Athenians after the terrible disruptions of war. Building public squares in Athens and opening his own gardens to the public, Cimon basked in praise.

Cimonian Imperialism.   For more than a decade—from about 476 to 463 BCE—Cimon commanded most of the operations of the Delian League against the Persians, pushing them from their remaining strongholds in the Aegean and thereby extending membership in the confederation. His brilliant victories raised Athens to new heights of power and secured the political eclipse of Themistocles. During these years Cimon virtually dominated the foreign policy of Athens. His success against the Persians prepared the way for the slow transformation of the Delian League into what is now termed the Athenian Empire.

Although attacks were made against a number of Persian garrisons in Thrace, which were then settled by Athenians, a new policy emerged when Cimon decided to force Carystus—a small Greek state in southern Euboea—into the league. Naturally that action alarmed many Greeks. Athens had now begun to acquire subject states in addition to the naval and tributary allies of the confederacy. When the island of Naxos decided to withdraw from the Delian League because of such Athenian aggression, Cimon promptly crushed the Naxians and compelled them to embrace a democratic constitution and to rejoin the confederation as a subject state without voting rights in the assembly. Noting that Naxos was the first of the nominal allies to be enslaved, the historian Thucydides reports that aggressive Athenian imperialism spread fear among all the other Greek states.

Perhaps in an attempt to allay the fears of the allies by returning to the fundamental purpose of the league, Cimon prepared a huge force of ships to attack the Persians in the southeastern Mediterranean. Here the Persians were restoring their naval capability with Phoenician vessels, the obvious intention being to resume the war in Ionia. Cimon led the league forces against them in a battle fought near the mouth of the Eurymedon River on the south coast of Asia Minor about 468 BCE, virtually annihilating the enemy fleet and ending the attempted comeback. He then continued his policy of welding the maritime confederacy into the Athenian Empire.

Apparently Cimon had decided to take control of the mining and timber interests in the northern Aegean. The large island of Thasos had established on the nearby Thracian mainland profitable gold mines, now threatened by the Athenian colonization in the area. Thasos seceded from the league. Then the Athenians pressed a siege of Thasos and ravaged the island state, compelling the Thasians to forfeit their colonies and mines on the adjacent Thracian shore as well as their fleet, all of which passed to the control of Athens. Moreover, Thasos was forced to tear down its walls and become a subject ally of Athens. The growing harshness of the Athenian imperial policy signaled that no member of the Delian League was free to withdraw.

Cimon's Pro-Spartan Policy Leads to His Disgrace (466–461 BCE).   The war issue declined in importance after the Persian defeat, with many Athenians starting to grumble about Cimon's antidemocratic and pro-Spartan sympathies. Meanwhile, in 466 BCE, the helots revolted in Sparta after a disastrous earthquake leveled the city. Two years later the Spartans—having been unable to quell the uprising—appealed to their allies for assistance, especially the Athenians, for the old Hellenic League had never been dissolved. The anti-Spartan democratic leader Ephialtes and the young noble Pericles advocated neutrality because Athenian supremacy in Greece would be assured if the helot insurrection ruined Sparta. Yet Cimon, whose policy was Hellenic unity, favored the request and persuaded the Athenians to dispatch a military force to aid Sparta as a means of winning undying Spartan gratitude. Acting as the chief *strategos*, Cimon assumed command of four thousand hoplites sent to Messenia for the expedition. The rebels had taken refuge atop a well-fortified peak, Mount Ithome, rising in majesty from the lower Messenian plain. Assisting the Spartans in besieging the mountain, the Athenians proved inept and unpredictable in their loyalties. Friction developed, and the Spartans abruptly sent the Athenians home. Cimon returned with his troops to Athens but could not evade responsibility for the fiasco. The disgrace cost him his influence. Ephialtes and the populist party quickly gained control of Athenian affairs. Determined to free Athens of its Spartan faction, Ephialtes and his political allies succeeded in ostracizing Cimon in 461 BCE, leading to the flowering of democratic government. Cimon's principle of friendship and shared leadership with Sparta had been repudiated, though many of his other goals—including Athenian imperialism—remained intact. The policies of Cimon had led inexorably to empire, transferring so-called

naval allies on one pretext or another to tribute-paying subjects. Only the large islands of Lesbos, Chios, and Samos still retained their status of allies of the highest
rank. Moreover, at the time of Cimon's ostracism most of Greece was divided between two powerful leagues, Peloponnesian and Delian.

Ephialtes' Reforms (462–461 BCE).   In the meantime Ephialtes, mentor of Pericles,
launched an attack against the Council of Areopagus, still a bastion of conservative
privilege. The Areopagus seems to have been the dominant body in the aristocratic
state before the era of Solon, but the body had declined in influence under the Pisistratids and had become even less significant with the introduction of lot for the
appointment of archons (former archons made up the council's membership)
around the turn of the fifth century BCE. The archons were chosen by lot from five
hundred candidates elected by the demes, an innovation that emphasized the influence of the board of ten generals (*strategoi*) because the *strategoi* continued to be
elected. Yet the Areopagus remained the only permanent body in the government.
Although Ephialtes and Pericles are said to have pushed through a series of laws
limiting the power of the Areopagus between 462 and 461 BCE, the specific measures employed to weaken the old council remain debatable. Perhaps at this time
the Areopagus was deprived of its authority to supervise the conduct of the chief
magistrates and its right to review the constitutionality of laws passed by the *ekklesia*—two powers the council had certainly lost by the late fifth century BCE, when
the Council of Five Hundred exercised the privilege of supervising magistrates, and
the *heliaea*—the citizens sitting as a court of appeal—safeguarded the law against il-
legal decrees. Thus Ephialtes' reforms seem to have deprived the Areopagus of all of
its powers except that of trying cases of homicide and sacrilege, which by reason of
religious conservatism would not be taken away. Apparently the action to weaken
the council stirred bitter conservative opposition against Ephialtes, and he was
soon assassinated. Yet his reforms remained, and hereafter the Athenian government would revolve around three powerful institutions: the popular assembly (*ekklesia*), the democratic Council of Five Hundred, and the ten generals (*strategoi*).

THE AGE OF PERICLES (c. 461–429 BCE)

After the death of Ephialtes in 461 BCE, populist leadership fell to Pericles. Guiding Athens through its heyday of power and cultural achievement, Pericles was
both an imperialist who extended Athenian influence and the preeminent architect of Athenian democracy. The term Age of Pericles, commonly applied to this
fascinating phase of Athenian history, suggests his significance. Pericles enjoyed a
distinguished aristocratic ancestry, for his father was Xanthippus, the commander
of the Athenian navy at Mycale, and his mother, Agariste, was a member of the
great Alcmaeonid clan and a niece of the reformer Cleisthenes, who had promoted
the popular assembly as the main constitutional power of the state. A patron and
associate of artists and thinkers throughout his life, Pericles had been instructed
during his youth in music by Damon, who became one of his political advisers, and
in philosophy by Anaxagoras of Clazomenae, who came to Athens at a young age

and played a vital role in introducing the Athenians to the study of philosophy. While Pericles preferred the company of these and other creative geniuses—exemplified by the great dramatist Sophocles and the master sculptor Phidias—he generally enjoyed the ability to persuade the ordinary people of Athens to accept his advice. He had served as Ephialtes' able lieutenant in the leadership of the Alcmaeonids, and Plutarch reports that Pericles soon became the most influential politician in Athens.

Periclean Democracy.   Pericles was reserved and even haughty in manner—the Athenians nicknamed him the Olympian Zeus—but he was incorruptibly honest and usually above flattery. The legislative program he promoted served to consolidate his popular support and to enlarge the scope of the Athenian democracy. Pericles is thought, for example, to have sponsored a measure in 457 BCE allowing the *zeugitai*—Solon's third income class—to serve as archons. The college of archons and hence the Areopagus were now open to many additional Athenians. Eventually even the poorest class, the *thetes*, became eligible for the office.

Theoretically, any citizen could now aspire to the archonships, but in practice only the wealthy participated in governmental affairs because there was no remuneration for duties performed. Accordingly, Pericles sponsored a measure of enormous importance to the development of Athenian democracy, authorizing the use of part of the money derived from the tributary allies to pay citizens for political or judicial services. Henceforth jurors, archons, and members of the Council of Five Hundred received a daily stipend of sufficient value to enable them to leave work and devote some time to state business, and the practice was eventually extended to soldiers and sailors. Bitterly attacked by the antidemocratic forces, the reform meant that Athenian citizenship bestowed both economic benefits and political power. In 451 BCE Pericles promoted legislation restricting citizenship to men of Athenian parentage on both sides of the family, not merely through the father, the previous practice. Apparently this was aimed at wealthy Athenian men who married rich women from other states, following the example of Pericles' own maternal grandfather. By discouraging marriage between citizens and aliens, the legislation not only closed an important avenue for establishing good relations with other city-states but also encouraged a more belligerent attitude toward them and their citizens, thereby producing increased tensions that often led to war.

Although denying political rights to the noncitizen groups—resident aliens, slaves, and women—Athenian democracy permitted the active participation of the entire citizen body in its political life, a rare practice in antiquity. This system valued government by amateurs, or ordinary citizens, and shunned the practice of entrusting individuals with great power over a long period. By the 440s BCE the state was paying some twenty thousand Athenian citizens for their contributions to the polis, though only for those days actually spent in public service. Active participation in the Athenian democracy required an earnest commitment of time and energy. Men came from every part of Attica to participate in governmental affairs, often walking several hours each way, though we should not forget that the political activity of citizens was made possible by the labor of noncitizen groups.

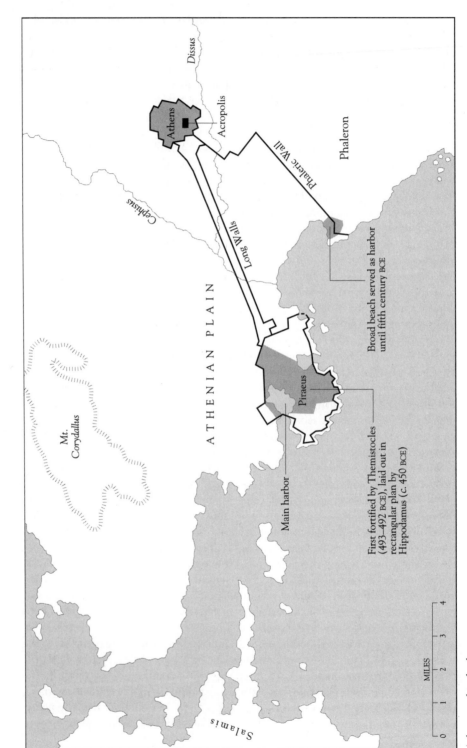

Athens and its harbors.

Periclean Imperialism and Foreign Policy.   Now politically preeminent, Pericles set out to make Athens the dominant state in Greece. He and his supporters from the democratic end of the political spectrum were firmly imperialistic and committed to securing Athenian leadership in the Hellenic world and Athenian control over Greek trade. The first step in this program was to build the Long Walls connecting Athens with its port on the promontory of Piraeus, a distance of more than four miles. These parallel walls, which were about two hundred yards apart, safeguarded access to the sea by providing a corridor through which overseas grain and other supplies could be brought to Athens when the city was under siege. The walls made Athens an isolated fortress that could survive indefinitely on seaborne provisions, provided the Athenian fleet continued to control the Aegean Sea.

The supply of grain was essential to Athens and other Greek cities because few states grew enough of the crop to feed themselves. The main Greek sources were the regions of the Black Sea, Egypt, Italy, and Sicily. The Athenians controlled the Black Sea trade through the colonies they had planted on the rich grainfields of the Thracian Chersonesus and through their domination of Byzantium on the straits of the Bosporus. Both the Chersonesus and Byzantium had been in the hands of the Persians for a number of years but were brought into the Delian League and thus under Athenian rule after the Persian Wars. In the meantime Pericles also pushed to dominate Greek trade with Egypt and with Italy and Sicily.

Pericles had no one to fear but Sparta in strengthening the Athenian hold over the Aegean trade. We saw that the Spartans had recently snubbed the Athenians by dismissing the Athenian hoplites sent to offer help against the Messenians at Mount Ithome, thereby kindling a defiant anti-Spartan foreign policy in Athens. Sparta had been weakened by the helot revolt, and its army was still bogged down around Mount Ithome. Athens thus repudiated the old alliance between the two states, for Pericles planned the development of a land empire on the Greek main-land as a buffer zone to challenge the Peloponnesian League of Sparta.

War of 460–445 BCE.   About 460 BCE the Athenians embarked on a period of in-tense military activity against various Spartan allies and soon with Sparta as well. This amounted to a declaration of war against Sparta and is commonly called the First Peloponnesian War, forerunner of the famous Peloponnesian War erupting in 431 BCE. To isolate central Greece from Spartan influence, Pericles moved to re-place Theban domination in the region with Athenian influence and occupation. Moreover, he obtained the support of northern Greece by bringing Thessaly into the alliance. Sparta countered by sending forces into Boeotia to boost the power of Thebes and won a battle over the Athenians at Tanagra about 457 BCE but failed to follow up the victory. After the Spartans returned home, the Athenians easily defeated the Thebans, thus drawing into the Delian League the various states within the regions of Boeotia (except Thebes), Phocis, and Locris.

Around 460 BCE Pericles had formed alliances with Argos, the main eastern Peloponnesian city, and Megara, an important town on the Isthmus of Corinth, to impede Spartan action beyond the Peloponnese. The Athenians gained mastery over the Isthmus through their alliance with the Megarians, who had seceded from the Peloponnesian League because they were unable to throw off Corinthian domination or to secure aid against Corinth from Sparta. Control of the small state of Megara greatly aided the Athenians, giving them access to the Gulf of Corinth through the Megaran port of Pegae. Meanwhile, also around 460 BCE, the surviving rebellious helots on Mount Ithome had surrendered and were permitted to leave the Peloponnese. Athens had settled them under its protection at the recently captured port town of Naupactus, a natural stronghold on the northern side of the entrance to the Gulf of Corinth. By thus taking control of the gulf and its valuable western trade, the Athenians incurred the implacable hostility of Corinth, now potentially bottled up.

Aegina Subject to Athens (458 BCE).   The prosperity of Aegina, the greatest rival to Athenian trade because of its location in the Saronic Gulf, was likewise threatened by the aggression and commercial expansion of Athens. When Corinth and Aegina then teamed up to fight Athens about 459 BCE, Pericles bid the Athenians "to remove Aegina as the eyesore of the Piraeus," according to Plutarch. Meanwhile the Athenian fleet was tied up in Egypt helping Egyptian rebels oppose Persian control. Rather than suspend the Egyptian campaign, Pericles called in ships from the allies to fight Aegina. In 459 BCE the Athenians landed on the island, and the following year the city surrendered and tore down its protective walls. Aegina was then forced into the Delian League as a tributary state. In the meantime the Corinthians had invaded Megara, believing the Athenians would respond by lifting their siege of Aegina to bring support to their recent ally. Instead the Athenians dispatched to Megara an army composed of boys and old men, an unusual force that succeeded in repelling the invasion.

Treasury of Delian League Transferred to Athens after Naval Losses in Egypt (c. 454 BCE).   The Athenians met with their first reversal in Egypt, where a Persian army put down the revolt and inflicted enormous damage to the Athenian fleet about 454 BCE, a great blow to Athenian power and pride. Pericles used the worsening situation in Egypt as an excuse to move the treasury of the Delian League from Delos to Athens, probably arguing that the Greek fleet was too weak to protect the Aegean from Persian aggression. The treasury consisted of the huge sum of five thousand talents, and the funds became a reserve from which Athens might borrow.

The Five-Years' Truce with Sparta (451 BCE) and the Peace of Callias (c. 449 BCE). The Egyptian disaster had shaken Pericles' leadership, however, and advocates of a pro-Spartan policy were gaining popularity in Athens. Then, probably to present a united front against the Persians, Pericles sponsored a motion to bring his old rival Cimon back from exile. In 451 BCE Cimon negotiated the Five-Years' Truce with Sparta, one condition being the Athenian renunciation of its treaty with Argos, and the defenseless Argives promptly signed a treaty with their traditional Spartan enemies. The following year Pericles sent Cimon to Cyprus with two hundred triremes—apparently a new fleet—to pursue the continuing war with Persia. Though Cimon died shortly before the battle, his forces won a great victory over the enemy, yet the Athenians were now so involved at home against Sparta and other states that they were agreeable to peace with Persia. An envoy named Callias (brother-in-law of Cimon) is said to have negotiated a formal peace treaty—the so-called Peace of Callias—with the Persians about 449 BCE. Scholars have debated the authenticity of a formal treaty for generations, but most modern historians accept the idea that Callias negotiated an agreement between Athens and Persia to end hostilities. Tacitly, at least, the Persians agreed not to intrude in Greek waters or to harass the Greeks of Asia Minor, thereby finally signifying an end to the Persian Wars. Although the Persian king never officially recognized the loss of his possessions in Asia Minor—many of which continued to pay him taxes on agricultural land—the Greeks were thereafter free of Persian assaults.

Pericles' Abortive Plan for a Panhellenic Congress (c. 448 BCE).   Peace meant unemployment for sailors, and Pericles began a great public building program on the Acropolis, partly to alleviate the loss of pay. About this time he sent envoys throughout Greece to invite delegates to a Panhellenic Congress at Athens, with the lofty stated objectives of restoring the Greek temples destroyed by the Persians and securing the freedom of the seas. Pericles' shrewd intention was to win for Athens the leadership of the Greek world and the right to police the seas. Spartan opposition was strong, and the plan came to nothing. Athenian aggression had made Panhellenism, or Greek unity, an unpopular concept. In the meantime Pericles proposed to the Athenians that they should use league funds to rebuild their own ruined monuments rather than to reconstruct temples throughout Greece.

Loss of the Land Empire (447–446 BCE).   In the years following the Peace of Callias, Athens consolidated its control over the maritime empire, but trouble was brewing in the land empire in central Greece. Athens had tried to ensure the loyalty of its allies in central Greece by establishing democracies and expelling oligarchic factions. The impending storm soon broke, however, and the Athenians lost their land empire almost overnight. Encouraged by Thebes, the determined citizens in most of the states of Boeotia overthrew their pro-Athenian democratic governments. When Athens attempted to recover the lost ground, its forces were cut to pieces at the Boeotian town of Coronea in 446 BCE, resulting in the loss of Boeotia. Meanwhile Phocis and Locris pulled out of the land empire and began supporting Sparta. Revolts broke out in Megara and Euboea, and the five-year truce between Athens and Sparta lapsed. A Spartan army led by King Pleistoanax advanced through Megara into Attica but soon withdrew—the king was probably bribed—leaving Athens free to crush the Euboean revolt. Athens continued to hold the islands of Euboea and Aegina, along with the rest of its great maritime empire, for the Athenians could not be defeated on the sea, but only Plataea and Naupactus remained of its land empire.

Promise of a Thirty Years' Peace (446 BCE).   At this critical juncture Pericles engineered a truce with King Pleistoanax of Sparta that was intended to last for thirty years. Although the exact terms of the Thirty Years' Peace between Athens and Sparta remain unknown, Athens made important diplomatic concessions such as renouncing claims in Megara (which had returned to the Peloponnesian League), recognizing the independence of Argos, and relinquishing control of mainland cities, with the exception of Plataea and Naupactus. The agreement was designed to freeze Greece for thirty years, preserving an Athenian power zone represented by the Delian League and a Spartan power zone represented by the Peloponnesian League. While Athens was recognized as supreme on sea and Sparta on land, trade between the cities of the opposing leagues was to be free of harassment from either side. Provision was made for the arbitration of all disputes between the two principals and their adherents, but no clear procedure was specified for the process. The equitable agreement secured for each side a much-needed respite from the exhaustive rigors of warfare. Yet both Corinth and Thebes seethed against Athens, making a lasting peace unlikely. Although Pericles had failed in his bold scheme to establish Athenian domination over strategic central Greece and the entire eastern Mediterranean, he had successfully built up an Athenian maritime empire recognized by both Persia and Sparta. He spent the following years strengthening the Athenian Empire and the fleet, for a Greece divided into two mutually antagonistic alliances did not bode well for the future.

Establishment of New Colonies (443–437 BCE).   The Thirty Years' Peace was unpopular in Athens, yet Pericles rallied to strengthen his hand against political opposition. From 443 until his death in 429, according to Plutarch, Pericles was elected general (*strategos*) every year, completely dominating affairs in Athens. After the peace with Sparta—which still had not fully recovered from its serious helot revolt and disastrous earthquake of the 460s—Athens was indisputably the leading Greek power, and Pericles extended the influence of the state by founding new colonies. In 443 he agreed to a Panhellenic enterprise, with colonists coming from Athens, the Peloponnese, and elsewhere to establish a Greek city called Thurii on the instep of southern Italy, not far away from the obliterated Greek city of Sybaris. The celebrated wealth of Sybaris had aroused intense jealously among other Greeks, and the city had been attacked and destroyed by the rival city of Croton near the end of the sixth century BCE, but the descendants of the Sybarites invited the Athenians and others to cooperate with them in building the new city. Two notables among the colonists sailing to Thurii were the historian Herodotus of Halicarnassus and the architect and philosopher Hippodamus of Miletus, the latter beautifying the place with wide straight avenues contrasting to the narrow crooked streets of most cities of the time. A respected Athenian Sophist named Protagoras compiled for the departing settlers laws based on those of Athens and other cities. When dissention broke out among the colonists after a few years, however, the non-Athenians gained control of the colony at Thurii and rejected Athenian leadership.

Pericles was more successful in extending Athenian influence elsewhere. He secured control of the coast of Thrace, for example, by founding Amphipolis and other new colonies. Settled in 437 BCE, Amphipolis was built on a site that commanded the important trade on the Thracian river Strymon, and thus Athens gained access to the metals, grain, and timber in the region. Pericles also increased Athenian presence in that great reservoir of wealth, the Black Sea region, to ensure control over its vital grain trade. Accordingly, he sailed around its shores on a magnificent detachment of the Athenian fleet, with the intention of cementing commercial ties that would render Athens independent of grain from Dorian Sicily. To secure that goal, he settled colonists around the rim of the Black Sea, brought the larger Greek cities of the area into the maritime empire, and made alliances with the native princes, especially in the Crimea, thereby beginning the process of Hellenizing the inhabitants of southern Russia and Ukraine.

The Organization of the Athenian Empire.   The nearly two hundred member states of the empire fanned out in a great semicircle along the coastline of the Aegean from Athens to southern Asia Minor. By the 440s all the Greeks realized that the Delian League had been transformed into an Athenian Empire. After a reorganization in 443 BCE, the subject states of the empire were grouped for purposes of tribute assessments into five districts: Ionia, the Hellespont, Thrace, Caria (southwestern Asia Minor), and the islands. In 438 BCE, however, Caria was merged with Ionia, and the remaining four districts survived until the last tribute assessment in Athens in 406 BCE. The amount of tribute was fixed by Athenian officials, and annually they issued tribute quota lists inscribed on blocks of marble. Tribute was collected by the dependent states and then paid to Athens, though a few powerful allies with a naval tradition supplied warships instead. The excess above the costs of imperial administration benefited Athens alone.

Athens virtually ignored its initial promise of autonomy for the members of the Delian League. Laws passed by the Athenian assembly, for example, required all members of the empire to use Athenian standards for coinage, weights, and measures. Athenian silver coinage became the customary medium not only for Greek exchange but also for trade with the Persian Empire. Athens made individual commercial agreements with many of its subject states, guaranteeing protection for their commerce through the power of the imperial fleet but turning their trade to Athens. Although Athens permitted any form of loyal government among its subjects—even tyranny—the internal political systems of the subject states generally reflected the Athenian preference for democracy.

Among the grievances of the dependencies was the Athenian policy of removing cases involving serious crimes or commercial treaties from local courts for trial in Athens. Another irritating Athenian practice was the establishment in strategic towns of special military colonies called cleruchies (*kleroukhoi*), which were regarded as an extension of the territory and power of Athens. Thus the settlers (cleruchs) kept their original Athenian citizenship. Tending to be arrogant and overbearing toward their reluctant hosts, the cleruchs—mostly impoverished Athenians—confiscated choice lands of the subject states and served almost as garrison troops in their new homes. The subject states also complained that Athens dominated their foreign relations. Moreover, they were annoyed that Athens consistently diverted funds for the naval defense of the league to its own use. Yet the empire brought many benefits to the Aegean world, including peace and prosperity, freedom from piracy, and—after the ending of hostilities with Persia—trade with Egypt, Mesopotamia, and even India.

The arbitrary conduct of Athens incited such bitterness that many of the subject states were eager to escape from the empire, though attempts at secession were met with harsh reprisals, exemplified by the cases of Naxos and Thasos some years earlier. The island of Samos dared to revolt in 441 BCE, the aristocratic party inciting rebellion among the citizens because Athens was attempting to impose a democratic constitution there. When the revolt spread to Byzantium, the Persians offered to aid the rebels. Pericles himself took command of the Athenian expedition sent to recover Samos, but the Athenians experienced nine months of arduous fighting before reducing the island to submission. Now Lesbos and Chios constituted the only remaining free partners of Athens. The Black Sea and the Aegean would continue to be Athenian waters, over which products from far-flung regions sailed to the harbor at Athens.

Notwithstanding Athens' willingness to employ naked force to control its empire, each dependent state included a pro-Athenian faction of generally middle- and lower-income citizens who favored democracy and the advantages of increased trade. The aristocratic landowners, on the other hand, usually opposed both the local democratic faction and Athenian domination. Meanwhile citizens in Attica also debated the advantages and disadvantages of imperialism. Conservative aristocrats criticized Pericles' harsh imperial policy and opposed his use of league funds, which had been contributed for defense but were used to adorn and rebuild Athens. They also wanted to turn back the democratic innovations of the past half century, pursue peaceful relations with Sparta, and strengthen the army rather than the navy. After a vote to ostracize Pericles failed in 443 BCE, however, imperialism ceased to be a political issue. Pride in the new material splendor of Athens and appreciation for its prosperity—both largely provided by the appropriation of the imperial treasury—simply laid the issue to rest.

CHAPTER X

THE PELOPONNESIAN WAR

The socioeconomic, intellectual, and artistic ferment of the Periclean Age, covered in the next three chapters, represents but a short period of cultural flowering between the Persian Wars and the Peloponnesian War. Lasting twenty-seven years, from 431 to 404 BCE, the Peloponnesian War was a deadly conflict between the Peloponnesians and the Athenians. We noted in chapter 9 that after the Persians had failed to conquer mainland Greece in the early part of the century, the rivalry between Athens and Sparta culminated in prolonged hostilities that ended with the Thirty Years' Peace in 446 BCE. The truce in fact lasted fewer than fifteen years before the disastrous Peloponnesian War broke out between the two powers, eventually engulfing most of the Greek world. The great tragedy of ancient Greece, the Peloponnesian War left both victor and vanquished on the verge of exhaustion and paved the way for the loss of Greek independence.

The Athenian historian Thucydides, who lived during the Peloponnesian War and began his perceptive chronicle at the point where Herodotus ended his narrative, argued in a famous passage that the underlying cause of the conflict was Spartan fear of Athenian expansion. Born about 460 BCE, when Pericles was reaching for political leadership of Athens, Thucydides was elected *strategos* in 424 BCE, eight years into the war. Failing to prevent the loss of the Athenian colony of Amphipolis to the Spartans, Thucydides was exiled. For twenty years he traveled and interviewed participants from both sides, obtaining detailed information he included in his vivid narrative. The greatest of all ancient historians, Thucydides was the first author to apply rationalistic standards of analysis to events. He pictured the war as a singular conflict having eternal significance, but he took great care to evaluate the accuracy of his sources and to let his readers know which statements were reliable and which could not be substantiated.

STEPS TO WAR (435–431 BCE)

RIVALRY BETWEEN CORINTH AND ATHENS

Athens and Sparta, each heading an extensive confederacy, stood for opposing ideals of government and social organization. A number of incidents before the outbreak of hostilities had increased the discord between the Peloponnesian League, led by the Spartans, and the Delian League, led by the Athenians. We saw that Thucydides identified the underlying cause of the Peloponnesian War as Spartan fear of the extension of Athenian power. Athens had already eradicated the autonomy of a number of Greek states and threatened many others. Sparta's ally Corinth grew to detest democratic, expansionist Athens. The Corinthians were alarmed that their polis had been hemmed in both east and west by the Athenians and that their traders had been driven from one market after another by Athenian competition.

ATHENS INTERVENES IN THE WAR BETWEEN CORINTH AND CORCYRA (433 BCE)

Athens repeatedly violated the spirit of the Thirty Years' Peace, as revealed in famous incidents at Corcyra and Potidaea, two immediate causes of the Peloponnesian War. The lush island of Corcyra (modern Corfu), opposite Epirus in the Ionian Sea, had been colonized by Corinth some three hundred years earlier. Providing an anchorage on the crossing from mainland Greece to Italy and Sicily, Corcyra developed into a prosperous and moderately powerful maritime state but had grown hostile to Corinth and competed with its mother-city for the western trade. To make matters worse, Corinth and Corcyra took opposite sides in a savage civil war that broke out in 435 BCE between the ruling oligarchs and the democrats in a colony the two cities had founded jointly, Epidamnus in Illyria on the northwest coast of Greece. When war erupted between Corinth and Corcyra in 433 BCE, the frightened Corcyreans abandoned their traditional isolationism and appealed to Athens for help. The Athenians—contrary to the spirit of their peace treaty with Sparta—responded by sending ten triremes to the Ionian Sea. Apparently the Athenians feared that their grain trade with Sicily might be endangered if the important naval state of the Corcyreans came under Corinthian control. The Corinthians won the advantage in the ensuing naval engagement—the important battle of Sybota—but they sailed for home after twenty additional Athenian triremes arrived on the scene. The Athenians gained as an ally the only naval power in the western waters of Greece. Now they could call upon the aid of the Corcyrean fleet, the third largest of Greece. As a consequence of these developments, Corinth urged Sparta to declare war against Athens.

ATHENIAN INTERFERENCE IN POTIDAEA (432 BCE)

Athenian policy in the Potidaean affair struck the Corinthians as equally belligerent. Potidaea, although founded as a Corinthian colony in the Macedonian Chalcidice, had been enrolled as a subject state in the Delian League following the Persian Wars. In spite of its dependence on Athens, Potidaea was still governed by magistrates sent out annually from Corinth, thereby increasing the rivalry and tension between the Corinthians and the Athenians. In the meantime King Perdiccas I of Macedonia—furious over Athenian aggression on his coast—promoted rebellion against Athens in Potidaea and the other cities of Chalcidice. The Potidaeans became implicated in the intrigues, and in 432 BCE the Athenians began to bully Potidaea, demanding that the city expel the Corinthian magistrates, tear down its walls, and give hostages to Athens. When the desperate Potidaeans appealed to the Corinthians and the Spartans for help, Corinth sent them an unofficial force of two thousand Peloponnesians. By the end of the summer of 432 BCE an Athenian army that included the philosopher Socrates and the future political leader Alcibiades was besieging Potidaea, thereby increasing the hatred of Athens by the allies of Sparta.

The Megarian Decree (c. 432 bce)

Pericles thought war was inevitable and thus decided to punish Megara for having aided Corinth against Corcyra. Megara, though bordering Attica, belonged to the Peloponnesian League and had long demonstrated animosity toward Athens. About 432 BCE Pericles sponsored the Megarian Decree excluding Megara from all ports and markets of the Athenian Empire, a clear violation of the peace treaty and a ruinous economic blow to the commercial interests of the beleaguered city. The decree served as a warning to the members of the Peloponnesian League what to expect if war broke out. Denouncing the decree as an attempt to starve them into submission, the Megarians joined the Corinthians in urging Sparta to declare war on Athens.

The Peloponnesian League Votes for War (432 bce)

Elderly King Archidamus of Sparta realized the possible consequences of a war with Athens and urged the Spartan assembly, meeting in private session, to save the peace and negotiate. Yet the assembly decided by a large majority that the Thirty Years' Truce had been broken, and the Spartans then made arrangements for the convening of delegates from the members of the Peloponnesian League to deliberate the possibility of war. A few weeks later, in the autumn of 432 BCE, the assembled delegates voted to inaugurate hostilities. Both sides began preparing for the coming armed conflict, which would have to await the arrival of better weather in the spring.

THE CONTESTANTS

The Athenian Alliance

At the beginning of the war the nucleus of the Athenian alliance was formed by maritime states: the Greek centers in western Asia Minor, the colonies on the north Aegean coast, most of the Aegean islands, and the Euboean cities. The islands of Chios and Lesbos still maintained a precarious autonomy. The alliance also embraced the islands of Corcyra and Zacynthus of western Greece. Of the few mainland allies of Athens, the most notable were Plataea in central Greece and

Naupactus in western Greece, the latter commanding the entrance to the Corinthian Gulf.

Pericles reported to the people that Athens, blessed with substantial military and financial resources, was better able to fight a long war than any of its enemies. Athens could count on the resources of its empire, annual tribute from its subject states, an enormous fund of six thousand talents of coined silver on the Acropolis, an army of twelve hundred cavalry and thirteen thousand hoplites, a reserve force of sixteen thousand fighters (older soldiers, boys, and resident aliens), and a fleet of three hundred triremes with well-trained crews. Although Attica lay open to invasion from both the Peloponnese and Boeotia, the Long Walls protected the vital supplies coming to Athens from Piraeus, and the Athenians themselves would be safe behind them. Pericles' strategy was to sacrifice the land without sacrificing the people. He planned to avoid land battles with the numerically superior Spartan hoplites and to bring Athenian farmers into the city for protection behind the Long Walls. Pericles realized that the bulk of the Peloponnesians were small farmers personally tilling their lands and thus unable to remain away from home for an extended period. The Athenians, on the other hand, were supreme at sea and could import supplies and also protect them from the enemy. In short, Athens could be taken neither by assault nor by starvation as long as its fleet remained intact. Pericles' strategy was not merely defensive, for he also planned to attack the coasts of the Peloponnese with the fleet, gradually cutting off trade and eventually gaining a favorable truce. The scheme of starving the enemy into submission was unrealistic, however, because a number of the Peloponnesian states produced a surplus of grain.

The Peloponnesian League

Unlike the Athenians, the Peloponnesians had almost no public funds. The Corinthians suggested that the treasuries of Delphi and Olympia be utilized for the war effort, but the other allies repudiated the idea because of religious scruple. Early in the war the Spartans even sought financial assistance from the Persians, who thought Athens was invincible and thus rejected the request. Although Sparta lacked a fleet, the Peloponnesians were not without assets. They could call upon fifty thousand or more aggressive hoplites, their core formed by four thousand well-disciplined Spartans. Moreover, the league included every state of the Peloponnese except neutral Argos and Achaea, and the Achaean cities eventually joined. The alliance also embraced a number of communities beyond the Peloponnese: the town of Megara in the northeastern isthmus region; the central Greek districts of Boeotia, Phocis, and Locris; and a few states along the west coast. The Spartans and their allies could march from the Peloponnese to Boeotia across the territory of Megara, part of the land bridge between southern and central Greece. Communication with Boeotia was essential because the district bordered northwestern Attica. Led by the Thebans, all the Boeotians except the Plataeans were solidly behind Sparta. Thebes had long nourished a grudge against Athens for championing the independence of Plataea, and actual hostilities broke out with a Theban raid against the Plataeans in the spring of 431 BCE.

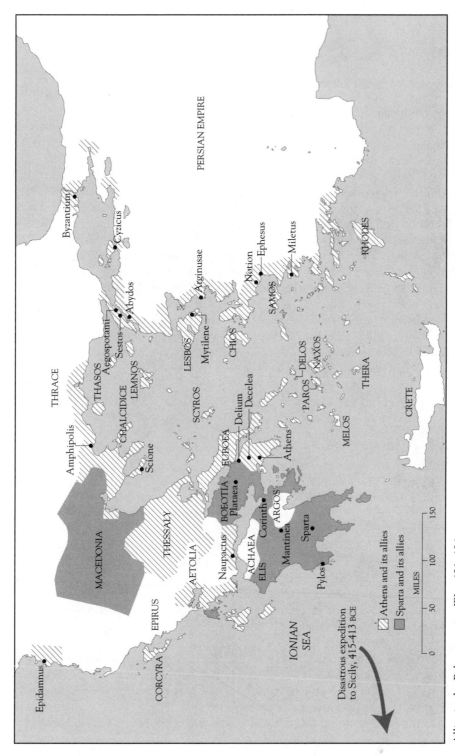

Allies in the Peloponnesian War, 431–404 BCE.

THE SEVERAL PERIODS OF WAR AND PEACE

The First Phase: The Archidamian War (431–421 bce)

The Peloponnesians Invade Attica (431 BCE).   The conflict developed during the first two years as each side had anticipated. In the spring of 431 BCE the Peloponnesians invaded Attica under the command of Archidamus, the venerable Spartan king, and the first ten years of the Peloponnesian War are often called the Archidamian War after him. The Peloponnesian army ravaged the deserted land for about a month and then withdrew. Pericles, with considerable difficulty, had managed to restrain the Athenian farmers from rushing out to confront the enemy when they saw their villages and fields going up in smoke. Meanwhile the Athenian fleet menaced the coast of the Peloponnese. In the winter of 431 BCE Pericles delivered a funeral oration eulogizing those who had been slain in battle and extolling the Athenian way of life, for which they had died. The speech, as reconstructed by Thucydides, is one of the most famous documents surviving from ancient Greece. Thucydides never claimed that the orations in his work are literally accurate. They simply detailed arguments appropriate for the occasion when the actual speeches were delivered. In Thucydides' rendering, Pericles exhorted citizens to love and support their city at a time when so much was at stake. Apparently his speech did not have the desired effect on everyone, for whenever the farmers were forced to find refuge behind the city walls, they gathered in groups to complain bitterly of their plight and to accuse Pericles of causing their losses.

The Plague (430–427 BCE).   A devastating plague, perhaps akin to typhus, broke out in the unsanitary refugee encampments and swept the city in 430 BCE. Thucydides observed that "the dead lay as they had died, one upon another, while others, hardly alive, wallowed in the streets and crawled about every fountain craving for water." Possibly a third of the population perished within the three-year course of the plague. While many Athenians became convinced that they had somehow offended heaven, others resolved to enjoy every conceivable pleasure of this transitory life. In the attendant hysteria, the Athenians turned bitterly against Pericles, tried him for embezzlement, and drove him from office. Relenting when other politicians failed to please them in conducting the war, the Athenians reelected Pericles *strategos*, but he too had contracted the pestilence and survived only a few months. Although his internal policies were more successful than his external ones, Pericles had never flinched from opposing the Athenians to their face when he believed it necessary. All too often the leaders who followed him were tempted to elevate popularity above principle.

The Leadership of Cleon (429–422 BCE).   The interests of great landowning families and small-scale farmers were undermined by the war, but a new class was rising to political and economic prominence. Shopkeepers and innkeepers were economically boosted by the influx of people from the countryside. Merchants readily sold the goods of artisans throughout the empire, while sailors received steady pay

This idealized marble portrait bust of the Athenian leader Pericles, who steered Athens through the height of its power and cultural achievement, dates to the Roman period but is probably a copy of a lost original bronze statue by the Athenian sculptor Cresilas. Artists often portrayed Pericles wearing a helmet in order to conceal his unusually elongated head. The original statue, no doubt taking the form of a godlike naked warrior, was set up on the Acropolis soon after Pericles' death in 429 BCE. British Museum, London.

for naval service. The advent of an empire dramatically increased the volume of public business and necessitated the creation of numerous new public officials, leading to a dilution of aristocratic control of state life. Moreover, scores of opportunities were created for contractors and shipbuilders. The vigorous new breed of entrepreneurs growing up outside the old nobility turned to a wealthy tanner of hides named Cleon as their leader. Thucydides viewed his actions with distaste and underestimated his importance. The Athenian comic playwright Aristophanes characterized him as a crowd-pleasing demagogue, a very persuasive speaker with a voice "like a mountain torrent." With Pericles' death, however, no orator in the Athenian assembly could summon the skill to oppose the bold planning of Cleon effectively, though a distinguished, conservative aristocrat named Nicias acted as his chief rival.

Meanwhile, after the plague had subsided, the Spartans resumed their pattern of annually invading Attica, while the Athenian fleet continued to achieve victories. Both sides resorted to grim atrocities. The Athenians, for example, vigorously pressed the siege of Potidaea for two years, and the beleaguered survivors were reduced to cannibalism before surrendering in the winter of 429 BCE. In the summer of 429 BCE the Peloponnesians marched against Plataea and massacred its defenders—most of the inhabitants had fled to Athens—after a grueling siege.

Attempted Secession of Mytilene (428 BCE).   We noted that the island of Lesbos was one of the two remaining states of the former Delian League retaining the status of an independent ally. Its wealth and naval strength were vital to Athenian success. In 428 BCE word reached Athens that Mytilene, the chief city on the island, had withdrawn from the alliance. The Athenian fleet blockaded the island until the people surrendered. When Cleon called for making a terrifying example of the Mytileneans, the assembly dispatched a warship carrying an order to massacre the adult male population and to enslave the women and children. The next day, however, some people as least had second thoughts, and the Athenians reconsidered the sentence. Cleon maintained that showing mercy would be a sign of weakness, but his conservative opponents, arguing for expediency, persuaded the Athenians they could govern the empire far more effectively by a display of calculated leniency. A second ship was thus sent to rescind the first order, arriving just in time to prevent mass butchery. The punishment of death was limited to the few Mytileneans most involved in the secessionist movement, but the land of the rebels were confiscated and divided among the Athenian colonists.

The Fortification of Pylos and the Capture of Sphacteria (425 BCE).   By this time a conservative peace party, led by the wealthy general and politician Nicias, wanted to negotiate a truce with Sparta. Although Nicias was devoutly religious, his timidity undermined his high principles. The radical democrat and aggressive imperialist Cleon, on the other hand, was prepared to extend the war recklessly, and he pushed the Athenians on the offensive. In 425 BCE a violent storm drove an Athenian fleet sailing to Corcyra and Sicily into the harbor of Pylos on the western coast of Messenia, only forty-five miles from Sparta. The brilliant general Demosthenes (not the orator of the same name), one of the commanders of the Athenian force, decided that Pylos would make an excellent base for raiding the Peloponnesian coast and encouraging the helots to revolt. When the storm subsided, he remained behind with five triremes and set out to fortify Pylos. Alarmed by the news that an Athenian contingent was actually established in southwestern Peloponnese, the Spartans sent their able general Brasidas on the offensive and stationed about 420 hoplites on the adjacent island of Sphacteria. Demosthenes countered by recalling the Athenian fleet and blockading the island, effectively marooning the hoplites.

In the face of this acute emergency, Sparta arranged a truce, the terms of which included temporarily turning over to the Athenians at Pylos all the Peloponnesian warships. Then Spartan envoys hastened to Athens, offering peace in return for the liberation of the stranded hoplites. Pericles had asked for nothing more than peace without concessions from Sparta, but now Cleon sternly insisted upon territorial gains. Thucydides regarded Cleon's refusal to negotiate seriously with Sparta at this time a fatal mistake, for Athens had been presented with the possibility of forging a lasting peace and winning the respect of the entire Greek world. After the failure of the negotiations, the Spartans asked for the return of the Peloponnesian fleet, according to the terms of the truce, but the Athenians broke their word and refused to hand over the ships. In the meantime when Cleon accused the Athenian generals of incompetence, the members of the assembly put him in charge of the entire Pylos campaign. Although he had never undertaken a military command, Cleon impetuously promised to lead a fleet to Pylos and capture the island of Sphacteria in twenty days. Helped by Demosthenes, Cleon quickly landed an overwhelming force on Sphacteria, and the exhausted surviving hoplites—including about 120 Spartans—surrendered rather than face annihilation. All Greeks would be stunned to hear that the Spartans had broken their long tradition of never surrendering under any circumstances. Cleon then fulfilled his pledge by returning to Athens with his prisoners within the twenty days. In the same year, with money urgently needed for the war effort, Cleon presumably approved a famous measure doubling or tripling the tribute imposed on the cities of the Athenian Empire, thereby increasing discontent among the subject states.

Brasidas.   With the Athenians now holding Spartan hostages, the Peloponnesians refrained from invading Attica, lest the prisoners be executed. Meanwhile the Athenians redoubled their coastal raids. Yet their euphoria proved short-lived indeed, for Athens began to lose ground almost immediately. Although a raid on the Corinthian coast was moderately successful, an attack on Megara in 424 BCE failed, thanks to the brilliant general Brasidas, now in command of the Spartan forces. Planning a vigorous offensive the same year in Boeotia, the Athenians were defeated by the Boeotians at Delium, the only large-scale land battle during the first phase of the war.

Brasidas, so brave and personable that even his enemies admired him, perceived the Athenian Empire was most vulnerable at spots that could be assailed by land. Marching without much difficulty through Boeotia, Phocis, and Thessaly, the energetic Spartan general soon appeared on the north Aegean coast, where most of the Delian League subject cities opened their gates to him. Then in a night attack in 424 BCE, he seized the vital Athenian colony of Amphipolis, which commanded the routes to inner Thrace and the Hellespont. Thucydides had been placed in command of a small fleet in the northern Aegean but failed to save Amphipolis from Brasidas. For this reason, the Athenians banished Thucydides, who lived in exile and concentrated on historical research for the next twenty years.

Death of Cleon and Brasidas (422 BCE).   The reversals of 424 BCE weakened Cleon and the rest of the war party in Athens, and in 423 BCE a truce was made with the enemy for the ensuing year, during which the proponents of peace in both Athens and Sparta hoped to negotiate a treaty. Yet the war leaders on each side—Cleon and Brasidas—continued to insist upon a decisive victory. As soon as the truce expired in 422 BCE, Cleon sailed to recover the rebellious communities in Chalcidice and, above all, the city of Amphipolis in Thrace. Although he enjoyed some success in Chalcidice, Cleon and his men were badly defeated at Amphipolis during a surprise charge led by Brasidas. Receiving mortal wounds, both Cleon and Brasidas fell in the engagement.

AN UNEASY TRUCE: THE PEACE OF NICIAS (421–415 BCE)

The two opposing sides were now completely exhausted, and each had lost its chief prowar leader of the day in battle. Thus the peace parties—headed by Nicias at Athens and King Pleistoanax at Sparta—negotiated a truce, which was signed in the spring of 421 BCE and was intended to last for fifty years. According to the terms of the Peace of Nicias, as the treaty is known, Athens agreed to liberate the prisoners captured on Sphacteria and to surrender Pylos and Cythera in return for the restoration of the city of Amphipolis and the former Athenian holdings on the north Aegean coast (these Chalcidic cities were to remain autonomous but pay tribute to Athens). Moreover, Athens was to retain several of its conquests in the Peloponnese and the Isthmus. After Sparta failed to persuade the citizens of Amphipolis to accept renewed Athenian control, however, Athens retaliated by retaining Pylos and other Peloponnesian acquisitions. Thus the two most important conquests of the war—Pylos and Amphipolis—were not restored.

In effect, the peace terms signaled a victory for the Athenians because their empire remained strong and largely intact. In its haste to come to terms with Athens, Sparta had ignored the claims of its allies. The Corinthians, Megarians, Boeotians, and Eleans refused to sign this agreement that gave the Athenians unfair advantages. Exemplifying its partiality, the treaty denied the Corinthians the right to recover two of their strategic colonies—Anactorium and Sollium—on the west coast of Greece. The refusal of the furious Spartan allies to sign the Peace of Nicias virtually destroyed the Spartan alliance.

Another concern for Sparta was that the truce made thirty years earlier with Argos—never its friend—was about to lapse. The Spartans feared the Argives might strike up an alliance with the Athenians. To prevent Argive aggression and a possible helot revolt, the Spartans nervously signed a fifty-year defensive alliance with Athens, much to the dismay and suspicion of the other Peloponnesian states. This defensive alliance was negotiated shortly after the signing of the Peace of Nicias. Now Athens and Sparta were not merely at peace but were also nominal allies. The two states did not invade one another's territories for six years, each being preoccupied with the serious problems left by protracted and grueling warfare. Meanwhile Argos—encouraged by Athens—established an anti-Spartan alliance with Corinth and several other former members of the Peloponnesian League.

Alcibiades.   While Nicias and the Athenian peace party firmly supported the Spartan alliance, the war party—led by the democrats—found a new leader in Alcibiades, the nephew and ward of Pericles and an intimate of Socrates. Unlike the great philosopher, however, Alcibiades developed a cynical attitude toward public morality. Through his mother he was related to the Alcmaeonids and through his father to a family of avid democrats. We hear from Plutarch of numerous infatuated men pursuing the teenage Alcibiades. Handsome, vain, rowdy, unprincipled, and notoriously licentious, the adult Alcibiades was feared, courted, and seduced by members of both sexes. He dreamed of seizing absolute power at Athens and thus made a demagogic play for popular support. Alcibiades rose in politics as the leader of the extreme democrats, his goal being to expand the Athenian Empire and to resume hostilities with Sparta, for he saw his way to power through war and conquest. His fellow citizens, though wary of his lust for personal power and honor, repeatedly voted him into high command.

The reckless Alcibiades helped to sabotage the recent Peace of Nicias by persuading the Athenians to form an anti-Spartan alliance with Argos. His intrigues soon drew Athens into a quadruple coalition with the Peloponnesian cities of Argos, Elis, and Mantinea. The provoked Spartans, led by King Agis, crushed a force of Argives, Mantineans, and Athenians in 418 BCE in the central Peloponnese. This victory rescued the prestige of the Spartans, on the wane since the disaster at Sphacteria, and enabled them to restore the Peloponnesian League. In the meantime the cunning Alcibiades temporarily allied himself with his chief rival Nicias to avoid ostracism.

Sack of Melos (416 BCE).   Not long afterward Alcibiades goaded the Athenians into attacking the Cycladic island of Melos, whose inhabitants were descended from Spartan colonists. Cleon had assessed Melos for tribute in 425 BCE, but the Melians courageously refused to pay and pursued a course of neutrality. This defiance was not forgotten in Athens, and in 416 BCE Alcibiades sent an expedition against the little island. The Melians, refusing demands they submit to Athenian rule, offered brave resistance but were starved into submission. The Athenians then butchered the adult men, sold the women and children into slavery, and repopulated the island with Athenian colonists.

The Second Phase of the War (415–404 BCE)

The Athenian Expedition against Syracuse (415–413 BCE).   By 415 BCE Alcibiades had conceived the fateful and grandiose scheme of creating a western branch of the Athenian Empire in Sicily. Most of the Sicilian east coast was Ionian, but not Dorian Syracuse, then the most powerful city in the western Greek world. An ally of Sparta, Syracuse was hostile to the Ionian Greeks of Sicily and southern Italy. The immediate opportunity for Athenian intervention came in 416 BCE, when the Sicilian city of Segesta—then at war with its neighbor Selinus—appealed to Athens for military aid.

An attack on Selinus would mean certain war with its ally Syracuse. Cautious Nicias opposed the scheme, arguing that sound strategy dictated a strong Athenian presence in the Aegean rather than undertaking a risky foreign adventure. Even if the Athenians succeeded in conquering Sicily, he reasoned, they lacked the power or resources to rule the island indefinitely. Alcibiades took an aggressive approach,

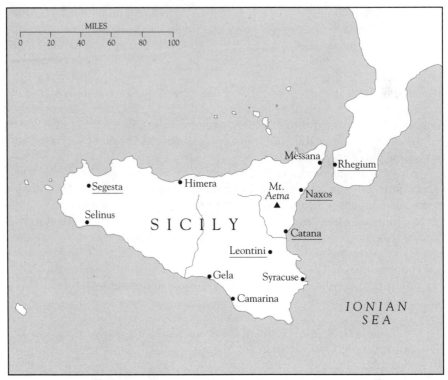

Sicily in the Peloponnesian War (the cities underlined supported Athens).

rallying the Athenians to the prospect of easy conquest and untold riches. The assembly, opting for war, foolishly partitioned command among three generals: Lamachus, Nicias, and Alcibiades. The veteran general Lamachus lacked sufficient political influence to counteract the other two commanders, the most powerful leaders in Athens. Nicias had been chosen against his will, while Alcibiades saw the appointment as an opportunity for his personal aggrandizement.

Athens was rocked by scandal shortly before the fleet sailed. Under cover of darkness, a group mutilated the religious images known as herms—stone pillars topped with a head representing the god Hermes and adorned on the front with a prominent, fully erect phallus recalling his connection with fertility—which were thought to protect Greek cities from danger. Herms stood in streets and squares, alongside roads, and in the doorways of temples and private houses. The mutilation was regarded as a religious sacrilege as well as a bad omen for the Sicilian enterprise, and many feared that the outrage was the prelude to an oligarchic revolution. Moreover, Athenians reacted with utter terror to the possibility that unknown conspirators were attempting to deprive the city of divine protection. Thus the mutilation was thoroughly investigated, but the culprits were not identified. Some thought the statues may have been desecrated by drunken youths. Suspicion also fell upon

Alcibiades. He was undoubtedly innocent of this charge and demanded an immediate trial. Yet his enemies, knowing he would probably win acquittal because many soldiers and sailors would serve as jurors, procured a postponement until his return. Their shrewd plan was to recall and prosecute him later, when his partisans would be absent.

The fleet thus set out for Sicily with charges still pending against Alcibiades. Thucydides describes the magnificence of the occasion. Practically the entire population of Attica gathered with tremendous enthusiasm at Piraeus on the day of departure in June 415 BCE. Then the trumpet commanded silence for the offering of solemn prayers and libations before sailing. Including the crews, at least twenty-seven thousand men put out to sea, the most ambitious foreign enterprise that had ever been undertaken by a Greek state, though few of the elated adventurers would ever see Athens again.

In compliance with the original Athenian objective, Nicias proposed executing a quick attack on Selinus as a means of relieving Segesta and then returning to Athens after making a show of strength along the coast of Sicily. Alcibiades, on the other hand, wanted to win as many states in Sicily as possible and then move against both Syracuse and Selinus. The experienced soldier Lamachus, whose plan was the most sensible, suggested an immediate attack on Syracuse before the city had time to make adequate preparations for war, thereby possibly opening the remainder of Sicily to the Athenians. When his fellow commanders rejected his proposal, Lamachus decided to avoid deadlock by backing Alcibiades' ambitious scheme. Much valuable time was then wasted in futile diplomacy with unenthusiastic Sicilian cities. When the Athenian ships finally approached Syracuse, Alcibiades was summoned back to Athens to face the charge of sacrilege. Realizing his condemnation and execution was a foregone conclusion, Alcibiades fled to Sparta, where he urged the Spartans to aid the Syracusans and to resume the war against Athens. Meanwhile the Athenians condemned him to death in absentia and confiscated his property.

Deprived of Alcibiades' leadership, the Athenian soldiers and sailors drifted toward disorganization and low morale, but they remained in Sicily and made preparations for the coming engagement. Nicias and Lamachus sought help from the native Sicels and sent an urgent plea to Athens for reinforcements, while Syracuse appealed for aid from Sparta and Corinth. The Athenian siege of Syracuse finally got underway in the spring of 414 BCE. By then the Syracusans were ready, and the Spartans—urged on by Alcibiades—had sent a contingent under Gylippus to aid them.

At first the Athenians had the better of the struggle. They blockaded the harbor of the city with warships and began putting up a wall to cut off the landward side, but Lamachus was killed in a skirmish during the construction. The ailing Nicias, the only remaining Athenian commander, then made the fatal mistake of not completing the wall. Thus the gifted Spartan general Gylippus was able to enter the city upon his arrival and take command of the Syracusan army, invigorating the men with a new confidence and leading them to capture the Athenian naval base.

Nicias, in danger of attack from the Syracusan fleet, urged Athens either to withdraw or to send substantial reinforcements. In the meantime Alcibiades exhorted the

Spartans to resume the war in Greece. Thus the Athenians debated whether to risk war on two fronts. In 413 BCE the assembly voted to take the gamble and dispatched a fleet to Syracuse under the able command of Demosthenes, but after the lives of many Athenians were squandered in a costly night contest, the two commanders decided to raise the siege. On the very night selected for the retreat, however, an eclipse of the moon occurred, terrifying many of the soldiers, and Nicias—the senior general—heeded the advice of soothsayers that the Athenians not leave the harbor until twenty-seven days had elapsed. Never had a celestial observance been more disastrous, for the soothsayers' advice proved fatal. During the twenty-seven days of waiting, the Syracusans firmly blockaded the Athenian fleet with a line of ships across the harbor mouth. Thucydides' riveting account of the last battle in the harbor is famous for the power of its imagery. Despite the determined effort of the Athenians to break out of the harbor, they were driven to the shore and their fleet burned and destroyed. More than forty thousand thirst-crazed men—most levied from the subject states of Athens—then attempted to escape by land, abandoning their sick and wounded and leaving their dead unburied. After hideous loses at the hands of the pursuing Syracusans, the survivors surrendered. Their harried generals were tortured and executed, and the surviving seven thousand men were reduced to imprisonment in stone quarries, where they suffered extraordinary agonies. Eventually they were sold into slavery. The reckless invasion had cost Athens the worst defeat in its history. Besides suffering a grotesque loss of life, Athens saw the crippling of its navy, the chief source of its military might. Without doubt the Sicilian disaster marked the beginning of the end for the great city.

The Last Years of the War (413–404 BCE).   When word reached Athens of the military calamity, stunned grief was followed by agonizing fear for survival. Athens, its prestige shattered, was now saddled with a depleted treasury and a disintegrating empire, while the rest of the Greek world regarded the Athenians as oppressors. In the meantime Sparta had renewed the war in Greece just before the Athenian defeat at Syracuse. This final phase of the Peloponnesian War began when the Spartans, on the advice of Alcibiades, occupied and fortified an old deme called Decelea in northeastern Attica, in sight of the walls of Athens itself. The danger to Athens was serious. Spartan forces now devastated Athenian farmland year-round, while thousands of slaves fled to Decelea, putting a stop to the flow of silver to Athens from mines in the Laurium district. Distressed Athens became increasingly reliant on food imported by sea.

Sparta sought funds to rebuild its fleet by coming to an understanding with Persia. In return for promised funds, Sparta agreed that the Persians could reassert their authority in the Greek cities on the coast of Asia Minor. In 412 BCE the Persians began sending money to the Spartans for shipbuilding. Now with Persia backing Sparta, the end for Athens seemed certain.

Athens Reorganizes and Its Allies Revolt (413–411 BCE).   Even after such crushing blows, Athens demonstrated its resilience by continuing to fight for another nine years. Yet many Athenians now advocated curbs on democracy to curtail the power of the assembly and council, both of which had endorsed the disastrous Sicilian expedition. Before the end of 413 BCE the Athenian had elected a committee of ten elderly counselors (*probouloi*) to advise the two bodies and to conduct the war with more responsibility and efficiency. Moreover, the Athenians employed emergency funds to construct new warships, for nearly three-fourths of the fleet had been lost in Sicily. They attempted to tackle their financial problems by abolishing the usual tribute on their subjects and instead imposing a flat customs tax of five percent on all imports and exports from or to the harbors of the empire. The remission of the tribute failed to satisfy the unhappy subject states, however, now seething with plots of rebellion. In the summer of 412 BCE Alcibiades sailed with a few Spartan ships to Chios—the last remaining free Athenian ally—and successfully engineered a revolt. As the winter of 412–411 BCE wore on, the Athenian Empire slowly unraveled amid revolts.

The Oligarchic Seizure of Power and the Dismantling of Athenian Democracy: The Rule of the Four Hundred (411 BCE).   After a hundred years of democracy, revolution broke out in Athens, with Alcibiades playing a directive role from afar. In 412 BCE Alcibiades had fled to Ionia from the enmity of King Agis of Sparta, whose wife he had reportedly seduced. Scheming for his restoration in Athens, Alcibiades apparently persuaded the Persian satraps to cut their subsidies to Sparta. Then, in the summer of the same year, he sent word to the officers of the Athenian fleet at Samos that Persian aid would be forthcoming if an oligarchy were established at Athens. The welcome prospect of receiving much-needed funds from Persia persuaded a number of the officers to become involved in an antidemocratic movement. Meanwhile the Athenian democratic leadership, whose imperial designs had brought on the ruinous war with Sparta, had already been discredited, and large numbers of the poorer, prodemocratic citizens were serving on the fleet at Samos. Backed by conservatives and farmers, the oligarchic party quickly gained strength in Athens. In 411 BCE several democratic leaders were assassinated by unknown knife wielders, intimidating both the assembly and democrats. The oligarchs then gained control of affairs by holding a meeting of the assembly more than a mile beyond the walls of Athens, thereby limiting attendance primarily to hoplites, mounted soldiers, and affluent men with full armor because the poorer, unarmed citizens were frightened by the possibility of encountering Spartan raiders. The assembly abolished all existing offices, decreed the ending of pay for government service—except in the military—and created a revolutionary oligarchic council known as the Four Hundred to serve as the executive body of the state. The assembly also authorized the establishment of the Five Thousand. As a means of eliciting moderate support, the oligarchs had promised that the Four Hundred would draw up a list of five thousand citizens, all of whom would be men of sufficient wealth to furnish themselves with full body armor. The Five Thousand were to serve as the voting citizens and ultimate governing body for the remainder of the war, but the Four Hundred had no intention of proceeding to the nomination of the Five Thousand and relinquishing their own power. Ruling through terror and fear, the Four Hundred established a violent guard of 120 youths to intimidate or murder their opponents, but the oligarchs failed to obtain what they most wanted—Persian gold—and they soon broke with Alcibiades.

The Establishment of the Five Thousand (411 BCE).   Meanwhile the sailors attached to the Athenian war fleet at Samos—who would have been disfranchised by the oligarchic plan—threatened to sail home and restore democracy unless the Four Hundred stepped aside. When the Peloponnesian fleet sailed in 411 BCE to aid the Euboeans, now eager to revolt, the thoroughly frightened Four Hundred sent out a small fleet from Athens that was badly defeated. The Athenians were terrified, for they had been dependent on Euboea for many essential supplies, they had few sea-worthy ships left in their harbor, and the fleet at Samos remained hostile to the oligarchic regime at Athens. Had the Spartans followed up their victory, they probably could have brought the war to a conclusion. Meanwhile the anxious Athenians called an assembly, which ousted the disgraced Four Hundred and turned the government over to the Five Thousand, those citizens able to furnish hoplite equipment. The number five thousand should be regarded as theoretical, however, because the actual number of men with full citizenship rights seems to have been closer to nine thousand. Thus the extremists had been replaced by moderate oligarchs. Both Thucydides and Aristotle praised the government of the Five Thousand—which operated through a complicated system of revolving committees—for its efficiency.

The Peloponnesians Attack the Athenian Black Sea Route (411–410 BCE).   In the meantime the sailors at Samos had recalled the now wiser and somewhat more mature Alcibiades, entrusting him with command of their fleet. He was soon faced with a serious challenge, for in the summer of 411 BCE the Peloponnesians sailed across the Aegean, intent on cutting the vital Athenian grain route with the Black Sea and destroying Athens by starvation. The Peloponnesians won the allegiance of the prosperous city of Cyzicus on the Propontis, but Alcibiades and other commanders acted quickly to reestablish control over the Hellespont. During the autumn of 411 BCE the Athenians defeated the Spartan fleet off Abydos. Then in the spring of 410 BCE Alcibiades overtook the Peloponnesian fleet near Cyzicus, thereby recovering the Hellespont and saving Athens from starvation. His notable success prompted Sparta to offer Athens peace, with each side keeping the territory then held, except the Athenians should return Pylos and the Spartans Decelea. The terms were stiff for Athens—Sparta would continue to occupy many cities in the Aegean and Asia Minor—but they far outweighed the possibility of inglorious defeat. Overconfident, the Athenian assembly rejected the Spartan peace proposal as insufficient.

Restoration of Democracy and the Final Exploits of Alcibiades (410–406 BCE).   The successes in the Hellespont by the prodemocratic fleet brought significant repercussions in Athens, swayed by the strong political voice of the men providing the crews. Prodemocratic Athenians, with hardly any bloodshed, managed to reestablish full democracy, thereby opening the assembly again to all adult male citizens and reinstating pay for public service. Although most of the subject states of the empire had revolted, Samos still remained loyal, and the army and navy carried on the war from that island base. Meanwhile Alcibiades, at the height of his popularity after having won several important naval victories, returned to Athens in 407 BCE amid loud shouts of joy and enthusiasm. The Athenians promptly gave him special powers of command. Sailing back to war, Alcibiades failed in a campaign to reconquer Ionia, and his enemies began to whisper that he intended to become a military tyrant. Soon, in 406 BCE, the Athenians were defeated in a naval battle off Notiom, a town north of Ephesus, where Alcibiades had left a subordinate in charge with explicit orders not to engage the Spartans. The fickle Athenians accused Alcibiades of endangering their forces by leaving an incompetent officer in charge. Rather than return home to face his enemies in an angry court of inquiry, he withdrew to a private fortress on the European shore of the Hellespont.

Cyrus the Younger Forms an Alliance with Lysander (408–407 BCE).   Sparta had entrusted its naval command for 408–407 BCE to Lysander, an exceptionally able general and politician. Lysander struck up a close friendship with Cyrus the Younger, then serving as viceroy of Asia Minor at the behest of his father, King Darius II, and thereby gained Persian financial backing for the rebuilding of the Spartan fleet. Meanwhile Athens won one final great sea battle in August of 406 BCE off the Arginusae islands, south of Lesbos, but a sudden storm arose that prevented the rescue of survivors and the recovery of the dead from disabled ships and the water. Great indignation arose in Athens at the news of the casualties, and the outraged assembly sentenced six of the victorious generals—two had fled—to death without a proper trial. Among the six victims was the younger Pericles, son of Pericles and his mistress Aspasia.

Peloponnesian Victory at Aegospotami (405 BCE).   Their many disasters notwithstanding, the Athenians still remained dominant at sea and were anxious to draw Lysander, who had resumed command of the Peloponnesian fleet after the battle of Arginusae, into a naval engagement. The resourceful Lysander had crossed the Aegean and captured Lampsacus, a city on the Hellespont in the northern Troad. He decided to make Lampsacus his headquarters, and the Athenians took up their position on the opposite side of the strait, operating from an open beach without harborage near the mouth of the Aegospotami River. For several days the Athenians sailed to Lampsacus each morning, but they were unable to lure the Peloponnesian fleet from its protected harbor. They would return in the afternoon to their unprotected base on the European side of the strait, where they beached most of their ships and went ashore. Alcibiades came down from his fortress to urge them to move to the protected harbor of Sestos, but he was snubbed and his advice ignored. The Athenians foolishly relaxed their guard when returning to the beach on the fifth day of the maneuvers. The watchful Lysander made a swift attack against their fleet. Because most of the Athenian crews were on land searching for provisions that afternoon in late August or early September of 405 BCE, their vessels fell into Lysander's hands without a struggle. The next day three or four thousand prisoners were

Combat scene, from an Attic red-figure amphora painted by the Suessula Painter, *c*. 400 BCE. Metropolitan Museum of Art, New York.

butchered in cold blood and their corpses denied funeral rites. Now that Lysander had thus cut the vital grain route from the Black Sea, his only remaining task was to take Athens itself.

The Fall of Athens (404 BCE).   As the Peloponnesian fleet proceeded toward Greece, the wily Lysander forced all the Athenians he encountered on the islands to return to Athens as a means of swelling the population because he intended to starve the city into submission. He arrived at Piraeus a few weeks later and blockaded the harbor. Meanwhile a Spartan army entered Attica to reinforce the garrison at Decelea. After enduring an eight-month siege by land and sea during the autumn and winter of 404 BCE, the starving Athenians capitulated. Both Corinth and Thebes clamored for the full destruction of Athens, which meant massacring the men and selling the women and children into slavery, the same fate the Athenians had so often inflicted on others. Yet the Spartan leaders resisted annihilating the city whose citizens had fought the Persian invaders with such valor. Much more critical was their desire to maintain Athens as a counterweight against the power of

Corinth, feared for its large navy and strategic location on the narrow land bridge connecting southern and central Greece, thus potentially controlling access to and from the Peloponnese. The prostrate Athenians accepted Sparta's severe terms for peace, including the destruction of the Long Walls and those of Piraeus, the forfeiture of all but twelve ships, the dissolution of what remained of the empire, and the pledge to become a subject ally of Sparta. The Athenians and their conquerors together pulled down the Long Walls to the music of the aulos—a wind instrument akin to the clarinet or oboe—and the Peloponnesians joyously proclaimed that liberty had been restored to the Greeks. Now Lysander would determine the course of events on the mainland and the Aegean islands. As the Athenians gave up their fleet and claims to empire, he sailed off to subdue Samos, the only remaining former Athenian possession that had not capitulated.

POSTWAR POLITICAL DEVELOPMENTS IN ATHENS

The Thirty Institute a Reign of Terror (404 bce)

The Spartans left a garrison in Attica to keep the peace and protect their interests. Whereas the Athenians had traditionally championed democratic government, the Spartans were avid supporters of oligarchy. Thus Athens—as a satellite of Sparta—would have to adopt some form of oligarchic rule. The moderate oligarchs in Athens were led by Theramenes, a leader in the government of the Five Thousand, but his proposals were pushed aside by the extreme oligarchs, foremost of whom was the aristocratic Critias, a noted poet and cynical politician backed by Lysander. Under intimidation from Lysander, a board of thirty ruling oligarchs was established as the ruling power. The Thirty, led by Critias and supported by Spartan troops, held Athens in complete subjection through a policy of merciless terrorism and corruption. When Theramenes protested their tactics, Critias compelled him to commit suicide by drinking hemlock. The Thirty—they fully deserved the nickname *Thirty Tyrants*—eventually executed about fifteen hundred Athenians, and many others fled to the hills. One of these was a moderate democratic politician named Thrasybulus, who took refuge in a frontier fortress and began organizing a military force to resist the government. After Thrasybulus defeated the Thirty in a major battle at Piraeus in 403 bce, they sought refuge in Eleusis.

Restoration of Athenian Democracy (403 bce)

In response to the democratic resistance at Piraeus, King Pausanias of Sparta soon appeared before Athens with an army, but he disapproved of Lysander's policies that were leading to a civil war and alienating most Athenians from any commitment to Sparta. The able king, who preferred keeping a loyal ally to maintaining an oligarchic government, permitted the restoration of democracy. Two years later, in 401 bce, the Athenians captured Eleusis and executed the survivors of the

Thirty. Athens had suffered ruinous disruptions from wartime conditions, however, and now survived as a weak, economically mutilated state. The Athenians had lost their Long Walls, their empire, their fleet, and at least half their population. Yet the complex portrait of the Athenians includes far more than victories and defeats in battle, for their astonishingly resilient and creative culture reflects great triumphs in art, literature, and philosophy as well as extraordinary developments in politics and society.

CHAPTER XI

PERICLEAN ATHENS: LIFE AND SOCIETY

The fifth century BCE in Athens remains one of the greatest epochs of cultural flowering in the history of western civilization. Historians commonly label a segment of the century the Age of Pericles, referring to the years from 443 to 429 BCE, when Pericles was the virtual ruler of Athens. Time limits cannot be rigidly fixed for the era called Periclean, however, for feats such as the construction of the Parthenon—begun in 447 BCE—should be included. Pericles' lofty vision of civilization helped to propel his community toward extraordinary political, social, and cultural achievements.

POLITICAL DEVELOPMENTS

ATHENIAN DEMOCRACY

Pericles Oversees the Completion of the Democratic Constitution.   Pericles was born to an aristocratic family. His mother descended from the famous Alcmaeonid clan and his father was a respected soldier-politician who served as an admiral at Mycale. Membership in a distinguished family was a distinct advantage in the democracy of ancient Athens because the citizens generally preferred to elect their political leaders from the aristocrats, some of whom had taken the lead in democratizing government in the late 500s and early 400s BCE. In this tradition, Pericles was an avid supporter of democracy and strongly favored the mass participation by the citizens in the political machinery of the state. With his lucid and persuasive speech, Pericles encouraged the Athenians to complete their democratic constitution. Athens became a full democracy in the Greek sense of the word, for all citizens—the adult Athenian males—were qualified to hold office and to direct state decisions by debate and vote in the assembly. Moreover, in 450 BCE Pericles had introduced the leading feature of his democratic reforms, the payment of regular salaries to state officials, so even poorer citizens could afford to serve in the government.

The Role of Social Classes in the Government.   Class differences were never fully eradicated in democratic Athens, though political rights became nearly equal. The aristocrats—the Eupatrids—consisted of the first two of Solon's four citizen classes based on income (the *pentakosiomedimnoi* and the *hippeis*), but in Pericles' day only a few financial officials were still restricted to the upper classes. Because the archonship became a paid office about this time, there was no good reason to restrict the position to the two wealthiest classes. Thus the third class, the *zeugitai*, became eligible for the post, and soon the fourth class, the *thetes*, as well. Yet the old income classes continued to function as a convenient means for determining the ability of a man to render financial and military service to the state. Certain public burdens, for example, were assigned to the wealthy rather than the poor, one of the ways ancient Greek society avoided direct taxes. Such public service was known as a liturgy (*leitourgia*) and was regarded by aristocrats as an honor and duty for which a man should not be paid. Men were selected, for example, to provide choruses for the dramatic performances at the festivals of Dionysus. The most costly of the liturgies was known as the trierarchy. Those men selected as trierarchs were obligated to sail on the triremes—each trireme carried one trierarch—as well as to collect crews for the vessels and to repair them at their own expense.

Athenian Citizenship.   In the fifth century BCE, as in the sixth, Athenian citizenship was based on membership in the demes, which were the townships, or smallest political divisions of Attica and hence the centers of local government. The members of the demes, as noted in chapter 5, elected local officials and oversaw the nominations for state office. Each deme maintained the list of its own members. A male was registered as a citizen in his father's deme upon reaching the age of eighteen, and he always kept his membership in his hereditary deme, even if moving to another. Moreover, each citizen took the name of his deme as the third element of his official name; for example, Pericles, of Xanthippus, Cholargus (son of Xanthippus, from the deme of Cholargus). The demes were divided among the ten artificial tribes inaugurated by Cleisthenes in the late sixth century BCE. The artificial tribes, in turn, were the basic units for the allocation of officials on boards and in the military service.

In earlier periods the sons of Athenian men and foreign women were regarded as citizens of Athens. Yet an unwillingness to share the profits of empire and the desire to keep Athenian blood pure, among other reasons, prompted Pericles to propose a law in 451 BCE that denied citizenship to sons of mixed marriages. Thus the Athenian citizen body was limited to the adult sons of Athenian parents. Had the law been enacted earlier, Pericles himself would not have been an Athenian citizen because his great-grandmother was Agariste of Sicyon.

The Population.   Population figures are difficult to estimate for the fifth century BCE, partly because the records of the various Greek states were concerned primarily with the duties of citizens rather than the counting of women, children, slaves, or resident aliens. No accurate record of figures for the population of Attica exists. Fragments of information suggest the population reached about 330,000 in the fifth century BCE, with around 50,000 citizens, 150,000 Athenian women and children, 30,000 resident aliens—known as metics—and 100,000 slaves.

The Assembly.   The mainspring of government in the Athenian democracy was the assembly, or *ekklesia*, which was open to all citizens and served as the sole legislative body and the sovereign political body of the state. The assembly embraced all citizens over the age of eighteen, but in practice attendance was generally limited to those over twenty because Athenian youths were obligated to participate in military training and garrison duty during their nineteenth and twentieth years. The estimate mentioned above suggests there were roughly 50,000 Athenian citizens in 431 BCE, but the assembly was usually attended by only about 5,000 residents of Athens or the immediate vicinity.

Although the assembly customarily met four times a month on the slopes of the Pnyx, the body might be convened daily in a crisis. The meetings opened with a solemn prayer and sacrifice, but if the proceedings were interrupted by a sign from heaven—exemplified by a storm or a shower—the assembly was dissolved immediately. A speaker presided over meetings of the assembly, a herald made the announcements, and a secretary kept records of the proceedings. Every citizen in Attica enjoyed the right to enter the debate, offer amendments, and vote, but usually the leaders of the various political factions or a generally recognized political leader such as Pericles carried the discussion. The assembly was responsible for electing the ten generals (the *strategoi*), revising the laws, enacting taxes—rare—and other financial measures, voting on war and peace, receiving embassies from foreign states, and making a multitude of other state decisions. Although powerless to initiate legislation, the assembly could ratify, amend, or reject any proposal submitted by the Council of Five Hundred or the various magistrates.

The Council of Five Hundred (Boule).   Each measure was brought to the assembly as a resolution (*probouleuma*) by the Council of Five Hundred. From this council, or *boule*, came the presiding officers of the assembly. Most of the significant powers formerly exercised by the conservative Council of the Areopagus were transferred to the Council of Five Hundred in 462 BCE. At that time the Areopagus lost its supervision over the laws and its right to punish officials violating them. Comprising the ex-archons of Athens, the Areopagus had steadily lost influence after the method of selecting archons was changed from election to lot in 487 BCE. Now the Council of Five Hundred determined the fitness of candidates for office and kept a strict watch over magistrates. Moreover, all the agencies of the government reported to the council. The council also supervised the construction of triremes and public buildings and prosecuted cases of treason before the assembly.

Although the citizens were sovereign through their power in the assembly, the administration of the government was carried out by the smaller, more manageable Council of Five Hundred. Yet, as noted in chapter 5, five hundred men were too many to keep in permanent session, and the fifty councilors from each tribe served as rotating executive committees known as prytanies when the council was not meeting. The prytanies—each met for one-tenth of the year—carried out the day-to-day business of the council. Through its prytanies, the Council of Five Hundred was in continuous session, and a third of the functioning prytany remained constantly on duty and in residence in the Tholos, the round building next to the meeting hall (the Bouleuterion) of the council.

The council was composed of fifty members from each tribe, chosen by lot for one year from citizens over thirty years of age. All such citizens were eligible to serve in the council, except that no man could be a member more than twice in his lifetime. Every citizen, besides being a continual member of the assembly, was almost certain to be chosen at least once in the course of his life as a member of the Council of Five Hundred. Had the members of the council held their terms for life, they could have exercised a virtual stranglehold over the government because of their control of many political affairs. Although their term of office was only a year, the members of the council still served as a brake on the *ekklesia* through their power to formulate measures to be considered by the popular assembly. After the assembly had expressed its will, however, the Council of Five Hundred dutifully supervised the magistrates in executing the *ekklesia*'s policy.

The Heliaea.   The ordinary Athenian citizen exercised control over the administration of justice through the law court known as the *heliaea*. Instituted by Solon, the *heliaea* functioned originally as a court of appeal from the decisions of the aristocratic archons. With the decline of the importance of the archonship, however, the *heliaea* developed into a criminal court of primary jurisdiction, though homicide cases continued to be tried in other courts. Every year 6,000 jurors (*dikasts*)— 600 from each tribe—were selected by lot from those citizens over thirty years of age who volunteered to be enrolled as candidates. The usual jury consisted of several hundred men, and decisions were rendered by majority vote. In the fourth century BCE odd numbers such as 501 were used to avoid a deadlock. The primary reason for the large jury was to make bribery difficult and to guard against intimidation. As an added safeguard against corruption, the jurors were not informed about the cases they would try until the beginning of actual proceedings.

The state did not initiate trials, but any citizen could bring a suit in his own interest or in the interest of the polis. The case first came before a public arbitrator in an attempt to settle the dispute out of court. Many cases were settled on an equitable rather than a legal basis through such arbitration, which served to lighten the work of the court, but those that could not be resolved in that manner went to the *heliaea*. The *heliaea* had no judge giving direction or advice to the jury, though an appropriate magistrate presided over each case. The jury decided the question of guilt and set the penalty. Jurors took an oath to render their decisions in accordance with the laws of Athens, and from the time of Pericles they received the modest pay of two (later three) obols for every day of duty. Because the fee was quite small, many of the volunteers for jury service were men who were too old for work.

Until the first half of the fourth century BCE, trial witnesses gave their testimony orally, but thereafter their testimony was taken beforehand by the magistrate in writing, and they merely gave assent when their statements were read aloud in court. Women, children, and slaves did not appear in court as witnesses. Written evidence of slaves was admissable, however, if given under torture. Every man had to plead his own case, that is, serve as his own lawyer, though he could employ a skilled orator to write his speech. The principals were allowed to question each other, and the members of the jury were authorized to ask questions to clarify points in the testimony. The chief weakness of the Athenian system of justice was that a jury might be too easily swayed by a skillful speaker. Religion and other emotionally charged issues were frequently interjected to influence the jury, and the reputation of the contestants was also important in determining the outcome. Yet the jurors, who lacked adequate legal training or experience, were expected to distinguish true from false statements. They heard no impartial summation by a judge and had no opportunity for discussion, for they were required to vote immediately at the close of the trial.

In the fifth century BCE a juror voted by placing a pebble or shell in an appropriate urn, one of the urns being used for the deposit of votes for an acquittal and the other for a conviction. No appeal was allowed. Some penalties were fixed by law, but in other cases—when the accused was convicted—each party submitted a proposed penalty and the jury decided which one to accept. Naturally, the penalty proposed by the accused was more lenient than that of the accuser. Public penalties were enforced by the magistrates, and customary penalties included fines, disfranchisement, confiscation of property, confinement in the stocks, exile, or death. Greek criminal law, however, did not utilize long terms of imprisonment as a penalty. In capital cases the sentence was carried out immediately after the announcement of the verdict.

The Generals and Lesser Magistrates.   The structure of the magistracies had not been changed since the time of Cleisthenes, but they had been considerably democratized by the inauguration of payment for government service, the introduction of appointment by lot (sortition) for most offices, and the great increase in the number of those serving the state in an official capacity. All the magistrates except military officers were paid. Historians estimate that of the roughly fifty thousand Athenian citizens, around twenty thousand men were on the payroll, including jurors, sailors, and soldiers. Tribute from the empire made this possible.

The state officials called archons were chosen by lot after 487 BCE. Selection by random chance often brought mediocre men to the fore and eclipsed the office. The nine archons, once the most important officials of the Athenian state, now generally enjoyed only narrow religious and courtroom duties. The archon eponymous (the first archon)—who had served as the chief magistrate until 487 BCE—remained the nominal head of state, continued to name the year, and retained jurisdiction over cases involving family matters. The archon *basileus* (the king archon) still exercised jurisdiction over the Eleusinian Mysteries, in addition to performing sacrifices and other religious duties of the former kings. The polemarch, who had commanded the army until 487 BCE, retained several religious duties, and he continued to be in charge of the funeral games held in honor of men killed in war. The six junior archons (the *thesmothetai*) still presided over a large number of legal cases and acted as recorders of judicial decisions. In short, the nine archons had become routine officials, though they retained significant sentimental importance in Periclean Athens. (In the fifth or fourth century BCE there were seven junior archons, the six *thesmothetai* and their secretary. The secretary had been added to raise the number of archons to ten, permitting one to be chosen from each of the ten tribes established by Cleisthenes.)

The highest magistrates and the chief executive officers of the administration were now the ten generals, the *strategoi*, who were elected annually by the assembly, but men demonstrating great ability might be reelected indefinitely. Pericles, for example, governed Athens by being elected *strategos* every year from 443 BCE to his death in 429 BCE. One general was chosen from each of the ten artificial tribes at first, but eventually they were elected from the entire citizen body without reference to tribes. Although the other magistracies had become weak under the impact of democracy, the *strategoi* were the exception. Combining military and political activities, the generals commanded the army and navy and presided over trials associated with military service. They attended to the defenses of the state and preparations for war. They enjoyed also the right of attending meetings of the Council of Five Hundred and recommending proposals to that body. Thus the office became a key position in the political life of fifth-century Athens. The only required qualifications were Athenian citizenship and the possession of land in Attica. Apparently they were unpaid, except when on active military service in wartime, and thus their office was liable to domination by wealthy families. The ten generals were theoretically equal, but the one with the strongest personality or the best oratorical skills tended to gain ascendancy over the others and to speak for the entire group. Although the *strategoi* functioned as the executives of the state, they were closely scrutinized by the council and could be prosecuted for failures in battle or for heavy combat losses. Such high-profile trials were often of a political nature, serving as tools of unscrupulous politicians.

The government included a host of other officials, most of whom were paid for their services. A few of the financial offices were filled by election and open only to members of the first two income classes, but the rest were chosen by lot and usually in boards of ten. All citizens had legislative duties, of course, but an Athenian might be chosen by lot to serve for a year on the boards as treasurers, auditors, supervisors of the grain supply, overseers of the roads, port superintendents, and other posts.

Finances.   Athens in the mid-fifth century BCE enjoyed an annual income of roughly one thousand talents (a talent was worth six thousand drachmas, and a drachma was the average daily wage of a skilled worker), an enormous sum for a Greek state at the time. About half of this amount came from the tribute paid by the subject states of the empire. Moreover, Athens received rent from leasing some of its property such as olive orchards, public buildings, pastures, and the silver mines at Laurium. Other sources of income included rent from leased land in the subject states, duties on imports and exports, market and harbor dues, a tax on resident aliens, court fees and fines, and confiscated property. All Greeks despised direct taxation as unbefitting a free people, and none was levied on Athenian citizens except in cases of dire emergency. Yet we noted that wealthy citizens were subject to various liturgies, that is, special public services that included major outlays such as providing a share of the cost for maintaining a vessel, or training and equipping of a chorus in the public festivals, or promoting various athletic events. Because the Athenians recognized the importance of acquiring and managing state funds, financial officials—always men of wealth—were elected rather than chosen by lot. Pericles himself was a careful financier, and Athens enjoyed a huge reserve of six thousand talents at the opening of the Peloponnesian War in 431 BCE.

The Debate about Athenian Democracy.   Governed by the whole body of its citizens (*demos*), Athens was a democracy by the standards of the ancient Greeks. Yet the forging of democracy did not mean changing common Greek assumptions about noncitizens or granting them rights. The Periclean citizen body was a closed and inaccessible group, with women, children, resident aliens, and slaves lacking political voice. Citizens in Athens and other Greek cities regarded women as members of a separate order following an essentially private rather than public life, and they viewed resident aliens and slaves as subordinate or inferior.

Although political discord was typical in Greek cities, the Athenian system of government worked reasonably well under Pericles. After his death Athenian democracy was often at the mercy of demagogues. Political leaders tried to survive by offering the masses various advantages and privileges, many of which were detrimental to the well-being of Athens. Meanwhile the fickle Athenian citizens were all too willing to oust their leaders, principled or otherwise, and they eventually repudiated almost every great leader of democratic Athens. For example, they fined Miltiades, ostracized Themistocles and Cimon, and even lashed out at Pericles from time to time, though he died in office. Perhaps we should not be surprised that a number of surviving literary sources express antidemocratic ideas. The great comic poet Aristophanes, who was active during the Peloponnesian War, penned plays ridiculing the politics, social attitudes, and philosophy of his day. Another critic of democracy was an anonymous aristocrat commonly called the Old Oligarch. About 430 BCE he produced a bitter satiric pamphlet against Athenian democracy, depicting the masses of the citizen body as ignorant men promoting aggressive imperialism and legislating for their own benefit. The Old Oligarch notes that the wealthy—identified as the best suited to govern—were exploited in the interests of the lower classes, and he refers to democracy as "rule of the worst."

Another view appears in Pericles' famous funeral oration, as freely reconstructed by the historian Thucydides. The speech was delivered at the public funeral honoring those who had fallen in battle during the first year of the Peloponnesian War. Instead of merely praising the dead, Pericles glorifies Athenian democracy, which he contrasts with the Spartan government permitting only a few to participate in any significant way. The speech expresses the idea that the Athenian system protects the collective interest of the entire state, not just the lower classes, as opponents charged. Thucydides puts emphatic words in Pericles' mouth: "Our constitution . . . favors the many instead of the few; this is why it is called a democracy. If we look to the laws, they afford equal justice to all in their private differences; if to social standing, advancement in public life falls to reputation for capacity, class considerations not being allowed to interfere with merit. . . ."

SOCIETY AND ECONOMY

SOCIAL CLASSES

The philosopher Aristotle, reflecting the view of the Greek aristocracy, observed that the precondition for a civilized life is leisure, which provides time to enjoy politics, education, and other noble pursuits of life. Educated Greeks regarded physical work as socially and morally degrading, an activity born of necessity. Even providers of specialized services such as teachers were denied high status in society. Yet earning a living was an inescapable routine for most Athenians, who performed labor for the powerful and wealthy.

Small-Scale Farmers.   Attica was dotted with small farms and shops at the outbreak of the Peloponnesian War in 431 BCE. Urban intellectuals seemed to take delight in ridiculing the large population of free farmers. Yet small-scale farmers, working their own land, formed the backbone of the Athenian democracy and the bulk of the hoplites in the army. They helped provide political stability during peacetime and fought bravely for the state in periods of war. The majority of the free farmers fell into the third income class of the *zeugitai*.

Aristocrats and Wealthy Merchants.   Although the characteristic Athenian farmer was the small landholder, aristocratic families possessed great ancestral estates in the country. Many lived in suitable villas and operated their holdings with the help of tenant farmers, hired laborers, and slaves. Others moved to the city, leaving their estates in charge of stewards. The leaders of the noble houses still dominated Athenian political life, for ordinary citizens chose among aristocrats when electing officials. After the Persian Wars, the aristocracy forged the Delian League to protect Greece from Persian power, though the alliance ultimately developed into what is now termed the Athenian Empire. A vast bureaucracy was established to keep records of the financial obligations of the cities of the empire and to administer tribute. Imperial revenues were used to rebuild the Athenian temples burned by the Persians. State projects were let out to private individuals contracting to perform work or provide supplies, with countless opportunities arising for business ventures. The creation of hundreds of new officials produced a non-noble wealthy class now undercutting aristocratic control of Athenian public and economic life. Shipbuilders produced large numbers of triremes for the navy, while contractors busied themselves with public works. Many investors opened factories and shops, which were concentrated in the Agora. In short, common people of wealth and influence increasingly entered the ranks of the first two income classes (*pentakosiomedimnoi* and *hippeis*).

Free Workers in the City.   The free workers in Athens consisted of hired laborers and artisans. Increasing employment opportunities in the city greatly benefited the landless *thetes*, the fourth income class, who worked as hired laborers on building projects and found an important role as rowers in the fleet. The majority of artisans in Athens fell within the third income class of the *zeugitai*. While some of them were herders who lived in Athens but led their sheep and goats out to pasturage during the day, others were farmers who went out in the morning to cultivate their nearby fields. Many of the *zeugitai* in Athens rented or owned houses where they conducted their trades as weavers, tanners, dyers, cobblers, blacksmiths, carpenters, retail dealers, or teachers. Archaeologists working along the south and west sides of the Agora have found evidence of a variety of crafts, including pottery, smithery, and sculpture.

The Metics.   Pericles, following a policy begun by Solon, encouraged foreigners to live and work in Athens. Known as metics (*metoikoi*, or dwellers among), the resident aliens abounded in the larger and more prosperous Greek cities, attracted by business opportunities. Most metics in Athens were Greeks from other states, but there were also Syrians, Phoenicians, Egyptians, and others. Not all foreigners living in Athens obtained the privileged status of the metic class. Each metic had to be sponsored by a citizen, who probably represented him in court. The metics were burdened with a special annual tax and were forbidden from owning land or voting but required to perform military services. They served in the army in separate divisions and were also employed as rowers in the fleet. In exchange, they were free to engage in trade and manufacturing, and they enjoyed the protection of Athenian law. Socially and economically diverse, the metic class controlled a large share of Athenian import-export and manufacturing ventures. Occasionally citizenship was conferred on a metic by special grant for meritorious service to the state. At Athens, a freed slave acquired the status of a metic.

Slaves.   The modern idea that all people are born equal would have been unthinkable in the ancient world. Aristotle seems to have expressed the general view when he noted in Book I of his famous work on political theory, the *Politics*, that a law of nature mandates the free to rule the slave, as the male rules the female. Slave labor was fundamental to the ancient Greek economy, and apparently few people—including slaves—imagined a society free of the brutal institution. Legally, slaves were pieces of property and could be bought, sold, or bequeathed. Whether male or female, slaves owed their masters labor and service, including sexual favors, if requested. Adult male slaves, purchased primarily for heavy labor, were in far less demand than women, teenagers, and children, purchased primarily for domestic service. Slaves were acquired in several ways. Some were born to slave mothers. A major source of slaves was war with foreign states, with victorious Greeks customarily selling non-Greek captives taken in battle as slaves while holding Greeks for ransom. Yet warring Greeks often enslaved defeated Greeks, a practice many Greeks found repugnant. We noted that the Athenians slaughtered the men and enslaved the women and children of Melos in 416 BCE. In time of peace, Greek pirates might return home with captives from Thrace, Scythia, and Asia Minor. Sometimes, slave dealers took unwanted infants left to die of exposure by their parents and reared them to be sold as slaves.

Much of the work performed by slaves in the ancient world would be done today by laborsaving machinery. Their treatment varied considerably. Huge gangs of the more intractable slaves were leased for work in the silver mines, where they were considered expendable and worked unmercifully to an early death. Yet self-interest at least prompted most owners to treat skilled slaves more humanely. Rural slaves labored at their owner's side on a small farm, or they worked under an overseer, himself a slave, on the large estates of the aristocrats. Slaves in the city were employed in every kind of work, particularly in domestic service in the wealthier households, where they did the cooking, cleaning, spinning, and weaving. Older domestic slaves accompanied boys to school and supervised their behavior. Others labored alongside citizens and metics at highly skilled crafts such as fluting the columns of the temples. Shopkeepers usually paid their slaves a small share of the profits. An enterprising slave might gain the confidence of his owner and be permitted to rent a shop, buy a woman, and start his own family. Some even amassed sufficient funds to purchase their freedom and win recognition as resident aliens.

Economic Organization

Farming Methods.   Early Greek farmers left fields fallow for at least a year after a season's cultivation, allowing the soil to replenish its nutrients. Yet by around 400 BCE they had discovered the process of rotation, or the growing of different crops in succession in the same field. Moreover, farmers facilitated continuous cultivation of the soil by the addition of manure and decayed vegetation. In the valleys farmers used crude plows to plant grain between rows of olive trees, though scant rainfall restricted the scale of its cultivation, allowing the Athenians to raise only about a quarter of the grain needed to feed the population of Attica. Grain crops were reaped by sickles and then trampled by oxen or asses, a rather inefficient and wasteful means of threshing. Farmers terraced the hills to plant vineyards, while they tended olive orchards in the valleys. Grapes and olives were the staple crops of Attica, and farmers reaped financial gains by exporting wine and olive oil. Animals were valuable for their dairy products, wool, and hides. Except during the great festivals, farmers butchered only unproductive, sick, or injured animals. Thus meat was rarely served at Greek meals. Small-scale farmers raised goats and horses, but few cattle, and they kept bees to supply the ready market for honey. Most of these freeholders operated their farms with the help of their families and two or three slaves.

Industry.   Athenian industry advanced greatly in the time of the tyrants—the sixth century BCE—largely because of the influx of metics from Ionia and elsewhere with their new ideas and skills. The sixth-century money economy produced workshops where goods were manufactured for the needs of expanding markets. Fifth-century Athens was one of the most important industrial cities in Greece and was particularly noted for its ceramics and shipbuilding. Pottery flourished for both domestic use and export, especially to the Black Sea region and Italy. Other items produced both for the domestic market and for export included furniture, textiles, weapons and armor, cutlery, musical instruments, leather goods, and bronze and marble sculptures. Heavy industry did not exist, however, and workers used only the simplest tools. Every product was essentially handmade because, except for the potter's wheel and a few simple devices, manufacturing machinery did not exist. A few wealthy men owned large industrial establishments with perhaps forty workers—the largest on record employed 120 shield-makers during the Peloponnesian War—but the typical shop included the owner and his family, a few apprentices, and perhaps one or two slaves. By this time specialization was becoming increasingly important, with artisans in metal, leather, wood, and pottery attaining an increasingly higher economic and social standing.

Interior of a cup showing a young sculptor carving a wooden herm. The suggestive positioning of the adult herm—its penis typically erect—between the thighs of the beardless youth reflects the prevalence of homosexual relations between Greek men and boys. Detail of an Attic red-figure kylix by Epictetus, c. 520 BCE. National Museum, Copenhagen.

Trade.   A tendency toward specialization and greater volume was not limited to industry, for the same pattern appeared in seaborne trade during the Periclean period. Grain was paramount in Athenian commerce and was imported primarily from the vast fields north of the Black Sea as well as from Egypt and Sicily. Although conducted by private enterprise, the grain trade was protected and regulated by the government as an essential component of Athenian survival. Ordinances stipulated that at least two-thirds of the grain imported on ships controlled by Athens had to be sold in the city, though the remainder could be exported to other Greek cities. Imported timber, vital for shipping and the navy, was subject to similar regulation. Other imports included iron, paint, dyes, hides, fish, salt, ivory, glassware, papyrus, metalwork, and linen. We noted that Athens dominated the pottery market, exporting its esteemed painted ware throughout the Mediterranean, while its leading agricultural exports were wine and olive oil. Athenian trade encompassed a huge area stretching from Ukraine and southern Russia to Egypt and from Syria to the western Mediterranean. With its merchants and seafarers sailing amazing distances, Athens was the leading commercial center of the Greek world. For safety, merchant and naval ships generally ventured out only during the period from May to mid-September, when weather conditions in the Mediterranean tended to be favorable. Nothing short of a drastic emergency could induce seafarers to sail during autumn or winter.

The bottom of the commercial scale was occupied by the small retail trader—essentially a peddler—who bought goods from manufacturers or importers and sold them, perhaps by hawking the wares on the street or from a booth in the Agora. Such a retailer was known to the Greeks as a *kapelos*. The *emporos*, on the other hand, bought large consignments of goods from manufacturers and took them by ship from city to city, trading them for local products on the docks. Although most trade was seaborne, some merchants followed the difficult roads to Delphi and Olympia to sell goods in the fairs accompanying the great festivals.

Banking.   The expansion of seaborne trade was closely tied to investment banking. Many Greek temples had provided banking services in an earlier day, taking deposits and lending money, but individual bankers and capitalists began to appear about this time. The first bankers were money changers selling Athenian coins to visiting merchants and foreign coins to people planning to travel abroad. By the end of the fifth century BCE they were accepting funds on deposit and lending part of the capital out again. While wealthy merchants floated loans from the bankers at high rates of interest to acquire goods to sell abroad, manufacturers borrowed funds to buy raw materials and slaves. Bankers also made large loans to contractors of public works and mining companies. Rich upstart merchants and traders, who were despised by the old aristocratic families, now spent lavishly on themselves. Partly in reaction, many aristocrats borrowed money to maintain a social position they could ill afford.

The Agora.   Much of Athenian life centered in the marketplace, or Agora, the large public square centered midway between the Acropolis and the Dipylon, or main city gate. The Agora was the site of shops, temples, and buildings of state. The latter included the Bouleuterion, the meeting hall for the Council of Five Hundred, and the Tholos, the circular building where the rotating executive committees (prytanies) of the council were lodged. The hub of economic activities, the Agora was the place that money changers set up their tables, farmers offered to sell their produce, artisans displayed their wares, and merchants sold their goods from home and abroad.

DAILY LIFE

Houses and Furniture

Design of Houses.   The rich intellectual and cultural life of Periclean Athens stood in sharp contrast to the simplicity of private life. The poorest houses consisted of a mere two rooms, but most Greek dwellings were built according to an inward-looking design, with rooms arranged in an informal, variable manner around a central courtyard. In the more expensive houses the courtyard—the dominant feature of the dwelling—might include a simple colonnade on one or more sides. Entered from the street by means of an inconspicuous doorway and a narrow passageway, the typical courtyard contained an altar of Zeus of the Courtyard and House (Zeus Herkeios), the supreme protector of the household. Religion was a vital concern of the Greeks, and the various parts of the Greek house—like the Roman dwelling— were thought to be protected by their respective guardian deities. Hestia, for example, was the guardian of the sacred hearth. Few remains of houses have been found in Athens, but excavations have revealed many at Olynthus, a major city of the Chalcidic peninsula in the northwestern Aegean. A new quarter of the city was laid out in a grid pattern about 432 BCE, with broad avenues lined with houses. The dwellings at Olynthus generally contained five to seven rooms. The kitchen was identified in some of the houses by its sacred hearth and a flue for carrying off the smoke, and archaeologists also discovered a number of bathrooms containing terra-cotta bathtubs large enough for a person to enjoy in a sitting position, though not reclining. Water heated in the kitchen was used to fill the bathtub and then scooped up from a depression at its foot and poured over the body. Housing in other cities tended to be less formal than in the new quarter at Olynthus.

Obtaining water for drinking, bathing, and cleaning was a major concern throughout the Greek world. The Athenians enjoyed a rudimentary municipal water supply, for Pisistratus had built a number of aqueducts linking Athens with nearby mountains. The water was first carried to reservoirs and then channeled to public fountains in various parts of the city. The fountains were the primary source of water, though the courtyards of some larger houses contained wells.

Most light and air on the inside of a Greek dwelling was admitted through the open doors of the rooms arranged around the courtyard. Although the outer walls of some rooms were pierced by a few small windows, such openings were rare on the ground floor. Many Greek houses rose two stories and employed packed clay or terra-cotta tiles for the pitched roof. Solid stone, expensive and difficult to work, was reserved for the construction of public buildings and temples. Houses, on the other hand, were constructed mainly of sun-dried bricks, which were inexpensive to manufacture, and the walls were often covered with stucco. The sun-dried brick walls offered excellent protection against the stifling heat of a Greek summer. Floors might be paved of stone or stucco, but the inhabitants of humbler dwellings walked on the bare earth. Because the winters of the Aegean region are relatively mild and short, the Greeks were not forced to create elaborate heating systems. They took the chill off a room with a movable charcoal brazier, wore woolens in cold weather, and sunned themselves in the courtyard whenever weather permitted. The hearth provided additional warmth.

Separation of the Sexes.   Separate quarters were provided for men and women in the houses of the upper classes, but the cramped dwellings of the poor made such a segregation of the sexes impossible. The principal room in an upper-class house was the men's dining room, which might have some simple painted decoration. This was also the room where the men entertained their guests and was usually placed close to the entrance, just off the street, so the guests would not risk encountering the women of the house. Large houses also included a kitchen, a bathroom, workrooms, and bedrooms. Sometimes one or two rooms of a house formed a separate unit that opened on the street and served as a shop, factory, or elementary school. The room (or rooms) set aside for women was known as the *gynaikonitis*, which formed the larger part of the house because men spent most of their day outside the dwelling. The women's division of the house was located in the rear and the upper

The women of the Greek household undertook all steps in the production of the family's clothing and other textiles, from spinning to weaving and sewing. This scene shows two women demonstrating their weaving skills on a warp-weighted vertical loom. They walk back and forth from one end of the loom to the other to weave in the crossthreads, with new woolen cloth emerging inch by inch under their fingers. Detail of an Attic black-figure lekythos (a tall, narrow-necked oil bottle) by the Amasis Painter, c. 560 BCE. Metropolitan Museum of Art, New York.

story—if there was one—where there also might be one or two bedrooms. The women worked wool in a major room of the *gynaikonitis*. Although slaves performed many chores in affluent households, the housewife—even if aristocratic—was expected to participate in the respected tasks of spinning and weaving.

Furniture.   The Greeks possessed little furniture. Usually fashioned of carved wood, their furniture is known chiefly from vase paintings and reliefs. Around the sides of the wall in the men's dining room were couches. When dining, the men reclined on the left elbow, reaching for the food that had been placed on tables in front of them. The Greeks also furnished their houses with chairs, some with grace-ful curved legs and a semicircular back. High-backed chairs known as thrones were reserved as seats of honor for the master of the house and his guests. A throne served also as the seat for the god in a temple, while thrones in public buildings were set aside for judges and leaders of the people. Other furniture in private houses in-cluded stools, footstools, three-legged tables, washbasins, and storage chests, but not closets or cupboards. Utensils were kept on the floor or hung on the walls. As in Minoan Crete, grain, wine, and oil were stored in huge jars. Beds, which were laced with leather straps, were similar to dining couches and were covered with woolen blankets and linen sheets. Nighttime darkness was dispelled by torches or small oil lamps.

FOOD AND WINE

The Greek diet was based on grain, oil, and wine. Athenians usually ate little or no breakfast, a light lunch—sometimes no more than a crust of bread dipped in wine—and a heavier meal, dinner, in the late afternoon. Even the dinner fare was plain, perhaps consisting of bread and goat cheese, a vegetable, a handful of olives, probably some fish, and then followed by nuts and figs or other fruit. Wheat and barley formed the mainstay of the diet of most Greeks, the former usually being baked as bread and the latter made into porridge. Next to the vital grains, the main staple of the diet was provided by many species of fish, which might be fresh, dried, or pickled. The most plentiful vegetables were peas, beans, garlic, leeks, and onions, while a large variety of wild plants were eaten as salads. Eggs and poultry were popular foods, but red meat was rarely eaten except at the time of religious festivals. Honey was employed as a sweetener. The most important beverage for adults and children was wine, usually diluted with water. The Greeks had no distilled alcoholic liquors, and beer was associated with barbarians. Al-though the fifth-century BCE Greek diet was frugal and plain, the fare was nutri-tious and vitamin-rich.

THE SYMPOSIUM

A main focus of aristocratic social life was the all-male, after-dinner drinking party known as a symposium, which took place in the men's dining room. Propped up on their left elbows, usually two to a couch, the male participants wore garlands of flowers and often perfume. First, they chose a ruler of drinking, who decided how much water should be mixed with the wine. Libations and prayers opened and ended the symposium. The servers and entertainers were usually young female and male slaves, selected for their beauty. The entertainers typically included pipe play-ers, dancers, acrobats, and mimes. Some females among the entertainers might be *hetairai* (companions), who were obliged to offer the male guests sexual favors. Sim-ilarly, reflecting ancient Greek aristocratic taste, the symposium was often pervaded by a homoerotic atmosphere that was expressed through various homosexual activi-ties between guests or between guests and slaves. Reclining together on a couch,

The symposium provided an opportunity for males to court and embrace while reclining on couches, as demonstrated by this scene on the interior of an Attic red-figure kylix, c. 475 BCE. Louvre, Paris.

two males might express affection for one another with kisses and embraces or more intimate physical contact.

The guests at the symposium also told riddles and fables, played games, and sang drinking songs. The jovial party could grow into a display of riotous intemperance and sometimes lasted until the morning hours. Yet the symposium had an intellectual component, for the ruler might select a philosophical or political topic for discussion. A loosely defined literary genre known as symposium literature developed, one form of which described the discussions of guests at symposia, exemplified by Plato's dialogue the *Symposium*. Plato idealizes the symposium's dual sexual-intellectual character. In his fictional account a symposium serves as the setting for a series of contrasting speeches on a single philosophical topic—love—but by morning all the disputants except the celebrated Socrates had fallen asleep.

ATHENIAN CLUBS AND ASSOCIATIONS

Like-minded members of the aristocracy enjoyed various clubs, founded for the pursuit of a common end. The poorer citizens and the resident aliens were also attracted to voluntary social associations. Known in Athens from the time of Solon, Greek clubs typically served a religious, economic, or political function, while having a prominent social aspect. A large number of associations were of a religious nature, promoting the cult of a hero or god. Merchant associations advanced commercial ends. Numerous guilds were made up of workers in the same industry or trade. Moreover, various shops served as social centers, where all the workers, including slaves, enjoyed a sacred meal paid for by the employer on important days of the religious calendar.

Clothing and Jewelry

Wearing apparel was made at home, with the same piece of homespun cloth often serving as a garment by day, a blanket by night, and a shroud in death. The loose-fitting clothing of men and women was outwardly quite similar. The traditional Greek woman's garment was the heavy peplos, a sleeveless, straight-hanging tunic, generally of wool, typically extending to the feet, with the material at the top pinned around the shoulders. The peplos was often worn over a lighter garment. In a probably unreliable account, Herodotus tells us women were forbidden to wear the peplos around the middle of the sixth century BCE because some of them murdered the bearer of an unwelcome message with the long pins used to fasten the garment at the shoulders. By the fifth century BCE the fashionable garment for both women and men was the chiton, a rectangular piece of linen or woolen cloth draped according to individual taste. Fastened at the right shoulder with a clasp, the chiton formed a tunic that could be belted at the waist. The feminine variety, arranged in elaborate folds, was fuller and longer than the masculine and the side was pinned or stitched together, for the respectable Greek woman concealed herself, though the man's body was visible on the open side.

Workmen and farmers favored a tunic extending to the knees or above. Soldiers wore a similar short tunic under their body armor. Older Greek boys wore the chlamys, a skimpy piece of oblong woolen cloth arranged over the left shoulder and fastened by a clasp on the right. The wearer frequently arranged the short chlamys to reveal rather than conceal his body. For outdoor wear both men and women threw on a woolen cloak, the himation, usually placed over the left shoulder and fastened with a brooch over the right, leaving the right arm free. To wear the himation with grace and ease was a mark of refinement. Many men in the fifth century BCE wore the himation with nothing underneath, draping the cloak in a number of ways with varying degrees of modesty. Travelers sometimes wore a low, broad-rimmed hat. Although poorer people went barefoot at all times, other Greek men and women wore footwear such as sandals, leather boots, soft shoes, and clogs. Because the streets were unusually dirty, Greeks left their footwear at the door when entering a house.

Men used rings both as signets and ornaments. Women, in contrast to the simplicity of their dress, wore a wide variety of jewelry, including rings, necklaces, bracelets, anklets, and earrings, the last varying from simple rings to elaborate pendants. Women also painted their faces and invariably wore their hair long, unless they were slaves or in mourning. They often favored elaborate coiffures, frequently confined in nets. Boys reaching puberty offered some locks of their hair to a deity. Athenian males, except short-cropped slaves, let their hair grow according to changing fashion or personal taste. Although men of an earlier day had grown their beards quite long, barbers in Periclean Athens kept facial hair neatly trimmed.

THE ROLE OF ATHENIAN WOMEN

Virtually all our knowledge about the lives of women in the ancient world comes from male sources, especially from Athens. A cautious reading of Greek myth and Homer suggests that a few aristocratic women of the Mycenaean civilization in the Late Bronze Age may have enjoyed a moderate degree of social freedom, but the mass of evidence from Classical Greece shows women as subservient and isolated. Apparently most Greek men of the privileged classes viewed women as irrational and passionate beings whose one absolutely necessary role was producing legitimate children. Bearing legitimate children was crucial in a society reserving citizenship for the legitimate children of citizens. Except for Plato, Greek philosophers imagined women as intellectually inferior to men. Aristotle argues in the *Politics* that "the slave has no deliberative faculty at all; the woman has, but it is without authority, and the child has, but it is immature." Throughout her life a woman remained the guardian of her closest male relative—father, brother, husband, or son—and played no political role in the city. A female child from a respectable urban family remained at home under the tutelage of her mother and nurse, learning the skills of spinning and weaving, cooking, managing the household stores, and overseeing the domestic slaves. Perhaps she was also taught to read and write, but the girl was usually married very early in life to a man who might be as much as twenty years older.

Men rarely married under the age of thirty in Athens, but their wives were often barely in puberty. The bride enjoyed no say in the choice and was betrothed to her prospective husband by her father or nearest male relative. Marriage was considered complete when the bride's father paid the groom a dowry, a significant and often burdensome expense. The principal ceremony for a family with means was the wedding feast, customarily celebrated at the home of the father of the bride. Afterward the veiled bride accompanied her husband to his house, followed by a procession of revelers. At the hearth of the dwelling the bride and groom knelt down under a shower of nuts and delicacies, symbolizing the plenty that would attend the couple. The bride and groom then entered the bridal chamber, amid much singing and ribaldry by well-wishers, and here the marriage was consummated. The bride was now a member of her new household.

A respectable woman never appeared in public unless accompanied by a male guardian or chaperone. Although the wife was allowed to visit female friends, her associations with men were limited to her closest male relatives. Most men in Athens probably would have agreed with Pericles' observation in his funeral oration, as reported by Thucydides, that respectable women should absolutely avoid being "talked about by men, whether in praise or criticism." Athenian men were determined to ensure the chastity of their women by keeping them at home to produce legitimate children. Moreover, a woman who stayed in the house retained her pale complexion, itself prized as a sign of feminine virtue. Only in religion were women permitted to participate in public life to any degree. Women were thought to enjoy close communication with the divine, and they joined in the various holy day celebrations of Athens. Athena was the patron of the city, where more than

This vase painting of a wedding procession shows the bride and groom riding in the front of the lead cart (central scene) to the groom's house after the wedding banquet in the house of the father of the bride. Relatives and guests accompany the couple. A figure, probably the mother of the bride, leads the way carrying torches, while a woman waits at the doorway of the groom's house with a torch in hand. Attic black-figure lekythos by the Amasis Painter, c. 540 BCE. Metropolitan Museum of Art, New York.

forty priesthoods were reserved for women. Apparently these religious duties were rooted in a prehistoric belief in the magical properties of female fertility. Besides participating in various religious celebrations with men, women congregated without men for the autumn festival Thesmophoria, held to ensure a good harvest by honoring Demeter, goddess of grain and fertility.

The inferior role of women in Athens was maintained in many ways. The husband and father, who was expected to control his family, enjoyed every authority over his household that law and custom could provide. He had the right to accept or disown a child at birth. If he chose the latter, the baby was left to die of exposure (girls were more often abandoned than boys), though sometimes a passerby would rescue the infant. The husband also controlled family property. We saw that the wife was confined by social custom to the *gynaikonitis*, or women's quarters, of the house and did not make an appearance when her husband brought guests home for dinner. Besides bearing legitimate children, the Greek woman's main obligations were to protect the house, produce clothes, and rear the young. A husband could divorce his wife by sending her back to her father, who could then arrange a second marriage for her. Women could not own property. In case of a divorce or the death of husband, the woman's new guardian claimed both the woman and her dowry. Intellectual companionship between an older, worldly husband and his secluded young wife was virtually impossible, yet the need for bountiful reproduction meant that most couples engaged in some conjugal relations. Moreover, many marriages evidently led to bonds of genuine devotion between husband and wife. When the husband had no guests for the evening or was not invited out for a dinner party, he and his wife might share each other's company, and affectionate family groupings show up repeatedly on vase paintings and sculpture.

Males played female roles on the stage, though the actors portraying women in Athenian tragedies and comedies often fascinated the audience by enacting feminine roles that were completely contrary to contemporary social custom. The comic poet Aristophanes even has women seizing the Athenian government in his play the *Ecclesiazusae*. Certainly, the segregation of women was most rigorously binding among the upper and middle classes, for the urban poor and the rural population could not afford to practice severe sexual separation. In lower-class circles women often assisted their husbands on farms, in the shops, in the booths of the marketplace, or they might be obligated to work for pay, particularly as spinners or as wet nurses.

Aspasia

Female Prostitutes (Hetairai).   Women rarely figure in ancient Greek history, but both Sappho and Aspasia represent notable exceptions. Sappho (discussed in chapter 7) was an aristocratic, early sixth-century BCE lyric poet from Lesbos who remains famous for her personal honesty and superb mastery of imagery. Aspasia, on the other hand, lived in fifth-century BCE Athens and was a resident alien from Miletus. Athenian public opinion allowed women of resident alien families a degree of latitude from the customary norms, and some of them served men as personal "companions," or *hetairai*. The word *hetairai* is an Athenian euphemism because the primary purpose of these women—whether slave or free—was not just to provide men with companionship but to offer them sexual favors for long or short periods outside marriage. Although some of the *hetairai* served as prostitutes in brothels, others were expensive courtesans. The most talented and attractive of them sometimes became the mistresses of men of distinction.

Aspasia was an educated and accomplished courtesan whose sparkling conversation and brilliant mind drew some of the most famous intellectuals of the day, including Socrates, into her circle. Pericles was one of her ardent admirers, and at Aspasia's prompting he divorced his wife. Aspasia became Pericles' mistress in 445 BCE—he was thirty years her senior—and she continued in that capacity until his death. She bore a son named Pericles, who lacked Athenian citizenship and legitimacy under his father's own law of 451 BCE, but he received both by special decree in 429 BCE. The younger Pericles was one of the six victorious generals executed after a storm prevented them from picking up sailors following the naval battle off the Arginusae islands in 406 BCE.

Frequently attacked on the stage in comedies, Aspasia was accused of prompting Pericles to steer Athens into the Peloponnesian War. Although she may have exercised some political influence behind the scenes, we should remember that as a foreigner and a courtesan, Aspasia was exempt from the customary restrictions imposed on respectable women. Both sexes gossiped about her, and she was eventually prosecuted on a charge of impiety—the true motive was political—but was acquitted after Pericles made an impassioned plea for mercy. He even broke down and wept, and the spectacle swayed the jury to save her. Following Pericles' death, Aspasia shifted for herself, ending her days as the madam of a house of prostitution.

EDUCATION

Ancient Greek education was designed less for developing intellectual curiosity than for imparting physical and mental abilities benefiting the state. In Athens a girl's education—conducted by her mother and trusted servants—focused on spinning, weaving, cleaning, and other skills intended to make her a good housewife, though vase paintings indicate some girls attended elementary schools that were separate from those of boys. Sparta granted women of citizen rank a degree of independence unknown in other major Greek city-states, with young females appearing scantily clad or nude in ritual events and athletic training. The Spartan practice of physical training for girls, which was shocking to other Greeks, was designed to strengthen the female body for childbearing.

An Athenian boy was named on the tenth day after his birth. During the next observance of the Apaturia—the autumn festival celebrated by the social associations known as the phratries—his father declared an oath on his legitimacy. His name was then inscribed on the rolls of the phratry, thus assuring the boy's citizenship. Although he remained under the guidance of his mother and nurse for the first several years of his life, an Athenian boy of citizen rank began attending school about the age of seven. There were no state-funded schools, but the cost of attending private schools was low because teachers were usually lightly esteemed free men barely eking out a living from educational fees. Corporal punishment was widely employed, and pupils lived in constant dread of their teachers. Boys from wealthy families were accompanied to school by a *paidagogos*, an elderly and trusted slave who supervised and protected the boy but did not take part in the actual instruction. The *paidagogos* also taught the boy to wear his clothing to best advantage, to walk through the streets with a confident bearing and an easy stride, and to conduct himself in an honorable and becoming manner both at school and at play.

Although boys of lesser means pursued education for no more than the three or four years required to learn basic skills, the rest continued for as many as ten years in elementary school. Most pupils attended three schools, for there were three branches of elementary education: gymnastics, letters, and music. A boy normally started the day with training in gymnastics to develop both his physique and the competitive spirit essential to the successful warrior. Greeks regarded the training of the body as important as the education of the mind, and athletics assumed an increasingly important role as the boy approached young manhood. Training in gymnastics took place at a sports ground known as a gymnasium—from *gymnos* (naked)—for an athlete was usually nude, his glistening body covered with oil and his foreskin tied over the tip of his penis with a string, apparently a means of protection from injury. Greek men were naked not only when exercising but also when competing in most games. The naked boys at the gymnasium were taught to wrestle

The brutal one-on-one sport called pankration combined boxing and wrestling with kicking, strangling, twisting, and nearly every other conceivable assault by hands, feet, and body. Only biting and gouging were forbidden. This vase painting shows the victor, on the right, striking the head of his opponent, who raises a finger to acknowledge defeat. Interior of an Attic red-figure kylix by Epictetus, *c.* 510 BCE. Agora Museum, Athens.

and box in a palaestra, a low building with a central courtyard. Their training outside the palaestra included running, jumping, discus throwing, javelin throwing, and archery.

Education in letters began with reading, writing, and simple arithmetic. Boys learned to write by using a sharp point to inscribe the alphabet on small, wax-covered wooden tablets, which were easy to erase. After gaining more proficiency, pupils wrote with pen and ink on the more expensive Egyptian papyrus. They spent much of their time copying and learning by heart passages of poetry selected to mold character and teach them great lessons of patriotism from the deeds of past heroes. The revered Homeric epics were favored, but Hesiod, Theognis, and others were also popular.

Instruction began in music—which included the works of the lyric poets—about the thirteenth year. The profound moral influence the Greeks attributed to music proper made this art an essential part of education. All but the poorest boys learned to play the lyre and to accompany the singing of lyric verse, and every Athenian gentleman was expected to be able to sing a song after dinner. Unfortunately, knowledge about the Greek system of musical notation remains obscure, and scholars have been unable to reconstruct the musical settings. The two principal instruments were the aulos, a loud reed pipe that was usually played in pairs by one performer, and the lyre, a stringed instrument plucked with the fingers and commonly including a sound box made of a tortoise shell. The lyre was the instrument of the schoolboy and the amateur, while the professional musician played a variant known as the kithara, of larger and more solid construction than the lyre and known for a deep resonance that carried in the open air.

Although Greek education placed considerable emphasis on listening and reciting from memory, vases from the sixth and fifth centuries BCE show boys and occasionally girls as well learning the skills of reading and writing. This scene portrays a standing boy reading a wood-backed wax writing tablet, which would have been inscribed with a stylus, while his seated teacher reads from a papyrus scroll. Interior of an Attic red-figure kylix, c. 430–420 BCE. Louvre, Paris.

On his eighteenth birthday, a youth was enrolled in the list of citizens in his deme and legally became a man and a full citizen of Athens. The state then required him to undergo an intensive two-year period of training for war, and he spent one year at Piraeus and another on the frontier. Similar programs were common in other Greek states.

GREEK HOMOSEXUALITY

As noted in chapter 7, ancient Greek statues of naked male youths (kouroi) contrast with statues of draped female figures (korai). Except for special occasions, respectable women remained at home and were clothed from head to foot. To discourage a rash of suicides among the young women of the Ionian city of Miletus, those who threatened to kill themselves were deterred by the shocking warning that they would be carried to their graves shamefully naked. Except for certain philosophers, most Greeks of the priveleged class regarded the body as the essential being of a person, the soul a mere shadow. The Greeks considered themselves living reflections of divinity, and males employed their naked bodies to inspire both poets and warriors. The male nude derived much of its iconography and power from the reverence accorded the phallus in Greek antiquity. A man's physical excellence was thought to be concentrated in his sexual organs. Men admired the phallic strength of other males and formed strong relationships with them. Aristotle argued in Book VIII of the *Nicomachean Ethics* that the relationship between a husband and wife is that between a superior and an inferior order and that true friendship is possible only between equals. Marriage in such a setting was largely an

Depiction of a girl playing the aulos, a musical instrument usually made from two reed pipes, from an Attic red-figure stamnos (two-handled storage vase) by the Chicago Painter, *c.* 450 BCE. South African Museum, Cape Town.

institution for procreating children, while love was thought to represent a more exalted standard, one that embodied friendship, courage, and nobility of character.

Ancient Greek art clearly reveals the form of this love. Hundreds of surviving Greek vase paintings depict older males conversing with younger males, offering them love gifts, or entreating them. Others show a man touching the genitals of a youth, performing intercrural (between the thighs) copulation with him, or penetrating him anally. In ancient Greece a senior partner commonly expressed his love for a junior partner who had reached puberty or adolescence. A Greek boy who had attained the age of puberty was known as an ephebe (*ephebos*), though later at Athens the word came to mean members of a military academy. The older man was expected to initiate the relationship, and love between the two often embodied both admiration and sexual attraction and was harmonious with Greek social values. The Greeks staunchly defended an intimate bonding between an older and younger man as a vital component of a sound education. Although romantic love was largely excluded from marriage, a male was free to seek erotic encounters with a courtesan or find both love and sex in a relationship with a youth. The strong erotic fantasy of Greek men for boys is reflected in the depiction on vase paintings of short thin penises for both men and youths, probably an assimilation of the adult male to the young male. This ideal is dispensed with when the penis is erect, for then it is depicted in normal size. Another example of the consistent tendency to

This vase painting of a man with an ephebe strongly suggests a romantic connection between the two. Interior of an Attic red-figure kylix, c. 490 BCE. Staatliche Antikensammlungen und Glyptothek, Munich.

assimilate adult males to boys is signified in vase paintings by the virtual elimination of chest and pubic hair on adult men. Moreover, gods such as Apollo are always portrayed in vase paintings and statues as eternally youthful and beautiful males (the Greeks did not make the English distinction between *handsome*, usually applied to males, and *beautiful*, usually applied to females).

In order to attract a suitable lover, adolescent boys dressed in an enticing and revealing manner. An ambitious youth endeavored to form a relationship with a distinguished and highly respected man who would bring honor to his name. The older man sought to compliment himself by attracting a boy with a noble mind and a beautiful body. Enjoying an intensity of affection not normally found in a Greek marriage, the pair were proud to be seen together walking through the streets of Athens. The symposium—from which respectable women were excluded—offered an opportunity to form liaisons both sexual and spiritual between men and youths. The love between two males—the older being perhaps in his twenties or thirties or even older—was thought to enhance the intellectual development of the younger and to elevate his character. Such relationships were considered entirely natural and respectable and were idealized by the priveleged classes. Upon growing up, however, the younger partner usually graduated from pupil to friend. Romantic love between males of the same age was generally frowned on as a rebellion against the social order, for sexual relations were considered seemly only between a social superior and a social inferior, between a dominant partner and a subordinate one. Only in the realm of the gods could such bonds between males last indefinitely. A number of the gods, as noted in chapter 6, were romantically captivated by youths. The beauty of the shepherd boy Ganymede had even aroused almighty Zeus, who took the form of an eagle and swept him away to Mount Olympus to become his cupbearer and lover.

ATHENIAN RELIGION

Civic Festivals

Athenians paid due reverence to the gods at mealtime, on leaving and returning home, and on festal occasions. Religion offered a framework of explanation for human experience and permeated all phases of Athenian life. Although the Greeks usually worshiped the same gods—Zeus, Hera, Apollo, Artemis, Athena, Demeter, Dionysus, and others (discussed in chapter 6)—the cults of these deities varied from polis to polis. Festivals or appropriate rites helped guide devotees through the great human transitions of birth, puberty, adulthood, and death. One class of public festivals prepared youths to become warriors or maidens to become mothers. Other festivals were concerned with events of the agricultural year (fertility celebrations in honor of Demeter or Dionysus), civic pride (exemplified by the observance of the Panathenaea on the birthday of the city's patron goddess Athena), divine protection during times of danger, homage to ancestral heroes, and so forth. Thus the pattern of life at Athens was regulated by the great state festivals that honored the deities preserving the city, and this spiritual recreation consumed about seventy days a year.

The Priesthoods

Religious activity in Athens was essentially a matter of cult performance rather than dogmatic belief. Although professional priests conducted sacred rites, they did not formulate doctrines, unlike their counterparts in Egypt and elsewhere. Most Athenian priests served part-time and were engaged in other occupations, except during festivals. The growth of democracy had altered the forms of religious expression in Athens, for the vast majority of cults formerly controlled by aristocratic families had been absorbed by the public calendar. Only a few priesthoods remained the privilege of certain aristocratic families. Most priests were now salaried magistrates, and even the king archon, who presided over sacrifices in Athens, was elected annually by lot. Worship focused on the rite of sacrifice, which the Greeks regarded as the essential avenue to divine favor. Sacrifices of domestic animals preceded all major events of public and private life and involved the belief that the god somehow fed on the victim.

The Greek Mysteries

Many Greeks sought additional outlets for their religious devotion by turning from the essentially civic religion to the mysteries, in which the beliefs and rites were kept hidden or secret from all except initiates. Promising a better lot in the afterlife, these Greek cults included the Eleusinian, Dionysiac, and Orphic mysteries. The Dionysiac rites, which attracted women particularly, had been tamed but still included intoxicated revelry and downright obscenity. Meanwhile other Greeks were embracing new mystery cults and deities introduced by foreigners, including the Cabiri, a small group of chthonian divinities venerated for promoting fertility and protecting seafarers. Phallic symbols and sacrificial pits played a part in these mysteries, which probably originated in the ancient kingdom of Phrygia in central Asia Minor as a cult of underground spirits. Worship of the Cabiri was brought to the Greek mainland from the northern Aegean island of Samothrace, a main center of the cult.

Cybele.   Inhabitants of Asia Minor had long worshiped a great mother-goddess, Cybele, whose chief sanctuary was in Phrygia. The cult spread in all directions, and by the fifth century BCE Cybele was known in Greece, where she was associated with Demeter and often called simply Meter, or Mother. Cybele was a goddess of mountains and of wild nature, for she personalized the earth in its primitive and untamed state. The parent of gods as well as humans and animals, Cybele enjoyed power over procreation. She was also responsible for curing (and sending) disease and protecting her followers in war. She was associated in myth with her young subordinate lover named Attis, who was lured into infidelity and bled to death after castrating himself to avoid further transgressions. Flowers sprang from his drops of blood, perhaps suggesting resurrection.

Devotees of Cybele achieved a mystical communion with her by participating in ecstatic rites. Her priests were eunuchs who, like Attis himself, castrated themselves as a great act of devotion to the goddess. During worship the emasculated priests engaged in frenzied dancing and made rousing music with drums, cymbals, and horns. The early spring festival honoring Cybele also commemorated Attis, the prototype of the eunuch priest, and culminated with an ecstatic celebration of his sacrifice.

CHAPTER XII

PERICLEAN ATHENS: ART, LITERATURE, AND PHILOSOPHY

Periclean Athens witnessed an amazing interplay of continuity and innovation that produced cultural triumphs in art, literature, and philosophy. The Parthenon and other temples proclaimed the grandeur of the city. While sculptors excelled in creating images of harmonious gods and humans, talented painters adorned walls with appealing and naturalistic figures and scenes. Periclean Athens was recognized also as an intellectual center, attracting writers and philosophers from the other cities of Greece. Athens was acclaimed for its tragic drama, which apparently developed from a religious performance of song and dance by a chorus. Rowdy comedy also found expression on the Athenian stage, with plots drawn chiefly from the social and political life of the time. In the meantime Thucydides, generally credited as the greatest historian of the Greco-Roman world, played an active role in Athenian life until he was banished for losing an important northern outpost during the Peloponnesian War. He employed his exile to write a detailed history of the war. Unlike Herodotus, born a generation earlier, who viewed history as an interaction of divine and human forces, Thucydides was disposed to regard human decisions and actions as the chief cause of historical events. Meanwhile philosophers wrestled to comprehend the nature of the gods, the universe, and humankind. The great philosopher Socrates developed a famous question and answer method for demolishing the views of his opponents. His focus on ethical inquiry and quest for wisdom attracted a diverse circle of young men wishing to learn from him, including Plato, whose celebrated writings made the name Socrates immortal.

ART

ARCHITECTURE

The art of Classical Greece may be divided roughly into two parts: the Early Classical phase, from about 480 to 450 BCE, and the High Classical phase, from about 450 to 400 BCE, the latter embracing the Age of Pericles. Fifth-century Athens remained a maze of narrow streets bordered closely by simple houses of sun-dried brick. In a climate and society where men spent so much time outside, houses were rather insignificant, but public buildings—especially temples—reflected state wealth and prestige. During the second half of the century Pericles, through his

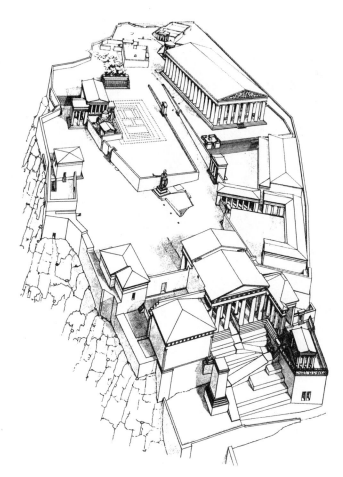

A restored view from the northwest of the Athenian Acropolis in the late fifth century BCE. Around mid-century, Pericles prompted the Athenians to construct resplendent new buildings on the Acropolis to replace those destroyed by the invading Persians three decades earlier.

constitutional post of *strategos,* devoted much energy to his goal of glorifying Athens both as a political power and as a cultural ideal. He persuaded the Athenians to undertake great building projects reflecting the majesty and greatness of his beloved city. Pericles used funds the Delian League had contributed for the war against Persia for this aggrandizement and fortification of Athens, the greatest program of state patronage in Greece until the Hellenistic Age.

The Athenian Acropolis.   Athenian devotion centered on the great rock of the Acropolis, whose steep slopes could be approached only on the western side. Cimon, who had started rebuilding the city, had constructed a huge retaining wall along the southern edge of the summit of this lofty hill, which honored the gods, especially the city goddess Athena. Devotees in a procession to honor Athena on the Acropolis traveled along the Sacred Way, which began at the Dipylon Gate and passed through the Agora before reaching the base of the Acropolis. The faithful made a sharp ascent up the western slope of the Acropolis—not the easier zigzag

Reconstruction of the west façade of the Parthenon, Athens, the centerpiece of the great fifth-century building program on the Acropolis and the epitome of the Doric order. Work began in 447 BCE, the temple was dedicated in 438 BCE, and the pedimental sculpture was in place by 432 BCE. The architects, Ictinus and Callicrates, incorporated gentle, almost imperceptible curves in the structure to enhance the visual response, thereby avoiding a boxlike appearance and creating a sense of dynamic tension. The steps of the magnificent temple displayed dedicatory plaques and over-life-size statues honoring various citizens, while the figures of the west pediment portrayed the mythical contest between Athena and Poseidon for the land of Athens.

path of today—and then passed through a monumental gateway, the Propylaea, to the holy ground beyond. They continued on the Sacred Way past the great bronze statue of Athena the Defender (*Promachos*), now totally lost, created by the acclaimed sculptor Phidias and erected in the 450s BCE in celebration of the final defeat of the Persians. The armored statue was about thirty feet high, and the point of its spear and the crest of its helmet were visible to mariners entering the Athenian harbor complex of Piraeus. The pilgrims then curved around to the eastern entrance of the Parthenon.

The Parthenon.   Among the buildings the Persians destroyed when sacking the Athenian Acropolis in 480 BCE was the temple dedicated to Athena the Virgin (*Parthenos*). Construction of the Parthenon, as the rebuilt temple came to be called, was directed by the architect Ictinus (famous also for his temple of Apollo at Bassae in Arcadia) and his assistant Callicrates. The two erected the great temple between

The west façade of the Parthenon today.

447 and 432 BCE of Pentelic marble, which takes on a rich cream color after exposure to the weather. Both the sculptor Phidias—who designed most of the ornamentation—and the painter Polygnotus participated in the planning of the
Parthenon. The marble blocks employed for building the temple were dressed so
carefully that no mortar was required for closing the joints, which originally were
virtually invisible to the naked eye.

The Parthenon, measuring about 228 by 101 feet, is justly regarded as the epitome of Doric temples (architectural terms are explained in chapter 7). The Doric
order was gloriously exploited in this structure of overwhelming breadth and
grandeur to reflect the ancient Greek values of harmony and proportion. The pediments rose in a graceful angle, bringing the height of the building to 65 feet. The
entire inner structure was surrounded by an immense peristyle of eight columns at
the ends and seventeen on the sides. The inner structure included a porch with six
extra columns at each end, creating the impression of a closely packed grove of
columns. The naos (or cella) was originally divided by a solid wall into two main
rooms. The eastern, larger chamber—framed by a two-tiered Doric colonnade—
held the great statue of Athena Parthenos, while the western, smaller room opened
off the back porch and served as a treasury. The western room was originally called
the Parthenon, or Chamber of the Virgin, and eventually the name was loosely applied to the entire building.

Simple yet vibrant, the Parthenon is a paramount example of Greek genius in
architecture. The architects rigorously applied a wide number of small but deliberate divergences from mathematical regularity, thereby subtly curving lines that

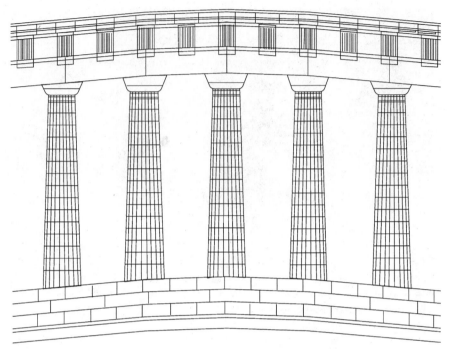

Diagram in exaggerated proportion of the horizontal curvature of the Parthenon.

were customarily straight and inclining vertical members that were usually perpendicular. The matchless Doric columns lean somewhat toward the interior, while the stylobate (the top part of the stepped base upon which the columns rest) gently curves upward and is more than four inches higher at the center than at the corners. Moreover, the slight swelling at the middle of the shafts of the columns was considerably refined from that of Archaic buildings. Such architectural techniques create a visually gratifying response in the viewer, for the subconscious mind clearly perceives the outwardly almost imperceptible curves and variant dimensions, making the structure seem to be an organic, pulsating entity rather than a heap of dead stones. When Athenians looked up at the Acropolis, the holy edifice of the Parthenon seemed almost to hover between heaven and earth in calm majesty.

Phidias.   Carved by seventy or eighty sculptors under the direction of Phidias and in accordance with his overall plan, the sculpture of the Parthenon depicted the legendary story of Attica. Phidias was the greatest sculptor of the fifth century BCE, and the Parthenon sculptures—many of which are in London—are strikingly lifelike and successfully convey the illusion of movement and potential action. The naos housed one of Phidias' chief masterpieces, a colossal gold and ivory statue of Athena Parthenos, some forty feet high. Although the magnificent cult statue is long since lost, marble copies and descriptions by ancient writers provide some idea of its ap-

Reconstruction of the eastern, larger chamber of the Parthenon, framed by a
two-tiered colonnade and housing Phidias' majestic gold and ivory statue of
Athena Parthenos, the Virgin, standing some forty feet high. This model
of the statue in Toronto is based on ancient descriptions and miniature
representations from Roman times. The flesh parts were fashioned of ivory,
while the dress was made of gold plates fitted over a wooden core. A shallow
pool of water reflected light on the statue and provided humidity for the
ivory. Royal Ontario Museum, Toronto.

pearance. The flesh parts were made of ivory, while the drapery was of pure gold over
a wooden frame. Guardian of Athenian power and victory, Athena Parthenos was
richly adorned as a warrior deity in the full panoply of battle. A shallow pool of water
in the floor before the statue provided humidity to protect the ivory in the dry climate of Athens and also served to reflect light on the goddess' features.

The extensive and varied sculptural ornamentation of the Parthenon was produced by a team under the general direction of Phidias. Most of the metopes of the temple have been seriously damaged or destroyed, but the marble figures gracing the finest surviving examples—carved in high relief—almost seem to erupt from their restrictive frames. The metopes designed for the south side of the building represent scenes from the mythical battle between the Thessalian tribe of the Lapiths and the Centaurs, wild Thessalian creatures with the upper half of a man and the legs and body of a horse. The splendid metope illustrated here, *c.* 447–438 BCE, shows a powerful Lapith leaping forward to seize with his left hand the neck of a wounded and writhing Centaur while raising his right hand to deliver the fatal blow. The Lapith's vibrant human torso is beautifully framed by the intricate folds of his cloak, originally painted. British Museum, London.

The Parthenon's metope panels, carved in dramatic high relief, portray combats between the Lapiths and Centaurs (part-horse, part-human creatures who battled the Thessalian human tribe of Lapiths), the Gods and Giants (primeval monsters unsuccessfully rebelling against Zeus and the other deities), and the Greeks and Amazons (mythical female warriors). These were favorite themes of the Greeks, who enjoyed extolling the triumph of the rational and civilized over the irrational and barbaric. A few surviving metopes on the north side depict highlights from the siege and capture of Troy. The two pediments were adorned with figures in the round, with the eastern showing Athena, attended by other gods, springing from the head of Zeus at her birth, and the western depicting the great contest between Athena and Poseidon to determine whose gifts would win the favor and worship of the Athenians.

The Parthenon Frieze.   A novel feature of the Parthenon was a 525-foot-long frieze. Celebrating imperial Athens and carved in low relief, the relief ran around the outer wall of the naos and portrayed a version of a familiar Athenian scene, the

The frieze erected around the outside of the central block of the Parthenon, carved in low relief, exemplifies the temple's rich sculptural decoration. To improve visibility, the frieze was brightly painted and slightly tilted toward the spectators below. Most scholars agree the frieze represents the important Panathenaic Procession, celebrated annually and with greater elaboration every four years, when the Athenians carried to the Acropolis a new peplos to drape on an old Archaic statue of Athena. Thus Phidias and his team audaciously decorated the new temple with both mortals and deities, doubtless provoking criticism from many conservative Greeks. Illustrated here are two vigorous young riders on spirited horses from the west frieze of the Parthenon, 447–438 BCE. Reflecting the frieze's extraordinarily high standard of execution, the cloak of one rider flies out behind him to suggest rapid forward motion. British Museum, London.

dignitaries and people of Athens marching in the Panathenaic Procession to carry the great embroidered peplos to Athena. Young horsemen, girls, women, and officials make their way to the Acropolis on the west frieze. The procession became slower and more solemn on the east end, where great deities were seated, apparently the guests of Athena at her great festival. The frieze exemplifies the Phidian style of sculpture, which successfully created the illusion of space and rounded form. We should not underestimate the use of color here and elsewhere in Greek sculpture and architecture. The entire Parthenon must have radiated with color. Patterned moldings were colored and perhaps even marble column shafts and walls. The backgrounds of the pediments were painted bright blue, while those of the metopes and friezes were in red. The hair, eyes, lips, skin, and dress of the figures were also colored. The addition of metal attachments for details, such as reins and bridles, not only reflected light but also added additional hues that helped to clarify the design.

The Panathenaic frieze shows the participants at the head of the procession coming into the presence of seated dieties. This detail of the east frieze of the Parthenon, *c.* 447–438 BCE, catches Poseidon, Apollo, Artemis, Aphrodite, and Eros during an informal moment, a novel treatment of sacred figures. Reminding the viewer of a human mother, Aphrodite extends her left arm to point out something of importance to her son Eros. Acropolis Museum, Athens.

Period of Alteration and Neglect.   The great temple underwent many vicissitudes in the later Christian era, becoming in turn an Orthodox and a Roman Catholic church. When Athens fell under the control of the Ottoman Turks in the fifteenth century CE, the Parthenon was converted to a mosque but eventually was used also as a powder magazine. A Venetian bombardment in 1687 detonated the gunpowder, and the resulting blast blew out the walls of the naos, shattering many columns and much of the rest of the venerable building.

The Elgin Marbles.   By the opening of the nineteenth century, when Greece was still ruled by the Ottoman Empire, the Parthenon had suffered centuries of decay and was surrounded by rubble. The British ambassador to the Ottoman court at Constantinople—Thomas Bruce, the seventh earl of Elgin—set out to rescue what sculpture he could from additional damage. Gaining permission from the Ottoman government to remove many sculptures, Lord Elgin arranged for their shipment to the safety of London. Most of the sculptures of the pediments and the great frieze of the Parthenon remain, controversially, in the British Museum in London, where they are popularly known as the Elgin Marbles. Here they have been preserved and have profoundly influenced art historians and other scholars. Some twenty years after the Elgin Marbles were shipped off to London, the Greeks finally won their independence from the Ottoman Turks. Archaeologists eventually restored the outer columns of the Parthenon, and a program of conservation continues.

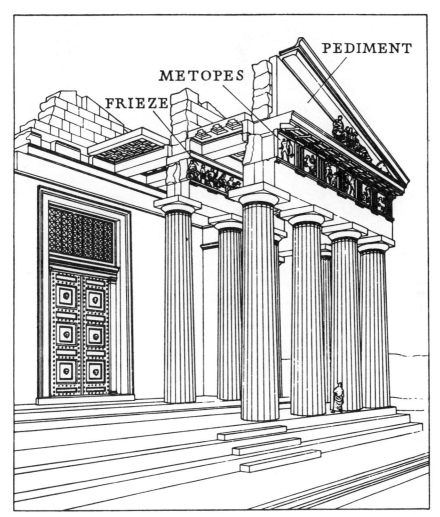

PEDIMENT

METOPES

FRIEZE

Reconstruction of the east front of the Parthenon, showing the original position of the sculptural decoration.

The Propylaea.   Immediately after the completion of the Parthenon, Pericles commissioned the monumental entry gate called the Propylaea, a splendid edifice at the western end of the Acropolis. Designed by Mnesicles and begun in 437 BCE, the Propylaea was constructed of rich Pentelic marble, with color contrast provided by occasional courses of black Eleusinian limestone. Mnesicles' complex plan, which combined Doric and Ionic elements, included a central pedimented Doric portico, or porch, of six columns facing west and massive wings extending on either side. The structure was still under construction at the outbreak of the Peloponnesian War, however, and the south flanking wing was never completed. The Propylaea

The spacious and complex Propylaea served as a new monumental entrance to the sacred ground of the Athenian Acropolis. Designed by the architect Mnesicles and constructed between 437 and 432 BCE, the structure was graced with a templelike façade of six Doric columns at either end. Planning was partly determined by the steeply sloping site. Two wings of unequal size flanked the front of the building, the north one housing a picture gallery that displayed works by some of the leading artists of the fifth century BCE. Both the Propylaea and the Parthenon were built of rich Pentelic marble, quarried on the slopes of Mount Pentelicon east of Athens.

disguises the irregular terrain and transforms what would have been a barren entrance among rude rocks into a magnificent colonnaded portal to the sacred precinct beyond. Pedestrians could approach the impressive western portico using either of two great staircases, while a central ramp between the two stairways allowed horses or sacrificial animals to reach the Doric portico. Along the roadway that passes through the central hall of the Propylaea are two rows of lofty Ionic columns. After their steep climb, worshipers could rest in these magnificent surroundings before proceeding to the holy buildings beyond. A room to the left displayed paintings on wooden panels, while a small porch to the right contained statues.

Temple of Athena Nike.   Athens, with its Aegean orientation, was receptive to influence from the eastern Greeks on the coast of Asia Minor, and splendid structures of the Ionic order are found on the Acropolis. The Athenians developed an affinity for this order with its graceful, slender columns topped with capitals in the form of a volute, or a double scroll. One of the last projects of rebuilding on the Acropolis was the diminutive but exquisite Ionic Temple of Athena Nike (Athena as Victory), constructed on the bastion to the right of the Propylaea under the direction of Callicrates in the late fifth century BCE. Athenian leaders of the late sixth cen-

The exquisite little Ionic temple of Athena Nike (Athena as Victory), designed by Callicrates, was erected c. 427–424 BCE to the right of the Propylaea on what used to be a Mycenaean bastion. The name of the building sent an unmistakable message of warning to anyone approaching the Acropolis. A highly visible parapet was added around the three edges of the bastion about 410 BCE and decorated with fine refliefs of Victories (Nikai) in elaborate, seemingly transparent draperies pressed close to the body.

tury had popularized the identification of Athena with Nike, the goddess—or personification—of Victory, but the temple was erected in the hope rather than the possession of victory, for the tragic death struggle with Sparta was in progress.

The amphiprostyle plan of the little temple included a square naos with four Ionic columns on each portico and two entrance pillars flanked by bronze grilles. A continous frieze, carved in a flamboyant style with swirling drapery and vigorous

Construction of the complex temple called the Erechtheum did not begin until 421 BCE, with work later interrupted for several years but finally completed in 406 BCE. The elegant asymmetry of the building contrasts sharply with the notable balance of the adjacent Parthenon. The Ionic Erechtheum enclosed various shrines and sacred precincts of a host of deities and demigods associated with the legendary past of Athens, most notably Athena, Poseidon, and Erechtheus, the last a mythical Athenian king believed to have established the worship of Athena on the Acropolis. The Erechtheum is particularly celebrated for its Porch of the Maidens, graced by six beautifully draped female figures, today called caryatids, functioning as supporting columns for the roof.

movement, depicts gods in the front and battles on the back and sides. One scene shows Greeks fighting Persians, almost certainly at the battle of Marathon. Surrounding the temple was a low stone balustrade, built at a slightly later date, decorated in relief with Victories (Nikai) shown separately or bringing sacrificial animals to Athena.

The Erechtheum.   Finally, the Erechtheum was built on the northern edge of the Acropolis during the last quarter of the fifth century BCE. The temple was named for Erechtheus, a mythical king of Athens, and was constructed on the spot where Poseidon was thought to have killed him. Although Erechtheus was the son of Earth, he had been reared by Athena, and his cult was associated with that of the great Athenian goddess. The Erechtheum was sacred to Erechtheus, Poseidon, and Athena in her capacity of guardian of the city (Athena Polias). The elegant Ionic temple was built of Pentelic marble, while its surrounding frieze consisted of white marble figures set against black Eleusinian limestone, later completely shattered. The structure has a complex shape, necessitated in part by the need to build around many holy spots and objects, including an altar of Poseidon and Erechtheus, the mark of Poseidon's trident, and the miraculous olive tree Athena had brought forth from the ground by the touch of her spear, the last protected by an open enclosure. A challenge was presented by the irregular and sloping terrain, reflected by a ten-foot difference in the levels of the sacred spots. The solution produced one of the most unusual buildings in the history of Greek architecture.

Essentially, the temple encloses four chambers—two with different floor levels—and supports four porticoes and four entrances. Six Ionic columns frame the main entrance on the east end. The building is flanked on the north by a porch sacred to Poseidon and on the south by the justly famous Porch of the Maidens, the latter inaccessible from outside. Six draped female figures known as caryatids support the roof of the Porch of the Maidens, performing their function as columns with exquisite grace. To arrest destruction by air pollution, the remaining originals (Lord Elgin carted off one of the caryatids to London) have been moved to the Acropolis Museum and replaced on the porch by copies of the originals. The eastern chamber of the Erechtheum housed the most venerated image of Athena, the olive-wood image of Athena Polias draped in a woven robe. A golden lamp, which required refilling only once a year, stood before the image. Celebrated for its Ionic grandeur, the architecturally provocative Erechtheum broke with the austere restraint of the past and marked a transition to the more elaborate buildings of the fourth century BCE and the Hellenistic period.

Environs of the Acropolis.   Standing on the southern slope of the Acropolis were the open-air theater of Dionysus—home of Athenian tragedy and comedy—and the adjoining roofed odeon of Pericles, a music hall constructed at the instigation of the great Athenian politician. A theater, associated with the cult of Dionysus, became an essential cultural feature of every Greek city. The theater of Dionysus was constructed in Athens fairly early in the fifth century BCE, augmented in Pericles' time, and rebuilt in the last third of the fourth century. Greek theaters were set in the slope of a hill, creating a vast auditorium. The theater of Dionysus contained superimposed rows of seating made of beaten earth and wood, until fourth-century builders put up the stone replacements visible today. These stone seats were curved and extended like a fan from the circular orchestra, where actors and chorus would perform. In the middle of the orchestra stood the *thymele*, a small round altar of Dionysus. Behind the orchestra was the *skene*, a long structure used for storing properties and from which the actors emerged at the appropriate time. Also standing at the base of the southern slope of the Acropolis was a temple to Asclepius, god of healing. The presence of springs and the southern exposure made this a natural site for a curative sanctuary.

The Areopagus, a hill northwest of the Acropolis, was the meeting place of the famous council of the same name. Rising west of the Areopagus was the low hill of the Pnyx, the usual place of meeting for the assembly. To the northwest of the

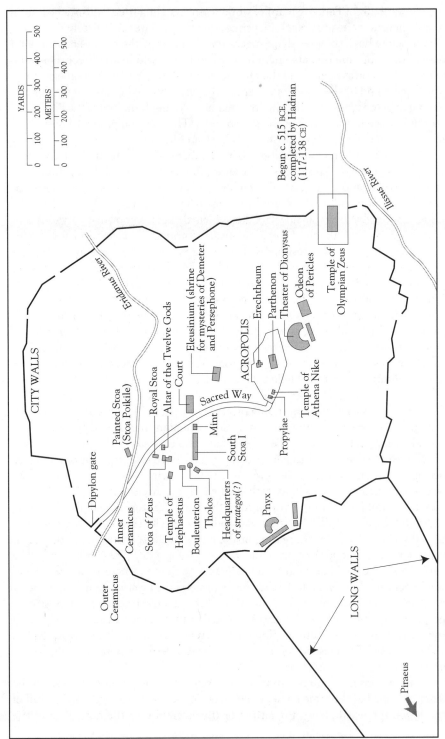

Athens in the late fifth century BCE.

Acropolis lay the Agora, a large open square containing shops, temples, and buildings of state. An agora formed the heart of every major Greek city and served as a favorite gathering place of freeborn males. The public buildings of the Athenian Agora included the splendid Painted Stoa (Stoa Poecile), constructed mainly of limestone, which displayed wall paintings of mythological and patriotic subjects, now entirely lost. The scenes were painted on large wooden panels by notable Athenian artists—Polygnotus, Micon, and Panaenus—and included the sack of Troy and the Battle of Marathon. Beyond the Agora lay the inner Ceramicus, the potters' quarter, its name derived from the production of ceramics. The houses of the Athenians crowded around the base of the Acropolis and spread out to the north and west.

The promontory of Piraeus—situated about four miles southwest of Athens—accommodated the largest and safest harbor complex on the Greek mainland. During his archonship Themistocles had made Piraeus the port of Athens in place of the inadequate open beach of Phaleron. Pericles commissioned Hippodamus of Miletus, who later laid out the colony of Thurii in southern Italy, to redesign Piraeus. Hippodamus gave the thriving naval base a grid pattern, a plan already known in Ionia, and he built huge dockyards for ships and warehouses. Then Pericles connected Piraeus with Athens by the Long Walls. The city of Athens had already been enclosed by the wall of Themistocles, about five miles in circumference, soon after the expulsion of the Persians. People entered Athens through a dozen gates, principally the Dipylon Gate in the northwest, where the city wall adjoined the potters' quarter. The outer Ceramicus beyond the Dipylon Gate contained the Athenian cemetery, which has yielded celebrated monuments to archaeological exploration. Just northwest of the gate was the Academy, an olive grove and popular exercise ground named for a local hero whose shrine was nearby.

SCULPTURE OF THE EARLY CLASSICAL PERIOD: THE SEVERE STYLE (c. 480–450 BCE)

The notable but short Early Classical period between the close of the Archaic period and the opening of the High Classical period in the Age of Pericles witnessed a remarkable transformation in Greek art. Sculpture in the Early Classical period (c. 480–450 BCE) is often termed the Severe Style because figures are characterized by expressions of dignity and self-control. The Severe Style reflected the Greek belief that their moral underpinnings had given them the resolve to repulse the Persians. Seizing this idea, sculptors sought to ennoble human figures and endow them with a sense of strength, resilience, and harmony. They broke with Archaic rigid symmetry to produce naturalistic standing youths, popular in Greek athletic society with its homosexual overtones. The Archaic smile gives way to an expression of utter calm, even when a Greek figure is confronted with anguish or danger. While hair remains stylized, a Severe Style statue evokes the effective image of a real person whose structure counterbalances upward- and downward-pressing forces, thereby creating the Classical equilibrium of rest in movement and movement in rest. In contrast to the Archaic kouroi, figures stand in a relaxed position, with the weight seemingly resting on one leg. Thus Severe Style statues stand at ease, like

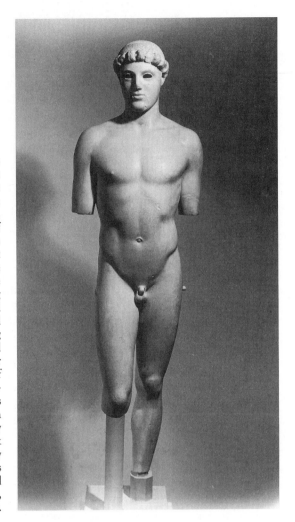

The *Critius Boy,* named for its similarity to the work of the sculptor named Critius, was dedicated on the Athenian Acropolis around 480 BCE. Emancipated from the rigidity of the Archaic kouroi, the statue has the weight shifted to the straight left leg, the right being bent at the knee, resulting in a tilt to the pelvis and a corresponding adjustment of the head and shoulders. The sculptor's skilled rendering of a relaxed, standing boy suggests an integrated and lifelike—though not altogether realistic—organism capable of acting spontaneously. This under-life-size marble statue represents the so-called Severe Style (a term often applied to the Early Classical phase of Greek sculpture), characterized by its calm, grave expressions and more successfully rendered physiques. Acropolis Museum, Athens.

actual people, and clearly distinguish between the leg supporting the weight of the body and the unburdened free leg serving as a prop and helping the body to maintain its balance. Art historians employ the Italian word *contrapposto* (set against) to describe the balanced, nonsymmetrical stance of these statues.

Critius Boy.   The earliest explicit example of the Severe Style is the famous *Critius Boy,* found in rubble on the Athenian Acropolis. Carved about 480 BCE and thought to be in the style of the sculptor Critius, the freestanding statue is now in the Acropolis Museum. The boy's weight is carried by his straight left leg, while his right leg is unburdened. Thus the sculpture has created a natural stance, with the

Although the magnificent Doric temple of Zeus at Olympia collapsed at the end of antiquity, excavations have rescued a large part of its lavish marble sculpture expressing the Severe Style. The west pediment, illustrated here, was completed about 460 BCE, its mythical scene celebrating the triumph of human civilization over savagery. The violent action focuses on the battle between the Lapiths and Centaurs at the wedding banquet of the Lapith king Pirithous. The Centaurs were regarded as creatures of ungovernable sexual appetite, ready to pounce on anyone, of either sex, whose beauty aroused them. Excited from drinking wine at the banquet, the Centaurs attempt to carry off the Lapith women and boys, provoking the bitter struggle depicted here. The brawl has attracted the attention of the central figure of the ensemble, stern-face Apollo, standing impassively but majestically stretching out his right arm to impose his divine will on the unruly Centaurs. Olympia Museum.

left leg pressing into the hip, thereby producing a tilt to the pelvis and a slight incline of the head and shoulders. A true harmony of forms has finally emerged in Greek sculpture, for we sense that we are in the presence of an integrated organism, a boy capable of movement and force and endowed with lifelike skin and muscles.

Battle of Lapiths and Centaurs: The West Pediment of the Temple of Zeus at Olympia. The fullest surviving sculptural ensemble of the Severe Style comes from the Temple of Zeus at Olympia, an imposing Doric structure completed by 456 BCE. The figures that graced the pediments were cut entirely in the round by artists whose names are lost to us. The west pediment represented the popular subject of the battle of Lapiths and Centaurs. The Lapiths were mythological warriors of Thessaly, while the Centaurs were imagined as fierce and oversexed creatures, male human above the waist and male horse below. The best-known myth about the Centaurs is their battle with the Lapiths. Invited to the wedding feast of the Lapith king Pirithous, the Centaurs drank too much wine and attempted to abduct the women—including the bride Hippodamia—and the boys. Apollo, the god of light and reason, appears at the center of the ensemble to bring order out of the chaos. Austere and autocratic, Apollo stands in majestic isolation with his arm outstretched to command the Centaurs to halt their ferocious attack. Apollo clearly portrays the Severe Style. His features are placid, his body still, yet his powerful physique suggests a gathering of forces. As a god, he wills the Lapith victory over the frenzied scene of violence created by the bestial Centaurs. Among the groups of struggling figures, most of the humans also display calm expressions—even the violated bride—symbolizing the popular Greek theme of the defeat of the wild and barbaric at the hands of the civilized.

Hollow-Cast Bronze Statues.   By the end of the Archaic period hollow-cast bronze had begun to replace marble for freestanding sculpture. The major achievement of

A Centaur attacks a Lapith woman, from the west pediment of the temple of Zeus at Olympia, *c.* 460 BCE. The struggling woman sharply elbows the head of the brutal Centaur, now grimacing in pain. Her face betrays no trace of emotion or distress, characteristic of this phase of Greek sculpture, though she twists forcefully from the grip of the violating creature. Most of the human figures seem composed despite the terrible assault, with only the frenzied Centaurs reduced to snarling and raging. Olympia Museum.

creating hollow metal statues, which have much greater tensile strength than those of marble, accelerated the drive of sculptors to create freer poses and to narrate the

Detail of the head and torso of the splendid statue of Apollo, from the west pediment of the temple of Zeus at Olympia, c. 460 BCE. Embodiment of reason and order, the imposing god calmly presides over the Lapith defeat of the Centaurs, his expressionless face reflecting the Severe Style. Olympia Museum.

human figure more convincingly. Parts of the figure were made separately and later assembled. Each part was first modeled in a thin layer of wax over a clay core and then covered with clay. Firing the whole melted away the wax and hardened the clay to form a mold, into which molten bronze was poured. Later, after a period of cooling, the clay covering was broken away, leaving the bronze. Sculptors inlaid the eyes of the figures with brilliant glass or colored stone. Hair, teeth, lips, and nipples were slightly gilt, adding richness and warmth to the face and upper torso. The statues exhibited a rich sheen, for they were kept bright and shiny, and thereby were prevented from taking on the dark patina so admired on bronzes today. Of the many thousands of hollow-cast bronze statues that must have been produced, only a tiny number survive. This can be explained, in part, by the scorn of the later Christians, who regarded the works as nothing less than biblically condemned idols and thus destroyed as many as they could. Most of the bronze statues escaping Christian eradication were melted down for utilitarian purposes when metal became scarce in the Middle Ages. The so-called Classical Greek statues in museums are almost all marble copies. Varying greatly in fidelity and lacking the vigor of the bronze originals, they were produced to satisfy the Romans' thirst for decorating their villas and public places with reproductions of famous Greek statuary. The translation from bronze to marble usually resulted in the disfigurement of statues by the addition of unsightly tree trunks to bear the great weight of the stone and struts between arms and body to strengthen weak points. These mass-produced imitations in stone are largely responsible for the widespread notion that Greek statues carried a vacant stare and were colorless and even insipid. As noted, the Greeks painted their stone statues, including the eyes, lips, hair, clothing, and skin (suntanned for men and gods, lighter for women and goddesses), while they colored the background of sculptured relief either red or blue.

The Artemisium Zeus.   Of the few surviving Severe Style bronzes, the finest have been found in the sea. The commanding presence of an over-life-size figure of the nude Zeus—its style indicates a date around 460 BCE—was brought up early in the twentieth century from the waters off Cape Artemisium in Greece. Thus an ancient shipwreck rescued the bronze masterpiece from perishing later in the melting pot or at the hands of the Christians. His arms outstretched, the god is poised for a moment before hurling his weapon (the thunderbolt) to enforce his divine will. His hair and beard are still stylized, but his limbs and musculature vibrate with a new power and intensity, creating a dramatic silhouette.

Myron: The Discobolus.   Besides Phidias, the most notable Greek sculptors of the fifth century BCE were Myron and Polyclitus, both celebrated for their bronze athletes, known to us only through numerous Roman copies, mainly in marble. Ancient sources suggest Myron was born in Attica and worked around the mid-fifth century. His famous *Discobolus* (Discus Thrower) shows an athlete at the high point of his backswing, his motion arrested for a moment before turning to hurl the discus. The placid face and idealized features are characteristic of the Severe Style. Judging from Roman copies, the bronze original (about 450 BCE) was composed in one plane—almost a freestanding relief—and was meant to be viewed only from the front. From other angles, the copies appear extremely flat. Myron enjoyed a reputation for extraordinary naturalism in animal sculpture. Ancient authors relate that his famous statue of a cow on the Acropolis could be mistaken for real flesh and bone.

This over-life-size figure of Zeus in motion was recovered from the sea off Artemisium, the north cape of the Greek island of Euboea, where the piece must have gone down in an ancient merchant ship bound for elsewhere. A Severe Style bronze, whose style indicates a date around 460 BCE, the work captures the majesty and awe of divine power. The striding god stretches out his arms to aim and hurl his weapon, the thunderbolt, underscoring the lightness and strength of hollow-cast bronze statues. National Museum, Athens.

SCULPTURE OF THE HIGH CLASSICAL PERIOD (450–400 BCE)

Polyclitus: The Doryphorus.   Polyclitus, a native of Argos, was a leading sculptor in the third quarter of the fifth century BCE, though his works are known only from literary reports or dry Roman copies. He was famous in the ancient Greek world for creating kouroi of idealized athletes. Polyclitus wrote a lost treatise, the Canon, on his system of striving for ideal proportions in the rendering of nude athletes. He

Ancient writers suggest the sculptor Myron, who spent much of his working life in Athens, enjoyed a reputation for catching figures in an instant of vigorous action. His celebrated bronze *Discobolus* (Discus Thrower), *c.* 450 BCE, is known to us only through a variety of Roman copies, recognized from a detailed description of the original by Lucian, an author of the second century CE. In this marble copy, we see the athlete in the moment just before he lets the discus fly, his powerful body and limbs forming two intersecting arcs, though his serene face betrays no hint of vigorous physical and mental concentration. Composed in one plane, the figure was meant to be viewed from the front and appears extremely flat from other angles. The Roman copyist added the supporting marble tree trunk, an unnecessary feature for the original bronze. Museo Nazionale delle Terme, Rome.

embodied this principle in his much-copied *Doryphorus* (Spear Bearer), which portrayed a powerful youth striding forth shouldering a spear. Although the impressive physique bears a sharply defined U-shaped pelvic groove, an unrealistic convention, the subtle organization of body parts and sensitive modeling combine to create a relaxed pose and a sense of natural movement not achieved previously. The statue's right leg bears the full weight of the body, thrusting the right hip outward,

Polyclitus of Argos was acclaimed for his harmoniously designed statues of standing naked males, especially athletes. He wrote a lost treatise, the *Canon*, or Rule, describing his concern for representing the standing male nude with ideal proportions and anatomical accuracy. Polyclitus embodied these principles in a famous statue called the *Doryphorus* (Spear Bearer). Although the bronze original of about 440 BCE is lost, we recognize its dynamic balance and subtle rhythm of relaxed and tense limbs in many Roman copies, generally of marble. This prosaic marble copy, one of the most complete, shows the broadshouldered youth standing naturally, resting his weight on the right leg, the left relaxed and supported only by the toes. He grasped a spear with his left hand while letting his right arm hang by his side. Museo Nazionale, Naples.

while the shoulders are tilted in the opposite direction and the head is slightly inclined. The stone tree trunk behind the right leg was added by the copyist to support the heavy marble statue but was not required in the bronze original.

Phidias.   The versatile Athenian sculptor Phidias, active from about 465 to 425 BCE, excelled in producing harmonious gods and humans. He and his associates represented the human figure as divine, the divine as human. In antiquity Phidias'

The east pediment of the Parthenon, 437–432 BCE, illustrated the birth of Athena from the head of her father Zeus, attended by the other Olympian gods. The sculpture is now fragmentary, ravaged by invaders and other assaults. Particularly noteworthy are three majestic marble goddesses, illustrated here, carefully designed to fit under the sloping cornice of the pediment. Perhaps representing Hestia, Dione, and Aphrodite, the first two goddesses are seated, while the third reclines with her arm supported in the lap of the second. The Phidian school adorned the figures with profoundly sensuous swirling drapery, clinging to the bodies to reveal the form beneath. British Museum, London.

two most celebrated masterpieces were his colossal cult statues of Zeus at Olympia and Athena in the Parthenon. Both were fashioned of gold and ivory over a wooden core, with adornments in silver, copper, enamel, paint, glass, and jewels. Inferior later copies fail to convey the grandeur the ancients attributed to them. Today Phidias is better remembered for his work on the Parthenon. He must have at least designed the so-called Elgin Marbles in the British Museum, which include substantial fragments of the figured frieze that ran around the outer wall of the naos of the temple. Placed high above the floor and intended to be viewed in relatively dim light, the frieze was brightly painted and carved in low relief to prevent deep obscuring shadows. Most scholars regard the frieze as a depiction of the Panathenaic Procession, the most important ceremony in ancient Athens. Phidias' harmonious design for the procession to Athena combines figures on foot and others on horseback, a novel depiction up to this time on a Greek religious building of human activity rather than mythological scenes. Some devout Athenians must have regarded the great frieze as nothing less than sacrilege.

Phidias designed sculptured drapery to reveal rather than to conceal the body of both males and females. Much of the drapery produced for the carved figures at the Parthenon appears almost transparent and clinging, the so-called wet-drapery technique, for which Phidias is justly famous. Essentially Phidian in style, the *Three Goddesses* from the east pediment of the Parthenon recline gracefully as a group and slope to fit within the downward movement of the architecture. The deep folds of their swirling drapery catch dramatic shadows, alternately revealing and con-

A reconstruction of the *Three Goddesses*, originally brightly painted, from the east pediment of the Parthenon.

cealing the bodies underneath. The relief of a Nike adjusting her sandal represents another notable example of the wet-drapery technique. Executed in the Phidian style about 410 BCE, the figure is from the low wall that surrounded the little temple of Athena Nike. Nike's drapery clings to her supple form as though drenched with water. The concealed kore tradition seems quite alien to these sculptures whose transparent veils reveal and enhance the female body.

Mosaics, Painting, and Pottery

Polygnotus.   The art of mosaic, as practiced by the ancient Greeks, consisted of fitting colored stones together to form a design or picture. The technique was used occasionally in fifth-century BCE Greece to produce patterns or scenes on floors, with artists pressing natural pebbles into wet cement. As for the painting of major scenes and portraits, our knowledge is confined to literary descriptions, paintings on pottery, and rare original examples. Greek and Roman writers suggest revolutionary artistic changes occurred during the second quarter of the fifth century BCE, with talented painters turning away from simple, uniform compositions. Polygnotus and Micon produced major paintings, probably on whitened wooden panels, to adorn the interior walls of public buildings in Athens and Delphi. The prime artist was Polygnotus of Thasos, who came to Athens in the time of Cimon and enjoyed high social standing. The Athenians praised him for an epic scene of the fall of Troy, lost to us, at the Painted Stoa. Polygnotus employed four basic

This exquisite marble relief of a Nike (Victory) adjusting her sandle, *c.* 410 BCE, graced the south side of the parapet built around three sides of the temple of Athena Nike on the Athenian Acropolis. The piece illustrates the Phidian style of clinging drapery at its most transparent, as if drenched with water. Acropolis Museum, Athens.

colors and obtained additional values by mixing them. He abandoned the insistence on profile stances and conveyed a sense of space by distributing groups of figures on different levels, freeing them from a single ground line. We hear from literary sources that Polygnotus was able to express nuances of motion convincingly and to create facial expressions showing a wide range of human emotions. The Roman writer Pliny the Elder credited him with enlivening the faces of figures by parting their lips and also with originating seemingly transparent or translucent drapery.

The Niobid Painter.   The red-figure technique, discussed in chapter 7, continued to dominate vase painting in fifth-century Athens. While some painters clung to stiff Archaic conventions during the first half of the century, others such as the Niobid

The painter Polygnotus of Thasos, whose compositions have all perished, was comparable in importance with the sculptor Phidias. Literary sources suggest Polygnotus' many innovations included conveying space and depth more realistically, partly by freeing figures from a single ground line. Vases decorated by the so-called Niobid Painter reflect the Polygnotan method of placing figures one above another in a natural setting. The Niobid Painter's modern nickname comes from this unsigned Attic red-figure krater, c. 460 BCE, one side of which shows the deities Apollo and Artemis slaying the children of Niobe, with the figures distributed over the surface of the vase in various postures. In myth Niobe, the mother of at least a dozen children, boasted that she was superior to the goddess Leto, who had borne only two offspring, Apollo and his twin sister, Artemis. To punish the arrogant affront to their mother, Apollo and Artemis hunted down with bow and arrow all the children of Niobe, who wept ceaselessly until Zeus turned her to stone. Louvre, Paris.

Painter chose calm Classical scenes. The Niobid Painter, apparently inspired by the new wall-painting compositions of Polygnotus, placed his figures one above another to suggest space and depth.

The Achilles Painter.   An echo of Polygnotus' use of color survives in the so-called white-ground vases. The technique resembled red-figure, though the vessel was first covered with a slip of very fine white clay to provide a light surface for painting.

Figures adorning the Achilles Painter's vases are thought to resemble those of Polygnotan wall paintings. The quiet grandeur of his style graced a number of white-ground lekythoi, the tall, one-handled flasks containing perfumed oil that were commonly offered as gifts to the dead, either placed in or laid above the grave. One of the finest by this painter, illustrated here, shows a Muse playing a lyre on Mount Helicon, with a nightingale beside her. The neatly rendered inscription praises the beauty of the youth Deiopeithes. Attic white-ground lekythos, c. 440 BCE. Antikensammlungen, Munich.

The range of colors remained severely limited because few colored glazes known to the Greeks could survive the intense heat of a kiln. Daily handling of these vases tended to destroy the applied slip, and thus the white-ground technique, employed initially mostly on the interior of cups, was reserved almost exclusively in the later fifth century for tall, cylindrical oil vases (lekythoi) used for grave offerings. Foremost among the painters of the white-ground vases was the Achilles Painter—named for his red-figure amphora in the Vatican Museums—who produced quiet, idealized figures.

LITERATURE

TRAGEDY

Origins and Early History.   Athenian drama marks the pinnacle of Classical literature. Tragic drama undoubtedly evolved from the choral song and dance to Dionysus called a dithyramb, performed by a chorus of men wearing masks to portray the satyrs associated with the god. Apparently tragic drama began in Athens in the sixth century BCE, when one of the performers separated himself from the chorus to converse with its leader, a development ascribed in antiquity to a shadowy figure named Thespis. With the gradual transformation of a choral performance into tragedy, actors played multiple roles and entered into dialogue with the chorus leader and with other actors. The presentation of tragedy became a regular feature at the annual Athenian festival called the City (or Great) Dionysia. Aeschylus is said to have added a second actor in the early fifth century BCE, thereby subordinating the chorus to the dialogue and producing dramatic tension through the interplay of confronting figures. Sophocles completed the process by adding a third actor. Actors, all male, played both male and female parts. They wore masks (with wigs attached) and could easily assume different roles by merely changing their masks behind the *skene*, the building used for the changing of costumes and forming a background for plays. The masks immediately identified the character to spectators as young or old, male or female, happy or sad, and other standard types. Violent deeds were always performed offstage and reported by a messenger. Providing a dazzling effect, a crane (*mechane*) could be manipulated to bring actors playing gods or heroes through the air onto the stage to decide the final outcome. From the Greek *mechane* came the Latin expression *deus ex machina* (god from the machine), still used to mean a contrived solution to the entanglements or the difficulties of a play by the sudden and unexpected introduction of a character, device, or event.

The City Dionysia.   As noted, the fifth century BCE witnessed the incorporation of tragic drama as a regular feature of the City Dionysia, the early springtime festival honoring Dionysus. Represented by an old-wooden statue, the god made his ceremonial entry into Athens in a preliminary procession before the festival proper began. The grand opening procession two days later included both citizens and resident aliens, with many participants carrying huge erect phalluses, the Dionysiac fertility symbol. Others drove before them great numbers of cows and bulls to be sacrificed at the sacred precinct adjacent to the theater of Dionysus on the lower south slope of the Acropolis. During the several following days of festivities the Athenians enjoyed parades, ceremonies, choral contests, feasting, and riotous drinking. Three days of theatrical performances took place in the theater of Dionysus, sanctified by the presence of the statue of the god.

The chief archon chose three poet-composers to enter the annual competition, each presenting three tragedies and one satyr play. Essentially a form of mythological burlesque, the satyr play featured a clownish chorus in the guise of satyrs—all with prominent attached tails and phalluses—providing bawdy comic relief after the often grim horrors of the tragedies. Every theatrical performance contributing to the greater glory of Dionysus was partly financed by a liturgy, a form of state service requiring wealthy citizens to bear the cost of public activities. A committee of ordinary citizens chosen by lottery judged the plays and awarded first, second, and third prizes to the three playwrights.

The popular use of a female chorus and strong individual female characters in Greek tragedy demanded a transition from masculine to femine identity, for males played the female parts. A number of vase painters focused on the compelling theme, exemplified by this scene of chorus-men preparing for female roles. The youth on the left has already donned the everyday dress of a young woman as well as a female mask—complete with attractive hair enclosed in a fashionable headscarf—and now practices theatrical gestures suitable to the role. The young man on the right, who is putting on the usual calf-length boots, soon will cover his head and face with the female mask on the floor. Attic red-figure amphora, c. 450 BCE. Museum of Fine Arts, Boston.

Greek tragedy drew mostly on stories from myth. The characters were not or-dinary human beings but gods and heroes played by actors speaking in verse, while the chorus provided the important musical element. The performance was normally religious in the sense that the fifth-century tragic poet focused on the complex relationship of gods and people and the influence of supernatural powers on human destiny. The dramatist employed the famous Greek stories as vehicles for discussing contemporary social and ethical issues and existential questions like mortality and time. Tragedy borrowed heavily from Homer, notably the theme of the destruction of a hero or some other lofty protagonist. Regardless of their greatness, these figures exhibited flaws bringing them to ruin. The more sophisticated Greek tragedies identify the cause of this downfall as hubris, extreme arrogance or dishonorable behavior inviting the retribution of the gods to balance the scales of justice.

Aeschylus (c. 525–456 BCE).   The three great tragic poets of fifth-century Athens were Aeschylus, Sophocles, and Euripides. Aeschylus, the earliest, was born of noble parentage at Eleusis in Athenian territory and died in Sicily. Few facts are known of his life, but he fought for Greece at Marathon and probably also at Salamis. Aeschylus produced his first tragedy about 499 BCE, and he won first prize at the drama festival in 484 BCE, thereafter enjoying many more victories. He is credited with adding a second actor, making true dialogue possible and reducing the role of the chorus. An extremely prolific playwright, Aeschylus wrote more than eighty plays, though only seven have survived, of which *Prometheus Bound* is of disputed authenticity. The playwright is remembered for his lofty theology and his interest in profound moral problems like crime and punishment. The greatest of his plays are concerned with catastrophic human struggles against divine justice. In defending the law established by Zeus, the gods strike down the person afflicted with deadly hubris.

In dark and wonderful language, Aeschylus focuses on his vision of divine justice in the *Oresteia*, one of the greatest works of western literature and the only complete Greek tragic trilogy to have survived. Its three plays form a continuous story. The first, *Agamemnon*, tells of the victorious king returning home from the Trojan War to be treacherously murdered by his faithless wife, Clytemnestra, and her lover, Aegisthus. In the second play, the *Libation Bearers*, Agamemnon's son, Orestes, at last avenges the death by slaying his mother and her paramour in obedience to the express command of the god Apollo. For the crime of matricide, however, Orestes arouses the wrath of the Furies, horrible female spirits punishing crimes committed between kin, who hound him mercilessly from one town to the next. In the third play, the *Eumenides*, Apollo directs Orestes to go to Athens to seek justice from Athena. The goddess impanels the venerable Athenian law court of the Areopagus to try the case, with both Apollo and the Furies presenting their sides. Athena gives her verdict in favor of Orestes when the votes are tied, but she mollifies the threatening Furies by establishing their cult in Athens. Thus they acquire benevolence and are to dwell in Athens as Eumenides, the kindly ones, without relinquishing their punitive side.

Aeschylus' *Persians* is the only surviving Greek historical tragedy. The action takes place entirely at the Persian court after the defeat of Xerxes, son of Darius, at the crucial sea battle at Salamis. Aeschylus ascribes the Greek victory to the intervention of the gods and, astonishingly, treats the defeated Persians with respect. After opening with a chorus of Persian elders expressing concern about the fate of the expedition, the play relates the terrifying forebodings of Atossa, the mother of Xerxes. A messenger then arrives and announces the Persians have been defeated at Salamis and recounts the appalling details of the battle. The ghost of former king Darius appears to explain that rash Xerxes had overstepped the boundaries upheld by Zeus and warns that the Persians must never again attack Greece. The humiliated Xerxes returns, blaming himself for the destruction of the glorious Persian state. The tragic hero of the play, he has unwittingly brought about his own catastrophe.

Prometheus Bound, whose authenticity is questioned by some scholars, is the surviving play of a trilogy. In myth, the Titan Prometheus, who had stolen fire from heaven to bestow on mortals, championed humankind against Zeus. Outraged at Prometheus' defiance, almighty Zeus commanded that Prometheus be chained to a rock for eternity and made to endure endless punishments. This is the point at which the play actually begins. During its course we learn that Prometheus is the benefactor of mortals, having given them numbers, metallurgy, ships, speech, intellect, and the healing arts. Prometheus is visited by the maiden Io, who had been seduced by Zeus and transformed into a heifer by his jealous wife, Hera. Io is continually tortured by a pursuing gadfly. Prometheus predicts to Io that Zeus will be overthrown by one of his own sons but refuses to name the mother to whom the child will be born. Finally, infuriated Zeus sends lightning and thunder and an earthquake that swallows Prometheus. One of the puzzling problems about the play is the depiction of a tyrannical Zeus, unlike the upholder of a just order familiar elsewhere in Aeschylus. Apparently in the two lost plays of the trilogy Zeus becomes reconciled with Prometheus and exercises moral responsibility toward humanity.

Sophocles (c. 496–406 BCE).   Sophocles was the son of a wealthy manufacturer of armor in an outlying Athenian village. After the Greek naval triumph at Salamis, the teenage Sophocles was honored with the assignment of leading the dance of youths, naked and anointed, at the victory celebration. Ancient writings testify not only to his beauty and courteousness but also to his many friends, including Pericles, Herodotus, and Euripides. Sophocles was elected to several high administrative and military offices, which gives some credence to the biographical tradition of his magnetic personality. In terms of his work as a playwright, he was the second great tragic writer of the fifth century BCE. Sophocles won his first competition at the City Dionysia in 468, defeating the old master Aeschylus. He wrote more than one hundred and twenty plays in his long career, though merely seven tragedies and one satyr play survive. Ancient sources credit him with playing a crucial role in the development of Greek theater by making several important changes in the way tragedy was performed. Most important, he is said to have added a third actor, providing scope for increasing the complexity of the plot. Sophocles broke with the usual practice of presenting tragedies as connected trilogies, instead producing three tragedies on different subjects at the same contest. He is said to have enlarged the chorus from twelve to fifteen and to have introduced painted backdrops as scenery. Sophocles was also celebrated for his use of dramatic irony, skill in creating suspense, mastery of dialogue, and beautiful choral lyrics.

Ancient sources rank Sophocles as the preeminent Greek dramatist, unrivaled in his ability to construct plots and delineate character, praised for his portrayals of individuals trapped by agonizing human conflicts and dreadful mental pain. While Aeschylus' characters demonstrate virtually no individual traits, Sophocles shifts to probing studies of human nature. The characters of Sophocles are famous for their heroic splendor, yet also for their helplessness and mortality. They find themselves torn between obeying human and divine law. The victim of such a dilemma must face terrible punishment, whichever law is obeyed. Sophocles' characters often fall into the very calamity they are trying to avoid and bring about the exact reversal of their good intentions. Yet these terrible contests with misfortune endow them with dignity and wisdom.

Sophocles' *Oedipus Tyrannus* (*Oedipus the King*), also known as *Oedipus Rex*, remains the most widely performed of all existing Greek tragedies. Perhaps written shortly after 430 BCE, the play concerns the personal disaster of Oedipus. During the course of the play certain events occurring before the start of the action are recalled. Oedipus, son of King Laius and Queen Jocasta of Thebes, was born under a dread prophecy by the Delphic oracle that he would kill his father and marry his mother. Laius tried to thwart the divine will by driving a spike through the infant's ankles and then instructing a servant to expose him on a mountainside. Yet the servant took pity on the baby and gave him to a Corinthian shepherd, who carried the infant to the childless king and queen of Corinth. King Polybus of Corinth named the little boy Oedipus (swollen footed) from the injury to his ankles. The boy grew up believing the king and queen of Corinth were his true parents.

As a young man Oedipus consulted the Delphic oracle and was informed that he would kill his father and marry his mother. Attempting to escape this fate, he vowed never to return to Corinth while the king and queen of the city were alive. He decided to make a new life for himself elsewhere. Taking the road from Delphi to Thebes, he fell into a dispute with a stranger at a crossroads and killed him, not knowing this was Laius, his actual father. Oedipus arrived at Thebes at a time when the city was being terrorized by the Sphinx, a monstrous creature with the head and breasts of a woman and the body of a winged lion. She challenged every Theban passing her way with a riddle: "What goes on four legs at morning, two at noon, and three at evening?" The Sphinx ate the passersby when they failed to solve the riddle. Oedipus confronted her and realized that the correct answer was a human being, for the riddle referred to the three ages of life: infancy, maturity, and old age (when leaning on a staff might be necessary). The defeated monster committed suicide. Acclaimed by the Thebans as their king, Oedipus became the husband of the newly widowed queen, Jocasta, his mother. He had now unknowingly fulfilled the prophecy by killing his father and marrying his mother. This union produced four children, all of whom were doomed to unhappy ends.

As the action opens, we find happily married Oedipus wisely ruling Thebes, but a plague now ravishes the city. Oedipus promises to rescue his people. When

This scene from Sophocles' *Antigone*—his famous tragedy examining the eternal conflict between moral obligation and human law—shows Antigone brought by two guards before Creon, mythical king of Thebes who condemns her to be sealed alive in a tomb. Detail of a south Italian (Lucanian) vase by the Dolon Painter, *c.* 370–380 BCE. British Museum, London.

the oracle of Apollo declares the pestilence is caused by the presence of the slayer of Laius, Oedipus vehemently calls on the unknown culprit to declare himself. He begins an investigation and gradually uncovers the dreadful truth by interrogating witnesses. Jocasta hangs herself in remorseful agony and Oedipus puts out his eyes with pins from her dress. He abdicates his throne and departs into self-imposed exile, divine retribution for his patricide and incest. At the end of his life Sophocles returned to the exiled king with his play *Oedipus at Colonus.* Oedipus has wandered to Colonus, an outlying Athenian village (and Sophocles' home), where he is called by the gods and disappears from mortal sight, with the power to protect Athens and perform miracles.

Around 441 BCE Sophocles wrote *Antigone,* relating the final calamity of the royal house of Thebes. At first, Oedipus' two sons, Eteocles and Polynices, quarrel about who should occupy the throne but finally agree to reign in alternate years. Eteocles refuses to relinquish the throne after ruling a year, however, and Polynices leads a foreign army to Thebes in an attempt to depose his brother. The two rivals slay one another in single combat. Succeeding to the kingship, their uncle Creon forbids anyone to bury the corpse of the invader under pain of death, thereby denying Polynices a resting place in the afterlife. Yet Polynices' sister Antigone defies the order of the new king and carries out the funeral rites. Caught in the eternal conflict between sacred duty and the authority of the state, Antigone claims she has an overriding duty to choose kinship and divine will over human law. As punishment, the king condemns her to be sealed in a tomb and left to die, though she is engaged to his son Haemon. Creon finally comes to realize the consequences of contravening divine law but arrives at the tomb too late, for Antigone has hanged herself, and Haemon then takes his own life in front of his father. Returning to the palace, the king learns that his wife, Eurydice, has killed herself as well. Creon is left broken and alone. Sophocles, in examining the struggles of humankind against the inscrutable ways of the gods, suggests that the laws of the state fall before the superior claims of universal moral obligation.

Euripides (c. 485–406 BCE).   The youngest and most controversial of the three great Athenian tragedians of the fifth century, Euripides withdrew from the bitter Athens of the late Peloponnesian War for Macedonia, where he died. He wrote some ninety plays but, failing to enjoy the kind of admiration accorded to the works of Aeschylus and Sophocles, won only four first prizes. Supposedly reclusive and irritable, Euripides was not active in public affairs. He was associated with several of the itinerant teachers known as the Sophists (discussed later), who aroused strong reactions among their contemporaries. They gained a reputation for teaching techniques of persuasion and argument without regard for truth or morality. Many Greeks, especially those of more conservative views, regarded them as subverters of virtuous conduct and religious tradition.

By chance, seventeen of Euripides' tragedies and one of his satyr plays have come down to us intact. They show his remarkable originality and inventiveness. Euripides asked brooding questions about the political, social, artistic, and philosophical ideas of his time. Most of his surviving plays were produced while the Peloponnesian War was in progress. Although Euripides championed the cause of Athens in his earlier plays, his later works boldly protest war and its horrors. The Peloponnesian War left many Greeks skeptical about the existence of divine government in the affairs of the world. Euripides shared that attitude, even casting scorn on hallowed myths and envisioning the gods as irrational beings flawed by the same uncontrollable passions as humans. Indeed, his portrayal of capricious, irrational supernatural forces operating in the world has its counterpart in his view of the irrational in individual humans. He is famous for his profound probing of human nature and, above all, human irrationality and madness.

Euripides frequently illustrated the suffering of women, rare for a Greek writer of the period. The *Trojan Women* (or *Troades*)—the surviving play of a trilogy about the Trojan War—details the courage and unspeakable suffering of the female captives after the fall of Troy. They retain a dignity that is lost by the bullying victors, who pass them around as trophies of war. The tragedy was performed in 415 BCE, at the height of the Peloponnesian War, and clearly reflects Euripides' concern about the brutality of warfare on the human spirit.

Euripides scorned false ideas of female docility and often focused on the driving passions of women, especially their loves and hates. In *Medea*, one of his most celebrated plays, Euripides tells the poignant story of a wronged woman who has surrendered everything for her beloved. Medea is an extraordinary figure, a sorceress and the daughter of the king of Colchis on the Black Sea. She fell passionately in love with Jason when he arrived in Colchis in search of the fabulous Golden Fleece. At great risk she helped him gain possession of the fleece and murdered her own brother to delay the pursuing party. Jason and Medea settled in Corinth and produced two children. As the play opens, Jason has betrayed Medea for a marriage to the daughter of the king of Corinth. Medea becomes deranged with anger and seeks a hideous vengeance. First, she sends the princess a poisoned robe that consumes her flesh. The king dies in agony from the same poison while trying to save his daughter. As a final revenge on Jason, Medea stabs both of their young children to death. Through his towering poetic artistry, Euripides tempts us to sympathize with Medea, despite her monstrous deeds. At the end of the play Medea confronts Jason, now reduced to wretchedness, in bitter triumph. Driving a magic chariot above the stage, she then flies away to take refuge in Athens.

In his final years Euripides wrote *The Bacchae (Bacchants)*, an unforgettable portrayal of the Dionysiac spirit. The play centers on the frenzy that characterizes Dionysus and his worshipers. The Bacchants are Asian maenads—portrayed by males—who form the chorus and are crucially involved in the action of the play. When Dionysus, accompanied by the maenads, returns from Asia to his native Thebes to establish his ecstatic cult, King Pentheus resists. The god's vengeance is swift and terrible. Dionysus bewitches the ruler, persuading him to dress in feminine clothing and spy on the Dionysiac rites of the women in the mountains. The intoxicated and shrieking worshipers, led by none other than the king's mother, Agave, mistake Pentheus for a mountain lion and tear him to pieces. Pentheus' mother carries his head in triumph but gradually comes to realize what she has done, a scene virtually unrivalled for sheer horror. *The Bacchae* defies certain interpretation. Whether the play is a warning against the destructive cruelty of the gods and their religion or a celebration of the elemental power of the Dionysiac cult, its cumulative effect is overwhelming.

COMEDY

The origins of comedy are obscure. Aristotle relates in the *Poetics*, his treatise on literary criticism, that comedy came from improvisations connected with the coarse songs of those accompanying the phallus in the Dionysiac cult. The genre developed much the same way as tragedy, with alternations between performance of the actors and choral song. Yet in comedy there were fewer formal restrictions, for the comic poet sometimes used more than three actors and was not bound by a few standard stories. The plot was drawn almost exclusively from the social and political life of Athens rather than mythological themes. By modern standards Athenian comedy was rowdy, even pornographic.

Comedy was not established as a competition at the City Dionysia until around 488 BCE, though its riotous origins were much older. Performances were staged by

440 BCE at the Lenaea, an annual Dionysiac festival celebrated in midwinter. The comedies produced in Athens during the fifth century were subsequently known to the ancients as Old Comedy, which represented a blend of political and social commentary, personal abuse heaped on individual Athenians, and unabashed slapstick comedy. The players wore grotesque masks, and their costumes included exaggerated phalluses and bellies for comic effect. A typical play of Old Comedy has a tripartite structure: a burlesque debate between the chorus and a character, an address (the parabasis) by the chorus to the audience on behalf of the comic poet, and a series of farcical scenes toward the end.

Aristophanes (c. 450–385 BCE).   The only surviving plays of Old Comedy are those of Aristophanes, who tells us much about public opinion during the Peloponnesian War. Recognized in antiquity as the greatest classical comic playwright, Aristophanes probably came from an aristocratic family and apparently identified with the basically antiwar sentiment of the landowning class, which had suffered greatly from the Peloponnesian War. He made no secret of his contempt for the costly conflict and mocked the excesses of Athenian democracy. In his eleven surviving plays, Aristophanes holds up countless named individuals to ridicule, though the significance of many of them is lost on the modern reader.

The *Knights,* performed in 424 BCE, savagely attacks the leading politician of the day, Cleon, accusing him of corrupting the assembly for his own glory and profit. The comedy describes his replacement by a sausage vendor, an even greater scoundrel. The Athenians awarded Aristophanes first prize for this play but, ironically, reelected Cleon to office shortly afterward. In the *Clouds,* performed in 423 BCE, Aristophanes depicts a dutiful Athenian father whose son has plunged him into embarrassing debt. He enrolls the young man in the school of Socrates (who in real life refused to found a school) to learn the art of argument and thereby win any lawsuits resulting from his debts. Essentially, the comedy is an amusing diatribe against the Sophists. Falsely categorizing Socrates as a Sophist, Aristophanes maliciously attacks the great philosopher as a corrupt teacher who threatens traditional religion and social morality. Socrates spent much of his life criticizing the Sophists, and this bizarre depiction of him has led to various interpretations. Apparently Aristophanes is drawing the portrait from the popular image of an intellectual. Aristophanes' attack on Socrates made a lasting impression on the Athenians, contributing eventually to the death of the philosopher.

The antiwar comedy *Lysistrata,* performed in 411 BCE, is named for an imaginary Athenian woman who convinces her female companions to seize the Acropolis and its financial reserves, thereby preventing males from squandering further funds on the Peloponnesian War, now turning calamitously against Athens. Then they team with the women of Sparta in an agreement to withhold sex from the men to coerce them to end hostilities. The women take an oath to make every attempt to sexually arouse the men but then to withdraw from their advances—a wild improbability in fifth-century Greece. Much of the action revolves around extremely risqué humor. Clearly, behind the wit of the comedy lies Aristophanes' strong yearning for peace.

The *Frogs*, which won first prize at the Lenaea in 405 BCE, was performed barely a year before Athens' final defeat in the Peloponnesian War. Aristophanes employs the brilliant comedy to attack Euripides—who had died a few months earlier—suggesting the skeptical attitude of his plays has the potential to undermine the morality and future of Athens. The comic protagonist is the god Dionysus, who fears the withering of Athenian tragedy following the death of Euripides and descends to the underworld to bring him back. When crossing the River Styx, the god hears an unseen croaking chorus of frogs singing their famous refrain: "Brekekekex, ko-ax, ko-ax; Brekekekex, ko-ax, ko-ax." In the underworld he witnesses a long contest between Euripides and Aeschylus, each attacking the other's lines with mockery and parody. Aeschylus proves to be the greater playwright, and Dionysus decides to bring him to Athens to restore tragedy to its old dignity and thereby inspire the Athenians to their former might and glory.

HISTORY

Herodotus (c. 484–425 BCE).   The earliest known prose literary works stemmed from the need to express thoughts with precision. Prose was adopted first to convey ideas in philosophy, later for historical writing. An important pioneer in the writing of history, as noted in chapter 7, was the aristocratic Hecataeus of Miletus, who penned a prose work on the legendary pedigrees of privileged Greek families and a travel book describing the world known to him. The second half of the fifth century BCE witnessed the appearance of another native of Greek Asia Minor, Herodotus of Halicarnassus, who has continued to shape western historical writing to this day. Herodotus mentions the geographical work of his predecessor Hecataeus with disdain but apparently borrowed freely from the treatise. A descendant of an aristocratic family and born a Persian subject, Herodotus gained an appreciation for foreign cultures. He investigated local customs and gathered a wealth of information by traveling widely in the Greek world and beyond, visiting Egypt, Palestine, Phoenicia, Mesopotamia, and the Black Sea region. Herodotus must have spent some time in Athens, where his friendship with Sophocles is well documented, and is said to have joined the Athenian-sponsored colony of Thurii in southern Italy, living there the remainder of his life.

His voluminous historical narrative on the Persian Wars, written in the graceful Ionic dialect, is the earliest surviving Greek work in prose. Herodotus termed his search for understanding *historia* (inquiry), a Greek word that has provided English with the word *history*: the investigation and analysis of the past. Herodotus offers the reader the result of his inquiry, in order to preserve a record of the extraordinary deeds of both Greeks and non-Greeks. Divided by later editors into nine "books," his riveting account is our major written source for the epic contest between the Greeks and Persians and its antecedents, which Herodotus traces to the subjugation of the Ionian Greeks by King Croesus of Lydia. The work passes on to Croesus' misconceived attack on Persian territory and then offers the history of the Persian Empire, telling of the reigns of Cyrus, Cambyses, Darius, and Xerxes, who expanded their realm westward and came into conflict with mainland Greece.

Herodotus, by virtue of his systematic factual investigation concerning the development of the conflict and his delightful style, earned the title accorded to him in antiquity, "the father of history." Reflecting the spirit of Homer and aristocratic Greece, he viewed excellence and glory as the proper goal of human activity, while avoiding the usual narrow Greek attitude toward foreigners, admiring Egyptian achievements and giving a sympathetic account of the lands and peoples of the Persian Empire. Much of what we know about Egypt and Persia in the decades before the Peloponnesian War comes from Herodotus, who provides a storehouse of information about places, peoples, customs, and monuments. His vast narrative derives sometimes from written records but usually from personal observations and what was told to him on his astonishing range of travels. Herodotus was always prepared to recount a good story and let the reader decide on its reliability. When opinions conflicted, he simply included them all, whether fanciful or factual. Despite his inclusion of myths, oracles, dreams, hearsay, short stories, sexual escapades, and similar motifs, Herodotus is the first known writer attempting to explain historical cause and effect. He organized his material around a grand unifying theme and exhibited remarkable narrative skill. As a writer, Herodotus was never surpassed in antiquity.

Thucydides (c. 460–400 BCE).   A wealthy aristocrat, Thucydides played an active role in Athenian life until he was exiled in 424 BCE for failing to prevent the Spartan capture of Amphipolis. Usually regarded as the greatest historian of the ancient world, Thucydides used his exile to produce a detailed account of the Peloponnesian War. He aimed for the utmost accuracy and traveled widely through the theaters of war searching for evidence from eyewitnesses. Thucydides did not live to complete his account, which breaks off in mid-sentence describing events of 411 BCE. The extant parts of the work were divided into eight "books" by later scholars.

Thucydides' great innovation was to write about the political and military events of his own time. Unlike Herodotus, Thucydides avoided tall tales and refused to explain human events through divine intervention, though he recognized the strong influence of belief on human affairs. He is considered more accurate than Herodotus in matters of chronology and is famous for distinguishing between the long-term and immediate causes of the war. Thucydides' chief weakness is his refusal to offer differing accounts of different eyewitnesses, forcing readers to trust his own judgment. Presenting no alternatives to his choice of facts, Thucydides produced a narrative with huge gaps in economic, social, and religious matters. The most striking feature of his history is the use of speeches—exemplified by the funeral oration of Pericles—which were generally composed by Thucydides himself and put in the mouths of historical characters to indicate their views and objectives prior to making crucial decisions. Pessimistic about the nature of society, Thucydides explains war and politics in terms of an inherent human drive for self-advantage and power over others. He saw the Peloponnesian War as inevitable from Sparta's growing fear of Athens, which arrogantly overreached itself with tragic consequences for the Greek world.

SCIENCE AND PHILOSOPHY

To the Greeks, philosophical investigation included both science and what we call philosophy. They hardly distinguished between the two. Greek philosophers were searching for ultimate truth and viewed science as one of their tools rather than a separate discipline. Thus the methods of science continued to be largely speculative. Although scientific progress was delayed because empirical observation was ranked behind speculation, the Greeks accumulated a considerable body of practical knowledge in fields such as physiology, anatomy, engineering, metallurgy, navigation, and astronomy.

Astronomy

Meton of Athens.   In the fifth century BCE astronomy was primarily concerned with the quest for a dependable calendar. The traditional Athenian calendar was lunar, the year beginning in summer. Because the twelve lunar months equaled only 354 days, an intercalary (or inserted) month was added to the calendar at intervals to harmonize the lunar and solar year, but the corrections were made rather haphazardly. Meton of Athens is famous for introducing a calendar that brought the lunar calendar into approximate correlation with the solar year by adding intercalary months at specified intervals in a nineteen-year cycle. Meton's calendar was employed for dating astronomical observations, not as a reform of the regular civil calendar that regulated the religious festivals of Athens.

Medicine

Hippocrates of Cos.   The greatest Greek scientific advances of the fifth century BCE were in the field of medicine, though Greek snobbishness toward manual labor downgraded the status of the practitioner while elevating that of the medical theorist with unsoiled hands. Most Greeks of the day still regarded disease as a visitation from the supernatural and sought cures through both magic and religion. Shrines of healing gods and heroes dotted Greece and were the focus of pilgrimages by countless sick people seeking cures. The most successful cult of this kind was that of Asclepius, god of healing, who was popular in Athens and elsewhere, with each of his temples serving as a hospital. The usual method of healing was by incubation, whereby the patient slept overnight, to be visited and cured by the deity in dreams. Asclepius' priests, who claimed to be descendants of the god, acquired a basic knowledge of medicine through practice and observation. They often advised various therapies such as exercise, bathing, and changes in diet. Both Epidaurus (in the northeastern Peloponnese) and Cos (an island in the eastern Aegean) were famous centers of the cult in the fifth century BCE.

Cos was the home of a highly skilled school of physicians, one of whom was Hippocrates (*c*. 460–380 BCE), considered the founder of scientific medicine and medical ethics, though we know little about him. Of the sixty medical treatises preserved under his name—the so-called *Hippocratic Corpus*—possibly none was written by Hippocrates himself. Many of the works represent the efforts of his pupils and later physicians. Although these efforts reveal an established body of medical practice based on solid observation, all kinds of medical doctrines have been associated with Hippocrates. He or one of his followers advocated the view that the human body contains four humors (blood, phlegm, yellow bile, and black bile), influenced by Empedocles' theory that the cosmos is made up of four elements (earth, air, fire, and water), discussed below in conjunction with philosophy. The Hippocratic school taught that the ascendant humor determines the temperament of each individual—blood (sanguine), phlegm (phlegmatic), yellow bile (choleric), or black bile (melancholic)—and that an excess of any humor causes illness. The curative process consisted of restoring the natural harmony of the humors, by bloodletting, for example, if the physician decided the patient suffered from an excess of blood. The theory that the four humors must be kept in balance in order to maintain good health underlay medical practice and blocked additional advances down to the eighteenth century. Yet Hippocrates and his followers formulated the fundamental principle of medicine that illnesses result from natural rather than supernatural causes. Much of the emphasis seems to have been on diet and regimen. The physicians of the Hippocratic school also employed drugs, set broken bones, and even performed minor operations (not internal surgery). They were mindful also of the importance of cleanliness in medical procedures and adhered to strict ethical principles. One Hippocratic treatise, *On the Sacred Illness*, concludes that epilepsy was not of divine but natural origin, while another, *On Airs, Waters, and Places*, describes the effects of climate and environment on human health and psychology.

PHILOSOPHY

Heraclitus: The Last of the Great Pre-Socratic Philosophers Living in Ionia.   As noted in chapter 7, thinkers coming from the intellectually advanced region of Ionia in Greek Asia Minor created philosophy in the sixth century BCE as they wrestled to comprehend the nature of the gods, the physical universe, and humankind. The last of the great Ionian philosophers was Heraclitus of Ephesus, who lived toward the end of the century. In his search for reality, Heraclitus was impressed by the constant change he observed around him and postulated that the world was in a perpetual state of change and conflict, flux and decay. Yet Heraclitus also observed balance and order in the universe and argued that cosmic reason—Logos—causes and regulates all physical processes and human intelligence.

Parmenides: The Concept of Being.   The pioneering Greek thinker Parmenides of Elea (*c.* 515–440 BCE), who lived in his native city in southwest Italy, rejected Heraclitus' notion of perpetual change. The philosophers prior to Parmenides had sought to show that the world is derived from a single everlasting principle, but he denied that an eternal prime substance can divide itself and change. In this vein, Parmenides postulated Being, an eternal primeval substance that is immovable, unchangeable, and indivisible. He went on to suggest that although the visible world appears to our senses to change, it does not, for matter—which is eternal and indestructible—has neither a beginning nor an end. Parmenides argued that in thinking, we must postulate something that *is* because that which *is not* cannot be thought and cannot be. Thus absolute nonexistence is an unthinkable void, and the universe cannot be in a state of constant flux because "Being exists and nonbeing does not exist." Reality, then, does not come into being or move or change, and empty space does not exist. What is—Being—is uncreated and never perishes. Clearly, Parmenides' philosophy challenged scientific observation based on sensory perception—empiricism—for he argued that the real world is not what we see and feel around us but what we perceive by mental contemplation alone.

Empedocles: The Four Elements.   Belonging to the western Greek world in Sicily, Empedocles of Acragas (*c.* 493–422 BCE) was an influential philosopher who also enjoyed success as a politician, poet, and healer. He sought a way out of the impasse created by the conflict of views between Heraclitus and Parmenides. Empedocles postulated four unchanging elements: earth, air, fire, and water. These produce the changing material of observed reality. The four elements are combined and separated by two forces: Love (the principle of unification) and Strife (the principle of disunification), which together cause creation, destruction, and re-creation. Thus Empedocles accepted Parmenides' assertion that Being is eternal, but he also argued for change, which he viewed as a mixture and separation of the four permanent elements by the two forces. Empedocles' concept of the four elements, adopted by Aristotle, became the standard four elements of later Greek philosophy and remained a basic theory of the universe until modern times.

Anaxagoras: Mind Acting on the Seeds.   Empedocles' postulation of the four elements was controverted by Anaxagoras of Clazomenae, a late pre-Socratic philosopher who was born about 500 BCE in Ionia but spent about thirty years in Athens, where he became the teacher and friend of Pericles. Eventually Pericles' enemies indicted Anaxagoras on charges of impiety, but the philosopher saved himself by taking flight. The outrage was caused by his declaration that the sun is a red-hot stone somewhat larger than the Peloponnese, a theory that would logically contradict the existence of Helios, the god personifying the sun. Anaxagoras also taught that the moon was torn from the earth and reflects the light of the sun. He is said to have written only one book—now lost—and his views are extremely difficult to reconstruct from the sometimes contradictory references by later writers. Like his Ionian predecessors of the previous century, Anaxagoras speculated about the ultimate substance from which all things are made, suggesting that the entirety of matter is composed of small particles he called "seeds," which formed a primeval mixed mass at the beginning of the world. The cosmic Mind (*nous*) served as a moving cause by forcing the seeds to separate and form the universe, each substance of which contains every sort of seed, though in varying proportions. Hence Anaxagoras moved beyond Empedocles' four elements to innumerable ones, and beyond his governance by the two forces—Love and Strife—to direction of all things by eternal Mind, which initiates cosmic motion. In short, he regarded Mind as the principal cause of change and cosmic order.

Leucippus and Democritus: The Atomists.   Scholars cannot easily distinguish the teachings of the first of the Atomists—the shadowy Leucippus of Miletus—from that of his distinguished pupil Democritus of Abdera in Thrace. Born about 460 BCE and said to have lived to an extraordinarily advanced age, Democritus was a prolific writer on numerous subjects. Although only brief fragments of his work survive, Democritus apparently adhered closely to the philosophical system of his master, an atomic theory of matter that was later adopted by the Hellenistic philosopher Epicurus. Democritus was another philosopher seeking a way out of the impasses created by the conflicting conclusions of Heraclitus and Parmenides. As noted, Parmenides postulated that reality is imperishable, single, motionless, and indivisible, and that empty space is nonexistent. While Democritus conceded Parmenides' idea that what exists is unchanging, he asserted that reality consists not of the Parmenidean eternal primeval substance—Being—but of atoms. Democritus believed that all things, including the human soul, are composed of these atoms, imperceptibly small particles that possess the indivisible character of Parmenides' Being but that move eternally. The Atomists reasoned that because there is motion, empty space must exist, thereby refuting Parmenides' denial of void. They postulated that the universe is made up of both atoms and empty space, and the former fall endlessly through the latter. Through their movement in space, atoms combine to produce matter—the origin of the world and human society—but the resulting combinations are continually disintegrating and entering new forms. Thus the universe is in a state of continual flux. Essentially, his atomic theory was based on speculation rather than on a scientific hypothesis supported by empirical evidence and should not be regarded as the cornerstone of modern science. Because atoms and space were the only things whose existence Democritus recognized, his philosophy was thoroughly materialistic and thereby rejected by many of his contemporaries as atheistic.

The Sophists.   Although Greek religion provided emotionally satisfying rites for worshipers, its attempt to explain the nature of the world was based not on any systematic theology but on myths that were vulnerable to rational criticism. Philosophical speculation tended to fill the intellectual vacuum left by religion. Although the pre-Socratic philosophers from Thales to Anaxagoras refrained from directly opposing the old religious traditions, their view of the world offered the Olympian gods little scope. Few people who were attracted to Ionian and later pre-Socratic philosophy seriously maintained that Zeus hurled thunderbolts or that Poseidon caused earthquakes. Moreover, the traditional religious, economic, and political structure of the Greek way of life was disrupted by the Persian Wars, followed by a growing sense of disillusionment that culminated in the tragedy of the Peloponnesian War. The educated classes were losing their faith in the gods and traditional moral standards. In the meantime the philosophers failed to agree among themselves, and many thinking people increasingly viewed the philosophical quest to understand the nature of the world as absurd.

With trust in the supernatural waning, the Sophists gained influence. They went from city to city, instructing wealthy teenage boys for hefty fees in a wide range of subjects, including rhetoric (the art of persuasion through public speaking), which was highly valued in the arena of politics. Skills in communication were mandated by the rise of democracy, for political success depended on influencing the assembly and law courts and holding one's own in discussion or debate. Before Plato wrote certain of his dialogues, the name Sophist (sage or expert) did not carry its present negative connotation. These men, who tended to gravitate to Athens, considered serious philosophical points irrelevant, instead teaching their students to win arguments with rhetorical cleverness. They promised that their pupils would develop the ability to speak persuasively on any subject and to argue convincingly both sides of a case. Thus their goal was to subordinate purely theoretical learning to its practical usefulness, teaching what is most likely to bear political fruit rather than what is most likely to be true. While some of them were brilliant teachers, others were unscrupulous charlatans.

The Sophists professed to teach *arete*, or excellence and efficiency in the conduct of public and private life. The most famous Sophist, Protagoras (c. 490–420 BCE), was a native of the Greek city of Abdera in Thrace. He visited Athens on occasion and became associated with Pericles, who selected him to draft a law code for the Athenian colony of Thurii in southern Italy. Protagoras was famous in antiquity for his doctrine that "man is the measure of all things," generally understood to mean there are no absolute truths, whether religious or scientific, apart from what people believe. The implication of such moral relativism is that humans created religion to satisfy their needs. "As to the gods," he is credited with having expressed an agnostic attitude: "I cannot know whether they exist or not; too many obstacles are in the way—the obscurity of the subject and the shortness of life."

Clearly, the Sophists rejected philosophical speculation about the world as irrelevant, turning instead to teach methods of living successfully. Some Sophists recommended the uncritical acceptance of a state's moral and legal codes as a means of achieving success, though others encouraged disobedience of all ethical and legal restraints blocking the pursuit of human goals. This destructive emphasis attracted the increasingly cynical and individualistic youths of Athens and other cities. Yet those Greeks who clung to the old traditions were incensed by such notions that seemed to undermine religion, morality, society, and the state. The more conservative of the traditionalists adopted an intense anti-intellectualism that struck out at the Sophists and anyone else identified with deviance from customary orthodoxy.

Socrates (469–399 BCE).   The celebrated Socrates has exercised enormous influence on western thought, although he wrote nothing. Our information about his philosophy comes mainly from four sources of widely divergent views: Plato, Xenophon, Aristotle, and Aristophanes. Both Plato and Xenophon were pupils of Socrates, but the two differ significantly about their beloved mentor. Plato belonged to the inner circle of Socrates' students, while Xenophon—despite his statement to the contrary—did not. Apparently Xenophon failed to grasp fully the principles of his teacher, and most scholars regard Plato as the more reliable source for information on Socrates' ideas and character. Yet Plato's dialogues idealize Socrates and probably carry his philosophy far beyond his original thought. Aristotle, who was born after the death of Socrates, learned most of what he knew of the great philosopher from Plato, his own teacher. Aristophanes, in his comedy the *Clouds,* portrays Socrates as the foremost of the Sophists, the group of teachers the dramatist thought were corrupting the noble youth of Athens. Socrates certainly used sophistic verbal techniques and, like the Sophists, was contemptuous of unexamined orthodoxy, but he charged no fees for his teaching and spent much of his time criticizing the Sophists. He believed people can achieve happiness by living a moral life and stood his ground against the cynical expediency of the Sophists. The distorted Socrates of the play probably should be viewed as a composite figure representing the popular view of intellectuals in the late fifth century. This false caricature made a lasting impression on the Athenians, however, contributing eventually to the great philosopher's death.

Socrates was an ordinary Athenian citizen whose mother was a midwife and father a stonecutter or sculptor. He may have worked at his father's trade for a while, though in a sense he practiced his mother's profession, for Plato has Socrates describing himself as one who assists at the birth of ideas. During the Peloponnesian War he served twice as a hoplite, distinguishing himself by his bravery and physical endurance. His marriage late in life to Xanthippe, whom several sources describe as irascible, produced two sons.

Indifferent to comfort and luxury, Socrates neglected his worldly affairs to devote himself to philosophy. He was encouraged in this endeavor by an oracle of Apollo declaring him the wisest of all men. The philosopher took the god's message seriously and apparently believed he had been chosen for a divine mission. The Platonic Socrates often speaks of being guided at intervals throughout his life by a small inner voice (*daimonion*), warning him against taking some particular action.

Plato portrays Socrates as an eccentric figure of unattractive appearance—paunchy, balding, pug-nosed, and shabbily dressed—who was ridiculed by his fellow Athenians and frequently compared to the wise but grotesque, horse-eared woodland deity Silenus. Yet Socrates was also a man of profound vitality and force. He attracted a diverse group of devoted friends, including aristocratic young men seeking intellectual training that would serve them in public life. Invariably professing ignorance (the famous Socratic irony), Socrates demonstrated to others their own ignorance by his unique method of cross-examination, which has become known as the Socratic method. The philosopher was a familiar figure at the Athenian sports grounds, frequented by males of leisure, where he would stop chance acquaintances or passersby and engage them in conversation, leading them by a series of probing questions about goodness, truth, justice, law, piety, and other subjects into a reevaluation of their ideas and definitions. The pointed questions caused the exasperated victims to contradict themselves hopelessly, and they were eventually brought by the same method to new conclusions. Socrates was able to show thereby that most popular notions are inconsistent and untenable. The Socratic method greatly irritated adults who were humiliated before a company of bystanders, but Socrates' aristocratic young pupils—Plato, Xenophon, Alcibiades, Critias, Charmides, and others—delighted in seeing the hapless victims respond with contradictory answers that made them appear foolish. Yet Socrates had a higher purpose, for he believed that infants are born with immortal souls possessing knowledge, which can be recalled later in life only through the probing questions. Thus Socrates professed to help uncover rather than to impart information.

If we can accept the Socrates of Plato's dialogues as the real philosopher, then we encounter a great and noble thinker attempting to better the ethical quality of the Athenians. He appears as the chief character in many of the dialogues, carrying out his penchant for cross-questioning people to reveal true knowledge. Socrates' goal was to achieve wisdom, which could be gained by discussion or quiet contemplation. The most important of his convictions was that each individual is endowed with a soul that commands the body. Perhaps Socrates was the first European to understand the soul as an intellectual and moral force causing a human to act rightly or wrongly. Before his time, most Greeks regarded the soul as a vaporous force—breath—necessary for physical life but not the source of actions or the seat of consciousness. Socrates also systematically examined questions of morality and the conduct of life, believing that moral virtue (another meaning of the Greek word *arete*) could be drawn from the soul. He deplored the Sophists' equation of *arete* with worldly success and their dictum that might makes right. "It is better to suffer injustice than to do it," claims a Socratic doctrine that indicates how far the philosopher went in rejecting the moral skepticism of the Sophists and the popular morality of his day.

The Platonic Socrates reasoned that happiness comes from living a life of virtue, itself equivalent to knowledge (that is, self-knowledge, in accordance with the Delphic command to "know thyself"). Virtue, then, depends on knowledge, through which one perceives the Good. How does virtue depend on knowledge of the Good? Socrates argued that to know the Good—a supreme and unchanging principle—is to desire it. Thus by turning the "eye of the soul" to a compelling vision of the Good, it can be realized. Socrates reasoned, in other words, that no one who knows the Good will deliberately lead an unethical life. Although proper action comes from knowledge, moral perfection is not just a form of behavior but a consistent attitude of mind springing from the vision of the Good.

In the quest for the Good, Socrates attaches much importance to inspiration by physical beauty. Young men and boys who possess both good looks and nobility of character, he reasoned, can offer one a faint glimpse of the Good through the desire (*eros*) they provoke. He argued that such desire springs from the response of an older man to the beauty of a younger male, but knowledge of the Good rather than sexual gratification becomes the goal—the purpose—of *eros*. We hear from Plato, who perhaps wishes to present Socrates as a figure beyond ordinary humanity, of one detached from tormenting sexual desires: On one occasion when Alcibiades tried to arouse Socrates sexually, the philosopher resisted, treating *eros* as love for the beautiful youth's soul rather than the attributes of his body. Although the Platonic Socrates frequently professed to be in love with Alcibiades, he never allowed himself to be seduced by the young man. Yet he thought that unfulfilled desire for a youth has a profound purpose, for in Plato's *Symposium, eros* becomes a force draw-ing one to the Good. In the philosophy of the Platonic Socrates, then, an inward response to the stimulus produced by a young man's beauty can be an initial step toward the beatific vision of the Good. Thus Socrates seems to have inaugurated the view that the world is teleological, the idea that all nature works toward a pur-pose, a concept that was dominant in the later philosophy of Aristotle. Everything is ordered for the best, and there is an appropriate purpose for all movement and endeavor.

Many Athenians thought that Socrates' ideas and methods were in part respon-sible for the rot they perceived among the rising generation. In 399 BCE Socrates was brought to trial on the double charge of introducing new gods and corrupting the minds of young men. The philosopher was around seventy years old at the time and had been asking his questions for as long as most people could remember, but he became a victim of the vengeful frustration sweeping Athens after its defeat in the Peloponnesian War. Most of his aristocratic friends were either dead or discredited. Meanwhile the restored democracy was decidedly anti-intellectual. Socrates had often criticized the practice of choosing officials by lot—a mainstay of the Athenian democracy—and was known for his hostility to democracy in general, questioning the ability of the masses to govern wisely and apparently favoring government by a worthy ruling class. Behind the official charges also lay the old Athenian hostility toward intellectuals as well as the resentment of prominent citizens who had been humiliated by the Socratic method.

Concerning the first charge, Socrates was outwardly orthodox in his religious observances. Available evidence suggests the charge was not clearly formulated and was designed simply to provoke popular hostility against the philosopher. The sec-ond charge—that he corrupted the minds of the youth—seems to represent the heart of his indictment, for government officials no doubt considered some of his young friends dangerous and knavish. Alcibiades, who recently had been killed in Asia Minor by Persians at Spartan request, had been a pupil and intimate friend. Alcibiades was remembered for his personal ambition and treacherous intrigues. Critias and Charmides, considered even more dissolute than Alcibiades, had be-longed to Socrates' inner circle. These two men eventually became members of the oligarchic Thirty Tyrants and were killed during the forcible restoration of Athen-ian democracy.

After the trial of Socrates, the jury voted for the death penalty. Athenian law gave Socrates the right to make a counterproposal for a less severe penalty, with the jury then choosing one of the two sentences. Socrates might have saved his life by proposing a true compromise, such as exile, but instead argued before the court that the Athenians should punish him by providing him with free meals at public expense for the rest of his life. Infuriated by his flippant defiance and un-willingness to take the matter seriously, the jury confirmed the death sentence by an even larger majority than the original vote. Meanwhile the solemn celebration of the Delian festivals prevented his execution for thirty days, during which time he was confined. Socrates still could have escaped into exile, as urged by his friends and perhaps preferred by his accusers, but he refused to disobey the law. His last hours and death are described in Plato's dialogue *Phaedo*. After making a libation to the gods, he serenely drank the fatal hemlock and died with the cheerful observation that finally he would discover for himself the truth about the afterlife. Across the centuries, his forceful personality still discloses itself, for the great philosopher's ideas lived on in the heart and mind of Plato, his close friend and wisest disciple, who spent the rest of his life making the name Socrates immortal.

CHAPTER XIII

The Greek City-States Lose Political Autonomy in the Fourth Century bce: From Spartan Domination to the Rise of Macedonia

The fall of Athens at the end of the poisonous Peloponnesian War in 404 BCE was followed by violence, social demoralization, political corruption, intellectual confusion, and economic ruin. This chapter covers the major political developments of the fourth century, notably the erosion of the Greek city-state system. The early fourth century BCE saw the Spartans abandon their traditional isolationism for an adventure in imperialism, replacing the former Athenian empire with an unimaginative Spartan version ruling its newly acquired cities through subservient native oligarchies or proud Spartan governors. The Greek world watched warily as the Spartans proved insufferably arrogant in victory and demonstrated a harsh willingness to exploit their new subjects. Growing resentment fueled the emergence of a successful challenger state, Thebes, which dismantled Sparta's empire but later became easy prey for the able and tireless king of Macedonia, Philip II, who extended his power and became the undisputed ruler of Greece in 338 BCE.

PERIOD OF SPARTAN DOMINATION (404–371 BCE)

LYSANDER AND THE FORMATION OF THE SPARTAN EMPIRE (404–403 BCE)

The competent commander Lysander, introduced in chapter 10, continued to dominate Spartan policy after the Peloponnesian War. He substituted a system of unpopular Spartan control in most of the Greek cities hitherto allied with Athens. In some of these Lysander set up oligarchies, as in Athens, while in others he established Spartan military governors (harmosts) supported by menacing garrisons. Lacking much acquaintance with trading ventures, the Spartans could not provide the Aegean world with the economic vitality enjoyed by the Athenian empire. To pay the tremendous costs of military operations on land and sea, Sparta demanded heavy tribute from its subject states. The old Spartan allies, especially Thebes and Corinth, gained few economic advantages from the creation of a Spartan empire and seethed in resentment for having been deprived of the spoils of victory. Meanwhile many Spartans came to see Lysander's power as a threat to their time-honored government and kingship, and he was temporarily pushed aside from political leadership in 403 BCE.

REVIVAL OF ATHENS (404–403 BCE)

Athens was distressed by repeated attacks during the Peloponnesian War, its thin soil depleted by enemy ravages, its country dwellings and barns destroyed, and its industry left on the verge of ruin. After losing the war in 404 BCE, the city fell under the control of Sparta through the eight-month-long despotic rule of the Thirty Tyrants. A functioning democracy was restored in 403, though Athens remained a dependency of Sparta. The revived assembly rejected a conservative proposal to limit the franchise to property owners as well as a suggestion to enfranchise aliens who had fought for democracy. The assembly also restored the Periclean law of 451, which limited citizenship to those with both an Athenian mother and an Athenian father. Earlier, the law had been relaxed and then discarded altogether. Meanwhile the city had suffered grievous commercial blows from the loss of its empire. Merchant ships had perished along with triremes, causing a widespread collapse of trade routes. Yet the Athenians achieved an astonishing recovery in the early fourth century BCE through sheer resolve and effort.

GROWING TENSION BETWEEN SPARTA AND PERSIA: THE MARCH OF THE TEN THOUSAND (401–400 BCE)

The history of Spartan diplomacy with Persia during this period is tangled with bewildering rivalries and intrigues. Darius II died in 405 BCE and was succeeded by his elder son, Artaxerxes II. The new king foolishly permitted his brother Cyrus the Younger, who was suspected of plotting to take the throne, to return to Sardis as viceroy for Asia Minor. Cyrus' friendly cooperation with Lysander had helped to ensure victory for Sparta in the Peloponnesian War, and the Spartans encouraged his scheming to topple the new Persian king. Cyrus recruited more than ten thousand Greek mercenaries—mostly veterans of the Peloponnesian War—and placed them under a Spartan commander. Among the recruits was Socrates' former pupil Xenophon, who had found life in Athens precarious after the restoration of democracy. As told in Xenophon's lively *Anabasis* (expedition to the interior), Cyrus marched inland to Mesopotamia in 401 BCE with the Greek mercenaries and a large number of regular contingents from Asia Minor, a total force of perhaps twenty thousand. When Cyrus reached the town of Cunaxa, not far from Babylon, he found his brother waiting. The Greeks fought bravely in the face of a larger Persian force, but the purpose of the expedition was lost when Cyrus was killed in battle.

The Greek commanders were lured to the Persian camp on the pretext of negotiations and ruthlessly murdered, so the endangered mercenaries quickly elected new generals—including Xenophon—who decided that the Greeks should not return the way they came but instead head north for the Black Sea through completely unfamiliar territory. The heroic Greek retreat out of the heart of the Persian Empire was plagued by attacking tribesmen, wrenching winter weather, and countless other vicissitudes. Advancing by sea and by land, however, the famous Ten Thousand finally made their way to Byzantium on the European side of the Bosphorus. After taking service under a Thracian prince—who cheated them of their pay—they eventually joined a Spartan crusade against Persia.

THE WAR BETWEEN SPARTA AND PERSIA (400–386 BCE)

The War in Asia Minor and the Exploits of King Agesilaus (400–394 BCE).   Fearing retaliation by Persia, the Greeks of Asia Minor sought help from Sparta. The daring of the Ten Thousand had led to a new view of the weakness of the Great King, and the Spartans were anxious to regain their former reputation as guardians of Greek liberties. In 400 BCE they dispatched to Asia Minor a force composed of what remained of the Ten Thousand (roughly six thousand troops), several thousand Peloponnesians, and about one thousand freed helots. After the Spartans managed to liberate a number of Greek cities, King Artaxerxes grew weary of the provocations and prepared for full-scale warfare. Thus in the spring of 396 BCE Sparta was obliged to send a large army of Peloponnesian allies and freed helots to Asia Minor under the command of the new Spartan king, Agesilaus, a brilliant tactician who had succeeded his older half-brother Aegis II in 399 BCE, with the aid of his former lover Lysander. Aegis' young son Leotychides, who would have been king under normal procedure, was rumored to be the child of Alcibiades, and Lysander argued that the kingship should be awarded to Agesilaus. Thus Agesilaus secured the succession largely through the continuing influence of Lysander, who hoped to control the king for his own ends. Yet in Asia Minor the able Agesilaus, a dominant Spartan figure in the first half of the fourth century, began to disregard Lysander's advice. To avoid additional personal humiliation, Lysander obtained permission from the king to withdraw on a mission to the Hellespont.

Improvising a cavalry and reorganizing the infantry, Agesilaus conducted a spectacular two-year campaign in western Asia Minor. He defeated the satrap Tissaphernes, who was then accused by the Persians of slackness in his conduct of operations and executed, as well as the satrap's replacement Tithraustes. Although the Persians were unable to withstand the Greeks in battle, their garrisons remained intact within secure fortresses. Then events in Greece suddenly called Agesilaus home, but his successes in Asia Minor suggested to many Greeks that they had the ability, if unified, to conquer the entire Persian Empire.

The Corinthian War (395–386 BCE).   The coalition defeating Athens in the Peloponnesian War did not long survive its victory, undermined by Sparta's oppressive rule and expansionism in Asia Minor and Greece. The Persians dispatched an envoy to distribute gold on the Greek mainland to encourage an alliance against Sparta. The response was vigorous and immediate. Allied with Persia, all of central Greece—most notably Athens and Thebes—as well as the Peloponnesian states of Corinth and Argos formed an anti-Spartan coalition and attacked the Peloponnese in 395 BCE, beginning what is called the Corinthian War. The Athenian historian Xenophon, who was present at some of the events, describes the course of the war with strong pro-Spartan sympathies in his valuable but biased work *Hellenica,* one of the principal sources for mainland Greece in the period following the Peloponnesian War. In 395 BCE Lysander invaded Boeotia at the head of a Spartan-allied army but was defeated and killed by the Thebans. Then in 394 BCE the Athenian admiral Conon, commanding a Persian-Athenian naval force, destroyed a Spartan fleet off Cnidus, a prosperous Greek city on the southwestern coast of Asia Minor. Accordingly, the Spartans lost control of the Aegean. Eventually Conon landed triumphantly at Athens and contributed much Persian gold for the rebuilding of the Long Walls and the construction of a new Athenian fleet. With the completion of these projects, Athens resumed a major role in international politics. Meanwhile the Spartans warned the Persian king that his subsidies were being used to restore an Athenian empire.

The King's Peace (386 BCE).   Having been summoned home from Asia Minor, King Agesilaus raced through Thrace, Macedonia, and Thessaly to Boeotia, where he overwhelmed the anti-Spartan allies in 394 BCE on the plain of Cornea. Yet Sparta's situation was precarious, with its fleet destroyed and its opponents strengthened by Persian ships and gold. Sparta once again cut a deal with Persia. In a treacherous betrayal of its long-standing claim to be the defender of Greek freedom in Asia Minor, Sparta negotiated a peace settlement with the Great King acknowledging Persian control of Ionia in return for permission to restore Spartan leadership in Greece without Persian interference. For his part, King Artaxerxes had become concerned about growing Athenian power. Athens had already reoccupied the Aegean islands of Lemnos, Imbros, and Scyros, besides launching its new navy, paid for with Persian gold. Artaxerxes transferred his financial support from Athens to Sparta, enabling the Spartans to construct a new fleet. Once deprived of Persian finances, Athens and its war-worn allies could offer little resistance to the king's terms. Moreover, the Athenians were terrified to hear that Sparta had seized the Hellespont with eighty triremes and cut off their lifeline to the wheat trade through the Black Sea. The terms of the King's Peace imposed by Artaxerxes were humiliating. Ionia and Cyprus were returned to Persia and all other Greek cities (except Athenian-controlled Lemnos, Imbros, and Scyros) were to be autonomous, thereby crushing Athens' new Aegean federation and lessening the possibility of an anti-Persian coalition. Enforcement of the peace was left to the Spartans, and Artaxerxes vowed to wage war against anyone who did not accept the terms. Thus the Persians had finally won through gold and diplomacy many of their designs against the Greek world, while Sparta and Agesilaus had gained tremendous power in mainland Greece by sacrificing the Greeks of Asia Minor. Perhaps after their difficult experiences under Athenian and Spartan control, the Ionian cities found some consolation in the comparative peace and prosperity provided by Persian rule. Meanwhile the Athenians continued to criticize the Spartans for the noxious treaty that meant abandoning the Greek settlements in Asia Minor, and Athenian orators urged the Greeks to unite and liberate Ionia, an appeal bearing fruit in the later conquests of Alexander the Great.

Brutal Enforcement of the King's Peace: The Period of Spartan Intervention in Greece (386–371 BCE)

The Spartans Forge an Empire (386–379 BCE).   With Persian backing, King Agesilaus and his Spartan followers used their dominant position to enforce the terms of the peace on the mainland. They eradicated all Greek confederations except the Spartan-headed Peloponnesian League. Accordingly, the Spartans dissolved the Boeotian League, an ancient combination headed by Thebes. They split up the important Arcadian city of Mantinea into villages dependent upon Sparta and brutally suppressed the democracies among their allies. The Spartans also struck at the notable Chalcidian League, then flourishing on Chalcidice, the triple peninsula projecting from Macedonia. Grouped around the common capital of Olynthus, the league functioned as a great federal union, with member cities sharing citizenship and laws. Yet federalism had no place in a world ruled by Sparta. Claiming to act as the guardians of the autonomy clause in the King's Peace, the Spartans dissolved the Chalcidian League by force in 379 BCE and enrolled its separate communities as Spartan allies, though the ultimate beneficiary of this aggression was Macedonia.

In 382 BCE, the same year they launched their campaign against the Chalcidian League, the Spartans demonstrated their willingness to adopt any policy to further their power. A Spartan army on the way to the Chalcidic peninsula was encamped near the city of Thebes. The commander eagerly accepted a suggestion by a Theban oligarchic leader that the Spartans seize the Theban acropolis, suppress democracy, and install a pro-Spartan government. Thus Thebes was taken by treachery and occupied by a Spartan force, sparking outrage throughout Greece. The ruthless King Agesilaus argued in favor of this bludgeoning of a city at peace, and the leader of the Theban democrats was hustled off to Sparta for execution, though some three hundred of his followers escaped to Athens. Meanwhile the pro-Spartan oligarchs now controlling Thebes entered the Spartan alliance. The Theban takeover was just another example of how Sparta—under the pretext of safeguarding the autonomy of the Greek cities—had converted free states to subjects and carved out an empire that included the Peloponnese, Megara, Boeotia, Locris, Phocis, and part of Thessaly as well as the former members of the Chalcidian League. Despite its power and successes, arrogant Sparta utterly failed to provide Greece with tranquility or unity.

Liberation of Thebes (379–378 BCE).   At dusk one evening in the winter of 379 BCE seven Theban exiles and their leader Pelopidas slipped back into Thebes with workers returning from the fields. Two evenings later the same men, now disguised as heavily veiled female pipers and dancers, attended a drinking party for the leaders of the pro-Spartan, oligarchic government established in the city. When the merriment was well under way, the costumed men slew their hosts and then rallied the townspeople to expel the Spartan garrison. Thus the Theban democracy was restored. For a number of years thereafter the most prominent figures in Theban politics were the dashing Pelopidas and his confederate Epaminondas, both of whom enjoyed exceptional military and political abilities. Defying the tradition of Spartan military invincibility, the two managed to liberate Boeotian towns from Spartan garrisons.

Formation of the Second Athenian League (378–377 BCE).   Athens had remained neutral at first in the conflict between Sparta and Thebes. Then the Spartan harmost in the south-central Boeotian town of Thespiae set out with troops one night in an attempt to recapture Piraeus for Sparta in the early hours of morning. Badly underestimating the distance of his march, however, he found himself far from his objective at dawn and retraced his steps, destroying property as he proceeded. Faced with the possibility of Spartan attack, Athens formed a defensive alliance with Thebes in 378 BCE. The Athenians also proceeded to organize a new league—which modern historians call the Second Athenian League—for defense against Sparta. The Second Athenian League received constitutional sanction when the Athenian assembly passed a resolution in 377 BCE providing for a restored confederation, but denying membership to any state owing allegiance to Persia. Many safeguards were provided to prevent the sort of repression Athens' allies had suffered in the preceding century. Thus Athenians could neither own land in an allied state (a prohibition of the detested cleruchy) nor collect tribute, though member states were expected to contribute ships and money when needed. The allied states sent their representatives to a council (*synedrion*) at Athens, in which the Athenians alone enjoyed no part, yet each resolution had to pass both the *synedrion* and the Athenian assembly to be binding, an arrangement making Athens equal to its collective allies. Moreover, the Athenians exercised executive power over the league and were responsible for commanding military expeditions, but the member states were guaranteed local freedom and autonomy. Although the new Athenian League was popular among the allied states for a while and survived for forty years, the confederacy was clearly much weaker than the old Delian League.

Revival of the Theban League and the Decline of Sparta (378–371 BCE).   As the Theban leaders Pelopidas and Epaminondas fought to free the towns of Boeotia, one by one, from the Spartan garrisons, a restored Boeotian League was organized for defense against Spartan attack. Two military expeditions led by King Agesilaus against defiant Thebes in 378 and 377 BCE met inglorious failure, signaling the approaching end of Spartan dominance. The powerful new Theban army included the Sacred Band, an elite contingent of three hundred troops serving as the formidable backbone of the federal forces. The Sacred Band consisted of paired male lovers fighting side by side. Trained by Epaminondas in new military tactics, the members of the Sacred Band were sworn either to die in battle or to conquer, and each fighter exercised extreme valor in warfare both to protect his beloved and to demonstrate to him his prowess. After many years of seeming invincibility, the Sacred Band would fight and die in a last valiant stand for Thebes when facing Philip II of Macedonia in 338 BCE.

Although Spartan aggression was checked by the powerful military combination of Thebes and Athens, the new allies failed to reach an agreement for concerted action and drifted into an uneasy relationship. The boisterous Thebans left the conduct of the war to Athens and concentrated on enhancing their own might and territory. They began meddling in the politics of the region of Phocis, for example, and they seized the city of Plataea—an honored old Athenian ally in southern Boeotia—whose survivors found refuge in Athens. Another cause for stress on the Greek mainland was the emergence of new aggressive states such as Thessaly, ruled by Jason of Pherae, who hoped to unite all of Greece under his hegemony and then to launch an offensive against Persia. Although the other Greeks were greatly alarmed, the threat from the north ended suddenly with Jason's assassination in 370 BCE, before he could put his plan into effect. Meanwhile the increasing power of Thebes had actually pushed Athens and Sparta closer together.

Peace Conference of 371 BCE.   Delegates from the major Greek states attended a peace conference in 371 BCE and agreed that the best hope for a lasting peace lay in a declaration of friendship between Athens and Sparta, including their sworn agreement not to interfere in local political disputes. War-weary Athens and Sparta once again agreed on a proclamation of peace. The arrangement included formal Spartan recognition of the Second Athenian League, in return for acknowledgement of Spartan hegemony in the Peloponnese, and Sparta consented to withdraw its garrisons from central Greece. Athens signed for its league and Sparta for the Peloponnesian League, but at the last moment King Agesilaus of Sparta—determined not to recognize the Boeotian League—stubbornly challenged the right of Epaminondas to sign for the Theban allies, for the Spartans believed the success of the peace plan depended upon curtailing the growing power of Thebes. After discussions broke down, the opposing sides reconvened on the battlefield. The quest for peace had come to nothing.

Battle of Leuctra (371 BCE).   In the course of the ensuing war between Thebes and Sparta, the Theban army demonstrated its new military tactics during an incredible battle in 371 BCE at Leuctra in northern Boeotia. Sparta enjoyed clear numerical superiority at Leuctra, marshaling ten thousand hoplites (seven hundred of which were Spartans) against six thousand Thebans and other Boeotians. The Spartan hoplite phalanx stood twelve deep, supported by cavalry. After the well-trained Theban cavalry dispersed the Spartan horse with relative ease, the Theban phalanx was thrown against the enemy. Traditionally, Greek armies had achieved victories on their right wings. Yet Epaminondas' brilliant tactic was to deepen and strengthen his left wing, constituted with hoplites massed fifty shields deep. The left wing advanced ahead of the other Theban units in a slanting formation. Led by the crack Sacred Band of sworn lovers, the strengthened left wing charged forward on the double. While the Spartans were rallying to stop the charge of this wing, Epaminondas successively sent his center and right to overwhelm them. The Spartans were led by one of their kings, Cleombrotus I, who was struck down and killed during the engagement, along with four hundred of his seven hundred Spartan hoplites.

The survivors fled in panic and disarray, stunned that the Spartan phalanx had been crushed for the first time in Greek history. Sparta could not afford to suffer a diminished population of even a few hundred men, and the city never recovered from the calamitous defeat at Leuctra. Characterized by its thirty-three years of inefficiency and brutality, Spartan hegemony had finally come to an astonishing end.

THEBAN SUPREMACY (371–362 BCE)

DISMANTLING OF THE SPARTAN EMPIRE (370–366 BCE)

Leuctra changed everything overnight. For the next nine years Spartan domination was replaced by that of Thebes, its power ultimately resting upon leadership of the Boeotian League. In 370 BCE the great Theban military genius Epaminondas proceeded to dismantle the Spartan empire. He invaded the Peloponnese and helped the Arcadians throw off Spartan control. Then he encouraged the cities of the reorganized Arcadian League to build a new federal capital called Megalopolis, the Great City, which was surrounded by a long double wall. Located near the northwestern border of Laconia, strongly fortified Megalopolis was clearly intended to serve as a barrier against Spartan aggression. Epaminondas and his pillaging army advanced southward and penetrated the Spartan homeland until reaching the marshy banks of the Eurotas River, across which lay Sparta, where the inhabitants could clearly see the enemy campfires. Panic spread among the Spartans at the prospect of degrading capture. Realizing that attacking Sparta would entail unbearable losses, however, Epaminondas eventually made his way into the region of Messenia, an especially poignant victim of Spartan domination. Here he freed the helots and, as part of his strategy to contain Sparta, founded a strongly fortified town on the western slopes of Mount Ithome—Messene—to serve as the capital of the liberated territory. The loss of Messenia was a major economic blow to the Spartans, depriving them of a major source of food. Next Epaminondas arranged for Arcadia, Messene, and Argos to enter into alliances, which resulted in the blocking of roads leading from the north and west of Sparta. By 366 BCE the famous Peloponnesian League had ceased to exist, and the tradition of invincible Spartan power had been forever shattered.

EXPEDITION TO THESSALY (364 BCE)

Thebes basked in the brilliance of its two great leaders, the general Epaminondas and his collaborator Pelopidas. The latter had twice intervened in the internal wars of Thessaly by leading expeditions there in 369 and 368 BCE. Then in 364 BCE Pelopidas responded to an urgent appeal from the Thessalian cities for aid against Jason's brutal nephew Alexander of Pherae, who had succeeded to power. An ally of Athens, Alexander was employing ruthless means to maintain his control. Before Pelopidas could leave Thebes for Thessaly, however, an eclipse of the sun darkening the heavens was interpreted as a sign of coming evil, casting great fright over his departure. When his forces met Alexander in battle on rolling Thessalian hills, the Thebans steadily pushed the enemy from its position, yet the death of Pelopidas prevented a complete Theban victory. When Thebes dispatched an army to Thessaly the following year to avenge the death of one of its national heroes, Alexander was defeated, confined to his own city of Pherae, and obliged to submit to Theban authority. In the meantime, following Pelopidas' untimely death, Epaminondas had assumed political leadership at Thebes itself. First he reorganized the towns of Thessaly into a league under Theban authority. Then, in an attempt to increase Theban influence throughout the Greek world, Epaminondas took the bold step of challenging Athenian supremacy at sea by embarking on a great program of shipbuilding.

The Battle of Mantinea and the Disintegration of Theban Dominance (362 BCE)

Alarmed by growing Theban power, Athens rallied to the assistance of Sparta. The Athenians and the Spartans found support for their anti-Theban policy among the cities of the Arcadian League, which were thoroughly disgruntled after being forced to make alliances with Thebes and to convert their oligarchic governments into democracies. When the Arcadian cities broke away from Epaminondas' coalition, he rushed to the Peloponnese and met his opponents at the battle of Mantinea in Arcadia in 362 BCE. Here he faced a combined force drawn from Sparta, Athens, Elis, and Achaea. Epaminondas was fully aware of the significance of the coming battle, for a Theban victory might permit Thebes to extend its control over the entire Greek mainland. The brilliant general won handily with the same tactics employed at Leuctra but fell mortally wounded in the closing moments of battle. Now with the death of its last great leader, Thebes disintegrated as a power, and the exhausted Greeks were faced with general chaos. Accordingly, they made peace—impotent Sparta abstained—but a political vacuum of divisive Greek states now replaced the Theban hegemony. The Boeotians could only daydream about their former influence as they returned to their fields, for the Boeotian League had been reduced once again to a small landlocked confederation. The one stable power in Greece, Sparta, already had been ruined, and the way lay open for future conquest from the north.

THE DECLINE OF THE ATHENIAN ALLIANCE: THE SOCIAL WAR (357–355 BCE)

Athens alone among the former belligerents retained a modicum of its former vitality, but the Athenians had repeatedly broken promises to members of the Second Athenian League. Added concerns were raised when the inhabitants of some islands were once again forced to submit to the jurisdiction of Athenian courts. Moreover, many Athenians still thought of the league as a source of wealth, and despised cleruchies reappeared in Samos and at Potidaea. Meanwhile the native ruler of Caria in southwest Asia Minor, Mausolus, supported rebellious schemes among the various Athenian allies. Although Mausolus (whose splendid tomb was counted among the Seven Wonders of the World) was officially a Persian satrap, he functioned almost as an independent ruler, while wisely acknowledging the over-lordship of the Persian king by paying tribute regularly. Mausolus especially coveted several of the great islands in the Athenian alliance and thus fanned opposition to the policies of Athens. In the autumn of 357 BCE revolts broke out, led by the eastern Aegean islands of Rhodes, Cos, and Chios, with the support of the rich city of Byzantium. This rebellion of the allies of Athens is generally known as the Social War. After a series of naval defeats, the Athenians were compelled to recognize the independence of these centers of opposition, and soon Lesbos and other states broke away. Lacking its most important eastern members, the Second Athenian League now consisted of only a few harbors in the north and some tiny Cycladic islands. With the virtual collapse of the Second Athenian League, Athens faced ruin. The Athenians and other Greeks no longer enjoyed the means or the will to defend themselves against aggressors, and soon the Macedonians would devour them.

CARTHAGE AND THE WESTERN GREEKS

CARTHAGE

Located on the coast of North Africa across from Sicily, Carthage was founded by settlers from the Phoenician city of Tyre around 800 BCE as an anchorage and trading post for Phoenician merchant ships making the long voyage to Spain. The Carthaginians continued to observe the Phoenician religion established by the earliest colonists. Maintaining continually burning fires in their sanctuaries, the Carthaginians worshiped traditional Phoenician deities such as Astarte and Baal, and in times of drastic crisis they propitiated heaven by resorting to the sacrifice of children, a practice giving them a reputation for extreme cruelty. One potential weakness for oligarchic Carthage was its military system, for the army was composed chiefly of mercenaries hired from various western Mediterranean peoples. Citizens, though serving as officers in the army and known for their skills in sailing, were generally exempt from military service.

Blessed with a combination of good harbors, strategic location, and fertile hinterland, Carthage grew to become a great city, eclipsing even celebrated Tyre. The Carthaginians controlled the sea routes between the eastern and western basins of the Mediterranean and also monopolized trade in the western part of the great sea. Carthage was the most successful of all the Phoenician colonies and eventually brought other Phoenician settlements in the western Mediterranean under its hegemony, while managing also to subdue the native tribes on its eastern and western borders, thus establishing authority in North Africa from Cyrenaica (eastern Libya) to the Atlantic Ocean. Later the Carthaginians employed their feared navy to establish rule over the island of Sardinia and southern Spain. Meanwhile settlers from Carthage occupied the western side of Sicily. Reaching the height of its power in the fourth and third centuries BCE, Carthage slammed against the Greeks in western Sicily and attempted to dominate the entire island. In 409 BCE Carthage dispatched a great naval force to Selinus on the southwest coast of Sicily, capturing and sacking the city—the westernmost Greek settlement on the island—after a ferocious siege lasting nine days. Several days later the assailants obliterated Himera on the north coast.

SYRACUSE

The most powerful Greek city-state on Sicily, Syracuse watched these military developments with great alarm. The disastrous Athenian naval expedition against democratic Syracuse in 415 BCE had thrown the city into turmoil. Now the Carthaginian campaign in Sicily increased the panic, and the ruthless Dionysius I employed demagogy to gain power about 405 BCE. Dionysius remained the city's tyrant until his death in 367 BCE. Although he preserved a semblance of democracy, Dionysius arranged for his inner circle to be elected to the most important offices of state. Meanwhile he maintained his authority with a huge mercenary force of more than ten thousand soldiers recruited from many Greek territories. Dionysius gave magnificent Syracuse an enormous girdle of fortifications. His navy included more than three hundred warships, and his engineers devised catapults that threw large stones several hundred yards, the first Greek siege artillery. Although achieving only varying degrees of success in fighting the Carthaginians, Dionysius managed to confine them to the western third of Sicily. The dynamic Dionysius, a brilliant soldier, elevated Syracuse as the controlling power in the greater part of Sicily and much of southern Italy. Still not content, he decided to expand his realm by founding settlements on both shores of the Adriatic, thereby bringing that sea into his sphere of influence. The Syracusan economy flourished under his leadership, and he seems to have enjoyed wide support at home.

Despite his notorious cruelty, Dionysius was a patron of literature and the arts and fancied himself a great dramatist. His plays were generally considered mediocre, though courtiers who dared to criticize them ended their days toiling in the quarries. Plato, in his search for the ideal state, visited Dionysius' court. He was unimpressed but struck up an intimate friendship with the tyrant's kinsman Dion.

The great tyrant was succeeded in 367 BCE by his son Dionysius II, who lacked his father's ability and was no match for the intrigues of the Syracusan court. His ambitious uncle Dion invited Plato to become Dionysius' tutor, perhaps hoping to increase his influence over the young man. Yet Plato, whose goal was to help Dionysius become a philosopher-king, eventually returned to Athens as court conspiracies between the supporters of Dion and Dionysius mounted. The feuding ultimately dismantled the Syracusan empire through war and massacre, with bands of unemployed mercenaries slaying and plundering as they roved across the landscape. Meanwhile the Carthaginians, encouraged by the disorder, were on the march in Sicily. Finally, in 344 BCE the desperate Syracusans appealed for help to Corinth, their mother city and ally in Greece. The Corinthians sent them a courageous aristocratic general named Timoleon, who ended the civil strife in Greek Sicily and pushed the Carthaginians back into their strongholds on the western coast. Timoleon also established a moderate oligarchy on the Corinthian model in Syracuse and organized a federation to keep peace in Sicily. His work accomplished, the general relinquished power and spent his final years in Syracuse as a revered private citizen, dying in 334 BCE. His achievements were fleeting, however, for within a generation another strong man, Agathocles, seized power in Syracuse, first as tyrant and later as king.

THE LEGACY OF PHILIP II
AND THE MACEDONIANS

Macedonia before the Fourth Century bce

The fragmentary sources before the reign of Philip II give us an incomplete picture of the history of the kingdom of Macedonia on the northern fringe of ancient Greece. A pastoral country inhabited by peasants, shepherds, and powerful landholding nobles, Macedonia consisted of several fertile river valleys separated by mountains. Apparently the population of mixed Illyrian, Thracian, and Greek descent spoke an obscure dialect of Greek, bore Greek names, and worshiped Greek gods. Essentially a large tribal kingdom, Macedonia differed in many ways from the small, self-governing city-states fashioned by the Greeks to the south. At the beginning of the fifth century Macedonia remained a loose federation of regions giving various degrees of allegiance to the king. Because the Macedonians were beleaguered by raids from both Thrace and Illyria, they were concerned with defense and had preserved a warrior king of the Homeric tradition to lead them in battle. The power of the ruler was tempered by custom as well as the prerogatives of powerful nobles, who must have influenced major decisions of state. Apparently another of their functions was to affirm the succession of a new king, usually an adult son designated by his father, the late ruling king. Royal assassinations were common in Macedonia, resulting partly from the absence of primogeniture and from the kings' practice of polygamy, which produced rival claimants to the throne by different wives. On occasion the nobles must have blocked a child or weak claimant deemed unable to command troops successfully in battle. Fighting for supremacy in the Macedonian valleys and highlands, the hardy nobles still practiced the blood feud. Although the Greeks of the city-states regarded the heavy drinking bouts and murderous dynastic intrigues of the Macedonians with contempt, the kings aspired to be fully Hellenized and maintained military and economic contacts with their Greek neighbors.

The kings of the fifth century BCE attempted to forge a powerful state from the loose Macedonian federation. One ruler, the ruthless Archelaus (c. 413–399 BCE), established Pella as his capital while augmenting his military strength by training infantry and building forts and roads. He made good use of the new army and roads to establish his authority over the upland chieftains, who had a history of challenging kingly rule. He also increased Macedonian trade by selling lumber to the Athenians for their ships and sought to foster Hellenization in his land. The royal family claimed Greek descent from no less a figure than Heracles, and Archelaus maintained a sufficiently polished court to attract the Athenian tragic playwright Euripides, who died in Macedonia.

Philip II and the Consolidation of Macedonia (359–354 bce)

Macedonia experienced a period of bloody dynastic struggles and invasions during the first half of the fourth century BCE. The brief reign of Perdiccas III, for example, came to an abrupt end when the king lost his life in 359 BCE fighting the Illyrians—a large tribal group inhabiting the east Adriatic coast and its hinterland—who had overrun his western frontier. Among the several claimants seeking the throne at the death of Perdiccas was his younger brother Philip, then about twenty-three years old. Although the evidence is confused, perhaps Philip was initially regent for Perdiccas' son Amyntas, who was only a child, later pushing his nephew aside to seize the crown for himself. Meanwhile he skillfully eliminated pretenders. Philip II (359–336 BCE) was thoroughly familiar with Greek politics because as a teenager he had been taken to the powerful city of Thebes, where he served as a royal hostage to guarantee a treaty with Macedonia. Philip's time in Thebes (probably 369–367) gave him an opportunity to learn military tactics and political lessons from Epaminondas and Pelopidas, both of whom he greatly admired, and to observe the Sacred Band of the Theban army at close quarters, an adventure apparently leaving him with a burning desire to transform Macedonia into the preeminent military power in the Greek world.

Inauguration of Military Reforms (359 BCE). Philip's position was perilously weak in 359 BCE, and he needed time to grapple with the dangers facing the throne and the state. His chief concern was to save the kingdom from hostile powers. A genius at achieving advantage by compromise and intrigue, Philip bought temporary breathing space by bribing invaders—the Paeonians from the north and the Thracians from the east—to withdraw from his territory, though the Illyrians remained for the time being in the west. He then pushed through a crash military training program and created a formidable standing army of professional soldiers. The king inspired devotion and loyalty in his troops by training closely with them. Assisted by his most reliable general, Parmenio, Philip introduced compulsory service, requiring every region of Macedonia to furnish its quota of men. He built his formidable army with units of heavy infantry, light infantry, and cavalry. The undisciplined army of the past had consisted chiefly of cavalry—the royal Companions—drawn from the nobility. Philip's most important military reform was his reorganization of the infantry by creating a uniformly equipped phalanx, which employed the highly effective tactics of Epaminondas. The heavily armed Macedonian infantrymen carried lighter armor than the Greek hoplites, but instead of using the short stabbing spear of the hoplite—wielded with one hand—they employed both hands to hold a long pike (*sarissa*). Thus Philip's deadly phalanx consisted of a solid body of infantry bristling with thrusting pikes and forming an impregnable wall of iron. Space between the infantrymen was dramatically increased to allow greater mobility and free

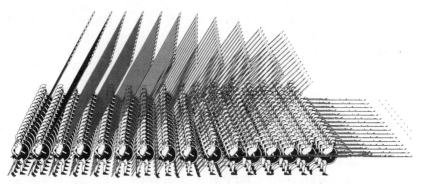

The Macedonian phalanx depended on unflinching discipline for its success
in inflicting hideous carnage. In battle the first five ranks extended their wall of
formidable long pikes, while the shoving multitude behind raised theirs as a bristling
barrier against arrows. The task of the phalanx was to pin the enemy, permitting the
cavalry to strike the decisive blow.

use of the dreaded Macedonian pike. Drawn up in sixteen ranks, the phalanx relied
upon its sheer weight and pushing power to bear down heavily upon opponents.
Philip increased the effectiveness of the phalanx by the addition of various sorts of
light-armed troops, including archers and slingers. Yet the Companion cavalry remained the elite force of the Macedonian army. In battle the primary task of the infantry was to pin the front line of the opposing force, while the calvary would strike
the decisive blow by attacking the opponent's flanks. Aided by the light-armed
troops, the cavalry also protected the vulnerable flanks and rear of the Macedonian
phalanx. Philip's army operated as a formidable instrument of his will and helped to
foster national sentiment in the turbulent outlying regions by drawing men from
these territories into his infantry. Meanwhile many nobles in the cavalry began to
reside in Pella rather than on their country or highland estates, a trend further reducing the traditional separatist tendencies of the country.

*The Extension of Macedonia Proper and the Acquisition of Vital Gold and Silver Mines
(358–354 BCE).*   Philip's efforts paid off handsomely in 358 BCE, when he crushed
the Paeonians and forced them to acknowledge Macedonian overlordship. Immediately thereafter he decisively defeated the Illyrians and used his victory to annex the
previously independent principalities of Upper Macedonia. He also inaugurated a
series of measures designed to provide sufficient resources for adopting an imperialistic policy. Two important goals in this regard were obtaining precious metals and
pushing the boundaries of Macedonia toward the sea to obtain revenue and shipping
outlets. Rich deposits of precious metals lay just inside Thrace on Philip's eastern
frontier, though he would be hard put to hold any captured mines there without
gaining control of the commercially wealthy city of Amphipolis, a former Athenian
colony on the north Aegean coast of Thrace. Calling upon his remarkable diplomatic skills, Philip came to a secret understanding with the Athenians, promising to
restore Amphipolis to Athens in exchange for the city of Pydna—the people of

Pydna knew nothing of their betrayal by Athens—but the cunning king planned to keep both. In 357 BCE Philip seized territory that included Amphipolis and the rich gold and silver mines of the Mount Pangaeus district. He fortified an old city near Mount Pangaeus and renamed it Philippi after himself, the prototype of the many Philippis and Alexandrias founded by Macedonian rulers in the Hellenistic period. Athens declared war on Philip over the capture of Amphipolis, though hostilities trailed off because the Athenians were entangled in the Social War.

The newly acquired mines of Mount Pangaeus are said to have increased Philip's annual income by the enormous sum of one thousand talents of gold and silver—no other state of mainland Greece enjoyed such wealth—and constituted the economic foundation of his power. These revenues enabled the king to maintain a large mercenary army, unify his country with roads, and fashion a diplomacy based largely on massive expenditures. Now Philip could bribe Greek politicians south of Macedonia to represent his interests or could pay traitors to deliver up besieged cities. He gave his name to the famous gold coins coming from the mines—the handsome Philippi—used by Macedonian envoys to bend cities to his will.

Meanwhile Philip was still threatened from the east, especially by the Greeks of the northwest Aegean region known as Chalcidice and by the Athenians holding the cities of Potidaea and Methone on his nearest coast. Philip was anxious to prevent the Chalcidian League, headed by the city of Olynthus, from challenging Macedonia, for he feared that the Olynthians might turn to their old enemy of Athens and form a pact against him. Thus when Philip captured Potidaea in the Chalcidice in 356 BCE, he ceded the city to the league in return for an alliance. Philip's seizure of Methone in 354 BCE rounded off his kingdom along the Thermaic Gulf, at the cost of his right eye.

Marriage to Olympias (357 BCE).   Philip had found an ally against Illyria in the northwest, mountainous kingdom of Epirus, a political backwater for most of Greek history, and cemented the alliance in 357 BCE by marrying the young Epirote princess Olympias, his third and by far most famous wife, who became the mother of the great Alexander two years later. Powerful, bearded Philip was said to be consumed by desire for drink, women, and, at times, boys. Like many other rulers of the day, he took wives to engender sons and secure alliances. His relationship with the tempestuous, beautiful Olympias was never easy, though she did not oppose his liaisons. She fiercely protected the status of her son Alexander, with whom she developed an intense bond, and was passionately devoted to snake handling and the orgiastic rites of the Dionysiac cult.

Conquest of the Greek Cities (356–338 BCE)

Philip Gains a Firm Foothold in Central Greece: The Third Sacred War (356–346 BCE). Meanwhile central Greece was convulsed by a decade-long Sacred War. The conflict erupted when the Phocians were charged with cultivating lands sacred to Apollo at Delphi, the great religious center in the heart of their territory. Egged on by Thebes, the Delphic Amphictony—the interstate board responsible for administering Apollo's sanctuary at Delphi—declared war against tiny Phocis for sacrilegious trespassing. The Phocians, traditional members of this same amphictiony, were backed by both Athens and Sparta, but neither state offered them much aid. Although ostensibly fought to defend the rights of Apollo, the Sacred War was fed by the traditional hatred of Thebes and Phocis, and the religious nature of the conflict incited many Greeks to join this terrible conflagration rather than unite against their common threat from Macedonia. Meanwhile the Phocians impetuously seized the treasure at Delphi to finance their military operations. Hiring vast numbers of mercenaries, they fielded a force of around ten thousand men that pushed into Thessaly and Boeotia and achieved more victories than losses. In 356 BCE the Delphic Amphictony (the Thessalians controlled half of its votes) foolishly appealed for aid to Philip, who was then occupied in the north, but he marched south in 352 BCE—posing as the champion of Apollo—and eventually drove the Phocians from Thessaly. Reorganizing the Thessalian League to further his own imperialistic ambitions, with the right to levy troops from its members, Philip had taken advantage of the Greek disarray to bring all of Thessaly under his sway.

Conquests in Thrace and Chalcidice (351–349 BCE).   Meanwhile Philip had employed his considerable resources—bribes, deceptions, and military power—to subjugate the Thracian seacoast, gobbling up towns one by one and incorporating them into his growing kingdom. Many Greeks remained blind to the danger, but in 351 BCE Demosthenes, the greatest Athenian orator, vainly appealed to his fellow citizens for stronger opposition to Philip in a speech known as the *First Philippic* (from the name of the king). In the same year Philip set out to absorb his last independent neighbor, his ally the Chalcidian League, for the Chalcidic peninsula blocked a large part of his kingdom from the sea. Although the citizens of Olynthus decided to fight and appealed to Athens for aid, Philip had thwarted such intervention by fomenting a revolt against Athenian authority in Euboea. Meanwhile Demosthenes, ever mindful of the rising Macedonian threat, pleaded with the Athenians to send immediate relief in his three *Olynthiac Orations*. In 348 BCE Philip finally captured and destroyed Olynthus, betrayed by his paid traitors. He sacked many other cities in the area, killing or enslaving countless people, while acquiring the splendid harbors of the Chalcidice that were vital in the Aegean trade. The Athenians sent reinforcements too late to save Olynthus and then utterly failed to rouse allies against Macedonia.

Philip Triumphs: The Peace of Philocrates (346 BCE).   Philip had razed Olynthus as a warning to other Greeks. He employed diplomacy to convince most Athenian leaders that cooperation with Macedonia would best serve their interests, and in 346 BCE they dispatched an embassy to Macedonia to conduct peace negotiations. The Peace of Philocrates, which took its name from the chief Athenian negotiator, was a great victory for Philip. Philocrates somehow managed to convince his fellow envoys—of whom the most notable were Demosthenes and Aeschines—that Macedonia wanted no quarrel with Athens. The treaty called for the mutual recognition of the current possessions of each state, and a defensive alliance was also concluded.

Thus Athens and Macedonia became allies, and Phocis—which had relied upon promises of Athenian assistance—was left to its dreadful fate. Philip immediately brought the Sacred War to an end by invading Phocis, burning and plundering its towns. The Phocians were then expelled from the Delphic Amphictony, and their two votes were transferred to Philip and his descendants. Thus Philip, the man many Greeks had once ridiculed as a barbarian and a drunkard, was not only publicly acknowledged as a Greek but also took his place in the most venerable Greek religious association. The champion of Apollo and the overlord of Thessaly, Philip was well on his way to becoming the captain of Greek affairs.

The Ascendancy of the War Party in Athens (346–340 BCE).   When the Peace of Philocrates was being negotiated, Philip enjoyed the support of a strong pro-Macedonian party in Athens. In his open letter to Philip—the *Philippus*—the aged rhetoric teacher Isocrates urged the Macedonian king to lead the Greeks in a military crusade against the Persians and plant Greek colonies in Asia Minor. The letter must have come as a propaganda blessing to Philip, who was determined to persuade the Greeks to accept Macedonia as their leader and guardian of their interests. Meanwhile the anti-Macedonian party was gaining influence in Athens. Demosthenes, who was perfectly willing to distort facts to arouse the Athenians against Philip, returned to the attack and warned that democracy would wither under Macedonian hegemony. Demosthenes had become a bitter enemy of the more restrained politician Aeschines, who now argued that Athens could not fight without allies and certainly would be defeated in a war against the Macedonians. When Demosthenes initiated a trial against his rival in 343 BCE on the charge of having taken bribes from Philip and betrayed Athens in the negotiations preceding the Peace of Philocrates, Aeschines was acquitted by a very small majority. Earlier in the same year, Demosthenes and his associates had brought a charge of treachery against Philocrates, who then fled from Athens in fear of aroused public opinion, only to be condemned to death in his absence for contempt of court. The members of the now powerful anti-Macedonian party, led by Demosthenes and others, were determined to resist Philip's future attempts at expansion, and by 340 BCE Athens had formed a considerable coalition to defend Greece against the king, including Corinth, Megara, Euboea, Phocis, Achaea, and the northwest Greek states of Acarnania and Leucas. Most of the Peloponnesian states held aloof, as did Thebes, still grateful for Macedonian help against Phocis.

Philip Expands His Hegemony and Prepares for War (345–340 BCE).   Unable to become overlord of the leading Greek states through diplomacy, Philip carried out a determined campaign between 345 and 340 BCE to extend his power through other means. He gained full control of Epirus in 342 BCE by placing Olympias' younger brother Alexander on the throne. Next he strengthened his hold on Thrace and Thessaly. By 340 BCE Philip had advanced eastward against the northern shore of the Propontis (the modern Sea of Marmara), planning not only to complete his conquest of Thrace but also to cut off the Athenian grain lifeline from the Black Sea. The two chief cities on the northern coast, Perinthus and Byzantium, had already abandoned their alliance with him to join the anti-Macedonian coalition formed by Athens. His first objective was to crush the troublesome duo. When he laid siege to Perinthus in the spring, the Byzantines and the Persians immediately sent aid to the beleaguered city, though Athens still hesitated in declaring war. The Perinthians—now reinforced with additional arms and men—offered ferocious resistance, and Philip eventually turned away to hasten eastward toward the walls of Byzantium. There he commandeered an Athenian merchant fleet of 180 grain-laden vessels in the late summer of 340 BCE, thereby bringing the diplomatic contest between Athens and Macedonia to a conclusion and forcing the outbreak of war. Athens dispatched a fleet to aid Byzantium in the early spring of 339 BCE. Demosthenes, who was now in full charge of the war, had roused the Athenians over the years with additional orations against Philip: the *Second Philippic* (344 BCE), the *Third Philippic* (341 BCE), and the *Fourth Philippic* (341 BCE). Meanwhile the Byzantines, reinforced by Athenian naval power, fought valiantly to repel Philip, and in the late spring the king was forced to withdraw from the region.

The Battle at Chaeronea (338 BCE).   For the time being the war between Athens and Macedonia smoldered, but Philip looked forward to leading a united Greek invasion against Persia and decided to force the Athenians to meet him in a great land battle in Greece, not at sea, where they would enjoy superiority. Thus he used his new position in the Delphic Amphictony to stir up trouble. On the pretext of a Sacred War against the Locrian town of Amphissa—accused of trespassing on the sacred land of the Delphic Apollo—Philip marched south into Greece. At last Demosthenes managed to win over Thebes and a number of smaller states, now provoked by Philip's proximity. The battle was fought at Chaeronea in northern Boeotia during the summer of 338 BCE. Each side numbered about thirty thousand men, though the armies of Athens, Thebes, and other allies were no match for the battle-hardened Macedonian forces. Philip's young son Alexander commanded the cavalry flanking the left wing of the formidable Macedonian phalanx, and in a thundering charge he attacked the elite Theban Sacred Band of sworn lovers, who fought and died where they stood in a last brave stand for Thebes. Meanwhile Philip, on the right, feigned retreat. Pursuing him in a haphazard fashion, the Athenians broke and ran into headlong flight when Philip ordered the Macedonian phalanx to turn and advance. By evening one thousand Athenians had fallen and two thousand had been taken prisoner. Chaeronea made Philip the undisputed master of Greece, with the exception of Sparta, which had not participated in the decisive battle. The old city-states of Greece—Athens, Sparta, Thebes, Corinth, Argos, and the rest—had long known one another as friends and foes, enjoying a common history and heritage. Now most Greeks must have regarded the Macedonians as intruders and upstarts in their midst.

THE LEAGUE OF CORINTH (337–336 BCE)

Although free to reorganize Greece as he wished, Philip treated the Athenians with respect, sending Alexander to Athens with the ashes of their dead and releasing their prisoners. The king had always maintained a genuine admiration for the cultural pre-eminence of Athens, and he realized that future enterprises might depend on the co-operation of the city and its powerful warships. Moreover, a protracted siege of Athens could bring Persia and many Greek states to its support. Thus Philip offered the Athenians conciliatory peace terms, which they accepted with some gratitude and set up a statue of him in the Agora. Athens retained its constitution and its territory, while extremist anti-Macedonian politicians such as Demosthenes escaped punishment. In return for this leniency, Athens was required to become Macedonia's ally, to join a new Hellenic union that Philip proposed, and to dissolve its maritime league. The Athenians knew they had come off well and now heeded moderate leaders, who realized the wisest course was to offer Philip cautious cooperation.

All the Peloponnesian states submitted to Philip except Sparta. He ravished Laconia and trimmed off part of its frontier to strengthen and enlarge Messenia, Arcadia, and Argos, though he did not attack the city of Sparta itself. Philip was most severe in his treatment of Thebes, which at the end had ignored treaty obligations to him. Thus Thebes was stripped of all its power in Boeotia and was garrisoned by Macedonians, with former democratic leaders being executed or exiled.

Having made considerable progress in arranging the affairs of the various Greek states, Philip marched to Corinth and proceeded to organize what modern scholars call the League of Corinth. He invited all the states of central and southern Greece and many of the Aegean islands to send delegates to Corinth to discuss the arrangements. Only Sparta—pitifully weak but defiant—refused to attend. The League of Corinth was essentially a union of Greek states bound by treaty obligations to preserve a common peace with one another. The legislative body of the organization was a representative council, and the executive was the king of Macedonia. Although Macedonia was not an actual member of the league, Philip and his descendants were to function as its military commander and head (*hegemon*) for life. Thus the League of Corinth served as an important instrument for imposing Macedonian domination on Greece. The terms of the treaty called for each state to be autonomous, exempt from attack by other Greek cities, and free to sail the seas. Moreover, arrangements were made to arbitrate disputes. Philip intended for the treaty to end the political and economic unrest that had caused so many disruptions in the past. Only then could he fulfill his great underlying aim for the league: a united Greek war against Persia.

Death of Philip (336 BCE).   Philip persuaded the delegates of the newly established League of Corinth to declare a war of revenge on Persia and then sent an advance force of ten thousand men into northwestern Asia Minor in the spring of 336 BCE. Yet Philip was not to lead in that enterprise, for he was removed from the scene by an untimely death. The final year of the king's life was overshadowed by domestic clashes. As customary among Macedonian rulers, Philip practiced polygamy. The stormy Olympias had presented him with two children, Alexander and Cleopatra. A crisis loomed in 337 BCE when the king was seized with passion for a young Macedonian noblewoman, another Cleopatra, who was the niece of his trusted general Attalus, and he announced his intention of marrying her. We hear that Philip imparted a new light on his love match by questioning Olympias' marital fidelity and encouraging unfounded rumors that Alexander might be illegitimate, an insult that could endanger the normal succession. These claims suggest an atmosphere of distrust had arisen between Philip on the one hand and Alexander and Olympias on the other. The story continues, on uncertain authority, that at the wedding feast of Philip and Cleopatra, Attalus drank heavily of wine and then recklessly—or perhaps in calculation—invited the nobles to pray to the gods for a legitimate heir to the throne. Alexander immediately threw his drinking cup in the face of the general for having insulted both his mother and himself, whereupon Philip drew his sword in fury to silence his son. Reeling under the influence of wine, however, the king fell sprawling, and Alexander taunted him with insults. Pella was no longer the place for Alexander and Olympias. Alexander accompanied his mother to her home in Epirus, and then went into exile himself among the warlike Illyrians, enemies of Macedonian kings, though he eventually reappeared at Pella upon the invitation of Philip.

In 336 BCE Olympias returned to Macedonia for the wedding of her brother, King Alexander of Epirus, to her daughter, Cleopatra. Philip, who had adroitly arranged the wedding, received gold wreaths from the guests. The second day began with a dazzling religious procession, which was headed by richly adorned statues of the twelve Olympian gods accompanied by a godlike image of Philip. Macedonian tradition regarded the kings as descendants of Zeus, and the most prestigious rulers were worshiped after death. When Philip himself finally entered alone, wearing a white ceremonial cloak, a disgruntled young noble named Pausanias sprang forward and stabbed him to death. Several years earlier Philip had discarded Pausanias as a lover in favor of another handsome youth, whereupon the former referred to the latter as a paid prostitute. To disprove the insult, the new lover saved Philip's life at the expense of his own in battle. Meanwhile Attalus devised a humiliating retribution for Pausanias, inviting him to his house for a banquet and getting him dead drunk. Then he and all his guests took turns raping Pausanias, after which Attalus' slaves subjected the wretched youth to the same treatment in the stable yard. When Pausanias complained to the king about the repeated sexual assaults, Philip refused to act against his father-in-law and brilliant general. Thus Pausanias bore a grudge against Philip at the time of the assassination, though he is unlikely to have acted without assistance and encouragement from others. The youth could offer no evidence for his murderous assault because he was killed on the spot. Although the ultimate source of the assassination remains a matter of speculation, there were whispers that either Olympias or Alexander, or both, were involved. Alexander immediately asserted his claim to the succession and was acknowledged king by assembled Macedonians. His rivals and foes were gradually all slain. The relentless Olympias seized and murdered the young widowed queen and her infant daughter (most modern historians discount the tradition that she had also given birth to a baby boy, said to have been killed in the purge), while Alexander sent an assassin to the front in Asia Minor to dispose of Attalus. Thus began the reign of Alexander III, called the Great, whose meteoric career was founded on the celebrated accomplishments of his father. The remarkable Philip had transformed a peripheral kingdom into a formidable power and established Macedonian hegemony over Greece.

CHAPTER XIV

CULTURAL DEVELOPMENTS IN THE FOURTH CENTURY BCE

Culturally, the fourth century may be said to have begun with the fall of Athens in 404 BCE and to have ended with the death of Alexander the Great in 323 BCE. Fourth-century social institutions suffered greatly under the impact of wars, plots, assassinations, and foreign interventions. The writing of history and poetry shows notable decline, but economic life was far from moribund, and many efforts in oratory and art matched earlier achievements. Athens, despite its diminished political power, remained at the center of Greek intellectual life during this period, with the bedrock of Western philosophy emerging in the thought of Plato and Aristotle.

ECONOMIC LIFE REFLECTS THE GROWING PROMINENCE OF THE RICH

Cynical attitudes acquired in the struggle for survival during the horrors of the Peloponnesian War had released many Greeks from the traditional sense of obligation to the state, with rich citizens generally failing to give to the polis on the scale of their predecessors. The fourth century witnessed entrepreneurs making huge fortunes in commerce, industry, real estate, and banking, their wealth affording comforts and luxuries undreamed of in an earlier day. Many of them began looking beyond the polis for economic opportunities and investments. A sign of the times was the separation of the population into extremes of wealth and poverty, a development paralleled by a significant decline in the power of ordinary citizens. Self-sustaining Greek farmers, for example, had loyally rendered military service when their lands were being devastated by the Peloponnesian War. Lacking the capital to reconstruct their property after the conflict, many of these landowners sold their holdings to the wealthy and then either slipped into the class of landless tenants or moved to the cities and lived on state doles, while clamoring for redress. Meanwhile the wealthy few were buying up even the small workshops in the city, and the people of moderate means became fewer and fewer as the century passed. Thus in Athens the proportion of *thetes*, the hired laborers, rose from forty-five percent of the population in 431 to fifty-seven percent in 322. Party strife and class warfare continued unabated under these circumstances and more than once gave rise to revolution and bloodshed.

ART

Fourth-century Greek art reveals a lingering classicism gradually moving toward the artistic spirit of the succeeding Hellenistic period. The individualism of the day is clear, with the grave and serene beauty of fifth-century art almost vanishing as artists concentrate on the problems and emotions of individuals. Thus the art of the century is often described as pre-Hellenistic rather than Classical.

POTTERY AND PAINTING

The fourth century was transitional in terms of pottery decoration. Potters, particularly those of Athens, had ceased to produce fresh vase paintings by the end of the fifth century, turning instead to an ornate style with large, brightly colored figures pushed into crowded compositions. By the end of the fourth century figured ware had almost disappeared in the Greek world, partly because the upper classes could afford to purchase metalware. Moreover, artists increasingly turned from painting the vessel to working its surface by ribbing, impressed decoration, and other methods of adornment.

Reflecting a trend beginning in the fifth century, artists now favored wall paintings or panel paintings, which served as decoration for the interior walls of public buildings and the houses of the wealthy and powerful. Two methods of painting were in vogue: encaustic (employing pigment mixed with melted wax) and tempera (employing pigment mixed with egg yolk). Fourth-century artists demonstrated a new sense of the fundamentals of anatomy, the relation of figures to space, and the effects of light on surfaces. Greek painting seems to have reached its height during the century, and literary sources tell of many great artists, though their work is lost. Apelles of Colophon, later of Ephesus, produced portraits of Philip, Alexander, and their circle. His painting of Aphrodite rising from the sea, wringing out her hair, was celebrated in antiquity for its naturalism.

ARCHITECTURE

Fewer temples were constructed during the fourth century, partly because most of the earlier sacred buildings remained serviceable. As noted, the Doric and Ionic orders had reached their height in the temples of the fifth century, though an important fourth-century variation of the Doric order was realized in the temple of Athena Alea at Tegea in the Peloponnese, designed by the famous sculptor Scopas of Paros. The columns across each end and flank were quite slender. Scopas adorned the interior walls of the usually long naos with engaged Corinthian half columns.

The late fifth century had witnessed the birth of the Corinthian order. Probably used for the first time by Ictinus in the temple of Apollo at Bassae in the highlands of southwestern Arcadia, the Corinthian column is characterized by a bell-shaped capital decorated with spirals and stylized acanthus leaves. According to legend, the design of the Corinthian capital was inspired by the sight of acanthus leaves growing from a basket set upon a grave column. Until roughly 330 BCE

A new type of architectural order appeared before the end of the fifth century BCE: Corinthian, distinguished from the Ionic order chiefly by its more ornate capital, which is bell shaped and decorated with carved spirals and acanthus leaves. Apparently this splendid example from Epidaurus in the northeastern Peloponnese served as the masons' model for the capitals of the Tholos, a round building of the mid-fourth century BCE. Archaeological Museum, Epidaurus.

the order was employed only for interior colonnades, afterward for exterior work as well. Although not used extensively by the Greeks, lush Corinthian columns were widely exploited by the Romans.

Tholoi.   Another distinctive form of Greek architecture was the circular building, the tholos, which reflected a new emphasis in the fourth century on the interior space of buildings. The circular plan of the tholoi seems to have been inspired by the tholos tombs of the Mycenaeans. Although the tholoi were used for various purposes, apparently a number were linked to the cult of dead heroes. Famous tholoi stood at Delphi and the Peloponnesian city of Epidaurus.

Buildings in Asia Minor.   Architecture flourished in fourth-century Ionia, where designers were motivated by their quest for elaborate ornamentation and grandeur. They adhered closely to the Ionic order—Asia Minor was the home of the style—and produced a number of notable buildings, such as the elegant temple of Athena Polias at Priene, designed by the architect Pythius to honor the goddess in her attribute of Polias, the protector of the polis. Pythius strongly objected to the use of the Doric order in sacred buildings because of the complications arising from the spacing of the corner triglyphs. Dedicated by Alexander the Great in 334 BCE, the temple at Priene served as a model for many subsequent sanctuaries.

Temple of Artemis at Ephesus and the Mausoleum at Halicarnassus.   The southwestern shore of Asia Minor was the setting of two magnificent monuments that the ancient Greeks ranked among the Seven Wonders of the World: the massive temple of the goddess Artemis at Ephesus and the gigantic Mausoleum at Halicarnassus. From Ephesus the worship of Artemis had spread throughout the Mediterranean basin. Her Archaic temple at Ephesus burned to the ground the night that Alexander was born in Macedonia, so we are told, but the Ephesians immediately started building another on the same scale. Although its exact appearance is impossible to reconstruct, the temple was of great size and included a double exterior colonnade of tall Ionic columns that produced vivid alternations of light and shade. In both the Archaic building and its successor, some of the lower column drums were embellished with reliefs depicting figures of mythology. The sumptuous temple fell upon calamitous times in the Christian era, and only a few remains of the temple and its sculpture survive.

The Mausoleum at Halicarnassus—nearly 150 feet high—was designed as the resting place of Mausolus, satrap of Caria, who unwittingly gave his name to a particular kind of stately monument used for the entombment of the dead. Work began on the tomb during the lifetime of Mausolus and continued after his death in 353 BCE under the direction of his grief-stricken sister and incestuous wife, Artemisia, who succeeded him as ruler and, legend says, drank his ashes mixed with wine. The Mausoleum was another structure designed by the architect Pythius of Priene. Pliny the Elder gives us a rather vague description and relates that four famous sculptors, including Scopas, contributed to its abundant and spectacular sculptured decoration. The massive tomb dominated the entire city of Halicarnassus (modern Bodrum on the Turkish coast), and the design foreshadowed Hellenistic architecture through its fusion of Greek and eastern elements. Although its precise appearance remains uncertain, the Mausoleum included a lofty rectangular base, which may have receded upward from the ground in three huge steps. This substructure supported an Ionic colonnade topped by a roof in the form of a stepped pyramid, itself crowned by a great marble quadriga, or chariot drawn by four horses harnessed

Conjectured reconstruction of the unique Mausoleum at Halicarnassus, designed as
a great tomb for Mausolus, who ruled the mountainous region of Caria in southwest
Asia Minor as a virtually autonomous satrap until his death in 353 BCE. The non-
Greek Mausolus commissioned Greeks to design and decorate his magnificent tomb,
which beautifully combined Greek and eastern elements and was ranked by the
ancients as one of the Seven Wonders of the World.

abreast. Unfortunately, the Mausoleum was badly damaged, perhaps by an earthquake, in the thirteenth century of our era and then thoroughly plundered by the
Knights of Saint John in the late fifteenth century. The knights used many blocks

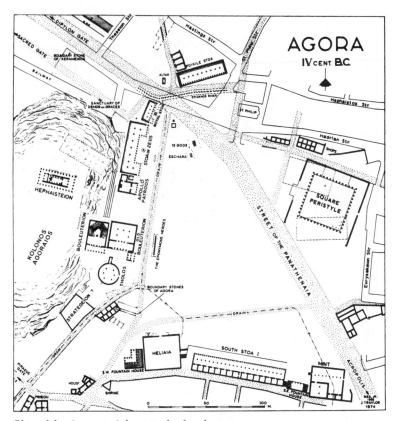

Plan of the Agora at Athens in the fourth century BCE.

and pieces of the relief sculpture as building materials for the improvement and extension of their nearby castle. Excavations have recovered a number of sculptures and remains from the castle and the actual site of the great tomb.

Buildings of the Athenian Agora.   A popular gathering place in a Greek city was the agora, a large open space used for socializing and conducting political, commercial, judicial, or religious business. The Agora of fourth-century Athens was a place of architectural splendors, though space prohibits enumerating all its secular and sacred structures. The main civic buildings stood along the west side. The Tholos in the southwest corner had been constructed about 465 BCE as an office building and a dining place (a kitchen was attached) for the use of the prytany, the executive committee on duty from the *boule,* or Council of Five Hundred. One third of the members of the committee on duty stayed at the Tholos day and night to ensure that responsible officials might always be on call. Both the Bouleuterion, where the Council of Five Hundred met, and the Old Bouleuterion, used at this time for storing records, were immediately north of the Tholos. The Bouleuterion, erected in the late fifth century BCE, formed a compact auditorium, its seats built in a semicircle around a speaker's place. In front of the Old Bouleuterion stood a long pedestal supporting statues of the ten eponymous heroes. *Eponymoi* were those who gave their name to something. When Cleisthenes divided the Athenians into ten artificial tribes, the Delphic oracle chose ten Attic heroes as *eponymoi*, the name-giving ancestors for the so-called tribes. The pedestal bearing the statues also served as a bulletin board for public announcements. North of the council buildings stood the temple of Apollo Patrous, where citizens were registered and magistrates took their oaths of office. Destroyed by the Persians in the fifth century, the temple was not restored until the fourth.

Much of the social and commercial activity of the Agora took place in the various stoas. A Greek invention, the stoa is essentially a building with a rear wall from which a roof slopes to a long open colonnade along the front. The many possible elaborations on this simplest form include the addition of an interior colonnade, rooms behind the wall, wings, or a second story. Stoas provided shade and shelter for a wide range of activities, including business engagements, shopping, civic responsibilities, and philosophical discussions. Several stoas were constructed in the Agora during the fifth century BCE. One of these, the Stoa of Zeus, which was north of the temple of Apollo, was noted for having projecting wings that broke its straight façade. The Stoa of Zeus was built late in the century just south of the famous sixth-century Royal Stoa (or King Archon's Stoa), the office of the magistrate known as the king archon, or *basileus*. Stoas provided an excellent setting for displaying famous paintings, along the back wall, and the Stoa of Zeus was celebrated for its murals by the painter-sculptor Euphranor, who was applauded for his use of color and the majestic bearing of his figures. His paintings at the Stoa of Zeus included the twelve Olympian gods and the depiction of a cavalry battle between the Athenians and the Thebans.

The Doric temple of Hephaestus, which is well preserved thanks to its conversion to a church during the Middle Ages, was erected on a slope west of the buildings mentioned above and dominated the western side of the Agora. Southwest of the Tholos stood a building identified as the Heliaea, where jurors met to hear legal cases. Immediately to the east of the Heliaea the Athenians erected what is now called South Stoa I, a long double-aisled colonnade in front of a row of sixteen magistrates' offices. Finally, the north side of the fourth-century Agora was dominated by the Painted Stoa (Stoa Poecile), a public hall constructed of various limestones before the middle of the fifth century. Decorated by Polygnotus and others with famous paintings of historical and mythological battle scenes on large wooden panels, the Painted Stoa became a favorite haunt of philosophers in Hellenistic times, including Zeno of Citium, whose followers became known as Stoics, their name derived from this very stoa where he so often taught.

The architectural fashion during the later Hellenistic period was to regularize the shape of an agora into a rectangle. King Attalus II of Pergamum, in gratitude for his education in Athens, provided funds for that purpose in the mid-second century BCE, and a great two-story stoa of Pentelic marble was constructed along the east edge of the Athenian Agora. The colonnade on each level of the Stoa of Attalus was backed by a series of rooms, probably serving as prestigious state or

Reconstruction of the beautiful Painted Stoa (Stoa Poecile) in the Agora at Athens, c. 450 BCE, named after its large painted wooden panels depicting great historical and mythological battles involving the Athenians. Created by Polygnotus of Thasos and other celebrated artists of the day, the paintings were still in place when the Greek travel writer Pausanias visited Athens six centuries later. The architects graced the front of the Painted Stoa with a simple colonnade of Doric columns and erected inside a row of Ionic columns to support the roof, an early example of order mixing in Athens.

business offices. This magnificent monument of exceptional design was completely rebuilt in the mid-twentieth century by the American School of Classical Studies in Athens.

The Theater of Dionysus.   The famed Greek theater of Dionysus on the southeast slope of the Athenian Acropolis was rebuilt—this time with stone—in the 330s BCE and renovated several times in the Roman era. The theater could accommodate an amazing fourteen to seventeen thousand spectators, and twelve radiating stairways divided the tiers of seats into thirteen wedge-shaped sections. The first two rows were thronelike seats of honor reserved for the priests and officials of Athens.

SCULPTURE

The idealizing style of fifth-century sculpture continues into the fourth, with figures retaining tranquil expressions, generally transparent drapery (though often rendered as agitated heavy folds swirling over limbs and torso), and an easy stance. While clearly remaining in the Classical tradition, fourth-century sculpture exhibits a lessening of restraint and tends toward a deceptive realism in the rendering of facial expression and musculature. Social and political changes were reflected in art, as in literature and philosophy. With Greek civic ideals of the fifth century crumbling under the dual impact of the Peloponnesian War and the erosion of the polis, the old balance between the citizen and the city-state weakened. The Greeks began to lose their traditional assurances concerning the gods and hallowed customs, leading to a greater interest in the individual. This individualism shows up in sculpture, with patriotic and sacred themes increasingly replaced by personal subjects. Numerous portrait statues of prominent fourth-century men reflect the growing interest in the individual, while the decline of religious fervor is revealed in the humanizing of the sculptures of the gods. The humanizing tendency also meant that figures in the round became more popular than reliefs, and many of the more notable works of sculpture were entirely disassociated from any particular building.

Striking innovations were introduced in technical methods, for sculptors increasingly employed the drill to make deep incisions in marble, impractical when they depended entirely upon the hammer and chisel. The use of the drill made possible the deeper folds of drapery and the heavy masses of hair on many fourth-century statues. Sculptors were also breaking with the old tradition of composing for one main viewpoint, usually frontal, and now created figures that encouraged the viewer to walk around them, achieved by the twist of the body or by a marked contrast between the direction of the gesture and that of the gaze. Most anatomical problems had been solved in carving the nude by the fourth century, when sculptors increasingly focused on a naturalistic depiction of the naked human body. Homosexual idealism and the profound fascination with the male form had declined with the erosion of civic pride. Fullscale female nudes first appear in the fourth century. The goddess Aphrodite was progressively undressed. Her statues had been veiled with closely clinging drapery in the fifth century, but they are sometimes naked in the fourth. Meanwhile many sculptors sought to create a deliberate and provocative sensuality in both their male and female nudes. The overall result of these various tendencies was a loss of the grandeur and dignity of fifth-century art.

Praxiteles, Scopas, and Lysippus.   Three artistic geniuses dominated the sculpture of the fourth century BCE: Praxiteles of Athens, Scopas of Paros, and Lysippus of Sicyon. The Athenian sculptor Praxiteles, who returned to the use of marble for many of his greatest pieces, gained fame for the grace and softness of his style. The best-known surviving work of the period is the provocative *Hermes and Dionysus,* found in the temple of Hera at Olympia, a sculpture of such high quality that some scholars take the piece to be the original executed by the great Praxiteles himself and dismiss the strong suspicion that it is an exceptionally fine copy. The sculptor used translucent marble to represent a youthful Hermes supporting most of his weight on one leg in a sensuous leaning pose of relaxed languor that creates a pronounced reverse S-curve. Although Hermes is represented as a powerful figure, his thrusting right hip, delicate facial features, and dreamy expression give him a graceful feminine quality. On his left arm, the half smiling god holds the infant Dionysus, who reaches for something, probably a bunch of grapes Hermes

Fourth-century sculptors demonstrated an increasing enthusiasm for dreamy facial expressions, sinuous poses, and naturalistic drapery. The acclaimed Athenian sculptor Praxiteles, who worked in the mid-century, returned to marble for many of his major works. He was famous for his beautiful nudes, exemplified by this provocative marble statue representing Hermes carrying the infant Dionysus, found in excavations of the temple of Hera at Olympia. At first commonly regarded as an original from the sculptor's own hand, the statue is probably an exceptionally fine copy of a Praxitelean work of around 340 BCE. The superb figure of Hermes seems characteristic of the style of Praxiteles, with its smoothly modeled face, deep-set eyes and dreamy gaze, expressive mouth, freely tousled hair, fluid modeling of bone and muscle, and pronounced sinuous curve and outthrust right hip. The overall effect of this luminous softness almost suggests casual indolence, a notable secularizing of the Olympian gods. Battered by the Peloponnesian War and other difficulties, the Greeks had begun to take traditional conceptions of divinity less seriously. Clearly, a wide gulf separates the fourth-century artistic presentation of deity from that of the fifth. Archaeological Museum, Olympia.

was dangling in his missing right hand. The statue conveys the tenderness of the adult for the child, and Dionysus seems to respond with affection and trust, an appeal to the strictly human rather than the divine realm. The humanizing of the two gods and the humor of the scene, assuming Dionysus is reaching for grapes, could not have been missed by the Greek viewer. The sculptor polished away all sharp edges from the features of the figures, creating fluid surfaces with a deliberately blurred effect, in contrast to the rough masses of hair and deep folds of the drapery.

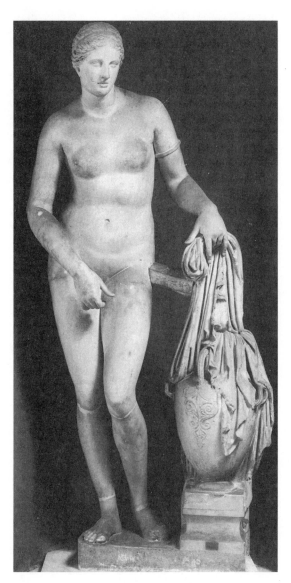

Praxiteles took the unprecedented step of making a cult statue of an entirely nude Aphrodite, purchased by the prosperous Greek city of Cnidus in southwest Asia Minor. Many people sailed to Cnidus just to see the goddess of love in her open circular shrine, where they could admire her from all sides. The social climate of the fifth century BCE had discouraged portraying the female form with outright erotic appeal. Although the sculptor has imposed a degree of modesty by representing Aphrodite—who has disrobed for bathing—shielding her pelvis from some intruder's gaze with her right hand, our encounters with the grand sculptured deities made in the previous century leave us totally unprepared for this startling view of the divine in an intimate moment. Ancient writers lavishly praised the figure's beauty, acclaimed by the Roman writer Pliny the Elder as the most beautiful statue in the world. The endless and rather mechanical Roman copies fail to convey the quality of the lost original of about 340 BCE. The best known among them, illustrated here, is now in the Vatican. Vatican Museums, Rome.

Praxiteles' most famous work in antiquity was his revolutionary marble statue of Aphrodite, carved for her sanctuary at the city of Cnidus in Asia Minor. He popularized the nude female statue through this piece, known only from inferior Roman copies. The *Aphrodite of Cnidus*, said by ancient sources to have been dazzlingly beautiful, may have been the first fully undraped state of the goddess and was certainly one of the earliest Greek statues of a female nude. Viewers were supposed to imagine that the goddess had been surprised during her bath by an intruder, and she reacts with token modesty by partially blocking the sight of her genitalia with

This bronze original known as the *Marathon Boy*, cast around 340 BCE, was retrieved from an ancient shipwreck near Marathon. The work is celebrated for its expression of dreamy adolescent melancholy. We cannot explain why the boy gracefully raises his right hand high and what object might have been on his left. The pronounced S-curve and flowing musculature reflect the Praxitelean style, and some scholars suggest the under-life-size *Marathon Boy* comes from the great sculptor's own hand. The eyes are inset limestone, with glass pupils, while the nipples are inlaid with copper. National Museum, Athens.

one hand, but her penetrating gaze and slight smile were said to betray a hint of encouragement. Praxiteles was entranced with the depiction of appealing physical attributes and made a profound impact upon the art of his day by setting a new standard of sensuous beauty for both male and female nudes.

Although Praxiteles derived his fame mainly from the use of marble, he also made superb bronzes. A magnificent bronze statue of a youth, often referred to as the *Marathon Boy*, was recovered from an ancient shipwreck off Marathon. The controlled rhythm of the piece suggests the Praxitelean style and may be a late work of Praxiteles or at least someone in his circle. An action statue, the youth's gestures are

The robust and vigorous work of Scopas of Paros contrasts with the untroubled beauty of Praxitelean art. An architect as well as a sculptor, Scopas designed the great Doric temple of Athena Alea at Tegea in Arcadia. Fragmentary heads from the temple's pedimental sculpture, which was executed by Scopas or under his supervision, epitomize intense power and unbridled psychological tension. The head illustrated here, probably either Heracles or his son Telephus, shows an anguished hero with deep-set, heavily shadowed eyes, wearing a lion-skin headdress, *c.* 340 BCE. National Museum, Athens.

unexplained, but he gazes at an object formerly held in his extended left hand, while his right is raised high in a graceful movement. The boy exhibits the undulating pose for which Praxiteles was noted, and his naturalistic eyes are made of white lime-stone with glass pupils, while his nipples are inlaid with copper. In this work, one of the few surviving Greek bronzes, the sculptor has deftly captured an expression of

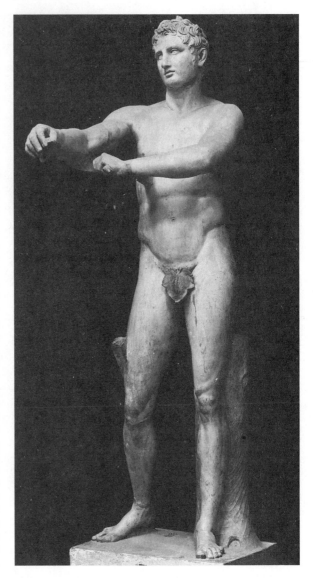

The third principal sculptor of the fourth century was the innovative Lysippus of Sicyon, active from about 370 to 310 BCE. Preferring to work in bronze, Lysippus abandoned the somewhat stocky Polyclitan proportions in favor of a slimmer physique and smaller head that gave his figures the appearance of greater height, a new canon adopted in a more limited way by Praxiteles. Lysippus' proportions are evident in this Roman marble copy in the Vatican of his original bronze *Apoxyomenus* (Body Scraper) of about 330 BCE, portraying a young athlete scraping oil from his body after exercising. In a drive for greater naturalism, the sculptor has broken completely with the one-view frontality of most fifth-century statues. By having *Apoxyomenus* thrust his arms into what might be regarded as the observer's space, Lysippus claims a revolutionary spatial independence for the statue, which offers no single optimum viewpoint and can be appreciated only by walking around the whole. The fig leaf is a modern addition. Vatican Museums, Rome.

dreamy adolescent melancholy, a bittersweet mood first appearing in Greek art in the fourth century BCE.

Scopas of Paros, a contemporary of Praxiteles, worked on the elaborate sculptured decoration of the Mausoleum at Halicarnassus and served as the architect of the temple of Athena Alea at Tegea in Arcadia. Scopas is known for a robust and vigorous style of sculpture. The dramatic sculptures surviving from the pediments of the temple of Athena Alea at Tegea are thought to have been executed either under his supervision or partly by his own hand. Despite their mutilations, fragmentary heads from the temple reveal an impassioned upward gaze, heavily furrowed brows, and sunken eye cavities producing dark shadows around the eyes, features giving the pieces an intensely emotional and pained expression. Scopas was celebrated in his day for portraying passion and strenuous action, and the wide staring eyes and facial expressions of the heads generate considerable psychological tension in the viewer.

The prolific Lysippus of Sicyon, last of the principal sculptors of the century, took up the athletic themes favored by Myron and Polyclitus, but he was a highly innovative artist who broke completely with the one-view frontality of most fifth-century statues. Lysippus also completed the evolution of the naked standing male. Ancient writers praise him for abandoning the somewhat bulky proportions of Polyclitus for a slim physique and smaller head, designed to make his statues look taller. Yet this was a general trend in late fourth-century sculpture, exemplified by the slender Praxitelean statues. Working entirely in bronze, Lysippus produced numerous pieces characterized by their delicate modeling and precision of detail. One of his standing male nudes is represented by a Roman marble copy in the Vatican, the *Apoxyomenus*, which shows a young athlete, after exercising, scraping oil from his body with an S-shaped cleaning implement called a strigil. The sculptor portrays the athlete rocking from one foot to another and thrusting his arms into the viewer's space. The twisting pose of the *Apoxyomenus* offers no single optimum viewpoint and can be fully appreciated only by walking around the whole. Its fig leaf is a modern addition. At the height of his career Lysippus was invited to become the court sculptor of Alexander the Great, and ancient tradition relates that he alone was allowed to execute bronze portraits of the king. The transforming designs of Lysippus and his two great predecessors, Praxiteles and Scopas, clearly foreshadow the sculpture of the succeeding Hellenistic period.

ROYAL MACEDONIAN TOMBS

With the shift of political power north to the kingdom of Macedonia in the fourth century, we are on the threshold of an era when commissions come from king-emperors rather than city-states, a change dictating the future of Greek art. Excavations of a number of Macedonian tombs have shed considerable light on fourth-century Greek painting and other arts. The most remarkable discoveries have come from the royal cemetery near the village of Vergina (ancient Aegae), traditional burial place of Macedonian kings. Of the three tombs found here, two were previously untouched. Although debate continues over the identification of the royal occupants, the tombs have yielded rare examples of original pre-Hellenistic paintings of high quality, including a panoramic view of a hunt and, above all, a robust mural portraying the abduction of Persephone by Hades. The main scene of the latter shows the terrified Persephone desperately flinging her arms back toward her distraught companion as the god's chariot whisks her away to the underworld. The emotional facial expressions would have been unthinkable a century earlier. One tomb housed numerous pieces of extraordinary splendor made of gold, silver, bronze, and ivory. Its richly equipped antechamber contained a woman's ashes consigned to an exquisite gold casket and wrapped in protective fabric that was finely decorated with floral patterns and woven in purple on a gold background. Her gold casket also held a magnificent gold diadem of rare beauty and intricate design.

LITERATURE AND RHETORIC

POETRY AND DRAMA

The erosion of the city-state and, consequently, its civic and religious obligations influenced every aspect of Greek culture, including literature. The fourth century created far less poetry. Earlier, much verse had been composed in the service of the state and had taken popular forms such as choral song and drama. The decline in poetry writing reflected a shift of emphasis from civic responsibilities to fulfillment of social and private concerns. Although tragedies continued to be written for the Athenian festivals, they were so lacking in originality that the state encouraged restaging the masterpieces of the Age of Pericles.

Middle Comedy (c. 404–323 BCE).   Comedy, which maintained much of its former vigor, was less restricted in form than tragedy and thus could more easily reflect the changes in the temper of life coming with the fall of Athens in 404 BCE and the loss of imperial power. While the Old Comedy of the fifth century had emphasized personal attacks on well-known individuals and political issues of the day, fourth-century Athenians occupied a much weaker polis and thus were less confident and less tolerant of unbridled political and social criticism. With the progressively tamer Middle Comedy of the fourth century, overtly political satire gives way to mythological burlesque and scenes from daily life. Ribaldry generally disappears. Meanwhile the role of the chorus is considerably diminished (exemplified by the discontinuance of its direct address, or parabasis, to the audience to reveal the poet's intentions), and the heavily padded costume and the prominent phallus of Old Comedy is now gone.

Aristophanes lived into the fourth century. His last plays reveal the changes in comedy, for he abandons political attacks and concentrates instead on social themes. He seems to relish poking fun at women. The plot of his comedy *Ecclesiazusae (Women in the Assembly)* centers on a group of women who have fastened on false beards and seized political power in Athens, introducing a social order based on the communal holding of property. Aristophanes discloses in his last surviving comedy, *Plutus (Wealth),* performed in 388 BCE, what sort of a world would exist if the god of wealth—Plutus—were cured of his blindness and could give his bounty to the deserving. Yet when Plutus recovers his sight and redistributes wealth, the result is comic confusion both in heaven and on earth. The rich old woman loses her gigolo because now he has ample funds without her payments. The new order is to the detriment even of almighty Zeus. Much experiment was taking place in such plays during the period, and typical plots of Middle Comedy revolve around young men in love, lost children, courtesans, philosophers, and gluttons. Stock characters of this sort formed an important element in New Comedy, written from the last quarter of the fourth century until the end of the third.

History.   We saw that poetry yielded its place to prose as the predominant form of literature in the fourth century. This was the great century of Greek prose writing in history, oratory, and philosophy. The historians of the fourth century BCE were notable for their attention to the new individualism of society, often writing biographies of prominent figures. Thus Theopompus of Chios, formerly a pupil of the Athenian orator Isocrates in the art of rhetoric, penned the *Philippica,* whose fifty-eight books focus on the life and times of Philip of Macedonia. Written on a grand scale, the *Philippica* reflects Isocrates' contention that history should serve politics by propelling the Greeks into a union against the Persians. Ephorus of Cyme in Asia Minor, also a pupil of Isocrates, wrote a voluminous history of Greece down to 340 BCE, with large sections devoted to accounts of Egypt and Persia. Although surviving today only in fragments, the works of Theopompus and Ephorus served as indispensable sources for later authorities such as Polybius, Strabo, and Plutarch.

Xenophon (c. 428–354 BCE).   Most of our knowledge of the early fourth century rests on the prolific works of Xenophon. Born of a wealthy Athenian family of pronounced conservative inclination, Xenophon became a disciple of Socrates, against whose advice he went to Asia Minor as one of the Greek mercenaries in the service of the Persian prince Cyrus the Younger. Xenophon participated in Cyrus' daring attempt to depose Artaxerxes II, king of Persia, as noted in chapter 13. After Cyrus lost his life in 401 BCE trying to wrest the throne from his brother at Cunaxa, near Babylon, Xenophon served as one of the generals of the beleaguered Ten Thousand Greeks making their way through unfamiliar Persian territory to the Black Sea. His *Anabasis,* already mentioned, immortalized the epic journey and serves as a valuable source for Greco-Persian interaction.

Xenophon's background and participation in the discredited Socratic circle gave him little enthusiasm for democracy. He demonstrated strong pro-Spartan sympathies. Exiled from Athens, he spent most of the remainder of his life in the Peloponnese, where he produced a large and versatile literary output, mostly historical narratives, Socratic texts, and technical treatises. His seven-book *Hellenica* is a Greek history that continues the unfinished narrative by Thucydides, who breaks off abruptly at 411, and brings the account up to 362 BCE. Although his effort is respectable, Xenophon fails to equal the sweeping historical perspective and penetrating analysis of his predecessor, and his admiration of the discipline and order of Spartan society—in contrast to that of Athenian—seems excessive. His *Memorabilia,* four books of memoirs about Socrates, contains dialogue scenes in which the great philosopher converses with various named individuals, from politicians to courtesans. Xenophon refutes the charges advanced at the trial of Socrates but portrays him as a colorless moralist and fails to grasp the depth of his ideas. Most contemporary scholars turn to Plato as a more reliable witness for information about the life and thought of Socrates. Although Xenophon was not a profound thinker, his writing is lively and entertaining, and his diverse treatises shed light on the views and pursuits of a conservative upper-class Greek in the fourth century.

ATHENIAN RHETORIC

We find impressive prose in surviving examples of fourth-century Athenian rhetoric (also called oratory). For the ancient Greeks, rhetoric was the art of persuasion through public speaking. The Greeks relished speeches, both as speakers and as listeners, and rhetoric was regarded as a vital skill for any active citizen in a democratic state. Political success in the restored democracy of Athens depended on influencing the assembly and law courts or the crowds gathered at the great festivals. The Athenian law courts were packed not only with disputants having commercial grievances but also with politicians charging one another with corruption or treason. Aristophanes had satirized this litigiousness in his fifth-century comedy the *Wasps*. There were no lawyers, for the laws were simple and easily comprehended. Professional speechwriters usually wrote orations for clients to memorize and then deliver in court. Lysias and Isaeus were two of the most brilliant practitioners of this art in Athens. Lysias (c. 459–380 BCE), son of a Syracusan metic, was noted for his smooth, clear style. As a metic, Lysias was forbidden from pleading in court personally but was much in demand because he composed speeches helping his clients to speak naturally and to express their own personalities convincingly. Isaeus (c. 420–350 BCE), who was active in Athens and may have been an Athenian, was reportedly a pupil of the orator Isocrates and a teacher of the great Demosthenes. An expert on the Athenian law of inheritance, Isaeus composed speeches persuasively expounding his points through simple and lucid language.

Isocrates (436–338 BCE).   Rhetoric reached full maturity with Isocrates, who was born into a wealthy Athenian family and studied under the famous Sophist leader Gorgias and others during the Peloponnesian War. Isocrates began his professional life as a speechwriter for litigants in the law courts and at some point established a school on the island of Chios to teach practical politics and rhetoric. He went far beyond teaching skills in composing and delivering speeches, preparing students for all phases of public life. Thus he emphasized the broadly rounded education of the Sophists, though he condemned their radical toppling of standards. Youths—many of whom became famous—came from all over Greece during a forty-year period to study under him. One of Isocrates' achievements was to mold the oration into a formal work of art through the grace and melodious language of his prose, which greatly influenced the Roman orator and writer Cicero. Isocrates frankly admitted he lacked the strong speaking voice and confident temperament needed for addressing a large audience and rarely, if ever, uttered the speeches he wrote. Thus most of his orations should properly be termed essays, for they were intended to be read rather than delivered. Presumably, they had some influence on public opinion, and they provide us with valuable information on fourth-century political concerns.

Isocrates devoted his career to solving the political, economic, and social problems of the Hellenic world at a time when the city-state was in a state of marked political decline. The Greeks seemed recklessly bent on destroying their way of life through the constant wars among the city-states. Alarmed, Isocrates argued they should form a political union for their very survival, a Panhellenic ideal he advocated throughout his life. He also vigorously promoted another Panhellenic goal, a Greek crusade against the Persians, whom he regarded as deadly enemies. The *Panegyricus*, published in 380 after a ten-year period of composition, demanded that the Greek states unite, with Athens as the leading maritime power and Sparta as the leading land power. The purpose of this Panhellenic union was to wage war on the common enemy of Persia in order to liberate the Greeks of Asia Minor. Isocrates eventually despaired that the Greeks would come together under the shared hegemony of Athens and Sparta, however, and turned his pleas for leadership to a number of eminent men throughout the Greek world and finally to Philip II of Macedonia. In 346 Isocrates published his famous *Philippus*, calling on the Macedonian king to lead the Greek states against Persia. Despite his plea for Philip's guidance, Isocrates remained a loyal Athenian to the end, believing Athenian cultural achievement would guarantee a glorious role for the city in the new Greece. In the *Panathenaicus*, written when he was ninety-four, Isocrates praises the achievements of Athens and contrasts the city favorably with Sparta. In local Athenian politics, Isocrates advocated curbing the growing individualism of his day by restoring traditional aristocratic ethics and checking the ills of democracy by reviving the guiding power of the Areopagus.

Demosthenes (384–322 BCE).   The most notable of the Athenian orators and probably the greatest in antiquity was Demosthenes, the eloquent defender of Greek freedom against Philip of Macedonia. Left fatherless in childhood and deprived of inherited wealth by the mismanagement and dishonesty of guardians, he grew up nursing his wrath and longing for vengeance against those who had wronged him. His youth was plagued by poor health, an unsociable disposition, and a lack of interest in athletics, but behind his brooding nature lay an indomitable will. At the age of twenty-one Demosthenes brought an action against his guardians and eventually secured the remnants of his property. Meanwhile he entered the speechwriting profession and gained a favorable reputation, leading to his appointment as an assistant to prosecutors in public trials. He also began delivering speeches on issues of public importance. Enjoying an excellent ear for sound and rhythm, Demosthenes never sacrificed clarity for eloquence in his speeches, for he aimed to make convincing arguments. The cadence of Demosthenes' powerful language suggests a voice raised in a heated outburst and then quietly pleading with deep conviction. His orations strongly influenced the Roman Cicero.

Alarmed by the aggressions of Philip II in the northeast, Demosthenes in 351 BCE delivered the *First Philippic*, his initial speech identifying the Macedonian king—rather than Sparta or Persia—as the principal enemy of the Athenians. Demosthenes begs his fellow citizens to offer stronger opposition to Philip or risk losing their state's independence. The *Philippics* and his other political orations against Philip are among the greatest political speeches of antiquity, portraying the king's intentions toward Athens and the other Greek city-states as lethal. Yet

Demosthenes failed to persuade the majority of his fellow Athenians to heed his alarm. Demosthenes, who remained hostile to Philip and his successor Alexander the rest of his life, thought Greek freedom depended on retaining the traditional framework of autonomous states, among which Athens should exercise primacy.

The unquestioned courage of his zeal against Philip and later Alexander aroused much admiration for Demosthenes and his party. In 336 BCE the Athenians voted to present him with a golden crown (the Greeks often bestowed crowns as awards of merit) in recognition of his services to the state. Later, his implacable political enemy Aeschines, whom Demosthenes had accused of accepting bribes from Philip and betraying the interests of Athens, attacked him by bringing charges of unconstitutionality against the proposer of the award. Demosthenes defended his friend and his own political career in *On the Crown*, a masterpiece of effective argument and organization, winning such a resounding acquittal from the jury that the humiliated Aeschines retired to the island of Rhodes.

The last years of Demosthenes' life were troubled and embittered. Condemned for embezzlement, he escaped into exile. He was recalled home upon the death of Alexander the Great to help organize a revolt against Macedonian rule (the Lamian War, 323–322 BCE), but Athens was crushed, and Demosthenes died by his own hand to avoid being taken prisoner by the pursuing Macedonians. His renown rests mainly on his artful, rhythmic speeches, majestically ebbing and flowing and perfectly tailored to the subject matter of his discourse. Rather than flattering his audience, Demosthenes frequently showered listeners with contempt, derision, or criticism, for his entire political life revolved around his total commitment to the lost cause of Athenian freedom.

PHILOSOPHY

The fourth century was especially fertile for philosophical speculation, through which many intellectuals sought a purpose for life after the erosion of their confidence in the Olympian gods. Space does not permit sketching more than a bare outline of the thought of fourth-century philosophers. Two great geniuses of the period, Plato and Aristotle, founded the most important comprehensive philosophical systems of antiquity. Their ideas still exercise direct and profound influence.

The Minor Socratics

Euclides of Megara: The Megarian School.   During the generation following the death of Socrates several of his associates and others exaggerated certain aspects of his character or ideas as embodying the core of Socratic teachings and expanded them into systems of thought. His disciple Euclides of Megara (c. 450–380 BCE), founder of the Megarian school, attempted to synthesize the systems of Socrates and Parmenides. Euclides reportedly held that the Good was one thing existing under many names such as *wisdom, god,* or *intelligence.* In the hands of his successors this doctrine degenerated to a quibbling, fruitless sort of elementary logic.

Antisthenes: Forerunner of the Cynic Tradition.   Antisthenes (*c.* 445–360 BCE), the son of an Athenian father and a Thracian slave woman, was first educated by Sophists but later became Socrates' ardent disciple. After the death of Socrates, he practiced an exaggerated imitation of the great philosopher's austerity of lifestyle. Antisthenes founded a school near Athens in a gymnasium known as the Cynosarges. Following Socrates in holding that virtues can be taught, Antisthenes regarded the proper goal of life as the attainment of happiness *(eudaimonia)*, which comes from virtue *(arete)*. He was so taken with Socrates' ascetic habits and paucity of possessions that he identified virtue with self-denial and happiness with the avoidance of worldly goods and pleasures.

Diogenes: Cynicism.   The eccentric Diogenes of Sinope (*c.* 400–325 BCE) moved from his native Greek city on the south coast of the Black Sea to Athens in middle age and pursued a life marked by extreme asceticism and shocking actions designed to rouse others from complacent acceptance of social conventions. His unique behavior still provokes stories, perhaps apocryphal, that he slept in an overturned barrel (the famous "tub"), searched with a lamp in the daytime for an honest man, and once ordered Alexander the Great to stand out of his sunlight. Supposedly, Diogenes fulfilled all his physical needs and desires openly, even masturbating in public, defending the practice by saying he wished he could gratify hunger as readily, by merely rubbing his stomach. Apparently this tradition of shamelessness earned him the nickname the Dog *(Kyon)*. From this, his followers became known as the Cynics *(Kynikoi)*, or the Doglike. Diogenes lived in extreme poverty and rejected with utter contempt all proprieties and customs of society, for the Cynics proclaimed the supreme importance of individual freedom. Obviously Cynicism was a way of life rather than a formal school of theoretical philosophy. Individuals who are virtuous and happy, the Cynics believed, live in complete independence from material goods, comforts, and artificial pleasures. Moreover, they are citizens of the entire world and must be content to return to the ways of nature by renouncing all ties of family, friendship, and state. Such individuals are as happy wearing rags as fashionable finery and find contentment with the plainest food and simplest lodging, for nature will provide all necessities. Scorning the material and social values of most people, the Cynics disparaged society, education, and civilization as corrupting influences. Through their poverty, immodest behavior, and detachment from worldly ties, the Cynics sought tranquility from earthly concerns. While many elements of the movement were borrowed by the Stoics in the third century BCE, the Cynicism of Antisthenes and Diogenes persisted into the Christian period.

Aristippus of Cyrene: The Cyrenaic School.   A dissimilar philosophical posture was promoted by another associate of Socrates, Aristippus of Cyrene (*c.* 435–356 BCE), traditional founder of the Cyrenaic school. Apparently he was impressed by Socrates' ability to enjoy drinking wine at dinner parties, while avoiding being overcome by pleasure. Aristippus is said to have identified happiness with pleasure—the latter being the proper pursuit of life—and virtue with the self-discipline to resist being dominated by bodily gratification. Ancient evidence suggests he enjoyed a worldly and luxurious way of life. Later, Aristippus' ideas reappeared in a modified form in Epicureanism. The contrasting attitudes of the Cynic tradition and the Cyrenaic school persisted as polarizing beliefs into Christian times.

PLATO (427–347 BCE)

The preeminent disciple of Socrates, Plato, came from a distinguished aristocratic family of Athens and claimed descent on his father's side from the last king of Athens and on his mother's from the great social and political reformer Solon. Plato was a nephew of the ill-fated Critias, a leader of the oligarchs who had established the rule of the despotic Thirty Tyrants. Although Plato condemned the cruel acts and repression of the Thirty, he was sympathetic to this antidemocratic faction. He had been destined as a young man for an aristocratic political career, but the excesses of the Thirty and the demagoguery of the restored democracy turned him away from these ambitions. Becoming a devoted friend of Socrates several years before the fall of Athens in 404 BCE, he turned to the study of philosophy. The execution of Socrates in 399 BCE under the restored Athenian democracy had a profound effect on Plato. Disgusted with democracy and personally devastated, he fled from Athens and during the next twelve years is said to have traveled widely, journeying to Egypt, Cyrene, Italy, and Sicily. In Sicily he came under the influence of Pythagorean thought, which colored his writings. Seeking the ideal state, he was attracted to the court of Dionysius I, ruthless tyrant of Syracuse. Now about forty years of age, Plato became both teacher and lifelong friend of the ruler's young kinsman Dion. Surviving verse attributed to Plato and addressed to Dion suggests the relationship was also romantic and probably sexual. According to one story, the Sicilian stay abruptly ended when the despotic Dionysius took offense at Plato's criticisms and arranged for him to be sold into slavery. Plato, so the story goes, was released only after friends purchased his freedom.

The Academy.   Returning to Athens, Plato began teaching near a public park and gymnasium on the outskirts of Athens known as the Academy, which gave its name to his school. Although legally an institution for the worship of the Muses, Plato's Academy functioned as a school, and its students—of whom the most gifted was Aristotle—came from the entire Greek world. Never married, Plato devoted most of the remainder of his life to his work at the Academy, the first of the great philosophical schools in Athens, but interrupted his teaching to return to Sicily. When Dionysius I died in 367 BCE, Dion invited the sixty-year-old Plato to the intrigue-ridden Syracusan court to shape the young new tyrant, Dionysius II, into a philosopher-king. All these hopes were dashed by the growing discord between Dionysius and Dion. Meanwhile Plato left for Athens. The intense civil strife engendered by the rivalry between the two kinsmen would ultimately lead to the murder of Dion in 354 BCE and the dismantling of the Syracusan empire.

Plato presided over the Academy until his death at the age of eighty in 347 BCE. His chief aim was training potential leaders through a philosophical education. He believed that the wise individual in public service must have a broad range of knowledge, and to that end the Academy offered instruction in astronomy and mathematics, but the school is best remembered now for its contributions to the philosophical development of Platonism. The Academy remained one of the great intellectual centers of Greco-Roman civilization for more than nine hundred years, until the emperor Justinian—believing himself divinely appointed to protect the Christian religion—closed all non-Christian schools of philosophy in 529 CE.

The Dialogues.   The enormous influence of Socrates on Plato is reflected in the latter's writings. Plato does not appear in his own works, but instead expresses his point of view through Socrates. Although Plato agreed with Socrates that philosophical inquiry is best realized through an interchange of ideas, he did not follow his friend's example of rejecting the written word in favor of personal encounter. Yet Plato chose a style that was unusual in his day—prose dialogue—and based his writings upon the Socratic method of arriving at some important truth through a probing system of question and answer. Socrates had chosen the oral method because of its lack of restraint, and Plato attempted to recapture on the written page the informality that allows an argument to proceed without inhibition, for such philosophical debates draw the reader mentally into the dialogue as a participant. Plato's purpose in writing the dialogues was not only to defend Socrates against the verdict of the Athenian court but also to carry on the great thinker's philosophical inquiry.

We can follow the evolution of Plato's thought through his twenty-six dialogues, which express his philosophical themes through a rare combination of magnificent literary style and challenging content. To refer to all of these works as dialogues is misleading, however, for the *Apology* purports to be the speech made by Socrates at his trial, and a number of the others are essentially monologues. The dialogues do not respond to easy summary and are by no means systematic expositions of a complete philosophy that can be put forward as a final characterization of his position. Instead Plato introduces us to lively debates with a wide range of characters, many of whom were historical figures. Although scholars quibble about the dates of Plato's works and the order in which they were written, the dialogues have been arranged in three groups that are thought to represent successive periods. In the first group, we find Socrates as the most important figure, dramatically and convincingly overturning the errors of his opponents. Although the philosophy of Plato is difficult to separate from that of Socrates, most historians agree that the latter, as a historical figure, is chiefly represented in the dialogues of the first group. Three of these—the *Euthyphro, Apology,* and *Crito*—revolve around Socrates' life and behavior immediately before, during, and after his trial.

In the second group, although Socrates still remains the chief speaker, Plato expounds a number of his own theories through the mouth of his friend. Plato's masterpiece the *Republic* provides the classic explanation of his famous theory of forms, discussed below, and articulates a view of the ideal political community. In the *Symposium*, a dialogue with a heavy homosexual aura, Plato considers the nature of sexual love. The male initially seeks physical, then spiritual, beauty in the beloved. Thus male love becomes a source of the highest and noblest aspirations.

The modern notion of nonsexual, Platonic love is a distortion of the views of the philosopher, who believed two males could be inspired by their passion to nourish a spiritual, not just a sexual, union. In the *Phaedo*, which describes the last hours and the death of Socrates, Plato defends the belief in the divinity of the soul, a divinity that ensures its survival after the death of the body.

In the third group, the dramatic element dwindles, and Socrates assumes a position of lesser importance. There is very little actual conversation in the latter dialogues, for a chief speaker presents long expositions of philosophical doctrines to shadowy figures who make few comments. The *Theaetetus* is an inquiry into *episteme*, or knowledge, and the *Timaeus* considers the origin of the world. In the *Laws*, Plato's longest dialogue, he takes up again the question of the best constitution for a state and revises some of the ideas expressed in the *Republic*.

Plato's Revolutionary Concept of Reality: The Theory of Forms.   As noted, Plato concentrates on Socrates in the first group of dialogues. Socrates, whose philosophy is discussed in chapter 12, concerned himself with ethical matters, particularly with uncovering general definitions of ethical terms by asking probing questions. Socrates believed that through reason individuals can discover the Good, apprehension of which leads to virtue, for to become aware of the Good is to practice right conduct. Through apprehension of the Good, individuals also attain knowledge of the inner truth of the world. Thus virtue is equivalent to knowledge and is teachable.

Apparently Socrates did not define the Good, however, and one of Plato's aims was to define the nature not only of the Good but also of the soul, which becomes virtuous by apprehending the Good. Plato turned for guidance in this quest to the Pythagoreans, who argued that an eternal reality transcends our senses, a reality that can be expressed in numerical terms, for they believed numbers are the essence of all things. Like the Pythagoreans, Plato stresses the mathematical interpretation of nature. The Pythagoreans believed also in the immortality of the soul, which they viewed as a fallen divinity confined within the body and condemned to a cycle of transmigrations as humans, animals, and plants, until finally achieving release through purifying rites and abstinences. Plato was strongly influenced by these Pythagorean doctrines and the ethical teachings of Socrates.

Plato's first task, then, was to define the nature of the Good, and this led him to investigate the nature of knowledge, for Socrates taught that virtue is knowledge. Combining Socratic and Pythagorean principles, Plato derived his central doctrine of knowledge: the theory of forms (or ideas). Through this theory Plato sought to reconcile the opposing views of the followers of Heraclitus (what exists is in flux) and those of Parminedes (what exists is unchanging). Plato thought both systems are reflected in the universe, for he postulates that the changing principle functions in the realm perceived by the various senses and the unchanging principle in the realm of forms. He maintains, moreover, that the main feature of the world of sensory perception is its instability; everything within this realm is in constant change, an indication that knowledge of it is mere opinion. Thus through the eye, ear, nose, and other senses, an individual becomes acquainted with nothing more than the changeable realm of appearances. True knowledge, on the other hand, comes through discovering the ideal realm of immutable forms, attained through mathematics and especially philosophy. Geometers, for example, in discussing the properties of the circle or the square are not referring to their imperfectly drawn diagrams but to the eternal forms of the circle or square.

Thus Plato postulates a system of eternal realities, forms, that exist in a separate realm beyond the shifting objects and events revealed by our senses. Plato taught that every material thing on earth is an imperfect reflection or copy of these perfect forms. For example, we see a single tree, but in the realm of forms there is a perfect tree—the form of tree—and each single earthly tree is merely an inferior copy. A form corresponds to all objects and concepts that we can conceive such as houses, desks, beds, living things, colors, shapes, beauty, goodness, and justice. Thus the forms are perfect archetypes that are imitated by the changing copies, and the forms alone are the proper objects of knowledge, for encounters with their pale reflected copies in the world of sense—however real we may think them—are as variable and changing as shadows.

At this point the question naturally arises, with what faculty does a person know the Good and the forms? The answer to Plato is that the human soul preexists before its incarnation in the body and has apprehended the realm of forms before its embodiment. Thus the imperfect copies on earth—perceived through the senses—remind the soul of the perfect archetypes. This principle means that knowledge of the form behind the particular appearance on earth is simply recognition of a truth known in a preexistent state. That is why the Socratic method of asking probing questions and subjecting the answers to logical analysis is essential to uncover the truth the soul already possesses.

The forms owe their existence to the one supreme form, the Good, the source of all being and truth. Although the first and highest principle of reality, the Good is not a god. In the *Timaeus* Plato introduces the figure of a Divine Craftsman. He suggests that the limitations of human intelligence preclude genuine knowledge of the universe outside the realm of the forms, and so his Divine Craftsman is not intended to be a literal but a plausible figure. Plato postulates that the Divine Craftsman is the self-moving source of the motions of the heavens and the creator of the sensible universe. Using a preexistent formless material, the Divine Craftsman made the universe in accordance with the pattern of the forms. Thus the Craftsman molded the world in imitation of the forms, making everything in the cosmos resemble them as closely as possible. The Craftsman should not be viewed as any sort of monotheistic divinity, however, for this being calls subordinate deities into being to aid in the work of creation.

The Problem of Evil and the Afterlife: Transmigration.   The object of the *Phaedo* is to justify belief in the immortality of the soul. Plato presents the soul as having three parts: reason, spirit or resolution, and appetite. Through reason, the most important part, the soul is reminded of its divine existence before incarnation in a human body. Spirit or resolution is a natural ally of reason in its struggle to keep the various appetites within bounds. The part of the soul that Plato calls appetite is disorderly and seeks worldly and sexual gratification. Only with great difficulty can reason bring appetite under its control. Additionally, the soul has a driving force, desire (*eros*), the motivating principle behind all human thought and action. Whichever part of the soul gains mastery over the individual determines the aim of desire. Thus its power can be directed toward lust by appetite, toward fame or honor by spirit, or toward the forms by reason. As noted, the quest for the forms occurs when desire for mortal beauty is channeled into passion for the form of beauty. When, on the other hand, appetite seizes control of reason and spirit, the constant attempt to gratify its unending cravings will lead to greater pain than happiness.

Plato inherited from the Pythagoreans the concept of transmigration, the belief that at death the soul survives to enter another body. His dialogues feature several accounts in mythical terms of the punishment of the soul and of its purification during the intervals between successive incarnations. Souls that have not sought the Good do not enjoy blessings in the next life. Near the end of the *Republic* we learn through a mythic vision that a thousand years elapse between each human death and the succeeding rebirth of the soul. This period is spent either above in a heavenly abode enjoying the delights and beauties merited by the past life or below in a lowermost abyss of the underworld (Tartarus) reaping punishments for offensive behavior, a clear warning to act justly in this life.

Plato's Political Theory: The Republic.   All the aforementioned philosophical elements find expression in Plato's masterpiece, the *Republic*, which begins with an ethical problem: What is the nature of justice in the individual? Plato, through words he attributes to Socrates, argues that the nature of justice in the individual can be discerned by first examining justice on the larger scale of the state. Thus he insists that the well-ordered state is justice writ large. Plato ultimately develops an analogy between the human soul and the state, arguing that the former reflects the latter because each operates under the same principles.

In the *Republic* Plato describes an imaginary, justice-embodying state, the parent of many utopias conceived by later thinkers. This perfect state is not a democracy, a political system Plato blames for many evils of his day. He views the masses of people as incapable of governing the state justly. His ideal state—profoundly aristocratic—is a Greek city-state that assigns to each person a position according to natural aptitude. Thus its population is divided into three general classes corresponding to the tripartite soul. The first class consists of the rulers, a small group of individuals whose education, wisdom and character permit them to perceive clearly the realm of forms and to be guided by the Good. The souls of the rulers are governed by the element of reason, of course, and they are to function as philosopher-kings. They are motivated solely by the knowledge of the Good, a reflection of the underlying assumption in the *Republic* that goodness is the aim of the state and that ethics cannot be divorced from politics. Hence Plato insists in Book V, through the words of Socrates, that cities will not know rest from their ills "until philosophers are kings."

A second class consists of the warriors, the defenders of the state. For this purpose Plato proposes to employ those whose souls are governed by spirit or resolution, endowing them with the courage and loyalty to protect the state. A third class consists of the workers, the producers of the necessities as well as the luxuries of the state. Appetite governs the souls of the workers—the large majority of the population—who will serve as farmers, manufacturers, artisans, or traders, thereby carrying on economic activities necessary for the survival of the community. Their motivating drive is love of gain. The workers are to be told the Noble Lie that the class division reflects divine will. This deliberately fictional justification for the stratification of society is designed to induce the workers to accept their inferior status in society.

The division of the population into the three classes is to be made on the basis of natural aptitude rather than birth or wealth. The assignment of all individuals to their respective classes occurs only after they have received an education, which is provided by the state to ensure its proper form and content. Those enjoying sufficient ability progress to the next educational level. Men and women, Plato insists, should have the same education and follow the same pursuits. Plato's view of the role of women represents a startling departure from the traditional practice in ancient Greece. Although he regarded women as inferior to men (his *Timaeus*, for example, has men who fail in their lives becoming women in the next birth), Plato argues that women should be permitted to hold any position in society for which they are qualified, even that of warrior or ruler.

Education will include mathematics, music, literature, and physical training. Yet all literature must be expurgated, leaving only edifying matter that ennobles the mind and instills fearlessness. Plato regarded poetry as particularly harmful to the young because the genre frequently creates unflattering portraits of both gods and heroes, and hence he suggested banning the study of most poets, including Homer and Hesiod. Likewise, he disapproved of drama in education. Thus students will not enact tragedies or comedies, for what could be worse, he wonders, than a future warrior or ruler playing the role of a woman or a slave? Music too must be strictly controlled by the authorities to ensure that only rhythms and harmonies suitable for the training of warriors are heard in the state. In short, education should not aim at objective truth but character building. One of the main goals of the educational process will be to sort individuals according to the categories mandated by their predominating soul elements. The workers should be chosen early from those demonstrating aptitude only for practical training, the warrior class from those making more progress in their education. A few selected students will go on to study philosophy, the avenue to contemplation of the Good.

Plato refers to the philosopher-kings and warriors collectively as the Guardians. To prevent disunity from arising in the state through the competition of powerful families, Plato forbids the Guardians from having families. All women of the class are to be held in common to all Guardian men, while children are to be held in common and reared in state nurseries. Parents will never know the identities of their own children, nor children know that of their parents. The Guardians must practice selective breeding, for Plato complains that people carefully breed dogs and horses but foolishly rely upon pure chance to produce warriors and rulers. Sexual relations will be confined to special mating festivals, with couples paired by the rulers to produce strong, healthy children. Likewise, the Guardians will own no private property, and their needs will be provided for by the rest of the community. The Guardians in the Platonic state will not be burdened by individual rivalry and quests for possessions, both eliminated by their vision of the Good. Yet the workers, motivated by want of material gain, will be permitted to own property and have families.

As the individual soul functions virtuously when its three elements are in proper relation, the political state functions virtuously when its three classes agree about who should rule and who should obey. Justice then is the virtue attained in the state when the three classes act in harmony, each performing its proper task. From this Plato turns to the original question of justice in the individual. As the harmony of the three classes produces a just state, the harmony of the three elements of the soul (reason, spirit, and appetite) produces a just individual.

In the central part of the *Republic* Plato turns to explain the theory of the forms in several ways, including the famous Allegory of the Cave. Socrates asks his friends to imagine a group of prisoners who have been chained since childhood in a subterranean cave with their backs to its entrance. Unable to turn even their heads, they can look only in front of them. Men behind them are carrying models of human beings and animals on their heads, and a fire behind this group casts shadows of the objects on the wall in front of the prisoners. For the chained men, who cannot see either the people behind them or the models, the shadows are the only realities. If one of the prisoners were unfettered and permitted to look upon the models being carried, at first he would regard the objects as an illusion and think reality lay in the shadows. Only slowly would he learn to appreciate the true reality. Likewise, humans are imprisoned by their senses, until released by the study of mathematics and philosophy, an arduous upward road to knowledge of the realm of the forms and the Good. Thus education involves a complete turning of the soul from the realm of appearance and change to the realm of the eternal forms.

The Laws.   Abandoning hope that citizens of a city would voluntarily inaugurate the radical state proposed in his *Republic,* Plato substituted a different political system in his late dialogue the *Laws,* which has a trio of elderly men in Crete discussing the laws that will govern a projected Greek city-state. Plato portrays the community of the *Laws* living under a highly authoritarian order, with complete obedience to the laws guaranteeing the stability of the state and the moral goodness of its citizens. The rigidity of the system is exemplified by the provision that only mature and reliable citizens will be permitted to travel. In the *Laws* the family becomes a recognized institution for all classes, with monogamous marriage strictly enforced. Plato insists people should be ashamed of their sexual activity, whether legitimate or not, and should make every effort to conceal such participation in order to reduce the power of sexual desire. He goes on to demand, through a speaker, rigorous suppression of the practice of homosexuality, a remarkable change for a man who had moved in the homoerotic aura pervading the Socratic circle and had stressed in the *Symposium* that male love between a man and a youth inspires an ennobling passion for the forms and the Good. This new doctrine of homosexual suppression, if adopted, would have required a massive restructuring of Greek belief and practice.

Plato relates in the *Laws* that all citizens will own property, but they are to be taxed at the rate of almost 100 percent on incomes above a modest statutory limit. Although the philosopher now favors a mixed constitution combining elements of democracy and authoritarianism, the chief aim of the government is to ensure that all subjects obey the rigid laws. The citizen body will consist of 5,040 men, with each member supporting his family by cultivating two parcels of land, while resident foreigners will enjoy exclusive jurisdiction over trading and teaching. Plato also proposes a rigid state theology, with the denial of any major divine truth being a grave crime. Thus atheists must be either converted or executed. Significantly, Plato's beloved Socrates—who never would have been tolerated in a city like this—makes no appearance in the *Laws*. The work can be read as evidence of an old man's despair concerning the enlightenment of humanity and his pain over the erosion of the Greek city-state.

A number of subsequent thinkers synthesized Platonic ideas and other elements of Greek philosophy, resulting in a movement now called Neoplatonism. Developing in the Roman Empire in the third century CE, Neoplatonism strongly influenced many Latin writers, non-Christian and Christian alike. To the latter, Plato's concept of the Good seemed to foreshadow Christian monotheism, and for centuries his teachings enjoyed great prestige as a medium for presenting Christian doctrines.

ARISTOTLE (384–322 BCE)

After Plato died in 347 BCE at the age of eighty—pen in hand, according to tradition—the Academy continued under less able masters. The next great achievements in philosophy were realized elsewhere. Plato's greatest pupil, Aristotle, retained a lasting veneration for his teacher's genius, though he rejected certain Platonic principles. Unlike Plato, he was not an Athenian citizen. Born in a minor town known as Stagirus (later Stagira) in Chalcidice, Aristotle was the son of Nicomachus, court physician to Amyntas II of Macedonia. His family belonged to the hereditary medical guild in the service of Asclepius, the god of healing, and Aristotle probably acquired his passionate interest in biology and physical science from his father. He entered the Academy at the age of seventeen and remained for nineteen years, eventually being allowed to teach and to work in relative independence on his research. Although profoundly influenced by Plato's thought and personality, he demonstrated less concern than his teacher with mathematics and more with empirical data.

Aristotle left Athens with a number of friends and followers when Plato died, accepting an invitation from a former fellow student at the Academy named Hermias, Greek ruler of Assos and other villages around Mount Ida in northwest Asia Minor. Hermias had acquired valuable mining interests that allowed him to purchase the title of prince from the Persian king. Aristotle and the others in his community advised the ruler on political matters. Aristotle must have formed a close friendship with Hermias, for he married the ruler's niece and adopted daughter

Pythias. Apparently Aristotle began his extensive zoological inquiries during his three years at Assos, and in 344 BCE he moved to Mytilene on the nearby island of Lesbos, where he indulged his passionate interest in marine biology.

A sudden change occurred in 342 BCE, when Aristotle was summoned to Pella to act as tutor to the thirteen-year-old crown prince of Macedonia, Alexander, who was destined to conquer the Persian Empire. We lack direct evidence about Aristotle's opinion of his royal pupil, though their relationship was not close in later years. Apparently his teaching focused on Homer and the dramatists, employing the model of epic heroes such as Achilles to reveal the embodiment of Greek valor. No doubt Aristotle also instructed the young prince in the fields of politics and scientific investigation. Alexander, who clearly absorbed some of his teacher's great scientific curiosity, took along a host of scientists on his Persian campaign.

The Lyceum.   In 335 BCE, after Alexander had inherited the throne, Aristotle returned to Athens to found his own school in rented buildings (as an alien he could not buy real estate) outside the city wall on the grounds of a gymnasium known as the Lyceum. Here he accumulated a considerable library and encouraged his students to embark on research projects covering a wide range of fields. The members of the school became known as the Peripatetics, probably from *peripatoi,* the colonnaded walks where Aristotle often lectured while strolling with his students. Aristotle maintained a natural history museum at the Lyceum to help illustrate his lectures, which seem to be the basis of his surviving works in technical and unadorned language. One great difference between the Lyceum and the rival Academy was that the scientific curiosity of the Platonists centered on mathematics but that of the newer school lay in biology and empirical research.

We hear that Alexander supported the Lyceum handsomely. With his sudden death in 323 BCE, however, anti-Macedonian feeling erupted in Athens, bringing Aristotle under attack. Charged with impiety, Aristotle refused to follow Socrates' example of waiting in the city for trial, supposedly remarking that he was saving the Athenians from committing a second sin against philosophy. He fled to the Macedonian-garrisoned city of Chalcis, where he died the next year at the age of sixty-three.

Works.   From Plato's principles, Aristotle gradually developed his own, sometimes diverging from and sometimes refining the views of his old teacher. Aristotle was bent on discovering knowledge, both theoretical and practical. For almost two millennia, down to the sixteenth century and beyond, he exercised an unparalleled influence on European science and philosophy. Although a huge number of separate treatises were attributed to him in antiquity, only fifty or so have survived under his name, and modern scholars accept only about half of these as authentic. All the works that were actually published by Aristotle—mostly popular writings for the general public—have been lost except for brief fragments. The surviving works were meant for use only in Aristotle's school and were written as an aid in presenting lectures. Apparently these lecture notes were not adequately published until the first century BCE, when an editor grouped them as treatises. Thus Aristotle did not have the privilege of editing or fully developing points in these writings, and at times the treatises seem to lack unity or any clear progression of thought. Many show signs of addition or revision. Works written at different stages of Aristotle's life, moreover, have been lumped together under one title. Consider, for example, the *Metaphysics* (after the *Physics*), a collection of writings that editors thought should be read after Aristotle's books on *Physics* (the science of nature, or *physike*). Finally, the language of the works is often dry and notoriously difficult.

The scope of Aristotle's thought cannot be covered briefly, for no single work of his—in contrast to Plato's *Republic*—furnishes a comprehensive foundation of his philosophy. Aristotle, unlike Plato, was empirically oriented and spent much time on a systematic effort to collect data as a basis for understanding natural phenomena. His great achievement was to systematize and reduce to writing the knowledge that the Greeks had accumulated up until his time. Aristotle's writings—unparalleled in their dimensions—were virtually an encyclopedia of learning. He investigated and wrote in the fields of logic, physical science, psychology, biology, metaphysics, ethics, political philosophy, and literary arts. Thus he was the leading expert of his day in almost every field of knowledge. No one before his time had seen the need to classify and write down such a vast compass of knowledge. Consequently, Aristotle lacked a guide in many areas of his endeavor. Imagine, for example, his difficulty in organizing the treatise called *Parts of Animals* without a book on animal parts to steer his research.

Works on Logic: The Organon.   Aristotle was not the first to comprehend the importance of the form of statements and their relationship to one another. Socrates, for example, had inquired into the nature of definition, and Plato had regarded dialogue as the appropriate form for philosophical argument. Yet Aristotle was a pathfinder in the discipline of logic, or the art of reasoning. His six treatises in the field came to be grouped in the sixth century CE under the general title *Organon*—the Greek word for instrument—because in these narratives Aristotle identifies logic as the *instrument* of knowledge. Hence Aristotle treats logic as the preliminary instrument to be applied in the study of each branch of knowledge. The best known and most influential of these treatises is *Prior Analytics*, in which Aristotle offers a general account of what represents a valid argument and what does not. He argues that the heart of logic is the syllogism, his treatment of which provided the basis of teaching formal logic until the beginning of the twentieth century. A syllogism is a deductive argument of three propositions: a major premise, a minor premise, and a conclusion. The following are two examples of valid syllogisms:

> All animals are mortal;
> All humans are animals;
> Therefore all humans are mortal.

> All humans are wise;
> All Greeks are human;
> Therefore all Greeks are wise.

Clearly, an argument does not prove anything just because it is a *valid* syllogism, though it must be a valid syllogism to offer a proof. Aristotle realized that in any attempt to arrive at scientific truth the reasoning must be valid and the premises true. Hence Aristotle relates that if the premises are true in a syllogism, then the conclusion is necessarily true. His chief aim in developing the syllogism was not just to assure consistent reasoning, but to provide an instrument for scientific demonstration.

Works on the Philosophy of Nature and Natural Change: The Physics.   Aristotle's eight-book *Physics* would be more accurately described as lectures on nature and natural change. He thought the most striking aspect of nature was change, and his physics may be regarded as that discipline having for its subject the study of phenomena that are changeable. Many of Aristotle's ideas—though modified to fit the thought and needs of his later admirers—dominated medieval science and theology. One of these was the concept he calls substance, which refers to anything that exists. Thus by substance he meant an individual thing such as Socrates or Bucephalus (Alexander's horse) or this horse or this dog or this man. Clearly, the concept of substance can refer either to an individual thing or to a species. Moreover, any given substance has an essence, or essential definition, that cannot be separated from its particular qualities. A table (substance), for example, may be round or square or rectangular or some other shape, yet the essential definition remains the same. Its shape and other nonessential characteristics constitute what Aristotle calls accidents. A substance can gain or lose accidents (color, size, shape, weight, and so forth) without losing its identity. An individual, for example, may be young or old, yet the substance of that person remains the same. Thus a substance can undergo many changes and still retain its identity, but not if the changes mean losing the characteristics constituting its essential definition. If, for example, a dog is defined as an animal that is capable of barking, then loss of the ability to bark would entail loss of caninity.

Hence Aristotle postulates that for every substance there is a fixed set of characteristics—the form—constituting its nature. The form of Socrates, in other words, is that which makes him what he is. Yet every substance has another intrinsic element besides form, and that is matter. Matter is the basic stuff making it possible for the form to have existence at all. A bronze statue of a duck, for example, has a duck as its form and bronze as its matter. Matter is the element that makes change possible, for everything in the material world has the possibility of becoming something else. Aristotle says that change consists of matter acquiring a new form. Thus change occurs if the bronze sculpture of a duck is remolded into a chicken. This leads us to one of Aristotle's fundamental doctrines, that of actual and potential being, for he says a thing can be one thing actually and numerous other things potentially. For example, a mature oak is the actuality of which the undeveloped matter of the acorn was the potentiality. A brick is the actuality of which the matter of clay was the potentiality. Thus the potential is eternally changing into the actual.

Additionally, Aristotle postulates that each individual thing has Four Causes (principles enabling it to exist): the material cause (the stuff from which it is made or generated), the formal cause (the blueprint that determines its form), the efficient cause (the agent responsible for producing it), and the final cause (the purpose, *telos*, for which it came into being). Hence Aristotle held the teleological view that everything in nature exists for an end or purpose. The purpose of Phidias' famous gold and ivory statue of Zeus in the temple at Olympia, for example, was the greater glory of Zeus.

Works on "First Principles and Causes": The Metaphysics.   In the *Metaphysics*, Aristotle's goal is to develop a science of things that *never* change, and he thereby investigates the basic principles of reality and the highest level of knowledge. He argues that these "first principles and causes" are the true foundation of wisdom, for they provide knowledge of reality. As noted, the title *Metaphysics* was not used by Aristotle but was applied by editors to this collection of his writings centuries after his death. On occasion Aristotle did refer to this branch of his inquiry as "first philosophy" because of its fundamental importance in the scheme of his thought. In the *Metaphysics*, Aristotle discusses the question of the ultimate source of motion and change in the universe—he says every movement or change in the world implies a mover—and in Book 12 finds it to be the eternal Unmoved First Mover, which may be identified as the philosophical equivalent of the god or gods of popular religion. Aristotle's god is not a personal deity involved in the affairs of this world, however, and the philosopher seems to have left no place in his thought for individual immortality. The Unmoved Mover, whose single activity consists of rapt self-contemplation, is not the creator of the world—which has existed from all eternity—but is the sole immaterial substance of the universe and is without possibility of change or motion. Yet all things in the universe desire to associate themselves with the Unmoved Mover. The stars of the outermost sphere of heaven enjoy an *intelligence* that causes them to strive for the Unmoved Mover's absolute perfection, and they imitate that perfection by moving eternally in a circle, the most perfect motion. Their movement is communicated to lesser things and serves as the source of all motion. In that sense the Unmoved Mover is the ultimate cause of all movement in the universe, from bodies in the heavens to living things on the earth.

Plato identified the only real world as the realm of unchanging eternal forms, which are known by the soul. Moreover, the only reality of the perceived world is through its participation in the forms. Plato was a rationalist who believed that reality can be grasped by reason, which reminds us of what we already know. Aristotle, on the other hand was an empiricist. Although not postulating that all knowledge is limited to perceptible things, he holds that perception is the only direct path to reality. Thus Aristotle says that knowledge is won by building upon perception itself. He ignores Plato's idea that the soul can reveal the forms, for his natural scientific bent led him to teach that the things we perceive by our senses are the primary realities. Aristotle accepts the existence of the forms, though not in a transcendent realm, and suggests they are characteristics of particular things in this world. Explaining that the forms have no independent existence on their own account, Aristotle refuses to reduce material things to pale reflections of the forms. Thus the forms do not exist apart from things but in them. Accordingly, the forms exist only in relation to matter (except in the case of the Unmoved Mover, which is pure form and exists independently of matter). For Aristotle, then, the real world is the one of concrete things we perceive. Although the things of the world change and perish, they contain a constant reality. In short, forms are realized in matter.

Works on Physiology, Astronomy, Biology, and Psychology.   Aside from astronomy, mathematics, and medicine, the Greeks had almost no scientific tradition or method of scientific inquiry. They often made unsupported hypotheses in fields where direct observation and experimentation could have rendered verifiable knowledge. Aristotle attempted to counter this tradition by observing the world rather than merely speculating about it. Yet he had to contend with the mass of false information then in circulation and sometimes accepted unsupported hypotheses. Aristotle's physiological knowledge was poor, for he regarded the heart as the seat of intelligence and the brain as an organ for regulating the temperature of the blood. Moreover, he insists that women have fewer teeth than men and that eels are spontaneously generated from putrid mud. Knowledge of astronomy was greatly limited without the telescope. Although Aristotle proposes in *On the Heavens* that the earth is spherical, his cosmology (the branch of philosophy dealing with the origin and structure of the universe) rested upon the false notion that the heavenly bodies move in perfect circles around a stationary earth located at the center of the universe. He maintains that these heavenly bodies are attached to concentric, transparent spheres. Aristotle goes on to postulate that the movement of the spheres is communicated to them by the rotation of the outermost stars, mentioned earlier, that move in a perfect circle in their intelligent desire to imitate the perfection of the Unmoved Mover. This cosmology shaped western thought to the sixteenth century and beyond.

Biology was Aristotle's key discipline, as mathematics had been for Plato. The first great biologist of history, Aristotle gathered vast amounts of information about both animals and plants. His greatest contribution to the field was the observation and classification of animals, though he often complained that many small creatures were impossible to scrutinize within the limits of human vision. The largest of his works in biology is the *History of Animals* (a better translation would be *Inquiry into Animals*), a four-book introduction to the anatomy, physiology, and behavior of all sorts of animals.

Aristotle's psychology is closely tied to his biology. The purpose of psychology, Aristotle insists, is the study of the nature of the soul (*psyche*). He argues that the soul is the principle endowing organic things with life, and hence a body without the life-giving soul is merely dead matter. Thus a soul makes a potential living body—whether plant, animal, or human—an actual living body. In *On the Soul*, Aristotle investigates the functions of the soul and postulates that the body (matter) and the soul (form) unite as one substance, and thus the soul—being inseparable from the body—perishes with the body's demise. This concept is in sharp contrast to Plato's idea that the body imprisons the soul. Aristotle goes on to say the human soul is above those of animals and plants, for it alone possesses the faculty of reason. Yet the human soul has an irrational part that opposes the rational part, and the problems of morality arise from the conflict between the two. If the rational element of the soul guides and controls the irrational element, the individual will live a virtuous and happy life.

Works on Ethics and Politics.   Aristotle considered both ethics and politics practical rather than theoretical disciplines, for he thought that knowledge of these two prompts individuals to act properly and live happily in society. His most important and best known ethical work is the ten-book *Nicomachean Ethics*, named after his son Nicomachus. Aristotle's ethics is teleological (concerned with end or purpose). He insists that the end of humankind is to live flourishing, happy lives. The pursuit of happiness or well-being is closely tied to virtue, the purpose of which is to obtain the supreme good for one's life. Virtue is defined as an intermediate course, the *golden mean*, between two extremes of behavior, excess and defect, or excessive indulgence and ascetic denial. The virtue of courage, for example, is the mean between the vices of foolhardiness (excess) and cowardice (defect). The idea of the golden mean is simply a reaffirmation of the traditional Greek ideal of *sophrosyne*, meaning "nothing too much," the insistence on human moderation in thought, word, and deed. While Aristotle argues that happiness comes from virtuous action, the highest happiness springs from following the ultimate virtue, namely, activity in accordance with reason. Thus the highest form of happiness, the supreme way of life, consists of a life of intellectual contemplation.

While Aristotle discusses the nature of individual happiness in the *Nicomachean Ethics*, he treats the state as one of the chief means through which the individual can attain happiness in his *Politics* (perhaps a better translation would be *Life in a Polis*). The *Politics*, as suggested, is concerned with the polis, which Aristotle regards as the political institution having the greatest potential for fostering human happiness or well-being, and throughout the work he is concerned with the state in this sense. Although the independent polis was doomed by the advance of the Macedonians, cities and civic pride continued to flourish within the Macedonian imperial system.

The *Constitution of the Athenians* is the sole surviving example of a massive investigation, which Aristotle directed, of 158 Greek city-state constitutions. His political theories were based, in part, on these extensive surveys. Aristotle argues in the *Politics* that "man is by nature a political animal" (that is, intended to live in a polis). Thus an individual's natural goal or purpose—*telos*—is to live in a polis, a city-state like Athens or Sparta. Human beings realize their full social nature and potential only through participation in a city-state. The ideal polis, though large enough for self-sufficiency, is a small agricultural city-state containing everything necessary for its citizens to live the good life. All the citizens know each other personally, so they can determine who is worthiest of holding public office, and all participate directly in the government. Aristotle insists, moreover, that a proper system of education, law, and political institutions will lead to moral perfection for the citizens. He argues that human beings have always lived in communities of some sort and that the polis had developed from the family, or rather the household, through the village to the complex city-state. Ridiculing Plato's plan to abolish marriage and the family in the idealized state, Aristotle argues that the family preserves life. Thus he recognizes the necessity of maintaining families, as well as private property, which should be used for the common good, for he disapproves of the unlimited accumulation of material wealth as an evil influence that overwhelms restraint and moderation.

Aristotle may shock modern readers in the first few pages of the *Politics* by attempting to justify slavery. The institution was part of the traditional order throughout antiquity and was accepted by most people without question. A fundamental component of the ancient Greek economy, slave labor was the basis of many celebrated Greek advances. Aristotle goes to some pains to argue that slavery is in accord with nature's design. He insists that human beings fall into two groups, those endowed with the reason to act on their own and those lacking the capacity. He says the latter group, natural slaves, should be subservient to the former and told what to do. Yet Aristotle took great care to distinguish between those barbarians (non-Greeks) who became slaves by nature and those Greeks who became slaves by military conquest, a mode he rejects. Thus Aristotle proposes that the slave force should be drawn strictly from the barbarians. While arguing that slavery is necessary to provide labor, Aristotle seems strangely prophetic in suggesting that the institution might be unnecessary if the shuttle of a loom could "weave of itself" and other tools and machines could perform their function automatically at human bidding. Yet Aristotle has no doubt that natural slavery is a moral institution, for he conceives of the natural slave as an individual who profits by the control of a superior mind and is elevated by association with the family of the owner.

Concerning the status of women in the state, Aristotle does not share Plato's view of their political ability. He argues women are defective both in intellectual and moral capacity and thus must be debarred from full citizenship. Although concluding they should enjoy a limited freedom and education, Aristotle insists they must be governed by men and quotes with approval a line from Sophocles: "Silence is a woman's glory." Just as the family is ruled by the father as patriarch, the state must be governed by men. Aristotle regards citizenship is a full-time occupation and says full citizenship must be limited to the men of the leisured classes.

Aristotle argues that a state can be ruled well through three forms of government: *monarchy* (rule by one man), *aristocracy* (rule by a few men), and *polity* (rule by all men meeting a certain property requirement). The ideal form would be a monarchy governed by a man of exceptional virtue, but such a person is rarely found. The second best form would be an aristocracy governed by several men of true excellence, also rarely found. The best easily obtainable form is a polity governed by a large number of citizens. Each of these good forms, however, can degenerate into a corrupt form: monarchy into *tyranny* (unjust rule in the interests of one man), aristocracy into *oligarchy* (selfish rule in the interests of the wealthy few), and polity into *democracy* (mob or party rule in the interests of the poorer classes). None of these corrupt forms provides for the general welfare of the members of the state.

Aristotle tells us every state has three classes—one rich, one poor, and one in the middle—and that a practical way of organizing its government is to establish a mean between rule of the rich (oligarchy) and rule of the poor (democracy) by making those in the middle supreme. Rule by the middle class provides a mixed constitution combining some of the features of oligarchy and democracy. Aristotle points out that the members of the middle class, drawn from moderate landholders and fairly prosperous citizens, tend to be the most stable and law-abiding citizens of the polis, and they make excellent administrators because they are able to prevent either of the extremes from dominating the state for their own interests. Thus the best form of government, *practically speaking,* is a fusion of oligarchy and democracy.

Turning to advocate eugenic measures intended to improve Greek offspring, Aristotle argues that the government should fix the age of marriage to bring forth healthy infants. If the parents are too young, they are more likely to produce female and weak children, disappointing in the masculine society of ancient Greece. Deformed infants must not be allowed to live, Aristotle insists, but children should not be exposed merely to prevent the population from expanding. He argues that the proper course of action when a state or family is burdened with an excess of children is to procure an abortion "before sense and life have begun in the embryo."

Aristotle closes the *Politics* with a discussion of education. He insists that education should be compulsory for all citizens—though not for women—to train them for ruling the state through the proper molding of their intellectual and moral capabilities. Because neither slaves nor manual laborers—farmers, artisans, and shopkeepers—are capable of participating in affairs of government, they will be barred from becoming citizens in a well-governed polis. Male children destined for citizenship, on the other hand, will be trained from birth to enhance their minds and bodies. The purpose of teaching is to produce good citizens. This aim is essentially moral, and hence the polis must have complete control over education as a means of inculcating goodness in its potential citizens. Education will include reading and writing for practical benefits, gymnastics to foster the virtue of courage, and music to promote leisure. The concept of leisure is of fundamental importance to Aristotle. To be a citizen requires the exercise of leisure, which does not mean chasing amusements, but rather pursuing activities that cultivate the mind.

Works on Rhetoric, Aesthetics, and Literary Criticism.   Space does not permit examining Aristotle's contributions in rhetoric, art, and literary criticism in any detail. His *Rhetoric,* in three books, makes use of traditional rhetorical methods, but Aristotle analyzes oratory in terms of its purpose, which is the ability of the speaker to persuade through the appropriate arrangement of words and the invention of arguments. The speaker can persuade the members of the audience to look upon him favorably, Aristotle instructs, by whipping up their emotions and convincing them of his virtue and other sterling qualities.

The *Rhetoric* and the fragmentary *Poetics* are the two treatises providing the most complete information about Aristotle's aesthetic theories. As noted, Plato regarded any particular man as a copy of the eternal form of man, and thus he says that a statue or portrait of a particular man—like Socrates—represents nothing more than a copy of a copy. Hence Plato was contemptuous of certain kinds of art for being merely imitations of terrestrial things, which themselves are but pale reflections of the forms. By making a copy of a copy, he says, the artist leads us one step further from the truth than does a pale reflected copy of an eternal form. Although Aristotle agrees with Plato that art was a matter of imitation, he insists the forms exist only in particular things and that the artist is justified in translating the forms into art. Hence Aristotle maintains that art does impart information about nature.

Aristotle's *Poetics* continues to enjoy an unsurpassed reputation in the field of literary criticism. Written to analyze the methods of the art of poetry, the *Poetics* survives only in the part covering tragedy, which Aristotle regards as the most advanced form of poetry. Unlike Plato, who censures poetry as a dangerous stimulant, Aristotle argues that the genre benefits humanity. He insists poetry is "more philosophical" than history and hence of greater intrinsic value, for the historian is concerned with particular persons and events of the past, while the poet's domain is general truths of universal experience that are closer to reality than historical records. Aristotle argues that all the arts—poetry, drama, music, dance, painting, and the like—are based on the principle of imitation *(mimesis)*, or the human desire to represent the actions and lives of people. After briefly distinguishing between comedy, tragedy, and epic poetry, Aristotle goes on to say that tragedy—enhanced by appropriate artistic language—is an imitation of serious human action. Using Sophocles' *Oedipus Tyrannus (Oedipus the King)* as a prime example, Aristotle seems to say, although this interpretation is disputed, that the plot of a tragedy should arouse strong responses of both pity and fear as a means of providing a cleansing *(katharsis)* of these very emotions from the souls of the spectators, thereby producing a pleasurable experience of liberation.

Knowledge of Aristotle's philosophy almost disappeared in the west with the closing of the philosophical schools in the sixth century CE. Yet his works were preserved in Arabic versions, Latin translations of which passed to western Europe in the twelfth and thirteenth centuries, becoming in St. Thomas Aquinas (1225–1274) a set of doctrines to be applied mechanically to the articulation and defense of Christian theology. By systematizing and adapting Aristotle to the needs of the Catholic Church, St. Thomas revolutionized Christian thought. Aristotle's influence persists in modern times. In every branch of philosophy his thought remains a vital force. Indeed, he systematized immense tracts of knowledge and method, thereby establishing the major and still accepted divisions of philosophy. Aristotle's work in science was epoch-making, for he laid the foundation for empirical research. His thought enriches the western intellectual heritage in numerous other ways, exemplified by our frequent use of considerable scientific and philosophical terminology derived from his writings. In short, Aristotle can fairly be judged as the most influential western thinker prior to the nineteenth century.

CHAPTER XV

ALEXANDER THE GREAT

Philip II of Macedonia had transformed his frontier kingdom into a strong military state that dominated Greece through the League of Corinth, but his assassination in 336 BCE elevated twenty-year-old Alexander III as king. The Greeks were jubilant, not only regarding the new monarch as too young to equal his father's brilliant military efficiency but also hoping he would intrude less in Greek affairs. They realized Alexander had been educated by Aristotle and trusted he would direct much of his attention to learning. Yet Alexander shared with his father a taste for battle and would ultimately reject Aristotle's vision of the city-state as the ultimate unit of civilization. Under Alexander's leadership, the Macedonians and Greeks carried out the great war of revenge Philip had planned against the Persians, a relentless conquest making the young ruler a legend in his own lifetime, for he carved out the largest empire the world had ever seen, stretching from Greece and Egypt across the vast landmass of western Asia to the plain of the river Indus.

The enigmatic figure of Alexander still attracts and repels the human imagination. Much of twentieth-century scholarship was dominated by an idealistic view of the great conqueror but now generally focuses on his aggressive pursuit of personal fame and glory through untold blood and horror. Yet who can deny that Alexander was a man of his time—not ours? Muscular and compact, he was a strikingly handsome youth with classic features captured best, Plutarch tells us, by the sculptor Lysippus, who often portrayed Alexander's liquid and melting glance and slight leftward inclination of his neck, a distinguishing characteristic imitated later by many of the king's friends and successors. A thoroughly charismatic figure, Alexander was famous for his unbridled ambition, indomitable will, and tireless energy. To later ages, he was a figure of myth to be ranked virtually with the gods. Whereas Philip had acted cautiously and never struck without careful preparation, headstrong Alexander, a man of extremes and contractions, often took extraordinary risks to solve problems through immediate action. Apparently some inner compulsion drove him to conquer the world and to seek majesty and godlike glory.

Alexander's conquests vastly extended the domain of the Greek language and Greek institutions. His subjugation of the Persian Empire brought changes of such magnitude that scholars use the term Hellenistic to describe the enlarged Greek world—famous for its Macedonian monarchies—emerging after his storied career. Although we should not forget that the Greeks and their neighbors, particularly of

This marble representation of a youthful Alexander the Great assimilates him to the fresh-faced ephebic ideal with its balanced facial proportions and subtly modeled flesh, while the deep-set eyes tinge the expression with melancholy and the mane of lionlike hair suggest virility. The study, deftly conveying a fusion of masculine and feminine, is possibly an original work by the Athenian sculptor Leochares, c. 338–334 BCE. Acropolis Museum, Athens.

Egypt and Asia Minor, had long influenced one another culturally, Alexander's military mission to the east led to the imposition of Greek cultural enclaves on an alien world. In the meantime the economic center shifted from the Greek peninsula to the Aegean islands and the nearby coasts of Asia and Africa, while the tradition of independent city-states yielded to larger political units and to absolute monarchy. The word Hellenistic customarily refers specifically to the period following the death of Alexander in 323 BCE and leading into the Roman era, yet perhaps more logically should begin with his invasion of Asia in 334 BCE. After all, he initiated in some sense the opening up of an enormous area of the world to increased Greek influence. Following Alexander's untimely death, his sprawling realm was soon torn apart by the struggles of his Macedonian generals and their sons and successors to carve out great kingdoms for themselves.

ALEXANDER'S YOUTH

Alexander shared certain personality traits of his parents, both of whom could demonstrate unbounded passion, violence, and cruelty. His mother Olympias not only fostered in young Alexander a burning dynastic ambition but also convinced him that his conception resulted from her impregnation by Zeus, king of the gods. Apparently he believed his miraculous origins included in some sense both an earthly father and a divine father. Like his earthly father Philip, Alexander exhib-

This marble head of a youth is thought to represent Alexander's intimate companion Hephaestion. From a commemorative or funerary monument in the eastern Mediterranean, reportedly Megara, c. 325–320 BCE. The J. Paul Getty Museum, Malibu.

ited raw shrewdness and the ability to scheme with cold calculation. Homer was his boyhood idol, and he longed for such a poet to sing his own praises. Early in life, encouraged by his mother, Alexander set the goal for himself of winning such unbounded fame that his name would be as honored as that of the Homeric hero Achilles. Through his mother he traced his ancestry to Achilles and through his father to the demigod Heracles. Alexander saw himself as a second Achilles, and much of his behavior betrays an attempt to emulate his reputed forebears.

The love of women never played a leading part in Alexander's life. His inseparable companion from childhood was Hephaestion, described in later reports as the great love of Alexander's life. All indications are that the bond between the two was exceptionally deep and close, and contemporaries referred to Hephaestion as the Patroclus to Alexander's Achilles, the Homeric friendship that fourth-century Greeks regarded as having a strong sexual component. Hephaestion generally shunned personal ambition in the interest of being Alexander's constant companion and confidant.

In 340 Philip left on his campaign against Byzantium, first formally appointing sixteen-year-old Alexander as regent. No sooner had he departed than the young prince was faced with a rebellion by a Thracian tribe. Alexander dashed northward, defeated the rebels, and renamed their main center of population Alexandropolis, the first of the Alexander cities. Alexander again proved his mettle as a warrior when, at the age of eighteen, he led the victorious Macedonian cavalry charge at Chaeronea in 338. Alexander was but twenty when he became king at the time of his father's assassination in 336. He then prepared to carry out

Philip's plans to conquer Asia Minor, but the new ruler gradually enlarged the program of his father, not stopping until he had pushed into the distant plain of the Indus.

CONSOLIDATION IN EUROPE (336–335 BCE)

ALEXANDER ESTABLISHES HIS POSITION IN MACEDONIA, THESSALY, THERMOPYLAE, CORINTH, THRACE, AND ILLYRIA (336–335 BCE)

The murder of Philip quickly threw the integrity of his kingdom into doubt. Alexander's rivals and enemies were eliminated. Inspired by the Homeric Achilles, Alexander spent the remainder of his short life winning a reputation for tactical genius and personal prowess, but he could not begin his mission before showing the Greeks that he was a worthy successor of his father. The Greeks were grumbling over Macedonian hegemony, and the spellbinding Demosthenes had persuaded the Athenians to declare a day of public thanksgiving over the assassination of Philip. Hearing of these inclinations to revolt in Greece, Alexander descended upon the south with lightning speed. In Thessaly he won the right to succeed his father as the head of the Thessalian League. He reminded the Thessalians that he and they were joined by their common heroic descent from Achilles and Heracles. At Thermopylae he summoned a meeting of the Delphic Amphictony and gained succession to his father's seat. He then marched on Corinth, where he summoned envoys for a meeting of the League of Corinth. Before the end of the year 336 the league had named him lifetime *hegemon*, or commander in chief of its land and naval forces. With Greece firmly under his control, Alexander left Corinth and turned to the restless tribes on his northern frontier. The Triballians, a tribe in Thrace, and the Illyrians on the western side of the Balkan range were causing most of the trouble. Early in 335 Alexander moved swiftly to extend his control northward through Thrace to the Danube and westward to the Adriatic Sea in brilliant campaigns that clearly demonstrated to Philip's veteran generals the military genius of their young king.

THE DESTRUCTION OF THEBES (335 BCE)

Meanwhile the new Persian king, Darius III (336–330 BCE), was aware of the danger presented by Alexander, and his envoys offered the Greek states large sums of gold to revolt from the Macedonian hegemony. During this period a rumor swept through Greece that Alexander had been killed in Illyria, prompting the Thebans to revolt and slay some of his officers. Alexander raced down into Greece and appeared without warning before the gates of Thebes. After the city fell, Alexander and his Boeotian confederates made an example of the Thebans, massacring the men, selling the women and children into slavery, and leveling the entire town except for temples and the house of the poet Pindar. The other Greek states immediately made profuse protestations of loyalty. In the future the terrorized Greeks would offer Alexander far less trouble.

THE CONQUEST OF THE
PERSIAN EMPIRE (334–330 BCE)

With the sullen fidelity of the Greeks assured, Alexander made active preparations for the invasion of Persia. The Greeks offered him scant cooperation, and many of them longed for a Persian victory. The Persian fleet of 400 ships controlled the sea and vastly outnumbered the Macedonian fleet of about 160 ships. Thus the confrontation would be on land, where Alexander's army would face Persian opponents who enjoyed much greater wealth and numbers. The Persian king had demonstrated a seemingly strong position through diplomacy and gold, but his empire was slowly disintegrating into its heterogeneous components during the fourth century BCE. A weakened Persia could not effectively oversee its satraps, with the result that the more aggressive of these officials sometimes attempted to establish autonomous principalities. Moreover, Egypt had managed to defend its independence from 404 down to 343, though recently the country had been restored to Persian control at great cost. By this time the Persians had abandoned their traditional, practical policy of offering religious toleration to subject peoples, thereby sapping loyalty and encouraging revolts. Thus the Jews, Egyptians, Babylonians, and others would greet Alexander as a liberator who had come to restore their age-old customs and ways of life.

Meanwhile Darius III had advanced from obscurity to the Persian throne in 336 through a series of palace intrigues and murders that left intense hatred and rivalry among the nobles of the court. The new king lacked a viable sense of purpose, while the Persian army, no match for the powerful Macedonian phalanx, had made scarcely any progress in the art of war for over two centuries. Persian soldiers were burdened with obsolete equipment and traditional tactics long superseded elsewhere by more effective methods. The usual Persian soldier was outfitted with a turban, quilted tunic, trousers, and a wicker shield, whereas the more heavily armed Macedonian employed a bronze helmet, cloth tunic, sturdy breastplate, and heavy round shield. From the beginning of the fourth century the Persian kings had relied increasingly on Greek mercenaries to form the bulk of their infantry.

ALEXANDER CROSSES THE HELLESPONT (334 BCE)

Assembling a formidable army of roughly 32,000 infantry and 5,000 cavalry in the spring of 334, Alexander soon crossed the Hellespont to invade northwest Asia Minor. He joined his invasion army with an advance force sent by Philip in the spring of 336. Alexander's entire complement totaled almost 50,000. Philip had organized the Macedonian army into three main divisions: phalanx, light infantry, and heavy cavalry. The strength of Alexander's army lay chiefly in the heavily armed Macedonian cavalry and the disciplined phalanx of Macedonian foot soldiers, the former numbering about 2,000 and the latter about 12,000. Diversity was achieved for tactical purposes by the addition of other contingents. The tribal peoples on the Macedonian frontiers had furnished Alexander with light-armed troops such as javelineers, archers, and slingers, while Thessaly had provided him with members of its well-trained cavalry. The League of Corinth sent fighters used mainly for garrisons and communications, and the army also included a large number of mercenaries. The close coordination of the light support troops and the cavalry with the phalanx, as originated by Philip, largely explains the overwhelming power of the Macedonian army. The striking arm in a pitched battle was Alexander's magnificent cavalry, its core made up of the so-called Companions, who were drawn from the most influential noble families of Macedonia. Meanwhile the famous Macedonian phalanx bristled with long spears and fought in open order, a good three feet separating the men. The long spear, or *sarissa*, of the Macedonian phalanx was a weapon strange to Greek troops but gave its wielders the advantage of the first blow in an engagement. Alexander's practice in battle was to strike with the Companions from the right to cover the unshielded side of the infantry, and the splendid Thessalian cavalry rode on the left. Moreover, both the right and left wings of the infantry were strengthened with light troops. Siege equipment played a vital role in Alexander's conquests. The army stripped walls of defenders with various siege engines, including battering rams, high towers on wheels, and powerful catapults firing arrows and stones.

Alexander's tough-minded, loyal general Antipater remained behind as his viceroy in Macedonia and Greece. The king also left at home his turbulent mother Olympias, who despised her son's deputy but could do little more than vehemently denounce him. Alexander chose Parmenio—then about sixty—as his chief of staff for the Asian expedition and conferred command of the cavalry on Parmenio's son Philotas. Many of Alexander's generals were veterans trained by Philip, and they readily followed their daring king. Alexander invaded Asia with a thirty-day supply of provisions, an enormous amount for an ancient army, expecting to supplement this from Asian sources by quickly winning victories. The brash young ruler was short on money but intended to fill his war chests with the plunder of Asia. Although careful in his strategic and logistical planning, he rashly embarked on the campaign childless and unmarried. If he lost his life in Asia, Macedonia would face a devastating struggle for the succession.

Alexander entered Asia Minor with a vast staff of surveyors, engineers, architects, biologists, artists, court officials, and historians. Aristotle's nephew Callisthenes was present as Aristotle's publicist and sent back incredibly favorable reports of the conqueror to impress the Greeks. Although his patron put him to death in the eighth year of the campaign under bizarre circumstances, Callisthenes left an unfinished narrative that apparently influenced a number of later historians to adopt Alexander's preferred image of himself. More reliable sources for the expedition came from the official journal penned by Alexander's secretary Eumenes of Cardia and the memoirs of the Greek engineer Aristobulus as well as the history written by Alexander's friend and bodyguard Ptolemy, later king of Egypt. All accounts by actual participants are now lost, known only through scattered quotations incorporated in the works of later writers. Of the surviving, well-preserved sources, that of the Greek historian Arrian, a native of Bithynia in Asia Minor, stands out for the clarity of its prose. Most scholars regard his *Anabasis of Alexander*, written in the second century CE, as the most reliable extant account of the conqueror's life and

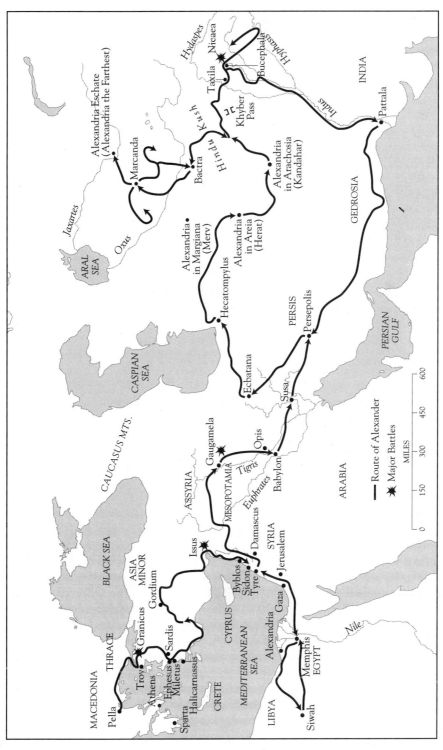

Alexander's conquest of the Persian Empire, 334–323 BCE.

campaigns. Additional information about Alexander comes chiefly from three ancient writers, all of whom should be treated critically: the Greek biographer and
philosopher Plutarch, the Greek historian Diodorus Siculus, and the Roman writer
Curtius Rufus.

The Conquest of Asia Minor (334–333 bce)

First Victory: The Battle of Granicus (334 BCE).   The first act of Alexander in Asia
Minor was to hold a festival at the site of Troy, where he ran naked to offer a garland on the tomb of Achilles, while Hephaestion did likewise for the tomb of Patroclus, Achilles' intimate friend in the *Iliad*. These actions not only identified the
bond of Alexander and Hephaestion with the great Homeric epic but also served as
a symbolic beginning of another divinely sanctioned war in Asia. Rejoining his
army, Alexander encountered a Persian force of some forty thousand men—half of
whom were Greek mercenaries—which the Persian satraps of Asia Minor had positioned behind the little river Granicus. Alexander fought in the thick of this crucial battle but nearly lost his life on the threshold of his extraordinary penetration
of Asia, for a Persian came up from behind and prepared to strike him down with a
raised scimitar. A quick thrust by the Macedonian commander Cleitus saved
Alexander from a mortal blow, an act that would seem ironic six years later when
the king killed the loyal veteran during a drunken brawl.

Alexander's bold charge across the river asserted his military superiority over
the Persians. His acts following the battle of Granicus promoted loyalty to himself
and high morale among his troops, who were spellbound by his fearlessness during
the engagement and deeply moved afterward by his practice of commending each
soldier individually and visiting the wounded—this despite his own injuries—gestures he would make throughout his career of conquest. Like his father, Alexander
aimed at the complete annihilation of opposing forces. Most of the Greek mercenaries serving the Persians were massacred, though two thousand were sent off to
labor in Macedonia as slaves.

The Submission of the Aegean Coast (334 BCE).   The victory at Granicus allowed
Alexander to occupy the neighboring parts of Asia Minor without a blow. He then
marched south toward the satrapy of Lydia, home of an ancient civilization that
had once greatly influenced the Greeks. When the invaders entered Lydia, Sardis
and other important cities submitted and were rewarded with the confirmation of
their traditional privileges and ancestral Lydian laws. Leaving a Macedonian satrap
in Lydia, Alexander then turned back to the coast to take the cities of Ionia. He
feared that Darius might use his huge fleet to transfer the war to the Greek mainland and then persuade the Greeks to fight against the Macedonians, so Alexander
developed the brilliant plan of weakening the naval strength of his opponents by
conquering first the coastal regions of the empire, thereby denying them anchorage.
As he proceeded southward along the coast of Asia Minor, Alexander was hailed as
a deliverer by the democrats in the Greek cities, though the governing oligarchs
continued to support the Persian cause. Everywhere he overthrew oligarchies and

established democracies. The people of Ephesus massacred their oligarchs at the approach of Alexander, and he entered the city in triumph. The artist Apelles painted Alexander at Ephesus and set the work up at the temple of Artemis, showing the king mounted and wielding the thunderbolt of Zeus. When Alexander advanced to Miletus, he encountered resistance from the Greek commander, but Macedonian siege engines soon forced surrender. Alexander then disbanded his treasury-draining fleet, rendered virtually useless by Athens' refusal to lend assistance. His future military operations would be restricted to the land.

South of the Greek cities lay the satrapy of Caria and its spectacular Greek seaport Halicarnassus, where the Persians had long ruled through a native dynasty. Halicarnassus was the site of the splendid tomb of the ruler Mausolus, counted among the Seven Wonders of the World (monuments the Greeks celebrated for their size or grandeur). Alexander succeeded in taking the resisting city after an extended siege. He reinstated the legitimate ruler, Ada, who had been driven out as satrap by her own brother, and allowed her to adopt him as a son, thereby gaining a legitimate claim to Caria. Most Greeks despised non-Greeks as barbarians, yet Alexander's promotion of Ada typifies his prudent policy of organizing conquered territory by sharing rule with local figures. Maintaining the Persian system of satrapies, he generally awarded military authority to Macedonians but often left civil matters in the hands of loyal natives who enjoyed local support.

Alexander at Gordium (333 BCE).   After receiving the submission of maritime cities along the southwest coast as far as the Pamphylian shore, Alexander turned north and followed a semicircular route through the mountainous central region of Asia Minor until he reached Gordium, the old capital of Phrygian kings. The entire western half of Asia Minor was now his. Gordium possessed an ancient wooden wagon supposedly driven by the mythical founder of the Phrygian dynasty. Local legend held that whoever could unfasten an intricate leather knot (the ends were concealed) on the yolk of the wagon was destined to rule Asia. Such a story appealed to Alexander's romantic imagination. According to the most familiar account of the event, Alexander hacked through the famous Gordian knot with his sword to fulfill the prophecy.

About this time Darius placed his resourceful Greek general, Memnon of Rhodes, in command of the Persian fleet. Memnon launched a successful counteroffensive in the Aegean but died in June while blockading the city of Mytilene on Lesbos, a serious blow to the Persian cause. Earlier, before the battle of Granicus, Memnon had urged the Persians to avoid a pitched battle by retiring into the interior, systematically destroying crops and settlements on their way, thereby forcing the precariously provisioned Alexander back into Europe. Yet the proud Persian generals had rejected the foreigner's brilliant scorched-earth plan.

The Battle of Issus (333 BCE)

Early in 333 Alexander occupied Cilicia in southeast Asia Minor, securing the capital of Tarsus, and then advancing into Syria. At Tarsus, while hot and tired, Alexander bathed in the icy waters of the river Cydnus and contracted a fever that nearly took his life. His recovery took months. Meanwhile Darius III was approaching. The Persian king decided to take a stand at Issus on the Mediterranean shore in northern Syria. Alexander lured Darius and his numerically superior forces onto a battlefield that was too narrow for the vast Persian army to fight effectively. Leading the heavy cavalry on the right wing, Alexander charged into the Persian left wing. This life-and-death struggle at the battle of Issus, fought in November, witnessed the Persians giving way before the stabbing lances of the Macedonians, whereupon Darius fled, leaving his mother, wife (who was also his sister), and daughters behind in Alexander's hands. Alexander and Hephaestion came to their tent. The queen mother, Sisygambis, mistaking the taller Hephaestion for Alexander, began to prostrate herself before him until her frantic attendants made signals of her error. Mortified at her blunder, she began again with Alexander, who then is reported to have raised Darius' mother up and told her she had made no mistake, for Hephaestion was also Alexander. Ancient writers emphasize that Alexander treated his royal captives with extreme deference, and when the Persian queen Stateira died in his camp as a prisoner, he honored her rank with a magnificent funeral.

The Conquest of Syria, Palestine, and Egypt (333–331 bce)

The Capture of Tyre (332 bce).   Alexander's immediate financial problems had been solved by the battle of Issus, for he had captured the money the Persian king had brought for the campaign. Rather than pursue the defeated Darius, who managed to make his way to Babylon, Alexander continued his strategic plan. The Persians still controlled the sea and could incite trouble among the unruly Greeks at Alexander's back. Thus he spent the winter of 333 and most of the following year besieging the Persians' remaining port cities, from the coast of Syria to Egypt. The northern cities of Aradus, Byblos, and Sidon opened their gates immediately to Alexander, but the strongly fortified island city of Tyre—the chief Persian naval base—held out for seven months. During the siege of Tyre in 332 Alexander's men constructed a causeway about half a mile long into the bay. When the causeway neared the stronghold, Tyrian missiles inflicted grave casualties, so Alexander summoned naval support from Aradus, Byblos, and Cyprus to protect his engineers. Finally, the Macedonians bombarded Tyre into submission with powerful stone-hurling catapults, followed by a terrible massacre of the military population and sale into slavery of most of the rest, a warning against resisting the conqueror. Darius frantically sent an offer to cede all Persian territory west of the Euphrates in return for peace, but unbending Alexander rejected the Persian overture. He insisted his victory at Issus had already established him as king of Persia. He was now firmly committed to conquering the entire Persian Empire. Historians often criticize Alexander for his response because Darius' offer contained most of the new territory that the Greeks would effectively govern for any substantial length of time.

Alexander in Egypt (332–331 bce).   Alexander marched south toward Egypt. The strongly fortified city of Gaza, situated on the strategic route from Asia to Egypt, re-

Silver tetradrachm, or four-drachma coin, representing Alexander as an inspired deity, with upturned eyes and the horns of the Greco-Egyptian god Zeus Amon, whom he claimed for his divine father. Issued by the Hellenistic ruler Lysimachus of Thrace in the early third century BCE, the coin was probably based on portraits in Alexander's lifetime, which doubtless bore some resemblance to him but were partly idealized to present the exalted image he wished his subjects to see. British Museum, London.

sisted the conqueror bravely, but the Persian garrison fell after a bitter siege of two months. Twice wounded during the siege, furious Alexander massacred the fighting men wholesale and sold the women and children into slavery. By contrast, he then entered Egypt in triumph, the ancient country welcoming him with open arms. Alexander flattered the Egyptians by assuming the titles of a native king and by sacrificing to their gods. One of his chief acts while in Egypt was the laying out a city near the northwest corner of the Nile Delta. He named the new foundation Alexandria after himself. With its excellent harbors, Alexandria served as a great shipping and military center, the most important of Alexander's city foundations. His engineers would lay out at least five additional cities, all now long gone, on important trade routes in central Asia.

Alexander had always attached great importance to oracles. Hearing that his reputed ancestors Perseus and Heracles had visited the famous oracle of the chief Egyptian god Amon at the western oasis of Siwah, Alexander sought glory for himself by making the dangerous pilgrimage deep into the desert. At the oasis the prophet of the god received Alexander and greeted him, according to one account, as "Son of Amon," for as king of Egypt he was officially divine. The Macedonians and Greeks had long identified Amon with Zeus, under the name of Zeus Amon, and stories began to circulate among them that Alexander had been hailed as Son of Zeus. Apparently Alexander's pilgrimage to the oracular seat made a profound impression on him. Thenceforth he turned increasingly toward his divine sonship of Zeus Amon as a means of binding all his subjects to his rule.

Alexander deliberately manipulated his public image to indicate his divine origins. Most of his surviving portraits are posthumous. All are idealized—his exact appearance eludes us—conveying the message that the young ruler enjoyed a special relationship with the gods. While Greek men prized the smooth bodies associated with youth, they traditionally wore beards as a sign of virility. Except for Zeus and Poseidon, their gods were without facial hair, being depicted in art as the young adolescents so admired by Greek men. In Greek male erotic fantasy, in other words, the gods represented the beauty of the boy. Yet Alexander wore no beard, an unusual preference that may have been encouraged by his mother's whispered tales of his birth and ancestry. He fostered an image of divine sonship by remaining smooth faced, thereby encouraging ordinary mortals to perceive both his sacred mission and his hallowed relationship with Mount Olympus. His practice of shaving soon set a fashion. The depiction of Alexander's eyes, besides his shaved face, helped create the image of his divine sonship. A figure of his exalted status, a hero with a mortal mother and a divine father, was thought to have the power to see into heaven, and Alexander was often depicted in art or on coins staring upward into the divine realm. Finally, he was frequently shown on coins and elsewhere with the ram's horns of the Greco-Egyptian god Zeus Amon. Thus Alexander was disposed to see himself as Son of Zeus, a claim troubling many of his more conservative courtiers.

The Conquest of Babylonia and Persis (331 BCE)

The Decisive Battle: Gaugamela (331 BCE).   Alexander's conquest of Egypt completed his control of the entire eastern Mediterranean coast. In 331 he returned to Tyre, appointing a Macedonian satrap for Syria, and then advanced to the east to face Darius, who had prepared frantically for the decisive battle during the two years since the battle of Issus. Cut off from the Greek mainland, the Persian king was unable to recruit fresh Greek mercenaries but had levied a huge army from what remained of his empire. Darius stationed his forces on the broad, flat plain of Gaugamela, not far from the site of the ancient Assyrian capital of Nineveh and near the river Tigris. He had chosen the battleground this time, attempting to take maximum advantage from his numerically superior forces. Darius planned a battle based on his strong cavalry. Moreover, he hoped to cut Alexander's army to pieces with his two hundred chariots, armed with long scythe blades projecting from the ends of the wheel hubs. The chariots—antiquated weapons by this time—proved tactical failures, partly because the Macedonian light infantry attacked their horses, but the battle lasted much longer than the Persian fiasco at Issus and created a blinding cloud of dust. Darius launched a massive cavalry attack against both wings of Alexander's forces. With the departure of the cavalry, the Persians allowed a gap to open in their infantry line. At the head of a wedge-shaped formation, Alexander immediately rushed through the opening with his Companion cavalry and part of the phalanx, leading them straight for Darius himself. The terrified Persian king took flight in his chariot, just as at Issus, with Alexander recklessly abandoning the battlefield in a failed attempt to catch him. The battle continued, but soon all the Persian army was in retreat, despite having inflicted heavy losses on the invading enemy. The battle of Gaugamela (often called the battle of Arbela after the nearby

A Persian soldier recoils from a Macedonian in this detail from the sumptuous Alexander Sarcophagus commissioned in the late fourth century BCE by one of the local Hellenized rulers of the Phoenician metropolis of Sidon. The finest and most elaborate funerary monument surviving from the Hellenistic period, the sarcophagus preserves much of the added color on its narrative scenes, all carved in high relief, commemorating Alexander's conquest of the Persian Empire. The many-figured Alexander Sarchophagus is famous for its magnificent sense of movement, probably inspired by the bold sculpture of Lysippus. Archaeological Museum, Istanbul.

city) broke the power of Darius. His flight completed the demoralization of his army, and his empire was now at the mercy of the Macedonian conqueror. Although Darius and a ragged remnant of followers struggled eastward over rugged mountain passes toward Ecbatana (modern Hamadan) in Media, the way was open for Alexander to advance southward to secure the great capitals of the Persian Empire.

Alexander Captures the Persian Capitals (331–330 BCE).   Alexander entered Babylon without opposition and was invested with all the titles of the old Babylonian kingship. From Babylon, he headed southeast and took Susa without resistance. He then occupied the heartland of Persia, where Persepolis quickly fell to him. Alexander confiscated the royal treasury in each capital. Thus the colossal wealth of the Persian rulers passed into his hands. He put a considerable amount of this coin and bullion into circulation, largely by making lavish gifts to his officers and soldiers, an

In 330 BCE Alexander greatly antagonized his new subjects by inflicting merciless destruction on the city of Persepolis, traditional burial place of Persian kings and site of solemn religious festivals, even burning down its magnificent palace complex erected chiefly by Darius I and Xerxes. Illustrated here are the still impressive ruins of the many-columned audience hall, or Apadana, and one of its relief-decorated monumental stairways, built about 500 BCE by Darius I. The architecture and ornamentation of the vast palace complex are discussed at length and illustrated with reconstruction drawings in *The Ancient Near East,* the first volume of this series.

influx of treasure that would dramatically change the economy of the ancient world in the Hellenistic period. Alexander treated Persepolis—the traditional burial place of Persian kings and site of solemn religious ceremonial—with shocking harshness, turning the helpless city over to his troops, who wildly sacked houses, cut down men, and enslaved women. Alexander also torched the magnificent royal palace complex built chiefly by Darius I and Xerxes. Some sources suggest this tragic destruction was the final act in the Panhellenic campaign of revenge against Persia, while others say Alexander set the fire during a drunken revel. Yet he also increasingly adopted the dress of a Persian king, probably to encourage the Persian elite to collaborate, though such gestures aroused great resentment among the xenophobic Macedonians. In the spring of 330 BCE Alexander invaded Media and hastened to Ecbatana, its capital, where he expected to find Darius, but the Persian had escaped with his few remaining loyal troops and a group of his nobles.

The Death of Darius (330 BCE).   Darius fled northward to the shore of the Caspian Sea and then turned eastward toward the province of Bactria (corresponding roughly to what is now northern Afghanistan). Although Alexander followed in almost reckless forced marches, the conquering Macedonian never saw Darius alive again. Darius' ambitious cousin Bessus, the satrap of Bactria, thought the tottering Persian throne might be saved if he supplanted the now completely broken king. A plot was formed. Bessus and other nobles bound Darius in chains, set him in a covered wagon, and hurried him off as a prisoner along the road to Bactria, an act prompting the last remnant of the king's troops to scatter. When the swiftly pursuing Alexander drew near, the nobles stabbed Darius and fled, leaving the last of the venerable Achaemenid line mortally wounded. He was dead when when Alexander reached the wagon. Alexander, profoundly moved by the sight of the royal corpse, reverently threw his cloak over the body and ordered the burial of Darius with full regal honors beside his storied Persian ancestors at Persepolis. Alexander then acted as an avenger on behalf of the slain king, ordering the punishment of the regicides. By conquest, Alexander had taken most of the Persian Empire, though no essential Macedonian interests lay behind this vast seizure of land.

SUBDUING THE EASTERN EXPANSES AND MAKING THE ARDUOUS TREK BACK (330–323 BCE)

THE CONQUEST OF THE NORTHEAST FRONTIER AND THE INDIAN CAMPAIGN (330–325 BCE)

Alexander regarded himself as the rightful successor of Darius on the Persian throne, and he even addressed the Persian queen mother Sisygambis as his adopted mother. To symbolize his new role, Alexander sometimes wore Persian royal attire in the presence of his eastern subjects. He also adopted Persian court ceremonial. Despite the reported advice of Aristotle that he act toward the Persians and other barbarians as a master over slaves, Alexander realized he could not hold freshly conquered territory without some sort of integration of his new subjects into his administration and army. Such policies led to serious conflicts with the Macedonians, especially among the older men who had served Philip. They deeply resented the growing influence of the despised eastern nobles and were shocked and horrified to see Alexander appear in Persian dress.

Alexander spent the first four years after Darius' assassination capturing the eastern satrapies of the old Persian Empire. He began by pushing into central Asia after Bessus, who had fled into his native Bactria and had proclaimed himself Persian king. Yet Alexander was forced to turn southward to impose his authority on the province of Aria, whose satrap had taken to the field for Bessus. After securing the unruly satrapy, Alexander ventured further south to Drangiana, where he met no substantial resistance, and then turned northeastward, finally approaching Bactria by crossing the snowy high mountain range now known as the Hindu Kush in the spring of 329. His soldiers suffered keenly from the bitter cold and lack of provisions during the tortuous crossing and had to feed upon raw mule flesh.

The Conquest of Bactria-Sogdiana (329–327 BCE). When Alexander pressed near the Bactrian capital of Bactra (modern Balkh), Bessus fled across the river Oxus (Amu Darya) and retired to Sogdiana (corresponding roughly to Uzbekistan and Tajikistan), the extreme northeastern satrapy of the old Persian Empire. Alexander entered Bactra in triumph, and pursued Bessus into Sogdiana, where the fugitive was soon captured. In a tribunal of Medes and Persians, Alexander prosecuted Bessus for treason in killing Darius and rebelling against himself. Bessus was scourged and then mutilated in Persian fashion, his nose and ears cut off, before he was hustled off to Ecbatana for a gruesome execution.

The northeastern population strongly resisted accepting Alexander as king, and in the years 329 and 328 BCE he grimly fought his way through hostile territories. His understanding of the geography of the area was severely limited. Passing the Caspian Sea in the pursuit of Darius, Alexander had thought the huge lake might be a gulf of Ocean, the outer sea the Greeks and Macedonians conceived as ringing the earth, itself regarded as southern Europe, western Asia, and North Africa. The Greeks and Macedonians vaguely took the Hindu Kush and its spurs for an extension of the Caucasus, the mountains between the Black and Caspian Seas. Upon finally arriving at the northeastern limit of the Persian Empire on the river Jaxartes, Alexander mistakenly identified the river as the Tanais (the modern Don), which he knew empties into what is now called the Sea of Azov and is thus connected with the Black Sea. Beyond the Jaxartes lay the steppe land of central Asia, but Alexander thought he was gazing on an extension of that part of Europe inhabited by the Scythians. He began drawing up plans for a new Greek city beside the river, which was to be called Alexandria the Farthest (Alexandria Eschate), as a bulwark against the "Scythians" and then turned to the conquest of Bactria and Sogdiana. He finally crushed the fierce resistance of the powerful Sogdian noble Spitamenes, whose nomad allies across the Jaxartes ultimately killed him. They sent his head to Alexander as a peace offering in the winter of 328 BCE.

Worsening Relations with the Macedonian Nobles. Alexander was now regularly employing Asians in his army, reflecting his political strategy of attempting to reconcile his new Asian subjects to his rule. Following that policy, he married Roxane, the captivatingly beautiful daughter of a defeated Sogdian noble. Alexander had never shown much interest in women, though fanciful stories of later legend transformed this diplomatic matrimonial bond into a fabled love match. The king, who began to take more Persians into his army and administration, announced that thirty thousand young Asians of exceptional strength and beauty would be trained in Macedonian arms and tactics and incorporated as a separate military unit. Alexander's willingness to bring Asians into his service, coupled with his adoption of Persian dress and customs, resulted in heated opposition from some of his generals, especially those who had served under Philip. They bitterly complained of having undergone deadly toils and risks only to see the despised barbarians assuming lofty roles.

The Conspiracy of Philotas (330 BCE).   The disagreement poisoned relations between Alexander and certain of the Companions. Between 330 and 327 several of Alexander's associates were executed for treason. The autumn of 330 saw Philotas, son of Parmenio, accused of complicity in a conspiracy against the king's life. When Philotas was brought before the army for trial in Macedonian fashion, he was found guilty of treason and slain. His father, Parmenio, had accompanied Alexander into Asia as the second in command, but Alexander now regarded him as too dangerous to be left alive and sent his subordinates orders to put him to death immediately. The old general was simply cut down from behind as he turned to read the death warrant handed him.

The Murder of Cleitus.   A year or so later, as Alexander modeled his life more and more on that of a Persian king, the clash between Macedonian and Persian customs exploded with elemental violence in Sogdiana. One night Alexander and his closest associates were drinking at a banquet. Cleitus, an older veteran who had saved the king's life at the battle of Granicus, began to give vent under the influence of heady wine to his long-restrained indignation. When Cleitus taunted Alexander for his Persian practices—even calling him "son of Amon, not Philip"—the king was seized with fury and ran his old friend through with a pike. Alexander refused all food for three days in desperate remorse, but his contrition hardly allayed the discontent of the Macedonians for the outright murder.

The Conflict over Proskynesis.   Many of Alexander's closest associates clung to the old Macedonian concept that the king was first among his noble peers and hated the new self-aggrandizement. Nothing better illustrates their distress than the matter of *proskynesis,* the Greek term for the homage performed before the Persian king by his subjects, expressed in various ways, ranging from blowing a kiss from a standing position to complete prostration before the ruler. After his return to Bactra, Alexander attempted to introduce among the Macedonians and Greeks this Persian form of court protocol. Macedonians and Greeks performed the ceremony only to gods, and they mocked the Persians for their customary obeisance to Alexander. Yet the king rashly decided to bring the two groups into uniform practice. He held a small dinner party for his Macedonian and Greek friends, each guest having allegedly agreed beforehand to make the *proskynesis* before Alexander and then to come forward to receive a kiss. Offering proof of his long devotion, Hephaestion acted first. Everything went smoothly until the court historian Callisthenes, Aristotle's nephew, who had glorified Alexander and propagated his claim to divine paternity, refused to do obeisance to the king on the grounds that a mortal may not receive divine honors that would be construed as worship. In turn, Alexander refused to offer him a kiss. Callisthenes then defiantly called out to the king: "Well, I go away the poorer by a kiss." The unpleasant incident demonstrated that the Macedonians would resist the king on the point of the ceremony. Although

Alexander finally agreed to confine the practice to his Asian subjects, Callisthenes would pay for thwarting his will.

The Conspiracy of the Pages.   The historian was soon charged with complicity in another plot on the life of Alexander, this time by the royal pages, sons of prominent Macedonian nobles who were enlisted for personal service to the king and for military training. The sensational plot is said to have begun after one of the pages took the king's prerogative of first shot at a boar during a hunting party, and Alexander ordered that he be flogged for the offense. Humiliated and outraged, the boy persuaded his lover and several dissident pages to join him in an unsuccessful attempt at seeking revenge. Callisthenes, who served as tutor and friend of many of the pages, was suspected of involvement and brutally executed.

The Invasion of India (327 BCE).   Alexander and his army left Bactra in 327 and struggled to recross the snow-clad passes of the Hindu Kush to invade India, where Persian rulers had claimed loose suzerainty. To the Greeks and Persians alike, India was the land of the Indus, essentially modern Pakistan. Alexander's goal was simply to expand his Asian empire, though he knew nothing of the great land masses stretching east to the Pacific Ocean. Alexander conceived of ancient India as a relatively small peninsula jutting eastward into Ocean, where he would gain a sea route back to the Caspian Sea and beyond.

The Battle of the Hydaspes (326 BCE).   Alexander's first encounters with the inhabitants of India were reassuring. In Sogdiana he had been visited by Taxiles, the powerful ruler of the pivotal territory between the Indus and the Hydaspes (modern Jhelum), with its capital at Taxila just east of the Indus. Taxiles made overtures to Alexander to obtain aid against his rival Porus, the king of the country beyond the Hydaspes. Alexander entered into an alliance with Taxiles and made him a vassal prince. Then Alexander divided his forces, sending the trusted Hephaestion— along with Taxiles and the baggage train—through the famed Khyber Pass (the chief mountain pass between modern Afghanistan and Pakistan). While Hephaestion headed to the Indus to build a strong pontoon bridge—no mean feat—Alexander conquered the difficult mountainous region in the north, punishing resistance with massacre and enslavement. In the spring of 326 Alexander and his army crossed the new pontoon bridge over the Indus and entered the territory of his ally Taxiles. After staging a round of lavish sacrifices and athletic games, Alexander made meticulous preparations to fight King Porus, Taxiles' deadly foe, who took the desperate gamble of resisting the most powerful army the ancient world had ever known.

About mid-May Alexander found the larger army of Porus drawn up with two hundred elephants and three hundred chariots on the east bank of the river Hydaspes. After much diversionary maneuvering to confuse the enemy, Alexander led a major part of his army over an uncontested but dangerously flooded crossing several miles upstream under cover of a stormy night. Then he marched down to meet the Indian force, while one of his generals remained to hold the bank opposite Porus. The beleaguered Indian ruler's trump card was his elephants, for untrained

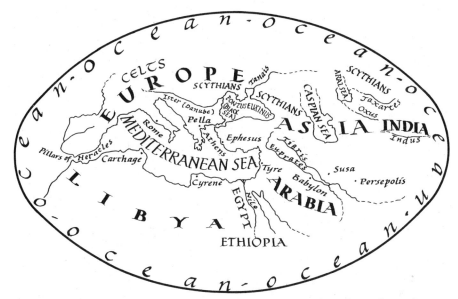

Alexander's view of the world in 327 BCE. Deriving his concept from the teaching of Aristotle, Alexander believed that an outer sea, Ocean, encircled and delimited the Earth, itself conceived as southern Europe, western Asia, and North Africa.

horses are terrified of the beasts. Porus hoped the elephants could annihilate the enemy cavalry and trample down his assailants. Yet Alexander managed to lure the Indian horsemen into a preliminary battle and soon rolled them back upon the great beasts. Then the Macedonian phalanx attacked, using their lethal long spears to hack and madden the elephants. Meanwhile the rest of the army crossed the Hydaspes and attacked the Indians from the rear. A terrible massacre was halted only by Porus' surrender. His bravery and noble bearing impressed Alexander, who greatly expanded his territory. In return, Porus became his faithful ally. Coins proclaimed the victory to the Greek world. A magnificent silver decadrachm (ten-drachma coin), minted in Babylon, portrays Alexander on horseback attacking Porus and his driver on a retreating elephant, while the reverse has Alexander standing in triumph wielding the thunderbolt of Zeus and receiving a wreath of victory from Nike.

The Death of Bucephalas.   Alexander's beloved stallion Bucephalas died after the battle from age or wounds. A celebrated tale tells of his boyhood taming of the horse. We hear that Bucephalas had been offered at a high price to Philip, but no one could mount the rearing Thessalian stallion until the young prince—then not more than eight or nine—ran forward and calmed the animal, then jumped on and thundered away. Alexander and Bucephalas became inseparable. The horse had borne his human companion on countless campaigns, and Alexander gave faithful Bucephalas a state funeral, leading the cortege himself. The Macedonians must have regarded the death as an evil omen.

Alexander's Exhausted Troops Refuse to Advance beyond the Hyphasis (326 BCE).
After the battle Alexander planned two new defensive cities on opposite sides of
the river, one named Nicaea (Victory) at the site of his triumph, the other named
Bucephala in honor of his great horse. Alexander then continued his eastward drive
until reaching the river Hyphasis (modern Beas) in July 326 during the monsoon
rains, but his ambition was not yet satisfied. Local native rulers must have told him
of the Ganges river system to the east, and he probably intended to extend his conquests there, but his troops were now exhausted and miserable from incessant heat
and rain, hazardous river crossings, dreadful disease, and grueling battles. The broken remnant who had followed him from home had endured years of campaigning
and had marched well over eleven thousand miles. Thus his men, seeing no predictable limit to his conquests, refused to advance. Like his venerated Achilles,
Alexander withdrew to his tent and sulked for three days, while silence reigned in
his camp. Finally he yielded, and the soldiers erupted with wild joy and tears of
gratitude at the prospect of seeing their homes again. Yet the humiliated Alexander
never forgave them for preventing his advance to Ocean, where he had planned to
build great port cities that would unify his realm economically and produce remarkable prosperity. Before he left, he built twelve huge altars of dressed stone honoring
the gods that had brought him so far. His great expedition had reached its easternmost point.

The Massacre of the Mallians (325 BCE).   Back at the Hydaspes River, Alexander
threw himself into the construction of a huge fleet of eight hundred to one thousand ships. He did not return to Babylon by the fastest or easiest route, deciding instead on an arduous campaign of conquest and exploration down the Hydaspes and
Indus, beginning in November 326, with a joint land and river expedition. Alexander defeated many hostile tribes during the descent but nearly lost his life storming
a walled city of the powerful Mallians. He had ordered his soldiers up a couple of
scaling ladders, but they hesitated in the face of a shower of missiles from above, so
the king himself dashed up first, accompanied by a mere handful of aides. The
Macedonians now realized their king was in grave danger and clamored up in such
numbers that both ladders broke. Alexander's friends urged him to jump down from
the wall, but his response was to leap down among the enemy, where he was gravely
wounded in the chest by an arrow, eventually fainting from the loss of blood. When
the frantic Macedonians finally broke through a gate, they went berserk in a brutal
slaughter of the population to the last of the women and children, marking the end
of all local resistance. Alexander himself nearly died. He could never resist the
temptation of danger and had again acted as a daring warrior rather than a responsible general, though the wound temporarily relieved the bruised relations with his
troops.

THE LONG JOURNEY BACK TO BABYLON (325–323 BCE)

At the apex of the Indus delta, Alexander ordered the building of a city to serve as
the Indian terminus for a sea route to the Persian Gulf. At last the king had reached

an ocean. Although he was actually standing upon the banks of the Indian Ocean, Alexander viewed the body of water as part of Ocean, the great sea ringing the earth. He intended to employ the newly discovered ocean—the southernmost point of his realm—to link his empire together. Unfinished tasks included exploring the sea route to Babylon and conquering all territories between India and Persia. Alexander decided again on a double journey, by land and sea. He dispatched the fleet, commanded by his friend Nearchus, to sail along the coast of the Indian Ocean to the Persian Gulf.

The Catastrophic March through Gedrosia (325 BCE).   Trusting in his own invincibility and seeking additional glory, Alexander recklessly set out in early autumn to lead part of his forces through the enormously dangerous and dreadful route of the Gedrosian Desert in what is now southern Pakistan and southeastern Iran. The march through the waterless, sandy desert resulted in staggering losses of life. Because the searing heat rendered daytime marching impossible, the exhausted army plodded on through the sand at night. The scarcity of food and water resulted in the butchering and devouring of countless horses and mules. An appalling number of men died in great agony, though Alexander tried to shore up morale by sharing all privations with his men. He dismounted, for example, and trudged alongside his troops. When some soldiers found water and offered it to Alexander in a helmet, he praised them but dramatically poured the life-sustaining liquid into the sand, an act of sacrifice that momentarily reinvigorated the army. His admiral Nearchus also had misfortunes, though the fleet came through unscathed. At length, in the spring of 324, Alexander's forces were reunited near the entrance to the Persian Gulf. Alexander was gratified that Nearchus' impressive voyage of exploration had proven the existence of a sea route to India. The king ordered a festival of thanksgiving that included not only sacrifices to the gods but also gymnastic and musical contests. Then Alexander proceeded to the Persian royal city of Susa, which he had left six years earlier on his way to Ecbatana and the east.

The Embezzlement by Harpalus.   As he proceeded northwestward toward Susa by way of Pasargadae and Persepolis, Alexander heard that a number of his leading officials had seized money or power for themselves during his long absence. Eight satraps and generals were summarily deposed and executed. Meanwhile Alexander's old friend Harpalus, the chief financial officer of the empire, fled to Athens with a huge embezzled fortune and a private army of six thousand mercenaries. Ancient sources suggest that the turmoil resulted from a deterioration of Alexander's character. Arrian says he now welcomed any accusation, reliable or otherwise. Although court politics and jealousies played a role in the upheaval, the Roman historian Curtis Rufus correctly recognized that most victims of the king's wrath had mistakenly assumed that Alexander would not survive in the east and embarked on a policy of plundering his empire.

The Marriages at Susa (324 BCE).   As noted, Alexander found Persians and the Persian culture useful to his cause. This helps explain the famous five-day mass wedding ceremony of east and west at Susa. The king set the example by taking two additional wives, one of whom was Stateira, eldest daughter of Darius, while Hephaestion married her sister Drypetis. Alexander also arranged for more than eighty leading Macedonians to marry daughters of the Persian nobility. The splendid marriage ceremonies for the king and officers were performed in the Persian manner—the Bactrian rite had been used in the case of Roxane—under a gigantic royal tent. Alexander offered wedding presents to any soldiers among the ranks who would legalize their casual unions with native women, and Arrian reports that more than ten thousand men complied. Alexander looked forward to the births from these unions, probably hoping the mixed offspring would help undercut old regional and family loyalties, thorns to monarchs in both Asia and Macedonia. Yet Alexander's senior staff as well as the rank and file were becoming more and more disgruntled by his willingness to distance himself from his Macedonian heritage and alarmed by his increasingly despotic rule and behavior. Most of them strongly opposed his plan to govern his realm in some sort of collaboration with the conquered. Their unease was heightened by the arrival of the thirty thousand Asian youths from the northeast satrapies, specially trained in Macedonian weaponry and discipline. The members of the new body were called the *Epigoni* (Successors), a tactless name suggesting Alexander regarded them as heirs of the Macedonian phalanx, an idea that infuriated the Macedonians.

The So-Called Mutiny at Opis (324 BCE). The culmination of the antagonisms occurred in the summer of 324 at Opis, a small settlement on the great river Tigris north of Babylon. There Alexander announced that he would discharge and send home all Macedonian veterans unfit for active service because of age or injury. The stunned soldiers, interpreting the declaration as rejection, demanded that the king discharge them all. Underneath the expressed resentment lay deep fear that Alexander would stay in Asia and never return to Macedonia and that they would become a small minority in a great Persian army. In the general outcry some Macedonians shouted furiously that the king should go campaigning in the future with his father Amon, thereby publicly ridiculing the most hallowed experience of Alexander's inner religious life. Enraged and humiliated, Alexander leapt down from his platform—followed immediately by Hephaestion and other officers—and sprang into the crowd, seizing about thirteen ringleaders and dispatching them to immediate execution. A horrified silence fell. Alexander then harangued the men for their ingratitude, finally discharging all the Macedonians from the army and demanding they tell everyone at home how they had abandoned their king in the heart of Asia. After secluding himself for two days in his palace, the unyielding Alexander summoned the most capable Persian leaders and offered them high military commands. They were to rank as his "Kinsmen" and alone enjoy the honor of greeting him with a kiss. The Macedonians—struck by remorse at this threatening turn of events—rushed weeping to the palace and begged for reinstatement. Alexander, also shedding tears, relented and allowed the Macedonians to come forward and kiss him as a sign of the restoration of fraternal relations.

The Banquet at Opis (324 BCE). The triumphant king sealed the reconciliation with a lavish banquet, said to have been attended by more than nine thousand guests. The entire throng of Macedonians, Persians, and other peoples of the empire made one libation at the sound of a trumpet. Alexander himself prayed that harmony should prevail between the Macedonians and Persians as partners in government. Macedonians who had threatened to desert just days earlier were now joined in prayer with the Persians on behalf of the very goal they had opposed. Alexander realized the survival of his Asian empire depended on peaceful coexistence between the Macedonian conquerors and the Persian conquered. After the reconciliation in the late summer of 324, Alexander had his way and discharged the veterans who were unfit for fighting, thereby lessening the Macedonian element in the army. He liberally rewarded the men and sent them back to Macedonia under the leadership of Craterus. To prevent family discord at home, Alexander retained their offspring born to Asian women, promising to educate the sons at his expense in the Macedonian fashion and to train them as a new generation of soldiers loyal to him alone. Meanwhile the king proceeded to fill the vacancies in his Macedonian units with Persians.

The Exiles' Decree (324 BCE).   Alexander now faced an urgent problem. Roving bands of embittered former mercenary soldiers from Greek cities who had served the old Persian Empire threatened the security of his Asian realm. He issued a decree to the cities of European Greece requiring them to permit their exiles to return home. His call for the return of vast numbers of exiles to their communities provoked much resentment, in part because the Greeks viewed the decision as a blatant violation of the internal autonomy of their city-states. For his part, the king must have hoped the Exiles' Decree would both bring about the resettlement of a large floating population and provide him with entrenched, loyal supporters in the various Greek cities.

Alexander's Deification by the Greek States (324 BCE).   About this time, according to a probable tradition, Alexander sent messages to the mainland Greek states requesting they honor him as a god incarnate. Scattered reports indicate Philip had strongly flirted with divinity. Alexander himself had long been acknowledged as Son of Zeus, but divine sonship fell short of divinity. Alexander was profoundly influenced by the divine kingship of Egypt and quite possibly believed in his own divinity, for his whole career reveals a preoccupation with emulating gods and heroes. Perhaps he also envisioned a political purpose in this: uniting his entire empire through a common cult. The deification of the living was rare but not unknown in the Greek world—Lysander had enjoyed divine pretensions—and apparently the Greeks raised no great objection in the case of Alexander. Cults were established and persisted long after his death. The god-king concept became a potent political and religious force in the Hellenistic world and served as the chief unifying element of the Roman Empire.

Hephaestion's Death (324 BCE).   Alexander spent the summer and early winter of 324 at the magnificent Median capital of Ecbatana. The greatest sorrow of his life occurred here when his lifetime companion Hephaestion suddenly died from fever and drinking. For a day and a night Alexander lay weeping upon Hephaestion's body, refusing food and drink, his friends finally dragging him off by force. Inconsolable and half mad in his grief, Achilles mourned for his Patroclus. Thus the king sheared his hair, just as his hero Achilles did at the news of the death of his beloved Patroclus in the *Iliad*. Alexander's terrible heartache took violent forms, exemplified by his execution of the unfortunate attending physician. The king silenced all musical instruments in camp and proclaimed mourning throughout the empire. He knew there would never be another Hephaestion.

Babylon (323 BCE).   Late in the year Alexander roused himself sufficiently from his consuming sorrow to set out for Babylon, designated as the capital of his empire, and arrived in the spring of 323. Here he laid plans for further exploration and conquest, including a circumnavigation of the Arabian peninsula. He still envisioned exploring the Caspian Sea to locate Ocean, which he thought would provide a northeast passage to India. Meanwhile Alexander ordered a colossally expensive funeral and tomb for the embalmed body of Hephaestion. Artisans came from far and wide to erect and decorate the tomb, designed as a ziggurat, or traditional Mesopotamian pyramidal structure topped with a shrine, though no trace of such an edifice has even been found. The king longed to establish a divine cult for Hephaestion, but the oracle of Amon at the oasis of Siwah, responding to the king's request, announced that a hero cult would suffice. Alexander then interred his fallen companion with kingly honors and offered him a sacrifice of ten thousand animals, thereby inaugurating the cult of Hephaestion, which survived for centuries.

Alexander's Death (323 BCE).   Although he was broken by the death of Hephaestion, Alexander managed to finalize plans for the naval expedition to Arabia. Many farewell banquets with prodigious drinking bouts lasted until late at night. Brooding and self-destructive, Alexander had been drinking heavily for months, sleeping off the effects by day, which gave his physicians cause for alarm. After one night of drinking unmixed wine the king came down with a high fever. Ancient rumors ascribing the fever to poisoning were challenged by both Arrian and Plutarch, and most modern scholars also find them unpersuasive. The illness progressed over the course of about ten days. At first Alexander continued each day to offer the customary sacrifices and to make preparations for the Arabian venture, but he was too debilitated by grief, old wounds, and drunken escapades to throw off the raging fever and was finally left unable to utter a word. Rumors spread that he was dead or dying, and the Macedonian rank and file forced their way past guards at the palace gates. When his bewildered troops silently filed past his bedside, Alexander struggled to greet each with a faint nod or look of recognition. On June 10, 323 BCE, Alexander closed his eyes forever. Not yet thirty-three, he had reigned twelve years and eight months. About two years passed before the funeral procession of Alexander commenced its long journey from Babylon, with the royal body encased in a coffin of beaten gold and embedded in precious spices. The huge, opulent funeral carriage, designed by skilled Greek artisans, was laboriously pulled by mules and preceded by road builders smoothing its passage. Kings of Macedonia were customarily buried at Aegae (modern Vergina), the old capital of the kingdom, but Alexander's body was not conveyed to the traditional royal burial site, nor to the

Siwah oasis to be buried with his "father," as apparently he had requested. The Macedonian general Ptolemy sidetracked the physical remains, which offered great potential as a symbol of power, to Memphis in Egypt and subsequently transferred the body to Alexandria. Here he kept Alexander on display in a glass coffin housed in a magnificent tomb erected for that purpose, the conqueror's embalmed body attracting countless pilgrims over the years.

ALEXANDER'S LEGACY

Alexander had been consumed with yearning to achieve the virtually impossible and reach the ends of the earth. Incredible stories were told of him even in his own lifetime, and ultimately his true personality was lost in legend. His powerful will inspired an extraordinary body of literature known as the Alexander Romance, which began to form soon after his death. The Alexander Romance is a bizarre fictionalized account of his career that is interspersed, on occasion, with apparently genuine material. The extraordinary tales surrounding his name had an enormous impact in medieval times, with Alexander portrayed as a superhuman figure. Even today, his eternally fascinating personality and qualities remain elusive and subject to debate. Bred as a king and warrior, the flesh and blood Alexander raped a vast land, yet achieved acclaim and immortality by inspiring people through the ages to believe the legend he helped engineer.

Part of his success resulted from inheriting his father's solid power base, but Alexander himself was among the greatest military geniuses of history, covering more than eleven thousand miles in his eleven years of campaigning without once losing a battle. His explorations and marches added significantly to western geographical knowledge. Although he retained the impetuousness of his youth and his passionate nature could take him to extremes of generosity or ferocity, he was obsessed with excelling and emulating Achilles and Heracles. Alexander firmly believed in the superiority of Greek civilization. He found his inspiration in the heroic age and always carried a copy of the *Iliad* during his meteoric career of conquests. The Greeks were astounded by his exploits and grateful for his overthrow of the Persian Empire, carried out on the pretext of righting the wrongs inflicted on Greece during the Persian invasions of the early fifth century BCE. For their part, the Persians knew their rule had provided western Asia two centuries of peace and promoted magnificent cultural forms. They saw Alexander as a butcher and exploiter who brooked no opposition in destroying much of their remarkable world to gain wealth and territory.

Alexander adapted much of the Persian system in administering the conquered territory. Thus he imposed his own satraps upon the former Persian provinces, but he also founded a network of cities on the Greek pattern that were dominated by Hellenic mercenaries supported by hostile native agricultural workers. He adopted the weight standard of Athens for his fine coinage, issued to facilitate trade throughout his empire and permit large-scale economic exploitation of the Near East. He took steps also to transform his Macedonian army into a mixed force—of which

Persians should form part—owing loyalty only to himself. Yet his plans for a limited integration of Macedonians and Persians to help unify the empire turned out to be a failure, for the Macedonians detested the idea, and his successors repudiated the concept. Almost to a man, they rejected the Persian wives they had taken in the mass-marriage ceremony at Susa. If Alexander had lived, how far he could have succeeded in the difficult task of coordinating the rule of his realm is impossible to judge. The most significant link binding his vast territories was his dynamic personality, and the death of Alexander—so soon after his insatiable conquests—doomed the empire to rapid political fragmentation.

Alexander had made no arrangements for the succession and had already lost the power of speech by the time he realized the gravity of his final illness, though legend claims the dying king whispered the empire should go to "the strongest." Months earlier, after the death of Hephaestion, Roxane had become pregnant. The son she subsequently bore was Alexander's only legitimate heir, the unfortunate Alexander IV. Alexander was also survived by his mentally impaired half-brother Arrhidaeus. The surviving generals had debated the question of his succession. Some of them pressed the claims of Roxane's unborn child (should she deliver a boy), but the infantry opposed the offspring of a Persian woman and supported Arrhidaeus. The army almost came to open warfare over the succession but finally agreed on a compromise: Arrhidaeus should become king as Philip III, and if Roxane's child turned out to be a boy, then Philip and the infant should share the throne. Meanwhile the pregnant Roxane is said to have engineered the killing of both Stateira, Alexander's second wife, and Drypetis, Hephaestion's widow. When Roxane produced a son a few months later, Philip III and young Alexander IV became joint rulers, with Alexander's last senior commander Perdiccas acting as regent. In the absence of the old focus of loyalty engendered by the charismatic personality of Alexander, however, the surviving cast of characters soon would be embroiled in deadly struggles erupting from their personal ambitions and intrigues.

CHAPTER XVI

THE SUCCESSORS OF ALEXANDER THE GREAT

As a foreign overlord, Alexander established colonies and imposed Greek culture in Egypt and southwest Asia. A veneer of Greek culture spread rapidly in the aftermath of his conquests and, influenced by native traditions, produced a mixed culture that historians call Hellenistic. The term Hellenistic also customarily refers to the period in Greek and Near Eastern history after Alexander's death and leading into the Roman era. The early Hellenistic period saw Alexander's generals struggling to carve out their own domains from his improvised empire. This tortuous period ultimately produced three rich, warring kingdoms ruled by Macedonian monarchs, none of whom was a member of a traditional royal family. The Ptolemies controlled Egypt and at various times part of Asia Minor, the Seleucids took over the bulk of the old Persian Empire, and the Antigonids ruled Macedonia. The Seleucids gradually lost various territories of their huge realm both in the east and the west. In the west, for example, the Attalids carved out an influential kingdom in western Asia Minor, with its capital at Pergamum. Gone was the society centering on the old world of the Greek polis, now replaced by large, culturally diverse states headed by kings who ruled native populations autocratically.

THE POWER STRUGGLES OF THE SUCCESSORS (323–276 BCE)

PERDICCAS TRIES TO MAINTAIN UNITY THROUGH HIS REGENCY (323–321 BCE)

Alexander's death was followed by a fierce contest for power by his ambitious Macedonian generals, who are called the Successors (or the Diadochi). At first, the struggles centered on the attempts of Perdiccas, Alexander's last senior commander, to maintain a nominally unified empire on behalf of the legitimate royal heirs. Perdiccas claimed that dying Alexander had given him his signet ring and thus his authority. Yet his fellow officers demanded a high price indeed for acknowledging his central role in governing the state: the distribution of the satrapies of Alexander's empire among themselves, though formally these regions were to remain within the empire. Perdiccas summoned a council in Babylon to announce the decisions. As virtual regent, if not in name, Perdiccas would remain in Babylon and oversee the administration of Asia. The elderly Antipater retained his position as viceroy of Macedonia and the conquered land of Greece, where he had performed loyally since Alexander's army left for Asia in 334, though his relations with the king soured at the end. Ptolemy successfully bargained to become satrap of Egypt, rich in resources and generally defensible through its relative isolation. Antigonus the One-Eyed, a towering figure with a commanding voice and older than any of the rest except Antipater, was confirmed in his command of Phrygia and other areas in central Asia Minor. The still unconquered satrapy of Cappadocia in eastern Asia Minor was granted to Alexander's secretary, Eumenes of Cardia, one of the few Greeks to gain an important appointment. This potential prize was contingent on Eumenes' gaining control of the area. Minor figures received the less important districts, the most significant of which was Thrace, turned over to Lysimachus. Each of these scheming, able generals would soon assume the prerogatives of an independent sovereign.

Revolts in Bactria and Greece (323–322 BCE).   Almost immediately rebellions broke out in Bactria and Greece. The military settlers in Bactria, lying on the eastern edge of the empire, were miserable so far from home. When they revolted on hearing of Alexander's death and began a homeward march, some 23,000 strong, Perdiccas dispatched one of his eastern satraps against them. The rebellion was crushed with extreme violence, but Bactria would remain a difficult land for the Macedonians to govern. Greece, where Antipater was disliked for having supporting oligarchs and tyrants, also was engulfed in turmoil at this time. Even while Alexander was alive and making his greatest conquests, Sparta had led a revolt against Macedonian dominance in 331, though Antipater quickly quelled the rebellion. News of Alexander's death precipitated a formidable rising in some of the mainland Greek states, led by Athens, the so-called Lamian War. Demosthenes returned to Athens from exile in jubilation, but Antipater—collaborating with the Macedonian general Craterus— was finally victorious, his triumph signaling the end of Athens as a serious military or political force in Greece. Antipater imposed a Macedonian garrison and an unpopular oligarchy on the city, now tightly bound to Macedonia and left without even the pretense of an alliance. Meanwhile Demosthenes was condemned to death and took poison rather than fall into Macedonian hands.

The Coalition against Perdiccas (322–321 BCE).   Despite the success in Greece, the jealous ambitions of the Macedonian generals brought about a rapid deterioration of their initial arrangement. Perdiccas took control of the kings, but Antipater insisted their rightful place was in Macedonia. Until his death, Antipater remained outwardly loyal to the Macedonian dynasty and continued to hold the throne for the co-monarchs, Philip III and young Alexander IV. Meanwhile the dowager queen Olympias, anxiously watching events from her homeland in Epirus, attempted to salvage the empire on behalf of her grandson Alexander IV. She detested Antipater, for he had thwarted her attempted interferences during Alexander's lifetime and probably played a part in her decision to resume residence in Epirus. Thus she resorted to various means to create a rift between Perdiccas and Antipater, thereby hoping to reestablish her influence in Macedonia. Olympias set out to win an alliance with Perdiccas by offering him the valuable hand of her widowed daughter Cleopatra, Alexander's sister. The Successors, playing the risky game of dynastic politics, tenaciously pursued marriage ties with the royal family of Philip II. Perdiccas thought the proposed match might clear the way for his attainment of unrivaled power. First he intended to divorce his new bride Nicaea, Antipater's daughter. Meanwhile Philip's redoubtable daughter Cynane complicated matters further by pushing her young daughter Adea forward as a bride for Philip III. Perdiccas took fright over this and ordered the assassination of Cynane, but the Macedonian soldiers reacted so violently to the spilling of royal blood that he was compelled to allow the marriage. The ambitious new queen made a bid for the loyalty of the troops by assuming the traditional Macedonian royal name Eurydice.

Perdiccas, now increasingly isolated, was compelled to form an alliance with Eumenes. The former's grasping for power soon provoked a coalition against him by the commanders Antipater, Craterus, Lysimachus, and Antigonus, united in their fear that Perdiccas might frustrate their own ambitions. Meanwhile Ptolemy had enhanced his position in Egypt by seizing the embalmed corpse of Alexander. Perdiccas had sent the body to be buried in the royal cemetery at Aegae (modern Vergina) in Macedonia, but Ptolemy cunningly sidetracked the funeral procession to Memphis until he could build a great tomb for Alexander in the capital city of Alexandria. Ptolemy realized that Alexander's body—which elicited unquestioned veneration—could legitimize his power. He soon threw his support behind the anti-Perdiccan alliance. Perdiccas now saw Ptolemy as a deadly rival and, leaving the government in the hands of Eumenes, invaded Egypt in the summer of 321. After more than two thousand of Perdiccas' men drowned in a Nile disaster, which provoked grave discontent in the army, a group of his own officers assassinated him.

THE STOPGAP REGENCY OF ANTIPATER (321–319 BCE)

Antipater had declared war and invaded Asia Minor with Craterus in 321. Craterus fell in battle against Eumenes, whom the other generals now regarded as virtually an outlaw. Despite his advanced age—he was nearly eighty—Antipater assumed the vacant office of regent. He bestowed the satrapy of Babylonia on Seleucus, one of Alexander's minor generals, and relied on Antigonus to overwhelm Eumenes. Antipater returned to Europe with the two kings, Philip III and Alexander IV, thus removing the court to Macedonia. To bind Antigonus closer to him, Antipater gave his daughter Phila (the widow of Craterus) in marriage to Antigonus' son Demetrius—a youth of sixteen—despite the fifteen-year difference in their ages.

THE END OF A DYNASTY (319–310 BCE)

Antipater's death in 319 witnessed the rapid demise of legitimately constituted authority. He had passed over his son Cassander and chosen the aging Polyperchon to succeed him as regent. War immediately broke out between Cassander and

Polyperchon. The latter alienated Antipater's influential friends by inviting Olympias to return to Macedonia and take responsibility for her young grandson Alexander IV. She took her time, not returning to Pella until 317. Meanwhile Cassander, Ptolemy, and Antigonus came together in a coalition against Polyperchon. Cassander gained control of Athens, which he ruled for the next ten years through an Aristotelian philosopher, Demetrius of Phaleron, whose policies favored the rich. In the spring of 316 Cassander marched on Macedonia, driving Polyperchon out, but Queen Eurydice—the wife of Philip III—joined Cassander and proclaimed him regent. Thus Cassander backed Philip III against Alexander IV. In the bitter power struggle for Macedonia, Olympias soon engineered the death of Philip III and Eurydice, but when Cassander returned to Macedonia shortly afterward, he blockaded the old queen and the remaining members of the court, including Alexander IV and Roxane, in the ill-provisioned fortress of Pydna. Olympias' mercenaries turned to cannibalism and surrendered only on condition that her life be spared, yet she was tried and executed, dying with proud defiance. Cassander, hoping to strengthen his claims, married Thessalonice, a half sister of Alexander. Polyperchon, on the other hand, gradually lost control of his possessions and disappears from the historical record. Meanwhile Eumenes, who claimed that the spirit of the deified Alexander resided in his camp as divine leader, remained steadfastly loyal to the principle of legitimacy. His Macedonian soldiers betrayed him in 316, however, and he was handed over to Antigonus, tried, and put to death. Although the legitimate kingship was still represented by Alexander IV, Cassander kept the young king and Roxane closely guarded for several years until he deemed the time ripe to execute both mother and son about 310, ending the male line of the Macedonian dynasty. Thereafter the unity of Alexander's empire would no longer be preserved even in name, for the various generals had attained sufficient power to declare themselves independent sovereigns.

ANTIGONUS STRUGGLES TO BRING THE EMPIRE UNDER HIS CONTROL (316–301 BCE)

After the defeats of Eumenes and Olympias, Antigonus—despite his age—fought constantly to reunite and rule Alexander's enormous empire. Antigonus and his dynamic son Demetrius gained control of most of Alexander's Asian territory. His military success and increasing power provoked a coalition against him by the four secessionist Successors: Ptolemy in Egypt, Cassander in Macedonia, Lysimachus in Thrace, and Seleucus, who claimed vast tracts in Asia. Thus began a long, complicated struggle, with Antigonus and Demetrius fighting their foes in Syria, Asia Minor, Greece, and the Mediterranean. In 307 Demetrius liberated Athens from Cassander's minion Demetrius of Phaleron, who then hurried off to Alexandria. Antigonus assumed the title of king both for himself and his son in 306, and soon Ptolemy, Cassander, Lysimachus, and Seleucus also took the royal title, another step in the breakup of the empire.

Demetrius' Siege of Rhodes (305 BCE).   Meanwhile the war continued unabated. In 305 Demetrius began his famous siege of the island of Rhodes. His effort wasted a

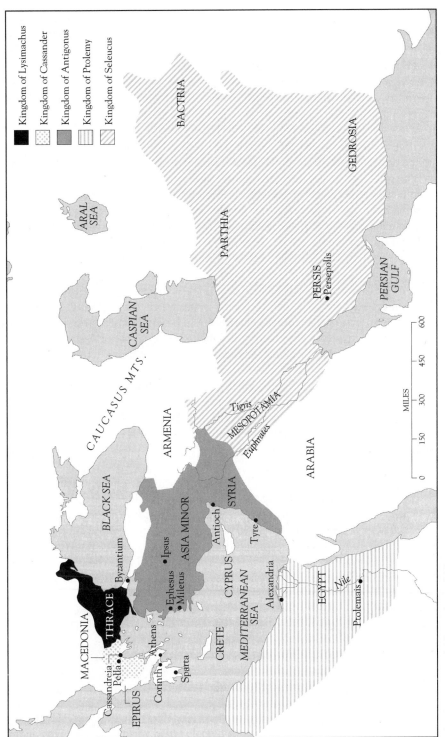

The Successors of Alexander in 303 BCE.

Legend:
- Kingdom of Lysimachus
- Kingdom of Cassander
- Kingdom of Antigonus
- Kingdom of Ptolemy
- Kingdom of Seleucus

BACTRIA

GEDROSIA

ARAL
SEA

PARTHIA

PERSIS
• Persepolis

PERSIAN
GULF

CASPIAN
SEA

CAUCASUS MTS.

ARMENIA

MESOPOTAMIA

Tigris

Euphrates

ARABIA

BLACK SEA

Byzantium

ASIA MINOR

SYRIA

• Ipsus

• Antioch

Ephesus
Miletus

CYPRUS

Tyre

MACEDONIA

THRACE

Cassandreia
Pella

Athens

Corinth

Sparta

EPIRUS

CRETE

MEDITERRANEAN
SEA

Alexandria

EGYPT

Nile

• Ptolemais

MILES

0   150   300   450   600

full year and ended in utter failure. The Rhodians taunted him as Poliorcetes, or the Besieger of Cities, and later commemorated their victory by erecting the Colossus of Rhodes, a great bronze statue of Helios—around one hundred feet tall—which stood beside the harbor entrance until 227, when the towering figure was felled by a devastating earthquake. The Colossus—counted among the Seven Wonders of the World—did not bestride the mouth of the harbor, contrary to general belief.

The Battle of Ipsus (301 BCE).   The decisive battle of the war took place in the summer of 301 at Ipsus in southern Asia Minor, where Antigonus and Demetrius, now tagged Poliorcetes, faced the armies of Seleucus and Lysimachus. Demetrius impetuously rode too far in pursuit of the enemy's cavalry and was cut off from returning by their elephants, thus weakening his father's position. The aged Antigonus was killed during the course of the battle, helplessly crying, "Demetrius will come and save me."

Division of the Spoils (301–276 BCE)

Antigonus death marked a major turning point, for the bid to maintain a central power was over, and Alexander's empire would be dismembered irrevocably into separate states. In a new allotment of the spoils, the kingdom of Antigonus was divided among the victors. Lysimachus added Asia Minor to his Thracian domains, and Seleucus took Syria. Yet Demetrius Poliorcetes remained alive and still master of part of Greece. He profited not only by dissension among his enemies but also by the death of Cassander to seize Macedonia in 294. Although Demetrius the Besieger was eventually driven out of the kingdom by Lysimachus, his son Antigonus Gonatas—as he became known—established the stable Antigonid dynasty in Macedonia in 276.

The Battle of Corupedium (281 BCE).   Ptolemy's wife Eurydice—daughter of Antipater—bore a number of children, including Ptolemy Ceraunus. His third wife, Eurydice's niece Berenice I, who had been his mistress for many years, enjoyed notable influence at court. Ptolemy favored his son by Berenice, the later Ptolemy II Philadelphus, as his successor. To place the succession beyond dispute, Ptolemy appointed Ptolemy II as joint ruler in 285. The ailing old king died in 283 or 282. Ptolemy's death heightened the rivalry between Seleucus and Lysimachus over Asia Minor. A domestic drama ultimately led to hostilities between the two. Lysimachus was strongly influence by his third wife Arsinoë II, who persuaded the aging king to put his son Agathocles to death on suspicion of treason, to the advantage of her own children. Thereupon the executed son's widow Lysandra and her brother Ptolemy Ceraunus—both of whom were children of Ptolemy I by Eurydice—incited Seleucus to challenge Lysimachus. In 282 Seleucus invaded Asia Minor, and Lysimachus fell fighting him early the next year at Corupedium near Sardis. Having finally taken Asia Minor, the seventy-seven-year-old Seleucus—the last of Alexander's companions—now aimed at winning Macedonia. He launched a vigorous campaign but was assassinated by Ptolemy Ceraunus, who wanted the throne for himself. The murder left Seleucus' son Antiochus I as king in the eastern territories, while Ptolemy Ceraunus managed to acquire the kingship in Macedonia for a brief, violent reign.

The Invasion of the Gauls (279 BCE).   Two years later massive waves of fierce Celtic-speaking Gauls pushed southward from central Europe to penetrate the weakened frontiers of Thrace and Macedonia. They killed everyone in sight. Ptolemy Ceraunus perished at their hands. One group established a kingdom in Thrace, while others who reached the sacred treasures of Delphi were beaten off by the Greeks. Another contingent of the invaders crossed the Hellespont to attack Asia Minor and were soundly defeated by Antiochus I, who consequently assumed the title of Soter, the Savior. He confined the surviving Gauls—or Galatians (as they were generally known to the Greeks of Asia from this time)—to a small region in central Asia Minor known thereafter as Galatia. Meanwhile Antigonus Gonatas defeated twenty thousand Gauls near Lysimacheia on the Thracian Chersonesus in 277, thereby winning much popular support for his accession to the kingship of Macedonia. The following year the grateful Macedonians accepted him as their king, and Antigonus established an enduring dynasty and devoted his energies to reviving the exhausted country.

CHAPTER XVII

THE HELLENISTIC KINGDOMS IN THE THIRD CENTURY BCE

Between 276 and 200 BCE three great Hellenistic kingdoms built after the destruction of Alexander's empire flourished in the eastern Mediterranean, each under its own dynasty, with the Antigonids ruling in Macedonia; the Ptolemies in Egypt and Palestine; and the Seleucids in Syria, Mesopotamia, and Asia Minor. In each kingdom the son or, in the case of Macedonia, grandson of Alexander's Successors occupied the throne: Antigonus Gonatus (Macedonia), Ptolemy II (Egypt and Palestine), and Antiochus I (Seleucid territories). The Hellenistic rulers not only consolidated their kingdoms but also maintained a balance of power, though the pattern was complicated by the emergence of lesser monarchies in the third century BCE. Native kingships appeared in Pontus, Bithynia, and Cappadocia, three districts that had escaped direct Macedonian conquest. Further east, seminomads from the steppes penetrated southward into the heterogeneous Seleucid lands in the middle of the century, marking the beginning of the Parthian kingdom, while a string of secessions from Seleucid control erupted about the same time from Bactria in the far east to the Attalid kingdom of Pergamum in the west. Other notable smaller powers in the Hellenistic world included the commercial republic of Rhodes and two rival leagues—the Aetolian and the Achaean—on the Greek mainland. Despite frequent friction, reasonable equilibrium prevailed until the Romans began absorbing the enormously rich Hellenistic kingdoms shortly after 200 BCE.

THE GREEKS AND MACEDONIANS IN THE HELLENISTIC KINGDOMS ABROAD

The wars of the Successors had been waged by professional generals and soldiers, the latter seeking good pay and plunder. They expected a bonus of land or money when discharged, at which time some returned to their homelands, while others settled in veterans' colonies in the new Hellenistic kingdoms. Here they enjoyed a privileged position and were soon joined by immigrants from Greece and Macedonia who hoped to reap economic benefits resulting from Hellenistic business and trading ventures. The settlers formed a new governing class, with many members winning high status and wealth, and a multitude of hostile native peoples in Asia and Egypt found themselves reduced to supporting these overbearing masters.

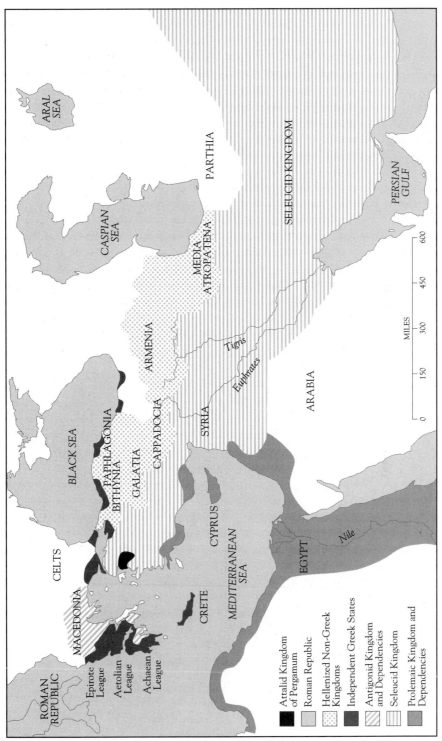

The Hellenistic world in 240 BCE.

PTOLEMAIC EGYPT

The Wealth of the Ptolemies

Ptolemy I took the title of king in 305, reckoned as the first year of his reign, and the honorary title Soter, or Savior, later. His fourteen successors, the Ptolemies, continued to rule Egypt until its incorporation in the Roman Empire in 30 BCE. Backed by a tiny Greco-Macedonian elite, the Ptolemies exploited the geographical advantages and traditional administrative machinery of the country to make their state the most powerful and prosperous of the Hellenistic kingdoms. The Greeks regarded Egypt as fabulously wealthy and had long traded with the country for wheat, linen, papyrus, and numerous articles produced by skilled artisans. Much of its economic prosperity stemmed from the abundant supply of wheat, wholly dependent on the annual flooding of the Nile and an intricate system of artificial irrigation. Following the example of the ancient Egyptian kings, the Ptolemies saw themselves as the sole proprietors of the entire wealth of the realm. Thus the sullen small-scale native farmers, who leased their land from the royal government, were severely taxed and forced to sell their produce to the state, which in turn sold much of the grain abroad at an immense profit. Ptolemy I Soter was largely preoccupied with defending the kingdom and used his great wealth to hire a strong army and navy.

A substantial number of Greek speakers had come to Egypt in the fourth century BCE as mercenaries and traders. Their numbers were dramatically swollen by mercenaries from all over the Greek world after Alexander founded Alexandria. The Ptolemies attracted additional Greek and Macedonian settlers by promising them important government posts and land allotments in return for military service, and the new immigrants inhabited not only the three Greek cities—Alexandria, Naucratis, and Ptolemais—but also Memphis, the ancient capital, and they settled on plots throughout the countryside, where as cleruchs they formed a large reserve army. Besides paying taxes, they also had the double duty of cultivating the land and serving in the army when needed. In Alexandria, the capital and chief Mediterranean port of the kingdom, a cadre of Macedonians and Greeks formed the citizen body and lived in the most important quarter, while Egyptians, Persians, and Jews coexisted in their own quarters and maintained their traditional societies and customs.

Expansionist Foreign Policy

Dispatching their hired mercenaries, the Ptolemies carried on an aggressive foreign policy against Macedonia and Syria. First they secured the western desert by taking Cyrenaica, usually ruled thereafter by a member of the Ptolemaic family. Egypt was particularly vulnerable from the north, where land invasions might come through Palestine, and this helps explain the frequent wars between the Ptolemies and Seleucids. The Ptolemies dreamed also of monopolizing the vital east—west trade routes of the Levant, the lands of coastal Asia Minor, and the eastern Aegean. Thus they initiated a bold naval policy leading to important gains in the area and then harassed the Seleucids from Asia Minor and the Macedonians in Greece from the Aegean. Meanwhile the Ptolemies took control of Palestine and the Phoenician seaports. The caravan routes from Arabia and Mesopotamia terminated in Phoenicia, corresponding roughly to modern Lebanon, a region whose celebrated cedar furnished the main building material for both naval vessels and merchant ships. The Ptolemaic occupation of Phoenicia and Palestine deeply affected both lands. Phoenicia, already Hellenized, now supplied the Ptolemies with fleets and revenues, while Palestine, ruled by a military governor, was partly urbanized. Although the colorful Greek way of life attracted many members of the Jewish aristocracy, the shepherds and small-scale farmers strongly resisted Hellenization. Meanwhile the Ptolemies fostered commerce with Ethiopia, dominated Nubia for its gold, and established close trading relations with the powerful Mediterranean port of Carthage.

Ptolemy II and Arsinoë II.   Expansion continued under Ptolemy I Soter and his successors Ptolemy II Philadelphus (282–246 BCE) and Ptolemy III Euergetes (246–221 BCE). Ptolemy II banished his first wife for plotting to kill him and then married his full sister Arsinoë II, who had originally been married to Lysimachus and then to her half-brother Ptolemy Ceraunus. The union of Ptolemy II and Arsinoë II, the first of a series of Ptolemaic brother-sister marriages, earned the king the title Philadelphus (Lover of his Sister), which he bore with pride. Brother-sister marriages among members of the royal family was an ancient Egyptian tradition, and many subsequent Ptolemies adopted the custom to reduce court intrigues and problems of succession. Although Arsinoë died within a few years, she had strongly influenced the king. Her career marked the chief period of Ptolemaic expansion and the most brilliant epoch of the royal court at Alexandria. Meanwhile Ptolemy II clashed with the Seleucids and won territory in Asia Minor and Syria. After the reign of Ptolemy III, however, the Ptolemaic empire virtually ceased expanding as a result of the growing power of the Seleucids and Antigonids.

GOVERNMENT

The Policy of Ruler Deification.   The Ptolemies, like other Hellenistic kings, employed military, spiritual, and administrative programs to maintain their huge domains. Militarily, the Hellenistic monarchs preserved power with Greco-Macedonian mercenaries. Spiritually, they endeavored to unify their diverse subjects through common bonds. Thus the Ptolemaic and the Seleucid rulers adopted the calculated policy of being deified as earthly benefactors and saviors. To the Egyptians, Ptolemy I was the son of the god Amon, but the king hesitated to seek acknowledgement of his official divinity from the reluctant Greeks and Macedonians. He did establish in Alexandria a cult of Alexander, whose body he had cunningly seized. The electrifying symbol of the embalmed conqueror lying in a coffin of beaten gold helped win the allegiance of Macedonian soldiers. When Ptolemy died in 283, his son and successor Ptolemy II proclaimed his father a god and, upon the death of the late king's widow Berenice I, set up a joint cult for the two as Savior Gods. Finally, in 271, Ptolemy II promoted the worship of the living members of the royal family, having both himself and his sister-wife Arsinoë II acclaimed divine. This was the time that he took the title Philadelphus. The subsequent Ptolemies continued the practice of emphasizing the divinity of the king and royal family, choosing titles to stress the characteristic attributes they wanted their Greek subjects to acknowledge. Thus the third Ptolemy was deified under the title Euergetes, or Benefactor, to promote the image of a protecting and benevolent king. Alexander the Great stood at the head of the royal cult, of course, with the Ptolemies regarded as successors to his divinity.

The Royal Court.   The rule of the Ptolemies was absolute and combined features of Macedonian and Egyptian kingship. The outward marks of the monarchy included not only the royal diadem and purple robes but also the ruler's portrait on coins. As noted, the Ptolemaic kings preserved their Macedonian bloodline through matrimonial unions with rival Hellenistic dynasties and by participating in brother–sister marriages. Ptolemaic queens often exercised tremendous independent power and ultimately acted as corulers, whereas Antigonid queens were virtually invisible and Seleucid queens much less powerful than their Ptolemaic counterparts. The first Ptolemy, who was Macedonian by birth and Greek by culture, created a governing class of Macedonians and Greeks. Yet with the loss of most Ptolemaic possessions outside Africa by the opening of the second century BCE, Egypt became relatively isolated from the Greco-Macedonian world. The Ptolemies began to adopt a more Egyptianized pattern of court life and the veneer of Greek influence was increasingly stripped away. Yet even the last ruler of the Ptolemaic line, Cleopatra VII, discussed at length in the final book of this series, exhibited all the cunning and political ambition of her Macedonian ancestors.

Administration.   The Ptolemaic administration revolved around the royal capital of Alexandria, cosmopolitan and flourishing, one of the great cultural centers of the Mediterranean world. Because the king's attention was concentrated on the extraction of wealth from the land, his most important official was the *dioketes*, the financial minister, whose authority gradually assumed preeminence over the other branches of government. Ptolemy II, who laid down the general lines of administration, kept the traditional division of Egypt into nomes, or provinces, about forty in number, each officially headed by a nomarch, or governor. Natives could aspire to the office, but the governorship had lost much of its power, and the actual functioning head of the nome was the *strategos* (general), who was responsible for maintaining order in the district. Although the Ptolemies issued edicts, they allowed the Egyptians to live under the old laws. Thus Egypt maintained two legal systems, one for the Macedonians and Greeks and another for the Egyptians. Civil suits between Egyptians were tried before native judges, but Greek-speaking judges traveled on circuit to hear the suits of Macedonians and Greeks.

Economy and Trade

Land Use, Agriculture, and Taxation.   The king enjoyed tremendous economic power, for the Ptolemies were the owners of Egypt in the ancient pharaonic tradition, and Egypt functioned as a huge royal business. Agriculture remained the basis of a highly planned economy, most of the productive land being leased to native farmers. Moreover, the king released large tracts of land to the powerful native temples—whose estates were worked under the supervision of the priesthood—and he granted additional estates to the high officials of the government. To foster loyalty among his Greco-Macedonian mercenaries, the king offered them land allotments. The Ptolemies obtained new land by draining Lake Moeris, lying west of the Nile, thereby winning a large district known as the Fayum for cultivation, and they spent a fortune improving the Egyptian irrigation system.

The entire economic life of the country was based on direct government control of all agriculture, industry, and trade. The king furnished seeds to the farmers—the main crops were wheat and barley—and collected his rent in produce. An additional tax was levied on farm animals such as horses, donkeys, camels, goats, sheep, and geese. The Ptolemies taxed their subjects rigorously at every opportunity, farming out the collection of revenues to private individuals who bid for the privilege at auction. The tax collectors reported directly to the finance minister at Alexandria, the *dioketes*, who supervised the whole economic life of the kingdom. The tax collectors were allowed to keep a certain percentage of the revenues for themselves, and apparently the system became the model for the later Roman practice.

Royal Monopolies.   Alexandria quickly became not only one of the chief markets for the supply of grain but also a great manufacturing center, exporting articles such as papyrus, linen, glass, jewelry, and cosmetics throughout the Mediterranean. The most important industries served as royal monopolies, with the government exclusively controlling the production and sale of olive oil, textiles, papyrus, and salt. Additionally, the king either owned or licensed businesses such as cosmetics, glass, pottery, and beer brewing. Although the Egyptians embraced beer as a beverage and sesame oil for cooking, the Greco-Macedonians preferred wine and olive oil. Accordingly, the Ptolemies introduced the cultivation of the grape and the olive, the former proving adequate but the olive groves failing to produce satisfactorily in the soil and climate of Egypt. Steep tariffs forced the Greeks and Macedonians to pay a high price for their imported olive oil.

Coinage.   Ptolemaic trade was supported by a sound coinage of gold, silver, and copper. Coinage in the Hellenistic period, as previously, was minted on different standards of weight in different places. The Antigonids and Seleucids coined to the Attic standard, adopted by Alexander himself, which became the footing for virtually an international coinage, but the new Ptolemaic coins were struck on a lighter standard. The Ptolemies created a monetary monopoly by excluding Seleucid and other foreign currencies from Egypt and requiring international traders to change their money upon reaching the kingdom. Ptolemaic rulers obtained gold from mines in the Nubian Desert, where prison gangs and prisoners of war labored under brutal conditions. They acquired silver from the Aegean as payment for grain, and copper arrived from the subject state of Cyprus. Copper coinage was widely used in the rural districts, where barter was never entirely abandoned, but bimetallic currency was employed for foreign trade. The entire Hellenistic world developed into one great market dominated by Greco-Macedonian or Hellenized merchants, and an evolved, cosmopolitan form of Greek called *koine,* or the common tongue, became by degrees the regular language for conducting business in Hellenistic Africa and Asia.

Trade.   While Carthage monopolized western Mediterranean commerce, the Ptolemaic fleet dominated trading activities in the eastern Mediterranean and the Red Sea. Moreover, Egypt served as a natural point of exchange for the products of Africa, India, and the Mediterranean world. The Ptolemies obtained spices, ivory, incense, coral, and rare woods from eastern Africa and southern Arabia not only for their own use but also for the valuable trade with the Aegean markets. They occupied Nubia and even traded as far south on the Nile as the city of Meroë (beyond modern Khartoum in Sudan), the capital of a partly Hellenized African kingdom bearing the same name. To encourage profitable trade with the east coast of central Africa as well as Arabia and beyond, Ptolemy II reopened an old canal between the Nile and the Red Sea, though this artery was soon choked with silt, and thereafter imported goods coming this way were brought overland from Red Sea ports.

The Ptolemies reaped huge profits from the trade with southern Arabia via the Red Sea. Yet for centuries the Nabataean Arabs had acquired great wealth by conveying luxury goods from India and spices from Arabia along a desert caravan route on the east bank of the Red Sea, with a terminus on the banks of the Mediterranean. The Ptolemies were anxious to dominate trade in the area and followed the Red Sea to explore routes in the Indian Ocean, but only in the early Roman Empire did Greek sailors learn a fact kept secret by their Arab counterparts for centuries: Monsoonal winds could be employed to carry ships to India and back.

ALEXANDRIA

Alexandria, royal capital of the Ptolemies, was a magnificent city of roughly one million inhabitants during its period of greatest glory. The bulk of Egyptian overseas trade passed through its famous double harbors, and a large part of Ptolemaic industry was concentrated in the city. Founded by Alexander on the western side of the Delta in accord with the best principles of Greek city planning, Alexandria was laid out with broad avenues crossing one another at right angles, intercepted at places with spacious squares and parks. The city was dotted with stately buildings in the Greek style, while its avenues were lined with lengthy colonnades. Ancient sources report that the most important thoroughfares were lit at night with torches, a rare practice in antiquity. The Ptolemaic court at Alexandria preserved many Macedonian institutions—exemplified by its Greek language and dress—but the influence of the old Egyptian and Persian courts remained significant, with an extraordinary number of officials and titles, eunuchs and slaves. On the walls of new temples, moreover, the Ptolemies appear in traditional pharaonic garb and style.

The Pharos.   The landmark of Alexandria was its famous lighthouse, or Pharos, the ancestor of all modern lighthouses. Now vanished, the Pharos stood on a small

In the spring of 331 BCE Alexander chose a reef-guarded strip west of the Nile's mouth to found Alexandria, destined to become one of the greatest cities of the ancient world. Towering over its wide avenues and dazzling monuments was the now-vanished Pharos, reconstructed here, a lofty lighthouse completed about 285 BCE and reckoned among the Seven Wonders of the World. The light from the fire maintained at the top was directed out to sea by an intricate mirror system and provided a welcome guide to mariners.

island of the same name at the entrance to the double harbor of Alexandria until an earthquake toppled its tower in 796 CE. The architect, Sostratus of Cnidus, employed white marble or limestone to construct the tower during the reigns of the first two Ptolemies. Rising more than four hundred feet from a terrace on the island, the Pharos was counted among the Seven Wonders of the World for its unsurpassed height. The imposing tower was crowned with a statue of Zeus the Savior. The light of the signal fire was directed out to sea by an intricate curved metal mirror and was visible from ships about twenty miles from shore.

Alexandria's Wealth Reflected in Its Buildings. As the capital of Ptolemaic Egypt, Alexandria supported a well-stocked zoo and was adorned with many splendid monuments and public buildings such as Alexander's tomb, bureaucratic offices, gymnasiums, and theaters. Poised between Africa and Europe, this city of diverse traditions provided fine temples sacred to Greek and Egyptian gods as well as a synagogue for the sizable minority of Jews. Royal palaces and their land occupied at least one-fourth of the city and contained magnificent gardens, statues, fountains, and shrines, including the royal necropolis centering on Alexander's rich tomb, though we hear that a late Ptolemy of the first century BCE, short of funds, replaced the conqueror's gold sarcophagus with one of glass.

The Museum and Library. With the advice of Demetrius of Phaleron, who had been driven from Athens, Ptolemy I planned and his son founded at Alexandria the greatest of all ancient institutions intended primarily for scholarship and research, the Museum (*Mouseion,* or Place of the Muses), with its vast Library containing everything of note ever written in Greek. Originally, as its Greek name implies, a museum was a shrine or center dedicated to the Muses, Greek goddesses presiding over poetry, music, dance, and all artistic and intellectual pursuits. Plato and Aristotle had organized their schools as associations for the cult of the Muses, and a museum became a place of education and research. The king's patronage supported writers and scholars at the Museum and Library at Alexandria. Yet all who could read were welcome at the Library, said to have eventually amassed nearly five hundred thousand rolls of papyri, a remarkable number of volumes for the time. Most of the vast collection of scrolls were consumed by flames during a desperate struggle between Egyptian troops and Julius Caesar's occupation forces in 47 BCE, however, and the Library was completely destroyed in the seventh century CE.

During the Hellenistic period the most talented scholars, poets, and artists were invited to live with tax-exempt status in Alexandria. These intellectuals associated with the Museum and Library helped to glamorize a regime that was essentially sordid. Alexandrian scholarship made a strong impact on many Greco-Roman authors as well as the fathers of the early Christian church. The Septuagint, a translation of the Hebrew Bible into Greek, was undertaken in Alexandria. Most of this work was completed before the Christian era and was prepared for the many Jews who had immigrated to Egypt and other Greek-speaking lands.

Municipal Government.   About one-third of the diverse population of Alexandria was made up of Greco-Macedonians, while the rest included Egyptians, Persians, Jews, Syrians, and Anatolians. The great city was divided into five quarters, with the various nationalities tending to congregate together. As noted, a large self-governing Greco-Macedonian colony occupied one quarter, and a similar group of Jews another. The Greco-Macedonian males were reckoned as citizens of the city and were known as the Alexandrians. They elected magistrates and passed laws through their assembly and council, but the Jews enjoyed privileges of self-administration for their large community. Meanwhile the entire city was under the direction of a governor appointed by the king.

DECLINE OF PTOLEMAIC EGYPT (246–30 BCE)

Apparently most Egyptians despised the ruling Greco-Macedonians, who had appropriated the best land and grown wealthy at native expense. Ptolemy III Euergetes (246–221 BCE) attempted to gain support by making additional concessions to the Egyptian priests. His successor Ptolemy IV Philopator (221–205 BCE) managed to win a decisive victory over the Seleucids in 217 at the battle of Raphia on the coast of southern Palestine. Yet the triumph was achieved only by using twenty thousand native troops, whose success stimulated a nationalist movement, with the Egyptians revolting for decades afterward. Meanwhile the kings neglected their foreign possessions, and by the end of the third century BCE their control of the empire began to crumble. In the period from about 200 to 80 BCE the Ptolemaic state was weakened by dynastic conflicts and considerable corruption. The Seleucids captured Phoenicia and Palestine by 197, with the Ptolemies losing all their possessions in the Levant except a few posts on the mainland coast and the island of Cyprus. Stripped of most territories outside Africa, Ptolemaic Egypt became increasingly isolated from the Greek political world. Moreover, Greek culture in the kingdom represented only a thin veneer overlying the storied Egyptian civilization. The last years of Ptolemaic Egypt witnessed extraordinary chaos and decay, though the Ptolemies continued to rule until 30 BCE, the end of the reign of Cleopatra VII, when the kingdom finally fell to Rome.

THE SELEUCID KINGDOM

GRADUAL FRAGMENTATION

Seleucus I (312–281 BCE).   Egypt was a defensible and compact realm centering on the Nile valley and the Delta. The rival kingdom of the Seleucids stood in sharp contrast, its size fluctuating dramatically and its rulers, despite their vast eastern territories, often drawn westward into costly conflicts with the Ptolemies. Seleucus I Nicator (the Conqueror), who had served as cavalry commander under Alexander, gained the satrapy of Babylon after Alexander's death. Losing his satrapy in 316 BCE, he fled to Egypt but regained his holdings through a spectacular campaign in 312, the year from which the Seleucid era begins. Seleucus succeeded in wresting control of the largest area among the Hellenistic kingdoms. Although he acquired the bulk of the old Persian Empire, his descendants found themselves struggling to control its diverse peoples, proud heirs of ancient traditions and customs. At its greatest extent the Seleucid kingdom reached from the Hellespont to the Indus, yet provincial governors and local rulers fostered rebellious movements that gradually fragmented the realm. In 303 Seleucus I was forced to abandon his Indian holdings to a remarkable native king named Chandragupta (known to the Greeks as Sandracottus), founder of the Mauryan empire in ancient north India, in exchange for five hundred war elephants. Seleucus employed the elephants in his struggles to gain territory in the west, fighting for eleven years before putting down rival claimants for the control of Syria. His victory in 301 over Antigonus and Demetrius at the battle of Ipsus, as noted in chapter 16, finally gave him rule over Syria, and in 281 he advanced into Asia Minor, defeating and killing Lysimachus at Corupedium. Seleucus then took control of western Asia Minor and claimed the vacant throne of Macedonia and dominion over Thrace but was assassinated when he invaded Europe. Most subsequent rulers of the dynasty were named either Seleucus or Antiochus.

Antiochus I (281–261 BCE).   Seleucus I was succeeded by his son Antiochus I Soter, who renounced his father's ambitions in Macedonia but was preoccupied with nearby Ptolemaic Egypt. The Seleucids and the Ptolemies carried on a seemingly endless struggle over their shared frontier in the Levant, fighting for Palestine, Phoenicia, and coastal Asia Minor. Disorder was rife in Asia Minor at the accession of Antiochus I in 281. The Greek cities on the coast, asserting that Alexander had restored their independence, attempted to play off Seleucid and Ptolemaic rivalry to their own advantage. Elsewhere in Asia Minor numerous petty rulers made themselves independent. The disarray in Asia Minor was exploited by the wealthy Greek city of Pergamum on the north-central west coast of Asia Minor. About fifteen miles from the Aegean and commanding the fertile valley of the river Caïcus, Pergamum revolted from Seleucid rule and established a small rival kingdom in the third century BCE. This new domain threatened Seleucid interests in northwest Asia Minor and beyond.

Meanwhile the Gauls invaded central Asia Minor in 279 and formed the Celtic enclave of Galatia in the Hellenistic world. In northern and central Asia Minor, much of which had not been directly attached to Alexander's empire, the Seleucids failed to prevent the rise of Hellenized native states in Cappadocia, Pontus, and Bithynia. By this time the Seleucids were also struggling to exercise authority over territories east of the Euphrates, and their rebellious governors in Bactria (corresponding roughly to northern Afghanistan) formed a new independent kingdom around 250 BCE. Farther west a seminomadic people—the Greeks and Romans called them Parthians—came from east of the Caspian to occupy the Seleucid satrapy of Parthia. A new Iranian state called Parthia began to form under King Arsaces, and eventually the Parthians gained control of an area from the Euphrates to the Indus, with Ecbatana as their capital. The Parthian rulers proudly claimed to be the successors to the Persian kings.

Thus the Seleucid kingdom was thrown back on its central and western territories, Mesopotamia and Syria. The Seleucid heartland lay in Syria, where the great capital of the kingdom was located on the left bank of the Orontes, Antioch-on-the-Orontes, an important commercial city noted for its luxuries and sensual pleasures. Seleucid Syria stretched from the Orontes to Mesopotamia, a fertile and well populated region straddling the vital trade routes to Asia Minor and strategically located for keeping a guarded eye on the Ptolemaic territories of Phoenicia and Palestine, both of which, as noted, would be incorporated in the Seleucid realm by 197 BCE. While Antioch served nominally as the capital of the kingdom, the Seleucids had also built a new eastern subcapital near Babylon on a bend of the Tigris, Seleucia-on-the-Tigris, across from the small settlement of Opis, where Alexander held his famous banquet of reconciliation with the army. The heir apparent usually lived in Seleucia, from which the eastern satrapies were governed, and the city enjoyed tremendous prosperity as the terminus of the caravan routes from India and eastern Iran.

GOVERNMENT OF THE SELEUCID EMPIRE

Court and Administration.   The Seleucids faced countless difficulties governing their vast and complex kingdom, whose administration was less efficiently organized and necessarily far less centralized than the more homogeneous Ptolemaic Egypt. The kings tried to impose their rule on the great diversity of peoples within their domains with the help of the bureaucracy and army. Seleucus I established a monarchy in the Macedonian tradition, ruling personally through edicts that were carried out by his high officials—selected chiefly from his kinsmen and friends—who distanced themselves from the native populations they governed. For about two generations Persians, Syrians, Jews, and others were almost completely excluded from the ruling class and even later represented but a fraction of the whole. Thus the Seleucids generally reversed Alexander's policy of limited collaboration with local leaders.

The royal court was essentially Macedonian, interspersed with eastern features. The king's finance minister acted as a virtual prime minister. The empire was divided into many small satrapies, each controlled by a Macedonian or Greek governor, but financial administration remained under direct royal control. In remote areas or those places where national sentiment ran high, native rulers or local nobles enjoyed autonomy in return for paying occasional tribute and providing military assistance. Yet the immensely wealthy Seleucids inherited extensive holdings of their own known as the King's Land, partly occupied by small-scale farmers paying taxes and by military colonists rendering armed service for the privilege. Meanwhile the Seleucids initially conciliated native priests, especially those of Babylon, through lavish gifts amounting to bribery, but the later kings incurred priestly hostility by plundering temples for funds to battle the armies of Rome.

Establishment of Greek Cities and Royal Cults. To boost royal authority and enhance prosperity, the kings planted a chain of Greek towns and cities—their most striking accomplishment—from the Mediterranean to Bactria. These grid-patterned cities carried Greek institutions and culture eastward. The settlements promoted trade—they were founded along the great trade routes—and served as the chief prop of the state, for their Greco-Macedonian inhabitants generally supported the Seleucid king and exploited his oppressed Asian subjects. The Seleucids set out to win allegiance from their Greco-Macedonian subjects by encouraging the establishment of ruler cults. Seleucus I claimed descent from Apollo, and his successors reigned as living gods, taking titles such as Epiphanes (God Manifest). Antiochus III organized a ruler-cult throughout the empire, with priests of the living king and his divine ancestors officiating in each province. Antiochus IV Epiphanes (175–164 BCE) identified local gods with Zeus. He failed to see the consequences, however, when he granted the petition of Hellenizing Jewish leaders to stamp Jerusalem with the forms of a Greek city, a move provoking the displeasure of conservative Jews. Later, when Jerusalem was strife ridden over dissension in the high priestly families, Antiochus received word that a rebellion was afoot and adopted punitive measures. He suppressed the Yahweh cult and installed Zeus in the Jerusalem Temple, a policy supported by the Hellenizing Jewish aristocracy but provoking the outbreak of an uprising in 167 BCE by the traditionalists under Judas Maccabeus—the Maccabean revolt—which soon turned into a vicious Jewish civil war, with anti-Greeks fighting pro-Greeks. Finally, in 142 BCE the Seleucid garrison was expelled from Jerusalem.

ANTIOCH

The old Greek cities of Asia Minor—exemplified by the trading and cultural centers of Ephesus and Miletus—had little in common with the Seleucid foundations in the East. These flourishing new cities were planned in relation to the great trade routes and remained commercially important in later ages. Seleucus I founded numerous cities, including Seleucia-on-the-Tigris and Antioch-on-the-Orontes, the latter named for his son Antiochus. Rich Antioch lay in northern Syria about fifteen miles from the mouth of the Orontes and enjoyed an excellent seaport known as Seleucia-in-Pieria. Antioch profited from its position on the ancient trade route between Mesopotamia and the Mediterranean. The city lay on the edge of a large fertile plain and exported local natural resources such as wine and olive oil. Built on the eastern bank of the Orontes in the shadow of the towering peaks of Mount Silpius, Antioch served as the empire's political capital, the site of the palace and court of the king. The great city was laid out in the familiar grid plan of the new Greco-Macedonian cities and supported an international population of Macedonians, Greeks, Syrians, Jews, and others.

Daphne.   The kings adorned Antioch with magnificent buildings, though not much of Seleucid Antioch has survived. Seleucus I opened a beautiful park about five miles away at Daphne, famous in antiquity for its natural springs supplying the city with water. The park was dedicated to the royal gods, especially Apollo, and the Seleucids celebrated lavish games in their honor at a great stadium there. Daphne was known also for its luxury, a tradition confirmed by the excavation of splendid house mosaics from the Roman period.

TRADE AND COINAGE

The lifeblood of the Seleucid Kingdom was trade. Although the huge realm was too diverse to achieve economic unity, the kings issued an abundant coinage, which was based on the Attic standard and stamped for a while with Alexander's portrait to emphasize Seleucid continuity with his rule. The Seleucids challenged the monetary and trading monopoly of the Ptolemies by excluding Ptolemaic coinage from their kingdom. They also developed trade routes that Alexander had planned to India and southern Arabia, thereby increasing their capacity to export luxury products. They protected these ventures with fleets stationed in the Persian Gulf and the Mediterranean, together with their army of regular soldiers and mercenaries. Greek was the official language of the kingdom. Aramaic continued as the vernacular in Syria, but anyone not speaking Greek was excluded from the ruling circle. As noted, an evolved form of Greek known as *koine* (the common tongue) was the most important language of commerce in Hellenistic Africa and Asia.

THE SELEUCIDS SUCCUMB TO ROMAN EXPANSION (c. 200–64 BCE)

Antiochus III (c. 242–187 BCE).   After the assassination of the able Seleucus I in 280, Seleucid Asia experienced several periods of weakness until its sixth ruler, Antiochus III, eventually surnamed the Great, ascended the throne about 242. The most remarkable of the Seleucid monarchs, Antiochus regained full control of the essential territory of the kingdom and compelled the rulers of Armenia, Parthia, Bactria, and western India to acknowledge his suzerainty. Apparently Antiochus then entered some sort of secret agreement with Philip V of Macedonia to conquer and divide between them various overseas possessions of Ptolemaic Egypt, weakened by the succession of the child-king Ptolemy V in 205. Although Antiochus had been defeated by Ptolemy IV at the battle of Raphia in 217, he succeeded in seizing Phoenicia and Palestine from the feeble grasp of young Ptolemy V at the opening of the second century BCE.

Antiochus' success was short-lived, however, for his aggression soon led to the direct intervention of Rome. Antiochus had designs on Europe and crossed the Hellespont in 196 to occupy Thrace. At this point the Roman Senate—already deeply suspicious of Antiochus—strongly warned him to desist. After protracted negotiations with the Senate, the Seleucid king lost patience and invaded Greece in 192. The Romans defeated him in Greece and western Asia Minor, and he was compelled to accept their terms for a peace treaty, which excluded the Seleucids from Greek Asia Minor and the Aegean. This treaty of Apamea (188 BCE) was a milestone in Rome's absorption of the Greek east. The later history of the Seleucids is intertwined with that of Roman expansion in the eastern Mediterranean, the kingdom melting away piece by piece until its last territory, Syria, was annexed as a Roman province in 64 BCE. So ended the second of the great Hellenistic kingdoms, though the Romans built their eastern provinces on its foundation.

THE GREEKS IN BACTRIA AND INDIA

The political history of the Greeks in Bactria and India remains obscure and rests chiefly on mediocre sources and surviving coins. Bactria, whose fertile uplands were watered by networks of irrigation canals, was an important satrapy of the Persian Empire. Although the Persian king had long ago settled Greeks on this fringe of his empire, partly as a buffer against incursion by northern nomads, the inhabitants fought heroically before finally submitting to Alexander. Following the conqueror's death in 323, Bactria passed to Seleucid control. The early Seleucids extensively colonized Bactria, which supported a far-eastern enclave of Greek culture, but the Greco-Macedonian governors began yearning for independence and eventually formed a breakaway kingdom. This achievement is generally ascribed to Diodotus, the first king, possibly as early as 256. Prospering from its central Asian trade routes, the Greco-Bactrian kingdom survived for more than a century and embraced what is now southern Afghanistan, western Pakistan, southern Uzbekistan, and southeastern Turkmenistan. This amazing land, almost entirely cut off from the main body of the Hellenistic world, produced a superb coinage showing rulers with startlingly realistic features, foreign to traditional Greek idealizing influences. Demetrius I (c. 200–185 BCE), for example, boldly presents himself as the conqueror of India in silver coins portraying him wearing an elephant-scalp headdress. Yet by 100 BCE the Greek presence in Bactria had been virtually eradicated by invasions of nomads from central Asia.

Earlier, in the second century, Greco-Bactrian kings had crossed the Hindu Kush and carved out a kingdom in ancient northwest India. Greeks ruled here until well into the first century BCE, long after the Greek mainland had succumbed to the control of Rome, though only one of these kings—Menander (c. 150–130 BCE)—has survived in Indian literature, under the name Milinda. Probably the greatest of the Indo-Greek kings, Menander was in some sense a convert to Buddhism. The last Indo-Greek king vanished about 55 BCE in the wake of incursions by fierce tribes from central Asia. By this time the Greeks in India, though considerably Indianized, had left their mark on the Buddhist sculpture of Gandhara, a prosperous region in ancient northwestern India. Hitherto Buddhists, like the earliest Christians, had refrained from portraying their master. The Gandhara school of sculpture was the first that dared to depict the Buddha in human form, an obvious Greek influence. Although the content of Gandhara sculpture is purely Buddhist, the form is largely Hellenistic, with customary Greek motifs used freely as decoration.

PERGAMUM OF THE ATTALID DYNASTY

The city of Pergamum enjoyed a commanding position in northwest Asia Minor. Sixteen miles from the Aegean Sea, Pergamum crowned an isolated, steep hill rising more than one thousand feet above the broad, fertile valley of the river Caïcus. When the governor of Pergamum, the eunuch Philetaerus, deserted Lysimachus and aided Seleucus I at the battle of Corupedium in 281 BCE, the Seleucid king rewarded him by recognizing his dynasty and granting him additional land as a vassal. Almost twenty years later, in 263, Philetaerus' nephew and successor Eumenes I defeated the Seleucid king Antiochus I in battle near Sardis and asserted his independence. Eumenes was succeeded by his cousin and adopted son Attalus I (241–197 BCE), who gained prestige through his victories over the Gauls. Having firmly established the reputation of Pergamum, he began using the royal title. The Pergamene kings commissioned numerous works of sculpture, discussed in chapter 19, to commemorate their role as protectors of Hellenism against the raids of the Galatians.

Rulers Cooperate with Rome and Amass Wealth

The dynamic Attalus I managed to gain control of most of the western coastline of Asia Minor, including several of the Greek cities. The Ptolemies encouraged the growth and independence of the Pergamene kingdom as a wedge between their two great enemies, the Seleucids and the Antigonids. Meanwhile Attalus I wisely pursued a policy of cooperating with Rome against the ambitions of Philip V of Macedonia. This strategy of friendship with Rome was continued by his son and successor Eumenes II (197–158 BCE), who resisted the threats of the Seleucid king Antiochus III and backed Rome in a conflict with him. As noted, Antiochus' occupation of Thrace in 196 BCE and his invasion of Greece in 192 provoked war, and the victorious Romans laid down peace terms that excluded the Seleucids from Greek

Asia Minor and the Aegean, driving them south of the Taurus Mountains. Rewarded for siding with Rome, Eumenes II gained most of Seleucid Asia Minor and the Thracian Chersonesus.

The royal dynasty of the Attalids amassed a substantial treasury, partly by taxing the peasants at a fixed rate, as did the Ptolemies, and by exporting goods such as wine, oil, grain, horses, gold, silver, and lead. Many slaves labored in their factories, making parchment from hides imported from the Black Sea area, creating prized Attalid brocade and other textiles, and manufacturing perfumes for personal or ritual use. The Attalids are also remembered for their interest in Greek philosophy and their fascination with various mystery cults. Moreover, the kings of Pergamum patronized learning—their great library was second only to that of Alexandria—and their wealth was reflected in the magnificent temples of the city.

THE CITY OF PERGAMUM

The Attalids spent lavishly to transform Pergamum—the most thoroughly excavated of the Hellenistic capitals—into an architectural masterpiece and cultural center that was modeled on Athens. The lofty acropolis and its descending terraces created a dramatic ensemble. Pergamum was linked to its acropolis by an agora, a gymnasium, and the sanctuary of Demeter, all constructed on intermediate levels. The focus of the summit of the acropolis was the fortress-palace of the Attalids, around which were grouped other notable structures, including a spacious theater nestled into a hill, splendid temples, and the Great Altar, the last celebrated for its colonnade with projecting wings on either side of a broad central staircase. The west front of the Great Altar of Pergamum has been reconstructed in Berlin. The monument, erected by Eumenes II to glorify the victories of his father Attalus I against the Galatians and others, features a four-hundred-foot frieze portraying the *Battle of Gods and Giants* in the vigorous and highly dramatic sculpture typifying the Hellenistic period. The sculpture sets Attalus' success against the barbarian Galatians in the context of divine triumph over monstrous Giants.

Pergamum retained the constitution and institutions of a Greek city-state, with the Attalids posing as "first citizens" and occasionally even marrying commoners, yet in practice they intervened in the operations of the state at will. The Greeks detested the Attalid pretense at democratic rule and considered them untrustworthy instruments of Rome. The alliance with the Romans prolonged the independence of Pergamum only until 133 BCE, however, when the last Pergamene king, Attalus III, died and bequeathed his rich possessions to Rome.

THE NATIVE KINGDOMS OF CAPPADOCIA, PONTUS, AND BITHYNIA

Although the Seleucids realized the importance of Asia Minor as an outlet on the sea and fought strenuously for its western and southern seaboards, they took no firm steps to hold the wild mountainous terrain on its northern and southwestern fringes.

Thus Cappadocia, Pontus, and Bithynia split off under native dynasties into kingdoms with a veneer of Greek influence. Their determined kings, who claimed descent from Persian rulers, established eastern-style absolute monarchies.

Cappadocia—at one time designating the whole long plateau stretching from the Taurus Mountains in southwestern Asia Minor to the Black Sea—passed from Macedonian to Seleucid domination after the death of Alexander, but about 260 BCE the region was consolidated into a kingdom under a native ruler. Rugged Cappadocia, plagued by severe winters and much inhospitable terrain, remained generally Persian in outlook and culture, though a gradual Hellenization took place in urban areas. The nonurban population was ruled by quasifeudal lords or priests of the great temples.

About 300 BCE a Persian of noble ancestry named Mithridates won the northern part of Cappadocia—Cappadocian Pontus—which he joined with an adjacent district to form a new kingdom on the southern shore of the Black Sea that was eventually called simply Pontus. This was a mountainous country with fertile valleys. Its social and political structure resembled that of its southern neighbor. Like Cappadocia, Pontus remained generally Persian in outlook and custom, though its rulers cultivated friendly relations with the Seleucids.

The third native kingdom in northern Asia Minor was Bithynia, located west of Pontus on the southern shore of the Black Sea. The political history of Bithynia was characterized by efforts to preserve its independence and enlarge its territory. The population of the kingdom, largely of Thracian origin, was far more substantially Hellenized than Pontus, and the kings here founded a number of Hellenistic cities, but the extent to which Greek civilization penetrated the rural interior remains unclear. The Bithynians, who had eluded conquest by Alexander, made a number of prudent alliances to protect themselves from the Seleucids and others.

CELTIC GALATIA

About 278 BCE the Bithynians complicated the political life of Asia Minor by encouraging the migration of Celtic-speaking Gauls from the Balkan peninsula, where the Macedonian kings had been carrying on a difficult struggle against them. The Bithynians brought the Gauls over to protect themselves from the Seleucids, and these settlers penetrated far into Asia Minor and carved out a state south of Bithynia that became known as Galatia. The Galatians—that is, the Gauls in Galatia—remained Celtic in language and custom throughout the Hellenistic period. Their society, like that of the Celtic peoples of western Europe, was tribal and agricultural. The Celts were sources of fear and fascination not only for their size and physical beauty but also for their fierceness in battle, and the Galatians posed a constant threat to the peace of the surrounding countryside.

RHODES

The large Greek island of Rhodes, located off the southwest corner of Asia Minor, was a wealthy maritime state with a spectacular capital of the same name. Although

Alexander installed an unpopular Macedonian garrison on the island, the Rhodians reasserted their political independence after the partitioning of his empire, provoking the spectacular but unsuccessful siege in 305 BCE by Demetrius. The Rhodians commemorated their triumph by erecting the famous but short-lived Colossus, a towering statue of their patron god Helios, who was adorned with a halo of sun rays and held a torch provided with a beacon fire to aid ships at sea. Third-century Rhodes, secure on its island, was one of the few Greek powers enjoying genuine independence. Rhodes was ideally placed at the intersection of the great Mediterranean shipping routes to the Aegean and the Black Sea and to Italy and North Africa from Egypt, Cyprus, and Phoenicia. The island served as an international clearinghouse and distribution center for trade, particularly in grain and other essentials. A port tax on its transit business provided great wealth, and numerous foreign bankers and merchants came here to live and conduct their business. The wealthy deposited funds with the bankers of Rhodes for security against kingly requisitions or piracy. The Rhodians themselves carried on an extensive trade in wine—said to have been of mediocre quality—and archaeologists working over a wide area of the Mediterranean and the Black Sea have uncovered many fragments of wine jars, the handles stamped with the insignia of Rhodian magistrates.

The Rhodians generally maintained close ties with Ptolemaic Egypt to foil any resurgence of the Seleucids in Asia Minor and to prevent the Macedonians from gaining control of the Aegean. Hellenistic Rhodes outstripped Athens as the wealthiest Aegean port and by degrees its distinguished, powerful fleet became the largest in the eastern Mediterranean. This naval and commercial power enabled Rhodes to play an important role in defending the freedom of the seas. A code of maritime law, for example, was developed by the Rhodian merchant-traders, who enjoyed an enviable reputation for integrity in business. Indicative of the high repute of Rhodes, other countries of the Mediterranean made use of its sea laws to decide maritime disputes. The laws were eventually introduced into the Roman codes, from which they were later extracted to form the basis of the maritime regulations of modern Europe. The Rhodians had a vested interest in the suppression of piracy. They won strong applause after their navy took over this difficult task about the mid-third century BCE, when Ptolemaic Egypt was no longer able to police the high seas. In 220 BCE the Rhodian fleet compelled Byzantium to keep open the strategic waters leading to the Black Sea and its vital grain. Rhodes enjoyed such prestige and respect throughout the Greek world that when a major earthquake virtually destroyed the capital about 227 BCE, donations for the repair effort came from virtually all the Hellenistic powers in the Mediterranean.

Rhodes rejected the characteristic pattern of Hellenistic kingship for a benevolent naval aristocracy. The ruling families, who maintained a limited democracy, preserved many features of the old Greek city-states. The island remained virtually free of political or social strife because wealthy families distributed necessities to the needy. Moreover, the city was famous in the Hellenistic period for its schools of philosophy and art. Like Egypt and Pergamum, Rhodes sought the friendship of Rome to check the aggression of the Macedonians and the Seleucids. Yet the Rhodians ultimately alienated the Romans by offering insufficient help against the Macedonians in the Third Macedonian War (171–168 BCE). The Romans then stripped Rhodes of its commercial supremacy by developing the island of Delos as the new center of the eastern Mediterranean transit trade. Although Rhodes remained a prosperous haven of cultural activity, its power was broken and piracy again posed grave threats to ships at sea.

MACEDONIA AND GREECE

CONSOLIDATION: ANTIGONUS GONATAS (277–239 BCE)

Antigonus Acknowledged as King of Macedonia (277 BCE).   Macedonia, birthplace of Alexander, was spared the clash of cultures plaguing the Hellenistic monarchies of Asia and Egypt. Yet the political history of Macedonia was in utter confusion after the death of Alexander as one general after another endeavored to take the throne. Between 294 and 279 BCE Macedonia knew four kings—Demetrius Poliorcetes, Pyrrhus of Epirus, Lysimachus, and Ptolemy Ceraunus—with the first two being driven out, and Lysimachus killed by Seleucus I in battle. The chaos increased with the onslaught from the north of the Celtic Gauls, who had raided Rome a century earlier. Although the Gauls devastated the countryside and killed Ptolemy Ceraunus, a Macedonian deliverer was at hand. This was Antigonus Gonatas, son of Demetrius and grandson of the great Antigonus. After he defeated twenty thousand Gauls near Lysimacheia in 277, he secured control of the kingdom and ten months later was acknowledged as king. Antigonus Gonatas and his descendants—the Antigonid dynasty—ruled Macedonia until the country was conquered by Rome in 168 BCE. Meanwhile some of the Gauls—they were known to the Greeks of Asia as the Galatians—crossed into central Asia Minor and settled upon the uplands of Phrygia, an area that came to be called Galatia, where their descendants perpetuated their language and customs for at least seven centuries. The states of Asia Minor paid the Galatians tribute for more than thirty years after their arrival as the price of security from their devastating raids.

Policies.   Antigonus Gonatas was cautiously persistent, unlike his brilliant but impetuous father Demetrius the Besieger. Thus where Demetrius failed, Antigonus Gonatas eventually triumphed. He gave Macedonia peace and restored the old monarchy after the long disorders of the wars of the Successors. Antigonus Gonatas' practicality is reflected in his response to a poet who hinted at his divinity. According to Plutarch, the king replied that "the man who carries my chamber pot knows better."

Under Antigonus Gonatas and his descendants, Macedonian power rested on the citizen army, unlike the mercenary armies familiar to the Seleucids and the Ptolemies. Macedonia was the smallest and poorest of the three great Hellenistic states, and the Antigonids regarded control of Greece as essential to their security. Thus they kept garrisons at key geographic points—including Corinth, Chalcis on the west coast of Euboea, and Demetrias in Thessaly—described as the Fetters of Greece. In other Greek cities they supported pro-Macedonian governments. Although the Antigonids provoked the traditional Greek passion for freedom and autonomy, they generally respected the self-government of the cities of central Greece and the Peloponnese, while denying them any right to an independent foreign policy.

Intrigues of Ptolemy II to Overthrow the Macedonian Hegemony in Greece.   The Ptolemies, especially Ptolemy II Philadelphus, tried to counter the Antigonid policy in Greece by supporting the Greek desire for independence with gifts of money and grain, though never full-scale military aid. The intrigues of Ptolemy II bore fruit in 278 BCE when the ambitious Spartan king Areus started a revolt in the Peloponnese against Antigonus Gonatas, but the Peloponnesian coalition soon collapsed. Ptolemy then devised an anti-Macedonian scheme with Pyrrhus of Epirus, a king of considerable military talent who had attempted to conquer Macedonia in the 280s and later went to Italy to aid the Greek city of Tarentum (Greek Taras) against the Romans. Pyrrhus was eventually repulsed from Italian soil by Roman superiority, but then he made a new attempt to conquer Macedonia. Although his triumphal victories drove Antigonus Gonatas into eastern Macedonia, Pyrrhus suddenly moved off to the Peloponnese, where he ingloriously lost his life in a street fight at Argos in 272 BCE.

The Chremonidean War (267–262 BCE).   In 267 Ptolemy engineered a more serious threat to Macedonia by provoking Athens and Sparta to rise in the Chremonidean War, named after one of its principal instigators, the Athenian politician Chremonides. The war ended when Athens was starved into surrender in 262, marking its final attempt to regain a measure of the old power and prestige. Compelled to replace its democracy with a pro-Macedonian oligarchy, Athens remained a dependency of Macedonia until 229 BCE.

Naval Victories against Ptolemy II.   Having conquered Athens, Antigonus established a garrison in the Piraeus. Yet Ptolemy II still retained the upper hand in the Aegean, governing the importation of grain to the Greek cities. The Egyptian threat posed a serious challenge to Macedonian authority in Greece. Accordingly, Antigonus mounted a naval war against Ptolemy, enjoying two important victories in the Aegean around 258 and 245 BCE, thereby seriously limiting Egyptian sea power.

MACEDONIAN HEGEMONY CHALLENGED BY THE AETOLIAN AND ACHAEAN LEAGUES

The Aetolian League.   Besides his difficulties with Ptolemy II, Antigonus was plagued by the practice of Greek states combining into leagues to strengthen themselves and resist outside domination. The most effective leagues in the third century BCE were those of Aetolia in the western part of central Greece and of Achaea in the northern Peloponnese. The Aetolian and Achaean leagues emerged as leading players in the Greek resistance to the overlordship of Macedonia. For many centuries the Aetolians remained rugged mountain people divided by tribal feuds and known for brigandage and piracy. They plundered an extended area, reaching as far as the islands of the Ionian and Aegean seas. The Aetolian League came into existence in the early fourth century BCE as a national union of the towns and tribal units in Aetolia, but the confederation played only a minor role in Greek affairs until after the death of Alexander.

Expansionist Policies.   The Aetolian League ultimately adopted a policy of federal expansion and gained control of Delphi in 290 BCE, thus securing a controlling interest in the Amphictionic League organized around the important sanctuary of Apollo at Delphi. In 279, when the Gauls invaded Greece, the Aetolian League sprang into prominence, for the Aetolians practiced guerilla warfare to help repel the invaders, thereby winning new adherents. If persuasion failed, the Aetolians used force, and by the middle of the third century BCE they had overrun all of central Greece except Athens. They also gained control of certain places in the Peloponnese—including Elis, Tegea, and Mantinea—resulting in conflict with the Achaean League. Meanwhile the leaders of the Aetolian League did not curb its members from plundering both enemy and neutral states, a practice giving the confederation a bad name among other Greeks.

Government of the League: Sympoliteia.   Politically, the Aetolian League merged separate cities into a single state, thus creating what is described as *sympoliteia*. The term implies a double citizenship—local and central—and a sharing of political authority between the local and central governments. Thus the individual political communities in a *sympoliteia* retained their own identities and certain rights. This arrangement seemed advantageous to many Greeks who had witnessed large territorial monarchies dwarfing and threatening the old individual cities. The Aetolian League was headed by a general elected for a one-year term by an assembly of federal citizens, the men of military age. The assembly elected the other magistrates of the league and held two regular meetings each year to transact business but could be summoned additionally for special sessions. The federal government also included a council of one thousand deputies, in which the towns of the league were represented in proportion to their population. Apparently the council attended to many governmental concerns between meetings of the assembly. A standing committee of the council, along with the general, conducted day-to-day business of the league and functioned as the executive power.

The Aetolians Dominate the League: Isopoliteia.   The central government maintained full control over foreign policy, warfare, command of the army, and the minting of coinage. Yet each community—often not much more than a fort and its surrounding countryside—retained sufficient autonomy to govern its local affairs. The league incorporated peripheral and distant city-states by offering them *isopoliteia*, an exchange of reciprocal rights without unification and an exchange of potential citizenship for the citizens of each. Potential citizenship became actual only if a recipient took up residence in the city making the grant. Thus the considerable power of the league never passed out of the hands of the Aetolians proper. The organization and its powerful army of ten thousand fighters served as a bulwark against

Macedonian inroads into the Greek peninsula, though the Aetolian League was seldom reluctant to help the Antigonids undermine its arch rival, the Achaean League.

The Achaean League.   The Achaean League was an ancient institution developed by the relatively small and insignificant states along the southern shore of the Gulf of Corinth, communities traditionally hostile to Sparta. Its organization was similar to the Aetolian League, except each city enjoyed full membership upon entering, while still retaining local autonomy. The states of the league met in a council to decide matters such as foreign policy and defense. The chief executive was the general of the army, who served a one-year term and was eligible for reelection every other year.

Aratus of Sicyon.   The Achaean League gained stature in 251 BCE, when the politician Aratus of Sicyon brought his city into the confederation for defense against Macedonia. He soon became the dominant figure of the league. His anti-Macedonian policy won financial support for the confederacy from Ptolemy II, whom he visited personally. From 245 to 213 BCE Aratus was elected general of the confederacy every other year, and his political allies held the office during the alternative years. Aratus' fear of battle often prompted him to mount surprise attacks and ambushes—without a declaration of war—rather than fighting traditional pitched battles. Yet under his command the Achaean League became the dominant Peloponnesian power and expanded to take in Corinth, Arcadia, and eventually the entire northern Peloponnese.

The Spartan Revival: Agis IV and Cleomenes III

Agis IV (c. 244–241 BCE).   Events in Sparta eventually prodded Aratus to abandon his anti-Macedonian policy. Sparta had continued in its usual proud isolation until young Agis IV came to the throne about 244 BCE with dreams of reviving Spartan power through expansion in the Peloponnese. King Agis also sought to restore the ancient constitution of Lycurgus by introducing major social and economic changes, intended to enlarge a citizen body undermined by a few grasping families of extraordinary wealth. Proposing the cancellation of debts and a redistribution of land, the king was eventually put to death by the conservative ephors.

Cleomenes III (c. 235–222 BCE).   The Spartan revolution seemed doomed after the execution of Agis in 241 but was carried through fourteen years later by Cleomenes III, representing the other royal line, who discarded constitutional kingship and seized absolute power. Cleomenes had adopted ideals of social revolution from his wife Agiatis—widow of Agis—and adroitly carried out the program by hiring mercenaries, deposing the ephors, abolishing debts, redistributing land, and admitting four thousand *perioikoi* to full citizenship. Next, aiming at Spartan control of the Peloponnese, Cleomenes won a series of victories over the Achaean League, now faced with the prospect of complete extinction. Meanwhile Aratus, dreading the possibilities posed by the revival of Spartan power, appealed for help from Antigonus Doson, king of Macedonia.

MACEDONIAN HEGEMONY IN GREECE REIMPOSED: ANTIGONUS DOSON (227–221 BCE)

Antigonus Doson served for two years as regent of Macedonia on behalf of the child king, Philip V, but was granted the royal title in 227 BCE. The growth of the two rival leagues—the Aetolian and the Achaean—had rendered Macedonian control of Greece almost a thing of the past, and Antigonus was quite willing to cooperate with the Achaeans against the Spartans. In 224 he invaded the Peloponnese, organizing his allies into a Hellenic League (virtually a reconstituted League of Corinth) under Macedonian presidency. All of the states of the Greek peninsula except Athens, Sparta, some smaller cities, and the Aetolian League became members of the body. In 222 Antigonus defeated Cleomenes at Sellasia, some eight miles north of Sparta, and then entered Sparta, reducing the state to the status of an ally in the new Hellenic League. This was the first capture of the city in its long and defiant history. Clearly, the Macedonians had restored their hold over Greece. Meanwhile Cleomenes bade farewell to his ruined country and sailed off to Egypt, where he eventually committed suicide after failing in a brash attempt to stir up a revolution in Alexandria.

CONFLICTS WITH ROME: PHILIP V (221–179 BCE)

Antigonus Doson had engineered a great Macedonian triumph, but his sudden death in 221 BCE and left the crown to seventeen-year-old Philip V. Although an exceptionally able soldier, Philip was plagued by a volatile temperament and inconsistent policies. At his accession he overcame serious threats to his authority and then turned to challenge the dreadful military machine of the Roman Republic. Originally a small city-state like Athens or Sparta, Rome gradually won supremacy in Italy. In the third century BCE the Romans embarked on their career of conquest beyond Italy, challenging the Carthaginians for control of Sicily and finally emerging victorious in the First Punic War (264–241 BCE). Afterward, repeated pleas from Italian trading communities prompted the Romans to send an expedition across the Adriatic in 229 to eliminate nests of Illyrian pirates. They established a Roman protectorate on a stretch of the Illyrian coast opposite the heel of Italy and pushed their control northward in 219. Philip, humiliated by this incursion into his sphere of influence, entered an anti-Roman alliance with the Carthaginian general Hannibal during the Second Punic War (218–201 BCE). The Romans retaliated by making an alliance with the Aetolian League and declaring war on Macedonia, despite their ongoing struggle with Hannibal on Italian soil. Philip's catastrophic decision to back the Carthaginian general sealed the fate of the Antigonid monarchy. He fought two wars in Greece against Rome and the Aetolian League—the First and Second Macedonian wars (215–205 and 200–197 BCE)—the former bringing important strategic advantage only to Rome and the latter ending with Macedonian defeat. The Romans then confined Philip to Macedonia. His son and successor Perseus (179–167 BCE) provoked Roman hostility by extending Macedonian influence. After the Romans defeated Perseus in the Third Macedonian War (171–168 BCE), they imprisoned him and dismantled his kingdom. The rise of Rome as well as the fall of the Antigonids and other Hellenistic rulers is discussed at length in *Ancient Rome*, the concluding volume of the Harcourt Series on Ancient Civilizations. Needless to say, the states ruled by the Successors of Alexander were beset by such mutual hostility and rivalry that no Hellenistic power could unite them, and the mending of their fragmentation would fall to Rome.

CHAPTER XVIII

HELLENISTIC SOCIETY, RELIGION, PHILOSOPHY, AND SCIENCE

The Hellenistic period is usually regarded as the three-hundred-year span between the death of Alexander in 323 BCE and the beginning of the reign of the first Roman emperor, Augustus, in 31 BCE. Desire for Alexander's sprawling empire drove his Successors to repeated confrontation. Their autocratic descendants, who ruled native populations in vast states, pursued their intense rivalries through frequent warfare. Then, beginning in the late third century BCE, Rome threw a shadow over the entire eastern Mediterranean and gradually annexed the Hellenistic kingdoms one by one.

Admiration for the cultural accomplishments of Classical Greece has blinded many observers—both ancient and modern—to the remarkable creativity of the Hellenistic period. With the horizon of the Greek world stretching eastward to ancient India, Greeks and Macedonians traveled to faraway new homes as soldiers and settlers, thereby accumulating a considerable stock of historical and geographical information. They were generally tolerant in matters of religion, and eastern cults gained a new vitality. Many ordinary Greco-Macedonian men and women embraced emotional religious expressions, while a number of intellectuals turned to philosophy. New philosophical systems—exemplified by Epicureanism and Stoicism—searched for peace of mind and attracted individuals seeking tranquility in a turbulent world. The Hellenistic period is famous also for its triumphs in science, which made a number of modern scientific achievements possible. Meanwhile alien Greek cities planted in the east saw many cultural developments, which were often reserved for the enjoyment of the wealthy few.

SOCIAL AND ECONOMIC TRENDS

HELLENISTIC SOCIETY AND CITIES

A number of the variants influencing Hellenistic socioeconomic patterns were covered in chapters 16 and 17. Political and social life in the old Greek world was dominated by the polis, or city-state, but the Hellenistic age saw powerful absolute monarchies governing huge areas. During the late fourth century BCE thousands of Greeks and Macedonians settled in Asia or Egypt, creating enclaves of Greek language and culture. Scholarship now rejects the old flawed perspective that these Greco-Macedonian invaders and their Near Eastern subjects lived together harmoniously and created a brilliant new mixed culture. Indeed, Hellenistic cities firmly promoted the Greek way of life. Meanwhile tensions often flared between cities and monarchies, between Greeks and non-Greeks, between rich and poor.

Class Conflict and Economic Problems in Greece.   Many cities in Greece proper and the areas around the Aegean were weakened by emigration and made poorer by the shift of trade to Egypt and Asia. Meanwhile economic distress and great extremes of poverty and wealth bred class conflict and threats of social revolution, with the upper class living in constant fear of the lower class. Many members of the latter escaped from penury and social strife by emigrating southward and eastward to join new settlements or enlist in mercenary armies serving Hellenistic kings.

The Upper Classes of the Greek Mainland, the Aegean, and the Coastal Cities of Asia Minor.   The tone for society in the old Greek cities was set by the reasonably affluent men of the citizen class, who dominated the public offices and promoted their conservative and materialistic outlook. Civic loyalty prompted them to contribute money for the presentation of religious festivals, the construction of public buildings, and the furtherance of education. Materially, members of the Hellenistic upper classes were better off in certain respects than their Classical Greek counterparts, enjoying better diets, clothing, and housing. Merchants in Corinth continued to export fine bronze work, and both the island of Delos in the Aegean and the city of Ephesus on the coast of Asia Minor developed into wealthy trading centers. Prosperous Delian merchants of the second century BCE decorated the walls of their houses with striking wall paintings and paved their floors with handsome mosaics.

Slaves.   The number of slaves employed in domestic service and industry had increased appreciably by the Hellenistic period. The use of slaves for power and labor was taken for granted in preindustrial societies, and virtually no Greeks objected to the practice except when fellow Greeks were enslaved. Aristotle was not alone in arguing that slavery was necessary for the running of a democratic polis. Slaves played an essential role as artisans, entertainers, teachers, farmers, and miners. Those working in the mines tended to lead short, dreadful lives, but slaves serving in Greek households—judging from Athenian comedies of the period—frequently gained familiar places in the family setting and lived reasonably comfortable lives. Slaves were admitted to social and religious clubs, and those with special skills or training commanded high wages and were often able to purchase their freedom. Others were freed outright, a practice that had become much more common by the Hellenistic period. As a result of the proliferation of slavery, the wages of free laborers remained at the subsistence level or even lower.

Women.   The lives of women became more agreeable in the Hellenistic period. The royal courts, particularly at Alexandria and Pella, produced a group of ruling-class women who strongly influenced the world around them. Many Hellenistic queens were notable for achieving success in administration and diplomacy, while others were feared for their unscrupulous or even bloodthirsty acts. Native Egyptian

This vase bears a portrait in relief of the powerful, ambitious Ptolemaic queen Arsinoë II pouring a libation. After Arsinoë married her full brother Ptolemy II in the mid-270s BCE, her third marriage, the royal couple strengthened the monarchy by arranging to be worshipped as gods in their lifetimes. Numerous wine jugs decorated with likenesses of Ptolemaic queens, always depicted in Greek dress, were produced for devoted subjects wishing to pour libations in their honor. Faïence jug, c. 280–270 BCE. British Museum, London.

tradition far surpassed Greece in assigning high status to women. Queens of the Macedonian line in Egypt sometimes coruled with their husbands, to say nothing of building temples, founding cities, commanding armies, and encouraging art. Fiery Cleopatra VII—the last of the Ptolemaic monarchs of Egypt—was clearly the dominant figure in her kingdom. Such royal examples must have inspired wealthy women, at least, to reach for new opportunities, and parts of the Greek world saw females attaining a rudimentary education in imitation of the traditional curriculum for males. Women poets began to reappear. Erinna of Telos, an island in the Aegean, lived in the fourth century BCE and gained considerable fame from her verse. The changed status of women in the Hellenistic period must have been linked not only to the role of queens as models but also to the declining political importance of citizenship, polis, and public life, a development blunting the difference between the world of men and women.

New Cities in the East.   The Successors founded countless new cities, some reaching astounding populations. Three of them—Alexandria, Seleucia-on-the-Tigris, and Antioch—approached or even surpassed one-half million inhabitants. The development of city planning was an outstanding contribution of the age. Most new Hellenistic cities—exemplified by Alexandria—were laid out in squares with a rectangular grid of wide straight boulevards. The main streets customarily intersected in the center of the city, thereby creating four quarters, with separate quarters being maintained for Europeans and easterners. People gathered at the agora, the city's marketplace and civic center. In every city of consequence the agora attracted temples, theaters, public baths, and administrative buildings. Some cities enjoyed paved streets and sidewalks, while others ensured a plentiful supply of water by constructing facilities such as aqueducts and underground conduits.

Authoritarian Governments.   Numerous social changes accompanied the establishment of the Hellenistic states. Gone was the exercise of any significant municipal power by the citizens, this hallowed tradition replaced by authoritarian kings ruling through royal decree. The Hellenistic monarchs struggled to attract Greek and Macedonians settlers, regarding them as essential for the development and defense of the state. The old Greek polis served as the ostensible political model for the new Hellenistic cities, with the Greco-Macedonians permitted to retain a council and assembly for the administration of local affairs. Yet a royal governor was often in residence, and the astounding resources and power of the monarchies absolutely dwarfed those of the cities. Although the cities were nominally the allies of the king, in reality the monarch owned all the land surrounding them and subjected the population of each to taxation and conscription. Only an exceptional city-state like Rhodes, secure on its island, could aspire to an independent policy in the Hellenistic period, and even Rhodes was closely linked to the Ptolemies.

Wide Social Distinctions in Asia and Egypt.   Greco-Macedonian society demonstrated a clear hierarchy, particularly in the larger cities, where high officials lived in sumptuous residences and formed a privileged class of immense wealth. Because a truly independent city was rare, the wealthy often turned from the relative insignificance of local politics to focus on social and private life. Their clubs became more important to upper-class men than politics, and their civic concern was channeled into municipal beautification projects. Below this rich few an active professional class grew up, consisting of specialists such as soldiers, merchants, artisans, teachers, physicians, architects, and engineers. Meanwhile the efforts of the laboring class—virtually identical with the subjugated native population—made possible the pleasant lifestyle of the ruling Greeks and Macedonians. The natives formed the bulk of the population and included laborers, small-scale farmers, and slaves. Although the Egyptian priestly elite and royal scribes enjoyed considerable power and influence, Seleucid Asia permitted only a handful of Hellenized upper-class natives to gain even a minor post in the bureaucracy.

EDUCATION IN THE HELLENISTIC EAST

A System Fostering Social Distinctions.   The Greco-Macedonians clung to the Greek way of life in the Hellenistic cities and, to a lesser extent, in the military and rural colonies planted in the Seleucid east. While Athenian law was widely adopted—with modifications for local needs—the educational system was the most important Greek institution transported to the Hellenistic kingdoms. The educational system ensured that the young were immersed in the Greek culture of their forebears. From the age of seven to fourteen the boys—and sometimes the girls—attended privately funded schools, where they learned to read and write, use basic mathematics, and hone their skills in physical training. The young students practiced writing in sentences, some examples of which survive on papyrus fragments, revealing a decidedly antibarbarian and antifeminine content. Those students able to afford the expense then went on to a secondary school from the age of fourteen to eighteen and studied subjects such as Greek literature, geometry, and music theory.

The Gymnasium.   The educational capstone for the sons of the ruling class was the gymnasium. The Hellenistic gymnasium served as an athletic and educational institution for young men, principally those from eighteen to twenty years old. Young men attending a gymnasium were called ephebes (Greek *epheboi*), a term originally applied to boys who had reached the age of puberty but later to men between the ages of eighteen and twenty. In the gymnasium they underwent military training for one or two years and were additionally immersed in Hellenic values. Because the status of ephebe was highly valued socially, fathers made every effort to have their sons enrolled in a prestigious gymnasium. The gymnasium served also as the focus of Greek life and culture, providing a social club for adults as well as an avenue to material success. Thus Greekness was expressed primarily through the gymnasium. While the gymnasium was usually a private institution supported by regular gifts from wealthier citizens, including graduates, some were financially aided by royal endowment.

RELIGION

DEIFICATION OF THE PTOLEMIES AND THE SELEUCIDS

The Greeks, with whom we should now include the Macedonians, did not claim an inherent superiority in matters of religion. Accordingly, Hellenistic kings generally tolerated eastern cults throughout the ancient Near East and allowed freedom of worship. The Successors were all usurpers and sought to legitimatize their dynasties with religious support. Thus each dynasty adopted a special protector-god from among the Olympians: the Antigonids in Macedonia claiming descent from Heracles, the Seleucids from Apollo, and the Ptolemies from Dionysus. Additionally, the Ptolemies and the Seleucids established ruler cults to enhance their power and legitimacy among the Greeks, though the Antigonids in Macedonia shunned the deification of living rulers. The germ of the Greek form of king worship can be found in the hero cults that were bestowed after death on men of outstanding merit or reputation. The principle of king worship was advanced in 324 BCE when Alexander sent messages to the mainland Greeks requesting that they honor him as a god. They bowed to his will, though not without some derision, and thus set a precedent leading to the establishment of state cults of living Hellenistic kings. The Greeks in Egypt and Asia did not regard their monarchs with the same exalted sense of divinity long accorded the Olympians, nor should their worship of living rulers be confused with the traditional Egyptian elevation of each king as an incarnation of the sun-god, a practice continuing in Egypt under Hellenistic rule. Clearly, the complex significance of the ruler-cult is difficult to define, though one certain aspect was the formal recognition of royal power.

CHALLENGES TO TRADITIONAL GREEK RELIGION

The Fondness for Mystery Cults and Religious Associations.   The cities of the Aegean area still celebrated the traditional festivals of the Olympians and the civic cults with great intensity, and settlers and mercenaries coming to Hellenistic kingdoms brought their Greek gods with them. While the Greek cults remained weak on ethical teachings, their rituals were singularly appealing. Many gods in the pantheon served as patrons of cities, and the worship of these deities was backed by a long tradition of local patriotism. Although the state cults offered scant relief from a sense of sin and little promise of a future immortality, the Eleusinian and Orphic mysteries gave expression to doctrines of a new life after death. This was a time when a growing mood of individualism promoted personal fulfillment or personal salvation and posed a challenge to the traditional intense involvement with the civic community. Apparently the longing to fulfill individual needs prompted the formation of private religious associations, which emerged in every Greek community and enjoyed certain similarities with modern fraternal orders. The members of the associations—usually men of the same occupation—selected a patron deity for their protection. Living in a changing and bewildering world, the members looked after the welfare of individual fellow members during times of adversity. Thus the religious associations provided the warm brotherhood of a small group, in contrast to the more impersonal worship of the city deities.

Olympians Undermined by the Eclipse of the Greek Polis.   The Greeks did not forsake their old gods upon encountering powerful eastern deities. At Alexandria citizens took oaths by the Trinity of Zeus, Hera, and Poseidon. Immigrants in Egypt and Asia built temples and elected boards of priests to conduct worship, but they were cut off from their religious roots, resulting in some lessening of the influence of the traditional cults. Clearly, the Olympians had been closely associated with the polis, and the reduced power of the Greek cities helped to weaken ancient religious bonds and loyalties. Worship, now separated from its former settings, tended to sink back into emphasizing the mere forces of nature from which the gods had sprung. Meanwhile a number of Greeks were influenced by the late fourth-century writer Euhemerus of Messene, who wrote a novel of travel that could be interpreted as identifying the

Greek gods as mortals, mere heroes out of the past whose divinity rested simply on honors bestowed after death. Despite this, the cult of Aphrodite remained as important and popular as ever. Hellenistic rulers promoted the goddess, while Hellenistic queens identified with her.

The Impact of Philosophy, Abstract Powers, Magic, and Astrology.   Although many Greeks still fervently supported the established cults and practices, others turned elsewhere for solace or guidance. The intellectually robust took up philosophy, focusing on ethical values that could furnish a rule of life for the uprooted individual. Many others paid homage to the abstract goddess Tyche (identified with the Italian goddess Fortuna), who was thought to dispense both good and bad fortune. Tyche presided over whatever befalls a person or a city and was usually conceived as an independent force or even above the gods. Acting capriciously or blindly, Tyche was generally viewed as mere luck divorced from human effort. The mysterious power was thought to work obscurely, favoring one person or city but casting down another. Like Moira, Tyche was often identified with the inevitability of death. Ancient sources provide abundant evidence that many seekers of assurance were drawn irresistibly to magic or astrology, the latter revived in Babylon under the Seleucids and then coming westward to profoundly influence the European mind. Astrological lore was employed in Greek and Roman practice to determine the fate not only of kingdoms but also of rulers and lesser individuals. Meanwhile peddlers on the streets promised quick results to those who purchased their amulets and books containing magic charms and secret names.

Competition from the Eastern Cults.   Other than ambitious Hellenizers, few Egyptians or Asians adopted Greek religion in lieu of their powerful ancient faiths. Yet the Greek immigrants, geographically divorced from their religious heritage, found the eastern cults appealing. The ecstatic cult of Cybele, the great mother-goddess of Asia Minor, had already gained a foothold in the Greek world before Alexander, but the eastern deities with the most appeal in the Hellenistic period were two from Egypt, Sarapis and Isis.

The Chief Eastern Cults Borrowed by the Greeks

Sarapis.   The cult of Sarapis (usually Serapis in Latin) emerged from a cult at Memphis, where the sacred bull Apis—a living beast—was worshiped. When an Apis died, his mummified body was entombed in a huge sarcophagus alongside those of his predecessors, and a new Apis was chosen. Each Apis was identified after death with the god Osiris, the resurrected king and judge of the dead, and was then worshiped as Osor-Hapi (or Osorapis in Greek), a name formed by combining Osiris and Apis. The early Ptolemies established the worship of Sarapis (a version of the name Osor-Hapi) in Alexandria as a link between Egyptian and Greek religion, though the Egyptians soon reverted from the new syncretized cult to the native worship at Memphis. A temple sacred to Sarapis was known as a Sarapieion (or a Serapeum in Latin), the greatest of which stood in Alexandria, its cult statue taking the form of a huge seated man adorned with precious metals. Serapis was conceived as a combination of the Greek gods Zeus and Asclepius, the latter regarded as a great healer, and the Egyptian god Osiris. Retaining from Osiris an association with the underworld, Sarapis was also a worker of miracles, restorer of the sick, and patron of sailors. He gradually advanced through the Greek, later the Roman, world in the wake of the decline of the Olympians.

Isis. Many Greeks also adopted the goddess Isis, whose cult had enjoyed some prominence among fourth-century Greeks and became even more widespread in the second. Later, in the days of the Roman Empire, the worship of Isis eclipsed that of Sarapis. Isis was popular for her creative, nurturing, and healing roles. In Egyptian mythology she was the wife of Osiris, thereby becoming a power in the underworld. As a mother and a female, Isis was a source of warmth, comfort, protection, and love. Her cult involved a ritual of initiation into a new life on earth, with the devotee promised future happiness after death. Thus Isis' worship enjoyed an appeal similar to that of the Greek mysteries. Later, the worship of Isis rivaled Christianity. Although Christianity emerged victorious from the struggle, Isis strongly influenced the new religion through the figure of Mary.

Fusion of Greek and Eastern Deities. The Greeks, despite the popularity of Sarapis and Isis, were simply unwilling to abandon their traditional religion. Rather than incorporate native deities in their pantheon wholesale, the Greeks fused foreign divinities with their own to create composite figures—exemplified by Hermes Mithras and Zeus Amon—thereby associating the gods of east and west in prayer and religious ceremony.

JUDAISM

Among the Semitic-speaking peoples inhabiting the region of ancient Palestine on the east coast of the Mediterranean were the Jews, who ultimately carried their distinctive religious practices to the east and the west. Most Jews opposed Hellenic civilization on principle. They descended from the ancient Hebrews, discussed at length in *The Ancient Near East,* the first book of this series. The Jews were criticized for their exclusiveness and strict monotheism. Yet Judaism became widespread during the Hellenistic period, chiefly because Jewish immigrants flocked to various cities in the eastern Mediterranean, particularly Alexandria and Antioch, and eventually also to Rome. Meanwhile, beginning in the third century BCE, Jewish scholars working at Alexandria translated the Hebrew Bible into Greek—the version known as the Septuagint (abbreviated LXX)—which was read by Hellenized Jews and became the Old Testament of the Greek-speaking Christians.

From 538 to 332 BCE Palestine was under Persian control. Then Alexander seized Palestine from the Persians, bringing the country under direct Greek influence and thereby offending the monotheistic beliefs of the Jewish population. After Alexander's death, the Jewish territories in Palestine fell first under the control of Ptolemaic Egypt, then Seleucid Asia. When the Seleucid king Antiochus IV sought to impose Greek culture on all his subjects, he ran into stiff resistance from many Jews in Jerusalem, where in 167 BCE he attempted to eliminate the traditional Yahweh cult and enforce the worship of Zeus. Although he was supported by the Jewish aristocracy who had Hellenized, his policies provoked the conservative Jews to revolt under the leadership of the Maccabees. This violent religious and nationalistic uprising against Seleucid rule helped to create a fertile environment in Palestine for the later rise of Christianity.

PHILOSOPHY

The Academy and the Lyceum

While ordinary people in the Hellenistic period turned increasingly toward mystery and eastern cults, the intellectually oriented frequently sought answers in philosophy. Athens remained the center of philosophical study during the Hellenistic age, with the established schools founded by Plato and Aristotle continuing to flourish and enjoy influence. Yet Plato's Academy, under the successive direction of Speusippus and Xenocrates in the fourth century BCE, tended toward a narrow specialization in questions about ethics, and in the third century BCE the reputation of Aristotle's Lyceum also declined.

Cynicism and Skepticism

Cynicism: Proposal to Return to a State of Nature.   Hellenistic people found themselves adrift in a complex and distressful world of great kingdoms and huge cities, with traditional moral sanctions gravely weakened by the eclipse of the city-state and the emigration of many families, the old confidence replaced by a sense of helplessness. Thus the main emphasis in philosophy changed to provide a standard of conduct and a guide for living in a precarious environment marked by uncertainties about existing political and social systems. The ground for Hellenistic philosophy had been prepared by the fourth-century philosophies of Cynicism and Skepticism. Cynicism, as noted in chapter 14, was a school of thought adhering to the principles of Diogenes of Sinope, who taught that tranquility comes from personal virtue, an idea leading the Cynics to propose that humans return to a state of nature. Their way of pursuing the natural life was to demonstrate contempt for standards of religious piety and patriotism by withdrawing from society and discarding all conventions. Diogenes even proposed that the Cynics practice incest and cannibalism. A return to nature, then, meant a denial of all bodily comforts and civilized customs in exchange for the spiritual contentment derived from virtue. Many wandering Cynics clothed themselves in filthy rags, lived without adequate housing, subsisted mainly on bread they obtained by begging, practiced the utmost freedom of speech, and showed a total lack of social conscience by defecating, masturbating, and copulating in public, a deliberate display of shamelessness from which they got the name Cynics, or the Doglike. Declaring that all people are citizens of the world and owe no allegiance to any polis or state, they attacked the materialism of the Hellenistic cities and advocated an arrogant and self-conscious asceticism. Thus Cynicism remained a negative response to the ills of the day, offering no practical alternative to the existing social system. A widespread adoption of the philosophy's principles would have literally destroyed the bonds of society.

Skepticism: Denial of Knowledge.   The Skeptics, representing another negative answer to the social disruptions of the period, denied the possibility of any positive knowledge, for they argued that the human mind is incapable of apprehending reality, if such a thing even exists. Thus they suspended judgement on everything and fell into a self-destructive indifference toward life. Skepticism was formally founded by Pyrrhon of Elis (*c.* 365–275 BCE), who had accompanied Alexander on his expedition to India. There he is said to have encountered some native ascetics, to whose influence tradition ascribes many of his later philosophical views.

EPICUREANISM: A QUEST FOR TRANQUILITY AND FREEDOM

Epicurus.   The two most popular Hellenistic philosophies were Epicureanism and Stoicism, the former founded by Epicurus (*c.* 341–270 BCE), son of an Athenian schoolmaster who had settled on the island of Samos. About 306 Epicurus opened a school of philosophy in Athens, giving lectures in his house and garden. His school is frequently called simply the Garden. His doctrines, preserved relatively unchanged by his disciples for six centuries, were based on ethical precepts and grounded in the renewed interest of the day in natural science. Indicative of the latter, Epicurus revived the principle of Leucippus and Democritus—the Atomists—that the world was created by the movement of atoms, accidently combining as they fall downward through space to form the earth, plants, animals, and humans. Thus Epicurus identified the ultimate causative force in the universe as the random movement of atoms.

Epicurus acknowledged the existence of the gods and advocated honoring them with the traditional rites, but he suggested they live in perfect tranquility in a faraway heaven (conversing in Greek, of course) and did not interfere in human life. Epicurus argued that the human soul, like the body, is composed of atoms. Moreover, the body and soul are dissolved into their component atoms at death, and thereafter these minute entities are rearranged into new combinations. Hence there is absolutely no reason to fear either the gods or death, the dread of the two being the chief obstacle to tranquility and freedom. Epicurus suggested also that humans suffer greatly from religious sanctions that instill fear of punishment after death. He taught that punitive religion, while conveniently employed by governments to control the population, is nothing more than idle superstition. Because death might terminate an individual's existence at any moment, he argued that the sole aim of life should be pleasure. Yet Epicurus, unlike the Cyrenaics, was not advocating transitory sensual indulgence, for he taught that misery comes from overindulgence in drink or sex. Instead, pleasure means freedom from fearing the gods and death, and this tranquility of mind is obtained by withdrawing from worldly concerns in a closed community to study philosophy and to enjoy the companionship of a few friends. Thus the early Epicureans were encouraged to live a balanced life, reducing desires to the simplest minimum. Epicurus' relatively small group of followers—they included slaves and women—were directed to avoid entanglements in politics, a requirement making them extremely unpopular with those regarding citizenship as both a privilege and a duty. Moreover, the Stoics and, later, the Christians repeatedly attacked Epicurean teachings about the gods, the absence of divine providence, and the nature of the world. Ironically, the philosophy was so transformed at a later time by some of its Roman practitioners that the word *Epicurean* became associated with gluttony.

STOICISM: LIVING IN CONFORMITY WITH DIVINE REASON

Zeno and His Followers.   The only Hellenistic philosophy achieving a degree of practical success was Stoicism, which produced some of the most distinguished thinkers of antiquity. Zeno (c. 330–260 BCE), its founder, was a Hellenized Phoenician born on the island of Cyprus, but he settled in Athens as a young man. Influenced by various philosophies, notably Platonism and Cynicism, Zeno developed his own set of ideas, designed to make human lives reflect the order of the cosmos. In 302, lacking means to rent a lecture room, he began teaching in the public building called the Painted Stoa (Stoa Poecile), which gave its name to Stoicism. Here he walked up and down with his disciples expounding ideas covering all three divisions of philosophy formulated in Aristotle's Lyceum—logic, physics, and ethics—though strongly emphasizing ethics. Zeno's followers, Cleanthes of Assos (331–232 BCE) and Chrysippus of Soli (280–207 BCE), clarified and systematized his teachings, the latter bringing Stoic principles to the attention of the public through his prolific writings. The long history of the Stoic school is conveniently divided by scholars into three periods: the Early Stoa (from Zeno to the first half of the second century BCE), the Middle Stoa (second and first centuries BCE), and the Late Stoa (Roman Empire), with various modifications and divergences within each phase.

Divine Reason Permeates and Guides the Cosmos.   Many Stoic principles strike the modern reader as strangely ill defined and contradictory. Essentially, the Stoics based their physical doctrines on Heraclitus' idea that all material substance is derived from fire, while centering their philosophy on moral precepts. Epicurus had accepted the traditional Olympian gods but excluded them from any influence on human affairs. Zeno, on the other hand, postulated that the supreme power of the universe may be regarded variously as Divine Reason, Fiery Breath, Zeus, God, Providence, and the Logos, to mention just a few names employed by the Stoics. This Divine Reason not only governs the cosmos but also permeates the totality of matter, giving life and substance to the universe. Hence everything that is real is material. Even Divine Reason is material, although constituting a different form of matter, one that is constantly moving like breath or a heated air current. The Stoics said Divine Reason is fire. All humans have a spark of Divine Reason—a pure material substance by which they are animated—and hence their aim should be to live in absolute conformity with this guiding Providence. This did not mean, in the mold of the Cynics, practicing extreme asceticism or abandoning the duties and responsibilities of the civilized life. Indeed, Stoicism encouraged public activity, and the philosophy became immensely popular among Roman intellectuals for that very reason.

Universal Brotherhood of All People.   The Stoics argued that because all mortals contain an element of pure divinity, they are essentially kin, a view reflected in their doctrine of the essential brotherhood of all people, a principle strongly opposing distinctions of wealth and birth. Although the Stoics regarded humanity as a community standing in close relation to the divine, they viewed women as inferior to men. Zeno proposed that men abolish the private family and share women and children—a scheme similar to the community of wives described in Plato's *Republic*—but later Stoic thinkers in Roman times urged their adherents to practice monogamy and to rear their own children. Despite their idea of the essential brotherhood of all people, the Stoics lived in an age with no obvious alternative to cheap labor and accepted the practice of slavery, though arguing that even the most downtrodden slaves rule their own souls.

Use of Astrology and Allegorical Interpretations.   Because they regarded the world—endlessly being destroyed and recreated—as the product of ordered Divine Reason, the Stoics left no room for improvement in the cosmos. Hence what exists is good, what happens is divinely ordained. This doctrine, which was favored by Hellenistic and Roman rulers, justifies the existing social and political order. The Stoics believed also that all future events are predictable, for Divine Reason controls the universe through the stars. Accordingly, the Stoics retained practices such as astrology and divination. The Stoics also kept the gods of classical mythology but explained them away through wholesale allegorical interpretations, a trend influencing both Jewish and Christian thinkers to employ the same method to bring their scriptures into harmony with the doctrines they wished to promulgate.

Natural Law.   The Stoics also developed a strong notion of cosmopolitanism, the idea that all individuals are citizens of the same human community, sharing not only a universal brotherhood but also a universal law. The concept of universal or natural law reflects the Stoic belief that Divine Reason pervades everything in the universe with the principle of reason. The continual conformity of matter to this principle is what is meant by natural law, a universally valid but unwritten divine law that the Stoics regarded as superior to human law. Stoic moral philosophy focused on bringing human behavior into harmony with natural law, an idea encouraging many later authoritarian figures and governments, whether sacred or profane. The Stoic concept of natural law strongly influenced the development of Christian theology.

The Practice of Virtue Leads to Stoic Tranquility.   The ultimate aim of the Stoics was to achieve tranquility through the practice of virtue, that is, to live in conformity with Divine Reason. The human will has free choice in this matter, with the wise individual deciding upon virtue. The Stoics argued that those who live virtuously are indifferent to things over which they exercise no control. Hence virtuous individuals are indifferent to earthly passions, and they accept their adversities without complaint. Conditions such as poverty, illness, and death are part of the divine plan and remain immaterial to the virtuous individual, their presence or absence not disturbing Stoic tranquility. Thus virtue rests on two negative goals: submitting without complaint to unavoidable necessity and eliminating all emotions disturbing inner calm, the popular meaning of the term Stoic even to this day. Yet the Stoics did concede that some external circumstances in life are preferable to others—exemplified by wellness over sickness—and thus they permitted suicide during a painful terminal illness or other appropriate circumstance. Clearly, Stoicism was an intellectual creed appealing to a limited but influential segment of society, with ordinary people turning for comfort to the timeless rituals performed in the service of the gods of their forebears.

SCIENCE

The Hellenistic period was the golden age of Greek science, particularly in geography, mathematics, astronomy, medicine, and physics. When Alexander invaded the Persian Empire, he took along an impressive group of scientists. His enthusiasm for scientific discovery was shared by the Ptolemies, who established the Museum in Alexandria and made the city a new Greek center of learning. The Ptolemies were generous patrons of scientific research, supporting the work of about a hundred scientists at the Museum. Other important Hellenistic centers for scientific activity flourished at Pergamum in Asia Minor and Syracuse in Sicily. An enormous stimulus to Greek scientific endeavor was fostered by contact with Mesopotamian and Egyptian scientists. Babylonian astronomical works detailing discoveries made over several centuries were translated into Greek during the third century BCE. Greek scholars also became aware of the achievements of Babylonian and Egyptian mathematicians. Thus Hellenistic science benefited not only from a cross-fertilization of cultures but also, and more significantly, from the resources provided by royal patrons.

Pure Mathematics

Euclid and Archimedes.   Mathematical knowledge was basic to research in astronomy, geography, and physics. The most notable Hellenistic mathematician was Euclid, who lived sometime between 325 and 250 BCE and was possibly one of the scholars taking up residence at Alexandria. Euclid's fame rests on his celebrated thirteen-book textbook of mathematics, the *Elements*, which brought together much that already had been discovered and loosely proved but in a precise and systematic form. The first six books, covering topics in plane geometry, remained the standard textbook in the field for European and North American schools until the early twentieth century. The brilliant Hellenistic inventor and mathematician Archimedes of Syracuse, active in the second half of the third century BCE, developed new methods for measuring the sphere, the cone, and the cylinder, thereby advancing the field now known as solid geometry. Archimedes also established the best solution to the problem of the value of pi until modern times and prepared the way for the seventeenth-century development of integral calculus. Although Hellenistic scientists failed to devise an algebraic notation—their chief deficiency in mathematics—a substantial body of their rules and nomenclature remains standard.

ASTRONOMY

Aristarchus Proposes the Heliocentric Theory.   In the field of applied mathematics the interest of Hellenistic scientists was confined chiefly to astronomy. Aristarchus of Samos, working at the Museum in Alexandria during the first half of the third century BCE, had learned from earlier scientists that the earth turns on its axis, and he declared the revolutionary theory that the sun is some three hundred times larger than the earth. He argued against Aristotle's view that the earth is at the center of the universe. Instead, he proposed the heliocentric theory, that is, the earth and the other planets revolve around the sun, but this notion was so contrary to Greek religious beliefs that the Stoic philosopher Cleanthes called for the prosecution of the astronomer for impiety. Most ancient astronomers also pronounced against the brilliant Aristarchus, and supported the geocentric theory that the sun and planets circle around a stationary earth, for this view seemed more in accord with their observations. Their ability to decide the issue on the basis of observation was limited by the lack of a telescope and other instruments. The heliocentric theory was revived eighteen hundred years later by the great Polish astronomer Copernicus and confirmed by Galileo's use of the telescope.

Hipparchus Discovers the Precession of the Equinoxes.   Another notable Hellenistic astronomer was Hipparchus, who was born at Nicaea in Bithynia and spent most of his life at Rhodes. Active during the latter half of the second century BCE, Hipparchus was the chief proponent of the false geocentric theory, offering a complicated series of epicycles and eccentric circles to explain the apparent movements of the heavenly bodies. Yet he was not only the greatest of the Greek astronomers but also a brilliant mathematician, a genius transforming Greek astronomy from a theoretical to a practical science. His important contributions to astronomy included a remarkably accurate measuring of the length of the solar year and the lunar month, partly basing his work on Babylonian observations. His calculation of the length of the solar year was a mere six minutes and fourteen seconds at variance with the actual figure. Besides carrying out a systematic survey of the night sky, noting about 850 stars, Hipparchus invented several instruments, including a device for taking bearings.

His most famous legacy to astronomy was his discovery of the precession of the equinoxes. The term equinox refers to the two days of the year when the sun is directly above the earth's equator, but astronomers also use the designation to refer to either of two imaginary points where the sun's apparent path crosses the celestial equator (an imaginary line in the sky directly over the equator). The two equinoctial points slowly shift westward, about one degree every seventy years. This gradual movement—known as the precession of the equinoxes—results from a slight change in the direction of the earth's axis of rotation caused by the gravitational pull of the sun and moon. Hipparchus learned from observations taken by an earlier Greek astronomer (Timocharis) that a star in the constellation of Virgo had changed its position about two degrees from the autumn equinoctial point in the intervening period of approximately 160 years, thereby discovering the phenomenon of the precession of the equinoxes. Hipparchus even proposed a scheme for determining longitude by joint observation of a lunar eclipse throughout the Mediterranean area, but the idea was ruled out by the wars of his day.

Ptolemy.   The last great astronomer of Alexandria, Ptolemy worked in the second century CE to synthesize much of the Hellenistic work in astronomy. Ptolemy pronounced in favor of the geocentric theory, and his great treatise—usually called the *Almagest* from the name of its Arabic translation—was used for centuries as a standard textbook by Arab scholars. Through them the work passed into the west in the form of a fifteenth-century Latin translation. Although its geocentric view was discredited by the heliocentric system of Copernicus, many principles of the book still serve as the starting point for astronomical research.

Geography

Eratosthenes Maps the Known World and Computes the Circumference of the Earth. Western knowledge of geography greatly advanced with the campaigns of Alexander, and the Hellenistic Greeks notably contributed to the field by employing mathematics to calculate the size of the earth. The foremost name and pioneer in mathematical geography, Eratosthenes of Cyrene, accepted the invitation of Ptolemy III to become the head of the Alexandrian Library in the second half of the third century BCE. His scholarly output was prodigious, with treatises on mathematics, astronomy, music, philosophy, history, and literary criticism, though his greatest contributions were in geography. His detailed map of the world was the first based on a grid of meridians of longitude and parallels of latitude. Eratosthenes suggested that ships could reach India by sailing west across the Atlantic, and he concluded from the similarity of the tides in the Atlantic and Indian oceans that one could sail from Spain around Africa to India.

Eratosthenes' most celebrated achievement was his computation of the circumference of the earth. The sphericity of the earth had been enunciated in the fifth century BCE, but the estimation of its size remained mere guesswork. Eratosthenes discovered that when the sun was directly overhead at the city of Syene (modern Aswan) in Egypt, and thus produced no shadow there, it cast a $7\frac{1}{5}$ degree angle of shadow at Alexandria to the north. This was $\frac{1}{50}$ of a circle ($360 \div 7\frac{1}{5} = 50$), so the distance between the cities was $\frac{1}{50}$ of the earth's circumference. Using an estimate of 5,000 stades as the distance between the two cities, Eratosthenes then com-

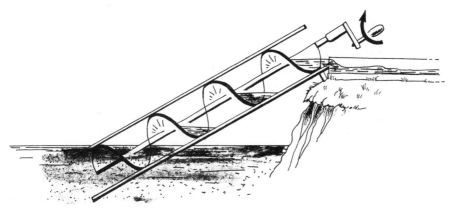

The third-century-BCE mathematician and technical genius Archimedes of Syracuse is credited with inventing the useful Archimedes' screw. A mechanical device for raising a continuous flow of water, it is said to have been first employed to irrigate fields in Egypt.

puted the earth's circumference as approximately 250,000 stades (5,000 × 50 = 250,000), which is thought to represent 24,662 miles, a figure only about 200 miles in error.

Physics

Archimedes' War Machines.   The Hellenistic period witnessed a wide gap between theoretical and applied science, between sublime intellectual achievement and technological development, for this was an age of slavery and cheap labor, with useful machinery often insufficiently appreciated. Yet some progress was realized, particularly in applying the principles of mechanics to military purposes. Archimedes, the celebrated mathematical genius from the Sicilian Greek city of Syracuse, invented a number of machines to frustrate the Romans in their seige of Syracuse in 213–212 BCE, but stories about the devices betray considerable embellishment. Fanciful accounts tell us that his catapults hurled rocks of sufficient size to sink the Romans' ships or leave their battle lines in disarray. We hear that Archimedes also invented a system of concave mirrors that concentrated the sun's rays with sufficient intensity on a very small spot to ignite Roman ships before they could enter the harbor. His grappling devices are said to have terrified the Romans by lifting their warships out of the water by the bow and dropping them back stern first. Popular history relates that the Roman capture of Syracuse was delayed for many months because the city-state was defended so well with Archimedes' astonishing war machines. When the enemy finally captured the city, Archimedes was struck down by a Roman soldier, reportedly after shouting at the man not to disturb the mathematical diagrams he had drawn in the sand.

The Archimedes' Screw.   In a more peaceful vein, Archimedes created a number of mechanical devices. We hear that he invented the screw for raising water, essentially a spiral pipe wound around a shaft and inclined at an angle of about forty-five degrees to the horizontal. If the lower end of the pipe is dipped in water, rotation will cause the liquid to rise in the pipe and overflow through the higher end. Archimedes is said to have fashioned the invaluable screw during a brief stay in Alexandria as a means of raising water from the Nile to irrigate fields. He is credited also with making an early orrery, a device for mechanically representing the motions of the sun, moon, and planets.

Archimedes' Principle.   Archimedes wrote the first scientific works on hydrostatics and statics. In hydrostatics—the branch of physics studying the properties of weights in standing fluids—he discovered the physical law of buoyancy that came to be called Archimedes' principle: a body immersed in fluid loses weight equal to the weight of the fluid displaced. Moreover, the volume of displaced fluid is equal to the volume of a body fully immersed in the fluid. We hear that his discovery was made after King Hieron II of Syracuse asked him to determine if a certain metal-smith had used adulterated gold in making a wreath commissioned for the dedication to a god. A famous story of questionable authenticity relates that Archimedes pondered the problem as he prepared to enter a bath at the gymnasium. Upon seeing the water overflow as he settled down, he suddenly realized that he could measure the volume of an irregular object such as the wreath by putting it into a vessel of water and then measuring the amount of displaced fluid. Delighted with his discovery, he ran naked through the streets of Syracuse shouting the famous "Eureka! Eureka!"—"I have found it! I have found it!" After a period of experimentation—this part of the story is probably true—he was able to demonstrate that the smith was honest.

Archimedes Invents the Compound Pulley.   In the field of statics, which deals with the relations of material bodies in equilibrium, Archimedes precisely formulated the principles of the pulley and the lever. Among his memorable inventions was the compound pulley. Plutarch relates the tradition that Archimedes, showing little effort, drew a fully laden ship toward himself by using the device. Although Archimedes was the most celebrated technical genius of antiquity, he considered his inventions trifling and preferred to devote his time to pure scientific research. Yet he demonstrated his faith in the unlimited power of science by boasting that he could move the earth if he had a lever of sufficient length and a firm place to stand. Finally, Archimedes was the greatest mathematician of antiquity, making monumental advances in solid geometry and preparing the way for integral calculus. Of his written effort, nine treatises survive in Greek and two others in late Arabic translation.

Ctesibius and Hero Create Various Mechanical Devices.   Although a world with an abundance of laborers did not encourage momentous inventions, the Hellenistic period witnessed the greatest proliferation of mechanical novelties in antiquity. Archimedes' ingenious contemporary Ctesibius, the son of a barber in Alexandria, was the first to invent devices depending on pneumatics—the action of air under pressure—fashioning not only an air gun but also a pump with a plunger and valve. He also created a water organ with a keyboard and the first accurate water clock, a

Hero of Alexandria designed a rudimentary steam engine in the first
century CE, with steam from a lower container of boiling water piped into a
hollow sphere that permitted release only through two bent nozzles on its
opposite sides, the thrust of the escaping steam making the sphere rotate.
Steam was not harnessed as a practical source of power until the Scottish
engineer and inventor James Watt introduced a dependable steam engine
in the eighteenth century.

great improvement over the sundial, which was worthless at night and on cloudy
days. Hero of Alexandria, who flourished in the first century CE, made a rudimentary steam engine, with steam from a cauldron of boiling water being piped into a

hollow ball and then escaping through two bent nozzles placed opposite each other, thereby forcing the ball to rotate. The device was a mere toy producing a rotary, not a reciprocating, motion. The effective use of steam as a form of power would not be developed until the invention of a dependable reciprocating engine by James Watt in the eighteenth century.

Medicine and Botany

Herophilus Breaks New Ground in Anatomy and Physiology.   The Hellenistic world was plagued with its share of quacks and greedy medical practitioners. Yet countless physicians earned gratitude by providing free treatment to the poor on a regular basis. The art of medicine continued to be associated with the Aegean island of Cos, where Hippocrates had labored to foster sound medical training in the fifth century BCE. Great medical strides occurred during the Hellenistic period, the work of Herophilus of Chalcedon being particularly noteworthy. Active in the early third century BCE, Herophilus was the greatest of the several anatomists working in Alexandria at the time. He relied upon systematic dissection of the dead and even extended this practice to the living, that is, vivisection, to advance knowledge about anatomy and physiology. The unfortunate subjects in the experiments were criminals delivered from prison by royal order. Performed for the first time in history, vivisections were regarded as a necessary cruelty that benefited many by making surgery safer. Herophilus and his circle also invented new surgical instruments and techniques. He solved the puzzle concerning the function of the brain, declaring—notwithstanding Aristotle's view—that the gray matter in the skull was the seat of intelligence. Herophilus made a detailed description of the brain, from which he traced the nervous system. Moreover, he discovered that observing the pulse rate is a useful tool in the diagnosis of illness.

Erasistratus Advances the Understanding of Physiology.   Erasistratus of Ceos, who lived in Alexandria about the middle of the third century BCE, followed the Hippocratic tradition of encouraging the body to heal itself by means of diet and air without the heavy use of drugs. Erasistratus was particularly productive in anatomical research. He discovered through dissections and vivisections that the heart is a pump, though mistakenly suggesting that the organ forced air—not blood—to every part of the body. Erasistratus' anatomical studies led him to distinguish between motor and sensory nerves, and he made important discoveries about digestion. Although he was the first to reject Hippocrates' humoral theory of disease and to condemn excessive bloodletting as a method of treatment, both of these were revived, unfortunately, by Galen in the second century CE.

Theophrastus Conducts Research in Botany.   The scientific study of botany originated in the Hellenistic period. The Greek philosopher Theophrastus, born at Eresus on the island of Lesbos but active in Athens, succeeded his teacher Aristotle as head of the Lyceum in the late fourth century BCE, maintaining the school's broad range of research. Much admired in antiquity, Theophrastus studied the botanical information made available by Alexander's campaigns in the East. Theophrastus did for botany what Aristotle had done for zoology by applying his teacher's methods to the study of plants. His two treatises, *History of Plants* and *Causes of Plants*, contain classifications and descriptions of approximately five hundred different species of botanical life. Theophrastus described in a rudimentary way the process of germination, and he understood the importance of climate and soil to plants. An empirical researcher rather than merely a speculative philosopher, Theophrastus produced an abundance of writings—most are lost—embracing virtually all branches of human knowledge. His *On Stones*, for example, remained the best systematic treatment of minerals until modern times. His interest in human behavior is reflected in his best-known surviving work, *Characters*, a collection of thirty razor-sharp sketches of eccentric or abnormal personality types.

CHAPTER XIX

HELLENISTIC LITERATURE AND ART

Scholars regard the third century BCE, before Rome began absorbing the eastern Mediterranean world piecemeal, as the golden age of Hellenistic literature and art. This was a time of profound learning, exemplified by the success of the remarkable scholars of Alexandria in analyzing and transmitting classical texts. Hellenistic literature and art generally reflected the great variety of tastes prevalent at the time, leading to striking cultural innovations, though many literary figures and artists who clung tenaciously to the Classical Greek tradition produced much that remains worthy of attention.

LITERATURE

THE READING PUBLIC

Literary lights of the period enjoyed wide acclaim. Hellenistic monarchs, particularly the Ptolemies, tapped their huge resources to endow literature and scholarship on an unprecedented scale. The Museum of Alexandria, the greatest of the ancient academies of learning, was established early in the third century BCE as a place of study and dwelling for scholars of literature and science, all of whom were chosen and endowed by the king. The Museum propelled Alexandria into the forefront of intellectual endeavor, even rivaling Athens for scholarly primacy. More men and women could read and write than at any earlier time, and the bulk of Hellenistic literature was intended for the general public. The demand for reading matter was great. Papyrus, produced under the royal direction of the Ptolemies, was plentiful for the manufacture of manuscript rolls, generally written in the new common form of Greek called *koine* (a modification of Attic, the dialect of Athens).

A number of schools—endowed by private benefactors—were established in the Hellenistic period. Provision was made for the education of girls. Women had enjoyed a limited emancipation after the Macedonian conquest, and a few even went on to advanced studies in the philosophical schools. Greek law still prohibited women from representing themselves in court, and although a widespread attitude characterized them as inept, this position was effectively challenged by the vigor of Ptolemaic and Seleucid queens and princesses. Men of letters began to take female readers into consideration, and a number of women writers emerged, occasionally achieving a measure of local fame from their compositions.

Literary Scholarship Advanced at the Alexandrian Library

The Hellenistic period was notable not only for the production of books but also for the building of libraries. The Library at Alexandria, generously endowed by Ptolemy II Philadelphus, eventually acquired a collection of nearly five hundred thousand manuscript rolls, the largest in antiquity. The intellectual endeavors of the librarians and literary specialists associated with them evolved into what is now called literary scholarship. These Greek scholars showed little interest in the literary achievements of the subjugated easterners, but they established authoritative texts of all the Greek authors at Alexandria, with more than one copy of any classic generally available for comparison. Zenodotus of Ephesus, the first librarian, produced a trustworthy text of Homer based on the best manuscripts and may have divided the *Iliad* and *Odyssey* into twenty-four books each—standard ever since—in place of continuous manuscript rolls. The technique of textual criticism was further developed by a number of his successors, exemplified by Aristarchus of Samothrace (215–145 BCE), who prepared a final and authoritative edition of the ever-popular Homer. The value of the great Library was enhanced considerably when the scholar-poet Callimachus of Cyrene (c. 305–240 BCE) compiled a 120-volume catalogue of the holdings, including a brief biography of each author.

Alexandrian Poetry

Alexandria served as the cultural center of the Greek world following the death of Alexander. The composition of Hellenistic verse was closely associated with the great city, thus the terms *Alexandrian poetry* and *Alexandrian poets*. The relative seclusion in which poet-scholars lived at the Museum had a restraining effect on their poetry, which was highly polished but lacked the soaring quality of an earlier day. With the gradual disappearance of the old noble families claiming to trace their ancestries back to traditional heroes, epic poetry based on ancient legends suffered some decline in popularity. Of the traditional styles of poetry—discussed in chapter 7—the Alexandrians favored the lyric form of Alcaeus and Sappho, for poets still sang of personal feelings, reinforced by musical accompaniment, about subjects such as men pursuing their favorite boys and individuals enjoying the pleasures of wine and food. The symposium, or drinking party, continued to flourish and provide an ideal setting for the lyric poetry of the day. Besides composing lyric verse, the Alexandrians experimented with a wide variety of novel meters. One of the new forms of poetry was the pastoral, combining the stylized with the spontaneous. Pastoral poems portray shepherds and cowherds singing the praises of love and friendship, often in subtle language and complicated meter.

Theocritus.   The father of pastoral poetry and the greatest poet of the Hellenistic period was Theocritus (c. 315–250 BCE), who was born in Sicily, lived for a while in Alexandria, and then settled on the island of Cos. His poems expressed a city dweller's delight with country life, extolling hills and streams, boughs of wild olives, songs of birds, and trees bearing apples and pears. The rustic simplicity of his verse appealed to the sophisticated urban readers of his day and influenced the Latin pastorals of Vergil two centuries later.

Callimachus.   One of Theocritus' rivals was the poet-scholar Callimachus, mentioned above, who was born late in the fourth century BCE at Cyrene on the North African coast. After studying in Athens, he lived at Alexandria and was appointed to a position in the Library. A prolific writer, Callimachus is credited with some eight hundred works on various subjects, all lost except some of his poems, a handful of hymns, and fewer than seventy epigrams. Callimachus opposed the epic form of poetry and often stated his preference for shorter compositions. Through his pen the terse epigram emerged as a literary genre and became very popular. Originally epigrams were nothing more than inscriptions on monuments or temple, but over time the form developed into very brief poems suggesting inscriptions through their precision and economy of language. Callimachus' epigrams, composed in clear and fluent language, reveal his passion for the love of boys and his fondness for wine. Witty and scholarly, Callimachus was the most admired poet of the Hellenistic period. His *Hymns,* which were composed for royal occasions, follow the example of the so-called *Homeric Hymns* in narrating episodes of the gods, but they seem devoid of religious fervor or emotion. His best-known work, now lost, was the *Aetia (Origins),* a four-book collection of elegies explaining the origins in myth or history of cults, festivals, customs, and names throughout the Greek world.

Apollonius Rhodius.   Ancient sources allege, probably falsely, that Callimachus became involved in a bitter literary dispute concerning poetic questions with his former pupil and intimate, Apollonius Rhodius (*c.* 295–215 BCE), head of the Library. Although apparently born at Alexandria, Apollonius is usually known by the surname Rhodius (Rhodian), referring to the Greek island city where he spent a period of his life. Apollonius is best known for his lengthy *Argonautica,* the only epic preserved from the Hellenistic age. The *Argonautica* tells the legend of Jason and the Argonauts in their quest for the Golden Fleece, the fleece of pure gold held by the king of Colchis. Apollonius excels in describing the romantic involvement of Jason and Medea, the daughter of the king. Several passages of verbal beauty present a sympathetic portrait of Medea, who retains magical powers but stands in sharp contrast to the violent creature in Euripides' tragedy. Apollonius was the first poet to use the power of romantic love as the central theme of an entire epic. His brilliant literary achievement enjoyed great popularity in later antiquity.

NEW COMEDY

Menander.   Drama was widely appreciated in Hellenistic cities, with actors traveling from place to place restaging the great plays of the fifth century BCE. Although new tragedies were still performed, they were of scant consequence and have completely disappeared. Yet comedy enjoyed a resurgence at Athens, where New Comedy developed in the late fourth century BCE. In New Comedy the chorus was reduced to performing interludes of dance and music between the usual five acts of

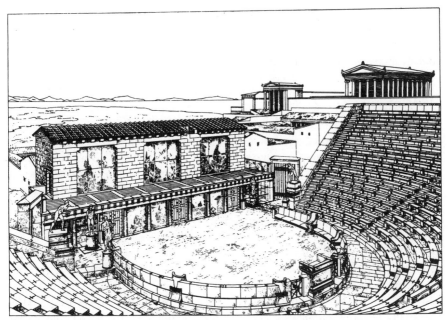

Stone theaters became a customary feature of Hellenistic cities. Illustrated here is a reconstruction of the Hellenistic theater erected at the small Greek coastal city of Priene in western Asia Minor. The design of theaters had changed noticeably since the Classical period, with the stage building (*skene*) given a handsome architectural form and moved forward, thereby cutting off part of the circular space formerly allotted to the orchestra, making it semicircular. Before the Hellenistic period, actors performed at orchestra level. The Hellenistic stage was raised above the orchestra, as in the modern theater, thereby curtailing contact between the actors on stage and the chorus, a reflection of the reduced importance of the latter. The new stage building employed large panels painted with scenery for both the stage front and the stage wall behind.

the play. Bawdy references to sex and elimination became rare, while the phallus was stripped from the costume of male characters. New Comedy adapted to changed conditions by transferring attention from politics to the private and family life of fictional individuals, and the genre was escapist to the extent that plays were constructed with happy endings. The leading writer of New Comedy was the Athenian Menander (*c.* 343–291 BCE), who skillfully reproduced stock characters—their typical masks made them easily identifiable—including the bullying father, the wealthy youth, the wronged heroine, the sly slave, the greedy parasite, the not-so-bad courtesan, the mercenary soldier, and the young lover. Many of his plots feature situations that are firmly rooted in comic tradition, exemplified by a long-lost child or a kidnapped daughter, with separated families finally reunited at the end after a dramatic recognition scene. Such plots would seem farfetched today, but were based on all-too-common practices in the ancient world. Ancient sources mention the exposure of infants, who were often reared as foundlings, and the abduction of uppercrust young men or women by pirates to sell them as slaves. Menander typically portrays his characters as credible and sympathetic individuals. His plays, often turning on an irregular love affair with a happy ending, excel in presenting the problems arising in personal relationships from ignorance and misunderstanding. His brilliant comedy influenced later writers in Latin, particularly Plautus and Terence.

HISTORY

Nearchus, Ptolemy, Aristobulus, and Callisthenes.   Hellenistic writers produced an enormous number of prose works—mostly lost or preserved only in fragments—on history, biography, geography, oratory, rhetoric, and other fields. Many individuals accompanying Alexander on his conquest of the Persian Empire wrote accounts of the conqueror's reign, though no one should expect such official histories to have been impartial or free of propagandist aims. All narratives by actual participants are now lost, known only through scattered quotations by later writers. Nearchus of Crete penned an account of his own voyage down the Indus and through the Indian Ocean to the Persian Gulf for a rendezvous with Alexander's army, blending exaggeration with sober fact. The Macedonian Ptolemy (the future king of Egypt) and the Greek Aristobulus (an engineer in the army) wrote influential, generally reliable histories, though both were inclined to eulogize Alexander and his army. Callisthenes of Olynthus, nephew of Aristotle, was the official historian in Alexander's campaign against the Persian Empire. His *Deeds of Alexander,* covering events at least to 330, must have included a great amount of sound material but was marred by incredible flattery and romantic exaggeration. The narrative influenced a number of later historians to adopt the conqueror's exalted image of himself. Yet Callisthenes opposed the abortive attempt of Alexander to persuade his Greco-Macedonian followers to adopt the custom of *proskynesis,* the Greek term for the homage performed before the Persian king by his subjects, and the historian was soon implicated in the Pages' Conspiracy and summarily put to death.

Cleitarchus and Arrian.   Another early historian, though probably not a member of the expedition, was the shadowy Cleitarchus of Alexandria. Cleitarchus penned an influential, less eulogistic history of Alexander that seems to have been based on firsthand reports. Although ancient critics rightly accused him of overlaying facts with wild legends and other deliberate distortions, he also included much reliable information. Of more importance, Cleitarchus was widely read, particularly in the Roman period, and his rather unflattering portrayal of Alexander's campaign was the source of the important "vulgate tradition" (large segments of the works of the later Greek historian Diodorus Siculus and the Roman historian Curtius Rufus). This *common* tradition supplements and sometimes corrects the respected Greek historian Arrian.

Ptolemy, Aristobulus, and Nearchus, mentioned above, served as the major sources for Arrian, a native of Bithynia in Asia Minor, who was employed as a Roman administrator in the Near East. In the second century CE Arrian wrote a thorough account in Greek of the conqueror's career, the *Anabasis of Alexander,* celebrated for the clarity of its prose. Most scholars regard the *Anabasis* as the most reliable surviving source for Alexander's reign. Disputes in Alexander scholarship stem principally from the inconsistencies between the "vulgate tradition" and what we may term the "court tradition" of Arrian.

Manetho and Berossus.   Increased geographical knowledge in the wake of Alexander's expedition reawakened interest in the history of the world abroad. In the third century BCE the Egyptian priest Manetho—discussed in the first book of this series—and the Babylonian scholar Berossus compiled histories of their countries for a curious Greek public, often intertwining fact and fiction.

Timaeus and Hieronymus.   The rich historical output of the Hellenistic period was also represented by competent Greek historians such as Timaeus of Tauromenium in Sicily, who wrote a monumental study of the western Greeks, and Hieronymus of Cardia in Thrace, who described the conflicts of the Successors and the establishment of the early Hellenistic kingdoms (his work was excerpted almost verbatim in the mammoth world history of Diodorus Siculus in the late first century BCE). The most celebrated Hellenistic Greek historians, Polybius of Megalopolis in Arcadia, narrated the history of the period that left Rome ruler of the Mediterranean world.

Polybius.   By general consent, Polybius of Megalopolis (c. 200–118 BCE) ranks as one of the greatest Greek historians of all times, bearing comparison with Herodotus and Thucydides. Polybius was a wealthy Arcadian aristocrat who played a leading role the Achaean League. After Rome crushed Macedonia at the battle of Pydna in 168, Polybius and one thousand other prominent Achaean citizens were deported to Italy and detained in various towns without trial. Yet Polybius was permitted to remain in Rome as a houseguest of the powerful Scipio family, thereby gaining admission to prestigious social and literary circles. He soon became a great admirer of Roman character and suggested that the Romans could bring a lasting peace to the Mediterranean world. The historian joined the Roman general Scipio Aemilianus, to whom he had become friend and adviser, in his campaign against Carthage on the coast of North Africa and was present at the destruction of the ancient city in 146 BCE, the concluding horror of the Punic Wars. The same year Polybius witnessed the razing of Corinth and the dissolution of the Achaean League for a rebellion against Rome, a clear demonstration the Romans would brook no opposition from Greece. He then helped to organize Macedonia as a Roman province.

Subsequently, Polybius wrote his forty-book *Histories*—we have the first five books intact and substantial fragments from much of the rest—to explain to the Greeks the rapid rise of Rome to supremacy in the Mediterranean world. Calling upon his immense knowledge of geography and warfare, Polybius originally envisioned detailing the history of Rome's expansion during a fifty-year period down to 168 (the ending of the Macedonian monarchy with the defeat at Pydna), but he revised the work to show how the Romans exercised their supremacy and extended the narrative to 146 (the destruction of Corinth and the reduction of Macedonia to a Roman province). Despite his excessive admiration of Rome and other flaws, scholars regard the narrative as essentially accurate and reliable. Polybius methodically analyzes the historical implications of bringing the western and eastern parts of the Mediterranean together under Roman rule. When no rational cause for an event can be identified, he invokes the hand of the supernatural agent Tyche, dispenser of both good and bad fortune. He attributes the success of Rome to its highly disciplined army and unique constitution, finding in the latter an admirable mixture of three elements: monarchy (the consuls), aristocracy (the Senate), and democracy (the popular assemblies). This theoretical model ignores the subtleties of Roman politics and the dominant role of the Roman nobility. While Polybius sees stability and harmony springing from the Roman use of a mixed constitution, he suggests the Greek willingness to change constitutions frequently has resulted in perpetual discord.

MUSIC

Poetry and music remained closely linked in the Hellenistic period, for verse was not intended for private reading but for occasions of musical performance. Enriching the fabric of life at all social levels, music was regarded as divine in origin and was central not only to public religious observance but also to other celebrations such as weddings and funerals. Uncertainties remain about the sound of Hellenistic music because too few musically annotated texts survive to reconstruct the musical settings employed by poets and dramatists. Invariably, choral singing was in unison or octaves. We know that music was an essential subject in Greek schools, and various musical instruments, especially the lyre, kithara, and aulos, appear frequently on vase paintings. Ancient sources tell us that soldiers marched to battle accompanied by song. Social events included appropriate songs such as joyful songs to celebrate childbirth, lamentations to express sorrow at death, work songs to lighten all manner of tasks, hymns to honor deities, and drinking songs to enliven symposiums. Although professional entertainers might render elaborate ballads at a symposium, the guests themselves enjoyed singing the *skolion*, or drinking song, which they performed after dinner as the cup was passed among them for toasts and libations to the gods. The word *skolion* (zigzag) refers to the custom of passing the cup and lyre back and forth to crisscross the men's dining room as each of the reclining guests sang in turn. Every guest was expected to have mastered an appropriate stock of songs, one example of which—discovered on a first-century BCE tombstone at Tralles in southwest Asia Minor—expresses a universal theme: "Oh laugh while you may,/ Keep toil and trouble at bay,/ For life is short and in its day,/ The night of death soon takes you away."

ART

The Hellenistic period witnessed a vibrant and complex artistic tradition of extraordinary variety. While Athens remained significantly creative, the focus of artistic innovation and patronage shifted to great capital cities like Alexandria and Pergamum. Meanwhile the sources of patronage changed from city-states and private citizens to Hellenistic monarchs commissioning public buildings and wealthy merchants embellishing their houses. Many individuals now regarded religion as intensely personal and sought direct and often ecstatic communication with eastern deities such as Isis or Cybele. Thus the traditional ideals of civic pride and civic religious devotion—the two great anchors of sublime Classical art—surrendered to the personal tastes and propaganda of the new ruling classes. With the eclipse of the Greek city-states and the decline of Greek religion, in other words, art lost its old primary role of fostering patriotic or religious inspiration. The combination of these various developments produced a far-reaching abandonment of restraint and a secularization of art, much of which was now intended to overwhelm, amuse, or even titillate the viewer. Despite the many innovations in architecture, sculpture, and painting, however, a number of Hellenistic artists continued to preserve the tradition of restraint that was so prized in the Classical period.

Town Planning

Hippodamian Planning.   In terms of architecture, the riches of the eastern kingdoms contrasted with the relative poverty of the Greek city-states. The new royal capitals and princely cities required planning on a monumental scale. Hellenistic kings, particularly the Seleucids, founded new cities in the Greek style to reassure the transplanted inhabitants that the Greek way of life was being preserved. When Hippodamus of Miletus, active in the mid-fifth century BCE, assumed responsibility for planning the port city of Piraeus for the Athenians and probably also for the Athenian-sponsored colony of Thurii in southern Italy, he employed a grid system with parallel streets intersecting at right angles. Although this rectangular system of town planning bears his name—Hippodamian planning—the method predates him in both Ionia and the Greek west. Yet Hippodamus apparently elaborated and refined the system, which offered an excellent pattern for Hellenistic cities. Accordingly, streets in new Hellenistic cities were laid out in a grid plan, after sites had been carefully chosen for the agora, theater, stadium, gymnasium, palaces, baths, and temples. On three sides of the agora stood long stoas. Varying in form from unpretentious to elaborate, a Greek stoa consisted essentially of a back wall from which a roof sloped to a colonnade along the front. Frequently a row of shops and offices opened up along the back wall, sometimes designed with two stories. Stoas provided people with shade and shelter when participating in the various activities of the agora.

Priene.   A classic example of Hellenistic public planning for a small city is offered by Priene in western Asia Minor. The Prienians moved to a more advantageous location in the fourth century BCE, choosing to build beneath a precipitous spur of Mount Mycale near the ancient mouth of the river Maeander. This site was opposite Miletus, home of Hippodamus. The new foundation was laid out in the late fourth century and built up in the third, with important second-century improvements. The site

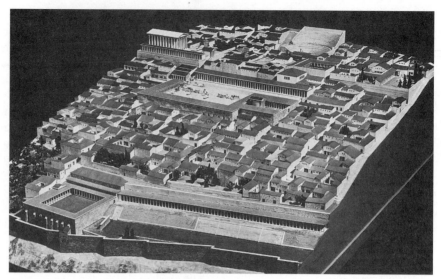

A remarkable application of Hippodamian planning took place at the compact city of Priene in western Asia Minor. The fourth-century Prienans moved their city to a more advantageous location beneath a high cliff near the mouth of the river Maeander (modern Menderes), imposing a grid plan on the difficult, steeply sloping terrain. The new city, laid out in the late fourth century, was developed appreciably in the third and provided with important improvements in the second. This model of Priene shows not only the grid plan but also the customary elements of a Greek city: agora (center), theater, main temple, gymnasium and stadium complex, other civic and religious buildings, and unpretentious dwellings. Staatliche Museen, Berlin.

has been beautifully excavated and the plan of its compact central area fully recovered, showing that a perfect Hippodamian plan was imposed on the irregular terrain of the steeply sloping hillside. From the neat grid of narrow streets—reduced in some places to flights of steps—the inhabitants gained a spectacular view of the land and sea. The public buildings were of solid marble, and the marble fortification walls enjoyed sufficient strength to withstand repeated assaults from siege engines. The terrain allowed water to be piped to a reservoir and then distributed to the public fountains of the city. The centrally located agora was enclosed on three sides with stoas, while its north side bordered a main avenue and served as a showcase for impressive civic buildings. The Ionic temple of the patron goddess of the city, Athena, and the theater were set higher on the city's steep slope, while the lower edge of the settlement was dominated by the gymnasium and stadium complex. The gymnasium contained lavatories and a lecture room, the latter's walls still bearing graffiti conveying the names of Hellenistic students. The acropolis was formed by the massive Prienian spur, soaring twelve hundred feet above the harbor and approached by a dizzying flight of steps cut into the naked rock.

Pergamum.   The wealthy city of Pergamum enjoyed a position of great strategic importance on the northwest coast of Asia Minor and became the capital of the

The magnificent Hellenistic city of Pergamum in western Asia Minor served as the capital and showcase of the Attalid kings, who gained royal status in the third century BCE and their greatest power and wealth in the second. Rising abruptly above the plain, the acropolis was built on great terraces, an ingenious adaptation of municipal planning to mountainous terrain. This model of the acropolis reflects the grandeur of the city's architectural ensemble. The striking theater, on the left, almost seems to cascade down the steep hillside. The nearby sanctuary of Athena, on the central terrace, was the religious center of Attalid Pergamum. The kings lavished funds on the sanctuary, which was surrounded by a two-story stoa and graced by an earlier, modest Doric temple of Athena. The terrace below supported the celebrated Great Altar, now in Berlin, a templelike masterpiece of the second century BCE. The lowest terrace provided room for an agora, while the uppermost reflects a building program of the early Roman Empire. Staatliche Museen, Berlin.

Attalid kings in the third century BCE. Admirably excavated, Pergamum offers a rich source for the study of Hellenistic art born of royal absolutism. The library was second only to that of Alexandria, and the city was famous both for its school of sculpture (discussed below) and its splendid architecture. Although the mountainous terrain rendered planning exceedingly difficult, Pergamum was magnificently accommodated to its site. The main entrance to the celebrated city was from the south through an arched gateway, from which the road led past the poorer dwellings and then a bustling lower agora. Next the road passed numerous workshops and, climbing ever higher, the houses of the wealthier citizens, finally reaching the entrance to the famed acropolis of the city. The buildings and sculpture of

In the second half of the third century BCE Pergamum demonstrated its military might by inflicting crushing defeats on a contingent of Celtic-speaking Gauls (or Galatians) who had crossed from Europe to terrorize Asia Minor, confining the survivors to a small region in central Asia Minor known thereafter as Galatia. The famous Great Altar, partly reconstructed in Berlin, was dedicated on the Pergamene acropolis around 175 BCE to glorify the Attalid victory over the Gauls. The altar proper stood on a huge stepped platform and was framed by an Ionic colonnade with projecting wings on either side of a monumental staircase. The podium below the colonnade carried a colossal marble frieze, carved in high relief, portraying the *Battle of Gods and Giants*, by which the gods successfully fought for civilization against barbarism, a theme clearly intended to symbolize the triumph of the Pergamenes over the Gauls. Reflecting the dramatic compositions favored in Pergamene sculpture, the frieze features twisting and turning figures who push into the observer's space with great intensity. Staatliche Museen, Berlin.

the magnificent acropolis, which rose almost one thousand feet above the surrounding countryside, gave the city its reputation as a second Athens. A seemingly endless series of ingenious terraces graced this lofty and sloping site. On the
lowest level of the acropolis was a spacious upper agora, above which the terraces
eventually culminated in the palace and arsenal of the city. Directly above this
upper agora was a marble-paved terrace, upon which stood the colossal masterpiece known as the Great Altar (partly reconstructed in Berlin). The altar itself,
which was accessible by a mammoth staircase, stood on a high platform in the
center of a court and was surrounded by a great Ionic colonnade. Erected about
180 BCE by Eumenes II to glorify the victories of his father Attalus I against the
Gauls (also known as the Galatians), the monument features a four-hundred-foot
encircling frieze portraying the *Battle of Gods and Giants*. The frieze, the most famous of all Hellenistic sculptural ensembles, suggests a parallel between the triumph of the gods and the success of the Attalids fighting the Gauls. The theme
was intended to symbolize also the triumph of Greek civilization over barbarity,
the victory of light and order over chaos and darkness.

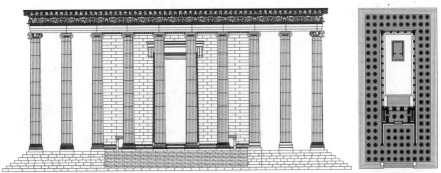

Illustrated here is a reconstruction of the façade (left) and the plan (right) of the mammoth, richly decorated Hellenistic temple of Apollo at Didyma, an oracular shrine south of Miletus on the west coast of Asia Minor. The Archaic temple had been destroyed by the Persians in the early fifth century BCE. One colorful story relates that when Alexander appeared at Didyma in 334 BCE, the sacred spring miraculously began to flow once again and the god to prophesy. Work began on a new temple around 300 BCE and dragged on for more than five centuries, but the grandiose structure was never finished. The plan of the temple is dipteral, that is, with double surrounding colonnades. The designers, like numerous others of the Hellenistic period, incorporated novel architectural features. The temple was open to the sky and thus lacked pediments and a roof. Narrow vaulted passages, dark and mysterious, led to Apollo's glorious light in the inner courtyard, which provided a dramatic setting for a small Ionic shrine protecting the cult statue of the god.

ARCHITECTURE

Temple of Apollo at Didyma.   Hellenistic architecture, in contrast to Classical, was constructed on an imperial scale and often emphasized dramatic and ingenious interior space, focusing attention away from exterior elements. Thus when Hellenistic kings erected colossal temples, their architects often greatly loosened rules governing Classical design, exemplified by the unique temple of Apollo at Didyma. Ten miles south of Miletus, Didyma was the site of an ancient oracular sanctuary of Apollo, one of the most important in Asia Minor. Although the Persians burned down the Archaic temple at Didyma in the early fifth century BCE, the oracle was refounded at the bidding of Alexander. A massive building project of unconventional design was inaugurated about 300 BCE to replace the destroyed predecessor. Excavations indicate that the grandiose and richly ornamented structure—though never quite finished—reflected the dramatic complexity of much Hellenistic architecture. The plan called for a vast enlargement of traditional design, with an encircling double colonnade and three rows of columns on the porch. The slender Ionic columns soared to a height of 64 feet. Numerous devotees came to the mammoth temple—measuring 358 by 167 feet—to consult Apollo. The grand doorway of the column-filled porch was elevated nearly five feet above the floor and thus could not be entered. Beyond the great doorway lay a rectangular room, perhaps functioning as a stage for Apollo's oracular response to be announced to anxious visitors, its roof supported by two freestanding Corinthian columns. Small doors from either side of

Among the great shrines raised to the glory of the gods, the enormous temple of Olympian Zeus in Athens, the Olympieum, was the most ambitious in European Greece. Construction began in the sacred area southeast of the Acropolis in the sixth century BCE, the plan specifying the Doric order, but the temple was left unfinished. The patronage of the Seleucid king Antiochus IV permitted resumption of work in 174 BCE, this time in the more modern Corinthian order, with the daunting project finally completed for the emperor Hadrian about 130 CE, nearly seven centuries after its inception. This view shows the majestic surviving Corinthian columns, with the Acropolis in the background.

the rectangular chamber opened upon stairways leading to the roof, perhaps for ritual purposes. From the porch, the visitor coming to consult the oracle could enter either of two dark, vaulted passageways sloping down and leading to a huge walled, roofless court blazing with Apollo's sunlight and lined with ornamental pilasters. At the end of the courtyard stood the actual shrine, a freestanding Ionic structure with the cult statue, within which the priestess took her seat by an oracular spring and entered into a state of ecstasy, her response interpreted by priests. Typical of much Hellenistic architecture, the immense scale of the temple and its emphasis on interior space and mystery produced an overwhelming emotional experience.

Temple of Olympian Zeus at Athens.   Although the Corinthian order was adopted in the fourth century BCE for interior columns gracing buildings such as the rebuilt temple of Athena at Tegea, the order became increasingly popular in the third and second centuries BCE, culminating with the prestigious temple of Olympian Zeus at Athens. Construction of this huge structure—almost equal in size to the temple of Apollo at Didyma—commenced without completion in the sixth century BCE. In 174 BCE the Seleucid king Antiochus IV engaged the architect Cossutius, a Roman citizen working

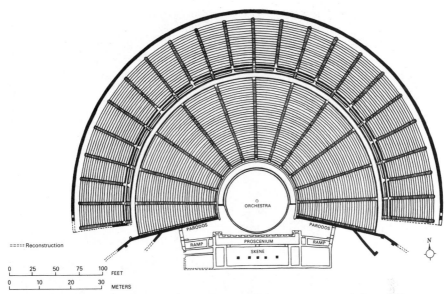

Plan of the theater at Epidaurus in the northeastern Peloponnese, erected about 350 BCE, the best preserved ancient Greek theater.

in the Greek style, to continue the work as a Corinthian temple, which meant abandoning the original plan specifying the Doric order. The temple was finally completed for the Roman emperor Hadrian (117–138 CE). Its Corinthian capitals, displaying luxuriant acanthus leaves that almost completely cover the bells, are thought to have exerted a strong influence on the Roman Corinthian order after the Roman general Sulla carried a number of the columns to Rome in the first century BCE.

Theater at Epidaurus.   The three main elements of a fifth-century Greek theater were seating, circular orchestra, and backdrop. The orchestra served as the center of dramatic action for both chorus and actors, with the former chanting and dancing and the latter performing around the altar of Dionysus in the center. In the Hellenistic period a raised stage was introduced behind the orchestra, elevating the actors, who gained access to the stage from the *skene*, a rectangular building serving both as an elaborate backdrop and as a dressing and mask-changing room. At first a tent (*skene*) had been employed for this purpose and thus the name. The natural auditorium of the hillside was provided with wooden benches for spectators. The fourth century witnessed the construction of the first stone theaters, celebrated for their aesthetic and acoustic refinement. The shape of the natural hillside was cut into a great semicircular auditorium. Seating was hewn from the natural rock of the hillside and neatly arranged in sections and tiers, with special front seats provided for dignitaries.

A large open-air theater of harmonious design was essential to any major Hellenistic city or sanctuary. Of the many theaters established or rebuilt in the fourth and third centuries BCE, the best preserved is at Epidaurus on the Saronic Gulf in the eastern Peloponnese. The seating extends around the circular orchestra like a

Floors paved with natural pebbles arranged to form pictoral designs were popular for decorating private houses in Greece during the fourth century BCE. At the end of the century pebble mosaics achieved greater realism by utlilizing a wide range of colors and shades. Outstanding examples come from the palatial houses at Alexander's birthplace of Pella in Macedonia. The finest pictorial masterpiece yet discovered at Pella, dated about 300 BCE and signed by the artist Gnosis, portrays two youths in billowing cloaks engaged in a stag hunt. The central scene, illustrated here, is framed in turn by an elaborate floral design and a rhythmic wave pattern (not shown). The mosaic depends on a painstaking arrangement of the closely packed pebbles to reproduce various views of the body convincingly. Treating each pebble like a separate brushstroke, the artist has succeeded in suggesting not only three-dimensional space but also the movement of light and shadow across the nude hunters and the animals. This mosaic, with its extraordinary use of light and shade to suggest volume, indicates the artist was abreast of contemporary developments in wall painting. In situ.

great fan and can accommodate some twelve thousand people, made possible by fifty-five rows of marble benches separated into huge wedges by radiating stairways. The theater at Epidaurus, which exhibits remarkable acoustics, remains in use for summer performances of Greek tragedy and comedy.

Private Houses and Pebble Mosaics. The dwellings of the rich and powerful—excellent examples survive at Delos and Pella—acquired a new architectural splendor in the Hellenistic period. Houses still faced inward, with the main rooms grouped around the courtyard in the Mediterranean manner, but they were larger and more lavishly appointed. Thick walls suggest many houses supported upper stories, now missing. The interior walls of a number of dwellings were decorated with painted murals, and the light-bathed central courtyard might be beautifully transformed by a colonnade and a mosaic pavement. The technique for creating pebble mosaics—made from natural river pebbles—evolved in the Classical period and reached the height of its refinement in the later fourth century BCE. Famous pebble mosaics graced the floors of mansions at Macedonian Pella, their wide range of colors and nearly life-sized figures portraying mythological stories on a grand scale.

SCULPTURE

Far more Hellenistic sculpture survives than Classical, partly because the output of statues multiplied enormously during the period. Most major statues were of bronze, though artists had become less reluctant to employ marble as a medium for freestanding statues. As noted in chapter 12, considerable Classical bronze work (and marble statuary) disappeared in the later Christian crusade against idols, and much that remained ended up in melting pots during the Middle Ages. Yet scholars can gain a reasonable overview of Hellenistic sculpture by examining the many surviving marble figures—generally not the best works of their day—and the later Roman copies.

The new cities demanded sculpture in astonishing quantities, resulting in sculptors traveling the vast Hellenistic world to accept commissioned projects. Many sculptors continued to embrace the Classical artistic tradition of idealizing figures through understated restraint, but others struck out in new directions, emphasizing naturalism, sensationalism, emotionalism, or eroticism. Hellenistic sculptors greatly expanded their range of styles and subjects—though bold steps in this direction had already been taken—focusing on themes such as anger, despair, sadism, drunkenness, or sleep. Striving to produce seemingly living bodies of flesh and blood, sculptors created figures ranging from the very young to the very old, from the appealing to the deliberately repellent. Appearing regularly in sculpture are decrepit peasants, gnarled old laborers, boisterous satyrs and centaurs, sexually ambivalent Hermaphrodites, lifelike athletes, and mortal women.

THE PERGAMENE SCHOOL OF SCULPTURE

Gallic Sculptural Groups. The most important Hellenistic schools of sculpture arose at Athens, Alexandria, Rhodes, and Pergamum. While some cities preserved a strong Classical tradition in the treatment of features and drapery, Pergamum produced pieces of exaggerated action and frequent contortions. The old serenity was abandoned for an expressive, even theatrical quality that is particularly marked in pieces portraying suffering or the perils of combat. The Attalids of Pergamum celebrated their defeat of the Gallic tribes in the 220s BCE by erecting at least two great bronze monuments on the Pergamene acropolis, with the Gauls rendered as noble in defeat. Statues from one of these sculptural ensembles are preserved in later Roman copies. The most complete are now in Rome, the famous *Gallic Chieftain Killing Himself and*

When the Attalids of Pergamum commissioned bold new sculptural ensembles in the late third century BCE to celebrate their earlier defeat of the Gallic tribes, the artists presented the Gauls as noble in defeat, reflecting the respect of the victors for the vanquished. This dramatic sculptural pair, portraying a Gallic chieftain defiantly turning the sword on himself after killing his wife to avoid capture and enslavement, is a Roman marble copy of an original bronze, dated about 230–220 BCE, from one of the Pergamene ensembles or another like them. The powerful and still vital Gaul and his dead wife form a typical Hellenistic pyramidal group, affording many effective viewpoints. This sculptural style is often termed Hellenistic baroque because of its theatrical, tumultuous, and flamboyant quality, an artistic expression known best from the Great Altar of Pergamum. Museo Nazionale dell Terme, Rome.

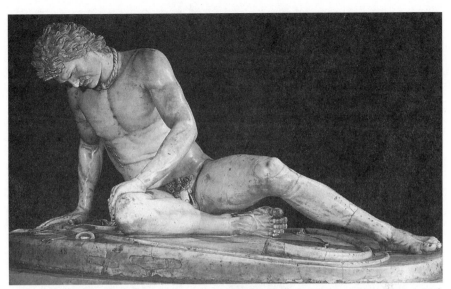

Scholars suggest the *Dying Gaul*, illustrated here, is another marble copy of a bronze original forming part of the great monument set up in Pergamum in the late third century BCE. This famous figure, a trumpeter, bravely confronts impending death by struggling to support his collapsing body with his right arm. With blood spurting from his spear-pierced chest, the Gaul looks despairingly at his mortal wound. Museo Capitolino, Rome.

His Wife in the Terme Museum and the *Dying Gaul* in the Capitoline Museum. Realizing his defeat and defiantly choosing suicide over surrender and enslavement, the Gallic chieftain has already killed his wife and now plunges the sword into his chest to avoid capture by the approaching Greeks. The twisting posture of the chieftain and the dark shadows cast by his limp wife's drapery heightens the sense of drama and pathos. The *Dying Gaul* is an excellent example of Hellenistic emotional expression. The figure, a trumpeter who is dying from a heavily bleeding chest wound, struggles to support himself with his right arm. Although the Gaul remains proud and defiant to the end, his anguished expression and the gaping wound suggest his death is imminent. The work places the defeated enemy on an unprecedented heroic plane and reproduces distinctive features of the Gauls, including their long hair and mustaches and their frequently worn torques (neck bands).

The Great Altar.   As noted, the Great Altar at Pergamum—partly reconstructed in Berlin—features a colossal encircling frieze representing the *Battle of Gods and Giants*, the violent combat through which the gods won victory for civilization, a theme clearly intended to symbolize the triumph of the Pergamenes over the Gauls. More than seven feet high and almost four hundred feet long, the celebrated frieze is second only to the Parthenon frieze as the largest sculptural ensemble of antiquity. The marble frieze would have been painted, making the huge naked figures stand out boldly. They are carved with such vigor and great depth that they seem almost detached from the background. The tumultuous narrative and raging battle

The Pergamene sculptural style reached its pinnacle with the extravagant decoration of the Great Altar, set up on the acropolis at Pergamum about 175 BCE (now partly restored in Berlin) to glorify the Attalid victory over the Gauls. The surface of the famous colossal encircling frieze depicts over-life-size figures, carved in high relief and no doubt originally colored, who twist and turn with extraordinary vigor and intensity into the space of the observer, the dramatic effect being further intensified by violent postures, anguished faces, and unruly hair. The time-honored subject of the frieze is the Gigantomachy, the battle of the gods—led by Zeus—against the rebelling Giants, with the Attalids drawing a parallel between the defeat of the Giants and the defeat of the Gauls. The scene of Athena battling Giants, illustrated here, shows the goddess seizing the hair of the winged Alcyoneus and wrenching him away from his mother, Gaea, or Earth, portrayed as a large figure rising from the ground, for the Giant could not be destroyed as long as he maintained contact with her. Athena's triumph is signaled by the Nike flying in from the right to crown her with a wreath of victory. Staatliche Museen, Berlin.

is amplified by the twisting bodies and swirling drapery seething around the monument, with some figures appearing to have fallen out of the frieze. They project threateningly, climbing and crawling up the very steps the worshiper also ascends to the sacrificial platform. The emotional intensity is heightened by expressions of extreme anguish and vivid depictions of death. From the frieze's shadow-obscured background, the figures seemingly erupt like bursts of light, revealing the intense contrast between Classical and much Hellenistic sculpture.

THE RHODIAN SCHOOL OF SCULPTURE

Nike of Samothrace (c. 200 BCE).   Another Hellenistic masterpiece, the *Nike of Samothrace*, was erected on a hill above the sanctuary of the Great Gods on the is-

An extraordinary Hellenistic masterpiece, the *Nike of Samothrace*, deftly conveys a fusion of power and grace. No doubt commemorating a great Hellenistic naval triumph, this marble statue personifying Victory was set up on a hill above the sanctuary of the Great Gods on the island of Samothrace around 200 BCE but now enjoys prominent display in the Louvre. The work imparts a strong sense of motion, showing the goddess alighting on the prow of a warship, her massive wings still outspread and her wind-whipped drapery pressing against her body. The theatrical mood was magnified by the setting, for the warship was originally placed in an elaborate reflecting pool of flowing, shimmering water. Louvre, Paris.

land of Samothrace around 200 BCE, perhaps by the Rhodians, no doubt in gratitude for a major naval victory. The statue, now gracing the Louvre, portrays the goddess

This famous group of Laocoön and his sons, discovered in Rome in 1506 with Michelangelo in attendance, has exerted considerable influence on western art. In the version of the story made famous by Virgil's *Aeneid*, after the Trojan priest Laocoön warned against drawing the wooden horse left by the Greeks within the walls of Troy, he and his two sons were crushed at an altar by giant sea serpents sent by gods hostile to the Trojans. The spectacular Laocoön group, with its contorted figures and anguished expressions, recalls the emotional intensity of the colossal frieze of the Great Altar of Pergamum and is most likely a marble version of a late-second-century-BCE Hellenistic masterpiece. The subject of endless scholarly debate, the Laocoön group has been attributed to three Greek sculptors from Rhodes (Hagesander, Athanodorus, and Polydorus), who provided superior reproductions for wealthy Roman buyers and worked perhaps as late as the early first century CE. Scholars have transferred certain elements of the composition from one position to another. An earlier restoration is shown here. Vatican Museums, Rome.

alighting on the prow of a warship, originally set in an elaborate reflecting pool of flowing water that created the illusion of waves slapping the sides of the vessel. Thus the Nike, or Victory, was central to a distinctive visual drama of the sort favored by many Hellenistic sculptors. Sea winds whip her drapery into splendid masses pressing against her body, producing a rich display of light and shade. The combination of outstretched, still beating wings and tempestuous drapery contributes to the unforgettable image of a goddess enveloped in an atmosphere of wind and sea.

Laocoön and His Sons *(first century* CE*)*.   Greek sculptors were in great demand to copy Classical and Hellenistic art for wealthy Roman patrons. Rhodian sculptors, perhaps working as late as the early first century CE, produced a superb marble copy of a mid-Hellenistic masterpiece, *Laocoön and His Sons,* which was discovered at Rome in 1506 and is now prominently displayed in the Vatican Museums. This famous group, reminding the viewer of the anguished Giants writhing on the frieze of the Great Altar of Pergamum, portrays the death of the Trojan priest Laocoön and his two sons for his vehement opposition to bringing the Greeks' enormous hollow wooden horse into Troy. The epic version of the story has the Trojans sealing their doom by ignoring the priest and moving the huge horse and its concealed warriors within their city walls. Meanwhile, as punishment for his warning, Laocoön and his two sons had already been enveloped and crushed by a couple of giant sea serpents sent by gods who favored the Greeks in the war against Troy. The desperate struggle of the priest and his sons against the death grip of the encircling coils is amplified by their contorted faces and agonizing cries, a striking example of Hellenistic emotional intensity.

Hellenistic Innovations in Portraying the Male and Female Nude

Sleeping Satyr (Barberini Faun) (c. 200 BCE).   Often rendered in novel ways, the nude was another major theme of Hellenistic sculpture. The *Sleeping Satyr (Barberini Faun)* in Munich, dated about 200 BCE and possibly an original, captures the unguarded pose of a young satyr consumed by drunken sleep, his troubled face betraying disturbing dreams and radiating a sense of tragic imprisonment. Satyrs were riotous woodland deities obsessed with pursuing sexual gratification. The sculptor has created an openly erotic anatomy by showing the well-formed, muscular satyr sprawled on a rock with his legs spread wide apart, thus deliberately focusing attention on his genitalia.

Aphrodite of Melos (Venus de Milo) (c. 150–125 BCE).   The female nude was also popular with Hellenistic sculptors. Praxiteles inaugurated the female nude with his celebrated *Aphrodite of Cnidus* in the fourth century BCE. Many Hellenistic examples combine even softer modeling with carefully blurred details, resulting in statues that are far more aggressively feminine than their predecessors. The partially draped *Aphrodite of Melos,* probably carved around 150–125 BCE, enjoys exceptional fame in this genre. This over life-size marble statue, one of the greatest treasures of the Louvre, was discovered at Melos and is better known today as the *Venus de Milo* (Milo being the Italian form of Melos). Although supporting a coldly Classical head in both expression and hairstyle, she is otherwise overtly sexual, her broad hips suggesting reproductive maturity, her small breasts suggesting youthfulness. The sculptor not only

The *Sleeping Satyr* (also known as the *Barberini Faun*) was probably made around 200 BCE and may be an original. Found in Rome in the seventeenth century, the statue was restored (with certain inaccuracies) by Bernini, the celebrated Italian Baroque sculptor. The figure does not represent a sleek Greek athlete but a drunken satyr sleeping fitfully in the wild. The sculptor has skillfully detailed muscles and veins to suggest vitality of this mythological being, a follower of Dionysus, and has pushed far beyond the sensuality of Praxiteles' works in the fourth century to create an openly erotic anatomy, for the widely spread legs of the satyr focus attention on his genitals, a frank invitation to voyeurism. Antikensammlungen und Glyptothek, Munich.

The over-life-size marble *Aphrodite of Melos* (*Venus de Milo*), dated 150–125 BCE, boldly explores the erotic character of the nude female form. The complex composition, clearly influenced by Late Classical sculpture, effectively combines a subtly twisting torso with a raised and advanced left leg. The most provocative element is the mass of naturalistic drapery clinging precariously to the hips. The sculptor deliberately tantalizes the viewer with the drapery, which appears unstable and ready to slip even farther down the body, imbuing Aphrodite with an overt sexuality not evident in Praxiteles' entirely nude statue of the goddess. Lourvre, Paris.

turned the torso of the massive body to the left, thus creating a twisting composition, but also chiseled the stone into the texture and appearance of warm human flesh. The naturalistic drapery encircling Aphrodite's hips appears unstable and ready to slip even farther down her body, creating a deliberate tantalizing effect that would be absent in an entirely nude version of the goddess.

PORTRAITURE

Roman copies and literary accounts show that sculptors created portraits of specific individuals in fifth-century Athens, examples including Pericles and Socrates, yet these were probably idealized types that were personalized to some degree. Alexander's

The members of the small Greek ruling class in Bactria, a vast region on the far-eastern fringe of the Hellenistic world, broke away from Seleucid rule around 230 BCE and maintained their prosperous kingdom and Greek presence for more than a century. Remarkably, the Greco-Bactrian rulers presented themselves on their coinage as they actually looked, including wrinkles and blemishes, thereby breaking new ground in royal portraiture. Illustrated here are coin portraits of Bactrian kings Antimachus, c. 185 BCE, and Eucratides I, c. 165-150 BCE. Antimachus, who is unknown apart from his coins, wears the distinctive Macedonian cap, or *causia*, with a royal diadem beneath, while Eucratides appears helmeted as supreme military leader. British Museum, London.

conquests encouraged both the concept of ruler portraiture and the demand for vast numbers of portraits at all levels. The king praised Lysippus for capturing his essence artistically and appointed him court sculptor. The portraits of Alexander tempered realism with idealized features to convey the image of inspired leadership that he wished his subjects to see. Lysippus' most celebrated portrait of the conqueror has disappeared, a tautly balanced bronze nude statue showing Alexander holding a spear and turning his head upward to the sky. An epigram inscribed on the base interpreted the work, stating that Alexander was looking upon Zeus while proclaiming, "I place the earth under my sway; you, O Zeus, keep Olympus." A sculptured fragment of the head of Alexander, attributed to Lysippus, was found in a shrine at Sparta and is now preserved at the Museum of Fine Arts in Boston. Wearing a lion-skin headdress, the youthful Alexander appears in the guise of his hero Heracles. Originally this fragment belonged to a complete statue, probably standing and nude except for the headdress. Numerous posthumous portraits of Alexander—commissioned by the rulers who promoted themselves as his Successors—appropriately rendered the extraordinary king as half god, half military genius. A vast number of portraits of the new Hellenistic monarchs appeared also, their statues, pictures, gems, and coins representing them as vigorous and often semidivine. Hellenistic coinage underwent a major change, with portrait heads of rulers and their families replacing the features of gods on the obverse, a tacit commentary on the assurance and conceit of these self-made autocrats. Although some Bactrian and Indian kings opted for a remarkable realism, the royal portraits elsewhere in the Hellenistic world were generally idealized, depicting the monarch as a youthful, clean-shaven, heroic figure, for which Alexander himself had set the standard.

PAINTING

Macedonian Tomb Paintings. Greek painting reached its zenith during Alexander's reign and the Hellenistic period. The artists of the day, who painted on walls or wooden panels, made great strides in the technique of rudimentary perspective and achieved considerable success in shading to suggest depth and roundness in their compositions. Royal Macedonian tombs discovered near Vergina (ancient Aegae), traditional burial place of Macedonian kings, have yielded rare examples of pre-Hellenistic wall paintings of high quality, notable for their vitality and brilliant color. As noted in chapter 14, the most remarkable of these paintings is a vigorous scene of Hades' abduction of Persephone. The character of monumental painting in the early third century is suggested by a Macedonian tomb at Levcadia. Its elaborate two-story façade includes engaged columns on either side of the doorway, symbolizing the entrance to the underworld. Between pairs of columns were painted four single figures: on the left of the door, the deceased in armor and the god Hermes to lead him to the underworld; on the right of the door, two judges of the dead. Subtle gradations of color create the illusion of volume and provide evidence of stylistic continuity between Hellenistic and Roman wall painting.

Roman Adaptations of Hellenistic Paintings. Although the great masterpieces of Hellenistic painting have perished, many of the murals and mosaic decorations at Pompeii and Herculaneum—Italian coastal towns suddenly buried under the deep volcanic of erupting Mount Vesuvius in 79 CE—were inspired by lost Greek originals. A painting from Herculaneum—*Heracles and Telephus*—is generally regarded an adaptation of an original Pergamene painting of the second century BCE. According to one version of the story, the infant Telephus was left to die of exposure

Scholars regard many paintings and mosaics from Pompeii and Herculaneum—Italian towns destroyed by the eruption of Mount Vesuvius in 79 CE—as Roman adaptations of lost Hellenistic originals. Notable among these is this beautifully composed wall painting from Herculaneum, *Heracles and Telephus,* thought to be a free copy of a Pergamene painting of the second century BCE. The mythical subject is Heracles' finding of his infant son Telephus (whom the Attalids treated as the founder of Pergamum, telling his story on the inner frieze of the city's Great Altar). One version of the myth has Telephus exposed in mountainous Arcadia but miraculously saved by wild beasts and suckled by a hind. The painting shows at the upper right a youthful winged figure (Nike or Iris), who has guided powerful Heracles to Telephus in Arcadia and now points out to him the wonder of his son nursing the deer. At the left sits the great brooding personification of Arcadia, while a young satyr behind her pauses in playing his pipes. The sensuous richness reflects the Hellenistic use of a range of light and shadow to model flesh, musculature, and drapery. Museo Nazionale, Naples.

in mountainous Arcadia but was miraculously suckled by a hind and thus saved. The painting shows Heracles, guided by a winged figure (Nike or Iris), discovering Telephus nursing the doe. A young satyr watches, while Arcadia is personified by a

By the mid-third century BCE, Hellenistic mosaicists were employing tesserae (tiny cubes of cut stone and glass) to provide a greater range of color and more naturalistic compositions. The technique was refined until artists developed brilliant pictorial masterpieces imitating the effects of painting. This exceptionally fine example, the *Alexander and Darius Mosaic*, decorated the floor of a sumptuous Roman mansion (the House of the Faun) at Pompeii around 100 BCE and is generally regarded as a reliable copy of a late-fourth-century monumental wall painting. Much of the scene has been obliterated, but the major figures remain relatively intact. The mosaic seems to portray the turning point in the crucial battle of Issus (333 BCE) between Alexander and Darius III. Although Alexander's forces were greatly outnumbered, he took the offensive and plowed through the Persian line. Wild-haired, helmetless Alexander charges from the left in pursuit of Darius and thrusts his spear through a Persian blocking his way. Darius, his face a mask of desperation, flees to the right in his huge chariot, utterly powerless to halt his reckless young opponent's remorseless conquest. Museo Nazionale, Naples.

stately seated female figure staring into space. The pictorial richness of this famous mural with its splendid figures and subtle shading from light to shadow clearly reflects the dazzling range of the Hellenistic artistic tradition.

Influence of Hellenistic Paintings on Roman Mosaics.   Pebble floors virtually disappeared after third-century Hellenistic artisans developed the lasting technique of fashioning brilliant mosaics from cubes of cut stone and glass (tesserae). Hellenistic mosaicists learned to create beautifully refined compositions exhibiting a wide range of colors and clearly defined contours, their works strongly influencing later Roman practitioners of the art. Various scenes in mosaics from Pompeii and Herculaneum are generally believed to be copies of lost Hellenistic paintings. The masterpiece known as the *Alexander and Darius Mosaic*, fashioned about 100 BCE, decorated the floor of the lavishly appointed House of the Faun at Pompeii. This famous mosaic depicts Alexander and Darius at the crucial battle of Issus and is generally regarded as a careful copy of a brilliant monumental wall painting of the fourth century, a view supported by the accurate representation of fourth-century arms and equipment on both sides. The reckless Alexander, wearing no helmet for protection, charges from the left into a nest of bristling spears to confront the Persian king, whose expression betrays his utter desperation as he flees to the right in his huge chariot to escape the Macedonian forces. This splendid translation of the original picture into the difficult medium of mosaic suggests the technical competence and magnificent composition achieved in Hellenistic wall painting.

THE HELLENISTIC LEGACY

The complex and innovative Hellenistic period differed in many respects from the old Greek world focusing on the polis. Although the cities of Aegean Greece remained vibrant cultural and commercial centers, their political independence and societal bonds were undermined by the increasing reach of autocratic monarchy. The privileged classes of the Greek world cooperated with the new Hellenistic monarchs emerging in the early third century BCE, when economic opportunities in faraway places invited unprecedented mobility and colonization. Male members of the Greek elite formed a powerful expatriated class and acquired exalted civilian and military positions, while other immigrants found ready employment as soldiers or petty bureaucrats. Women also enjoyed expanded horizons, though to a lesser extent than men, with opportunities being greatest for women of wealth, especially Hellenistic queens. The frequent urging by philosophers for safeguarding the traditional female role in family and social life suggests the altered position of women during this period. Meanwhile the enormous Hellenistic kingdoms, supported by the toiling majority, spread Greek culture widely, borrowing only modestly from the traditions of subjected native populations. The makers of the Hellenistic world, who admired yet sought to reshape their grand Classical traditions, established cultural patterns that remain vigorously influential to this day. They composed polished literary works in Greek—customarily in the standardized form called *koine*—which were read over a vast sweep of land from Sicily to the borders of India. They built beautifully planned cities whose great museums and libraries supported scholars laboring to transmit Greek texts and expand knowledge, thereby ensuring the survival of Greek literature from the fourth century BCE and earlier. They broke important new ground not only in art and philosophy but also in medicine and science. Their era might appear remarkably modern to the casual observer, with its superb science, diverse religion, widespread superstition, rampant materialism, strong cosmopolitanism, flamboyant art, and large-scale business activity.

Alexander's conquests and the Hellenistic period provided a rehearsal for the political unification of the Mediterranean world under the military might of Rome and its spiritual unification under the zeal of the Christian church, developments covered in *Ancient Rome*, the third volume of this series. Thus Alexander—forger of the largest empire the world had ever seen—had unwittingly prepared the way for the victorious march of an Italian city and a Near Eastern religion. Gradually, Rome annexed the Hellenistic world, though Hellenistic culture ultimately triumphed, for "conquered Greece took her fierce conqueror captive," in Horace's familiar phrase. Talented Greek architects, scientists, philosophers, and literary figures spread Hellenistic ideas and techniques throughout the Roman domains, while indelibly influencing Christianity. Then, in the fifth century CE, successive waves of Germanic tribes gained control of the western provinces of the Roman Empire, transforming them into separate barbarian kingdoms, the foundations of the modern states of western Europe. Meanwhile the intact Eastern Roman Empire, today usually called Byzantium, stubbornly survived despite shrinking borders until the determined Ottoman Turks captured its capital of Constantinople in 1453. Greek-speaking Byzantium, embracing a brilliant form of Hellenistic culture, bequeathed its rich civilization and Orthodox Church to the inhabitants of the Balkans and Russia. With the fall of Constantinople, many Byzantine scholars took flight westward to Italy, helping to inspire a new awareness of antiquity known as the Renaissance. Hellenistic thought and art had again triumphed in the western world.

BIBLIOGRAPHY

The following selection lists informative works in English, many with detailed references to foreign-language and more specialized studies. Some ancient sources in translation are included. Readers are encouraged to familiarize themselves also with the various scholarly journals presenting current research on ancient Greece.

GENERAL STUDIES

Adkins, Lesley, and Roy A. Adkins. *Handbook to Life in Ancient Greece*. Oxford: Oxford University Press, 1997.

Anderson, Warren D. *Music and Musicians in Ancient Greece*. Ithaca, N.Y.: Cornell University Press, 1994.

Barber, Elizabeth Wayland. *Women's Work: The First 20,000 Years: Women, Cloth, and Society in Early Times*. New York: Norton, 1994.

Biers, William R. *The Archaeology of Greece*. 2d ed. Ithaca, N.Y.: Cornell University Press, 1996.

Blundell, Sue. *Women in Ancient Greece*. Cambridge, Mass.: Harvard University Press, 1995.

Boardman, John. *Greek Art*. 4th ed. London: Thames and Hudson, 1996.

Boardman, John, ed. *The Oxford History of Classical Art*. Oxford: Oxford University Press, 1993.

Boardman, John, Jasper Griffin, and Oswyn Murray, eds. *Greece and the Hellenistic World*. Vol. 1 of *The Oxford History of the Classical World*. Oxford: Oxford University Press, 1988.

Burkert, Walter. *Greek Religion*. Cambridge, Mass.: Harvard University Press, 1985.

Cartledge, Paul, ed. *The Cambridge Illustrated History of Ancient Greece*. Cambridge: Cambridge University Press, 1998.

Cartledge, Paul. *The Greeks: A Portrait of Self and Others*. Rev. ed. Oxford: Oxford University Press, 1997.

Comotti, Giovanni. *Music in Greek and Roman Culture*. Baltimore: Johns Hopkins University Press, 1989.

Detienne, Marcel, and Jean-Pierre Vernant. *The Cuisine of Sacrifice among the Greeks*. Trans. Paula Wissing. Chicago: University of Chicago Press, 1989.

Dalby, Andrew. *Siren Feasts: A History of Food and Gastronomy in Greece*. London: Routledge, 1996.

Dihle, Albrecht. *A History of Greek Literature: From Homer to the Hellenistic Period*. Trans. Clare Krojzl. London: Routledge, 1994.

Easterling, P. E., and B. M. W. Knox, eds. *Greek Literature*. Vol. 1 of *The Cambridge History of Classical Literature*. Cambridge: Cambridge University Press, 1985.

Garland, Robert. *Daily Life of the Ancient Greeks*. Westport, Conn.: Greenwood, 1998.

Hornblower, Simon, and Anthony Spawforth, eds. *The Oxford Classical Dictionary*. 3d ed. Oxford: Oxford University Press, 1996.

Landis, John G. *Music in Ancient Greece and Rome*. London: Routledge, 1998.

Longrigg, James, ed. *Greek Medicine from the Heroic to the Hellenistic Age: A Source Book*. London: Duckworth, 1998.

Luce, J. V. *An Introduction to Greek Philosophy*. London: Thames and Hudson, 1992.

MacKendrick, Paul. *The Greek Stones Speak: The Story of Archaeology in Greek Lands*. 2d ed. New York: Norton, 1981.

Murray, Oswyn, and Simon Price, eds. *The Greek City from Homer to Alexander*. Oxford, 1990.

Pedley, John Griffiths. *Greek Art and Archaeology*. 2d ed. New York: Abrams, 1998.

Powell, Anton, ed. *The Greek World*. London: Routledge, 1995.

Riddle, John M. *Contraception and Abortion from the Ancient World to the Renaissance*. Cambridge, Mass.: Harvard University Press, 1992.

Sowerby, Robin. *The Greeks: An Introduction to Their Culture*. London: Routledge, 1995.

Stewart, Andrew. *Greek Sculpture: An Exploration*. 2 vols. New Haven: Yale University Press, 1990.

Talbert, Richard J. A., ed. *Atlas of Classical History*. London: Routledge, 1985.

Tomlinson, Richard. *From Mycenae to Constantinople: The Evolution of the Ancient City*. London: Routledge, 1992.

Vernant, Jean-Pierre, ed. *The Greeks*. Trans. Charles Lambert and Teresa Lavender Fagan. Chicago: University of Chicago Press, 1995.

West, M. L. *Ancient Greek Music*. Oxford: Oxford University Press, 1992.

THE AEGEAN CIVILIZATIONS OF MINOAN CRETE AND MYCENAEAN GREECE
(CHAPTERS 1–2)

Cambridge Ancient History. 3d ed, vol. 2, pt.1. *The Middle East and the Aegean Region*, c. *1800–1380 B.C.* Ed. I. E. S. Edwards et al. Cambridge: Cambridge University Press, 1973.

Cambridge Ancient History. 3d ed, vol. 2, pt.2. *The Middle East and the Aegean Region*, c. *1380–1000 B.C.* Ed. I. E. S. Edwards et al. Cambridge: Cambridge University Press, 1975.

Chadwick, John. *The Decipherment of Linear B*. 2d ed. Cambridge: Cambridge University Press, 1968.

Chadwick, John. *Linear B and Related Scripts*. Berkeley: University of California Press, 1987.

Chadwick, John. *The Mycenaean World*. Cambridge: Cambridge University Press, 1976.

Cunliffe, Barry, ed. *The Oxford Illustrated Prehistory of Europe*. Oxford: Oxford University Press, 1994.

Dickinson, Oliver. *The Aegean Bronze Age*. Cambridge: Cambridge University Press, 1994.

Ehrenberg, Margaret. *Women in Prehistory*. Norman: University of Oklahoma Press, 1989.

Evans, Arthur, Sir. *The Palace of Minos at Knossos.* 4 vols. and index. London: Macmillan, 1921–36.

Evely, Don, Helen Hughes-Brock, and Nicoletta Momigliano, eds. *Knossos, a Labyrinth of History: Papers Presented in Honor of Sinclair Hood.* London: British School at Athens, 1994.

Fitton, J. Lesley. *The Discovery of the Greek Bronze Age.* Cambridge, Mass.: Harvard University Press, 1995.

Forsyth, Phyllis Young. *Thera in the Bronze Age.* New York: Peter Lang, 1997.

Graham, James Walter. *The Palaces of Crete.* Rev. ed. Princeton: Princeton University Press, 1987.

Higgins, Reynold. *Minoan and Mycenaean Art.* New rev. ed. London: Thames and Hudson, 1997.

Hood, Sinclair. *The Minoans: The Story of Bronze Age Crete.* New York: Praeger, 1971.

Hood, Sinclair. *The Arts in Prehistoric Greece.* Harmondsworth, England: Penguin, 1978.

Hooker, J. T. *Mycenaean Greece.* London: Routledge, 1976.

Immerwahr, Sarah A. *Aegean Painting in the Bronze Age.* University Park: Pennsylvania State University Press, 1990.

Mallory, J. P. *In Search of the Indo-Europeans: Language, Archaeology, and Myth.* London: Thames and Hudson, 1989.

McDonald, William A., and Carol G. Thomas. *Progress into the Past: The Rediscovery of Mycenaean Civilization.* 2d ed. Bloomington: Indiana University Press, 1990.

Saggs, H. W. F. *Civilization before Greece and Rome.* New Haven: Yale University Press, 1989.

Sandars, N. K. *The Sea Peoples: Warriors of the Ancient Mediterranean, 1250–1150 B.C.* Rev. ed. London: Thames and Hudson, 1985.

Sasson, Jack M., ed. *Civilizations of the Ancient Near East.* 4 vols. New York: Scribner's, 1995.

Schliemann, Heinrich. *Mycenae.* London: John Murray, 1878.

Taylour, Lord William. *The Mycenaeans.* Rev. ed. London: Thames and Hudson, 1983.

Thomas, Carol G. *Myth Becomes History: Pre-Classical Greece.* Claremont, Calif.: Regina Books, 1993.

Wachsmann, Shelley. *Seagoing Ships and Seamanship in the Bronze Age Levant.* London: Chatham, 1998.

Ward, William A., and Martha Sharp Joukowsky, eds. *The Crisis Years: The Twelfth Century B.C. from Beyond the Danube to the Tigris.* Dubuque: Kendall/Hunt, 1992.

Warren, Peter. *The Aegean Civilizations: From Ancient Crete to Mycenae.* 2d ed. Oxford: Phaidon, 1989.

The Dark Age (Chapter 3)

Bouzek, Jan. *Greece, Anatolia and Europe: Cultural Interrelations during the Early Iron Age.* Jonsered, Sweden: Paul Aströms Förleg, 1997.

Coldstream, J. N. *Geometric Greece*. New York: St. Martin's, 1977.

Crouwel, J. H. *Chariots and Other Wheeled Vehicles in Iron Age Greece*. Amsterdam: Allard Pierson Museum, 1992.

Desborough, V. R. d'A. *The Greek Dark Ages*. London: Benn, 1972.

Donlan, Walter. *The Aristocratic Ideal in Ancient Greece: Attitudes of Superiority from Homer to the End of the Fifth Century B.C.* Lawrence, Kan.: Coronado Press, 1980.

Edwards, Mark W. *Homer, Poet of the Iliad*. Baltimore: John Hopkins, 1987.

Finley, M. I. *The World of Odysseus*. 2d ed. Harmondsworth: Penguin, 1979.

Homer. *The Iliad*. Trans. Richmond Lattimore. Chicago: University of Chicago Press, 1951.

Homer. *The Odyssey*. Trans. Richmond Lattimore. New York: Harper and Row, 1965.

Hurwit, Jeffrey M. *The Art and Culture of Early Greece, 1100–480 B.C.* Ithaca, N.Y.: Cornell University Press, 1985.

Lord, Albert Bates. *Epic Singers and Oral Tradition*. Ithaca, N. Y.: Cornell University Press, 1991.

Luce, J. V. *Celebrating Homer's Landscape: Troy and Ithaca Revisited*. New York: Yale University Press, 1998.

Morris, Ian, and Barry Powell, eds. *A New Companion to Homer*. Leiden: Brill, 1997.

Morris, Sarah P. *Daidalos and the Origins of Greek Art*. Princeton: Princeton University Press, 1992.

Osborne, Robin. *Greece in the Making,* 1200–479 BC. London: Routledge, 1996.

Snodgrass, A. M. *The Dark Age of Greece: An Archaeological Survey of the Eleventh to the Eighth Centuries B.C.* Edinburgh: Edinburgh University Press, 1971.

Whitley, James. *Style and Society in Dark Age Greece: The Changing Face of a Pre-Literate Society, 1100–700 B.C.* Cambridge: Cambridge University Press, 1991.

THE FERMENT OF ARCHAIC GREECE AND THE DEVELOPMENT OF ATHENS AND SPARTA (CHAPTERS 4–5)

Andrewes, Anthony. *The Greek Tyrants*. London: Hutchinson's University Library, 1956.

Aubet, María Eugenia. *The Phoenicians and the West: Politics, Colonies, and Trade*. Trans. Mary Turton. Cambridge: Cambridge University Press, 1993.

Boardman, John. *The Greeks Overseas: Their Early Colonies and Trade*. New ed. London: Thames and Hudson, 1980.

Burford, Alison. *Land and Labor in the Greek World*. Baltimore: Johns Hopkins University Press, 1993.

Cambridge Ancient History. 2d ed, vol. 3, pt.3. *The Expansion of the Greek World, Eighth to Sixth Centuries B.C.* Ed. John Boardman and N. G. L. Hammond. Cambridge: Cambridge University Press, 1982.

Carradice, Ian. *Greek Coins*. Austin: University of Texas Press, 1995.

Cartledge, Paul. *Sparta and Lakonia: A Regional History, 1300–362 B.C.* London: Routledge, 1979.

Demand, Nancy H. *Urban Relocation in Archaic and Classical Greece: Flight and Consolidation*. Norman: University of Oklahoma Press, 1990.

Dillon, Matthew, and Lynda Garland. *Ancient Greece: Social and Historical Documents from Archaic Times to the Death of Socrates (c. 800–399 BC)*. London: Routledge, 1994.

Fantham, Elaine, et al. *Women in the Classical World: Image and Text*. Oxford: Oxford University Press, 1994.

Ferguson, John. *Among the Gods: An Archaeological Exploration of Ancient Greek Religion*. London: Routledge, 1989.

Finley, M. I. *Early Greece: The Bronze and Archaic Ages*. Rev. ed. London: Chatto and Windus, 1981.

Fitzhardinge, L. F. *The Spartans*. London: Thames and Hudson, 1980.

Fornara, Charles W., and Loren J. Samons II. *Athens from Cleisthenes to Pericles*. Berkeley: University of California Press, 1991.

Garlan, Yvon. *Slavery in Ancient Greece*. Rev. ed. Trans. Janet Lloyd. Ithaca, N.Y.: Cornell University Press, 1988.

Grant, Michael. *The Rise of the Greeks*. New York: Scribner's, 1987.

Hansen, Mogens Herman, ed. *The Ancient Greek City-State*. Copenhagen: Munksgaard, 1993.

Hanson, Victor Davis. *The Other Greeks: The Family Farm and the Agrarian Roots of Western Civilization*. New York: The Free Press, 1995.

Hooker, J. T. *The Ancient Spartans*. London: J. M. Dent, 1980.

Jenkins, G. K. *Ancient Greek Coins*. 2d ed. London: Seaby, 1990.

Kennell, Nigel M. *The Gymnasium of Virtue: Education and Culture in Ancient Sparta*. Chapel Hill: University of North Carolina Press, 1995.

Kraay, Colin M. *Archaic and Classical Greek Coins*. Berkeley: University of California Press, 1976.

Manville, Philip Brook. *The Origins of Citizenship in Ancient Athens*. Princeton: Princeton University Press, 1990.

McGlew, James F. *Tyranny and Political Culture in Ancient Greece*. Ithaca, N.Y.: Cornell University Press, 1993.

Mitchell, Lynette G., and P. J. Rhodes, eds. *The Development of the Polis in Archaic Greece*. London: Routledge, 1997.

Murray, Oswyn. *Early Greece*. 2d ed. Cambridge, Mass.: Harvard University Press, 1993.

Patterson, Cynthia B. *The Family in Greek History*. Cambridge, Mass.: Harvard University Press, 1998.

Powell, Anton, ed. *Classical Sparta: Techniques Behind Her Success*. London: Routledge, 1989.

Snodgrass, Anthony. *Archaic Greece: The Age of Experiment*. London: Dent, 1980.

Stanton, G. R., ed. *Athenian Politics* c. *800–500 BC: A Sourcebook*. London: Routledge, 1990.

Starr, Chester G. *The Economic and Social Growth of Early Greece, 800–500 B.C.* Oxford: Oxford University Press, 1977.

Starr, Chester G. *Individual and Community: The Rise of the Polis, 800–500 B.C.* Oxford: Oxford University Press, 1986.

The Momentous Cultural Creativity of Archaic Greece (Chapters 6–7)

Amyx, D. A. *Corinthian Vase-Painting of the Archaic Period*. Berkeley: University of California Press, 1988.

Barnes, Jonathan. *Early Greek Philosophy*. Harmondsworth: Penguin, 1987.

Barnstone, Willis. *Greek Lyric Poetry*. Bloomington: Indiana University Press, 1967.

Boardman, John. *Athenian Black Figure Vases*. London: Oxford University Press, 1974.

Boardman, John. *Athenian Red Figure Vases: The Archaic Period*. London: Oxford University Press, 1975.

Boardman, John. *Greek Sculpture: The Archaic Period*. London: Oxford University Press, 1978.

Bryant, Joseph M. *Moral Codes and Social Structure in Ancient Greece: A Sociology of Greek Ethics from Homer to the Epicureans and Stoics*. Albany: State University of New York Press, 1996.

Bremmer, Jan N. *Greek Religion*. Oxford: Oxford University Press, 1994.

Burkert, Walter. *The Orientalizing Revolution: Near Eastern Influence on Greek Culture in the Early Archaic Age*. Trans. Margaret E. Pinder and Walter Burkert. Cambridge, Mass.: Harvard University Press, 1992.

Buxton, Richard. *Imaginary Greece: The Contexts of Mythology*. Cambridge, Mass.: Harvard University Press, 1994.

Coldstream, J. N. *Geometric Greece*. New York: St. Martin's, 1977.

Cook, R. M. *Greek Painted Pottery*. 3d ed. London: Routledge, 1997.

Dillon, Matthew. *Pilgrims and Pilgrimages in Ancient Greece*. London: Routledge, 1997.

Dodds, E. R. *The Greeks and the Irrational*. Berkeley: University of California Press, 1951.

Easterling, P. E., and J. V. Muir, eds. *Greek Religion and Society*. Cambridge: Cambridge University Press, 1985.

Emlyn-Jones, C. J. *The Ionians and Hellenism: A Study of the Cultural Achievements of Early Greek Inhabitants of Asia Minor*. London: Routledge, 1980.

Finley, M. I., and H. W. Pleket. *The Olympic Games: The First Thousand Years*. New York: Viking, 1976.

Fowler, Barbara Hughes, trans. *Archaic Greek Poetry: An Anthology*. Madison: University of Wisconsin Press, 1992.

Fränkel, Hermann. *Early Greek Poetry and Philosophy: A History of Greek Epic, Lyric, and Prose to the Middle of the Fifth Century*. Trans. Moses Hadas and James Willis. Oxford: Blackwell, 1975.

Garland, Robert. *Religion and the Greeks*. London: Bristol Classical Press, 1994.

Graf, Fritz. *Greek Mythology: An Introduction*. Trans. Thomas Marier. Baltimore: Johns Hopkins University Press, 1993.

Hesiod. *Theogony, Works and Days, Shield*. Trans. Apostolos Athanassakis. Baltimore: Johns Hopkins University Press, 1983.

Hurwit, Jeffrey M. *The Athenian Acropolis: History, Mythology, and Archaeology from the Neolithic Era to the Present.* Cambridge: Cambridge University Press, 1999.

Kirk, G. S., J. E. Raven, and M. Schofield. *The Presocratic Philosophers: A Critical History with a Selection of Texts.* 2d ed. Cambridge: Cambridge University Press, 1983.

Meiggs, Russell, and David Lewis. *A Selection of Greek Historical Inscriptions to the End of the Fifth Century B.C.* Rev. ed. Oxford: Clarendon Press, 1988.

Miller, Andrew M., trans. *Greek Lyric: An Anthology in Translation.* Indianapolis: Hackett, 1996.

Morford, Mark P. O., and Robert J. Lenardon. *Classical Mythology.* 6th ed. New York: Longman, 1999.

Morgan, Catherine. *Athletes and Oracles: The Transformation of Olympia and Delphi in the Eighth Century BC.* Cambridge: Cambridge University Press, 1990.

Mylonas, George E. *Eleusis and the Eleusinian Mysteries.* Princeton: Princeton University Press, 1961.

Nagy, Gregory. *The Best of the Achaeans: Concepts of the Hero in Archaic Greek Poetry.* Rev. ed. Baltimore: Johns Hopkins University Press, 1999.

Nilsson, Martin P. *Greek Popular Religion.* New York: Columbia University Press, 1940 (issued in paperback as *Greek Folk Religion.* Philadelphia: University of Pennsylvania Press).

Osborne, Robin. *Archaic and Classical Greek Art.* Oxford: Oxford University Press, 1998.

Page, Denys. *Sappho and Alcaeus.* Oxford: Clarendon Press, 1955.

Parke, H. W. *Festivals of the Athenians.* London: Thames and Hudson, 1977.

Podlecki, Anthony J. *The Early Greek Poets and Their Times.* Vancouver: University of British Columbia Press, 1984.

Seaford, Richard. *Reciprocity and Ritual: Homer and Tragedy in the Developing City-State.* Oxford: Clarendon Press, 1994.

Simon, Erika. *Festivals of Attica: An Archaeological Commentary.* Madison, Wis.: University of Wisconsin Press, 1983.

Swaddling, Judith. *The Ancient Olympic Games.* London: British Museum Publications, 1980.

Walsh, George B. *The Varieties of Enchantment: Early Greek Views on the Nature and Function of Poetry.* Chapel Hill: University of North Carolina Press, 1984.

Wilbur, James B., and Harold J. Allen. *The Worlds of the Early Greek Philosophers.* Buffalo: Prometheus, 1979.

THE MONUMENTAL TRIUMPHS AND FAILURES OF FIFTH-CENTURY GREECE:
THE PERSIAN WARS, THE ATHENIAN EMPIRE, AND THE PELOPONNESIAN WAR
(CHAPTERS 8–10)

Balcer, Jack Martin. *The Persian Conquest of the Greeks, 545–450 B.C.* Konstanz, Germany: Universitätsverlag Konstanz, 1995.

Cambridge Ancient History. 2d ed, vol. 4. *Persia, Greece, and the Western Mediterranean, c. 525 to 479 B.C.* Ed. John Boardman et al. Cambridge: Cambridge University Press, 1988.

Cambridge Ancient History. 2d ed., vol. 5. *The Fifth Century* B.C. Ed. D. M. Lewis et al. Cambridge: Cambridge University Press, 1992.

Casson, Lionel. *Ships and Seafaring in Ancient Times*. London: British Museum Press, 1994.

Cook, J. M. *The Persian Empire*. London: J. M. Dent, 1983.

Connor, W. Robert. *The New Politicians of Fifth-Century Athens*. Princeton: Princeton University Press, 1971.

Curtis, John. *Ancient Persia*. Cambridge, Mass.: Harvard University Press, 1990.

Ehrenberg, Victor. *From Solon to Socrates: Greek History and Civilization during the Sixth and Fifth Centuries* B.C., 2d ed. London: Methuen, 1973.

Fornara, Charles W., and Loren J. Samons II. *Athens from Cleisthenes to Pericles*. Berkeley: University of California Press, 1991.

Grant, Michael. *The Classical Greeks*. New York: Scribner's, 1989.

Green, Peter. *The Greco-Persian Wars*. Berkeley: University of California Press, 1996.

Hamel, Debra. *Athenian Generals: Military Authority in the Classical Period*. Leiden: Brill, 1998.

Hanson, Victor Davis, ed. *Hoplites: The Classical Greek Battle Experience*. London: Routledge, 1991.

Hanson, Victor Davis. *Warfare and Agriculture in Classical Greece*. Rev. ed. Berkeley: University of California Press, 1998.

Kagan, Donald. *The Archidamian War*. Ithaca, N.Y.: Cornell University Press, 1974.

Kagan, Donald. *The Fall of the Athenian Empire*. Ithaca, N.Y.: Cornell University Press, 1987.

Kagan, Donald. *The Outbreak of the Peloponnesian War*. Ithaca, N.Y.: Cornell University Press, 1969.

Kagan, Donald. *The Peace of Nicias and the Sicilian Expedition*. Ithaca, N.Y.: Cornell University Press, 1981.

Miller, Margaret C. *Athens and Persia in the Fifth Century* BC: *A Study in Cultural Receptivity*. Cambridge: Cambridge University Press, 1997.

Morrison, J. S., and J. F. Coates. *The Athenian Trireme: The History and Reconstruction of an Ancient Greek Warship*. Cambridge: Cambridge University Press, 1986.

Olmstead, A. T. *History of the Persian Empire: Achaemenid Period*. Chicago: University of Chicago Press, 1948.

Podlecki, Anthony J. *Perikles and His Circle*. London: Routledge, 1998.

Powell, Anton. *Athens and Sparta: Constructing Greek Political and Social History from 478 B.C.* London: Routledge, 1988.

Sage, Michael. *Warfare in Ancient Greece: A Sourcebook*. London: Routledge, 1996.

Sealey, Raphael. *A History of the Greek City States, ca. 700–338 B.C.* Berkeley: University of California Press, 1976.

Shaw, Timothy, ed. *The Trireme Project: Operational Experience, 1987–90: Lessons Learnt*. Oxford: Oxbow, 1993.

Spence, I. G. *The Cavalry of Classical Greece: A Social and Military History with Particular Reference to Athens*. Oxford: Clarendon Press, 1993.

LIFE AND CULTURE IN PERICLEAN ATHENS (CHAPTERS 11–12)

Aeschylus. *The Oresteia [Agamemnon, The Libation Bearers, The Eumenides]*. Trans. Robert Fagles. New York: Viking, 1975.

Aristophanes. *The Acharnians, The Clouds, Lysistrata*. Trans. Alan H. Sommerstein. London: Penguin, 1973.

Boardman, John. *Greek Sculpture: The Classical Period: A Handbook*. London: Thames and Hudson, 1985.

Bonner, Robert J., and Gertrude Smith. *The Administration of Justice from Homer to Aristotle*. 2 vols. Chicago: University of Chicago Press, 1930–38.

Cameron, Averil, and Amélie Kuhrt, eds. *Images of Women in Antiquity*. 2d ed. London: Routledge, 1993.

Camp, John M. *The Athenian Agora: Excavations in the Heart of Classical Athens*. Updated ed. London: Thames and Hudson, 1992.

Connolly, Peter, and Hazel Dodge. *The Ancient City: Life in Classical Athens and Rome*. Oxford; Oxford University Press, 1998.

Csapo, Eric, and William J. Slater, eds. *The Context of Ancient Drama*. Ann Arbor: University of Michigan Press, 1995.

Davies, J. K. *Democracy and Classical Greece*. 2d ed. Cambridge, Mass.: Harvard University Press, 1993.

Demand, Nancy. *Birth, Death and Motherhood in Classical Greece*. Baltimore: Johns Hopkins University Press, 1994.

Dover, K. J. *Greek Homosexuality*. Updated ed. Cambridge, Mass.: Harvard University Press, 1989.

Easterling, P. E., ed. *The Cambridge Companion to Greek Tragedy*. Cambridge: Cambridge University Press, 1997.

Euripides. *Medea, Hippolytus, The Bacchae*. Trans. Philip Vellacott. New York: Heritage Press, 1968.

Euripides. *Medea and Other Plays*. Trans. and ed. James Morwood. Oxford: Oxford University Press, 1998.

Farrar, Cynthia. *The Origins of Democratic Thinking: The Invention of Politics in Classical Athens*. Cambridge: Cambridge University Press, 1988.

Fornara, Charles W. *Herodotus: An Interpretative Essay*. Oxford: Clarendon Press, 1971.

Forrest, W. G. *The Emergence of Greek Democracy: The Character of Greek Politics, 800–400 B.C.* London: Weidenfeld and Nicholson, 1966.

Georges, Pericles. *Barbarian Asia and the Greek Experience: From the Archaic Period to the Age of Xenophon*. Baltimore: Johns Hopkins University Press, 1994.

Golden, Mark. *Children and Childhood in Classical Athens*. Baltimore: Johns Hopkins University Press, 1990.

Goldhill, Simon. *Reading Greek Tragedy*. Cambridge: Cambridge University Press, 1986.

Goldhill, Simon, and Robin Osborne, eds. *Performance-Culture and Athenian Democracy*. Cambridge: Cambridge University Press, 1999.

Green, J. R. *Theatre in Ancient Greek Society*. London: Routledge, 1994.

Halperin, David M. *One Hundred Years of Homosexuality: And Other Essays on Greek Love*. London: Routledge, 1990.

Herodotus. *The History*. Trans. David Grene. Chicago: University of Chicago Press, 1987.

Hibler, Richard W. *Life and Learning in Ancient Athens*. Lanham, Md.: University Press of America, 1988.

Hornblower, Simon. *A Commentary on Thucydides*. 2 vols. Oxford: Clarendon Press, 1991–96.

Hornblower, Simon. *Thucydides*. London: Duckworth, 1987.

Humphreys, S. C. *The Family, Women and Death: Comparative Studies*. 2d ed. Ann Arbor: University of Michigan Press, 1993.

Irwin, Terence. *Classical Thought*. Oxford: Oxford University Press, 1989.

Jenkins, Ian. *The Parthenon Frieze*. Austin: University of Texas Press, 1994.

Jordan, James N. *Western Philosophy: From Antiquity to the Middle Ages*. New York: Macmillan, 1987.

Jordan, William. *Ancient Concepts of Philosophy*. London: Routledge, 1990.

Jouanna, Jacques. *Hippocrates*. Trans. M. B. DeBevoise. Baltimore: Johns Hopkins University Press, 1999.

Just, Roger. *Women in Athenian Law and Life*. New York: Routledge, 1989.

Kagan, Donald. *Pericles of Athens and the Birth of Democracy*. London: Secker and Warburg, 1991.

Kerferd, G. B. *The Sophistic Movement*. Cambridge: Cambridge University Press, 1981.

Keuls, Eva C. *The Reign of the Phallus: Sexual Politics in Ancient Athens*. New York: Harper and Row, 1985.

Kraut, Richard. *Socrates and the State*. Princeton: Princeton University Press, 1984.

Loraux, Nicole. *The Invention of Athens: The Funeral Oration in the Classical City*. Trans. Alan Sheridan. Cambridge, Mass.: Harvard University Press, 1986.

Luce, T. J. *The Greek Historians*. London: Routledge, 1997.

Mark, Ira S. *The Sanctuary of Athena Nike in Athens: Architectural Stages and Chronology*. Princeton, N.J.: American School of Classical Studies at Athens, 1993.

McLeish, Kenneth. *The Theatre of Aristophanes*. London: Thames and Hudson, 1980.

Meier, Christian. *Athens: A Portrait of the City in Its Golden Age*. Trans. Robert Kimber and Rita Kimber. New York: Metropolitan Books, 1998.

Mikalson, Jon D. *Athenian Popular Religion*. Chapel Hill: University of North Carolina Press, 1983.

Mikalson, Jon D. *Honor Thy Gods: Popular Religion in Greek Tragedy*. Chapel Hill: University of North Carolina Press, 1991.

Morris, Ian, ed. *Classical Greece: Ancient Histories and Modern Archaeologies*. Cambridge: Cambridge University Press, 1994.

Oakley, John H., and Rebecca H. Sinos. *The Wedding in Ancient Athens*. Wisconsin: University of Wisconsin Press, 1993.

Ober, Josiah. *Political Dissent in Democratic Athens: Intellectual Critics of Popular Rule*. Princeton: Princeton University Press, 1998.

Osborne, Robin. *Classical Landscape with Figures: The Ancient Greek City and Its Countryside*. London: George Philip, 1987.

Parke, H. W. *Sibyls and Sibylline Prophecy in Classical Antiquity*. Ed. B. C. McGing. London: Routledge, 1988.

Parker, Robert. *Athenian Religion: A History*. Oxford: Clarendon Press, 1996.

Pomeroy, Sarah B. *Families in Classical and Hellenistic Greece: Representations and Realities*. Oxford: Clarendon Press, 1997.

Pomeroy, Sarah B. *Goddesses, Whores, Wives and Slaves: Women in Classical Antiquity*. New York: Schocken Books, 1975.

Rhodes, Robin Francis. *Architecture and Meaning on the Athenian Acropolis*. Cambridge: Cambridge University Press, 1995.

Roberts, J. W. *City of Sokrates: An Introduction to Classical Athens*. 2d ed. London: Routledge, 1998.

Robertson, Martin. *The Art of Vase-Painting in Classical Athens*. Cambridge: Cambridge University Press, 1992.

Romilly, Jacqueline de. *A Short History of Greek Literature*. Trans. Lillian Doherty. Chicago: University of Chicago Press, 1985.

Romilly, Jacqueline de. *The Great Sophists in Periclean Athens*. Trans. Janet Lloyd. Oxford: Oxford University Press, 1992.

Schaps, David M. *Economic Rights of Women in Ancient Greece*. Edinburgh: Edinburgh University Press, 1979.

Sealey, Raphael. *Women and Law in Classical Greece*. Chapel Hill: University of North Carolina Press, 1990.

Sophocles. *The Three Theban Plays [Antigone, Oedipus the King, Oedipus at Colonus]*. Trans. Robert Fagles. Harmondsworth: Penguin, 1982.

Stewart, Andrew. *Art, Desire, and the Body in Ancient Greece*. Cambridge: Cambridge University Press, 1997.

Stockton, David. *The Classical Athenian Democracy*. Oxford: Oxford University Press, 1990.

Strauss, Barry S. *Fathers and Sons in Athens: Ideology and Society in the Era of the Peloponnesian War*. Princeton: Princeton University Press, 1993.

Taplin, Oliver. *Comic Angels and Other Approaches to Greek Drama through Vase-Painting*. Oxford: Clarendon Press, 1992.

Thucydides. *The Peloponnesian War: A New Translation, Backgrounds, Interpretations*. Trans. Walter Blanco. Ed. Walter Blanco and Jennifer Roberts. New York: Norton, 1998.

Todd, S. C. *The Shape of Athenian Law*. Oxford: Clarendon Press, 1993.

Trendall, A. D., and T. B. L. Webster. *Illustrations of Greek Drama*. London: Phaidon, 1971.

Vlastos, Gregory. *Socrates, Ironist and Moral Philosopher*. Ithaca, N.Y.: Cornell University Press, 1991.

Webster, T. B. L. *Athenian Culture and Society*. London: Batsford, 1973.

Winkler, John J. *The Constraints of Desire: The Anthropology of Sex and Gender in Ancient Greece*. London: Routledge, 1990.

Zeitlin, Froma I. *Playing the Other: Gender and Society in Classical Greek Literature*. Chicago: University of Chicago Press, 1996.

Conflict and Achievement in Fourth-Century Greece (Chapters 13–14)

Aristotle. *The Complete Works of Aristotle: The Revised Oxford Translation*. Ed. Jonathan Barnes. 2 vols. Princeton: Princeton University Press, 1984.

Boardman, John. *Greek Sculpture: The Late Classical Period and Sculpture in Colonies and Overseas*. London: Thames and Hudson, 1995.

Borza, Eugene N. *In the Shadow of Olympus: The Emergence of Macedon*. Princeton: Princeton University Press, 1990.

Bryant, Joseph M. *Moral Codes and Social Structure in Ancient Greece: A Sociology of Greek Ethics from Homer to the Epicureans and Stoics*. Albany: State University of New York Press, 1996.

Cambridge Ancient History. 2d ed., vol. 6. *The Fourth Century b.c.* Ed. D. M. Lewis et al. Cambridge: Cambridge University Press, 1994.

Cartledge, Paul. *Agesilaos and the Crisis of Sparta*. London: Duckworth, 1987.

Clayton, Peter A., and Martin J. Price. *The Seven Wonders of the Ancient World*. London: Routledge, 1988.

Dillery, John. *Xenophon and the History of His Times*. London: Routledge, 1995.

Ellis, J. R. *Philip II and Macedonian Imperialism*. London: Thames and Hudson, 1976.

Errington, R. Malcolm. *A History of Macedonia*. Trans. Catherine Errington. Berkeley: University of California Press, 1990.

Hamilton, Charles D. *Agesilaus and the Failure of Spartan Hegemony*. Ithaca: Cornell University Press, 1991.

Hammond, N. G. L., et al. *A History of Macedonia*. 3 vols. Oxford: Oxford University Press, 1972–88.

Hammond, N. G. L. *The Macedonian State: Origins, Institutions, and History*. Oxford: Clarendon Press, 1989.

Hammond, N. G. L. *Philip of Macedon*. London: Duckworth, 1994.

Hansen, Mogens Herman. *The Athenian Democracy in the Age of Demosthenes: Structure, Principles, and Ideology*. Trans. J. A. Crook. Oxford: Blackwell, 1991.

Harris, Edward M. *Aeschines and Athenian Politics*. New York: Oxford University Press, 1995.

Hornblower, Simon. *The Greek World, 479–323 bc*. Rev. ed. London: Routledge, 1991.

Hunter, Virginia. *Policing Athens: Social Control in the Attic Lawsuits, 420–320 b.c.* Princeton: Princeton University Press, 1994.

Plato. *The Collected Dialogues of Plato, Including the Letters*. Ed. Edith Hamilton and Huntington Cairns. Trans. Lane Cooper et al. Princeton: Princeton University Press, 1961.

Ruzicka, Stephen. *Politics of a Persian Dynasty: The Hecatomnids in the Fourth Century B.C.* Norman: University of Oklahoma Press, 1992.

Sealey, Raphael. *Demosthenes and His Time: A Study in Defeat.* New York: Oxford University Press, 1993.

Sinclair, R. K. *Democracy and Participation in Athens.* Cambridge: Cambridge University Press, 1988.

Strauss, Barry S. *Athens after the Peloponnesian War: Class, Faction, and Policy, 403–386 BC.* London: Croom Helm, 1986.

Todd, S. C. *The Shape of Athenian Law.* Oxford: Clarendon Press, 1993.

Tritle, Lawrence A., ed. *The Greek World in the Fourth Century: From the Fall of the Athenian Empire to the Successors of Alexander.* London: Routledge, 1997.

Xenophon. *A History of My Times (Hellenica).* Trans. Rex Warner. Harmondsworth: Penguin, 1966.

ALEXANDER THE GREAT AND HIS SUCCESSORS (CHAPTERS 15–17)

Ager, Sheila L. *Interstate Arbitration in the Greek World, 337–90 B.C.* Berkeley: University of California Press, 1996.

Billows, Richard A. *Antigonos the One-Eyed and the Creation of the Hellenistic State.* Berkeley: University of California Press, 1990.

Billows, Richard A. *Kings and Colonists: Aspects of Macedonian Imperialism.* Leiden: Brill, 1995.

Bosworth, A. B. *Alexander and the East: The Tragedy of Triumph.* Oxford: Clarendon Press, 1996.

Bosworth, A. B. *Conquest and Empire: The Reign of Alexander the Great.* Cambridge: Cambridge University Press, 1988.

Cambridge Ancient History. 2d ed., vol. 7. *The Hellenistic World.* Ed. F. W. Walbank et al. Cambridge: Cambridge University Press, 1984.

Cartledge, Paul, and Anthony Spawforth. *Hellenistic and Roman Sparta: A Tale of Two Cities.* London: Routledge, 1989.

Cohen, Getzel M. *The Hellenistic Settlements in Europe, the Islands, and Asia Minor.* Berkeley: University of California Press, 1995.

Ellis, Walter M. *Ptolemy of Egypt.* London: Routledge, 1994.

Engels, David W. *Alexander the Great and the Logistics of the Macedonian Army.* Berkeley: University of California Press, 1978.

Gabbert, Janice J. *Antigonus II Gonatas: A Political Biography.* London: Routledge, 1997.

Grainger, John D. *Seleukos Nikator: Constructing a Hellenistic Kingdom.* London: Routledge, 1990.

Grant, Michael. *The Hellenistic Greeks: From Alexander to Cleopatra.* London: Weidenfeld and Nicholson, 1990.

Green, Miranda J., ed. *The Celtic World.* London: Routledge, 1995.

Green, Peter. *Alexander of Macedon, 356–323 B.C.: A Historical Biography.* Rev. ed. Harmondsworth: Penguin, 1974 (reprint, Berkeley: University of California Press).

Green, Peter. *Alexander to Actium: The Historical Evolution of the Hellenistic Age.* Berkeley: University of California Press, 1990.

Habicht, Christian. *Athens from Alexander to Antony.* Trans. Deborah Lucas Schneider. Cambridge, Mass.: Harvard University Press, 1997.

Hammond, N. G. L. *Sources for Alexander the Great: An Analysis of Plutarch's Life and Arrian's Anabasis Alexandrou.* Cambridge: Cambridge University Press, 1993.

Heckel, Waldemar. *The Marshals of Alexander's Empire.* London: Routledge, 1992.

Holt, Frank L. *Alexander the Great and Bactria: The Formation of a Greek Frontier in Central Asia.* 3d ed. Leiden: Brill, 1998.

James, Simon. *The World of the Celts.* London: Thames and Hudson, 1993.

Lewis, Naphtali. *Greeks in Ptolemaic Egypt.* Oxford: Clarendon Press, 1986.

Lund, Helen S. *Lysimachus: A Study in Early Hellenistic Kingship.* London: Routledge, 1992.

Mitchell, Stephen. *Anatolia: Land, Men, and Gods in Asia Minor.* 2 vols. Oxford: Clarendon Press, 1993.

Price, Martin Jessop. *The Coinage in the Name of Alexander the Great and Philip Arrhidaeus: A British Museum Catalogue.* 2 vols. Zurich: Swiss Numismatic Society with British Museum Press, 1991.

Pseudo-Callisthenes. *The Greek Alexander Romance.* Trans. Richard Stoneman. London: Penguin, 1991.

Rigsby, Kent J. Asylia: *Territorial Inviolability in the Hellenistic World.* Berkeley: University of California Press, 1996.

Roisman, Joseph, ed. *Alexander the Great: Ancient and Modern Perspectives.* Lexington, Mass.: Heath, 1995.

Stewart, Andrew F. *Faces of Power: Alexander's Image and Hellenistic Politics.* Berkeley: University of California Press, 1993.

Stonemen, Richard. *Alexander the Great.* London: Routledge, 1997.

Walbank, F. W. *The Hellenistic World.* Rev. ed. Cambridge, Mass.: Harvard University Press, 1993.

Wood, Michael. *In the Footsteps of Alexander the Great: A Journey from Greece to Asia.* London: BBC Books, 1997.

HELLENISTIC SOCIAL AND CULTURAL DEVELOPMENTS (CHAPTERS 18–19)

Bickerman, Elias J. *The Jews in the Greek Age.* Cambridge, Mass.: Harvard University Press, 1988.

Boyce, Mary. *A History of Zoroastrianism.* 3 vols. Leiden: Brill, 1975–91.

Downey, Susan B. *Mesopotamian Religious Architecture: Alexander through the Parthians.* Princeton: Princeton University Press, 1988.

Gabrielsen, Vincent. *The Naval Aristocracy of Hellenistic Rhodes.* Aarhus, Denmark: Aarhus University Press, 1997.

Green, Peter, ed. *Hellenistic History and Culture.* Berkeley: University of California Press, 1993.

Havelock, Christine Mitchell. *Hellenistic Art: The Art of the Classical World from the Death of Alexander the Great to the Battle of Actium.* 2d ed. New York: Norton, 1981.

Kuhrt, Amélie, and Susan Sherwin-White, eds. *Hellenism in the East: The Interaction of Greek and Non-Greek Civilizations from Syria to Central Asia after Alexander.* London: Duckworth, 1987.

Lloyd, G. E. R. *Methods and Problems in Greek Science.* Cambridge: Cambridge University Press, 1991.

Long, A. A. *Hellenistic Philosophy: Stoics, Epicureans, Sceptics.* 2d ed. Berkeley: University of California Press, 1986.

Longrigg, James. *Greek Rational Medicine: Philosophy and Medicine from Alcmaeon to the Alexandrians.* London: Routledge, 1993.

Martin, Luther H. *Hellenistic Religions: An Introduction.* New York: Oxford University Press, 1987.

Mikalson, Jon D. *Religion in Hellenistic Athens.* Berkeley: University of California Press, 1998.

Politt, J. J. *Art in the Hellenistic Age.* Cambridge: Cambridge University Press, 1986.

Pomeroy, Sarah B. *Women in Hellenistic Egypt: From Alexander to Cleopatra.* New York: Shocken Books, 1984.

Reid, Jane Davidson. *The Oxford Guide to Classical Mythology in the Arts, 1300–1990s.* 2 vols. Oxford: Oxford University Press, 1993.

Ridgway, Brunilde Sismondo. *Hellenistic Sculpture I: The Styles of ca. 331–200 B.C.* Madison: University of Wisconsin Press, 1990.

Smith, R. R. R. *Hellenistic Sculpture: A Handbook.* London: Thames and Hudson, 1991.

Thompson, Dorothy J. *Memphis Under the Ptolemies.* Princeton: Princeton University Press, 1988.

INDEX

References in italics denote illustrations.